Halsbury's
Statutory Instruments

VOLUME 10
Fifth Re-Issue

ISSUE DATE

This volume contains the Statutory Instruments which became available before
1 March 1986

United Kingdom	Butterworth & Co (Publishers) Ltd 88 Kingsway, LONDON WC2B 6AB and 61A North Castle Street, EDINBURGH EH2 3LJ
Australia	Butterworths Pty Ltd, SYDNEY, MELBOURNE, BRISBANE, ADELAIDE, PERTH, CANBERRA and HOBART
Canada	Butterworth & Co (Canada) Ltd, TORONTO and VANCOUVER
New Zealand	Butterworths of New Zealand Ltd, WELLINGTON and AUCKLAND
Singapore	Butterworth & Co (Asia) Pte Ltd, SINGAPORE
South Africa	Butterworth Publishers (Pty) Ltd, DURBAN and PRETORIA
United States of America	Butterworth Legal Publishers, ST PAUL, Minnesota; SEATTLE, Washington; BOSTON, Massachusetts; and AUSTIN, Texas D & S Publishers, CLEARWATER, Florida

Halsbury's Statutory Instruments

Being a Companion Work to
HALSBURY'S STATUTES

Prepared by
BUTTERWORTHS LEGAL EDITORIAL STAFF

VOLUME 10
Fifth Re-Issue

GAS
HIGHWAYS
HOUSING
HUSBAND AND WIFE

LONDON
BUTTERWORTHS
1986

Managing Editor
GILLIAN MATHER, LL.B.

This volume has been revised for the Fifth Re-Issue by
JOHN PITMAN, B.A., LL.M.

ISBN for the complete set of volumes: 0 406 04500 3
for this volume: 0 406 04603 4

Set in Great Britain by Cold Composition Ltd, Tonbridge, Kent.
and printed by The Whitefriars Press Ltd, London and Tonbridge

Table of Contents

References and Abbreviations used in this work

A list of references and abbreviations used in this work will be found in the preliminary pages of Volume 1

Gas

CHRONOLOGICAL LIST OF INSTRUMENTS

SI	Description	Remarks	Page
1972/1879	British Gas Corporation Regulations 1972	—	25
1974/847	Gas (Declaration of Calorific Value) (Amendment) Regulations 1974	Amend 1972/1878 (*qv*)	—
1976/1108	Compensation for Limitation of Prices (British Gas Corporation) Order 1976	—	26
1980/1782	Gas (Superannuation Scheme) (Winding Up) Regulations 1980	See Preliminary Note, "Pensions and staff compensation", p 5, *post*	—
1980/1851	Gas (Metrication) Regulations 1980	Amend 1972/1178, 1804, 1878 (*qv*) and the Gas Act 1972	—
1981/1611	Gas (Superannuation Scheme) (Winding Up) (Amendment) Regulations 1981	Amend 1980/1782 (*qv*)	—
1981/1764	Gas (Stock) (Amendment) Regulations 1981	Amend 1949/751 (*qv*)	—
1982/548	Gas Levy (Rate for 1982-83) Order 1982	—	26
1982/655	Gas (Consumers' Deposits) (Rate of Interest) Order 1982	—	26
1982/895	Oil and Gas (Enterprise) Act 1982 (Commencement No 1) Order 1982	See title Petroleum	—
1982/1059	Oil and Gas (Enterprise) Act 1982 (Commencement No 2) Order 1982	See title Petroleum	—
1982/1131	British Gas Corporation (Disposal of Offshore Oilfield Interests) Directions 1982	—	26
1982/1431	Oil and Gas (Enterprise) Act 1982 (Commencement No 3) Order 1982	See title Petroleum	—
1983/363	Gas Quality Regulations 1983	Amend 1949/789 (*qv*), 1972/1804 (*qv*)	27
1983/684	Gas (Meters) Regulations 1983	—	28
1983/967	British Gas Corporation (Transfer of Shares of Subsidiaries) Order 1983	—	33
1983/968	Gas Act 1972 (Modifications) Order 1983	—	33
1983/1096	British Gas Corporation (Further Disposal of Offshore Interests) Directions 1983	—	34
1983/1575	Gas Safety (Rights of Entry) Regulations 1983	—	34
1983/1667	British Gas Corporation (Transfer of Shares of Subsidiaries) (No 2) Order 1983	—	37
1983/1668	Gas Act 1972 (Modifications) (Amendment) Order 1983	Amends 1983/968 (*qv*)	—
1983/1749	Gas (Consumers' Councils) (Amendment) Regulations 1983	Amend 1972/1765 (*qv*)	—
1984/1358	Gas Safety (Installation and Use) Regulations 1984	Amend 1972/1178 (*qv*), 1983/1575(*qv*)	37
1984/1785	Gas (Meters) (Variation of Fees) Regulations 1984	Amend 1983/684 (*qv*)	—
1985/1149	Gas (Stock) (Amendment) Regulations 1985	Amend 1949/751 (*qv*)	—

INSTRUMENTS NO LONGER IN OPERATION

The following instruments, which were formerly included in this title, are no longer in operation:

SI		SI	SI		SI
1974/848	revoked by	1983/684	1978/1848	revoked by	1982/655
1975/1071	,, ,,	1983/684	1979/1224	,, ,,	1983/1246*
1975/1873	,, ,,	1983/1246*	1979/1257	,, ,,	1983/1247*
1975/1874	,, ,,	1983/1247*	1981/504	,, ,,	1983/684
1976/1882	,, ,,	1983/1375	1981/505	,, ,,	1983/1247*
1978/230	superseded by	1980/1851	1982/565	,, ,,	1983/684

*In the title Weights and Measures

CROSS REFERENCES

Acetylene	Explosives (Parts 1 and 3)
Alkali, etc, works	Public Health (Part 5)
Atmospheric pollution	Public Health (Part 5)
Census of production, exemption of gas undertakings	Trade and Industry (Part 1C)

PRELIMINARY NOTE

This title is mainly concerned with instruments made or having effect under the Gas Act 1972, Halsbury's Statutes, 4th edn Vol 19, title Gas (3rd edn Vol 42, p 466 *et seq*). A few instruments under other Acts are also included; see in particular those relating to the offshore oilfield interests and other subsidiaries of the British Gas Corporation, *viz* SI 1982/1131, 1983/967, 968 (as amended), 1096, 1667, pp 26, 33, 34, 37, *post*, which were made under the Oil and Gas (Enterprise) Act 1982, Halsbury's Statutes, 4th edn Vol 19, title Gas (3rd edn Vol 52, p 826 *et seq*), and also those relating to the underground storage of gas, *viz*, SI 1966/1375 and 1967/1167, pp 11, 16, *post*, which were made under the Tribunals and Inquiries Act 1971, Halsbury's Statutes, 4th edn Vol 10, title Constitutional Law (Pt 4), and the Gas Act 1965, *ibid*, 4th edn Vol 19, title Gas (3rd edn Vol 14, p 946 *et seq*), respectively.

Other relevant titles   A number of related instruments will be found in other titles of this work; see generally the list of cross-references above. The more important of the instruments concerned are mentioned below.

Civil Defence   Provision for ensuring the due functioning of gas undertakings in the event of hostile attack is made by the Civil Defence (Gas Undertakers) Regulations 1954, SI 1954/269, in the title Civil Defence.

Handling, etc, of compressed gases   Provisions of the Petroleum (Consolidation) Act 1928, Halsbury's Statutes, 4th edn Vol 35, title Public Health (3rd edn Vol 26, p 162 *et seq*), which deals with the handling and storage of petroleum, are applied by the Petroleum (Compressed Gases) Order 1930, SR&O 1930/34, in the title Petroleum, to vessels containing certain compressed gases, and the conveyance of such gases by road is regulated by the Gas Cylinders (Conveyance) Regulations 1931, SR&O 1931/679, as amended, in the same title; see also, in that title, the Compressed Gas Cylinders (Fuel for Motor Vehicles) Regulations 1940, SR&O 1940/2009. The construction of motor vehicles propelled by compressed gas is governed by reg 47 of the Motor Vehicles (Construction and Use) Regulations 1978, SI 1978/1017, in the title Transport (Part 2B).

Acetylene controlled as an explosive   By an Order in Council dated 2 February 1937, SR&O 1937/54, as amended, in the title Explosives (Part 1), the manufacture of acetylene declared by that order to be an explosive is prohibited except on premises and under conditions approved by the Health and Safety Executive; and by virtue of SI 1978/1723, in Part 3 of the same title, the importation of compressed acetylene is prohibited except under licence.

Factories legislation   The records to be kept of the examination of water-sealed gas holders under s 39 of the Factories Act 1961, Halsbury's Statutes, 4th edn Vol 19, title Health and Safety at Work (3rd edn Vol 13, p 445), are prescribed by the Gasholders (Record of Examinations) Order 1938, SR&O 1938/598, in the title Factories, Shops and Offices (Part 1B).

Transfer of ministerial functions   The minister responsible for the general control and supervision of the gas industry when it was nationalised in 1949 was the Minister of Fuel and Power, who was later re-named the Minister of Power by SI 1957/48. His functions were transferred to the Minister of Technology by SI 1969/1498, and subsequently to the Secretary of State (in effect the Secretary of State for Trade and Industry) by the Secretary of State for Trade and Industry Order 1970, SI 1970/1537. On the division of the Department of Trade and Industry into new departments in 1974 (in this connection, see the Secretary of State (New Departments) Order 1974, SI 1974/692), and the establishment, as one of them, of a Department of Energy, the functions concerned became, in effect, the responsibility of the Secretary of State for Energy. All the orders cited above are listed in the title Constitutional Law (Part 5).

Nationalisation of gas industry   The Gas Act 1948 (repealed) provided for the establishment of twelve Area Boards, covering the whole of Great Britain, with the principal duty of maintaining and developing an efficient gas supply for their areas, and substantially prohibited the supply of gas by other persons. The Gas Council was established as a central body with the general function of advising the Minister of Fuel and Power on questions affecting the gas industry and assisting the Area Boards. A Gas Consultative Council was also established for the area of each Area Board, with the function of considering and reporting on representations made by consumers.

The undertakings transferred under the Act of 1948 were the gas undertakings of the undertakers specified in s 15 of the Act; those undertakers with no functions other than the supply of gas were dissolved on the vesting date, while composite companies, local authorities and other undertakers with other functions continued in existence shorn of their gas undertakings. 1 May 1949 was appointed as the vesting date by SI 1949/392. Compensation was required to be paid by means of British Gas Stock issued in accordance with s 43 of the Act (see further Gas Stock Regulations 1949, SI 1949/751, p 6, *post*).

As in the case of other Acts effecting nationalisation, many of the provisions of the Act were left to be implemented by orders, regulations or other forms of subordinate legislation. All such instruments were formerly included in this title, but they have subsequently become spent either owing to the passage of time or (*eg*, in the case of instruments governing the Gas Council, Area Boards, and the Consultative Council) to the operation (discussed briefly *infra*) of the Gas Act 1972.

Reorganisation of gas industry   The Gas Act 1972, Halsbury's Statutes, 4th edn Vol 19, title Gas (3rd edn Vol 42, p 466 *et seq*), which repealed and replaced the Gas Act 1948, created a new structure for the gas industry in place of that established by the Act of 1948. The major change introduced was that, as from 1 January 1973 (*ie*, the day appointed for the purposes of the Gas Act 1972 by SI 1972/1440, listed at p 1, *ante*), responsibility for supplying gas passed from the Area Boards to the British Gas Corporation (*ie*, the body formerly known as the Gas Council). As from that date the Area Boards were dissolved and all their property, rights and obligations became vested in the Corporation. The Act also established consumers' bodies (namely the National Gas Consumers' Council and Regional Gas Consumers' Councils) to replace the former Area Gas Consultative Councils. For regulations relating to the Corporation, see the British Gas Corporation Regulations 1972, SI 1972/1879, p 25, *post*, and the Gas (Financial Year) Regulations

1972, SI 1972/1737, p 21, *post;* and with regard to the Gas Consumers' Councils, see SI 1972/1765, p 21, *post.*

The framework of the new structure created by the Gas Act 1972 is the sole concern of Part 1 of the Act; the other Parts re-enact, in conformity with that structure, provisions which had been contained in corresponding Parts of the Gas Act 1948. The gas supply code, formerly contained in Schedule 3 to the Gas Act 1948, is now re-enacted in Schedule 4 to the Gas Act 1972.

On 10 December 1985 the Gas Bill reached its second reading in the House of Commons. This measure, which is due to become law in the autumn of 1986, will effect the complete privatisation of the British Gas Corporation.

Gas charges and quality   Prior to nationalisation, statutory undertakers only were authorised to charge for gas according to the number of therms supplied, and other undertakers charged according to volume (*ie,* per cubic foot) or by some other method. By s 53 of the Act of 1948 (repealed) the thermal method was, in general, made compulsory for all Area Boards; and under s 25 (1) of the Gas Act 1972, Halsbury's Statutes, 4th edn Vol 19, title Gas (3rd edn Vol 42, p 488) (replacing s 53 of the 1948 Act) the method is now compulsory in repect of gas supplied by the British Gas Corporation (but see s 25 (7) of the 1972 Act). The method of calculating the number of therms supplied is prescribed by the Gas (Declaration of Calorific Value) Regulations 1972, SI 1972/1878, as amended, p 23, *post,* that number being calculated on the basis of the calorific value of the gas declared by the Corporation in accordance with those regulations.

The Gas Quality Regulations 1972, SI 1972/1804, as amended, p 22, *post,* and the Gas Quality Regulations 1983, SI 1983/363, p 27, *post,* prescribe (in pursuance of the Gas Act 1972, s 29B, which was inserted by the Oil and Gas (Enterprise) Act 1982, s 13, Halsbury's Statutes, 4th edn Vol 19, title Gas (3rd edn Vol 52, p 834)) standards of pressure, purity and uniformity of calorific value to be complied with by the Corporation and by persons other than the Corporation. By s 29B (3) of the Act the Secretary of State must appoint examiners to carry out tests of gas supplied through pipes. The Gas (Testing) Regulations 1949, SI 1949/789, p 7, *post,* prescribe the testing places and provide for the publication of the results of tests.

Gas Meters   The British Gas Corporation can require every consumer to take his supply through a meter, which is *prima facie* evidence of the amount supplied; see paras 7 and 10 of Schedule 4 to the Gas Act 1972, Halsbury's Statutes, 4th edn Vol 19, title Gas (3rd edn Vol 42, pp 523, 525). As from 1 January 1973 no meter may be used for the purpose of ascertaining the quantity of gas supplied unless stamped by a meter examiner in accordance with s 30 of the Act; but meters duly stamped under the enactments in force before that date are, however, deemed to be stamped under the section (para 15 (3) of Schedule 7). The standards with which a meter must conform to qualify for stamping are prescribed by the Gas (Meters) Regulations 1983, SI 1983/684, as amended, p 28, *post,* which also provide for the re-examination of meters whose accuracy is disputed and specify the fees for the examination or re-examination of a meter.

Safety regulations   Regulations may be made under s 31 of the Gas Act 1972, Halsbury's Statutes, 4th edn Vol 19, title Gas (3rd edn Vol 42, p 494), to secure the protection of the public from personal injury, fire, explosion or other dangers arising from the distribution or use of gas, see the Gas Safety Regulations 1972, SI 1972/1178, p 16, *post,* and the Gas Safety (Installation and Use) Regulations 1984, SI 1984/1358, p 37, *post.* These regulations are supplemented by the Gas Safety (Rights of Entry) Regulations 1983, SI 1983/1575, p 34, *post.*

Pensions and staff compensation   Responsibility for the establishment and maintenance of pension schemes for persons who are, or have been, employed in the gas industry now lies with the British Gas Corporation under s 36 of the Gas Act 1972, Halsbury's Statutes, 4th edn Vol 19, title Gas (3rd edn Vol 42, p 498); but by virtue of s 36 (3) and (4) old schemes (*ie*, schemes subsisting before 1 January 1973) are continued in force. See accordingly the Gas (Pension Scheme) Regulations 1949, SI 1949/744, as amended, *infra*, made under s 58 (repealed) of the Gas Act 1948, which empowered Area Boards and the Gas Council to establish pension schemes. The Gas (Pension Rights) Regulations 1950, SI 1950/1206, as amended, p 10, *post*, made under the same section, provide for the preservation of pension rights under schemes established by the transferred undertakers; by further regulations under s 58 of the 1948 Act, *viz*, SI 1961/816, 1964/328, 1968/415, 1972/630, and 1980/1782, as amended by 1981/1611, all listed at pp 1, 2 *ante*, provision has been made for the winding up of certain of such pension schemes. In connection with the operation of the graduated national insurance pension scheme (now wound up), certain gas superannuation schemes were modified by SI 1961/307, p 11, *post*.

Officers of the transferred undertakings, including the gas and coke associations transferred under s 62 of the 1948 Act, who lost employment or suffered loss or diminution of emoluments or pension rights as a result of nationalisation became entitled to compensation in accordance with the Gas (Staff Compensation) Regulations 1949, SI 1949/2289, as amended, p 10, *post*.

THE GAS (PENSION SCHEME) REGULATIONS 1949
SI 1949/744

NOTES
Authority These regulations were made on 13 April 1949 by the Minister of Fuel and Power under s 58 of the Gas Act 1948 (repealed) and all other enabling powers. They are continued in force by s 36 (3) of the Gas Act 1972, Halsbury's Statutes, 4th edn Vol 19, title Gas (3rd edn Vol 42, p 498), subject to any regulations which may be made by the Secretary of State under sub-s (4) of that section.
Commencement   23 April 1949.
Amendment The regulations have been amended by the Gas (Pension Scheme) (Amendment) Regulations 1950, SI 1950/742, with retroactive effect from 23 April 1949, and by the Gas (Pension) (Amendment) Regulations 1953, SI 1953/1525, the Gas (Pension Scheme) (Amendment) Regulations 1958, SI 1958/847 and the Gas (Pension Schemes) Regulations 1971, SI 1971/915.
General   These regulations, as amended, enabled any Area Board or the Gas Council for the purposes of s 58 (1) (*a*) of the Gas Act 1948 (repealed) to establish and administer any pension scheme or participate in any such scheme established by another of those bodies, or participate in pension schemes other than those established by the Boards or Council. Responsibility for the establishment and maintenance of pension schemes for persons who are, or have been, employed in the gas industry now lies with the British Gas Corporation under s 36 of the Gas Act 1972, Halsbury's Statutes, 4th edn Vol 19, title Gas (3rd edn Vol 42, p 498) but, by virtue of sub-s (3) of that section, old schemes (*ie*, schemes subsisting before 1 January 1973) are continued in force subject to any regulations which may be made by the Secretary of State.

Rights under pension schemes established by transferred undertakings have been preserved by the Gas (Pension Rights) Regulations 1950, SI 1950/1206, p 10, *post*. By reg 9 thereof nothing in those regulations is to prevent a person transferring, on such terms and conditions as may be agreed, to a scheme under these regulations.

THE GAS (STOCK) REGULATIONS 1949
SI 1949/751

NOTES
Authority   These regulations were made on 14 April 1949 by the Minister of Fuel and Power, with the approval of the Treasury, under s 43(2) of the Gas Act 1948 (repealed) and all other enabling powers. They continue to have effect as if made under s 21 (2) of the Gas Act 1972, Halsbury's Statutes, 4th edn Vol 19, title Gas (3rd edn Vol 42, p 484), by virtue of s 49 (2) of, and para 7 of Part II of Schedule 7 to, that Act.
Commencement   30 April 1949.
Amendment   These regulations have been amended by the Gas (Stock) (Amendment) Regulations 1959, SI 1959/807, the Gas (Stock) (Amendment) Regulations 1981, SI 1981/1764, and the Gas (Stock) (Amendment) Regulations 1985, SI 1985/1149 and by s 1 (3) of, and Part II of Schedule 1 to, the Family Law Reform Act 1969, Halsbury's Statutes, 4th edn Vol 6, title Children.
General   These regulations, as amended, govern the issue, redemption, transfer and management of British Gas Stock created by the Gas Council under s 43 of the Gas Act 1948 and (by virtue of s 49 (2) of, and para 7 of Part II of Schedule 7 to, the Gas Act 1972) by the British Gas

Corporation under s 21 of the Gas Act 1972, Halsbury's Statutes, 4th edn Vol 19, title Gas (3rd edn Vol 42, p 484).

In the regulations references to the British Gas Corporation are substituted for references to the Gas Council by s 49 (1) of, and para 19 of Part II of Schedule 6 to, the Gas Act 1972.

Summary *Issue and redemption* Stock is required to be created by, and issued pursuant to, resolutions of the Corporation and is to be redeemable. Redemption Fund Accounts are to be established to which sums are to be carried each year, and from these accounts sums are to be applied in redeeming stock according to the terms of its issue. There is provision for increasing annual payments to an account if it is likely to prove insufficient for redemption or if the Corporation desire to accelerate redemption. Sums standing to the credit of a redemption fund account may, in so far as they are not required to be applied in redemption, be applied in purchasing the stock to which fund relates, and when this is done consequential adjustments are to be made. The amount of any unclaimed stock is to be invested after three years from the date of redemption, and if still unclaimed after a further three years may be applied as the Secretary of State (*ie* the successor of the Minister of Fuel and Power referred to in the regulations) and the Treasury may approve, without prejudice to the rights of any person to recover that amount. A balance may be struck for the payment of interest on any day not more than thirty-seven days before the interest is payable; the person who is entered in the register on that day is entitled to the interest as against a transferee of the stock.

Registration and transfer The British Gas Corporation are to appoint a registrar who is to keep a register for each class of stock. The name and address of each holder from time to time and the amount of stock held by him are to be entered in the register, and proper entries therein are to be *prima facie* evidence. Each holder of stock is entitled to a stock certificate, which is *prima facie* evidence of title, and there is provision for replacing certificates that are worn out, damaged or lost. Stock is transferable by instrument in writing in any usual form executed by all parties; the transfer and stock certificate is to be delivered to, and may be retained by, the registrar. The Bank of England and the Stock Exchange have now established a computer-based system, known as the CGO Service, to facilitate the transfer of gilt-edged securities and by virtue of amendments made to these regulations by SI 1985/1149, listed *ante*, a CGO Service Member is allowed to transfer Gas Stock through that service. Such a transfer will be effective under the Stock Transfer Act 1982, s 1(2), Halsbury's Statutes, 4th edn Vol 30, title Money (Pt 1) (3rd edn Vol 52, p 1109) without the need for an instrument in writing. On the death of the holder stock standing in a register is transferable by his personal representative and the production of the grant of probate or letters of administration is to be accepted as sufficient evidence of the grant. A confirmation as executor may be accepted although not re-sealed in England.

A trustee holder may be described in a stock register as a trustee or as a trustee of a specified trust, but otherwise no notice of a trust may be entered in a register. Official descriptions may be entered in a register, and the holder of the office for the time being may then transfer the stock.

Payment Interest accounts are to be established, and interest is to be paid by warrants sent through the post to the stockholder's registered address, or, in the case of joint holders, to the address of the one whose name stands first on the stock register, or to such person and address as the holder or holders direct in writing. Redemption moneys are to be similarly paid. The due posting of a warrant is to be a good discharge to the Corporation and the registrar. Uncashed warrants that are defaced, lost or destroyed may be replaced by fresh warrants on application; any interest unclaimed for six years may be applied to such purpose as the Corporation think fit, without prejudice to the rights of any person to recover it.

Fees and miscellaneous The Corporation may make payment to the registrar of a fee, not exceeding 12½p, a condition of the registration of any transfer, probate or other document. The Forged Transfers Act 1891, s 1, as amended, Halsbury's Statutes, 4th edn Vol 30, title Money (Pt 1) (3rd edn Vol 5, p 99), is applied to the Corporation in relation to the stock. Stockholders are relieved from the need to inquire as to the regularity of the Corporation's proceedings or to see to the application of the money raised.

The Corporation and the registrar are deemed to be bankers within the meaning of the Bankers' Books Evidence Act 1879, Halsbury's Statutes, 4th edn Vol 17, title Evidence.

THE GAS (TESTING) REGULATIONS 1949
SI 1949/789

NOTES
Authority These regulations were made on 22 April 1949 by the Minister of Fuel and Power under s 55 of the Gas Act 1948 (repealed) and all other enabling powers. They, subsequently had effect, by virtue of the Gas Act 1972, s 49(2), Sch 7, Pt III, para 13(2), as if made under s 26(3) of that Act (repealed). Now, by virtue of the Interpretation Act 1978, s 17(2)(*b*), in the title Statutory Instruments, Vol 1, of this work, these regulations have effect as if made under the Gas Act 1972, s 29B(4), as inserted by the Oil and Gas (Enterprise) Act 1982, s 13(1), Halsbury's Statutes, 4th edn Vol 19, title Gas (3rd edn Vol 52, p 834).
Commencement 1 May 1949; see reg 6.
Amendment These regulations have been amended by the Gas Quality Regulations 1983, SI 1983/363, p 27, *post*.
Penalties The penalty for contravention of regs 1(2), 2, 3 and 3A of these regulations is prescribed by the Gas Quality Regulations 1983, SI 1983/363, reg 9, p 27, *post*.
Interpretation See reg 5 and notes thereto. References in the regulations to Area Boards must now be construed as references to the British Gas Corporation by virtue of s 49 (1) of, and para

19 of Part II of Schedule 6 to, the Gas Act 1972, Halsbury's Statutes, 4th edn Vol 19, title Gas (3rd edn Vol 42, pp 509, 546).

General Under these regulations tests are made by gas examiners to ascertain whether gas supplied by the British Gas Corporation is of the declared calorific value and conforms with the standards of quality prescribed by the Secretary of State. See, further, the Preliminary Note under the head "Gas charges and quality", p 5, *ante*.

1. Testing places (1) The places at which tests of the gas supplied by [any person supplying gas through pipes] for the purpose of ascertaining whether it conforms with the standards prescribed under section fifty-five of the Act are to be made by a person appointed by the Minister under subsection (2) of that section (in these regulations referred to as a "gas examiner") shall be those specified in directions given by the Minister.

(2) [Any person supplying gas through pipes] shall provide such premises, apparatus and equipment for the purpose of carrying out such tests as aforesaid as may be specified in directions given by the Minister, and shall maintain the same to the satisfaction of the Minister.

(3) Until it is otherwise provided by directions given under the foregoing paragraphs, the places at which tests are to be made of gas supplied by an Area Board and the premises, apparatus and equipment to be provided and maintained by an Area Board shall be the places, premises, apparatus and equipment prescribed by provisions in force immediately before the vesting date in relation to each undertaker whose property, rights, liabilities and obligations are vested in that Area Board.

NOTES
Amendment The words "Any person supplying gas through pipes" printed between square brackets in paras (1) and (2) were substituted by the Gas Quality Regulations 1983, SI 1983/363, p 27, *post*.
Standards prescribed *Ie*, the standards which are now prescribed by the Gas Quality Regulations 1972, SI 1972/1804, as amended, p 22, *post*, and the Gas Quality Regulations 1983, SI 1983/363, p 27, *post*.
Vesting date *Ie*, 1 May 1949 (Gas (Vesting Date) Order 1949, SI 1949/392).
Person appointed under s 55 (2) of the Act Any appointment having effect immediately before 1 January 1973 under and for the purposes of s 55 (2) of the Gas Act 1948 took effect as from that day as if made under and for the purposes of s 26 (2) of the Gas Act 1972 which is itself now repealed. All appointments now take effect as if made under s 29B (3) of the 1972 Act which was inserted by the Oil and Gas (Enterprise) Act 1982, s 13 (1), Halsbury's Statutes, 4th edn Vol 19, title Gas (3rd edn Vol 52, p 834).

2. Presence of . . . representatives at tests On any occasion on which a gas examiner tests the gas supplied by [any person supplying gas through pipes], a representative of [that person] may be present but he shall not interfere in any way with any test. The gas examiner shall, where the testing place is situated elsewhere than at the gasworks, give [any person supplying gas through pipes] reasonable notice of the time at which he will attend at the testing place.

NOTES
Amendment The words printed between square brackets in this regulation were substituted by the Gas Quality Regulations 1983, SI 1983/363, p 27, *post*. The words omitted where indicated in the heading to the regulation formerly referred to Area Boards and by virtue of the Gas Act 1972, s 49 (1) and Sch 6, Part II, para 19, Halsbury's Statutes, 4th edn Vol 19, title Gas (3rd edn Vol 42, pp 509, 546) this reference was to be construed as a reference to the British Gas Corporation. SI 1983/363 did not specifically alter this reference but the changes made to the text of the regulation have now rendered the reference otiose.

3. Publication of results of tests The Minister will, in respect of the tests of gas supplied by an Area Board in any part of the area supplied by them during any quarter, send to that Board, and to the Consultative Council for the area of that Board, a quarterly statement relating to the tests carried out in that part during that quarter, and that Board shall—

(*a*) cause the quarterly statement last issued relating to any such part as aforesaid to be made available to the public by exhibiting a copy thereof in a prominent position at each of their offices and showrooms within that part, and shall forward a copy to any consumer in that part of the area at his request; and

(b) cause the following notification to be printed on each consumer's gas account rendered after the issue of the first quarterly statement

"*Gas Act, 1948*

Regulations under the above Act require an Area Board to send to any consumer at his request a copy of a statement issued by [the Minister of Power] relating to the tests of the gas supplied to the consumer during the preceding quarter".

NOTES
Amendment As to the words "the Minister of Power", printed between square brackets, see note "The Minister" to reg 5, p 10, *post*.
Consultative Council These councils were formerly established under s 9 (repealed) of the Gas Act 1948.
Gas Act 1948 Repealed and replaced by the Gas Act 1972, Halsbury's Statutes, 4th edn Vol 19, title Gas (3rd edn Vol 42, p 466, *et seq*).

[3A. Publication of results of test—private suppliers The Secretary of State will, in respect of tests of gas supplied through pipes during any quarter by any person other than the British Gas Corporation carried out in the area of a Regional Gas Consumer's Council, send to the supplier and to the Council a quarterly statement relating to these tests, and the supplier shall—

(a) cause the quarterly statement to be made available to the public by exhibiting a copy thereof in a prominent position at each of their offices in the area and shall forward a copy to any owner or occupier of premises so supplied in the area at his request; and

(b) cause the following notification to be printed on each such owner or occupier's gas account rendered after the issue of the first quarterly statement:—

"*Gas Act 1972*

Regulations under the above require a supplier of gas to send to any owner or occupier of premises supplied at his request a copy of a statement issued by the Secretary of State relating to the tests of the gas supplied to such owner or occupier during the preceding quarter."]

NOTES
Amendment This regulation was inserted by the Gas Quality Regulations 1983, SI 1983/363, p 27, *post*.
Gas Act 1972 Halsbury's Statutes, 4th edn Vol 19, title Gas (3rd edn Vol 42, p 466 *et seq*).

4. Powers of entry Any gas examiner and, if duly authorised in writing for the purpose, any other officer of [the Ministry of Power] may enter on any premises of [any person supplying gas through pipes] for the purposes of section fifty-five of the Act.

NOTES
General Section 55 (4) (e) of the Gas Act 1948 was replaced by s 26 (3) (e) of the Gas Act 1972 which enacted that regulations could provide for conferring powers of entry on property of the British Gas Corporation for the purpose of deciding where tests are to be carried out and otherwise for the purpose of that section. The Gas Act 1972, s 26 was repealed by the Oil and Gas (Enterprise) Act 1982, ss 13 (2) and 37, and Sch 4, Halsbury's Statutes, 4th edn Vol 19, title Gas (3rd edn Vol 52, pp 834, 1082, 1101) and superseded by *ibid*, s 13 (1) which inserts a new s 29B in the 1972 Act. Accordingly the relevant law is now to be found in the Gas Act 1972, s 29B (4)(e), Halsbury's Statutes, 4th edn Vol 19, title Gas (3rd edn Vol 52, p 834) which states that regulations may provide for conferring powers of entry on property of persons supplying gas through pipes for the purpose of deciding where tests are to be carried out and otherwise for the purposes of that section.
Amendment The words "Any person supplying gas through pipes" printed between square brackets were substituted by the Gas Quality Regulations 1983, SI 1983/363, p 27, *post*. As to the words "the Ministry of Power" printed between square brackets see the note "The Minister" to reg 5, p 10, *post*.

5. Interpretation   (1) In these regulations the following expressions have the meanings hereby assigned to them respectively, that is to say:—

"the Act" means the Gas Act 1948;

"gas examiner" has the meaning assigned by paragraph (1) of regulation one;

"quarter" means the period of three months in any year beginning on the first day of January, the first day of April, the first day of July or the first day of October;

"the Minister" means [the Minister of Power].

(2) Expressions to which meanings are assigned by the Act or by these regulations shall, unless the context otherwise require, bear the same meanings in any instrument issued under the provisions of these regulations.

(3) The Interpretation Act, 1889, shall apply to the interpretation of these regulations as it applies to the interpretation of an Act of Parliament.

NOTES

The Minister   The words "the Minister of Power", printed between square brackets, were substituted for the words "the Minister of Fuel and Power" by SI 1957/48 in the title Constitutional Law (Part 5). They are now to be construed as referring to the Secretary of State (for Energy); see the Preliminary Note under the head "Transfer of ministerial functions", p 4, *ante*.

Gas Act 1948   Repealed and replaced by the Gas Act 1972, Halsbury's Statutes, 4th edn Vol 19, title Gas (3rd edn Vol 42, p 466 *et seq*).

Interpretation Act 1889   Repealed and replaced by the Interpretation Act 1978, printed in the title Statutory Instruments, Vol 1 of this work.

6. Commencement of citation   These regulations shall come into operation on the first day of May, nineteen hundred and forty-nine, and may be cited as the Gas (Testing) Regulations, 1949.

THE GAS (STAFF COMPENSATION) REGULATIONS 1949
SI 1949/2289

NOTES

Authority   These regulations were made on 8 December 1949 by the Minister of Fuel and Power under ss 60 and 62 of the Gas Act 1948 (repealed), and all other enabling powers. They continue to have effect by virtue of s 49 (2) of, and para. 21 of Part IV of Schedule 7 to, the Gas Act 1972, Halsbury's Statutes, 4th edn Vol 19, title Gas (3rd edn Vol 42, pp 510, 553).

Commencement   19 December 1949.

Amendment   These regulations have been amended by the Gas (Staff Compensation) (Amendment) Regulations 1951, SI 1951/1327 and modified by the Redundancy Payments Act 1965, s 44 (1), Sch 7 (repealed and replaced by the Employment Protection (Consolidation) Act 1978, s 130 (1), Sch 10).

Construction   Regulations in force immediately before 1 January 1973 and then applicable to the Gas Council or an Area Board have effect, as from 1 January 1973, as if for references to the Council or Board there were substituted references to the British Gas Corporation; see para 19 of Part II of Schedule 6 to the Gas Act 1972, Halsbury's Statutes, 4th edn Vol 19, title Gas (3rd edn Vol 42, p 546).

General   These regulations, as amended, required Area Boards and the Gas Coucil to pay compensation for loss of employment, loss or diminution of emoluments or pension rights consequent upon certain events. These events were the vesting by virtue of the Gas Act 1948 of the property, etc, of the former undertakers (a term defined for the purposes of the regulations to include the gas and coke associations), or the subsequent transfer of that property from one Area Board to another or from the Gas Council to an Area Board, or its subsequent disposal, or anything done under s 59 of the Act (which provided, *inter alia*, for modifying and winding up co-partnership schemes), occurring not later than 1 May 1959. The persons entitled to compensation are persons who after attaining the age of eighteen were continuously employed for at least eight years immediately preceding 1 May 1949 by one or more of the undertakers, or employed whole-time for the purpose of administering the transferred undertakings.

The regulations, by their nature, must now be obsolescent; and it appears from the Reports of the Minister of Fuel and Power for the years ended 31 March 1950 and 1951 that very few claims for compensation under the regulations were even then being made. Compensation payable could be immediate or substantive or residual.

THE GAS (PENSION RIGHTS) REGULATIONS 1950
SI 1950/1206

NOTES

Authority   These regulations were made on 21 July 1950 by the Minister of Fuel and Power under ss 58 and 62 of the Gas Act 1948 (repealed), and all other enabling powers. They are

continued in force by s 36 (3) of the Gas Act 1972, Halsbury's Statutes, 4th edn Vol 19, title Gas (3rd edn Vol 42, p 498), subject to any regulations which may be made by the Secretary of State under sub-s (4) of that section.
Commencement   1 September 1950. The regulations, however, have retroactive effect from the vesting date (1 May 1949; Gas (Vesting Date) Order 1949, SI 1949/392) or, as respects certain persons, from the date of the passing of the Gas Act 1948 (30 July 1948).
Amendment   These regulations have been amended by the Gas (Pension Rights) (Amendment) Regulations 1951, SI 1951/383, the Gas (Pension) (Amendment) Regulations 1953, SI 1953/1525 and the Gas (Pension Schemes) Regulations 1971, SI 1971/915 and modified by the Redundancy Payments Act 1965, s 44(1), Sch 7 (repealed and replaced by the Employment Protection (Consolidation) Act 1978, s 130 (1), Sch 10).
Construction   As to adaptation of references to the Gas Council and Area Boards, see the note, "Construction" to SI 1949/2289, p 5, *ante.*
General   These regulations, as amended, contain provisions as to the rights under existing pension schemes of employees of gas undertakings and gas and coke associations who by virtue of the Gas Act 1948 became employees of an Area Board or the Gas Council on the vesting date (1 May 1949) or who voluntarily entered such employment before that date. Schemes which are confined to employees of the transferred undertakings and associations are required to be continued in force by the appropriate Board or the Council subject to certain modifications, but, except in certain cases, no new members may be admitted. The modifications include provision entitling a member of a scheme (other than a scheme operated by insurance) to transfer to a scheme maintained under the Gas (Pension Scheme) Regulations 1949, SI 1949/744, p 6, *ante,* and, in the case of a scheme formerly connected with a co-partnership scheme, for the separation of the two schemes. A member of a transferred scheme who has left employment with a Board for employment with another Board or with the Council, or who has left employment with the Council for employment with a Board, may in each case transfer to the pension scheme established by the Board or Council employing him.
　With certain exceptions schemes not confined to such employees as aforesaid, including schemes involving local government funds, are to be divided. Such schemes cease to be applicable to transferred employees, but the Board or Council concerned is required to provide benefits corresponding to those which would have been provided under the schemes, and is entitled to receive a proportionate part of the assets. The excepted schemes are continued in force subject to a modification making eligibility for membership or benefits dependent upon gas board employment.
　The regulations also contain provisions enabling a member of a Board or the Council to reckon his service as service in their employment for pension purposes, and provide for the determination of questions arising under the regulations. Nothing in the regulations is to prevent a person transferring on such terms and conditions as may be agreed to a scheme approved under the Gas (Pension Scheme) Regulations 1949, SI 1949/744, p 6, *ante.*
　Former employees of gas undertakings and gas and coke associations who lost their pension rights as a result of nationalisation became entitled to compensation under the Gas (Staff Compensation) Regulations 1949, SI 1949/2289, p 10, *ante.*
Winding-up of transferred schemes.   Provision for the winding-up of specified transferred schemes has been made by SI 1961/816, 1964/328, 1968/415, 1972/630, and 1980/1782, as amended. The instruments are listed *ante,* and have effect under Gas Act 1972, s 36.

THE NATIONAL INSURANCE (MODIFICATION OF GAS SUPERANNUATION SCHEMES) REGULATIONS 1961
SI 1961/307

NOTES
Authority   These regulations were made on 21 February 1961 by the Minister of Power under s 69 (4) (repealed) of the National Insurance Act 1946, as extended by s 15 of the National Insurance Act 1959 (repealed). They subsequently took effect under s 110 of the National Insurance Act 1965 (now also repealed). As to their further operation, see below.
Commencement   3 April 1961.
General   These regulations modified certain gas superannuation schemes in connection with the operation of the graduated national insurance pension scheme, which was introduced by the National Insurance Act 1959 (repealed) and continued under the National Insurance Act 1965. The graduated pension scheme was discontinued, and the relevant provisions of the Act of 1965 were repealed, as from 6 April 1975 by the Social Security Act 1973, Halsbury's Statutes, 4th edn Vol 40, title Social Security (3rd edn Vol 43, p 866 *et seq*). The effect of the repealed provisions, and of these regulations, is, however, temporarily preserved for transitional purposes by the National Insurance (Non-participation—Transitional Provisions) Regulations 1974, SI 1974/2057, in the title National Insurance (Part 1).

THE GAS (UNDERGROUND STORAGE) (INQUIRIES PROCEDURE) RULES 1966
SI 1966/1375

NOTES
Authority   These rules were made on 3 November 1966 by the Lord Chancellor under s 7A of the Tribunals and Inquiries Act 1958 (repealed); they now have effect under s 11 of the Tribunals

and Inquiries Act 1971, Halsbury's Statutes, 4th edn Vol 10, title Constitutional Law (Pt 4), by virtue of s 18 (3) of that Act.
Commencement   1 December 1966; see r 1.
Interpretation   See r 3; and for construction of references to "the Minister", see the note "The Minister" thereto. The expression "the Act" is defined in r 2.

1. Citation and Commencement   These Rules may be cited as the Gas (Underground Storage) (Inquiries Procedure) Rules 1966, and shall come into operation on the 1st December 1966.

2. Application of Rules   These Rules apply to public local inquiries held by the Minister of Power in accordance with paragraph 8 of Schedule 2 to the Gas Act 1965 (hereinafter referred to as "the Act") for the purpose of inquiring into applications by gas authorities for orders authorising the storage of gas underground and (subject to the modifications set out in rule 13) to public local inquiries held in accordance with paragraph 12 of that Schedule.

NOTES
Minister of Power   See note "The Minister" to r 3.
Gas authorities   The reference must now be construed as a reference to the British Gas Corporation; see para 14 (1) of Schedule 6 to the Gas Act 1972, Halsbury's Statutes, 4th edn Vol 19, title Gas (3rd edn Vol 42, p 545).
Paras 8 and 12 of Schedule 2 to the Gas Act 1965   Halsbury's Statutes, 4th edn Vol 19, title Gas (3rd edn Vol 14, pp 982, 983). Consequential amendments to paras 8 and 12 have been made by para 14(12) of Schedule 6 to the Gas Act 1972.

3. Interpretation   (1) The Interpretation Act 1889 shall apply to the interpretation of these Rules as it applies to the interpretation of an Act of Parliament.
(2) Unless the context otherwise requires, expressions used in these Rules shall have the same meanings as in the Act.
(3) In these Rules—
"application" means an application made to the Minister for a storage authorisation order under paragraph 6 of Schedule 2 to the Act;
"applicants" means the gas authority making the application;
"appointed person" means the the person appointed by the Minister to hold the inquiry;
"inquiry" means a public local inquiry to which these Rules apply;
"the Minister" means the Minister of Power;
"statutory objector" means any person who, being entitled to be served with a notice of the application, has duly objected thereto in accordance with paragraph 7 of Schedule 2 to the Act and whose objection has not been withdrawn or disregarded in accordance with paragraph 8 of that Schedule.

NOTES
The Minister   References in these rules to "the Minister" must now be construed as references to the Secretary of State (for Energy); see the Preliminary Note under the head "Transfer of ministerial functions", p 4, *ante*.
Interpretation Act 1889   Repealed and replaced by the Interpretation Act 1978, printed in the title Statutory Instruments, Vol 1 of this work.
Paragraphs 6 to 8 of Schedule 2 to the Act   Halsbury's Statutes, 4th edn Vol 19, title Gas (3rd edn Vol 14, pp 981, 982).

4. Procedure before Inquiry   (1) The Minister shall as soon as may be notify the applicants of the substance of each objection received by him from a statutory objector and, so far as practicable, shall also notify the applicants of the substance of other objections.
(2) A date, time and place for the holding of the inquiry shall be fixed and may be varied by the Minister, who shall give not less than 42 days' notice in writing of such date, time and place to the applicants and to every statutory objector at the address furnished to the Minister:
Provided that—

    (i) with the consent in writing of the statutory objectors and of the applicants, the Minister may give such lesser period of notice as shall be agreed with the statutory objectors and the applicants and in that event he may specify a date for service of the statement referred to in paragraph (1) of rule 5 later than the date therein prescribed;

    (ii) where it becomes necessary or advisable to vary the time or place fixed for the inquiry, the Minister shall give such notice of the variation as may appear to him to be reasonable in the circumstances.

(3) The Minister may require the applicants—

(*a*) to publish in one or more newspapers circulating in the locality or localities in which the storage and protective areas are, such notices of the inquiry as he may direct;

(*b*) to serve notice of the inquiry in such form and on such persons or classes of persons as he may specify;

(*c*) to give such other notices of the inquiry as he may direct.

5. Statement to be served before Inquiry   (1) As soon as may be after receiving notification of the substance of the objections of statutory objectors and in any event (except where the Minister specifics a later date under proviso (i) to paragraph (2) of rule 4) not later than 28 days before the date of the inquiry, the applicants shall, unless they have already done so, serve on each statutory objector a written statement of the submissions that they propose to make at the inquiry and shall supply a copy of the statement to the Minister.

(2) Where a government department has expressed in writing to the applicants a view in support of the application and the applicants propose to rely on such expression of view in their submissions at the inquiry, they shall include it in the statement referred to in the last foregoing paragraph and shall send a copy of their statement to the government department concerned.

(3) Where the applicants intend to refer to or put in evidence at the inquiry documents (including maps and plans), their statement shall be accompanied by a list of such documents, together with a notice stating the times and place at which the documents may be inspected by any statutory objector; and the applicants shall afford every statutory objector a reasonable opportunity to inspect and, where practicable, take copies of the documents.

(4) The applicants shall afford any other person interested a reasonable opportunity to inspect and, where practicable, to take copies of their statement and of the other documents referred to in the last foregoing paragraph.

6. Appearances at Inquiry   (1) The applicants, statutory objectors and any persons on whom the Minister has required notice to be served under rule 4 (3) (*b*) shall be entitled to appear at the inquiry.

(2) Any other person may appear at the discretion of the appointed person.

(3) A body corporate may appear by its clerk or secretary or by any other officer appointed for the purpose by that body, or by counsel or solicitor; and any other person may appear on his own behalf or be represented by counsel, solicitor or any other person.

(4) Where there are two or more persons having a similar interest in the matter under inquiry, the appointed person may allow one or more persons to appear for the benefit of some or all persons so interested.

7. Representatives of Government Departments at Inquiry   (1) Where a government department has expressed in writing to the applicants a view in support of the application and the applicants have set out such a view in the statement referred to in paragraph (1) of rule 5, any statutory objector may, not later than 14 days before the date of the inquiry apply in writing to the

Minister for a representative of the government department concerned to be made available at the inquiry.

(2) The Minister shall transmit any application made to him under the last foregoing paragraph to the government department concerned, who shall make a representative of the department available to attend the inquiry.

(3) The said representative shall at the inquiry state the reasons for the view expressed by his department and shall give evidence and be subject to cross-examination to the same extent as other witnesses: Provided that the appointed person shall disallow any questions which in his opinion are directed to the merits of government policy.

8. Procedure at Inquiry   (1) Except as otherwise provided in these Rules, the procedure at the inquiry shall be such as the appointed person shall in his discretion determine.

(2) Unless in any particular case the appointed person with the consent of the applicants otherwise determines, the applicants shall begin and shall have the right of final reply; and the other persons entitled or permitted to appear shall be heard in such order as the appointed person may determine.

(3) The applicants and the statutory objectors shall be entitled to call evidence and cross-examine persons giving evidence, but any other person appearing at the inquiry may do so only to the extent permitted by the appointed person.

(4) The appointed person shall not require or permit the giving or production of any evidence, whether written or oral, which would be contrary to the public interest; but save as aforesaid and without prejudice to paragraph (3) of rule 7 any evidence may be admitted at the discretion of the appointed person, who may direct that documents tendered in evidence may be inspected by any person entitled or permitted to appear at the inquiry and that facilities be afforded him to take or obtain copies thereof.

(5) The appointed person may allow the applicants to alter or add to the submissions contained in the statement under paragraph (1) of rule 5 or to any list of documents which accompanied such statement, so far as may be necessary for the purpose of determining the questions in controversy between the parties, but shall (if necessary by adjourning the inquiry) give every statutory objector an adequate opportunity of considering any fresh submission or document; and the appointed person may make in his report a recommendation as to the payment of any additional cost occasioned by such an adjournment.

(6) If any person entitled to appear at the inquiry fails to do so, the appointed person may proceed with the inquiry at his discretion.

(7) The appointed person shall be entitled (subject to disclosure thereof at the inquiry) to take into account any written representations or statement received by him before the inquiry from any person.

(8) The appointed person may from time to time adjourn the inquiry and, if the date, time and place of the adjourned inquiry are announced before the adjournment, no further notice shall be required.

9. Site Inspections   (1) The appointed person may make unaccompanied inspections of the storage and protective areas before or during the inquiry without giving notice of his intention to the persons entitled to appear at the inquiry.

(2) The appointed person may, and shall if so requested by the applicants or any statutory objector before or during the inquiry, inspect the storage and protective areas or any part thereof after the close of the inquiry and, shall, in all cases where he intends to make such an inspection, announce during the inquiry the date and time at which he proposes to do so.

(3) The applicants and the statutory objectors shall be entitled to accompany the appointed person on any inspection after the close of the inquiry; but the

appointed person shall not be bound to defer his inspection if any person entitled to accompany him is not present at the time appointed.

10. Procedure after Inquiry   (1) The appointed person shall after the close of the inquiry make a report in writing to the Minister which shall include the appointed person's findings of fact and his recommendations, if any, or his reason for not making any recommendations.
(2) Where the Minister—
(*a*) differs from the appointed person on a finding of fact, or
(*b*) after the close of the inquiry takes into consideration any new evidence (including expert opinion on a matter of fact) or any new issue of fact (not being a matter of government policy) which was raised at the inquiry,
and by reason thereof is disposed to disagree with a recommendation made by the appointed person, he shall not come to a decision which is at variance with any such recommendation without first notifying the applicants and any statutory objector who appeared at the inquiry of his disagreement and the reasons for it and affording them an opportunity of making representations in writing within 21 days or (if the Minister has taken into consideration any new evidence or any new issue of fact, not being a matter of government policy) of asking within 21 days for the re-opening of the inquiry.
(3) The Minister may in any case if he thinks fit cause the inquiry to be re-opened, and shall cause it to be re-opened if asked to do so in accordance with the last foregoing paragraph; and, if the inquiry is re-opened, paragraphs (2) and (3) of rule 4 shall apply as they applied to the original inquiry, with the substitution in paragraph (2) of "28" for "42".
(4) In this rule "new evidence" includes any fact, information, or statement of opinion on a matter of fact which was taken into consideration by the Minister for the purposes of his decision upon the proposals submitted to him by the applicants in accordance with paragraph 3 to Schedule 2 to the Act and which was not disclosed at the inquiry in such a way as to give any person appearing at the enquiry an opportunity of dealing with it by way of cross-examination or otherwise.

11. Notification of Decision   (1) The Minister shall notify his decision, and his reasons therefor, in writing to the applicants, the statutory objectors and to any person who, having appeared at the inquiry, has asked to be notified of the decision; and, where a copy of the appointed person's report is not sent with the notification of the decision, the notification shall be ac-commmpanied by a summary of the appointed person's conclusion and recommendations.
(2) If any person entitled to be notified of the Minister's decision under the last foregoing paragraph has not received a copy of the appointed person's report, he shall be supplied with a copy thereof on written application made to the Minister within 28 days from the date of his decision.
(3) For the purposes of this rule "report" does not include documents, photographs or plans appended to the report.

12. Service of Notices by Post   Notices or documents required or authorised to be served or sent under the provisions of any of the foregoing Rules may be sent by post.

13. Inquiries held under Paragraph 12 of Schedule 2 of the Act   The following modifications shall be made in these Rules in their application to public local inquiries held in accordance with paragraph 12 of Schedule 2 to the Act, that is to say—
(1) "statutory objector" shall mean any person who, being entitled to be served with notice of the proposal to include additional land in the protective

area, has duly objected to that proposal and whose objection has not been withdrawn or disregarded in accordance with the said paragraph.

(2) The Minister shall not later than 28 days before the date of the inquiry (or such later date as he may specify under proviso (i) to paragraph (2) of rule (4) serve on each statutory objector a written statement of the reasons for the proposal to include additional land in the protective area.

(3) Any statutory objector may, not later than 14 days before the date of the inquiry, apply in writing to the Minister to make a representative of his department available at the inquiry; and on such application the Minister shall make a representative of his department available who shall at the inquiry answer questions in elucidation of the statement referred to in the last foregoing paragraph, not being questions which, in the opinion of the appointed person, are directed to the merits of government policy.

(4) Rule 9 shall apply to the additional land proposed to be included in the protective area as it applies to that area.

NOTES
Paragraph 12 of Schedule 2 to the Act   Halsbury's Statutes, 4th edn Vol 19, title Gas (3rd edn Vol 14, p 983).

THE GAS (UNDERGROUND STORAGE) (CERTIFICATES) (ENGLAND AND WALES) REGULATIONS 1967
SI 1967/1167

NOTES
Authority   These regulations were made on 26 July 1967 by the Minister of Power, the Minister of Housing and Local Government and the Secretary of State under para 7 of Schedule 3 to the Gas Act 1965, Halsbury's Statutes, 4th edn Vol 19, title Gas (3rd edn Vol 14, p 988) and all other enabling powers.
Commencement   1 September 1967.
General   These regulations govern the manner of making an application to the local planning authority under para 1 of Schedule 3 to the Gas Act 1965 for a certificate as respects planning permission; and the manner of making an application to the appropriate river authority under para 4 of that Schedule for a certificate as respects the grant of a statutory licence to abstract water. The regulations also govern procedure on appeal against certificates, and for obtaining information as to certificates.

THE GAS SAFETY REGULATIONS 1972
SI 1972/1178

NOTES
Authority   These regulations were made on 2 August 1972 by the Secretary of State under s 67 (repealed) of the Gas Act 1948; they now have effect under s 31 of the Gas Act 1972, as originally enacted, by virtue of s 49 (2), Sch 7, Pt III, para 16 of that Act. The said s 31 has now been substituted by the Oil and Gas (Enterprise) Act 1982, s 14, Halsbury's Statutes, 4th edn Vol 19, title Gas (3rd edn Vol 52, p 836).
Commencement   1 December 1972; see reg 1.
Amendment   These regulations are printed as amended by the Gas Safety (Rights of Entry) Regulations 1976, SI 1976/1882 (now revoked), the Gas (Metrication) Regulations 1980, SI 1980/1851, listed *ante*, and the Gas Safety (Installation and Use) Regulations 1984, SI 1984/1358, p 37, *post*.
Interpretation   See reg 2. References in the regulations to an Area Board must now be construed as references to the British Gas Corporation by virtue of s 49 (1) of, and para 19 of Part II of Schedule 6 to, the Gas Act 1972, Halsbury's Statutes, 4th edn Vol 19, title Gas (3rd edn Vol 42, pp 509, 546).
Penalties   See reg 8 of the Gas Safety (Rights of Entry) Regulations 1983, SI 1983/1575, p 34, *post*, as amended by the Gas Safety (Installation and Use) Regulations 1984, SI 1984/1358, p 37, *post*.

PART I
GENERAL

1. Citation and commencement   These regulations may be cited as the Gas Safety Regulations 1972 and shall come into operation on 1st December 1972.

2. Interpretation   (1) In these regulations—

"building regulations" means regulations under section 4 of the Public Health Act 1961;

"building standards regulations" has the same meaning as in section 3 (1) of the Building (Scotland) Act 1959;

"factory" has the same meaning as in the Factories Act 1961;

"gas appliance" means an appliance designed for use by consumers of gas to be used for lighting, heating, motive power or any other purpose for which gas can be used;

"governor" means a device for regulating the pressure of gas;

"heat input" means the gas consumption of an appliance expressed in terms of the quantity of heat supplied to the appliance in a specific time;

"installation pipe" means any pipe not being a service pipe for the use of gas on the premises of a consumer and includes any valve or cock inserted therein;

"meter bypass" means any pipes (including valves or cock inserted therein) through which a supply of gas may pass direct from a service pipe to an installation pipe without passing through a meter;

"meter control" means a valve or cock adjacent to and on the inlet side of a meter controlling the supply of gas from the Area Board to the consumer;

"meter governor" means an outlet pressure governor fitted between the meter control and the meter which is designed to operate at an inlet pressure [not exceeding 75 millibars];

"operating pressure" means the pressure of gas at which a gas appliance operates;

"outlet pressure governor" means a governor for automatic control of pressure of gas at a point on its outlet;

"pressure test point" means a fitting to which a pressure gauge can be connected;

"primary meter" means a meter connected to a service pipe, the index reading of which constitutes the basis of charge by the Area Board for gas used on the premises;

"purging" means the removal from a service pipe, meter or installation pipe or other gas fitting of all air and gas other than the gas to be supplied;

"secondary meter" means a meter which is not a primary meter;

"services" means pipes, drains, sewers, cables, conduits and electrical apparatus serving any premises;

"service governor" means an outlet pressure governor installed in a service pipe;

"service pipe" means the pipe between the gas main of the Area Board and a primary meter control for the use of gas on the premises of a consumer;

"service valve" means a valve or cock inserted in the service pipe outside a building for shutting off the supply of gas;

"sleeve" means a tubular case inserted in a prepared hole in a structure for the reception of a service pipe or installation pipe;

"temporary continuity bonding" means an electrical connection made to bridge a gap caused by the temporary absence of a continuous single gas pipe or any gas fitting to safeguard against the risk of fire, explosion or electric shock caused by contact with other services;

"thermal cut-off device" means a device designed to cut off automatically the flow of gas in the event of the temperature exceeding [95°C];

"venting" means the removal of gas from a service governor to the external air.

(2) References in these regulations to the supply of gas shall be construed as references to gas supplied by an Area Board to a consumer and references to the use of gas shall be construed as references to the use of gas so supplied.

(3) The Interpretation Act 1889 shall apply to the interpretation of these regulations as it applies to the interpretation of an Act of Parliament.

NOTES

Amendment   The words printed between square brackets in the definitions of "meter governor" and "thermal cut-off device" in para (1) were substituted by the Gas (Metrication) Regulations 1980, SI 1980/1851.

Building regulations   See now the Building Regulations 1985, SI 1985/1065, in the title Building and Engineering, which were made under the Building Act 1984, ss 1 (1), 3 (1) and 8 (2), and Sch 1, paras 1, 2, 7, 8, 10 and 11, Halsbury's Statutes, 4th edn Vol 35, title Public Health (3rd edn Vol 54 (2), pp 1332, 1334, 1338, 1441-1444).

Factory   For the meaning of the expression "factory" in the Factories Act 1961, see s 175 of that Act, Halsbury's Statutes, 4th edn Vol 19, title Health and Safety at Work (3rd edn Vol 13, p 562).

Interpretation Act 1889   Repealed and replaced by the Interpretation Act 1978, printed in the title Statutory Instruments, Vol 1 of this work.

PART II
INSTALLATION OF SERVICE PIPES

3. No person shall install a service pipe, service pipe fitting, service valve or service governor on any premises unless he is employed by an Area Board under a contract of service, a person approved in writing by an Area Board for the purpose or a person employed by such a person under a contract of service.

(2) Any person who installs a service pipe, service pipe fitting, service valve or service governor on any premises shall comply in so doing with the following provisions in this Part of these regulations.

(3) Where such a person carries out the installation in the performance of a contract of service his employer shall ensure that the following provisions in this Part of these regulations are duly complied with.

4.   (1) All service pipes, service pipe fittings, service valves and service governors installed shall be of good construction and sound material and of adequate strength and size to secure safety.

(2) All service pipes, service pipe fittings, service valves and service governors shall be installed and jointed in a sound and workmanlike manner and so as to be gastight.

5. Where—

(*a*) a service pipe is installed of internal diameter of 2 inches or more; or

(*b*) a service pipe is installed for the supply of gas to any premises where the nature of the premises or of any activity carried on or to be carried on upon the premises is such that the person who installs the service pipe knows or has reason to suspect that there is a special risk of personal injury, fire, explosion or other dangers arising from the use of gas; or

(*c*) a service pipe is installed which supplies more than one primary meter in a building,

a service value shall be fixed in the service pipe in a readily accessible position as near as practicable to the boundary of the premises through or to which the service pipe is laid and the position of the service valve shall be clearly indicated.

6. A service pipe shall not be installed in any position in which it cannot be used with safety having regard to the position of other nearby services and to such parts of the structure of any building through which it is laid as might affect its safe use.

7.   (1) No service pipe shall be installed in a cavity wall nor so as to pass through a cavity wall otherwise than by the shortest practicable route.

(2) Where a service pipe is installed so as to pass through any wall or is installed so as to pass through any floor of solid construction—

(*a*) the service pipe shall be enclosed in a sleeve; and

(*b*) the service pipe and sleeve shall be so constructed and installed as to prevent gas passing along the spaces between the pipe and the sleeve and between the sleeve and the wall or floor and so as to allow normal movement of the pipe.

(3) No service pipe shall be installed in an unventilated void space.

(4) No service pipe shall be installed under the foundations of a building or under the base of walls or footings.

8. All service pipes installed shall be constructed of material which is inherently resistant to corrosion or shall be protected against corrosion externally and, unless there is no risk of internal corrosion, internally.

9. No service pipe shall be connected to the gas main except by a suitable connector.

(2) Every service pipe installed shall be of such diameter as will permit it to be connected to the main without causing damage to the main.

10. All service pipes installed underground shall be installed in accordance with the following conditions—

(*a*) the pipes shall be bedded on firm ground throughout their length;

(*b*) the pipes shall be laid at such a depth as to ensure that there is no undue risk of accidental damage to the pipes or of damage by frost;

(*c*) the pipes shall not be laid in the same trench as other services unless the authorities responsible for those other services have first been consulted;

(*d*) where condensation of water is likely to occur the pipes shall be laid, where practicable, with a fall of at least one inch in ten feet from the meter to the gas main; and

(*e*) where condensation of water is likely to occur and such a fall is not practicable—

(i) a suitable vessel for the reception of any condensate which may form in any pipe shall be fixed to the pipe in a conspicuous and readily accessible position and means shall be provided for the removal of the condensate; and

(ii) a notice in permanent form to the effect that there is a vessel for the collection of condensate shall be fixed to the service pipe adjacent to the meter control.

11. All service pipes installed above ground shall be properly supported and so placed or protected as to ensure that there is no undue risk of accidental damage to the pipes.

12. No service pipe shall be installed in such a way as to impair the structure of any building nor so as to impair the fire resistance of any part of its structure.

13. Where both a service governor and a bypass to the governor are installed a governor shall be fitted on the bypass.

14. Where a service governor is installed and the pressure at which the gas will be supplied at the inlet of the governor [is not less than 75 millibars] a relief valve or seal and vent pipe of adequate size and capable of venting safely shall be installed in the outlet of the governor.

NOTES

Amendment   The words "is not less than 75 millibars" printed between square brackets in the regulation were substituted by the Gas (Metrication) Regulations 1980, SI 1980/1851, listed, *ante.*

15. A person who has installed a service governor shall forthwith after installation adequately seal the governor to prevent unauthorised persons interfering with it without breaking the seal.

16. A person who has installed a service pipe, service pipe fitting, service valve or service governor shall ensure—
  (*a*) that is it forthwith after installation adequately tested to verify that it is gastight and examined to verify that it has been installed in accordance with the foregoing provisions of this Part of these regulations;
  (*b*) that after such testing any necessary protective coating is applied to the joints of all service pipes installed;
  (*c*) that after complying with the provisions of sub-paragraphs (*a*) and (*b*) purging is carried out throughout every service pipe installed to the external air and throughout any gas fitting installed on a previous occasion through which gas could not flow at the time of installation; and
  (*d*) that immediately after such purging every service pipe which has been installed and is not to be put into immediate use is temporarily sealed off, capped or plugged at the meter control with the appropriate pipe fitting.

PARTS III-VI (**regs 17-48**) *(Revoked by the Gas Safety (Installation and Use) Regulations 1984, SI 1984/1358, p 37, post, and replaced by* Parts C-E *(regs 10-34) thereof).*

PART VII
REMOVAL, DISCONNECTION, ALTERATION, REPLACEMENT
AND MAINTENANCE OF GAS FITTINGS, ETC.

49. An electrical connection shall be maintained by means of temporary continuity bonding while a [service pipe or associated pipe fitting] is being removed or replaced until the work of disconnecting or connecting the [service pipe or associated pipe fitting], as the case may be, has been completed . . .

NOTES
Amendment   The words "service pipe or associated pipe fitting" printed between square brackets were substituted and the words omitted where indicated in this regulation were revoked by the Gas Safety (Installation and Use) Regulations 1984, SI 1984/1358, p 37, *post.*

50. A person who disconnects a [service pipe or associated pipe fitting] shall seal it off, cap it or plug it at every outlet of every pipe to which it is connected with the appropriate pipe fitting.

NOTES
Amendment   The words "service pipe or associated pipe fitting" printed between square brackets were substituted by the Gas Safety (Installation and Use) Regulations 1984, SI 1984/1358, p 37, *post.*

51. (1)   No alteration shall be made to a [service pipe or associated pipe fitting] (whether it has been installed before or after the date of coming into operation of these regulations) if as a result of such alteration there would have been a contravention of or failure to comply with any provision of [Part II] of these regulations if the [service pipe or associated pipe fitting] in question had been installed at the date of the alteration.
   (2) On every replacement of a [service pipe or associated pipe fitting] (whether it has been installed before or after the date of coming into operation of these regulations) the provisions of Part II . . . of these regulations shall apply to its replacement as they apply to its installation after the said date . . .
   (3) A person who makes any alteration to or replacement of a [service pipe or associated pipe fitting] subsequent to installation shall ensure that it is forthwith adequately tested to verify that it is gastight.

(4) A person who makes any such alteration of a [service pipe or associated pipe fitting] shall ensure that it is forthwith after such testing examined to verify that there would have been no such contravention of or failure to comply with any provision of [Part II] of these regulations as is referred to in paragraph (1).

(5) A person who makes any such replacement of a [service pipe or associated pipe fitting] shall ensure that it is forthwith after such testing examined to verify that it complies with such requirements of [Part II] of these regulations as apply to the replacement by virtue of paragraph (2).

[(6) A person who makes any such replacement of a service pipe shall ensure that, as soon as is reasonably practicable, any part of the old pipe which is not removed is disconnected as near to the main as is reasonably practicable.]

NOTES
Amendment The words printed between square brackets were substituted, the words omitted where indicated in this regulation were revoked and para (6) was added by the Gas Safety (Installation and Use) Regulations 1984, SI 1984/1358, p 37, *post*.

52. An Area Board supplying gas to any building shall at all times at their own expense keep all service valves inserted in the service pipes in proper working order.

PART VIII
PENALTIES

53. (*Revoked by reg 9 of SI 1976/1882. See now reg 8 of the Gas Safety (Rights of Entry) Regulations 1983, SI 1983/1575, p 34, post, as amended by the Gas Safety (Installation and Use) Regulations 1984, SI 1984/1358, p 37, post.*)

THE GAS (FINANCIAL YEAR) REGULATIONS 1972
SI1972/1737

NOTES
Authority These regulations were made on 14 November 1972 by the Secretary of State under s 48 (1) of the Gas Act 1972, Halsbury's Statutes, 4th edn Vol 19, title Gas (3rd edn Vol 42, p 508).
Commencement 1 January 1973.
General These regulations provide that the day on which the financial year of the British Gas Corporation ends shall be 31 March.

THE GAS (CONSUMERS' COUNCILS) REGULATIONS 1972
SI 1972/1765

NOTES
Authority These regulations were made on 17 November 1972 by the Secretary of State under para 5 (1) of Sch 3 to the Gas Act 1972, Halsbury's Statutes, 4th edn Vol 19, title Gas (3rd edn Vol 42, p 517), and all other enabling powers.
Amendment These regulations are amended by the Gas (Consumers' Councils) (Amendment) Regulations 1983, SI 1983/1749, listed, *ante*.
Commencement 1 January 1973.
General These regulations relate to the National Gas Consumers' Council and the Regional Gas Consumers' Council, established by the Gas Act 1972, (see s 9 thereof, Halsbury's Statutes, 4th edn Vol 19, title Gas (3rd edn Vol 42, p 476). They make provision as to the appointment and tenure of office of members of the Councils, the frequency and constitution of their meetings, voting minutes and evidence of proceedings, and the execution of documents by, or on behalf of, them. A member's appointment is for such term as may, prior to the appointment, be determined by the Secretary of State and is subject to any conditions notified to him in writing and to vacation of office on the decision of the Secretary of State. Each Council may determine its own quorum and their resolutions are to be passed by a majority of the votes of members present and voting. Any document requiring to be executed by or on behalf of a Council must be signed by the chairman and secretary of that Council or by such one or more of the members and officers of that Council as the Council may in any particular case determine.

THE GAS QUALITY REGULATIONS 1972
SI 1972/1804

NOTES
Authority These regulations were made on 27 November 1972 by the Secretary of State under the Gas Act 1972, s 26 (now repealed by the Oil and Gas (Enterprise) Act 1982, ss 13 (2) and 37 and Sch 4, Halsbury's Statutes, 4th edn Vol 19, title Gas (3rd edn Vol 52, pp 834, 1082, 1101) and superseded by s 13 (1) of that Act which inserts a new s 29B in the 1972 Act) and s 31, and Sch 7, para 13 (1), Halsbury's Statutes, 4th edn Vol 19, title Gas (3rd edn Vol 42, pp 494, 551), and all other enabling powers.
Commencement 1 January 1973; see reg 1.
Amendment These regulations are printed as amended by the Gas (Metrication) Regulations 1980, SI 1980/1851, listed, *ante*, and the Gas Quality Regulations 1983, SI 1983/363, p 27, *post*. They had previously been amended by the Gas Quality (Amendment) Regulations 1978, SI 1978/230, which were superseded by the Gas (Metrication) Regulations 1980, SI 1980/1851, the relevant part of which was itself superseded by the Gas Quality Regulations 1983, SI 1983/363, p 27, *post*.
Interpretation See reg 2.
General These regulations, as amended, prescribe standards of purity and smell to be complied with by the British Gas Corporation in transmitting or distributing, rather than supplying, gas.

PART I
GENERAL

1. Citation and commencement These regulations may be cited as the Gas Quality Regulations 1972 and shall come into operation on 1st January 1973.

2. Interpretation (1) In these regulations—
"the Act" means the Gas Act 1972;
"the Corporation" means the British Gas Corporation;
"a gas examiner" has the meaning assigned by regulation 7;
"quarter" means the period of 3 months in any year beginning on 1st January, 1st April, 1st July or 1st October;
"relative density", in relation to gas, means the ratio of the [mass] of a volume of gas when containing no water vapour to that of the same volume of air containing no water vapour under the same conditions of temperature and pressure;
"Wobbe number" means the number derived by dividing the calorific value of gas by the square root of the relative density of the gas.
(2) The Interpretation Act 1889 shall apply to the interpretation of these regulations as it applies to the interpretation of an Act of Parliament.

NOTES
Amendment The word "mass" printed between square brackets in the definition of "relative density" was substituted by the Gas (Metrication) Regulations 1980, SI 1980/1851, listed, *ante*.
Gas Act 1972 Halsbury's Statutes, 4th edn Vol 19, title Gas (3rd edn Vol 42, p 466 *et seq*).
Interpretation Act 1889 Repealed and replaced by the Interpretation Act 1978, printed in the title Statutory Instruments, Vol 1 of this work.

PART II (regs 3-9) (*Revoked by the Gas Quality Regulations 1983, SI 1983/363, p 27, post, and replaced thereby.*)

PART III
QUALITY OF GAS TRANSMITTED OR DISTRIBUTED BY THE CORPORATION

10. Purity The Corporation shall not transmit or distribute any gas which contains more than 3.3 parts per million by volume of hydrogen sulphide.

11. Distinctive smell The Corporation shall not transmit or distribute any gas which does not possess a distinctive smell.

12. Penalties   If the Corporation contravene any provision of the two foregoing regulations they shall be guilty of an offence and liable on summary
conviction to a fine not exceeding £400:
  Provided that the Corporation shall not be guilty of an offence in any case
in which they can show that the contravention was due to circumstances
beyond their control and that they took all reasonable steps to prevent the
contravention.

13. Exemptions   The Secretary of State may exempt the Corporation from
any provision of regulation 10, if he is satisfied that the safety of the public
will not be prejudiced in consequence of the granting of the exemption.

SCHEDULE   (*Revoked by the Gas Quality Regulations 1983, SI 1983/363,
and superseded by the Schedule thereto, p 28, post*).

THE GAS (DECLARATION OF CALORIFIC VALUE) REGULATIONS 1972
SI 1972/1878

NOTES
Authority   These regulations were made on 1 December 1972 by the Secretary of State under
s 25 (1) and (2) of the Gas Act 1972, Halsbury's Statutes, 4th edn Vol 19, title Gas (3rd edn
Vol 42, p 488), and all other enabling powers.
Commencement   1 January 1973; see reg 1.
Amendment   These regulations are printed as amended by the Gas (Declaration of Calorific
Value) (Amendment) Regulations 1974, SI 1974/847, and the Gas (Metrication) Regulations
1980, SI 1980/1851, both listed, *ante*.
General   These regulations prescribe the manner in which the number of therms supplied by
the British Gas Corporation to any consumer is to be calculated and make provision as to the
declaration of calorific value of gas supplied by the Corporation and the adjustment of charges
for gas where this value is altered.

1. Citation, commencement and interpretation   These regulations may be
cited as the Gas (Declaration of Calorific Value) Regulations 1972 and shall
come into operation on 1st January 1973.
  (2) The Interpretation Act 1889 shall apply to the interpretation of these
regulations as it applies to the interpretation of an Act of Parliament.

NOTE
Interpretation Act 1889   Repealed and replaced by the Interpretation Act 1978, printed in the
title Statutory Instruments, Vol 1 of this work.

2. Calculation of charges for therms supplied   Where the British Gas Corporation (hereinafter referred to as "the Corporation") charge for gas supplied
by them according to the number of therms supplied, the number supplied
to any consumer shall be ascertained by multiplying the number of cubic
[metres] of gas [supplied to the consumer] by the number of [Megajoules] in
the declared calorific value of the gas and dividing the product by [105.5].
  [(Note: Where gas is supplied through a meter measuring in cubic feet, the
number of therms supplied can be ascertained by multiplying the number of
cubic feet of gas supplied by the number of megajoules in the declared calorific
value and dividing the product by 3730.)]

NOTES
Amendment   The words "supplied to the consumer" printed between square brackets in this
regulation were substituted by the Gas (Declaration of Calorific Value) (Amendment) Regulations 1974, SI 1974/847, listed, *ante*. All other amendments printed between square brackets
were made by the Gas (Metrication) Regulations 1980, SI 1980/1851, listed, *ante*.

3. Original declarations of calorific value   (1) Whenever the Corporation
propose to commence to charge for gas supplied to any area according to the
number of therms supplied, they shall declare the calorific value of the gas

to be supplied thereto on and after the date on which the declaration is to take effect generally, by notice given at least three months before that date.

(2) A declaration of calorific value as aforesaid shall take effect, for the purpose of calculating the charge to be made for gas supplied to any consumer, immediately after the first reading of that consumer's meter on or after the date on which that declaration takes effect generally.

4. General alterations in declared calorific value   Whenever the Corporation propose to alter the declared calorific value of gas supplied to any area and to supply gas of a new calorific value to all consumers in that area on the same date, they shall declare the calorific value of the gas to be supplied to that area on and after the date on which the declaration is to take effect which shall be, unless the Secretary of State consents in writing to any other date, 1st January, 1st April, 1st July or 1st October in any year, by notice given at least one month previously.

5. Alterations in declared calorific value affecting consumers on different dates   (1) Whenever the Corporation propose to alter the declared calorific value of gas supplied to any area and to supply gas of a new calorific value to different consumers in that area on different dates, they shall declare the new calorific value of the gas to be supplied to that area on and after the date on which the declaration is to take effect generally, by notice given at least one month before the Corporation propose to supply any consumer with gas of that new calorific value.

(2) Subject to regulation 6, the new declaration of calorific value as aforesaid shall take effect, for the purpose of calculating the charge to be made for gas supplied to any consumer, immediately after the first reading of that consumer's meter on or after the date on which gas of that new calorific value is first supplied to that meter.

6. Calculation of charges   Where any alteration in the declared calorific value of gas as aforesaid occurs in the course of any period for which charges for any such gas are made to any consumer, charges to him shall be calculated in respect of that period in the manner prescribed in regulation 2 on the basis—
  (a) if the alteration increases the calorific value, of the declared calorific value in force immediately before such alteration;
  (b) if the alteration decreases the calorific value, of the declared calorific value as so altered.

7. Publication and service of notice   (1) The notice required by regulations 3 (1), 4 and 5 (1) (hereafter called "the notice") shall be given—
        (i) where the area to be supplied with gas is wholly or partly in England or Wales, in the London Gazette;
       (ii) where the said area is wholly or partly in Scotland, in the Edinburgh Gazette; and
      (iii) in one or more local newspapers having circulation areas covering the said area.

(2) The Corporation shall send a copy of the notice to the Secretary of State for Trade and Industry, the Regional Gas Consumers' Council or Councils for the area to be supplied with gas and, in the case of the notice required by regulation 3 (1), to every consumer in the area to be so supplied.

NOTES
Secretary of State for Trade and Industry   This is now to be construed as referring simply to the Secretary of State (the appropriate department being the Department of Energy), by virtue of the Secretary of State (New Departments) Order 1974, SI 1974/692, in the title Constitutional Law (Part 5); see also the Preliminary Note under the head "Transfer of ministerial functions", p 4, *ante.*

8. Form of notice and map   (1) The notice shall refer to all the local authority districts (or parts thereof) to be supplied with gas and the area to be so supplied shall be defined by reference to a map signed on behalf of the Corporation on which that area shall be clearly delineated by a green line.

(2) The Corporation shall send a copy of the said map to the Secretary of State for Trade and Industry.

(3) The Corporation shall keep the said map at appropriate premises of the Corporation, the address of which shall be specified in the notice, and shall ensure that it is open to inspection by any consumer at all reasonable times free of charge.

NOTES
Secretary of State for Trade and Industry   See the note to reg 7.

9. Declarations of calorific value before 1st January 1983   (1) Any declaration of calorific value made by an Area Board before 1st January 1973 in compliance with the Gas (Declaration of Calorific Value) Regulations 1949 as amended and expressed to take effect on or after 1st January 1973 shall be treated as from that date as a declaration validly made by the Corporation under these regulations.

(2) Where any declaration of calorific value is made before 1st January 1973 by a notice which refers to a map and the declaration has effect on or after 1st January 1973, the Corporation shall send a copy of the map to the Secretary of State for Trade and Industry as soon as possible after 1st January 1973, and the Corporation shall keep the map at appropriate premises of the Corporation and shall ensure that it is open to inspection by any consumer at all reasonable times free of charge.

NOTES
Secretary of State for Trade and Industry   See the note to reg 7.
Gas (Declaration of Calorific Value) Regulations 1949, as amended SI 1949/788 amended by SI 1951/2286.   Those regulations lapsed on the repeal of the enabling powers by the Gas Act 1972.

THE BRITISH GAS CORPORATION REGULATIONS 1972
SI 1972/1879

NOTES
Authority   These regulations were made on 1 December 1972 by the Secretary of State under s 1 (4) of the Gas Act 1972, Halsbury's Statutes, 4th edn Vol 19, title Gas (3rd edn Vol 42, p 469), and all other enabling powers.
Commencement   1 January 1973.
Summary   These regulations relate to the appointment and tenure of office of members of the British Gas Corporation (as to which, see the Preliminary Note under the head "Reorganisation of gas industry", p 4, *ante*), who are appointed by the Secretary of State, to the quorum and minutes of proceedings of the Corporation, and to the execution of instruments by them and the proof of documents. Each member is to hold and vacate his office in accordance with the terms of the instrument appointing him, and on ceasing to be a member he is eligible for re-appointment. A member may resign his office by giving the Secretary of State three months' written notice or such shorter notice as the Secretary of State may approve. The Secretary of State may from time to time satisfy himself that persons appointed or to be appointed members of the Corporation have no financial or other interest likely to affect prejudicially the exercise and performance of their functions as such. If the Secretary of State is satisfied that a member of the Corporation has been absent from its meetings for more than three months without its permission, or has become a bankrupt or made an arrangement with his creditors or is incapacitated by physical or mental illness or is otherwise unable or unfit to discharge his functions as such, the Secretary of State may declare that member's office vacant. A member of the Corporation who is in any way interested in a contract made or to be made by the Corporation, or by one of its subsidiaries, must disclose the nature of his interest at a meeting of the Corporation; and if he has disclosed such an interest he may not take part in any deliberation or decision on the contract concerned. The quorum of the Corporation is six. The Corporation must keep minutes of its proceedings. Its seal is to be authenticated by the signature of the secretary of the Corporation or of some other authorised person, and documents purporting to be executed or issued under it or by the secretary or an authorised person are to be received in evidence without further proof.

THE COMPENSATION FOR LIMITATION OF PRICES (BRITISH GAS CORPORATION) ORDER 1976
SI 1976/1108

NOTES
Authority This order was made on 9 July 1976 by the Secretary of State, with the approval of the Treasury and after consultation with the British Gas Corporation, under s 1 (1) of the Statutory Corporations (Financial Provisions) Act 1975, Halsbury's Statutes, 4th edn Vol 30, title Money (Pt 1) (3rd edn Vol 45, p 1042), and other enabling powers.
Commencement 10 July 1976.
General This order specified the amount of compensation to be paid to the British Gas Corporation for financial loss incurred in the financial year 1974-75 in consequence of their compliance with the national policy relating to limitation of prices.

THE GAS LEVY (RATE FOR 1982-83) ORDER 1982
SI 1982/548

NOTES
Authority This order was made on 7 April 1982 by the Secretary of State, with the consent of the Treasury, under the Gas Levy Act 1981, s 2 (2), Halsbury's Statutes, 4th edn Vol 19, title Gas (3rd edn Vol 51, p 991).
Commencement 1 May 1982.
General This order provided that the rate of gas levy payable by the British Gas Corporation for their financial year ending on 31 March 1983 was to be four pence per therm instead of the rate of five pence per therm specified by the Gas Levy Act 1981, s 2 (1) (c), Halsbury's Statutes, 4th edn Vol 19, title Gas (3rd edn Vol 51, p 991). By virtue of s 2 (3), (4) of that Act, if no rate is specified for any year subsequent to the year 1982-83, the rate of levy for that year is the same as the rate for the preceding year. No order has been made specifying a rate for any such year.

THE GAS (CONSUMERS' DEPOSITS) (RATE OF INTEREST) ORDER 1982
SI 1982/655

NOTES
Authority This order was made on 5 May 1982 by the Secretary of State, with the approval of the Treasury, under the Gas Act 1972, Sch 4, para 30 (2), Halsbury's Statutes, 4th edn Vol 19, title Gas (3rd edn Vol 42, p 534), and all other enabling powers.
Commencement 1 July 1982.
General This order increases from 7% to 10% per annum the rate of interest payable by the British Gas Corporation on every sum of 50p deposited with them by way of security under provisions of the Gas Supply Code contained in the Gas Act 1972, Sch 4, Halsbury's Statutes, 4th edn Vol 19, title Gas (3rd edn Vol 42, p 517) for every six months during which it remains in their hands. The provisions referred to are paras 2 (5) (b) (provision of a pipe or supply of gas), 3 (1) (provision of a new or enlarged main etc) and 7 (a) (provision of a meter). The Gas (Consumers' Deposits) (Rate of Interest) Order 1978, SI 1978/1848, is accordingly revoked.

THE GAS CORPORATION (DISPOSAL OF OFFSHORE OILFIELD INTERESTS) DIRECTIONS 1982
SI 1982/1131

NOTES
Authority These directions were made on 4 August 1982 by the Secretary of State, with the approval of the Treasury, under the Oil and Gas (Enterprise) Act 1982, s 11 (1), Halsbury's Statutes, 4th edn Vol 19, title Gas (3rd edn Vol 52, p 831), and all other enabling powers.
Commencement 31 August 1982.
General These directions require that the British Gas Corporation exercise their powers under the Oil and Gas (Enterprise) Act 1982, ss 9 and 10, Halsbury's Statutes, 4th edn Vol 19, title Gas (3rd edn Vol 52, pp 828, 829) so as to: (a) establish a subsidiary (Subsidiary A) with the principal object of searching and boring for and getting petroleum and make a scheme for transfer to subsidiary A of the property, rights and liabilities of the Corporation and Gas Council (Exploration) Ltd relating to four seaward areas, subject to rights of the Corporation to acquire petroleum from each of those areas; (b) establish four further subsidiaries and make a scheme for the transfer of the property, rights and liabilities of Subsidiary A relating to each seaward area to one of those subsidiaries; (c) establish a further subsidiary with the principal object of acquiring and disposing of petroleum and make a scheme for transfer thereto of the rights of the Corporation to acquire petroleum from each seaward area; (d) make provisions of a general nature in each scheme; and (e) provide for disposal of shares in the subsidiaries by engaging an independent petroleum consultant and compiling appropriate information.

THE GAS QUALITY REGULATIONS 1983
SI 1983/363

NOTES
Authority   These regulations were made on 9 March 1983 by the Secretary of State under the
Gas Act 1972, s 29B (1), (2) and (4) (inserted by the Oil and Gas (Enterprise) Act 1982, s 13
(1), Halsbury's Statutes, 4th edn Vol 19, title Gas (3rd edn Vol 52, p 834)) and s 42 (2), Halsbury's
Statutes, 4th edn Vol 19, title Gas (3rd edn Vol 42, p 503) , and all other enabling powers.
Commencement   12 April 1983; see reg 1.
Interpretation   See reg 2.
General   These regulations prescribe standards of pressure, purity and smell to be complied
with by any person supplying gas through pipes and a standard of uniformity of calorific value
to be complied with by the British Gas Corporation in supplying gas through pipes. These
standards replace those formerly contained in Part II of the Gas Quality Regulations 1972, SI
1972/1804, p 22, *ante*, which is accordingly revoked. The regulations also make provision for the
furnishing of information by persons other the British Gas Corporation supplying gas through
pipes and amend the Gas (Testing) Regulations 1949, SI 1949/789, p 7, *ante*, so as to apply those
regulations to such persons. Other provisions deal with penalties, exceptions to liability and
exemptions.

1. Citation and commencement   These Regulations may be cited as the Gas
Quality Regulations 1983 and shall come into operation on 12th April 1983.

2. Interpretation   In these Regulations—
   "the Act" means the Gas Act 1972;
   "the Corporation" means the British Gas Corporation.
   "quarter" means the period of 3 months in any year beginning on 1st
   January, 1st April, 1st July or 1st October;
   "relative density", in relation to any gas, means the ratio of the mass of a
   volume of the gas when containing no water vapour to the mass (expressed
   in the same units) of the same volume of air containing no water vapour
   under the same conditions of temperature and pressure;
   "Wobbe number" means the number derived by dividing the calorific value
   of gas by the square root of the relative density of the gas.

NOTES
Gas Act 1972 Halsbury's Statutes, 4th edn Vol 19, title Gas (3rd edn Vol 42, p 466 *et seq*).

3. Standard of pressure   No person shall supply any gas through any service
pipe having an internal diameter of 50 mm. or more, or through any main,
at a pressure less than that specified in Column 2 of the Schedule hereto in
relation to the range of Wobbe numbers specified in Column 1 of the Schedule
applicable to the gas supplied.

4. Standard of purity   No person shall supply through pipes any gas which
contains more than 5 milligrams of hydrogen sulphide per cubic metre.

5. Distinctive smell   No person shall supply through pipes any gas which does
not possess a distinctive smell.

6. Uniformity of calorific value   Where the Corporation charge for gas
supplied by them according to the number of therms supplied, they shall
maintain the calorific value of the the gas supplied at not less than the declared
value of the gas and, in particular they shall not cause or permit—
   (a) where there is a continuous record of the calorific value of the gas, the
   average calorific value of the gas in any quarter to be less than its
   declared calorific value, or
   (b) where there is no such continuous record, the average of the calorific
   values of the gas in any quarter shown by not less than six tests at each
   place at which gas is tested carried out by any person appointed by the
   Secretary of State under section 29B (3) of the Act to be less than the
   declared calorific value of the gas.

NOTES
Section 29B (3) of the Act   *Ie* the Gas Act 1972, s 29B (3), inserted by the Oil and Gas (Enterprise)
Act 1982, s 13 (1), Halsbury's Statutes, 4th edn Vol 19, title Gas (3rd edn Vol 52, p 834).

7. Information Any person other than the Corporation who supplies gas through pipes shall furnish to the Secretary of State any information which he may require as necessary or expedient for the purposes of section 29B of the Act.

NOTES
Section 29B of the Act *Ie* the Gas Act 1972, s 29B, inserted by the Oil and Gas (Enterprise) Act 1982, s 13 (1), Halsbury's Statutes, 4th edn Vol 19, title Gas (3rd edn Vol 52, p 834).

8. *(This regulation amends the Gas (Testing) Regulations 1949, SI 1949/789, p 7, ante.)*

9. Penalties Subject to Regulation 10 below, if any person contravenes or fails to comply with, any provision of Regulations 3 to 5 and 6 *(a)* and *(b)* and 7 above or, being a supplier of gas, Regulations 1 (2) and 2, 3 and 3A of the Gas (Testing) Regulations 1949, he shall be guilty of an offence and liable on summary conviction to a fine not exceeding £1,000.

NOTES
Gas (Testing) Regulations 1949 SI 1949/789, p 7, *ante.*

10. Exception as to liability No person shall be guilty of an offence by reason of any contravention, or failure to comply with, any provision specified in Regulation 9 above in any case in which he can show that any such contravention or failure was due to circumstances beyond his control and that he took all reasonable steps to prevent the contravention or failure, nor shall he be guilty of more than one offence by reason of any contravention or failure to comply with a particular provision specified in Regulation 9 above during any period of 24 hours in respect of gas tested by any person appointed by the Secretary of State under section 29B (3) of the Act at one place.

NOTES
Section 29B (3) of the Act *Ie* the Gas Act 1972, s 29B (3), inserted by the Oil and Gas (Enterprise) Act 1982, s 13 (1), Halsbury's Statutes, 4th edn Vol 19, title Gas (3rd edn Vol 52, p 834).

11. Exemptions The Secretary of State may exempt any person from any provisions of Regulations 3 to 5 above and the Corporation from any provision of Regulation 6 above in the case of the supply of gas to any premises for industrial purposes through any main not used for the supply of gas to other premises for other purposes.

12. *(This regulation revokes Part II of the Gas Quality Regulations 1972, SI 1972/1804, p 22, ante.)*

SCHEDULE   Regulation 3
PRESSURE OF GAS SUPPLIED THROUGH PIPES

Column 1	Column 2
Ranges of Wobbe Numbers	Pressure measured in millibars in excess of atmospheric pressure
Not exceeding 31	5 millibars
Exceeding 31 but not exceeding 40	10 millibars
Exceeding 40 but not exceeding 72	21.5 millibars
Exceeding 72	20 millibars

THE GAS (METERS) REGULATIONS 1983
SI 1983/684

NOTES
Authority These regulations were made by the Secretary of State under the Gas Act 1972, s

30 (2), (3), (6) (*a*), (*d*) and (*e*), Halsbury's Statutes, 4th edn Vol 19, title Gas (3rd edn Vol 42, p 493), and all other enabling powers.
Commencement See reg 1.
Amendment These regulations are printed as amended by the Gas (Meters) (Variation of Fees) Regulations 1984, SI 1984/1785, listed, *ante*.
Modification These regulations are modified by reg 21 (3) of the Measuring Instruments (EEC Requirements) Regulations 1980, SI 1980/1058, as substituted by the Measuring Instruments (EEC Requirements) (Gas Volume Meters) Regulations 1983, SI 1983/1246, and by reg 6 of the Measuring Instruments (EEC Requirements) (Gas Volume Meters) (Fees) Regulations 1983, SI 1983/1247, all in the title Weights and Measures.
Interpretation See reg 2.
General These regulations revoke and consolidate, with modifications, the Gas (Meter) Regulations 1974, SI 1974/848, and the amending SI 1975/1071, 1980/1851, reg 3 (4), 1981/504 and 1982/565. The regulations prescribe the national standards to which gas meters submitted for stamping or re-examination by a meter examiner must conform. Standards and tests are laid down for meters to be used for ascertaining the quantity of gas supplied within a range of densities. Provision is made for re-examination, in the case of disputes, of meters already stamped, for cancelling the stamp on any meter found on re-examination not to conform to prescribed standards and for the issue of appropriate certificates to the parties to the dispute. Changes are made in the scale of fees to be paid for the examining or re-examining of meters.

1. Citation and commencement   These Regulations may be cited as the Gas (Meters) Regulations 1983 and shall come into operation on 1st June 1983.

2. Interpretation   In these Regulations—
"the Act" means the Gas Act 1972;
"diaphragm meter" means a meter constructed so that it contains a flexible partition;
"meter examiner" means a meter examiner appointed under section 30 (3) of the Act.

NOTES
Gas Act 1972   Halsbury's Statutes, 4th edn Vol 19, title Gas (3rd edn Vol 42, p 466 *et seq*).

3. Prescribed standards for meters   (1) The standards with which a meter examiner is to be satisfied that a meter conforms so that he may stamp, or authorise the stamping of, the meter in accordance with section 30 (2) of the Act are as follows:—
(*a*) the meter is such that no gas or air will escape from it;
(*b*) in the case of any diaphragm meter, the meter, when used for the purpose of ascertaining the quantity of either gas or air passing through it—
   (i) at any rate of flow not less than 1/50th of the greatest rate of flow for which it is designed and not more than that greatest rate of flow, will register such quantity of gas or air as does not differ from the actual quantity of gas or air passing through the meter by more than 2 per cent of that actual quantity; and
   (ii) at the rate of flow specified in column 1 of Table A below which corresponds to the greatest rate of flow for which it is designed specified in column 2 of the Table, will register the passage of gas or air;

TABLE A

Column 1 *Rate of flow in cubic decimetres per hour*	Column 2 *Greatest rate of flow for which the meter is designed in cubic metres per hour*
15	Not exceeding 6
30	Exceeding 6 but not exceeding 25
60	Exceeding 25 but not exceeding 65
150	Exceeding 65

(c) in the case of a meter other than a diaphragm meter, the meter, when used for the purpose of ascertaining the quantity of either gas or air passing through it—

　(i) at any rate of flow not less than 1/5th of the greatest rate of flow for which it is designed and not more than that greatest rate of flow, will register such quantity of gas or air as does not differ from the actual quantity of gas or air passing through the meter by more than 1 per cent of that actual quantity; and

　(ii) at any rate of flow not less than the smallest rate of flow for which it is designed and less than 1/5th of the greatest rate of flow for which it is designed, will register such quantity of gas or air as does not differ from the actual quantity of gas or air passing through the meter by more than 2 per cent of that actual quantity;

(d) in the case of a diaphragm meter designed to operate at a pressure of not more than 1 bar, the mean difference between the pressure of air at the inlet of the meter and the pressure of air at the outlet of the meter, where air is passing through the meter at the greatest rate of flow for which it is designed, will not exceed the amount specified in column 1 of Table B below which corresponds to that greatest rate of flow specified in column 2 of the Table; and

TABLE B

Column 1 Mean difference in millibars	Column 2 Greatest rate of flow for which the meter is designed in cubic metres per hour
2.0	Not exceeding 16
3.0	Exceeding 16 but not exceeding 65
4.0	Exceeding 65

(e) in the case of any diaphragm meter, the difference between the pressure at the inlet of the meter and the pressure at the outlet of the meter, when air is passing through the meter at the rate of flow which is 1 per cent of the greatest rate of flow for which the meter is designed, will not exceed the amount specified in column 1 of Table C below which corresponds to that greatest rate of flow specified in column 2 of the Table.

TABLE C

Column 1 Difference in millibars	Column 2 Greatest rate of flow for which the meter is designed in cubic metres per hour
0.6	Not exceeding 65
1.0	Exceeding 65

(2) A meter shall be deemed to conform with a standard prescribed by paragraph (1)(b) or (c) above, notwithstanding that gas instead of air is passing through the meter, where the results of testing for that standard show that if it had been conducted with air passing through the meter—

(a) at a density of 1.2 kilograms per cubic metre, or

(b) in a case where the meter is marked in such manner as is approved by the Secretary of State so as to indicate that the meter is to be used only for the purpose of ascertaining the quantity of gas supplied to any person at a specified range of densities of which the lower limit exceeds 1.2 kilograms per cubic metre, at the higher and lower limits of that range,

the meter would have conformed with that standard.

(3) A meter shall be deemed to conform with a standard prescribed by paragraph (1)*(d)* or *(e)* above, notwithstanding that gas instead of air is passing through the meter, where the results of testing for that standard show that, if it had been conducted with air passing through the meter at a density of 1.2 kilograms per cubic metre, the meter would have conformed with that standard.

4. Re-examination of disputed meters   (1) Where there is a dispute between any person to whom gas is supplied and the person supplying the gas as to the accuracy with which a meter stamped under section 30 of the Act registered the quantity of gas supplied to that person and either party to the dispute requires a meter examiner appointed under that section to re-examine the meter, and the names and addresses of both parties to the dispute are communicated in writing to the meter examiner, it shall be the duty of the meter examiner on payment of the fee prescribed by any provision of Regulation 5 below to re-examine the meter.

(2) If a meter examiner, on re-examining the meter, is satisfied that the meter does not conform with the standards prescribed by Regulation 3 above, it shall be the duty of the meter examiner to cancel the stamp with which the meter is already stamped by defacing it.

(3) If a meter examiner on re-examining a meter is satisfied that the meter does not conform either with the standard prescribed by paragraph (1)*(b)*(i) or a standard prescribed by paragraph (1)*(c)* of Regulation 3 above, it shall be the duty of the meter examiner to give to each of the parties to the dispute a certificate signed by the meter examiner stating the degree exceeding the degree permissible for that standard to which the meter when re-examined registered erroneously.

(4) If a meter examiner on re-examining a meter is satisfied that the meter conforms either with the standard prescribed by paragraph (1)*(b)*(i) or the standards prescribed by paragraph (1)*(c)* of Regulation 3 above, it shall be the duty of the meter examiner to give to each of the parties to the dispute a certificate signed by the meter examiner stating that the meter when re-examined registered accurately.

(5) If a meter examiner on re-examining a meter is satisfied that the meter is so defective that he cannot examine it for conformity with the standard prescribed by paragraph (1)*(b)*(i) or the standards prescribed by paragraph (1)*(c)* of Regulation 3 above, it shall be the duty of the meter examiner to give to each of the parties to the dispute a certificate signed by the meter examiner stating that the meter when re-examined could not be so examined and to cancel the stamp with which the meter is already stamped by defacing it.

NOTES
Interpretation   References in this regulation to a meter stamped under section 3 of the Gas Act 1972 are to be construed as including references to a meter bearing the mark of EEC initial verification and references to a stamp are to be construed as including references to that mark; see reg 21 (3) of the Measuring Instruments (EEC Requirements) Regulations 1980, SI 1980/1058, as substituted by SI 1983/1246, in the title Weights and Measures.
Modification   Paragraph (1) of this regulation is modified in relation to a meter bearing the mark of EEC initial verification by reg 6 of the Measuring Instruments (EEC Requirements) (Gas Volume Meters) (Fees) Regulations 1983, SI 1983/1247, in the title Weights and Measures.

5. Fees   (1) Subject to the provisions of paragraphs (2) to (6) below, the fee to be paid to the Secretary of State for examining or re-examining by a meter examiner, with or without stamping, a meter described in column 1 of Schedule 1 to these Regulations used or intended to be used for ascertaining the quantity of gas supplied to any person shall be the corresponding fee specified in column 2 to that Schedule.

(2) Where the meter has not been delivered to the office of a meter examiner for the purpose of examination or re-examination, there shall be paid to the Secretary of State, in addition to any fee payable under paragraph (1) above, a fee equivalent to the amount of—

(*a*) all reasonable expenses, including incidental expenses, incurred by the meter examiner, and any other meter examiner assisting him in the examination, in travelling to and from the premises at which the meter is situated, in preparing for the examination of the meter or in dismantling any equipment used therefor; and

(*b*) a sum calculated at the rate of [£9.80] for every hour, or part of an hour exceeding thirty minutes, spent by the examiner and any such other meter examiner respectively in such travelling, preparing or dismantling.

(3) Where the meter is required to be re-examined by a party to such a dispute as is mentioned in Regulation 4 (1) above, there shall be paid to the Secretary of State, in addition to any fee payable under paragraph (1) or (2) above, a fee of [£1.50].

(4) Where the meter incorporates electro-mechanical compensating devices which cause its register to indicate the quantity of gas passing through it as if the gas were at a particular temperature or pressure or both, there shall be paid to the Secretary of State, in addition to any fee payable under paragraphs (1) to (3) above,—

(*a*) where the meter is a prototype submitted for approval of its pattern and construction or is a modified prototype so submitted which, prior to modification, had already been examined by a meter examiner, a fee of £300; and

(*b*) where the meter is not such a prototype or modified prototype, a fee of £30.

(5) Where the meter is marked in a manner referred to in Regulation 3 (2), there shall be paid to the Secretary of State, in addition to any fee payable under paragraphs (1) to (4) above—

(*a*) where the meter is a prototype submitted for approval of its pattern and construction not being a modified prototype so submitted which, prior to modification, had already been examined by a meter examiner, a fee of £2,000; and

(*b*) where the meter is such a modified prototype or is not a prototype so submitted, a fee of £200.

(6) Subject to the provisions of paragraph 8 (4) of Schedule 4 to the Act, any fee payable under paragraph (1), (2), (3), (4) or (5) above shall be paid to the Secretary of State on demand by the person who requires the meter to be examined or re-examined.

(7) Where any person requires the re-examination of any meter not owned by him through which gas is supplied to him and that meter, when examined on the premises at which it is situated for the purpose of ascertaining the quantity of the gas, is found to register erroneously to a degree exceeding the degree permissible under Regulation 3 (1) *(b)* (i) or *(c)* above, the owner of the meter shall pay to that person the amount of all fees paid by him under this Regulation.

NOTES
Amendment   The figures printed between square brackets in para (2) of this regulation were substituted by the Gas (Meters) (Variation of Fees) Regulations 1984, SI 1984/1785, listed, *ante*.

6. Revocations   The Regulations specified in columns 1 and 2 of Schedule 2 to these Regulations are hereby revoked to the extent specified in column 3 of the Schedule.

NOTES
The regulations in question are the Gas (Meter) Regulations 1974, SI 1974/848 and the amending SI 1975/1071, 1980/1851, reg 3 (4), 1981/504, and 1982/565.

SCHEDULE 1   Regulation 5(1)
FEES

Column 1 *Meter*	Column 2 *Fee*
	£
Prototype (not being a modified prototype) submitted for approval of its pattern and construction of—	
(a) a diaphragm meter	357.00
(b) a rotary positive displacement meter	840.00
(c) a turbine meter	950.00
(d) any other kind of meter	1500.00
Modified prototype so submitted of—	
(a) a diaphragm meter	35.70
(b) a rotary positive displacement meter	84.00
(c) a turbine meter	95.00
(d) any other kind of meter	150.00
Any meter (not being a prototype or modified prototype so submitted) with measuring capacity—	
(a) not exceeding 13 cubic metres per hour	[0.92]
(b) exceeding 13 cubic metres per hour but not exceeding 19 cubic metres per hour	[1.31]
(c) exceeding 19 cubic metres per hour but not exceeding 53 cubic metres per hour	[3.93]
(d) exceeding 53 cubic metres per hour but not exceeding 228 cubic metres per hour	[13.11]
(e) exceeding 228 cubic metres per hour	[32.77]

Note In this Schedule—
  (a)   "a modified prototype" means a prototype which, prior to modification, has already been examined by a meter examiner;
  (b)   "a rotary positive displacement meter" means a meter constructed so that it contains a rotating partition; and
  (c)   "a turbine meter" means a meter constructed so that it contains a turbine wheel.

NOTES
Amendment The figures printed between square brackets in the Schedule were substituted by the Gas (Meters) (Variation of Fees) Regulations 1984, SI 1984/1785, listed, *ante*.

SCHEDULE 2 (*This Schedule lists the instruments revoked by reg 6 of these regulations.*)

THE BRITISH GAS CORPORATION (TRANSFER OF SHARES OF SUBSIDIARIES) ORDER 1983
SI 1983/967

NOTES
Authority This order was made by the Secretary of State, with the approval of the Treasury, under the Oil and Gas (Enterprise) Act 1982, s 11 (5), Halsbury's Statutes, 4th edn Vol 19, title Gas (3rd edn Vol 52, p 831).
Commencement 1 September 1983.
General This order provides for the transfer of all the issued shares of British Gas North Sea Oil Holdings Ltd and British Gas (PAD) Ltd, wholly owned subsidiaries of the British Gas Corporation, to the Secretary of State for Energy and a nominee of his. The Oil and Gas (Enterprise) Act 1982, s 11 (5), Halsbury's Statutes, 4th edn Vol 19, title Gas (3rd edn Vol 52, p 831), provides that the shares transferred by the order shall vest in the Secretary of State for Energy and the nominee by virtue of the order. The said nominee is to be the Solicitor for the Affairs of Her Majesty's Treasury.

THE GAS ACT 1972 (MODIFICATIONS) ORDER 1983
SI 1983/968

NOTES
Authority This order was made by the Secretary of State, with the approval of the Treasury, under the Oil and Gas (Enterprise) Act 1982, s 11 (3), Halsbury's Statutes, 4th edn Vol 19, title Gas (3rd edn Vol 52, p 831).
Commencement 1 September 1983.

Amendment   This order was amended, as from 20 December 1983, by the Gas Act 1972 (Modifications) (Amendment) Order 1983, SI 1983/1668, listed, *ante*.
General   This order, as amended, provides that in its application to: (*a*) British Gas North Sea Holdings Ltd; (*b*) British Gas (Montrose) Ltd; (*c*) British Gas (Beryl) Ltd; (*d*) British Gas (NW Hutton and Hutton) Ltd; (*e*) British Gas (Fulmar) Ltd; (*f*) British Gas (PAD) Ltd; (*g*) British Gas North Sea Oil Exploration Acreage Ltd; and (*h*) British Gas North Sea Oil Exploration Participation Ltd, the Gas Act 1972, Halsbury's Statutes, 4th edn Vol 19, title Gas (3rd edn Vol 42, p 466 *et seq*), shall have effect as if ss 4 (1), (3) and (4) (duties of the Corporation as respect management of affairs), 5 (programmes for measures involving substantial capital outlay), 6 (3) (duties of the Corporation as respects guarantees), 14 (revenues of the Corporation and subsidiaries to cover outgoings and allocations to reserves), 18 (borrowing by wholly owned subsidiaries) and 19 (1) (*c*) (limitation on indebtedness of wholly owned subsidiaries) were omitted.

THE BRITISH GAS CORPORATION (FURTHER DISPOSAL OF OFFSHORE INTERESTS) DIRECTIONS 1983
SI 1983/1096

NOTES
Authority   These directions were made by the Secretary of State, with the approval of the Treasury, under the Oil and Gas (Enterprise) Act 1982, s 11 (1), Halsbury's Statutes 4th edn Vol 19, title Gas (3rd edn Vol 52, p 831), and all other enabling powers.
Commencement   12 September 1983.
General   These directions require the British Gas Corporation to establish two wholly owned subsidiaries: (*a*) Subsidiary I, a private company having as its principal object searching, boring for and getting petroleum; and (*b*) Subsidiary II, a private company having as its principal object the acquisition and disposal of petroleum. The directions also require, *inter alia*, the making of schemes to transfer to the Corporation (in the case of Subsidiary I) and to Subsidiary II, rights in respect of the acquisition of up to 51% of the petroleum rights to which the subsidiaries become entitled. Provisions are made for the eventual disposal of certain property, rights and liabilities and for the issue of debentures.

THE GAS SAFETY (RIGHTS OF ENTRY) REGULATIONS 1983
SI 1983/1575

NOTES
Authority   These regulations were made by the Secretary of State under the Gas Act 1972, ss 31 (1)-(4) and 42 (2), Halsbury's Statutes, 4th edn Vol 19, title Gas (3rd edn Vol 42, pp 494, 503), and all other enabling powers.
Commencement   21 November 1983; see reg 1.
Amendment   These regulations are printed as amended by the Gas Safety (Installation and Use) Regulations 1984, SI 1984/1358, p 37, *post*.
General   These regulations revoke and replace the Gas Safety (Rights of Entry) Regulations 1976, SI 1976/1882. The regulations provide for rights of entry of officers authorised by the British Gas Corporation (where gas is supplied by the Corporation) or by the Secretary of State (where gas is supplied by a person other than the Corporation) onto premises of consumers for the purpose of examining and testing gas fittings etc, and, where necessary to avert danger, disconnecting fittings and discontinuing the supply of gas. Provision is made for appeal to the Secretary of State against actions taken under these powers. Unauthorised reconnection of fittings or restoration of supply is prohibited; penalties are prescribed.

1. Citation and commencement   These Regulations may be cited as the Gas Safety (Rights of Entry) Regulations 1983 and shall come into operation on 21st November 1983.

2. Rights of entry, disconnection and discontinuance of supply   Any officer authorised by the relevant authority may, on the production of some duly authenticated document showing his authority, with such other persons (if any) as may be necessary—
   (*a*) enter any premises in which there is a service pipe connected with gas mains, for the purpose of inspecting any gas fitting on the premises, any flue or means of ventilation used in connection with any such gas fitting, or any service pipe or other apparatus (not being a gas fitting) which is on the premises and is used for the supply of gas or is connected with gas mains,
   (*b*) where he so enters any such premises, examine or apply any test to any such object as is mentioned in paragraph (*a*) above and (where the

object is a gas fitting) verify what supply of air is available for it, with a view to ascertaining whether the provisions of any regulations made under section 31 of the Gas Act 1972 have been complied with or whether the object is in such a condition, or (in the case of a gas fitting) the supply of air available for it is so inadequate, that it (or, in the case of a flue or means of ventilation, the gas fitting in connection with which it is used) is likely to constitute a danger to any person or property, and

(c) where in his opinion it is necessary to do so for the purpose of averting danger to life or property, and notwithstanding any contract previously existing, disconnect and seal off any gas fitting or any part of the gas supply system on the premises, or cut off the supply of gas to the premises or, if no such supply is being given, signify the refusal of the relevant authority to give or, as the case may be, allow such a supply.

NOTES

Gas Act 1972, s 31   Substituted by the Oil and Gas (Enterprise) Act 1982, s 14, Halsbury's Statutes, 4th edn Vol 19, title Gas (3rd edn Vol 52, p 836).

Relevant authority   This is defined by the Gas Act 1972, s 31 (9) (as substituted by the Oil and Gas (Enterprise) Act 1982, s 14, *ibid*, 4th edn Vol 19, title Gas (3rd edn Vol 52, p 836)) as meaning the British Gas Corporation or the Secretary of State, depending on whether gas supplied by the Corporation is involved or not.

3. Notification to consumer   (1) Where an officer authorised by the relevant authority takes any action in relation to any premises in the exercise of a power conferred by Regulation 2 *(c)* above, the relevant authority shall, within five clear working days after the action is taken, serve on the consumer a notice in writing—

(a) specifying—
   (i) the nature of the defect or other circumstances in consequence of which the power has been exercised; and
   (ii) the nature of the danger in question and the action taken in the exercise of the power; and

(a) stating—
   (i) that the consumer has a right to appeal under these Regulations to the Secretary of State against the action taken in the exercise of the power within the period of 21 days beginning with the date of service of the notice, or such longer period as the Secretary of State may at any time in any particular case allow;
   (ii) the grounds on which and the manner in which he can appeal; and
   (iii) the effect of Regulations 7 and 8 below.

(2) In this Regulation "working day" does not include a Saturday, Sunday or a bank or other public holiday.

NOTES

Relevant authority   See the note to reg 2.

4. (1) Where an officer authorised by the relevant authority takes any action in relation to any premises in the exercise of a power conferred by Regulation 2 *(c)* above, he shall at the same time affix prominently a notice of the effect of the relevant part of Regulations 7 and 8 below to, or to a part of the premises near to, the gas fitting or part of the gas supply system in question or, where he has cut off the supply of gas to the premises or signified the refusal of the relevant authority to give or, as the case may be, allow such a supply, to, or to a part of the premises near to, every primary meter therein, or, if there is no such meter, to a conspicuous part of the premises.

(2) In this Regulation "primary meter" means a meter connected to a service pipe for ascertaining the quantity of gas supplied through that pipe.

NOTES

Relevant authority   See the note to reg 2.

5. Appeals   The consumer on whom is served such notice as is mentioned in Regulation 3 above may, within the period of 21 days beginning with the date of service of the notice, or such longer period as the Secretary of State may at any time in any particular case allow, appeal to the Secretary of State against the action taken in the exercise of a power conferred by Regulation 2 *(c)* above on any of the following grounds, that is to say—
- (*a*) that the defect or other circumstances specified in the notice did not constitute a danger such as to justify the action taken specified in the notice;
- (*b*) that the defect or other circumstances so specified did not exist at the time the action was taken; or
- (*c*) that the defect or other circumstances so specified have ceased to exist.

6. (1) An appeal under Regulation 5 above shall be of no effect unless it is made by notice in writing given to the Secretary of State for the time being discharging the functions conferred by paragraphs (2) and (3) below at his principal office and indicates the grounds of the appeal.

(2) On any such appeal the Secretary of State may, if either the consumer or the relevant authority so desire, afford to each of them an opportunity of appearing before, and being heard by, a person appointed by the Secretary of State for the purpose.

(3) On the determination of the appeal the Secretary of State may direct that, subject to any right of the supplier to withhold supply—
- (*a*) any gas fitting or part of the gas supply system on the premises which has been disconnected under these Regulations either shall remain disconnected or shall or may be reconnected;
- (*b*) any supply of gas to the premises which has been cut off under these Regulations either shall remain cut off or may be restored; or
- (*c*) where the refusal of the relevant authority to give or, as the case may be, allow such a supply has been signified under these Regulations, the supplier either shall not give a supply of gas or shall or may cause gas to be supplied to the premises,

and may give such supplementary directions as he considers to be appropriate in consequence of the appeal.

7. Prohibition of reconnection or restoration of supply or causing a supply to be given   No person shall, except with the consent of the relevant authority or in pursuance of any directions given by the Secretary of State under Regulation 6 (3) above,—
- (*a*) reconnect any gas fitting or part of a gas supply system which has been disconnected by or on behalf of the relevant authority in the exercise of a power conferred by these Regulations where he knows or has reason to believe that it has been so disconnected; or
- (*b*) restore the supply of gas to any premises where it has been cut off by or on behalf of the relevant authority in the exercise of any such power and he knows or has reason to believe that it has been so cut off; or
- (*c*) cause gas from gas mains to be supplied to any premises where in pursuance of these Regulations the refusal of the relevant authority to give or, as the case may be, allow a supply to those premises has been signified and that refusal has not been withdrawn and he knows or has reason to believe that such refusal has been signified and has not been withdrawn.

NOTES
Relevant authority   See the note to reg 2.

8. Penalties   Any person contravening or failing to comply with any provision of these Regulations or the Gas Safety Regulations 1972 shall be guilty of an offence and liable on summary conviction to a fine not exceeding [£2,000].

NOTES
Amendment The figures printed between square brackets in this regulation were substituted by the Gas Safety (Installation and Use) Regulations 1984, SI 1984/1358, *infra*.
Gas Safety Regulations 1972 SI 1972/1178, p 16, *ante*.

9. (*This regulation revokes the Gas Safety (Rights of Entry) Regulations 1976, SI 1976/1882*).

THE BRITISH GAS CORPORATION (TRANSFER OF SHARES OF SUBSIDIARIES) (NO 2) ORDER 1983
SI 1983/1667

NOTES
Authority This order was made by the Secretary of State, with the approval of the Treasury under the Oil and Gas (Enterprise) Act 1982, s 11 (5), Halsbury's Statutes, 4th edn Vol 19, title Gas (3rd edn Vol 52, p 831).
Commencement 20 December 1983.
General This order provides for the transfer of all the issued shares of British Gas North Sea Oil Exploration Acreage Ltd and British Gas North Sea Oil Exploration Participation Ltd, wholly owned subsidiaries of the British Gas Corporation, to the Secretary of State for Energy and a nominee of his. The Oil and Gas (Enterprise) Act 1982, s 11 (5), Halsbury's Statutes, 4th edn Vol 19, title Gas (3rd edn Vol 52, p 831), provides that the shares transferred by the order shall vest in the Secretary of State for Energy and the nominee by virtue of the order. The said nominee is to be the Solicitor for the Affairs of Her Majesty's Treasury.

THE GAS SAFETY (INSTALLATION AND USE) REGULATIONS 1984
SI 1984/1358

NOTES
Authority These regulations were made on 23 August 1984 by the Secretary of State under the Gas Act 1972, ss 31 (1) (as substituted by the Oil and Gas (Enterprise) Act 1982, s 14, Halsbury's Statutes, 4th edn Vol 19, title Gas (3rd edn Vol 52, p 836)), 42 (2) and 45 (3), Halsbury's Statutes, 4th edn Vol 19, title Gas (3rd edn Vol 42, pp 503, 506), and all other enabling powers.
Commencement Partly on 24 November 1984 and fully on 24 February 1985; see reg 1.
Interpretation See regs 2, 10 and 24.
General These regulations impose requirements as to the installation and use of gas fittings for the purpose of securing that the public is so far as is practicable protected from personal injury, fire, explosion or other damage resulting from the use of gas supplied through pipes. The Gas Safety Regulations 1972, SI 1972/1178, p 16, *ante*, are further amended so that Parts III-VI cease to have effect and Part VIII is restricted in its operation to service pipes and their associated pipe fittings. The maximum fine for contraventions of or failure to comply with the provisions of the Gas Safety Regulations 1972 or the Gas Safety (Rights of Entry) Regulations 1983, SI 1983/1575, p 34, *ante*, is increased to £2,000 and the latter regulations are amended accordingly.

PART A
GENERAL

1. Citation and commencement (1) These Regulations may be cited as the Gas Safety (Installation and Use) Regulations 1984 and, except as provided by paragraph (2) below, shall come into operation on 24th November 1984.
(2) Regulations 8 (2) *(c)*, 12 (3), 14, 15 (3), 16, 17(2), 21 (3), 22, 29, 33 (3) and, so far as it relates to Regulations 23, 25 and 36 (2) of the Gas Safety Regulations 1972, 38 shall come into operation on 24th February 1985.

NOTES
Gas Safety Regulations 1972 SI 1972/1178, p 16, *ante*.

2. General interpretation and application (1) In these Regulations—
"emergency control" means a valve for shutting off the supply of gas in an emergency;
"flue" means a passage for conveying the products of combustion from a gas appliance to the external air and includes any part of the passage in a gas appliance ventilation duct which serves the purpose of a flue;
"gas appliance" means an appliance designed for use by a consumer of gas

for lighting, heating, motive power or other purposes for which gas can be used;

"installation pipe" means any pipe, not being a service pipe (other than any part of a service pipe comprised in a primary meter installation) or a pipe comprised in a gas appliance, for conveying gas for a particular consumer and any associated valve or other gas fitting;

"meter by pass" means any pipe and other gas fittings used in connection with it through which gas can be conveyed from a service pipe to an installation pipe without passing through a meter;

"primary meter" means a meter connected to a service pipe for ascertaining the quantity of gas supplied through that pipe;

"primary meter installation" means a primary meter and the pipes and other gas fittings used in connection with it, including any meter bypass, installed between the outlet of any service valve, or, if there is no service valve, the outlet of the service pipe and the outlet connection of the meter or the outlet of the common connection of the meter and any meter bypass or any other primary meter as the case may be;

"the responsible person", in relation to any premises, means the occupier of the premises or, where there is no occupier or the occupier is away, the owner of the premises or any person with authority for the time being to take appropriate action in relation to any gas fitting therein;

"service valve" means a valve for controlling a supply of gas incorporated in a service pipe and not situated inside a building;

"work", in relation to a gas fitting, means work of any of the following kinds, that is to say—

(*a*) installing the fitting;

(*b*) maintaining, servicing, permanently adjusting, repairing, altering or renewing the fitting or purging it of air or gas;

(*c*) where the fitting is stationary, changing its position;

(*d*) removing the fitting.

(2) For the purposes of these Regulations—

(*a*) the expression "gas fitting" does not include any part of a service pipe except any part comprised in a primary meter installation;

(*b*) any reference to installing a gas fitting includes a reference to converting any pipe, fitting, meter, apparatus or appliance to use gas supplied through pipes; and

(*c*) a person providing, for use in a flat or part of a building let by him, gas supplied to him shall not in so doing be deemed to be supplying gas.

(3) Noting in these Regulations shall apply in relation to the supply of gas to, or anything done in respect of a gas fitting at—

(*a*) a mine within the meaning of the Mines and Quarries Act 1954 or any place deemed to form part of a mine for the purposes of that Act; or

(*b*) a factory within the meaning of the Factories Act 1961.

NOTES
Mines and Quarries Act 1954 Halsbury's Statutes, 4th edn Vol 29, title Mines, Minerals and Quarries (3rd edn Vol 22, p 279 *et seq*).
Factories Act 1961 Halsbury's Statutes, 4th edn Vol 19, title Health and Safety at Work (3rd edn Vol 13, p 401 *et seq*).

PART B
GAS FITTINGS—GENERAL PROVISIONS

3. Qualification and supervision (1) No person shall carry out any work in relation to a gas fitting unless he is competent to do so.

(2) The employer of any person carrying out such work in the performance of a contract of service shall ensure that paragraph (1) above and the following provisions of these Regulations for the time being in force are complied with.

4. Materials and workmanship   (1) No person shall install a gas fitting unless every part of it is of good construction and sound material and of adequate strength and size to secure safety.

(2) Without prejudice to the generality of paragraph (1) above, no person shall install in a building any pipe for use in the supply of gas which is—

(*a*) made of lead or lead alloy; or

(*b*) made of a non-metallic substance unless it is—

   (i) a pipe connected to a readily moveable gas appliance designed for use without a flue; or

   (ii) a pipe entering the building and that part of it within the building is placed inside a metallic sheath which is so constructed and installed as to prevent, so far as is reasonably practicable, the escape of gas into the building if the pipe should fail.

(3) No person shall carry out any work in relation to a gas fitting otherwise than in a proper and workmanlike manner.

5. General safety precautions   (1) No person shall carry out any work in relation to a gas fitting in such a manner that gas could escape unless steps are taken to prevent any escape of gas which constitutes a danger to any person or property.

(2) No person carrying out work in relation to a gas fitting shall leave the fitting unattended unless every incomplete gasway has been sealed with the appropriate fitting so as to be gastight or the gas fitting is otherwise safe.

(3) Any person who disconnects a gas fitting shall, with the appropriate fitting, seal off every outlet of every pipe to which it was connected.

(4) No person carrying out work in relation to a gas fitting which involves exposing gasways which contain or have contained flammable gas shall smoke or use any source of ignition unless those gasways have been purged so as to remove all such gas or have otherwise been made safe from risk of fire or explosion.

(5) No person searching for an escape of gas from a gas fitting shall use any source of ignition.

(6) Where a person carries out any work in relation to a gas fitting which might affect the gas tightness of the gas supply system, he shall immediately thereafter test the system for gas tightness at least as far as the nearest valves upstream and downstream in the system.

6. Protection against damage   (1) Any person installing a gas fitting shall ensure that every part of it is properly supported and so placed or protected as to avoid any undue risk of damage to the fitting.

(2) No person shall install a gas fitting if he has reason to suspect that foreign matter may block or otherwise interfere with the safe operation of the fitting, unless he has fitted to the gas inlet of, and any airway in, the fitting a suitable filter or other suitable protection.

(3) No person shall install a gas fitting in a position where it is likely to be exposed to any substance which may corrode gas fittings unless the fitting is constructed of materials which are inherently resistant to being so corroded or it is suitably protected against being so corroded.

7. Existing gas fittings   (1) No person shall make any alteration to any premises which would affect a gas fitting in such a manner that, if the fitting had been installed after the alteration, there would have been a contravention or failure to comply with any provision of these Regulations in force.

(2) No person shall do anything which would affect a gas fitting or any flue or means of ventilation used in connection with the fitting in such a manner that the subsequent use of the fitting might constitute a danger to any person or property.

8. Emergency controls   (1) No person shall give a new supply of gas for use in any building unless there is provided an emergency control to which there is adequate access situated—
  (*a*) if there is a dwelling to be supplied with gas in the building—
      (i) as near as is reasonably practicable to the point where the pipe supplying the gas enters the dwelling, and also
      (ii) if the pipe supplying the gas enters the building at a place not comprised within a dwelling, as near as is reasonably practicable to the point of entry, or
  (*b*) if there is no such dwelling in the building, as near as is reasonably practicable to the point where the pipe supplying the gas enters the building.
  (2) Any person installing an emergency control shall ensure that—
  (*a*) any key, lever or hand wheel of the control is securely attached to the operating spindle of the control;
  (*b*) any such key or lever is attached so that—
      (i) the key or lever is parallel to the axis of the pipe in which the control is installed when the control is in the open position, and
      (ii) where the key or lever is not attached so as to move only horizontally, gas cannot pass beyond the control when the key or lever has been moved as far as possible downwards; and
  (*c*) either the means of operating the control are clearly and permanently marked or a notice in permanent form is prominently displayed near such means so as to indicate when the control is open and when the control is shut.
  (3) Where a person installs an emergency control which is not to form part of a primary meter installation, he shall immediately thereafter prominently display on or near the means of operating the control a notice in permanent form bearing the words "Gas Emergency Control"—
  (*a*) indicating that the consumer should—
      (i) shut off the supply of gas immediately in the event of an escape of gas in the building or dwelling, as the case may be, for which the control is provided;
      (ii) where any gas continues to escape after the emergency control has been closed, as soon as practicable give notice of the escape to the supplier; and
      (iii) not re-open the emergency control until all necessary steps have been taken to prevent gas from escaping again, and
  (*b*) stating—
      (i) the name of the supplier;
      (ii) the emergency telephone number of the supplier; and
      (iii) the date on which the notice was first displayed.

9. Electrical continuity—general   In any case where it is necessary to avoid danger, no person shall carry out work in relation to a gas fitting without first providing a suitable bond to maintain electrical continuity until the work is completed.

PART C
METER INSTALLATIONS

10. Interpretation of Part C   In this Part—
  "meter box" means a receptacle or compartment designed and constructed to contain a meter with its associated gas fittings;
  "secondary meter" means a meter for ascertaining the quantity of gas provided by a person supplied through a primary meter for use by another person.

11. Meters—general provisions   (1) No person shall install a meter on or under a stairway or in any other part of a building with two or more floors above the ground floor, where the stairway or that other part of the building provides the only means of escape in case of fire, unless the meter replaces an existing meter and sub-paragraph *(a)* or *(b)* of paragraph (2) below is complied with.

(2) No person shall install a meter in any building with no more than one floor above the ground floor on or under a stairway or in any other part of the building, where the stairway or that other part of the building provides the only means of escape in case of fire, unless—

(*a*) the meter is—
   (i)   of fire resisting construction; or
   (ii) housed in a compartment with automatic self-closing doors and which is of fire resisting construction; or
(*b*) the pipe immediately upstream of the meter or, where a governor is adjacent to the meter, immediately upstream of that governor, incorporates a device designed to cut off automatically the flow of gas if the temperature of the device exceeds 95°C.

(3) In paragraph (2) *(a)* above, the expression "fire resisting construction" means that, if the meter or the compartment housing the meter were subjected for 30 minutes to the furnace test described in British Standard BS 746 (Fire Tests on Building Materials and Structures) Part 8: 1972 (Test methods and criteria for the fire resistance of elements of building construction) ISBN: 0 580 07166 9 as amended by Amendment Slip No. 1 published 30th January 1976 and Amendment No. 2 published and effective 30th November 1981 or an equivalent test, the construction of the meter would not be so adversely affected that gas could escape in hazardous quantities.

(4) No person shall install a meter unless the installation is so placed as to ensure that there is no risk of damage to it from electrical apparatus.

(5) No person shall install a meter except in a readily accessible position for inspection and maintenance.

(6) Where a meter has bosses or side pipes attached to the meter by a soldered joint only, no person shall make rigid pipe connections to the meter.

(7) Where a person installs a meter and the pipes and other gas fittings associated with it, he shall ensure that—

(*a*) immediately thereafter they are adequately tested to verify that they are gas tight and examined to verify that they have been installed in accordance with any provisions of these Regulations in force; and
(*b*) immediately after such testing and examination, purging is carried out throughout the meter and every other gas fitting through which gas can then flow so as to remove safely all air and gas other than the gas to be supplied.

12. Meter boxes   (1) Where a meter is housed in a meter box attached to or built into the external face of the outside wall of a building, the meter box shall be so constructed and installed that any gas escaping within the box cannot enter the building or any cavity in the wall but must disperse to the external air.

(2) No person shall knowingly store flammable materials in any meter box.

(3) No person shall install a meter in a meter box provided with a lock, unless the consumer has been provided with a key to the lock clearly labelled "Gas Meter Box" in black capital letters on a yellow ground.

13. Governors   (1) No person shall install a primary meter or a meter bypass used in connection with a primary meter unless—

(*a*) there is a governor regulating the pressure of gas supplied through the meter or the bypass, as the case may be, which provides adequate automatic means for preventing the gas fittings connected to the downstream side of the governor from being subjected to a pressure greater than that for which they were designed;

(*b*) where the normal pressure of the gas supply is 75 millibars or more, there are also adequate automatic means for preventing, in case the governor should fail, those gas fittings from being subjected to such a greater pressure; and

(*c*) where the governor contains a relief valve or liquid seal, such valve or seal is connected to a vent pipe of adequate size so installed that it is capable of venting safely.

(2) Where a person installs a governor for regulating the pressure of gas through a primary meter or a meter bypass used in connection with a primary meter, he shall immediately thereafter adequately seal the governor to prevent its setting from being interfered with without breaking of the seal.

(3) No person except the supplier of the gas or a person authorised to act on his behalf shall break a seal applied under paragraph (2) above.

14. Meters—emergency notices (1) No person shall supply gas through a primary meter installed after the commencement of this Regulation unless he ensures that a notice in permanent form is prominently displayed on or near the meter—

(*a*) indicating that the consumer should—
   (i) shut off the supply of gas immediately in the event of an escape of gas in the consumer's premises;
   (ii) where any gas continues to escape after the supply has been shut off, immediately give notice of the escape to the supplier; and
   (iii) not re-open the supply until all necessary steps have been taken to prevent the gas from escaping again, and

(*b*) stating—
   (i) the name of the supplier,
   (ii) the emergency service telephone number of the supplier; and
   (iii) the date on which the notice was first displayed.

(2) Where a meter is installed in a building at a distance of more than 2 metres from, or out of sight of, the nearest upstream emergency control in the building, no person shall supply or provide gas through the meter unless he ensures that a notice in permanent form is prominently displayed on or near the meter indicating the position of that control.

15. Primary meters (1) No person shall install a prepayment meter as a primary meter through which gas passes to a secondary meter.

(2) Any person who first supplies gas through any service pipe after the commencement of this Regulation to more than one primary meter shall ensure that a notice in permanent form is prominently displayed on or near each primary meter indicating that this is the case.

(3) Where a primary meter is removed, the person who last supplied gas through the meter before removal shall—

(*a*) where the meter is not forthwith re-installed or replaced by another meter—
   (i) close any service valve which controlled the supply of gas to that meter and did not control the supply of gas to any other primary meter; and
   (ii) clearly mark any live gas pipe in the premises in which the meter was installed to the effect that the pipe contains gas; and

(*b*) where the meter has not been re-installed or replaced by another meter before the expiry of the period of 12 months beginning with the date of removal of the meter and there is no such service valve as is mentioned in sub-paragraph *(a)* (i) above, ensure that the service pipe for those premises is disconnected as near as is reasonably practicable to the main and that any part of the pipe which is not removed is sealed at both ends with the appropriate fitting.

16. Secondary meters Any person providing gas through a secondary meter shall ensure that a notice in permanent form is prominently displayed on or near the primary meter indicating the number and location of secondary meters installed.

PART D
INSTALLATION PIPES

17. Safe use of pipes (1) No person shall install an installation pipe in any position in which it cannot be used with safety having regard to the position of other pipes, drains, sewers, cables, conduits and electrical apparatus and to any parts of the structure of any building in which it is installed which might affect its safe use.

(2) Any person who connects an installation pipe to a primary meter installation shall, in any case where electrical cross-bonding may be necessary, inform the responsible person that such cross-bonding should be carried out by a competent person.

18. Enclosed pipes (1) No person shall install any part of an installation pipe in a wall or a floor or standing of solid construction unless it is so constructed and installed as to be protected against failure caused by movement.

(2) No person shall install an installation pipe so as to pass through a wall or a floor or standing of solid construction from one side to the other unless any part of the pipe within such wall, floor or standing as the case may be—
(*a*) takes the shortest practicable route; and
(*b*) is enclosed in a gastight sleeve and the pipe and the sleeve are so constructed and installed as to prevent, as far as is reasonably practicable having regard to paragraph (1) above, gas passing along any space between the pipe and the sleeve or between the sleeve and such a wall, floor or standing as the case may be.

(3) No person shall install any part of an installation pipe in the cavity of a cavity wall unless the pipe is to pass through the wall from one side to the other.

(4) No person shall install an installation pipe under the foundations of a building or in the ground under the base of a wall or footings.

(5) No person shall install an installation pipe in an unventilated shaft, duct or void.

19. Protection of buildings No person shall install an installation pipe in a way which would impair the structure of a building or impair the fire resistance of any part of its structure.

20. Clogging precautions No person shall install an installation pipe in which deposition of liquid or solid matter is likely to occur unless a suitable vessel for the reception of any deposit which may form is fixed to the pipe in a conspicuous and readily accessible position and safe means are provided for the removal of the deposit.

21. Testing and purging of pipes (1) Where a person carries out work in relation to an installation pipe which might affect the gastightness of any part of it, he shall immediately thereafter ensure that—
(*a*) that part is adequately tested to verify that it is gastight and examined to verify that it has been installed in accordance with those provisions of these Regulations in force; and
(*b*) after such testing and examination, any necessary protective coating is applied to the joints of that part.

(2) Where gas is being supplied to any premises in which an installation pipe is installed and a person carries out work in relation to the pipe, he shall also ensure that—
(*a*) immediately after complying with the provisions of sub-paragraphs *(a)* and *(b)* of paragraph (1) above, purging is carried out throughout every

installation pipe through which gas can then flow so as to remove safely all air and gas other than the gas to be supplied;

(b) immediately after such purging, if the pipe is not to be put into immediate use, it is sealed off at every outlet with the appropriate fitting;

(c) if such purging has been carried out through a loosened connection, the connection is retested for gastightness after it has been retightened; and

(d) every seal fitted after purging is tested for gastightness.

(3) Where gas is not being supplied to any premises in which an installation pipe is installed at a time when a person carries out work in relation to the pipe, no person shall supply gas to the premises unless he has caused such purging and other work as is specified in sub-paragraphs (a) to (d) of paragraph (2) above to be carried out.

22. Marking of pipes (1) Any person installing, elsewhere than in any premises or part of premises used only as a dwelling or for living accommodation, a part of an installation pipe which is accessible to inspection shall permanently mark that part in such a manner that it is readily recognisable as part of a pipe for conveying gas.

(2) The responsible person for the premises in which any such part is situated shall ensure that the part continues to be so recognisable so long as it is used for conveying gas.

23. Large consumers (1) Where the service pipe to any building having two or more floors to which gas is supplied or (whether or not it has more than one floor) a floor having areas with a separate supply of gas, has an internal diameter of 50 mm or more, no person shall install an incoming installation pipe to any of those floors or areas as the case may be unless—

(a) a valve is installed in the pipe in a conspicuous and readily accessible position; and

(b) a line diagram in permanent form is attached to the building in a readily accessible position as near as practicable to the primary meter indicating the position of all installation pipes of internal diameter of 25 mm or more, meters, emergency controls, valves, pressure test points, condensate receivers and electrical bonding of the gas supply systems in the building.

(2) In paragraph (1)(b) above "pressure test point" means a gas fitting to which a pressure gauge can be connected.

PART E
GAS APPLIANCES

24. Interpretation of Part E In this Part—

"flue pipe" means a pipe forming a flue but does not include a pipe built as a lining into either a chimney or a gas appliance ventilation duct;

"heat input", in relation to a gas appliance, means the gas consumption of the appliance expressed in terms of the quantity of heat supplied to the appliance in a specific time;

"operating pressure", in relation to a gas appliance, means the pressure of gas at which it is designed to operate.

25. Gas appliances—safety precautions (1) No person shall install a gas appliance unless—

(a) the appliance and the gas fittings and other works for the supply of gas to be used in connection with the appliance,

(b) the means of removal of the products of combustion from the appliance, (*c*) the availability of sufficient permanent supply of air for the appliance for proper combustion,

(*d*) the means of ventilation to the room or internal space in which the appliance is to be used, and

(*e*) the general conditions of installation including the stability of the appliance and its connection to any other gas fitting.

are such as to ensure that the appliance can be used without constituting a danger to any person or property.

(2) No person shall connect a flued domestic gas appliance to the gas supply system except by a permanently fixed rigid pipe.

(3) No person shall install a used gas appliance without verifying that it is in a safe condition for further use.

(4) No person shall install a gas appliance which does not comply with any enactment imposing a prohibition or restriction on the supply of such an appliance on grounds of safety.

(5) No person carrying out the installation of a gas appliance shall leave it connected to the gas supply unless the appliance can be used safely.

(6) No person shall install a gas appliance without there being at the inlet to it means of shutting off the supply of gas to the appliance unless the provision of such means is not reasonably practicable.

(7) No person shall carry out any work in relation to a gas appliance which bears an indication that it conforms to a type approved by any person as complying with safety standards in such a manner that the appliance ceases to comply with those standards.

(8) No person carrying out work in relation to a gas appliance which bears an indication that it so conforms shall remove or deface the indication.

(9) Where a person services a domestic gas appliance, he shall immediately thereafter examine—

(*a*) the effectiveness of any flue,

(*b*) the supply of combustion air,

(*c*) its heat input and operating pressure, and

(*d*) its safe functioning.

and forthwith notify the responsible person for the premises in which the appliance is situated of any defect.

26. Building legislation No person shall install a gas appliance unless the appliance and the gas fittings and any flue or means of ventilation to be used in connection with the appliance comply with—

(*a*) in the case of an installation in Greater London other than an outer London borough,

(i) any provision of the London Building Acts 1930 to 1939 and any byelaws made thereunder, and

(ii) any provision of the London Gas Undertakings (Regulations) Act 1939 and any regulations made thereunder;

(*b*) in the case of an installation in any part of England or Wales, any provision of regulations made or having effect under section 61(1) (power to make building regulations) of the Public Health Act 1936; or

(*c*) in the case of an installation in Scotland, any provision of regulations made under section 3(1) (building standards regulations) of the Building (Scotland) Act 1959,

which is in force at the date of installation.

NOTES

London Building Acts 1930-39 Halsbury's Statutes, 4th edn Vol 26, title London (3rd edn Vol 20, pp 66, 113, 136).

London Gas Undertakings (Regulations) Act 1939 1939 c xcix.

Public Health Act 1936, s 61(1) Repealed by the Building Act 1984, s 133(2) and Sch 7, Halsbury's Statutes, 4th edn Vol 35, title Public Health (3rd edn Vol 54(2), pp 1440, 1458) and replaced by ss 1(1) and (2) and 122(*a*) of that Act, *ibid*, 4th edn Vol 35, title Public Health (3rd edn Vol 54(2) pp 1332, 1434).

Building (Scotland) Act 1959 1959 c 24.

27. Flues (1) No person shall install a gas appliance to any flue unless the flue is suitably constructed and in a proper condition for the safe operation of the appliance.

(2) No person shall install a flue pipe so that it enters a brick or masonry chimney in such a way that the seal between the flue pipe and chimney cannot be inspected.

(3) No person shall connect a gas appliance to a flue which is surrounded by an enclosure unless that enclosure is so sealed that any spillage of products of combustion cannot pass from the enclosure to any room or internal space other than the room or internal space in which the appliance is installed.

(4) No person shall install a power operated flue system for a gas appliance unless it safely prevents the operation of the appliance if the draught fails.

28. Access No person shall install a gas appliance except in such a manner that it is readily accessible for operation, inspection and maintenance.

29. Manufacturer's instructions Any person who installs a gas appliance shall leave with the owner or occupier of the premises in which the appliance is installed all instructions provided by the manufacturer accompanying the appliance.

30. Room-sealed appliances No person shall install a gas appliance in a private garage or in a bath or shower room unless it is a room-sealed appliance.

31. Suspended appliances No person shall install a suspended gas appliance unless the installation pipe to which it is connected is so constructed and installed as to be capable of safely supporting the weight imposed on it and the appliance is designed to be so supported.

32. Flue dampers (1) Any person who installs an automatic damper to serve a gas appliance shall—
    (*a*) ensure that the damper is so interlocked with the gas supply to the burner that burner operation is prevented in the event of failure of the damper when not in the open position, and
    (*b*) immediately after installation examine the appliance and the damper to verify that they can be used together safely without constituting a danger to any person or property.

(2) No person shall install a manually operated damper to serve a domestic gas appliance.

(3) No person shall install a domestic gas appliance to a flue which incorporates a manually operated damper unless the damper is permanently fixed in the open position.

33. Testing of appliances (1) Where a person installs a gas appliance at a time when gas is being supplied to the premises in which the appliance is installed, he shall immediately thereafter test its connection to the installation pipe to verify that it is gastight and examine the appliance and the gas fittings and other works for the supply of gas and any flue or means of ventilation to be used in connection with the appliance for the purpose of ascertaining whether—
    (*a*) the appliance has been installed in accordance with these Regulations;
    (*b*) the heat input and operating pressure are as recommended by the manufacturer;
    (*c*) the appliance has been installed with due regard to any manufacturer's instructions provided to accompany the appliance; and
    (*d*) all gas safety controls are in proper working order.

(2) Where a person carries out such testing and examination in relation to a gas appliance and adjustments are necessary to ensure compliance with the requirements specified in sub-paragraphs *(a)* to *(d)* of paragraph (1) above, he shall either carry out those adjustments or disconnect the appliance from the gas supply.

(3) Where a person installs a gas appliance in any premises at a time when gas is not being supplied to the premises, no person shall supply gas to that appliance unless he has caused such testing and examination and adjustments as are specified in paragraphs (1) and (2) above to be carried out.

34. Unsafe appliances (1) No person shall use a gas appliance or permit a gas appliance to be used if at any time he knows or has reason to suspect—

(*a*) that there is insufficient supply of air available for the appliance for proper combustion at the point of combustion;

(*b*) that the removal of the products of combustion from the appliance is not being or cannot safely be carried out;

(*c*) that the room or internal space in which the appliance is situated is not adequately ventilated for the purpose of providing air containing a sufficiency of oxygen for the persons present in the room, or in, or in the vicinity of, the internal space while the appliance is in use;

(*d*) that any gas is escaping from the appliance or from any gas fitting used in connection with the appliance; or

(*e*) that the appliance or any part of it or any gas fitting or other works for the supply of gas used in connection with the appliance is so faulty or maladjusted that it cannot be used without constituting a danger to any person or property.

(2) Any person engaged in carrying out any work in relation to a gas main, service pipe or gas fitting who knows or has reason to suspect that any defect or other circumstance referred to in paragraph (1) above exists shall forthwith take all reasonably practicable steps to inform the responsible person for the premises in which the appliance is situated or, where that is not reasonably practicable, the supplier of gas to the appliance.

(3) In paragraph (2) above, the expression "work" shall be construed as if, in the definition of "work" in Regulation 2(1) above, every reference to a gas fitting were a reference to a gas main, service pipe or fitting.

PART F
MISCELLANEOUS

35. Escape of gas (1) If the responsible person for any premises knows or has reason to suspect that gas is escaping into those premises, he shall immediately take all reasonable steps to cause the supply of gas to be shut off at such place as may be necessary to prevent further escape of gas.

(2) If gas continues to escape into those premises after the supply of gas has been shut off or when a smell of gas persists, the responsible person for the premises discovering such escape or smell shall immediately give notice of the escape or smell to the supplier of gas to the premises.

(3) Where an escape of gas has been stopped by shutting off the supply, no person shall cause or permit the supply to be re-opened until all necessary steps have been taken to prevent gas from escaping again.

36. Penalty Subject to Regulation 37 below, a person contravening or failing to comply with any provision of these Regulations in force shall be guilty of an offence and liable on summary conviction to a fine not exceeding £2,000.

37. Exception as to liability No person shall be guilty of an offence by reason of any contravention of, or failure to comply with, Regulation 3(2), 4(1), 6(3), 14, 15(2) or (3), 16 or 33(1) in any case in which he can show that he took all reasonable steps to prevent that contravention or failure.

38. (*This regulation amends the Gas Safety Regulations 1972, SI 1972/1178, p 16, ante, and the Gas Safety (Rights of Entry) Regulations 1983, SI 1983/1575, p 34, ante*).

Goods, Sale Of

See the title Sale of Goods and Hire-Purchase

Harbours

Accounts of harbour undertakings	Transport (Part 7)
Associated British Ports	Transport (Part 7)
Discharge of oil into the sea	Shipping (Part 10)
Employment of dock workers	Employment (Part 3)
Harbour reorganisation	Transport (Part 7)
Modification of Factories Act 1961 for docks, wharves, quays, etc.	Factories, Shops and Offices (Part 1A)
Reception facilities for oil residues etc.	Shipping (Part 10)
Restrictions on carriage of explosives	Explosives (Part 3)
Restrictions on carriage of petroleum	Petroleum

Health

Health and safety at work	Factories, Shops and Offices
Health service	National Health Service
Health visitors	Medicine (Part 4)
Medical, dental, etc , professions	Medicine
Public health, regulation	Food and Drugs; Public Health

---

High Court

See, generally, the title Courts

Bankruptcy proceedings in High Court	Bankruptcy and Insolvency
Criminal proceedings in High Court	Criminal Law (Part 1)
Matrimonial causes	Husband and Wife (Part 2)

Highways

CHRONOLOGICAL LIST OF INSTRUMENTS*

*Certain instruments regulating vehicular and other traffic on roads in what was formerly the London traffic area, or designating parking places in central London, which are named in the Chronological List of Instruments for the whole work, contained in the Main Service Binder, and which were formerly included in this title, have now been excluded from the title. These instruments were:— SI 1958/659; 1969/395, 1132 and 2322; 1961/423, 424, 1692, 1912 and 1913; 1962/263, 1601 and 1602; 1963/194, 341, 469, 931, 1337, 1389, 1584, 1585, 1586 and 1823; 1964/113, 347, 1159, 1179, 1751 and 1914; 1965/160, 205, 235, 291, 293, 306, 383, 397, 437, 520, 523, 524, 545, 581, 606, 643, 726, 729, 731, 732, 739, 740, 765, 932, 933, 945, 954, 956, 957, 1017 and 1415; and 1966/1312. See further the Preliminary Note under the heads "Powers for regulating traffic" and "Parking places", pp 56, 58, *post*.

SI	Description	Remarks	Page
1971/1706	Special and Other Roads (Maps etc) Regulations 1971	—	94
1971/1707	Stopping up of Accesses to Premises (Procedure) Regulations 1971	—	95
1972/1705	Railway Bridges (Load-Bearing Standards) (England and Wales) Order 1972	—	97
1973/686	Walkways Regulations 1973	—	98
1973/2147	Boundary Bridges (Appointed Day) Order 1973	—	105
1974/142	Local Government (Road Traffic and Highways) (Transitional Provisions) Order 1974	—	106
1974/735	Walkways (Amendment) Regulations 1974	Amend 1973/686 (*qv*)	—
1974/1674	Motor Vehicles (Competitions and Trials) (Amendment) Regulations 1974	Amend 1969/414 (*qv*)	—
1976/721	Highways (Inquiries Procedure) Rules 1976	—	106
1976/1657	Motor Vehicles (Competitions and Trials) (Amendment) Regulations 1976	Amend 1969/414 (*qv*)	
1978/889	Removal and Disposal of Vehicles (Loading Areas) (Modification of Enactments) Regulations 1978	—	114
1978/932	Control of Road-side Sales Orders (Procedure) Regulations 1978	—	114
1978/1535	Control of Off-Street Parking (England and Wales) Order 1978	See title Transport (Part 2A)	—
1979/401	"Pelican" Pedestrian Crossings (Amendment) Regulations and General Directions 1979	Amend 1969/888 (*qv*)	—
1980/457	New Street Byelaws (Extension of Operation) Order 1980	See Preliminary Note under head "New streets and making up of private streets", p 55, *post*	—
1980/1185	Cycle Racing on Highways (Amendment) Regulations 1980	Amend 1960/250 (*qv*)	—
1982/1103	Motor Vehicles (Competitions and Trials) (Amendment) Regulations 1982	Amend 1969/414 (*qv*)	
1982/1163	Motorways Traffic (England and Wales) Regulations 1982	—	114
1983/374	Motorways Traffic (England and Wales) (Amendment) Regulations 1983	Amend 1982/1163 (*qv*)	—
1983/483	New Street Byelaws (Extension of Operation) Variation Order 1983	Amend 1980/457 (*qv*)	—
1983/1087	Highways (Road Humps) Regulations 1983	—	120
1984/288	Isles of Scilly (Refuse Disposal (Amenity) Act 1978) Order 1984	Applies the 1978 Act, ss 2(1), (2), 3(1)-(3), (5), (8), 4(1)-(3), (5)-(7), 5(1)-(4), 6(1)-(4), (6), (8), 10, 11 to the Isles of Scilly subject to specified modifications	—
1984/1431	Cycle Tracks Regulations 1984		123
1984/1479	Motorways Traffic (England and Wales) (Amendment) Regulations 1984	Amend 1982/1163 (*qv*)	—
1984/1933	Builders' Skips (Markings) Regulations 1984	—	126
1985/1177	Cross-Boundary Bridges (Appointed Days) Order 1985	—	126
1985/1320	London Traffic Orders (Anticipatory Exercise of Powers) Order 1985	See title Transport (Part 2B)	—
1985/1661	Removal, Storage and Disposal of Vehicles (Charges) Regulations 1985	—	126
1986/153	Metropolitan Roads Trunking Order 1986	See Preliminary Note under head "Types of highways", p 52, *post*	—
1986/154	Designation of Roads in Greater London Order 1986	See Preliminary Note under head "Types of highways", p 52, *post*	—
1986/181	Control of Parking in Goods Vehicle Loading Areas Orders (Procedure) (England and Wales) Regulations 1986	—	128
1986/183	Removal and Disposal of Vehicles Regulations 1986	—	128
1986/184	Removal and Disposal of Vehicles (Loading Areas) Regulations 1986	—	137

INSTRUMENTS NO LONGER IN OPERATION

The following instruments, which were formerly included in this title, are no longer in operation:

SR&O		SI	SI		SI
1927/21	lapsed[1]		1975/1894	revoked by	1985/1661
SI			1975/1949	spent[2]	
1959/1147	revoked by	1982/1163	1977/2003	lapsed[3]	
1961/705	,, ,,	1984/1575	1978/481	superseded by	1982/1103
1967/1900	spent[2]		1978/1345	revoked by	1986/184
1968/43	revoked by	1986/183	1978/1346	,, ,,	1985/1661
1971/1087	,, ,,	1982/1163	1978/1347	,, ,,	1986/181
1971/1705	lapsed[3]		1980/169	,, ,,	1985/1661
1971/2003	,, [3]		1981/989	,, ,,	1985/1661
1972/1099	,, [4]		1981/990	,, ,,	1985/1661
1973/685	,, [3]		1982/1682	,, ,,	1985/1661
1974/449	,, [5]		1982/1696	,, ,,	1985/1661
1975/1247	,, [6]		1984/1575	spent	

[1] Lapsed on partial repeal of enabling power by the Local Government, Planning and Land Act 1980, s 1(7), Sch 7, para 7.
[2] Spent on repeal of provisions of the Road Traffic Regulation Act 1967 by the Road Traffic Regulation Act 1984; now incorporated into the provisions of the 1984 Act.
[3] Lapsed on repeal of the Highways Act 1971 by the Highways Act 1980.
[4] Lapsed on substitution of enabling power by the Local Government, Planning and Land Act 1980, s 1(7), Sch 7, para 10.
[5] Lapsed on partial repeal of enabling power by the Local Government Act 1985, s 102(2), Sch 17, as from 1 April 1986; cf Sch 4, para 53 of that Act.
[6] Lapsed on partial substitution of enabling power by the Local Government Act 1985, s 8, Sch 5, Pt I, para 4(3), as from 1 April 1986.

CROSS REFERENCES

Access to the countryside	Open Spaces and Recreation Grounds
Advertisements, control of	Town and Country Planning
Carriage by road of:	
animals	Animals (Part 3)
dangerous substances	Public Health (Part 6)
explosives	Explosives (Part 3)
gas cylinders	Petroleum
goods and passengers	Transport (Part 2A)
petroleum and similar substances	Petroleum
radioactive substances	Trade and Industry (Part 1F)
Crown roads (Royal Parks)	Open Spaces and Recreation Grounds
Development affecting highways	Town and Country Planning
Dogs on highways	Animals (Part 7)
Driving licences	Transport (Part 2A)
Fixed penalty procedure	Transport (Part 2B)
Footpaths	Open Spaces and Recreation Grounds
Highways, noise insulation	Building and Engineering
Invalid carriages, use on highways	Transport (Part 2B)
Local authorities' traffic orders, procedure	Transport (Part 2B)
Motor vehicles, construction and use	Transport (Part 2B)
Off-street parking, control	Transport (Part 2A)
Private streets, construction and improvement	Town and Country Planning
Public path orders, procedure	Open Spaces and Recreation Grounds
Public rights of way	Open Spaces and Recreation Grounds
Public rights of way, extinguishment under Housing Acts	Housing
Public service vehicles	Transport (Part 2C)
Ribbon development	Town and Country Planning
Road traffic generally	Transport (Part 2)
Speed of traffic	Transport (Part 2B)
Stopping up of highways for planning purposes	Town and Country Planning
Street collections	Charities; Police
Traffic regulation orders, procedure	Transport (Part 2B)
Traffic signs	Transport (Part 2B)
Traffic wardens	Transport (Part 2B)
Transfer of functions	Constitutional Law (Part 5)
User of vehicles	Transport (Part 2B)
Statutory instruments generally, their validity, effect and termination	Statutory Instruments, Vol. 1

PRELIMINARY NOTE

Scope of the title   Legislation concerning roads and bridges is diffuse in character. It is the aim of this title to gather together those instruments which appertain to the creation, maintenance, classification and general use of roads and bridges. In general it is left to the title Transport to deal with the regulation of road traffic and of vehicles which may use the roads. Certain instruments made under traffic-regulating powers are, however, included in this title because they affect the user of roads; examples of such instruments are those relating to pedestrian crossings, traffic regulation on motorways, the removal of vehicles and motoring and cycling events on highways.

The table of cross-references printed at p 51, *ante*, indicates briefly the numerous special topics concerning roads and bridges which will be found in other titles.

In addition to the instruments listed at pp 49-50, *ante*, there exist very many orders relating to highways which, being of a local character, are outside the scope of this work. Nevertheless, in order to provide an adequate review of subordinate legislation regarding this subject, mention is made in the following paragraphs of some of the more important classes of local orders which may be made. Except where they are made by a local authority, such orders usually bear numbers in the SR & O/SI series and are included in the classified lists of local instruments which appear at the end of the official annual volumes of SR & O/SI.

Highway authorities and Ministers   The authorities who are to act as highway authorities for the various classes of highways are prescribed by Part I (ss 1-9) of the Highways Act 1980, Halsbury's Statutes, 4th edn Vol 20, title Highways, Streets and Bridges (3rd edn Vol 50 (1), p 462 *et seq*), as amended by the Road Traffic Regulation Act 1984 and the Local Government Act 1985. Consequent on the reorganisation of local government in the Greater London area by the London Government Act 1963, Halsbury's Statutes, 4th edn Vol 26, title London (3rd edn Vol 20, p 448 *et seq*) and outside that area by the Local Government Act 1972, *ibid*, 4th edn Vol 25, title Local Government (3rd edn Vol 42, p 841 *et seq*), transitional and other provisions, in connection with regulations, orders, etc, relating to traffic and highway matters, were made, respectively, by the London Traffic and Highways (Transitional Provisions) Order 1965, SI 1965/481, as amended, p 70, *post*, and the Local Government (Road Traffic and Highways) (Transitional Provisions) Order 1974, SI 1974/142, p 106, *post*. As to bridges, see also the Boundary Bridges (Appointed Day) Order 1973, SI 1973/2147, p 105, *post*, and the Cross-Boundary Bridges (Appointed Days) Order 1985, SI 1985/1177, p 126, *post*.

The responsible Minister, so far as legislation regarding roads and bridges is concerned, is now for most purposes the Secretary of State for Transport, by virtue of the Transfer of Functions (Transport) Order 1981, SI 1981/238, in the title Constitutional Law (Part 5); in relation to Wales, however, many of the functions concerned are exercisable by the Secretary of State for Wales by virtue of the Secretary of State for Wales and Minister of Land and Natural Resources Order 1965, SI 1965/319, in the same title.

Highways

Some of the principal instruments relating to highways are considered below under the following heads: I. Types of highways; II. Construction of roads; III. Stopping up and diversion; IV. New streets and making up of private streets; and V. User of Highways.

I. Types of highways   The meaning of "highway" at common law (see Halsbury's Laws, 4th edn Vol 21, para 1) is extended in the Highways Act 1980 to mean generally the whole or part of a highway other than a ferry or waterway, and where a highway passes over a bridge or through a tunnel, that bridge or tunnel is to be taken for the purposes of the Act to be part of the highway; see s 328 of that Act, Halsbury's Statutes, 4th edn Vol 20, title Highways, Streets and Bridges (3rd edn Vol 50 (1), p 791). The statutory types of highway include trunk roads (see ss 10, 11 of the 1980 Act), principal and classified roads (ss 12, 13) and special roads (ss 16-20). A special road may also be a trunk road or a classified road. A motorway is a form of special road. A further type of highway, in Greater London, was the metropolitan road, which was abolished, as from 1 April 1986, by the Local Government Act 1985. As from that date, metropolitan roads continue to be principal roads, but the Secretary of State is empowered by order to direct that a metropolitan road shall instead become a trunk road; see the 1985 Act, s 8, Sch 4, para 53 and the Metropolitan Roads Trunking Order 1986, SI 1986/153, listed at p 50, *ante*. Under s 8, Sch 5, Pt II, para 5 of that Act, the Secretary of State is empowered to designate roads in Greater London for the purpose of facilitating the movement of traffic; see the Designation of Roads in Greater London Order 1986, SI 1986/154, listed at p 50, *ante*.

Part II of the Highways Act 1980 (ss 10-23), which contains the principal provisions relating to classified roads and special roads, contains a number of provisions enabling the Secretary of State or highway authorities to make orders and schemes; see, *eg*, s 10 (2) (power to direct that a highway shall become or cease to be a trunk road), s 11 (power to direct that certain local and private Act functions with respect to trunk roads are to be exercisable in accordance with specified conditions), s 14 (powers as respects side roads which cross or join trunk or classified roads), s 16 (schemes for provision of special roads) and s 18 (supplementary orders relating to special roads). In addition, under s 12 (3), the Secretary of State may classify highways or proposed highways for which local highway authorities are the highway authorities in such manner as he may determine; such classification is effected administratively and not by statutory instrument. All orders and schemes made under Part II of the Act of 1980 are local, and therefore outside the scope of this work, with the exception of orders made under s 13 (1) changing the designation of principal roads to some other description and under s 17 (3) varying the classes of traffic specified in Schedule 4 to the Act (by reference to which the classes of traffic prescribed by a scheme under s 16 are to be designated); at the date of this volume, no orders under s 13 (1) or s 17 (3) have yet been made. The procedure to be followed in connection with the making of certain orders and schemes relating to special roads and trunk roads is prescribed by the Special Roads and Trunk Roads (Procedure) Regulations 1962, SI 1962/1319, p 61, *post* (see also the Special and Other Roads (Maps etc) Regulations 1971, SI 1971/1706, p 94, *post*); the manner of publication of a notice of opening of a special road (which is required by certain provisions of the Road Traffic Regulation Act 1984, Halsbury's Statutes, 4th edn Vol 38, title Road Traffic (3rd edn Vol 54 (2), p 1509 *et seq*) is prescribed by the Special Roads (Notice of Opening) Regulations 1962, SI 1962/1320, p 64, *post*; and the procedure to be followed at local inquiries held under para 7 or 14 of Schedule 1 to the Act of 1980 in connection with orders or schemes relating to trunk, special or classified roads is prescribed by the Highways (Inquiries Procedure) Rules 1976, SI 1976/721, p 106, *post*. Under reg 27 of the Town and Country Planning (Development Plans) Regulations 1965, SI 1965/1453, and reg 28 of the Town and Country Planning (Development Plans for Greater London) Regulations 1966, SI 1966/48, in the title Town and Country Planning, proceedings preliminary to the making of certain orders under Part II of the Act of 1980 may be taken concurrently with proceedings in connection with the approval, making or amendment of a development plan.

Public rights of way may be created by public path creation orders made by a local authority and confirmed by the Secretary of State under the Highways Act 1980, s 26, Halsbury's Statutes, 4th edn Vol 20, title Highways, Streets and Bridges (3rd edn Vol 50 (1), p 492); for the procedure on the making of orders, see the Public Path Orders and Extinguishment of Public

Right of Way Orders Regulations 1983, SI 1983/23, in the title Open Spaces and Recreation Grounds.

Footpaths over, through or under parts of a building may be created by agreements under the Highways Act 1980, s 35, Halsbury's Statutes, 4th edn Vol 20, title Highways, Streets and Bridges (3rd edn Vol 50 (1), p 500). For regulations relating to such footpaths, see the Walkways Regulations 1973, SI 1973/686, as amended, p 98, *post.*

Footpaths, or parts of footpaths, may be converted into cycle tracks by orders made by local highway authorities under the Cycle Tracks Act 1984, Halsbury's Statutes, 4th edn Vol 20, title Highways, Streets and Bridges (3rd edn Vol 54 (1), p 636). For the procedure to be followed in connection with the making of such orders and their confirmation, see the Cycle Tracks Regulations 1984, SI 1984/1431, p 123, *post.*

II. Construction of roads   The main power of the Secretary of State and local highway authorities to construct new highways is contained in the Highways Act 1980, s 24, Halsbury's Statutes, 4th edn Vol 20, title Highways, Streets and Bridges (3rd edn Vol 50 (1), p 490).

Power to make orders for the compulsory acquisition of land for highway construction is conferred, in particular by:—

(1) Sections 238 *et seq* of the Highways Act 1980, Halsbury's Statutes, 4th edn Vol 20, title Highways, Streets and Bridges (3rd edn Vol 50 (1), p 717 *et seq*).

(2) Section 218 of the Town and Country Planning Act 1971, *ibid*, 4th edn Vol 46, title Town and Country Planning (3rd edn Vol 41, p 1832) (see also, as to concurrent proceedings, s 219 of that Act and the Stopping Up of Highways (Concurrent Proceedings) Regulations 1948, SI 1948/1348, and reg 17 of the Town and Country Planning General Regulations 1976, SI 1976/1419, both in the title Town and Country Planning).

(3) Section 11 of the New Towns Act 1981, Halsbury's Statutes, 4th edn Vol 46, title Town and Country Planning (3rd edn Vol 51, p 2050) (see also, as to procedure, Schedule 4 to that Act, and the New Towns (Compulsory Purchase of Land) Regulations 1977, SI 1977/549, and the New Towns Compulsory Purchase (Contemporaneous Procedure) Regulations 1947, SR & O 1947/1353, both in the title Town and Country Planning.

The procedure for obtaining compulsory purchase orders is governed in most cases by the Acquisition of Land Act 1981, Halsbury's Statutes, 4th edn Vol 9, title Compulsory Acquisition, and forms are prescribed by the Compulsory Purchase of Land Regulations 1982, SI 1982/6, in the title Compulsory Acquisition in this work (see also, as to compulsory purchase under the Act of 1981, Part I of the Compulsory Purchase Act 1965, Halsbury's Statutes, 4th edn Vol 9, title Compulsory Acquisition).

Road humps   Highway authorities and the Secretary of State are empowered on certain conditions to construct road humps to control the speed of vehicles; see the Highways Act 1980, ss 90A-90F (as inserted by the Transport Act 1981, s 32, Sch 10), Halsbury's Statutes, 4th edn Vol 20, title Highways, Streets and Bridges (3rd edn Vol 51, p 998 *et seq*). As to consultation about proposals for, and the construction and maintenance of, road humps, see the Highways (Road Humps) Regulations 1983, SI 1983/1087, p 120, *post.*

III. Stopping up and diversion   The old common law writ "ad quod damnum" having fallen into desuetude, highways are in practice stopped up or diverted today only under statutory powers. In the case of a highway which is unnecessary, or which can be diverted so as to make it nearer or more commodious to the public, stopping up or diversion may be authorised by order of a magistrates' court under the Highways Act 1980, s 116, Halsbury's Statutes, 4th edn Vol 20, title Highways, Streets and Bridges (3rd edn Vol 50 (1), p 583) (see also, as to footpaths crossing or near to land leased for military purposes, s 13 of the Military Lands Act 1892, Halsbury's Statutes, 4th edn

Vol 3, title Armed Forces (Pt 6). If the inclosure of common land is proposed, highways through that land may be stopped up or diverted by means of a valuer's notice (s 62 of the Inclosure Act 1845, Halsbury's Statutes, 4th edn Vol 6, title Commons). The temporary closing of roads within the limits of an Order in Council authorising the execution of military manoeuvres may be ordered by two justices of the peace or a military officer duly authorised by them (see s 3 of the Manoeuvres Act 1958, Halsbury's Statutes, 4th edn Vol 3, title Armed Forces (Pt 6)).

In addition many enactments confer powers of making, approving or confirming orders for the stopping up or diversion of highways for a variety of purposes. Examples of such enactments are: the Defence Act 1860, s 40, Halsbury's Statutes, 4th edn Vol 3, title Armed Forces (Pt 6), the Land Powers (Defence) Act 1958, s 8, *ibid*, 4th edn Vol 20, title Highways, Streets and Bridges (3rd edn Vol 15, p 137), the Housing Act 1985, ss 294, 295, *ibid*, 4th edn Vol 21, title Housing, the Town and Country Planning Act 1971, ss 209-211, 214, *ibid*, 4th edn Vol 46, title Town and Country Planning (3rd edn Vol 41, pp 1822-1828), the Highways Act 1980, ss 14 (1)(*a*), 18 (1)(*c*), 118 and 119, *ibid*, 4th edn Vol 20, title Highways, Streets and Bridges (3rd edn Vol 50 (1), pp 478, 483, 585, 587), the Acquisition of Land Act 1981, s 32, *ibid*, 4th edn Vol 9, title Compulsory Acquisition, the New Towns Act 1981, s 16, *ibid*, 4th edn Vol 46, title Town and Country Planning (3rd edn Vol 51, p 2053) and the Civil Aviation Act 1982, s 48, *ibid*, 4th edn Vol 4, title Aviation. The procedure to be followed in connection with the making, etc, of extinguishment of right of way orders under the said s 32 of the Act of 1981 and of public path extinguishment and diversion orders under the said ss 118 and 119 of the Act of 1980 is prescribed by the Public Path Orders and Extinguishment of Public Right of Way Orders Regulations 1983, SI 1983/23 in the title Open Spaces and Recreation Grounds.

Under the Highways Act 1980, s 124, Halsbury's Statutes, 4th edn Vol 20, title Highways, Streets and Bridges (3rd edn Vol 50 (1), p 593), orders may be made for the stopping up of private means of access to premises from a highway where the means of access are likely to cause danger to, or to interfere unreasonably with, traffic on the highway; for procedure, see the Stopping up of Accesses to Premises (Procedure) Regulations 1971, SI 1971/1707, p 95, *post*. See also the 1980 Act, ss 125 and 126.

IV. New streets and making up of private streets Provisions relating to "new streets" are contained in the Highways Act 1980, Part X (ss 186-202), Halsbury's Statutes, 4th edn Vol 20, title Highways, Streets and Bridges (3rd edn Vol 50 (1), p 666 *et seq*). Under s 186, as amended, county, metropolitan district and London borough councils may, and if required by the Secretary of State, must, make byelaws for regulating the level, width and construction of new streets, the provision for the sewerage of such streets, etc. Such byelaws, or byelaws made under the Highways Act 1959, s 157, which the said s 186 replaces, are to cease to have effect ten years from the date on which they were made but the Secretary of State may by order extend this period (s 186 (8)). Byelaws in force immediately before the commencement of the Act of 1959 (*ie*, 1 January 1960) under an enactment corresponding to s 157 (which byelaws were saved by s 312 of, and para 31 of Schedule 24 to, the Act) were to cease to have effect on 30 April 1962 but this period might be extended by order under the 1959 Act, s 312 (6). The Highways Act 1980, Sch 23, para 11 provides that the repeal by that Act of the 1959 Act does not affect the operation of any order under the said s 312 (6) and any such order in force at the commencement of the 1980 Act (*ie* 1 January 1981) may be varied or revoked by the Secretary of State. The period was accordingly extended by successive orders made under the proviso to the said s 312 (6), *viz*, SI 1962/645, SI 1967/512, SI 1972/595, SI 1974/645, SI 1977/502 and SI 1980/457 (the last being varied by SI 1983/483, made under the 1980 Act, Sch 23, para 11). The combined effect of these orders (of which the last two are listed at p 50, *ante*) is to extend byelaws falling under s 312 (6) until 31 March 1986 unless such byelaws are revoked earlier.

The making up of private streets is governed by the Highways Act 1980, Part XI (ss 203-237), Halsbury's Statutes, 4th edn Vol 20, title Highways, Streets and Bridges (3rd edn Vol 50 (1), p 681 *et seq*). Certain matters arising under that Part of the Act are, by virtue of s 224, local land charges; as to the registration of local charges, see the Local Land Charges Act 1975, Halsbury's Statutes, 4th edn Vol 37, title Real Property (3rd edn Vol 45, p 1705), and the Local Land Charges Rules 1977, SI 1977/985, in the title Real Property (Part 2) in this work. A further instrument relevant to Part XI of the 1980 Act is the Town and Country Planning (Construction and Improvement of Private Streets) Regulations 1951, SI 1951/2224, as amended, in the title Town and Country Planning (having effect under s 232 of the Act).

V. User of highways   Power to make instruments regulating or restricting the user of highways is conferred by numerous enactments. The majority of such instruments apply only to vehicles, but in certain cases (*eg*, the "Zebra" Pedestrian Crossings Regulations 1971, SI 1971/1524, p 85, *post*) the rights of pedestrians are also affected, and certain instruments relate to animals on highways. Guidance for all road users is contained in the Highway Code, issued by the Secretary of State and obtainable from H M Stationery Office or through any bookseller. The revision and issue to the public of the Highway Code are statutory duties of the Secretary of State under s 37 of the Road Traffic Act 1972 (as substituted by the Transport Act 1982, s 60), Halsbury's Statutes, 4th edn Vol 38, title Road Traffic (3rd edn Vol 52, p 1462), and that section also lays down that failure to observe the code may be relied on in any legal proceedings as tending to establish or negative any liability which is in question.

Powers for regulating traffic   Some of the principal enactments under which instruments may be made for the regulation of traffic are mentioned below. As stated at p 52, *ante*, instruments made under traffic-regulating powers and which solely affect the user of vehicles are within the scope of the title Transport.

Under s 1 of the Road Traffic Regulation Act 1984, Halsbury's Statutes, 4th edn Vol 38, title Road Traffic (3rd edn Vol 54 (2), p 1513), as amended by the Local Government Act 1985, s 8, Sch 5, Pt I, para 4(2), which applies to roads outside Greater London, county councils or metropolitan district councils and, as respect trunk roads, the Secretary of State, may (subject to Sch 9, Pts I to III, which contain special provisions with respect to certain orders) make orders, called "traffic regulation orders", prohibiting, restricting or regulating the use of a road or any part of the width thereof by vehicular traffic or by such traffic of any class specified in the order, or by, or by any specified class of, pedestrians, either generally or subject to exceptions, and either at all times or at times, on days or during periods specified. In particular, provision may be so made (*a*) requiring vehicular traffic to proceed in a specified direction or prohibiting its so proceeding, (*b*) specifying the part of the carriageway to be used by traffic proceeding in a specified direction, (*c*) prohibiting or restricting the waiting of vehicles or the loading and unloading of vehicles, (*d*) prohibiting the use of roads by through traffic, or (*e*) prohibiting or restricting overtaking (see the 1984 Act, s 2). The Various Trunk Roads (Prohibition of Waiting) (Clearways) Order 1963, SI 1963/1172, p 68, *post*, and many other orders which are local and outside the scope of this work have effect under these powers. The procedure to be followed in connection with the making of orders under these powers is prescribed by the Local Authorities' Traffic Orders (Procedure) (England and Wales) Regulations 1986, SI 1986/179, and the Secretary of State's Traffic Orders (Procedure) (England and Wales) Regulations 1986, SI 1986/180, both in the title Transport (Part 2B).

As respects roads in Greater London, similar powers to make orders for controlling or regulating vehicular and other traffic (including pedestrians) are conferred, on local authorities (*ie* London borough councils or the Common Council of the City of London) or, in the case of trunk roads, the Secretary of State, or, with his consent, the local authority, by the Road Traffic Regulation Act 1984, s 6, Halsbury's Statutes, 4th edn Vol 38, title Road Traffic (3rd edn Vol 54 (2), p 1518), as amended by the Local Government Act 1985, s 8, Sch 5, Pt I, para 4 (3). In particular such orders may provide for any of the purposes, or with respect to any of the matters, mentioned in Schedule 1 to the Act of 1984, and for any other purpose which is a purpose mentioned in s 1 (1) (*a*) to (*f*) of that Act. In connection with the exercise of these powers reference should also be made to the special provisions contained in Sch 9, Pts I to III of the Act. Orders made or having effect under s 6 of the Act of 1984, being local, are outside the scope of this work. (Certain regulations relating to London traffic, which were made by the Minister of Transport under s 34 (repealed) of the Road Traffic Act 1960 and published as statutory instruments, were also formerly included in this title; see the note at the foot of p 49, *ante*.) The procedure to be followed in connection with the making of traffic regulation orders by London authorities is prescribed by the London Authorities' Traffic Orders (Procedure) Regulations 1986, SI 1986/259, in the title Transport (Part 2B).

Provision is made by the Local Government Act 1985, s 8, Sch 5, Pt II, Halsbury's Statutes, 4th edn Vol 25, title Local Government, concerning the exercise of traffic powers (including the making of such orders as are referred to above) in Greater London and the metropolitan counties.

Regulations with respect to the use of special roads may be made under the Road Traffic Regulation Act 1984, s 17 (2), Halsbury's Statutes, 4th edn Vol 38, title Road Traffic (3rd edn Vol 54 (2), p 1528), under which the Motorways Traffic (England and Wales) Regulations 1982, SI 1982/1163, as amended, p 114, *post*, now have effect.

Under s 7 of the Local Government (Miscellaneous Provisions) Act 1976, Halsbury's Statutes, 4th edn Vol 20, title Highways, Streets and Bridges (3rd edn Vol 46, p 701), highway authorities are empowered to make orders controlling road-side sales in order to avoid danger or facilitate the passage of traffic; the procedure to be followed in this connection is prescribed by the Control of Road-side Sales Orders (Procedure) Regulations 1978, SI 1978/932, p 114, *post*.

Pedestrian crossings   Pedestrian crossings are established (i) on roads other than trunk roads, by local authorities, subject to certain provisions as to consultation and the giving of notice (see the Road Traffic Regulation Act 1984, s 23, as amended, Halsbury's Statutes, 4th edn Vol 38, title Road Traffic (3rd edn Vol 54 (2), p 1534)); and (ii) on trunk roads, by the Secretary of State or by local authorities acting under delegated powers (see the 1984 Act, s 24 and the Highways Act 1980, s 6, Halsbury's Statutes, 4th edn Vol 20, title Highways, Streets and Bridges (3rd edn Vol 50 (1), p 466)). The "Zebra" Pedestrian Crossings Regulations 1971, SI 1971/1524, p 85, *post*, prescribe the manner in which crossings are to be indicated and govern their use by vehicles and pedestrians; and the "Pelican" Pedestrian Crossings Regulations 1969 (set out in Part II of SI 1969/888, p 76, *post*) provide a method of regulating traffic at pedestrian crossings by means of light signals and indicators for pedestrians which can be made to work by pedestrians pushing a button.

Street playgrounds   Under the Road Traffic Regulation Act 1984, ss 29, 30, Halsbury's Statutes, 4th edn Vol 38, title Road Traffic (3rd edn Vol 54 (2), pp 1538, 1539), as amended by the Local Government Act 1985, s 8, Sch 5, Pt I, para 4 (11), (12), s 102 (2), Sch 17, orders made by a local authority may prohibit or restrict traffic on a road set aside for use as a children's playground. The Local Authorities' Traffic Orders (Procedure) (England and Wales) Regulations 1986, SI 1986/179, in the title Transport (Part 2B), prescribe the procedure for the making of such orders by local authorities outside

Greater London while the making of such orders by local authorities in Greater London is regulated by the Secretary of State (see the 1984 Act, s 30 (6), as amended).

Obstructions in highways   Unreasonably obstructing a highway constitutes a nuisance at common law (for a statement of the circumstances in which an action will lie, see *Harper* v *Haden* (*G N*) & *Sons, Ltd*, [1933] Ch 298 at pp 304 *et seq*; see also *Dwyer* v *Mansfield*, [1946] 2 All ER 247; [1946] KB 437 and generally Halsbury's Laws, Vol 21, para 419 *et seq*. Wilful obstruction is also an offence under the Highways Act 1980, s 137, Halsbury's Statutes, 4th edn Vol 20, title Highways, Streets and Bridges (3rd edn Vol 50 (1), p 606), and parking a motor vehicle on the road so as to cause unnecessary obstruction is an offence under reg 122 of the Motor Vehicles (Construction and Use) Regulations 1978, SI 1978/1017, and reg 67 of the Motor Vehicles (Construction and Use) (Track Laying Vehicles) Regulations 1955, SI 1955/990, in the title Transport (Part 2B).

The removal of vehicles which have been illegally, obstructively or dangerously parked on roads or have been abandoned or have broken down and the disposal of abandoned vehicles are governed by the Road Traffic Regulation Act 1984, ss 99-103, as amended, Halsbury's Statutes, 4th edn Vol 38, title Road Traffic (3rd edn Vol 54 (2), p 1605 *et seq*), and ss 3-5 of the Refuse Disposal (Amenity) Act 1978, as amended, *ibid*, 4th edn Vol 35, title Public Health (3rd edn Vol 48, p 1203-1207) and by regulations made under those enactments, *viz*, the Removal and Disposal of Vehicles Regulations 1986, SI 1986/183, p 128, *post*. Compare SI 1978/889, p 114, *post* and 1986/184, p 137, *post*, which relate to the removal and disposal of vehicles standing in any part of a goods vehicle loading area while parking on that part is prohibited.

Restrictions on the deposit of builders' skips on the highway and provisions for their removal are contained in the Highways Act 1980, ss 139, 140, Halsbury's Statutes, 4th edn Vol 20, title Highways, Streets and Bridges (3rd edn Vol 50 (1), pp 608, 610); the Builders' Skips (Markings) Regulations 1984, SI 1984/1933, p 126 *post*, made under the said s 139, as amended, contain provisions as to the markings which must be carried by skips placed on the highway.

Parking places   The principal enactments relating to the provision by local authorities of parking places off highways or without payment on highways are the Road Traffic Regulation Act 1984, ss 32-41, Halsbury's Statutes, 4th edn Vol 38, title Road Traffic (3rd edn Vol 54 (2), p 1541 *et seq*). Orders made under these enactments are local and outside the scope of this work. The procedure to be followed in connection with the making of such orders by local authorities is prescribed by the Local Authorities' Traffic Orders (Procedure) (England and Wales) Regulations 1986, SI 1986/179, and the London Authorities' Traffic Orders (Procedure) Regulations 1986, SI 1986/259, in the title Transport (Part 2B). As respects London, attention is further drawn to the Restriction of Ribbon Development (Power to provide Parking Places) London, Order 1936, SR & O 1936/1088, in the title Town and Country Planning (which is saved so far as it applies to the City of London by the 1984 Act, Sch 10, para 13). The operation of public off-street parking in Greater London is regulated under the 1984 Act, s 43, Halsbury's Statutes, 4th edn Vol 38, title Road Traffic (3rd edn Vol 54 (2), p 1551), in non-metropolitan counties in England and Wales under the Control of Off-Street Parking (England and Wales) Order 1978, SI 1978/1535 (which now has effect under the 1984 Act, s 44) and in metropolitan districts in England and Wales under the Control of Off-Street Parking (England and Wales) (Metropolitan Districts) Order 1986, SI 1986/225 (made under the said s 44). Both of these instruments are included in the title Transport (Part 2A).

Provisions relating to parking places on highways where charges may be made are contained in the 1984 Act, ss 45-49, 51-55, as amended, Halsbury's Statutes, 4th edn Vol 38, title Road Traffic (3rd edn Vol 54 (2), p 1557 *et seq*). Subject to Sch 9, Pts I to III of that Act, such parking places are designated by "designation orders" made by local authorities under s 45, as amended; and by s 46, as amended, the local authority making a designation order must prescribe any charges to be paid for vehicles left in a parking place designated by the order and may make provision for regulating or restricting the use of any designated parking place. Orders made or having effect under these powers are local and outside the scope of this work (although certain orders designating parking places in central London, which were made by the Minister of Transport under s 85 (repealed) of the Road Traffic Act 1960 (as amended) and which were published as statutory instruments, were formerly included in this title; see the note at the foot of p 49, *ante*). The procedure to be followed in connection with the making of orders under ss 45, 46 and 49 (2) and (4) of the Act of 1984 by local authorities is governed by the Local Authorities' Traffic Orders (Procedure) (England and Wales) Regulations 1986, SI 1986/179, and the London Authorities' Traffic Orders (Procedure) Regulations 1986, SI 1986/259, referred to above.

Provision is made by the Local Government Act 1985, s 8, Sch 5, Pt II, Halsbury's Statutes, 4th edn Vol 25, title Local Government, concerning the exercise of traffic powers, including the making of such orders as are referred to above, in Greater London and the metropolitan counties.

Under the Road Traffic Regulation Act 1984, s 61, as amended, Halsbury's Statutes, 4th edn Vol 38, title Road Traffic (3rd edn Vol 54 (2), p 1575), orders may be made for controlling the parking of vehicles in areas used for loading or unloading goods vehicles; the procedure to be followed is governed by SI 1986/181, p 128, *post*.

Motoring and cycling events on highways The holding of competitions and trials involving the use of motor vehicles on public highways is governed by s 15 of the Road Traffic Act 1972, Halsbury's Statutes, 4th edn Vol 38, title Road Traffic (3rd edn Vol 42, p 1662) and by the Motor Vehicles (Competitions and Trials) Regulations 1969, SI 1969/414, as amended, p 74, *post*; and the holding of races and trials of speed on public highways between cycles is governed by s 20 of the said Act of 1972, Halsbury's Statutes, 4th edn Vol 38, title Road Traffic (3rd edn Vol 42, p 1665), and the Cycle Racing on Highways Regulations 1960, SI 1960/250, as amended, p 61, *post*.

Street works Provisions for mitigating obstruction caused by the execution of works in highways are contained in the Highways Act 1980, ss 156, 160, as amended, Halsbury's Statutes, 4th edn Vol 20, title Highways, Streets and Bridges (3rd edn Vol 50 (1), pp 627, 634). The Public Utilities Street Works Act 1950 (Commencement) Order 1951, SI 1951/1555 (listed at p 49, *ante*), appointed 26 October 1951 as the time from which the codes contained in Part I and II of the Public Utilities Street Works Act 1950, regulating the exercise of certain statutory powers relating to street works, were to have effect in relation to certain such powers (ss 15 (2) (*b*) and 24 (1) (*b*) of the Act, Halsbury's Statutes, 4th edn Vol 20, title Highways, Streets and Bridges (3rd edn Vol 15, pp 86, 97)). Under Schedule 2 to the Act of 1950, as amended, if a street, not being a maintainable highway, is likely to become a maintainable highway, the local highway authority may declare that it is likely to become such; such a declaration is a local land charge and is registrable in the local land charges register in accordance with the Local Land Charges Rules 1977, SI 1977/985, in the title Real Property (Part 2).

Miscellaneous Under s 5 of the Police, Factories, etc (Miscellaneous Provisions) Act 1916, Halsbury's Statutes, 4th edn Vol 33, title Police (3rd edn Vol 25, p 287), as amended, regulations may be made as to the collection of money in streets; as to such regulations, see the Preliminary Note to the title Charities under the head "Street collections".

Dogs on highways are required to wear a collar bearing the name and address of the owner by virtue of the Control of Dogs Order of 1930, SR &

O 1930/399, in the title Animals (Part 7). Under s 31 of the Road Traffic Act 1972, Halsbury's Statutes, 4th edn Vol 38, title Road Traffic (3rd edn Vol 42, p 1673), certain local authorities may make orders designating roads upon which dogs must be held on a lead; the procedure to be followed in connection with the making of such orders is prescribed by the Control of Dogs on Roads Orders (Procedure) (England and Wales) Regulations 1962, SI 1962/2340, as amended, p 64, *post*.

The carriage by road of animals is dealt with in the title Animals (Part 3) and the carriage of goods and passengers in the title Transport (Part 2A).

The carriage by road of particular substances may be regulated by statutory byelaw or other instrument. See, as respects explosives, byelaws made by the Secretary of State dated 20 September 1924, SR & O 1924/1129, and the Conveyance by Road of Military Explosives Regulations 1977, SI 1977/888, in the title Explosives (Part 3); as respects gas cylinders, petroleum-spirit, carbon disulphide, etc, see the relevant instruments in the title Petroleum; as respects radioactive substances, see the Radioactive Substances (Carriage by Road) (Great Britain) Regulations 1974, SI 1974/1735, in the title Trade and Industry (Part 1F); and as respects other dangerous substances, see the Dangerous Substances (Conveyance by Road in Road Tankers and Tank Containers) Regulations 1981, SI 1981/1059, in the title Public Health (Part 6).

Highway authorities are required in certain cases to insulate buildings (or to make grants for their insulation) against excessive noise caused by highway traffic or works; see the Noise Insulation Regulations 1975, SI 1975/1763, in the title Building and Engineering.

Bridges

Many statutes relating to highways apply also to bridges (see, *eg*, the Highways Act 1980, s 328 (2), Halsbury's Statutes, 4th edn Vol 20, title Highways, Streets and Bridges (3rd edn Vol 50 (1), p 791), and the definitions of "road" in the Road Traffic Regulation Act 1984, s 142 (1), *ibid*, 4th edn Vol 38, title Road Traffic (3rd edn Vol 54 (2), p 1644) and the Road Traffic Act 1972, s 196 (1), *ibid*, 4th edn Vol 38, title Road Traffic (3rd edn Vol 42, p 1834)), and only a few enactments confer powers for making instruments relating only to bridges.

Under the Highways Act 1980, s 93, Halsbury's Statutes, 4th edn Vol 20, title Highways, Streets and Bridges (3rd edn Vol 50 (1), p 559) the Secretary of State has power, on the application of the owners of a bridge or a local highway authority (or, in the case of a trunk road bridge, on his own initiative), to make an order as to the reconstruction, improvement or maintenance of the bridge. The procedure for making such orders is governed by certain provisions of the Act and by the Bridges Orders (Procedure) Regulations 1965, SI 1965/869, p 70, *post*.

By virtue of the 1980 Act, s 106, the Secretary of State may make orders or schemes for the construction as part of a trunk road or special road of a bridge over a tunnel under navigable waters and local highway authorities may make schemes for the construction of such a bridge or tunnel as part of certain highways. Such instruments are local and outside the scope of this work.

Under s 117 of the Transport Act 1968, as amended, Halsbury's Statutes, 4th edn Vol 20, title Highways, Streets and Bridges (3rd edn Vol 15, p 524), the Secretary of State may prescribe load-bearing standards for bridges carrying highways over railways, inland waterways, etc. This power has been exercised in respect of bridges over railways by the Railway Bridges (Load-Bearing Standards) (England and Wales) Order 1972, SI 1972/1705, p 97, *post*.

For provisions concerning agreements between authorities as to which of them was to be the highway authority for certain highways carried by bridges which cross local government boundaries, see the Boundary Bridges (Appointed Day) Order 1973, SI 1973/2147, p 105, *post*, and the Cross-Boundary Bridges (Appointed Days) Order 1985, SI 1985/1177, p 126, *post*.

THE CYCLE RACING ON HIGHWAYS REGULATIONS 1960
SI 1960/250

NOTES
Authority These regulations were made on 12 February 1960 by the Minister of Transport under s 13 (repealed) of the Road Traffic Act 1956 and all other enabling powers. The regulations continued to have effect, by virtue of s 267 (2) of, and para 1 of Sch 19 to, the Road Traffic Act 1960, as if made under s 12 (repealed) of that Act; and they now have effect, by virtue of s 205 (2) of, and para 1 of Sch 10 to, the Road Traffic Act 1972, as if made under s 20 thereof, Halsbury's Statutes, 4th edn Vol 38, title Road Traffic (3rd edn Vol 42, p1665).
Commencement 1 March 1960.
Amendment These regulations have been amended by the Cycle Racing on Highways (Amendment) Regulations 1963, SI 1963/929 and the Cycle Racing on Highways (Amendment) Regulations 1980, SI 1980/1185. They were previously modified by a number of instruments conferring special authorisations in respect of specified events; these are now all spent.
General It is provided by s 20 (1) of the Road Traffic Act 1972 that a person who promotes or takes part in a race or trial of speed on a public highway between cycles, not being motor vehicles, shall be guilty of an offence, unless the race or trial is authorised, and is conducted in accordance with any conditions imposed, by or under regulations under that section; for provisions as to prosecution and punishment of offences, see s 177 of, and Part 1 of Sch 4 to, that Act, as amended. The provisions which may be contained in regulations under s 20 are set out in sub-ss (2) and (3) and, under sub-s (4) of that section the chief officer of police may give traffic directions to prevent or mitigate consequent congestion, obstruction or danger.

These regulations, as amended (which apply in England and Wales), accordingly provide for the authorisation of the holding of races or trials of speed between bicycles or tricycles, not being motor vehicles, on public highways. The regulations distinguish between a race or trial of speed being a "time trial" (as defined) and any other kind of race or trial of speed (described as a "bicycle race"), and they provide that the holding of a time trial is authorised if notice of the proposal to hold the trial, containing prescribed particulars with respect to it, is given to the police not less than 28 days before the day on which it is to be held or begin, and that the holding of a bicycle race is authorised if it is held and conducted in accordance with certain conditions and the like notice as aforesaid with respect to the race is given. The conditions subject to which a bicycle race is authorised (referred to as "the standard conditions") are as follows:
  (i)   the number of competitors must not exceed in two, but not more than two, races selected in any one year by the British Cycling Federation, 84, and, in the case of any other race, 60;
  (ii) no part of the race must take place during the time between half an hour after sunset and half an hour before sunrise;
  (iii) where a competitor must pass the same point at least twice, the length of the intervening route must be at least ten miles; and
  (iv) where any length of the route is comprised in a public highway on which a speed limit of 40 mph or less is imposed, that length must not exceed 1½ miles and no part of it must be within three miles of any part of any other such length.
In the case of a time trial or such a bicycle race as aforesaid, of which the required notice has not been given or where the necessary particulars with respect to the trial or race have not been given, or where changes are proposed in the circumstances affecting the trial or race which affect the particulars which have been given, the police, if given notice of the particulars or, as the case may be, particulars of the said changes, may authorise the trial or race to be held. In the case of a bicycle race which is not a race proposed to be held and conducted in circumstances which comply with the above-mentioned standard conditions, the police may, if application is made to them and the like particulars as aforesaid with respect to the race are given to them, authorise the race to be held. The police may also impose conditions subject to which any bicycle race may be held and conducted.

Motoring events on public highways are governed by the Motor Vehicles (Competitions and Trials) Regulations 1969, SI 1969/414, p 74, *post*.

THE SPECIAL ROADS AND TRUNK ROADS (PROCEDURE)
REGULATIONS 1962
SI 1962/1319

NOTES
Authority These regulations were made on 22 June 1962 by the Minister of Transport under s 284 of the Highways Act 1959 (repealed) and all other enabling powers. They now have effect under the Highways Act 1980, s 324, Halsbury's Statutes, 4th edn Vol 20, title Highways, Streets and Bridges (3rd edn Vol 50 (1), p 787).
Commencement 10 July 1962; see reg 7.
Amendment See the notes to regs 1 and 4.
Interpretation See reg 6 and the note "Other expressions" thereto.
General These regulations (which are partly replaced by the Special and Other Roads (Maps etc) Regulations 1971, SI 1971/1706, p 94, *post*) prescribed the procedure to be followed in connection with the making of schemes under s 11 of the Highways Act 1959 authorising a special road, and supplementary orders relating to special roads under s 13 of that Act. The said ss 11

and 13 are now repealed and replaced by the consolidating Highways Act 1980, ss 16 and 18 respectively, Halsbury's Statutes, 4th edn Vol 20, title Highways, Streets and Bridges (3rd edn Vol 50 (1), pp 481, 483), and references to the said ss 11 and 13 must now be construed as references to the said ss 16 and 18.

1.   The centre line of any special road authorised by a scheme shall be indicated on a map on a scale of not less than six inches to the mile.

NOTES
Partial revocation   This regulation was revoked by reg 5 (1) of SI 1971/1706, p 94, *post*, in relation to schemes under s 11 of the Highways Act 1959 to which reg 3 of that instrument applied. The said s 11 is now replaced by the Highways Act 1980, s 16; see the head "General", p 61, *ante*.

2.   A section 13 order shall be made by reference to a plan on a scale of not less than 1/2500 and the plan shall show—
  (*a*) the route of any new highway or new private means of access to be constructed;
  (*b*) any highway or private means of access to be stopped up, or any length of highway or private means of access to be stopped up;
  (*c*) the diverted or realigned route of any highway to be diverted or realigned;
  (*d*) the route of any other highway to which the order relates.

3.   Every application to the Minister of Transport by a local highway authority for confirmation of a scheme or section 13 order shall be accompanied by the prescribed form containing the particulars required by that form and by any maps, plans and sections required by that form. The applicant authority shall also provide that Minister with any further information he may require, including maps, plans, sections and specifications.

NOTES
Section 13 order   This must now be construed as a reference to a s 18 order; see the head "General", p 61, *ante*.
Minister of Transport   This is now to be construed as a reference to the Secretary of State; see the Preliminary Note at p 52, *ante*.

4.   (*Lapsed*)

NOTES
This regulation lapsed on the repeal of the enabling provisions, *viz*, s 284 (2), (3) (*a*) and (*b*) and (4) (*a*) and (*b*) of the Highways Act 1959, by the Highways Act 1971. It had previously been amended by SI 1971/1706, p 94, *post*, and partially revoked by paras 1 (2) and 2 (2) of Sch 11 to the said Act of 1971 (repealed).

5.   The Special Roads (Procedure) Regulations 1950 are hereby revoked.

NOTES
Special Roads (Procedure) Regulations 1950   SI 1950/1850.

6.   The Interpretation Act 1889 shall apply for the interpretation of these Regulations as it applies for the interpretation of an Act of Parliament, and as if for the purposes of section 38 of that Act these Regulations were an Act of Parliament and the Regulations revoked by Regulation 5 were an Act of Parliament thereby repealed, and in these Regulations—
  "prescribed form" means the appropriate one of the forms set out in the Schedule to these Regulations;
  "scheme" means a scheme under section 11 of the Highways Act 1959;
  "*section 7 order*", "*section 9 order*" and "section 13 order" mean orders under those sections of the Highways Act 1959;

NOTES
The words printed in italics and those omitted where indicated by dots were relevant only to reg 4, which is no longer in force.
Other expressions   The expressions "local highway authority" and "special road" have the meanings assigned by the Highways Act 1980, s 329 (1), Halsbury's Statutes, 4th edn Vol 20, title Highways, Streets and Bridges (3rd edn Vol 50 (1), p 791).
Interpretation Act 1889   Repealed and replaced by the Interpretation Act 1978, printed in the title Statutory Instruments, Vol 1.
Highways Act 1959, ss 11 and 13   Repealed; see now the Highways Act 1980, ss 16 and 18 and the head "General", p 61, *ante*.

7. These Regulations shall come into operation on the 10th July 1962 and may be cited as "The Special Roads and Trunk Roads (Procedure) Regulations 1962".

THE SCHEDULE

FORM RELATING TO A SCHEME

Particulars to be furnished

1. Suggested name of special road and general description of route.

2. Class of traffic for which the special road is intended (by reference to Schedule 4 to the Highways Act 1959 as amended by the Special Roads (Classes of Traffic) Order 1961).

3. Precise points of:
(*a*) commencement, and
(*b*) termination of the special road.

4. Overall length of the special road, including lengths of existing roads, if any (in miles and to two places of decimals).

5. If the special road incorporates a section of existing road—
(*a*) name and classification number of the section;
(*b*) precise points of:
    (i) commencement, and
    (ii) termination of the section;
(*c*) length of the section (in miles and to two places of decimals);
(*d*) name of highway authority for the section.

6. Estimate of cost of the special road:

Land (including Accommodation Works)	£
Road Works	£
Bridge Works	£
Total ...	£

7. Full reasons for the proposals.

Maps, plans and section to be supplied

1. A map to a scale of not less than 6 inches to the mile, in triplicate, showing the ultimate centre line of the special road by means of a black band of not more than $\frac{1}{16}$ of an inch in width, the map to be up-to-date so far as detail is concerned within 220 feet of the centre line on each side of the line.

2. Where the special road is to be more than 10 miles long, a Key Plan to a scale of 1 inch to the mile showing the special road by means of a band of red colour $\frac{1}{32}$ of an inch wide, based on the ultimate centre line of the road.

3. A longitudinal section, in duplicate, on the centre line of the special road, to scales which should normally be 1/2500 horizontal and 1/250 vertical.

NOTES
Schedule 4 to the Highways Act 1959   Repealed; see now the Highways Act 1980, Sch 4, Halsbury's Statutes, 4th edn Vol 20, title Highways, Streets and Bridges (3rd edn Vol 50 (1), p 816).
Special Roads (Classes of Traffic) Order 1961   SI 1961/1210. Revoked and replaced by the Special Roads (Classes of Traffic) Order 1971, SI 1971/1156, itself superseded by the Highways Act 1980, Sch 4 (as to which, see the preceding Note).

FORM RELATING TO AN ORDER UNDER SECTION 13

Particulars to be furnished

1. Title of special road scheme or suggested name of special road to which the order relates.

2. Title of the proposed order.

3. Reference number of any map, plan or section referred to in the scheme to which the order relates.

4. Full reasons for the proposals.

Plans and section to be supplied

1. An engineering layout plan of the proposals to the minimum scale of 1/2500 together with a longitudinal section to scales of 1/2500 horizontal and 1/250 vertical.

2. A plan setting out diagrammatically the proposals contained in the order to the minimum scale of 1/2500, the plan to be up-to-date within the limits of the proposals.

NOTES
Order under section 13 This must now be construed as a reference to an order under section 18 (of the Highways Act 1980); see the head "General", p 61, *ante.*

THE SPECIAL ROADS (NOTICE OF OPENING) REGULATIONS 1962
SI 1962/1320

NOTES
Authority These regulations were made on 22 June 1962 by the Minister of Transport under s 20 (5) (repealed) of the Road Traffic Act 1960 and all other enabling powers. They subsequently had effect, by virtue of s 110 (2) of, and para 1 of Sch 8 to, the Road Traffic Regulation Act 1967, as if made for the purposes of s 1 (7) and certain other provisions of that Act (repealed). They now have effect under the Road Traffic Regulation Act 1984, ss 1 (4), (5), 6 (4), (6), Halsbury's Statutes, 4th edn Vol 38, title Road Traffic (3rd edn Vol 54 (2), pp 1513, 1518).
Commencement 10 July 1962.
General Section 1 of the Road Traffic Regulation Act 1984 (which confers powers to make traffic regulation orders outside Greater London) provides in sub-ss (4), (5) that the section shall not apply in relation to any part of a special road (as defined in s 142 (1) of that Act) on or after such date as may be declared by a notice published by the highway authority, in such manner as may be prescribed by regulations, to be the date on which it is open for use as a special road. Section 6 (which confers powers to make orders similar to traffic regulation orders in Greater London) makes similar provision in sub-ss (4), (6). These regulations (which revoke the Special Roads (Procedure) (Amendment) Regulations 1958, SI 1958/1848) provide that the notice in question shall, not less than seven days before the said date of opening, be published in at least one newspaper circulating in the area in which the special road, or the relevant part of the road, is situated and in the *London Gazette.*

THE CONTROL OF DOGS ON ROADS ORDERS (PROCEDURE) (ENGLAND AND WALES) REGULATIONS 1962
SI 1962/2340

NOTES
Authority These regulations were made on 19 October 1962 by the Minister of Transport under s 37 (repealed) of the Road Traffic Act 1962 and all other enabling powers. They now have effect, by virtue of s 205 (2), of, and para 1 of Sch 10 to, the Road Traffic Act 1972, as if made under s 31 (5) of that Act, Halsbury's Statutes, 4th edn Vol 38, title Road Traffic (3rd edn Vol 42, p 1673).
Commencement 1 November 1962; see reg 1.
Amendment These regulations are printed as amended by the Control of Dogs on Roads Orders (Procedure) (England and Wales) (Amendment) Regulations 1965, SI 1965/640.
Interpretation See reg 2.
General By s 31 of the Road Traffic Act 1972, as amended, certain local authorities are empowered to make orders designating lengths of road on which it is to be an offence to cause or permit a dog to be without its being held on a lead. These regulations prescribe the procedure to be followed in connection with the making of such orders.

1. These Regulations shall come into operation on 1st November 1962 and may be cited as the Control of Dogs on Roads Orders (Procedure) (England and Wales) Regulations 1962.

2. (1) In these Regulations the following expressions have the meanings hereby respectively assigned to them—

"the Act of 1960" means the Road Traffic Act 1960;

"local authority" means the council of a county borough or county district, the Common Council of the City of London or the council of a [London borough];

"Order" means an Order by a local authority under section 220 of the Act of 1960.

(2) The Interpretation Act 1889 shall apply for the interpretation of these Regulations as it applies for the interpretation of an Act of Parliament.

NOTES
Amendment   the words printed between square brackets in the definition of "local authority" were substituted for "metropolitan borough" by SI 1965/640.
Section 220 of the Road Traffic 1960   This is now to be construed as a reference to s 31 of the Road Traffic Act 1972, Halsbury's Statutes, 4th edn Vol 38, title Road Traffic (3rd edn Vol 42, p 1672).
Interpretation Act 1889   Repealed and replaced by the Interpretation Act 1978, printed in the title Statutory Instruments, Vol 1.

3. Before making an Order, a local authority shall—

(*a*) as well as consulting with the chief officer of police as required by subsection (4) of section 220 of the Act of 1960, also consult with such representative organisations as they think fit; and

(*b*) except as provided in paragraph (*a*) of Regulation 7 of these Regulations, publish a notice of their proposal to make the Order once at least in a newspaper circulating in the district in which are situated the roads to which the proposed Order relates.

NOTES
Chief officer of police   This expression is defined by s 62 of, and Sch 8 to, the Police Act 1964, Halsbury's Statutes, 4th edn Vol 33, title Police (3rd edn Vol 25, pp 370, 380).
Section 220 (4) of the Act of 1960   Now s 31 (4) of the Road Traffic Act 1972, *ibid*, 4th edn Vol 38, title Road Traffic (3rd edn Vol 42, p 1673).

4. Every notice published in accordance with the preceding Regulation shall be in the form and contain the particulars specified in Part I of the Schedule to these Regulations.

5. During the period commencing on the date on which the notice mentioned in Regulation 3 of these Regulations is first published in the newspaper in accordance with the provisions of that Regulation and ending immediately after the date by which objections to a proposed Order may be sent in writing in accordance with the said notice, a local authority shall cause—

(*a*) a copy of the said notice to be displayed in a prominent position on or near the roads to which the proposed Order relates, and in such other positions as the local authority think requisite for the purpose of securing that adequate information is given to persons using the said roads; and

(*b*) a copy of the proposed Order and a map clearly indicating in distinguishing colours or markings the said roads to be available for inspection at the offices of the local authority during the normal office hours of the authority.

6. When objections to a proposed Order are made in accordance with the notice mentioned in Regulation 3 of these Regulations, such objections and, if a public inquiry into the proposed Order is held, the report and recommendations of the person holding such inquiry, shall be considered by the local authority.

7. A local authority may cause a public inquiry to be held—

(*a*) after carrying out such consultations as are required by subsection (4) of section 220 and by paragraph (*a*) of Regulation 3 of these Regulations in which case the local authority may dispense with publication of the notice mentioned in that Regulation; or

(*b*) after complying with the provisions of the said Regulation 3.

NOTES
Section 220 (4)   *Ie*, s 220 (4) of the Road Traffic Act 1960, which is now replaced by s 31 (4) of the Road Traffic Act 1972, Halsbury's Statutes, 4th edn Vol 38, title Road Traffic (3rd edn Vol 42, p 1673).

8. When a public inquiry is to be held in pursuance of the foregoing Regulation, the local authority shall—

(*a*) publish a notice of the inquiry in the form and containing the particulars specified in Part II of the Schedule to these Regulations once at least in a newspaper circulating in the district in which the roads to which the proposed Order relates are situated;

(*b*) during the period commencing on the date on which the notice is first published in the newspaper in accordance with the preceding paragraph and ending immediately before the date on which the inquiry is to be held cause—

  (i) a copy of the said notice to be displayed in a prominent position on or near the roads to which the proposed Order relates, and in such other positions as the local authority think requisite for the purpose of securing that adequate information is given to persons using the said roads, and

  (ii) a copy of the proposed Order and a map clearly indicating in distinguishing colours or marking the said roads to be available for inspection at the offices of the local authority during the normal office hours of the authority; and

(*c*) if the inquiry is to be held in the circumstances mentioned in paragraph (*b*) of Regulation 7 of these Regulations, inform any person, who has objected to the proposed Order in accordance with the notice thereof mentioned in Regulation 3 of these Regulations and not withdrawn his objection, of the holding of the inquiry

9. (1) After a local authority have decided to make an Order, their decision to make the Order shall be notified in writing to the chief officer of police and, where any objection has been made to the Order in accordance with the notice mentioned in Regulation 3 or Regulation 8 of these Regulations and not withdrawn, to the person making such objection.

(2) Where any such objection has been made as aforesaid and not withdrawn, the local authority shall also notify in writing the person making the objection of their reasons for the decision to make the Order.

NOTES
Chief officer of police   See the note to reg 3.

10. Subject to the foregoing provisions of these Regulations, a local authority may make an Order and every Order so made shall bear the seal of the local authority duly authenticated in accordance with the Standing Orders made by the authority.

11. After an Order has been made by a local authority, the local authority shall—

(*a*) not later than fourteen days after the date of the making of the Order publish a notice thereof in the form and containing the particulars specified in Part III of the Schedule to these Regulations once at least in a newspaper circulating in the district in which are situated the roads to which the Order relates;

  (*b*) forthwith keep available for inspection at the offices of the local authority during the normal office hours of the authority a copy of the Order
and a map showing the roads to which the Order relates; and

  (*c*) forthwith take all such steps as are reasonably practicable to cause to
be erected on or near to the said roads signs in such positions as the
local authority may consider to be requisite for the purpose of securing
that adequate information as to the effect of the Order is given to
persons using the said roads:
     Provided that nothing in this paragraph shall apply in the case of an
Order containing no provision other than provision revoking any other
Order.

12. Where a local authority causes a public inquiry to be held in pursuance
of these Regulations, the person to hold the inquiry shall be selected by the
local authority from a panel of persons appointed by the Minister for the
purpose of holding public inquiries under these Regulations.

NOTES
The Minister   This (which originally meant the Minister of Transport, as stated in the recital of
powers at the head of these regulations) is now to be construed as referring to the Secretary of
State; see the Preliminary Note at p 52, *ante*.

13. (1) Any person interested in the subject matter of a public inquiry may
appear at the inquiry either in person or by counsel, solicitor or agent.
    (2) Any person so interested whether he proposes to appear at the inquiry
or not may forward in accordance with the appropriate notice specified in
Part II of the Schedule to these Regulations to the person holding the inquiry
for consideration at the inquiry any objection which he may wish to make in
relation to the subject matter of the inquiry.
    (3) The person holding a public inquiry may refuse to hear any person or
to consider at the inquiry any such objection, if he is satisfied that the views
of that person are or the objection is frivolous or that such views have been
adequately stated at the inquiry by some other person.

SCHEDULE

FORMS OF NOTICE RELATING TO ORDERS

PART I

Form of Notice of Proposal to Make an Order

    The (*a*)
    The (*b*)   Council propose to make
an Order under section 220 of the Road Traffic Act 1960 the effect of which will be to (*c*)
    Objections to the proposals must be sent in writing to the undersigned by (*d*)
                        (Name and address of Clerk to order-making Authority.)

PART II

Form of Notice of Public Inquiry

The (*a*)
    A Public Inquiry will be held by (*e*)
at (*f*)
to consider the proposal of the (*b*)   Council
to make an Order under section 220 of the Road Traffic Act 1960 the effect of which
will be to (*c*)
    Any person interested is entitled to be heard in person or by counsel, solicitor or agent and
any person whether he intends to appear at the inquiry or not may forward any objection to the
proposal to (*e*)
at the under-mentioned address.
                     (Name and address of Clerk to order-making Authority).

PART III

Form of Notice of Making of an Order

The (a)

On the (g)   the (h)
Council made an Order under section 220 of the Road Traffic Act 1960 the effect of which is
to (c)

(Name and address of Clerk to order-making Authority.)

NOTES
(a) Here insert title of the Order;
(b) Here insert name of Council proposing to make the Order;
(c) Here insert brief but accurate description of the effect of the Order;
(d) Here insert date not less than 21 days from the date of the first publication of this notice
      in the local newspaper;
(e) Here insert name of person holding inquiry;
(f) Here insert place, date and time at which public inquiry will be held, the said date being
      not less than 14 days from the date of the first publication of this notice in the local
      newspaper;
(g) Here insert date of making of the Order;
(h) Here insert name of Council making the Order.

NOTES
Section 220 of the Road Traffic Act 1960   See the note to reg 2.

THE VARIOUS TRUNK ROADS (PROHIBITION OF WAITING) (CLEARWAYS) ORDER 1963
SI 1963/1172

NOTES
Authority   This order was made on 28 June 1963 by the Minister of Transport under ss 26 (1),
(2), (3) and (5) and 28 (1) of the Road Traffic Act 1960 and all other enabling powers. It
subsequently had effect, by virtue of s 110 (2) of, and para 1 of Sch 8 to, the Road Traffic
Regulation Act 1967, as if made under s 1 (1), (2), (3) and (6) of that Act (repealed). It now
has effect under the Road Traffic Regulation Act 1984, ss 1 (1), (2), 2 (1), (2), 3 (2), (4),
Halsbury's Statutes, 4th edn Vol 38, title Road Traffic (3rd edn Vol 54 (2), pp 1513-1516).
Commencement   29 July 1963; see art 1.
Interpretation   See art 3.
Penalties   Persons who contravene this order, or who use a vehicle, or cause or permit a vehicle
to be used, in contravention of this order are liable on summary conviction to a fine not exceeding
level 3 on the standard scale; see the Road Traffic Regulation Act 1984, ss 5 (1), 98, Sch 7.
Traffic signs   Traffic signs indicating the effect of this order must generally comply with diagrams
642-647 in Part II of Sch 1 to the Traffic Signs Regulations 1981 (*ie* Part I of SI 1981/859, as
amended, in the title Transport (Part 2B)). See also the first note to art 3 of the present order.
General   This order prohibits the waiting of vehicles on certain extensive lengths of main carriageways forming part of trunk roads outside Greater London, subject to the exceptions specified
in art 5, and it also prohibits trading from vehicles on verges or lay-bys of those main carriageways.

1. Commencement and Citation   This Order shall come into operation on
the 29th July 1963 and may be cited as the Various Trunk Roads (Prohibition
of Waiting) (Clearways) Order 1963.

2. Revocation   The Orders specified in Schedule 2 to this Order are hereby
revoked.

3. Interpretation   (1) In this Order the following expressions have the meanings hereby respectively assigned to them:—
     "the Act of 1960" means the Road Traffic Act, 1960;
     "main carriageway", in relation to a trunk road, means any carriageway of
        that road used primarily by through traffic and excludes any lay-by;
     "lay-by", in relation to a main carriageway of a trunk road, means any area
        intended for use for the waiting of vehicles, lying at a side of the road
        and bounded partly by a traffic sign consisting of a yellow dotted line on
        the road, or of a white dotted line and the words "lay-by" on the road,
        authorised by the Minister under subsection (2) of section 51 of the Act
        of 1960, and partly by the outer edge of that carriageway on the same
        side of the road as that on which the sign is placed;

"verge" means any part of a road which is not a carriageway.

(2) The Interpretation Act 1889 shall apply for the interpretation of this Order as it applies for the interpretation of an Act of Parliament and as if for the purposes of section 38 of that Act this Order were an Act of Parliament and the Orders revoked by Article 2 were Acts of Parliament thereby repealed.

NOTES
Traffic sign consisting of a yellow dotted line, etc   A sign to indicate the edge of the carriageway at a lay-by is shown in diagram 1010 in Sch 2 to the Traffic Signs Regulations 1981 (*ie* Part I of SI 1981/859, in the title Transport (Part 2B)).
The Minister   See the note to art 7.
Road Traffic Act 1960   So far as this order is concerned, the Act of 1960 is replaced by the Road Traffic Regulation Act 1984, Halsbury's Statutes, 4th edn Vol 38, title Road Traffic (3rd edn Vol 54 (2), p 1509 *et seq*). The reference to s 51 (2) of the Act of 1960 is to be construed as referring to the 1984 Act, s 64 (2).
Interpretation Act 1899   Repealed and replaced by the Interpretation Act 1978, printed in the title Statutory Instruments, Vol 1.

4. Prohibition of waiting on main carriageways   Save as provided in Article 5 of this Order no person shall, except upon the direction or with the permission of a police constable in uniform, cause or permit any vehicle to wait on any of those main carriageways forming part of trunk roads which are specified in Schedule 1 to this Order.

NOTES
The primary purpose of this article is to facilitate the passage of traffic, and a breach of the article does not of itself confer on an aggrieved member of the public a right to claim damages in the absence of negligence; see *Coote and Another* v *Stone*, [1971] 1 All ER 657 (CA).
Police constable   Note the provisions in s 19 of the Police Act 1964, Halsbury's Statutes, 4th edn Vol 33, title Police (3rd edn Vol 25, p 343), conferring jurisdiction on special constables (as well as members of police forces).

5. Exceptions to Article 4   Nothing in Article 4 of this Order shall apply—
   (*a*) so as to prevent a vehicle waiting on any main carriageway specified in Schedule 1 to this Order for so long as may be necessary to enable the vehicle, if it cannot be used for such purpose without waiting on that carriageway, to be used in connection with any building operation or demolition, the removal of any obstruction or potential obstruction to traffic, the maintenance, improvement or reconstruction of the road comprising that carriageway, or the erection, laying, placing, maintenance, testing, alteration, repair or removal of any structure, works, or apparatus in, on, under or over that road;
   (*b*) to a vehicle being used for fire brigade, ambulance or police purposes;
   (*c*) to a vehicle being used for the purposes of delivering or collecting postal packets as defined in section 87 of the Post Office Act 1953;
   (*d*) so as to prevent a vehicle being used by or on behalf of a local authority from waiting on any main carriageway specified in Schedule 1 to this Order for so long as may be necessary to enable the vehicle, if it cannot be used for such a purpose without waiting on that carriageway to be used for the purpose of the collection of household refuse from, or the clearing of cesspools at, premises situated on or adjacent to the road comprising that carriageway;
   (*e*) to a vehicle waiting on any main carriageway specified in Schedule 1 to this Order while any gate or other barrier at the entrance to premises to which the vehicle requires access or from which it has emerged is opened or closed, if it is not reasonably practicable for the vehicle to wait otherwise than on that carriageway while such gate or barrier is being opened or closed;
   (*f*) to a vehicle waiting in any case where the person in control of the vehicle—
      (i) is required by law to stop;
      (ii) is obliged to do so in order to avoid an accident; or
      (iii) is prevented from proceeding by circumstances outside his control

and it is not reasonably practicable for him to drive or move the vehicle to a place not on any main carriageway specified in Schedule 1 to this Order.

NOTES
Section 87 of the Post Office Act 1953 Halsbury's Statutes, 4th edn Vol 34, title Post Office (3rd edn Vol 25, p 453).

6. Restriction of waiting on verges, etc No person shall cause or permit any vehicle to wait on any verge or lay-by immediately adjacent to a main carriageway specified in Schedule 1 to this Order for the purpose of selling goods from that vehicle unless the goods are immediately delivered at or taken into premises adjacent to the vehicle from which sale is effected.

7. Non-application of s 26 (4) of Act of 1960 The Minister is satisfied that, for avoiding danger to persons or other traffic using the roads to which this Order relates, it is requisite that section 26 (4) of the Act of 1960, as amended by section 12 of the Road Traffic and Roads Improvement Act 1960, shall not apply in relation to this Order.

NOTES
The Minister This (which originally meant the Minister of Transport, as stated in the recital of powers at the head of this order) is now to be construed as referring to the Secretary of State; see the Preliminary Note at p 52, *ante*.
Section 26 (4) of the Act of 1960, as amended This is now to be construed as a reference to the Road Traffic Regulation Act 1984, s 3 (1), Halsbury's Statutes, 4th edn Vol 38, title Road Traffic (3rd edn Vol 54 (2), p 1516). That subsection restricts the making of orders under s 1 of that Act, preventing access to premises on or adjacent to any road or to any other premises accessible only from the road; the statement contained in this article has effect as if made by virtue of s 3 (2) of that Act.

SCHEDULE 1
NOTES
This Schedule specifies 195 lengths of trunk roads the main carriageways of which are subject to the prohibitions contained in arts 4 and 6 of this order.

SCHEDULE 2 (see Article 2)
NOTES
This Schedule specifies the following orders revoked by art 2: the County of Lancashire (Peel) (Traffic Regulation) Order 1955, SI 1955/1037; the Trunk Road (Southport New Road, Tarleton) (Prohibition of Waiting) Order 1961, SI 1961/1925; and the Various Trunk Roads (Prohibition of Waiting) (Clearways) Order 1962, SI 1962/2735, and the amending SI 1963/814.

THE LONDON TRAFFIC AND HIGHWAYS (TRANSITIONAL PROVISIONS) ORDER 1965
SI 1965/481

NOTES
Authority This order was made on 16 March 1965 by the Minister of Transport under s 84 of the London Government Act 1963, Halsbury's Statutes, 4th edn Vol 26, title London (3rd edn Vol 20, p 531), and all other enabling powers.
Commencement 1 April 1965.
Amendment This order has been amended by the London Traffic and Highways (Transitional Provisions) (Amendment) Order 1966, SI 1966/236.
General This order (now largely obsolete) contains transitional and other provisions consequential on the London Government Act 1963 (see, in particular, Part II of that Act which deals with road traffic, highways and motor vehicles), in respect of regulations, orders and other instruments made and things done relating to traffic and highway matters and existing immediately before 1 April 1965 (*ie*, the date on which the Act of 1963 largely came into force).
    Other ancillary provisions in relation to highways and bridges, made under the same power as the present order, are contained in art 6 of the London Authorities (Property, etc) Order 1964, SI 1964/1464, in the title Local Government (Part 2).

THE BRIDGES ORDERS (PROCEDURE) REGULATIONS 1965
SI 1965/869

NOTES
Authority These regulations were made on 7 April 1965 by the Minister of Transport under

para 11 of Sch 11 to the Highways Act 1959 (repealed), and all other enabling powers. They now have effect under the Highways Act 1980, Sch 11, Halsbury's Statutes, 4th edn Vol 20, title Highways, Streets and Bridges (3rd edn Vol 50 (1), p 831).
Commencement   15 April 1965; see reg 1 (1).
Interpretation   See regs 2 and 3 and note to reg 2.
General   Under the Highways Act 1980, s 93, Halsbury's Statutes, 4th edn Vol 20, title Highways, Streets and Bridges (3rd edn Vol 50 (1), p 559), the Secretary of State has power, on the application of the owners of a bridge or a local highway authority (or, in the case of a trunk road bridge, on his own initiative), to make an order providing for the reconstruction, improvement or maintenance of the bridge, or of the highway carried by the bridge, or of the approaches to the bridge. An order under that section may provide for any of the matters specified in sub-s (3) thereof. The procedure for making such orders is governed by s 93 (2), (4), (5) and (7) of, and paras 7-10 of Sch 11 to, the 1980 Act, and by these regulations which take effect under para 11 of that Schedule.
By the 1980 Act, s 93 (6), that section applies to any bridge (not being a highway maintainable at the public expense) which carries a highway consisting of or comprising a carriageway over a railway, over a canal, river, creek, watercourse, marsh or other place where water flows or is collected or over a ravine or other depression, other than a bridge to which a right to levy tolls is attached (see also s 95 (9) of that Act which excludes bridges crossing the Manchester Ship Canal and owned by the canal company).

1.   (1) These Regulations shall come into operation on the 15th April 1965, and may be cited as "The Bridges Orders (Procedure) Regulations 1965".
(2) The Bridges Orders (Procedure) Regulations and Rules 1961 are hereby revoked.

NOTES
Bridges Orders (Procedure) Regulations and Rules 1961   SI 1961/635.

2.   (1) In these Regulations, unless the context otherwise requires, the following expressions have the meanings hereby respectively assigned to them—
"the Act" means the Highways Act 1959;
"the Minister" means the Minister of Transport;
"order" means an order under section 99 of the Act.
(2) The Interpretation Act 1889 shall apply for the interpretation of these Regulations as it applies for the interpretation of an Act of Parliament.

NOTES
Highways Act 1959   Repealed and replaced by the Highways Act 1980, Halsbury's Statutes, 4th edn Vol 20, title Highways, Streets and Bridges (3rd edn Vol 50 (1), p 452 *et seq*). For s 99 of the 1959 Act, see now s 93 of the 1980 Act.
Minister of Transport   This is now to be construed as referring to the Secretary of State; see also reg 3, *post*, and the Preliminary Note at p 52, *ante*.
Other expressions   The expressions "bridge", "land", "local highway authority" and "statutory undertakers" have the meanings assigned by the Highways Act 1980, s 329 (1). It should be noted, however, that s 93 of the Act applies only to the bridges mentioned in sub-s (6) of that section and that its application is also restricted by s 95 (9) of that Act. In connection with the expression "owners of the bridge" reference should also be made to s 95 (5) of that Act.
Interpretation Act 1889   Repealed and replaced by the Interpretation Act 1978, printed in the title Statutory Instruments, Vol 1.

3.   For the purposes of an application for an order in respect of a bridge in relation to which the functions of the Minister under the Act have been transferred to the Secretary of State by the Secretary of State for Wales and the Minister of Land and Natural Resources Order 1965, these Regulations shall have effect with the substitution for references therein to the Minister of references to the Secretary of State.

NOTES
The Minister   See the note "Minister of Transport" to reg 2, *ante*.
Secretary of State for Wales and Minister of Land and Natural Resources Order 1965   SI 1965/319, in the title Constitutional Law (Part 5). The transfer of functions to the Secretary of State effected by that order extends to Wales.

4.   Every application to the Minister for an order shall be signed by the applicants, and shall be accompanied—
(*a*) in the case of an application relating to a bridge which is not vested in the applicants by a notification stating in whom the bridge is vested;
(*b*) in the case of an application for an order which requires or authorises

the owners of a bridge or a highway authority to execute or construct any works—
    (i) by a map showing the land on or over which the works referred to in the application are proposed to be executed or constructed;
    (ii) by such plans, sections and specifications as may be necessary to indicate the position and dimensions of the bridge to which the application relates and by particulars of the works proposed to be executed or constructed;
    (iii) by a notification stating the names and addresses of any statutory undertakers likely to be affected by the proposed works;
  (c) in the case of an application for an order which does not require or authorise the owners of a bridge or a highway authority to execute or construct any works—
    (i) by a map showing the situation of the bridge to which the application relates and by such plans and specifications (if any) of the said bridge as may be necessary for the purposes of the application;
    (ii) by a notification stating names and addresses of any statutory undertakers likely to be affected by the proposed order.

5. At the same time as application is made to the Minister, notice in writing of the application (accompanied by copies of any plans, sections and specifications and particulars of any proposed works furnished to the Minister under paragraph (b) of Regulation 4 of these Regulations) shall be given by the applicants, in the case of an application relating to or affecting—
  (a) a bridge which is vested in the applicants, to every highway authority entitled to exercise with respect thereto the powers conferred by section 99 of the Act;
  (b) a bridge which is not vested in the applicants, to the person in whom the bridge is vested;
  (c) foreshore or tidal lands within the ordinary spring tides, or tidal waters, to the Minister of Defence for the Royal Navy;
  (d) the banks, bed or foreshore of any river, to every navigation authority and river board concerned with or having jurisdiction over the waters affected or the area comprising those waters;
  (e) any watercourse (including the banks thereof), or any drainage or other works, vested in or under the control of a river board or other drainage authority within the meaning of the Land Drainage Act 1930, as amended by any subsequent enactment, to that board or authority;
  (f) common or commonable land, to the Minister of Land and Natural Resources;
  (g) any churchyard burial ground or cemetery, to the Secretary of State for the Home Department;
  (h) land an interest in which belongs to Her Majesty in right of the Crown or of the Duchy of Lancaster, or to the Duchy of Cornwall, to the Crown Estate Commissioners;
  (i) land an interest in which belongs to a government department or is held in trust for Her Majesty for the purposes of a government department, to that department;
  (j) the Duchies of Lancaster or Cornwall, to the Duchy affected

NOTES
Notice See the note to reg 8.
Highway authority entitled to exercise . . . the powers conferred by s 99 of the Act Section 99 of the 1959 Act now replaced by s 93 of the Highways Act 1980; see the note to reg 2. As to the authorities in question, see the 1980 Act, s 95 (1)-(4) (s 95 (1) as amended as from 1 April 1986 by the Local Government Act 1985, s 8, Sch 4, Pt I, para 20, and as repealed in part from that date by *ibid*, s 102 (2), Sch 17).
Minister of Land and Natural Resources This is now to be construed as referring to the Secretary of State for Transport or, as respects Wales, the Secretary of State for Wales (see the Preliminary Note at p 52, *ante*.)
River board The references in this regulation to river boards are now to be construed as references to water authorities (by virtue of para 4 of Sch 3 (repealed) to the Water Resources

Act 1963 and s 9 of the Water Act 1973, Halsbury's Statutes, 4th edn Vol 49, title Water (3rd edn Vol 43, p 1833)).
Land Drainage Act 1930 Repealed and replaced by the Land Drainage Act 1976, Halsbury's Statutes, 4th edn Vol 22, title Land Drainage (3rd edn Vol 46, p 805); for the meaning of "drainage authority" in that Act, see s 17 (7) thereof.

6. The applicants shall furnish the Minister with a list of the authorities or persons to whom notice has been given in accordance with the foregoing Regulation, and with such further information relating to the application, including further plans, sections and specifications and particulars of any proposed works, as he may require.

7. The three next following Regulations shall apply only to orders to which paragraph 7 of Schedule 11 to the Act does not apply.

NOTES
Orders to which para 7 of Sch 11 to the Act does not apply Now replaced by the Highways Act 1980, Sch 11, para 7; see the note to reg 2. By para 7 (4) of Sch 11, that paragraph applies to an order which requires or authorises the owners of a bridge or a highway authority to execute or construct any works. Special provisions relating to the procedure for making orders to which para 7 applies are contained not only in that paragraph itself but also in paras 8-10 of Sch 11 to the Act.

8. Before making an order to which this Regulation and the two next following Regulations apply, the Minister shall—
  (*a*) prepare a draft of the proposed order;
  (*b*) in two successive weeks publish in one or more local newspapers circulating in the area in which the bridge to which the proposed order relates is situated a notice—
    (i) stating the general effect of the proposed order;
    (ii) naming a place in the said area where a copy of the draft order and of any map or plan referred to therein may be inspected free of charge at all reasonable hours; and
    (iii) specifying the time (not being less than twenty-one days from the date of the first publication of the notice) within which and the manner in which objections to the draft order may be made;
  (*c*) serve on all statutory undertakers appearing to him to be affected by the proposed order a notice stating the general effect of the order and that it is proposed to be made, and specifying the time (not being less than twenty-one days from the date of the service of the notice) within which and the manner in which objections to the draft order may be made.

NOTES
Order to which this Regulation . . . apply See reg 7.
Notice For general provisions as to notices, see the Highways Act 1980, ss 320-322, Halsbury's Statutes, 4th edn Vol 20, title Highways, Streets and Bridges (3rd edn Vol 50 (1), pp 785, 786).

9. (1) If no objection is duly made by any person who will be affected by the proposed order, or if all objections so made are withdrawn, the Minister, on being satisfied that the proper notices have been published and served, may, if he thinks fit, make the order with or without modifications.
  (2) If an objection duly made as aforesaid is not withdrawn, the Minister shall, before making the order, either cause a local inquiry to be held or afford to any person by whom any objection has been duly made as aforesaid and not withdrawn an opportunity of appearing before and being heard by a person appointed by the Minister for the purpose, and, after considering the objection and the report of the person who held the inquiry or the person appointed as aforesaid, may make the order either with or without modifications.
  (3) If any person by whom an objection has been made avails himself of the opportunity of being heard, the Minister shall afford to the local highway authority or to the owners of the bridge, and to any other person to whom

it appears to him expedient to afford it, an opportunity of being heard on the same occasion.

(4) Notwithstanding anything in the two last foregoing paragraphs, the Minister may require any person who has made an objection to state in writing the grounds thereof.

10.   As soon as may be after the order has been made the Minister shall publish in one or more local newspapers circulating in the area in which the bridge to which the order relates is situated a notice stating that the order has been made and naming the place where a copy of the order and of any map or plan referred to therein may be inspected free of charge at all reasonable hours, and shall serve a like notice and a copy of the order on any statutory undertakers on whom a notice was required to be served under Regulation 8 of these Regulations.

NOTES
Notice   See the note to reg 8.

THE MOTOR VEHICLES (COMPETITIONS AND TRIALS) REGULATIONS 1969
SI 1969/414

NOTES
Authority   These regulations were made on 19 March 1968 by the Secretary of State and the Minister of Transport under s 36 (repealed) of the Road Traffic Act 1962 (as read with the Secretary of State for Wales and the Minister of Land and Natural Resources Order 1965, SI 1965/319, in the title Constitutional Law (Part 5)), and under all other enabling powers. They now have effect, by virtue of s 205 (2) of, and para 1 of Sch 10 to, the Road Traffic Act 1972, as if made under s 15 of that Act, Halsbury's Statutes, 4th edn Vol 38, title Road Traffic (3rd edn Vol 42, p 1662).
Commencement   1 April 1969.
Amendment   These regulations have been amended by the Motor Vehicles (Competitions and Trials) (Amendment) Regulations 1974, 1976, 1978 and 1982, SI 1974/1674, 1976/1657, 1978/481 and 1982/1103. SI 1978/481 was superseded by SI 1982/1103.
General   It is provided by s 15 (1) of the Road Traffic Act 1972 that a person who promotes or takes part in a competition or trial (other than a race or trial of speed, which is prohibited by s 14 of that Act) involving the use of motor vehicles on a public highway shall be guilty of an offence unless the competition or trial is authorised, and is conducted in accordance with any conditions imposed, by or under regulations under that section. The provisions which may be contained in regulations under s 15 are specified in sub-ss (2) and (3) thereof; and for provisions as to the prosecution and punishment of offences under the section, see s 177 of, and Part I of Sch 4 to, the Act (as amended).
   These regulations (which revoke and replace the Motor Vehicles (Competitions and Trials) (England) Regulations 1965, SI 1965/1400, as amended by SI 1967/415, the Motor Vehicles (Competitions and Trials) (Wales) Regulations 1965, SI 1965/ 1414, as amended by SI 1967/176 and 439, and the corresponding regulations relating to Scotland) provide for the authorisation of such competitions and trials. (By virtue of the amending SI 1976/1657, the application of these regulations is now limited to events taking place only in England or England and Wales and to the English or English and Welsh parts of events which takes place in part in England or in England and Wales, and in part in Scotland.) The following types of events are authorised unconditionally:—
   (*a*)   an event in which the total number of vehicles driven by the competitors does not exceed 12 (being an event no part of which takes place within 8 days of any part of any other event in which the total number of vehicles driven by the competitors does not exceed 12 and where either the other event has the same promoter or the promoters of both events are members of the same club in connection with which the events are promoted);
   (*b*)   an event in which no merit is attached to completing the event with the lowest mileage and in which, as respects such part of the event as is held on a public highway, there are no performance tests and no route and competitors are not timed or required to visit the same places, except that they may be required to finish at the same place by a specified time;
   (*c*)   an event in which, as respects such part of the event as is held on a public highway, merit attaches to a competitor's performance only in relation to good road behaviour and compliance with the Highway Code (as to which, see the Preliminary Note at p 56, *ante*);
   (*d*)   an event in which all the competitors are members of the armed forces of the Crown and which is designed solely for the purposes of their service training.
   Events, other than listed above, may be authorised by the Royal Automobile Club as provided by the regulations, and the procedure to be followed and the information to be given on application to the RAC for authorisation of an event are prescribed. For authorisation of an event by the RAC a fee is to be paid, varying between £1.40 and £5.60 (depending on the length of the route of the event on the public highway) for each vehicle covered by the application for the authorisation of the event. Events, other than those listed above, are to be held subject to such of the conditions specified in the regulations as apply to the event. These conditions may be modified by the RAC to the extent specified, and the RAC may require events to be held subject to additional conditions.

Before authorising an event the RAC must (not less than 6 weeks before the date of the proposed event, or, if the event is to be held on more than one date, before the date on which the event is to begin) notify the chief officer of police of any police area in which the route of the event on the public highway lies, whether partially or wholly. The RAC is also under duty to consult with certain authorities before authorising certain events; and the considerations to which the RAC is to have regard when exercising its discretion to authorise an event are laid down.

Cycle racing on public highways is governed by the Cycle Racing on Highways Regulations 1960, SI 1960/250, as amended, p 61, *ante*.

THE "PELICAN" PEDESTRIAN CROSSING REGULATIONS AND GENERAL DIRECTIONS 1969
SI 1969/888

NOTES
Authority   This instrument was made on 30 June 1969 by the Secretary of State and the Minister of Transport under ss 23, 54 and 55 of the Road Traffic Regulation Act 1967 (repealed), and all other enabling powers. It now has effect under the Road Traffic Regulation Act 1984, ss 25, 64 and 65, Halsbury's Statutes, 4th edn Vol 38, title Road Traffic (3rd edn Vol 54 (2), pp 1535, 1577, 1579).
Commencement   11 July 1969; see para 1 of Part 1.
Amendment   This instrument is printed as amended by the "Pelican" Pedestrian Crossings (Amendment) Regulations and General Directions 1979, SI 1979/401.
Interpretation   See para 3 of Part I. The term "the Act of 1967" in this instrument refers (as stated in the recital of powers at the head of the instrument) to the Road Traffic Regulation Act 1967; this must now be construed as a reference to the Road Traffic Regulation Act 1984.
Penalties, etc   See the note at the head of SI 1971/1524, p 85, *post*.
General   The regulations contained in Part II of this instrument (which replace the Pedestrian Crossings (Push Button Control) Regulations 1967 (set out in Part I of SI 1967/178)) provide a new method of regulating traffic at pedestrian crossings by means of light signals and indicators for pedestrians which can be made to work by pedestrians pressing a push button in the indicators. Pedestrian crossings at or near which such light signals are placed and the presence and limits of which are marked in accordance with the provisions of these regulations are called " 'pelican' crossings". Other pedestrian crossings (or "zebra crossings") are governed by the "Zebra" Pedestrian Crossings Regulations 1971, SI 1971/1524, p 85, *post*. The present regulations prescribe the size, colour and type of the traffic signs which are to be placed at or near a "pelican" crossing, provide for the manner in which the presence and limit of such crossings are to be indicated, prescribe the warnings, information, requirements and prohibitions conveyed by the light signals concerned, and make provision as to the precedence of foot passengers over vehicles on, and as to the movement of traffic at and in the vicinity of, the crossings. See, further, the note to Part III of this instrument.

These regulations are applied, with modifications, by the Crown Road (Royal Parks) (Application of Road Traffic Enactments) Order 1977, SI 1977/548, in the title Open Spaces and Recreation Grounds.

PART I—GENERAL

1. Citation and commencement   This Instrument may be cited as the "Pelican" Pedestrian Crossings Regulations and General Directions 1969, and shall come into operation on the 11th July 1969.

2. Revocation   The Pedestrian Crossings (Push Button Control) Regulations and General Directions 1967 are hereby revoked as from 10th July 1971.

NOTES
Pedestrian Crossings (Push Button Control) Regulations and General Directions 1967   SI 1967/178.

3. Interpretation   (1) In this Instrument unless the context otherwise requires the following expressions have the meanings hereby respectively assigned to them—

"the appropriate Minister" means, in relation to a crossing established on a road in Scotland, Wales or Monmouthshire, the Secretary of State, and in relation to a crossing established on a road in England excluding Monmouthshire, the Minister of Transport;

"carriageway" does not include that part of any road which consists of a street refuge or central reservation, whether within the limits of a crossing or not;

"central reservation" means any provision, not consisting of a street refuge, made in a road for separating one part of the carriageway of that road from another part of that carriageway for the safety or guidance of vehicular traffic using that road;

"crossing" means a crossing for foot passengers established either—

(*a*) by a local authority in accordance with the provisions for the time being in force of a scheme submitted and approved under section 21 of the Act of 1967, or

(*b*) in the case of a trunk road, by the Secretary of State or the Minister in the discharge of the duty imposed on him by section 22 of the Act of 1967;

"one-way street" means any road on which the driving of vehicles otherwise than in one direction is prohibited at all times;

"'Pelican' crossing" means a crossing—

(*a*) at which there are traffic signs of the size, colour and type prescribed by Regulation 3 (1) of the Schedule 1 to the Regulations contained in Part II of this Instrument, and

(*b*) the presence and limits of which are indicated in accordance with Regulation 3 (2) of and Schedule 2 to the Regulations contained in Part II of this Instrument;

"stop line" in relation to the driver of a motor vehicle approaching a "Pelican" crossing means the white line indicating the approach to the crossing in accordance with paragraph 3 of Schedule 2 to the Regulations contained in Part II of this Instrument, which is parallel to the limits of the crossing and on the same side of the crossing as the driver;

"stud" means any mark or device on the carriageway, whether or not projecting above the surface thereof;

"vehicular traffic light signal", "pedestrian light signal" and "indicator for pedestrians" mean respectively the traffic signals of those descriptions prescribed by Regulation 3 (1) of the Schedule 1 to the Regulations contained in Part II of this Instrument.

(2) Any reference in this Instrument to a light shown by a signal or indicator is a reference to a light of constant intensity unless the contrary intention appears.

(3) Any reference in this Instrument to any enactment or instrument shall be construed, unless the context otherwise requires, as a reference to that enactment or instrument as amended, re-enacted or replaced by any subsequent enactment or instrument.

(4) The Interpretation Act 1889 shall apply for the interpretation of this Instrument as it applies for the interpretation of an Act of Parliament, and as if for the purposes of section 38 of that Act this Instrument were an Act of Parliament and the Instrument revoked by paragraph 2 of this Part of this Instrument were an Act of Parliament thereby repealed.

NOTES

Minister of Transport   This is now to be construed as a reference to the Secretary of State for Transport. See, further, the Preliminary Note at p 52, *ante*.

Sections 21 and 22 of the Act of 1967   Repealed; see now the Road Traffic Regulation Act 1984, ss 23 and 24, Halsbury's Statutes, 4th edn Vol 38, title Road Traffic (3rd edn Vol 54 (2), pp 1534, 1535). Section 23 of the 1984 Act (which replaced s 21 of the 1967 Act, as substituted by the Local Government, Planning and Land Act 1980, s 1 (8), Sch 7, Pt II, para 10 (1)) does not require schemes to be made; it empowers local authorities, subject to certain requirements as to consultation etc, to establish crossings on any roads in their area, other than trunk roads.

Interpretation Act 1889   Repealed and replaced by the Interpretation Act 1978, printed in the title Statutory Instruments, Vol 1.

PART II — REGULATIONS

1. Citation   The Regulations contained in this Part of this Instrument may be cited as the "Pelican" Pedestrian Crossings Regulations 1969.

2.   (*Amended the Pedestrian Crossings Regulations 1954, SI 1954/370 (now revoked*).)

3. "Pelican" crossings   (1) The provisions of Schedule 1 to these Regulations shall have effect as respects the size, colour and type of the traffic signs which are to be placed at or near a crossing for the purpose of constituting it a

"Pelican" crossing.

(2) The provisions of Schedule 2 to these Regulations shall have effect for regulating the manner in which the presence and limits of a crossing are to be indicated for the purpose of constituting it a "Pelican" crossing.

NOTES
Traffic signs   As to traffic signs generally, see the title Transport (Part 2B) in this work.

4. Variations in dimensions   (*Not printed.*)

NOTES
This regulation provides for slight variations in the dimensions specified in the diagrams contained in Parts II and III of Sch 1 and in certain of the markings specified in Sch 2.

5. Significance of traffic signs   Regulations 6 and 7 of these Regulations are made under section 54 of the Act of 1967 and shall have effect for the purpose of prescribing the warnings, information, requirements and prohibitions which are to be conveyed to traffic by the traffic signs of the size, colour and type prescribed by Regulation 3 (1) of and Schedule 1 to these Regulations.

NOTES
Section 54 of the Act of 1967   Repealed; see now the Road Traffic Regulation Act 1984, s 64, Halsbury's Statutes, 4th edn Vol 38, title Road Traffic (3rd edn Vol 54 (2), p 1577).

6. Significance of the vehicular traffic light signals   (1) The vehicular traffic light signal at a "Pelican" crossing shall convey the following information, requirements and prohibitions—

(*a*) the green light shall convey the information that vehicular traffic may proceed across the crossing;

(*b*) the amber light shall convey the prohibition that vehicular traffic shall not proceed beyond the stop line, or, if the stop line is not for the time being visible, beyond the vehicular traffic light signal facing such traffic on the side of the carriageway on which vehicles approach the crossing, except in the case of any vehicle which when the amber light is first shown is so close to the said line or signal that it cannot safely be stopped before passing the line or signal;

(*c*) the red light shall convey the prohibition that vehicular traffic shall not proceed beyond the stop line, or, if the stop line is not for the time being visible, beyond the vehicular traffic light signal facing such traffic on the side of the carriageway on which vehicles approach the crossing; and

(*d*) the flashing amber light shall convey the information that vehicular traffic may proceed across the crossing but that every foot passenger, if the foot passenger is on the carriageway within the limits of that crossing before any part of a vehicle has entered those limits, has the right of precedence within those limits over that vehicle, and the requirement that the driver of a vehicle shall accord such precedence to any such foot passenger.

(2) Vehicular traffic passing the vehicular traffic light signal in accordance with the foregoing provisions of this Regulation shall proceed with due regard to the safety of other users of the road and subject to the direction of any police constable or traffic warden in uniform who may be engaged in the regulation of traffic.

7. Significance of the traffic signs for pedestrians   (1) The traffic signs for pedestrians at a "Pelican" crossing shall convey to foot passengers the warnings and information mentioned in the following paragraphs of this Regulation.

(2) The pedestrian light signal shall convey to foot passengers the following warnings and information—

(*a*) the red light shown by the pedestrian light signal shall convey to a foot passenger the warning that he should not in the interests of safety use the crossing;

(*b*) the green light shown by the pedestrian light signal shall convey to a foot passenger the information that he may use the crossing and drivers of vehicles may not cause their vehicles to enter the limits of the crossing; and

(*c*) the flashing green light shown by the pedestrian light signal shall convey—

   (i) to a foot passenger who is already on the crossing when the flashing green light is first shown the information that he may continue to use the crossing, that vehicular traffic may proceed across the crossing, and that if he is on the carriageway within the limits of the crossing before any part of a vehicle has entered those limits he has the right of precedence within those limits over that vehicle, and

   (ii) to a foot passenger who is not already on the crossing when the flashing green light is first shown the warning that he should not in the interests of safety start to cross the carriageway.

(3) When the word "WAIT" shown by the indicator for pedestrians is illuminated it shall convey to a foot passenger the same warning as that conveyed by the red light shown by the pedestrian light signal.

(4) Any audible signal emitted by any device for emitting audible signals provided in conjunction with the indicator for pedestrians shall convey to a foot passenger the information that he may use the crossing and drivers of vehicles may not cause their vehicle to enter the limits of the crossing.

8. Movement of traffic and precedence of pedestrians   Regulations 9, 10, 11 and 12 of these Regulations are made under section 23 of the Act of 1967 and shall have effect with respect to the movement of traffic (including foot passengers) and the precedence of the foot passengers over vehicles at and in the vicinity of a "Pelican" crossing.

NOTES
Section 23 of the Act of 1967   Repealed; see now the Road Traffic Regulation Act 1984, s 25, Halsbury's Statutes, 4th edn Vol 38, title Road Traffic (3rd edn Vol 54 (2), p 1535).

9. Requirements with respect to the stopping of vehicles on the approach to a "Pelican" crossing   (1) Subject to the provisions of paragraph (2) of this Regulation, the driver of a vehicle shall not cause the vehicle or any part thereof to stop on the carriageway between—

(*a*) a "Pelican" crossing, the approach to which is indicated by a pattern of studs as provided in paragraph 3 of Schedule 2 to these Regulations, and

(*b*) the line of studs in that pattern situated furthest from the crossing, on the side of the road on which the pattern of studs is placed, or, if the road is a one-way street, on either side of the road.

(2) Nothing in paragraph (1) of this Regulation shall apply—

(*a*) so as to prevent a vehicle stopping on any length of road or any side thereof so long as may be necessary to enable the vehicle, if it cannot be used for such purpose without stopping on that length of road or side thereof, to be used in connection with any building operation or demolition, the removal of any obstruction to traffic, the maintenance, improvement or reconstruction of that length of road or side thereof, or the laying, erection, alteration or repair in or near to that length of road of any sewer or of any main, pipe or apparatus for the supply of gas, water or electricity, or of any telegraphic line as defined in the Telegraph Act 1878;

(*b*) so as to prevent a vehicle stopping on any length of road or any side thereof to enable the vehicle, if it cannot be used for such purpose without stopping on that length of road or side thereof to be used for fire brigade, ambulance or police purposes;

(*c*) to a pedal bicycle not having a side-car attached thereto, whether additional means of propulsion by mechanical power are attached to the bicycle or not; or

(*d*) to a vehicle stopping for the purpose of complying with a requirement or prohibition indicated by the vehicular traffic light signals at the crossing, or where the driver of the vehicle is obliged to stop in order to avoid an accident, or is prevented from proceeding by circumstances beyond his control

NOTES
Telegraph Act 1878   Repealed by the Telecommunications Act 1984, s 109(6), Sch 7, Pt I. See now the definitions of "telecommunication apparatus" and "line" in *ibid*, ss 4 (3), 10, Sch 2, para 1 (1) and Sch 2, para 28, Halsbury's Statutes, 4th edn Vol 45, title Telecommunications and Broadcasting (3rd edn Vol 54 (2), pp 2205, 2294, 2321).

10. Prohibition against the proceeding of vehicles across a "Pelican" crossing
When the vehicular traffic light signal is showing a red light, the driver of a vehicle shall not cause the vehicle or any part thereof to proceed beyond the stop line, or, if that line is not for the time being visible or there is no stop line, beyond the vehicular traffic light signal facing the driver on the side of the carriageway on which vehicles approach the crossing.

NOTES
In connection with this regulation, see *Sulston v Hammond*, [1970] 2 All ER 830 (whether notice of intended prosecution necessary where contravention of this regulation is alleged).

11. Precedence of pedestrians over vehicles on a "Pelican" crossing   When the vehicular traffic light signal at a "Pelican" crossing is showing a flashing amber light every foot passenger, if the foot passenger is on the carriageway within the limits of that crossing before any part of a vehicle has entered those limits, shall have precedence within those limits over that vehicle, and the driver of a vehicle shall accord such precedence to any such foot passenger.

12. Prohibitions against the waiting of vehicles and pedestrians on a "Pelican" crossing   (1) The driver of a vehicle shall not cause the vehicle or any part thereof to stop within the limits of a "Pelican" crossing unless either he is prevented from proceeding by circumstances beyond his control or it is necessary for him to stop in order to avoid an accident.

(2) No foot passenger shall remain on the carriageway within the limits of a "Pelican" crossing longer than is necessary for the purpose of passing over the crossing with reasonable despatch.

SCHEDULE 1 (See Regulation 3)
THE SIZE, COLOUR AND TYPE OF TRAFFIC SIGNS AT A "PELICAN" CROSSING
PART I

1. Traffic Signs   The traffic signs which are to be placed at or near a crossing for the purpose of constituting it a "Pelican" crossing shall consist of a combination of—
  (*a*) vehicular traffic light signals,
  (*b*) pedestrian light signals, and
  (*c*) indicators for pedestrians,
of the size, colour and type prescribed by the following provisions of this Schedule.

2. Vehicular traffic light signals   The vehicular traffic light signals shall be as follows—
  (*a*) three lights shall be used, one red, one amber, and one green;
  (*b*) the lamps showing the aforesaid lights shall be arranged vertically, the lamp showing the red light being the uppermost and that showing the green light the lowermost;
  (*c*) each lamp shall be separately illuminated and the effective diameter of the lens thereof shall be not less than 200 millimetres nor more than 215 millimetres;
  (*d*) the height of the centre of the lens in the lamp showing the amber light from the surface of the carriageway in the immediate vicinity shall be not less than 2·4 metres nor more than 4·0 metres:
    Provided that if the vehicular traffic light signals are placed at or near a crossing in accordance with this paragraph any additional vehicular traffic light signals placed over the carriageway shall be of such a height that the centre of the lens in the lamp showing the amber light from the surface of the carriageway in the immediate vicinity is not less than 6·1 metres nor more than 9 metres;
  (*e*) the centres of the lenses of adjacent lamps shall not be more than 360 millimetres apart;

(*f*) the lamp showing the amber light shall be capable of showing a steady light or a flashing light such that it flashes at a rate of not less than 70 nor more than 90 flashes per minute;

(*g*) The word "STOP" in black lettering may be placed upon the lens of the lamp showing a red light and no other lettering shall be used upon the lenses.

3. Pedestrian light signals   (1) The pedestrian light signals shall be of the size, colour and type shown either in Diagram 1 or in Diagram 2 in Part II of this Schedule.

(2) The height of the lower edge of the container enclosing the light signals from the surface of the carriageway in the immediate vicinity shall be not less than 2·1 metres nor more than 2·6 metres.

(3) The said signals shall be so designed that—

(*a*) the red figure shown in the said Part II of this Schedule can be internally illuminated by a steady light;

(*b*) the green figure shown in the said Part II of this Schedule can be internally illuminated by a steady light or by a flashing light flashing at a rate of not less than 70 nor more than 90 flashes per minute; and

(*c*) when one signal is illuminated the other signal is not illuminated.

4. Indicator for pedestrians   (1) The indicator for pedestrians shall be of the size, colour and type shown either in Diagram 1 or in Diagram 2 set out in Part III of this Schedule.

(2) The indicator for pedestrians shall be so designed and constructed that the word "WAIT" as shown in each of the said diagrams can be illuminated so that it appears in white letters on a blue ground and there is incorporated in the indicator a device (hereinafter referred to as "a push button") which can be used by foot passengers with the effect hereinafter described.

(3) A device for emitting audible signals may be provided in conjunction with an indicator for pedestrians.

5. Sequence of signals   (1) The vehicular traffic and pedestrian light signals and the indicators for pedestrians when they are placed at or near any crossing shall be so designed and constructed that—

(*a*) before the signals and indicators are operated by the pressing of a push button or as described in paragraph 6 of this Schedule the vehicular traffic light signal shows a green light, the pedestrian light signal shows a red light, the word "WAIT" in the indicator for pedestrians is not illuminated and any device for emitting audible signals is silent;

(*b*) when a push button is pressed—

(i) after the expiration of the vehicle period but before the vehicular traffic light signals are showing an amber light, the signals and indicators, unless they are working as described in paragraph 6 (*b*) of this Schedule, are caused to show lights in the sequences specified in descending order in column 1 in the case of vehicular traffic light signals, in column 2 in the case of pedestrian light signals and in column 3 in the case of the indicators for pedestrians of [either the table in Part IV or the table in Part V of this Schedule];

(ii) when the vehicular traffic light signals are showing an amber light or a red light, there is no effect;

(iii) when the pedestrian light signals are showing a flashing green light, the word "WAIT" in each of the indicators for pedestrians is illuminated immediately and the signals and indicators are caused to show lights in the sequence specified in sub-paragraph (i) of this paragraph at the end of the next vehicle period;

(iv) after the pedestrian light signals have ceased to show a flashing green light and before the end of the next vehicle period, the word "WAIT" in each of the indicators for pedestrians is illuminated and the signals and indicators are caused to show lights in the sequence specified in sub-paragraph (i) of this paragraph at the end of the vehicle period;

(*c*) the periods, during which lights are shown by the signals and the indicators, commence and terminate in relation to each other as shown in the columns of [either the table in Part IV or the table in Part V of this Schedule] as if each horizontal line therein represented one moment in time, subsequent moments occurring in descending order, but the distances between the horizontal lines do not represent the lengths of the periods during which the lights shown by the signals and the indicator are, or are not, lit.

(2) Where a device for emitting audible signals is provided in conjunction with an indicator for pedestrians placed at or near any crossing it shall be so designed and constructed that—

(*a*) when a push-button is pressed—

(i) after the expiration of the vehicle period but before the vehicular traffic light signals are showing an amber light, a regular pulsed sound is emitted throughout the period when the pedestrian light signals are showing a green light and the vehicular traffic light signals are at the same time showing a red light;

(ii) when the vehicular traffic light signals are showing an amber or red light, there is no effect;

(iii) when the pedestrian light signals are showing a flashing green light or at the end of this period and before the end of the next vehicle period, a regular pulsed sound is emitted throughout the period when the pedestrian light signals next show a green light and the vehicular traffic light signals next show at the same time a red light;

(*b*) the period, during which the audible signal is given, commences and terminates in relation to the periods during which the light signals specified in sub-paragraph (i) of this paragraph are given as shown in the columns in [either the table in Part IV or the table in Part V of this Schedule] as if each horizontal line had the significance specified in that paragraph.

(3) In this paragraph "vehicle period" means such period as may be fixed from time to time in relation to a "Pelican" crossing, which commences when the vehicular traffic light signals cease to show a flashing amber light and during which the vehicular traffic light signals show a green light.

6. Operation by remote control   The vehicular traffic light signals, pedestrian signals, indicators for pedestrians and any device for emitting audible signals, when they are placed at or near any crossing may be so designed and constructed that they can by remote control be made to operate—

(*a*)   as if a push button had been pressed,

(*b*)   so that the pressing of a push button has no effect, other than causing the word "WAIT" in each of the indicators for the pedestrians to be illuminated, until normal operation is resumed.

NOTES

Amendment   The words in square brackets in sub-paras (1)(*b*)(i), (1)(*c*) and 2(*b*) of para 5 were substituted by SI 1979/401.

PART II

NOTES

This Part contains two diagrams of the pedestrian light signals mentioned in para 3 of Part I of this Schedule. Diagram 1 shows a red standing figure and a green walking figure on black rectangular backgrounds (300 mm high and 200 mm wide), and Diagram 2 shows the same figures on black circular backgrounds (300 mm in diameter).

PART III

NOTES

This Part contains two diagrams of the indicator mentioned in para 4 of Part I of this Schedule. Each diagram shows a push button face assembly, which incorporates the words "Pedestrians. Push Button and wait for signal opposite" at the top, and the word "WAIT" in white letters on a blue background in the middle.

PART IV

Sequence of vehicular traffic light signals 1.	Sequence of pedestrian signals		
	Pedestrian light signals 2.	Indicator for pedestrians 3.	Audible signal 4.
Green light	Red light	The word "WAIT" is illuminated	None
Amber light			
Red light			
	Green light	The word "WAIT" is not illuminated	Regular pulsed sound
Flashing amber light	Flashing green light	The word "WAIT" is illuminated	None
	Red light		
Green light			

NOTES

The above table is referred to in para 5 of Part I of this Schedule.

[PART V

Sequence of vehicular traffic light signals 1.	Sequence of pedestrian signals		
	Pedestrian light signals 2.	Indicator for pedestrians 3.	Audible signal 4.
Green light	Red light	The word "WAIT" is illuminated	None
Amber light			
Red light			
	Green light	The word "WAIT" is not illuminated	Regular pulsed sound
Flashing amber light	Flashing green light	The word "WAIT" is illuminated	None]
	Red light		
Green light			

NOTES
Amendment   Part V of this Schedule was inserted by SI 1979/401; it is referred to in para 5 of Part I of this Schedule, as amended by SI 1979/401.

SCHEDULE 2 (See Regulation 3)
THE MANNER OF INDICATING THE PRESENCE AND LIMITS
OF A "PELICAN" CROSSING

Manner of indicating the limits of the crossing

1.   (1) Every crossing which is a "Pelican" crossing and its limits shall be indicated by two lines of studs across the carriageway or between the edge of the carriageway and a street refuge or central reservation in accordance with the following provisions of this paragraph.
   (2) Each line formed by the outside edges of the studs shall be so separated from the other line so formed that the distance between any point on one of those lines and the nearest points on the other line shall not be less than 2·4 metres nor more than 5 metres or such greater distance (not being more than 10 metres) [as may be appropriate having regard to the layout of the carriageway and the extent to which it is used by pedestrians];
   Provided that the foregoing provisions of this sub-paragraph shall be regarded as having been complied with in the case of any crossing which for the most part complies with those provisions notwithstanding that those provisions may not be so complied with as respects the distance from one or more points on one line to the nearest point on the other line, so long as the general indication of the lines is not thereby materially impaired.
   (3) The studs of which each line is constituted shall be so placed that the distance from the centre of any one stud to the centre of the next stud in the line is not less than 500 millimetres nor more than 720 millimetres, and a distance of not more than 1·3 metres is left between the edge of the carriageway central reservation or street refuge at either end of the line and the centre of the stud nearest thereto:
   Provided that the foregoing provisions of this sub-paragraph shall be regarded as having been complied with in the case of any line where most of the studs constituting it comply with those provisions notwithstanding that those provisions may not be complied with as respects one or more such studs, so long as the general indication of the line is not thereby materially impaired.
   (4) Studs shall not be fitted with reflecting lenses and shall be—
   (*a*)   white, silver or light grey in colour;
   (*b*)   square or circular in plan, the sides of a square stud and the diameter of a circular stud

not being less than 95 millimetres nor more than 110 millimetres in length; and

(c) so fixed that they do not project more than 15 millimetres above the carriageway at their highest points nor more than 6 millimetres at their edges.

2. A crossing or its limits shall not be deemed to have ceased to be indicated in accordance with the provisions of the foregoing paragraph by reason only of the discolouration or temporary removal or displacement of one or more studs in any line so long as the general indication of the line is not thereby materially impaired.

NOTES
Amendment The words in square brackets in para 1(2) of this Schedule were substituted by SI 1979/401.

Manner of indicating the vehicular approach to the crossing

3. (1) Subject to the following provisions of this paragraph, the approach for vehicular traffic to a "Pelican" crossing shall be indicated by a pattern of studs placed and white lines marked on the carriageway in accordance with the following provisions of this paragraph.

(2) On a road, not being a one-way street, and where the crossing is not a crossing which extends only between the edge of the carriageway and a street refuge or a central reservation, the pattern of studs and white lines shall be indicated on each side of the crossing and shall comply with the following requirements, the relevant dimensions being those shown without brackets—

(a) There shall be a transverse stop line 200 millimetres (300 millimetres) wide from the edge of the carriageway to the centre of the carriageway on the side of the carriageway on which vehicles approach the crossing, parallel to the line of studs indicating the limits of the crossing on the side of the crossing nearer to the approaching vehicles, and not less than 1·7 metres nor more than 2·0 metres from such line of studs.

(b) There shall be a longitudinal broken line 100 millimetres wide along the centre of the carriageway extending from the end of the transverse stop line away from the crossing and consisting of three (five) strips 4·0 metres (6·0 metres) long and two (four) gaps 2·0 metres (3·0 metres) long arranged alternately in such a manner that the first strip adjoins the transverse stop line.

(c) There shall be two rows of studs from the edge of the carriageway to the centre of the carriageway on the side of the carriageway on which vehicles approach the crossing, complying with the following requirements—

   (i) The two rows shall be parallel to each other.

   (ii) The row of studs further from the crossing shall be not less than 14·0 metres (23·5 metres) nor more than 16·0 metres (26.5 metres) from the line of studs indicating the limits of the crossing on the side of the crossing nearer to the approaching vehicles except where such distances would be inappropriate having regard to the layout and conditions at the place where the crossing is situated.

   (iii) If the edge of the carriageway and the longitudinal broken line are parallel at the places where the two rows of studs meet them the two rows of studs shall be straight and at right angles to the edge of the carriageway and in any other case the two rows of studs shall be curved as appropriate so as to meet the edge of the carriageway or the longitudinal broken line at a right angle.

   (iv) Each row of studs shall have the same number of studs.

   (v) The two rows of studs shall be not less than 300 millimetres nor more than 410 millimetres apart, measured between the centre of the studs.

   (vi) There shall be not more than 1·3 metres between the edge of the carriageway and the centre of the nearest stud thereto in each row.

   (vii) There shall be not less than 500 millimetres nor more than 720 millimetres between the centre of any stud in a row and the centre of the next stud thereto in that row.

   (viii) There shall be not less than 500 millimetres nor more than 720 millimetres between the centre of the longitudinal broken line and the centre of the nearest stud thereto in each row.

(3) On a road, being a one-way street, or where a crossing extends only between the edge of the carriageway and a street refuge or a central reservation, the pattern of studs and white lines shall be indicated on the side of the crossing on which vehicles approach the crossing and shall comply with the following requirements, the relevant dimensions being those shown without brackets—

(a) There shall be a transverse stop line 200 millimetres (300 millimetres) wide from one edge of the carriageway to the other, in the case of a crossing on a one-way street, or, in the case of a crossing which extends only between the edge of the carriageway and a street refuge or a central reservation, from that edge of the carriageway to the centre of the carriageway or to the edge of the central reservation, as the case may be, in each case parallel to the nearer line of studs indicating the limits of the crossing and not less than 1·7 metres nor more than 2·0 metres from such line of studs.

(b) There shall be a longitudinal broken line 100 millimetres wide along the centre of the carriageway extending from the centre of the transverse stop line in the case of a crossing on a one-way street, or, in the case of a crossing which extends only between the edge of the carriageway and a central refuge from the end of the transverse stop line away from the crossing and consisting of three (five) strips 4·0 metres (6·0 metres) long and two (four) gaps 2·0 metres (3·0 metres) long arranged alternately in such a manner that the first strip adjoins the transverse stop line.

(c)   There shall be two rows of studs from one edge of the carriageway to the other, in the case of a crossing on a one-way street, or, in the case of a crossing which extends only between the edge of the carriageway and a street refuge or a central reservation, from that edge of the carriageway to the centre of the carriageway, or to the edge of the central reservation, as the case may be, in each case complying with the following requirements—

(i)   The two rows shall be parallel to each other.

(ii)   The row of studs further from the crossing shall be not less than 14·0 metres (23·5 metres) nor more than 16·0 metres (26·5 metres) from the nearer line of studs indicating the limits of the crossing except where such distances would be inappropriate having regard to the layout and conditions at the place where the crossing is situate.

(iii)   If the two edges of the carriageway and the longitudinal broken line, or the edge of the carriageway and the edge of the central reservation, are parallel at the places where the two rows meet them, the two rows of studs shall be straight and at right angles to the edge of the carriageway and in any other case the two rows of studs shall be curved as appropriate so as to meet the edge of the carriageway, or the edge of the central reservation, or the longitudinal broken line, as the case may be, at a right angle.

(iv)   Each row of studs shall have the same number of studs.

(v)   The two rows of studs shall be not less than 300 millimetres apart nor more than 410 millimetres apart, measured between the centres of the studs.

(vi)   There shall be not more than 1·3 metres between the edge or centre of the carriageway, or the edge of the central reservation, as the case may be, and the centre of the nearest stud thereto in each row.

(vii)   Except in the case of the two studs in each row which lie one on each side of the longitudinal centre line, there shall be not less than 500 millimetres nor more than 720 millimetres between the centre of any stud in a row and the centre of the next stud thereto in that row.

(viii)   There shall be not less than 500 millimetres nor more than 720 millimetres between the centre of the longitudinal centre line and the centre of the nearest stud thereto in each row on each side thereof.

(4) In the case of a road on which a speed limit on the driving of motor vehicles is not in force by virtue of any enactment—

(a)   of 30 miles per hour or less, where figures appear in the last two preceding sub-paragraphs in brackets alongside other figures in relation to the dimensions of the pattern of studs, the figures in brackets shall apply in substitution for the said other figures;

(b)   of 40 miles per hour or less, where figures appear in the last two preceding sub-paragraphs in brackets alongside other figures in relation to the dimensions of the pattern of white lines, the figures in brackets shall apply in substitution for the said other figures.

(5) The transverse stop line may be omitted or its angle in relation to and its distance from the crossing varied and the longitudinal broken line may be omitted having regard to the layout and conditions at the place where the crossing is situate.

(6) The requirements of this paragraph shall be regarded as having been complied with in the case of any pattern of studs or white lines if most of the studs or the lengths of white lines comply with those requirements notwithstanding that one or more studs or some of the lengths of white line may not comply with those requirements so long as the general appearance of the pattern of studs or white lines is not thereby materially impaired.

(7) The approach to a crossing shall not be regarded as having ceased to be indicated by a pattern of studs or white lines in accordance with the foregoing provisions by reason only of the discolouration, temporary removal or displacement of one or more studs in the pattern of studs or a length of white line in the pattern of white lines so long as the general appearance of the pattern of studs or white lines is not thereby materially impaired.

(8) The provisions of sub-paragraph (4) of paragraph 1 of this Schedule shall apply to the studs mentioned in this paragraph as they apply to the studs mentioned in that sub-paragraph.

(9) Where the appropriate authority is satisfied in relation to a particular approach to a crossing that by reason of the existence at or near that crossing of a road junction which is on the same side of that crossing and on the same side of the road as that approach—

(a)   the application of Regulation 9 of the Regulations contained in Part II of this Instrument in relation to that approach will not be appropriate unless the pattern of studs by which that approach is to be indicated is varied as hereinafter provided, or

(b)   that the application of the said Regulation 9 in relation to that approach would be inappropriate even if the pattern of studs were varied as aforesaid,

then, in the case mentioned in (a) of this sub-paragraph, that approach shall be indicated in accordance with the foregoing provisions of this paragraph varied by the substitution for the distance of not less than 14.0 metres nor more than 16.0 metres specified in paragraph 3 (2) of this Schedule, or for the said distance of not less than 23.5 metres nor more than 26.5 metres, as the case may be, of such shorter distance (not being less than 9 metres) as the appropriate authority may think fit, and, in the case mentioned in (b) of this sub-paragraph, it shall not be necessary for that approach to be indicated in accordance with this paragraph:

Provided that for the purpose of the application of this sub-paragraph to a crossing which is on a road which is a one-way street the foregoing provisions of this sub-paragraph shall have effect as if the words "and on the same side of the road" were omitted.

In this sub-paragraph the expression "appropriate authority" means, in relation to an approach to a crossing which is on a trunk road in England, the Minister, and in relation to an approach to a crossing which is on a trunk road in Scotland, or Wales, the Secretary of State, and, in relation to an approach to any other crossing, the Council in whose scheme under section 21 of the Act of 1967 the crossing is for the time being included.

NOTES
The Minister This (which originally referred to the Minister of Transport) is now to be construed as referring to the Secretary of State for Transport; see the Preliminary Note at p 52, *ante*.
Section 21 of the Act of 1967 Repealed; see now the Road Traffic Regulation Act 1984, s 23, Halsbury's Statutes, 4th edn Vol 38, title Road Traffic (3rd edn Vol 54(2), p 1534). The said s 23 (which replaced s 21 of the 1967 Act, as substituted by the Local Government, Planning and Land Act 1980, s 1 (8), Sch 7, Pt II, para 10 (1)) does not require schemes to be made; it empowers local authorities, subject to certain requirements, to establish crossings on any roads in their area, other than trunk roads.

PART III — GENERAL DIRECTIONS
(Not printed.)

NOTES
This Part of this instrument contains the "Pelican" Pedestrian Crossings General Directions 1969 (which were given under s 55 of the Road Traffic Regulation Act 1967 (now repealed and replaced by the Road Traffic Regulation Act 1984, s 65, Halsbury's Statutes, 4th edn Vol 38, title Road Traffic (3rd edn Vol 54 (2), p 1579), and which replace the Traffic Signs (Push Button Controlled Crossings) General Directions 1967 (set out in Part II of SI 1967/178)). They provide for the number, placing and arrangement of vehicular traffic light signals, pedestrian light signals and indicators for pedestrians at a "pelican" crossing.

THE "ZEBRA" PEDESTRIAN CROSSINGS REGULATIONS 1971
SI 1971/1524

NOTES
Authority These regulations were made on 14 September 1971 by the Secretary of State for the Environment, the Secretary of State for Scotland and the Secretary of State for Wales under ss 23 (1) and (2) and 54 (1) and (2) of the Road Traffic Regulation Act 1967 (repealed), and all other enabling powers. They now have effect under the Road Traffic Regulation Act 1984, ss 25 and 64, Halsbury's Statutes, 4th edn Vol 38, title Road Traffic (3rd edn Vol 54 (2), pp 1535, 1577).
Commencement 29 September 1971; see reg 1.
Interpretation See reg 3.
Penalties, etc Persons who contravene these regulations, so far as they now have effect under the Road Traffic Regulation Act 1984, s 25 (*ie* so far as they contain provisions relating to crossings for foot passengers other than those prescribing traffic signs to be used in connection with such crossings), are liable on summary conviction to a fine not exceeding level 3 on the standard scale; see ss 25 (5), 98, Sch 7 (and for provisions as to disqualification and endorsement of licences, see s 98, Sch 7). Note also that under s 25 (6) for the purpose of a prosecution for a contravention of the regulations the crossing is to be deemed to be properly established and indicated unless the contrary is proved. Persons who contravene, or fail to comply with, these regulations in other respects are also liable on summary conviction to a fine not exceeding level 3 on the standard scale; see ss 98, 118, Sch 7.
    Contravention of these regulations may also give rise to a claim for damages; see *London Passenger Transport Board* v *Upson*, [1949] 1 All ER 60; [1949] AC 155 (HL).
General Pedestrian crossings on trunk roads are established by the Secretary of State or by local authorities acting under delegated powers (see the Road Traffic Regulation Act 1984, s 24, Halsbury's Statutes, 4th edn Vol 38, title Road Traffic (3rd edn Vol 54 (2), p 1535) and the Highways Act 1980, s 6, *ibid*, 4th edn Vol 20, title Highways, Streets and Bridges (3rd edn Vol 50 (1), p 466); crossings on other roads are established by local authorities after certain provisions as to consultation etc have been complied with (see the 1984 Act, s 23, Halsbury's Statutes, 4th edn Vol 38, title Road Traffic (3rd edn Vol 54 (2), p 1534)). The present regulations, which re-enact with amendments the Pedestrian Crossings Regulations 1954, SI 1954/370, as amended, continue to specify the manner in which crossings (commonly known as "zebra crossings") are to be indicated by marks on the carriageway and by traffic signs and to impose the same duties as respects the according of precedence by drivers of vehicles to pedestrians on zebra crossings.
    The regulations do not define the responsibilities of pedestrians and drivers in relation to crossings in all circumstances; in particular they do not deal with the problem of when a pedestrian should start to cross; the Committee on Road Safety are of opinion that it is impossible so to frame regulations (see para 5 of their Report published in February 1949 by HM Stationery Office). See further the notes to reg 8.
    Attention is also drawn to the "Pelican" Pedestrian Crossings Regulations and General Directions 1969, SI 1969/888, p 75, *ante*.
    These regulations are applied, with modifications, by the Crown Roads (Royal Parks) (Appli-

cation of Road Traffic Enactments) Order 1977, SI 1977/548, in the title Open Spaces and Recreation Grounds.

PART I — GENERAL

Commencement and citation
1.   These Regulations shall come into operation on the 29th September 1971 and may be cited as the "Zebra" Pedestrian Crossings Regulations 1971.

Revocation and savings
2.   (1) Subject to the provisions of the next two paragraphs, the Pedestrian Crossings Regulations 1954 and the Regulations amending those Regulations specified in Schedule 1 are hereby revoked and the said Regulations of 1954 as so amended are hereinafter referred to as "the Regulations of 1954".

(2) Where immediately before the coming into operation of these Regulations a crossing within the meaning of the Regulations of 1954 other than a zebra crossing has been indicated in accordance with Part I of Schedule 1 to the Regulations of 1954, then notwithstanding the revocation effected by the last paragraph the Regulations of 1954 shall continue to apply to that crossing until the 30th November 1973.

(3) Where immediately before the coming into operation of these Regulations, the approach for vehicular traffic to a zebra crossing has been indicated by a pattern of studs on a road in accordance with the provisions of paragraph 8 of Part II of Schedule 1 to the Regulations of 1954, then notwithstanding the revocation effected by paragraph (1) of this Regulation or any variation of a speed limit on that road that approach may until the 30th November 1973 continue to be so indicated so long as the said pattern of studs does not lie within a zebra controlled area or in the vicinity of such an area on the same side of the crossing as that pattern

NOTES
Pedestrian Crossings Regulations 1954   SI 1954/370.

Interpretation
3.   (1) In these Regulations, unless the context otherwise requires, the following expressions have the meanings hereby respectively assigned to them—
"the appropriate Secretary of State" means, in relation to a crossing established on a road in England excluding Monmouthshire, the Secretary of State for the Environment, in relation to a crossing established on a road in Scotland, the Secretary of State for Scotland, and, in relation to a crossing established on a road in Wales or Monmouthshire, the Secretary of State for Wales;
"appropriate authority" means, in relation to a crossing on a trunk road, the appropriate Secretary of State, and in relation to any other crossing the local authority in whose scheme submitted and approved under section 21 of the Act of 1967 the crossing is for the time being included;
"carriageway" does not include that part of any road which consists of a street refuge or central reservation, whether within the limits of a crossing or not;
"central reservation" means any provision, not consisting of a street refuge, made in a road for separating one part of the carriageway of that road from another part of that carriageway for the safety or guidance of vehicular traffic using that road;
"crossing" means a crossing for foot passengers established either—
(*a*) by a local authority in accordance with the provisions for the time being in force of a scheme submitted and approved under section 21 of the Act of 1967, or
(*b*) in the case of a trunk road, by the appropriate Secretary of State in the discharge of the duty imposed on him by section 22 of the Act of 1967;

but does not include a "Pelican" crossing within the meaning of the "Pelican" Pedestrian Crossings Regulations 1969;

"dual-carriageway road" means a length of road on which a part of the carriageway thereof is separated from another part thereof by a central reservation;

"give-away line" has the meaning assigned to it by paragraph 2 of Schedule 3;

"one-way street" means any road in which the driving of all vehicles otherwise than in one direction is prohibited at all times;

"stud" means a mark or device on the carriageway, whether or not projecting above the surface thereof;

"zebra controlled area" means, in relation to a zebra crossing, the area of the carriageway in the vicinity of the crossing and lying on both sides of the crossing or only one side of the crossing, being an area the presence and limits of which are indicated in accordance with Schedule 3;

"zebra crossing" means a crossing the presence and limits of which are indicated in accordance with the provisions of Schedule 2;

"uncontrolled zebra crossing" means a zebra crossing at which traffic is not for the time being controlled by a police constable in uniform or by a traffic warden.

(2) Any reference in these Regulations to a numbered Regulation or Schedule is a reference to the Regulation or Schedule bearing that number in these Regulations except where otherwise expressly provided.

(3) Any reference in these Regulations to any enactment shall be construed as a reference to that enactment as amended by any subsequent enactment.

(4) The Interpretation Act 1889 shall apply for the interpretation of these Regulations as it applies for the interpretation of an Act of Parliament, and as if for the purposes of section 38 of that Act these Regulations were an Act of Parliament and Regulations revoked by Regulation 2 were Acts of Parliament thereby repealed.

NOTES
Secretary of State for the Environment   This is now to be construed as a reference to the Secretary of State for Transport by virtue of the Transfer of Functions (Transport) Order 1981, SI 1981/238 in the title Constitutional Law (Part 5).
"Pelican" Pedestrian Crossings Regulations 1969   See Part II of SI 1969/888, as amended, p 76, *ante*. For the meaning of "pelican" crossing therein, see para 3 (1) of Part I of that instrument, p 75, *ante*.
Sections 21 and 22 of the Act of 1967   *Ie,* the Road Traffic Regulation Act 1967, as stated in the recital of powers at the head of these regulations. These must now be construed as references to the Road Traffic Regulation Act 1984, ss 23 and 24, Halsbury's Statutes, 4th edn Vol 38, title Road Traffic (3rd edn Vol 54 (2), pp 1534, 1535). Section 23 of that Act (which replaced s 21 of the 1967 Act, as substituted by the Local Government, Planning and Land Act 1980, s 1 (8), Sch 7, Pt II, para 10 (1)) does not provide for schemes to be submitted and approved but for local authorities to be empowered to establish crossings on any roads in their area, other than trunk roads, after certain requirements as to consultation etc have been complied with.
Interpretation Act 1889   Repealed and replaced by the Interpretation Act 1978, printed in the title Statutory Instruments, Vol 1

PART II
MARKS, SIGNS AND OTHER PARTICULARS
AS RESPECTS ZEBRA CROSSINGS

Zebra crossings
4.   (1) The provisions of Part I of Schedule 2 shall have effect for regulating the manner in which the presence and limits of a crossing are to be indicated by marks or studs on the carriageway for the purpose of constituting it a zebra crossing.

(2) The provisions of Part II of Schedule 2 shall have effect as respects the size, colour and type of the traffic signs which are to be placed at or near a crossing for the purpose of constituting it a zebra crossing.

Zebra controlled areas and give-way lines
5.   (1) Subject to paragraph (3) of this Regulation, the provisions of Schedule 3 shall have effect as respects the size, colour and type of the traffic signs

which shall be placed in the vicinity of a zebra crossing for the purpose of constituting a zebra controlled area in relation to that crossing and of indicating the presence and limits of that area.

(2) A give-way line (included among the said signs) shall, where provided, also convey to vehicular traffic proceeding towards a zebra crossing the position at or before which a driver of a vehicle should stop it for the purpose of complying with Regulation 8.

(3) Where the appropriate authority is satisfied in relation to a particular area of carriageway in the vicinity of a zebra crossing that, by reason of the layout of, or character of, the roads in the vicinity of the crossing, the application of such a prohibition as is mentioned in Regulation 10 or 12 to that particular area or the constitution of that particular area as a zebra controlled area by the placing of traffic signs in accordance with Schedule 3 would be impracticable, it shall not be necessary for that area to be constituted a zebra controlled area but, if by virtue of this paragraph it is proposed that no area, on either side of the limits of a zebra crossing (not on a trunk road), is to be constituted a zebra controlled area by the 30th November 1973, a notice in writing shall be sent by the appropriate authority before that date to the appropriate Secretary of State stating the reasons why it is proposed that no such area should be so constituted.

Variations in dimensions shown in Schedule 3
6.   Any variations in a dimension specified in the diagram in Schedule 3 or otherwise specified in that Schedule shall be treated as permitted by these Regulations if the variation—
>   (*a*)   in the case of a dimension of 300 millimetres or more, does not exceed 20% of that dimension; or
>   (*b*)   in the case of a dimension of less than 300 millimetres, where the actual dimension exceeds the dimension so specified, does not exceed 30% of the dimension so specified, and where the actual dimension is less than the dimension so specified, does not exceed 10% of the dimension so specified.

Lamps for illumination of pedestrians at crossings
7.   (1) Where the appropriate authority is safisfied that the presence of a foot passenger—
>   (*a*)   at the end of a zebra crossing, being an end at or near which a globe has been placed in accordance with paragraph 2 of Part II of Schedule 2, or
>   (*b*)   on a street refuge or central reservation on such a crossing, being a refuge or reservation on which a globe has been placed in accordance with the said paragraph 2,

should be better indicated during the hours of darkness as defined in the Road Transport Lighting Act 1957 the authority may provide a lamp (showing a white light) beneath the globe so as to illuminate during the said hours any such foot passenger.

(2) Every such lamp shall be so arranged that the lowest part thereof is not less than 2 metres above the surface of the ground in the immediate vicinity and that the source of the illumination given thereby is not visible to drivers of approaching vehicles.

NOTES
Road Transport Lighting Act 1957   Repealed; by virtue of s 82 of the Road Traffic Act 1972, the expression "hours of darkness" was defined as the time between half-an-hour after sunset and half-an-hour before sunrise. This definition was repealed by the Road Traffic Act 1974, s 24 (3), Sch 7, but s 9 (4) thereof, Halsbury's Statutes, 4th edn Vol 38, title Road Traffic (3rd edn Vol 44, p 1355) provides for the expression to continue to be so construed.

PART III
REGULATIONS GOVERNING USE OF ZEBRA CROSSINGS AND ZEBRA CONTROLLED AREAS

Precedence of pedestrians over vehicles

8. Every foot passenger on the carriageway within the limits of an uncontrolled zebra crossing shall have precedence within those limits over any vehicle and the driver of the vehicle shall accord such precedence to the foot passenger, if the foot passenger is on the carriageway within those limits before the vehicle or any part thereof has come on to the carriageway within those limits.

For the purpose of this Regulation, in the case of such a crossing on which there is a street refuge or central reservation the parts of the crossing which are situated on each side of the street refuge or central reservation as the case may be shall each be treated as a separate crossing.

NOTES
This regulation imposes an absolute duty on the driver to allow the foot passengers to proceed, and it is quite immaterial whether there is any evidence of negligence or failure to take reasonable care on the part of the driver (*Hughes* v *Hall*, [1960] 2 All ER 504 (not followed, however, in *Levy* v *Hockey* (1961), 105 Sol Jo 157)). It is, moreover, irrelevant that the driver might have been genuinely misled into thinking that the foot passengers were stopping to allow him to pass (*Neal* v *Bedford*, [1965] 3 All ER 250). See also, however *Burns* v *Bidder*, [1966] 3 All ER 29; [1967] 2 QB 227 (no absolute duty).

It is the duty of a motorist approaching a crossing to drive in such a way that he could stop if there was a pedestrian whose presence on the crossing was hidden by other traffic (*Lockie* v *Lawton* (1959) 57 LGR 329, following *Gibbons* v *Kahl*, [1955] 3 All ER 345; [1956] 1 QB 59, and distinguishing *Leicester* v *Pearson*, [1952] 2 All ER 71; [1952] 2 QB 668, as a "very special case") "It is the duty of motorists to be able to stop before they get [to the crossing] unless they can see that there is nobody on the crossing" (*per* Lord Goddard, CJ, in *Gibbons* v *Kahl, supra*). The duty is unqualified, and it makes no difference whether the vehicle which masked the pedestrian from the motorist was on the off side or the near side of the road (*Lockie* v *Lawton, supra*, at p 331, *per* Lord Parker, CJ).

Limits of an uncontrolled crossing See reg 4 (1) and Part I of Sch 2. The limits of the crossing are the striped area (*Moulder* v *Neville*, [1974] RTR 53, following *Hughes* v *Hall, supra*, where the limits were held to be the studs bordering the striped area).

If the foot passenger is on the carriageway It was held in a case under the similar wording of earlier regulations that they applied only to a pedestrian who was already upon the crossing and did not refer to the case of a pedestrian suddenly stepping from the footpath onto the crossing when it was clearly unsafe to do so; and that to such a case the common law of principles of negligence applied (*Chisholm* v *London Passenger Transport Board* [1938] 4 All ER 850; [1939] 1 KB 426, CA). See also *Sparks* v *Edward Ash Ltd*, [1943] 1 All ER 1; [1943] 1 KB 223 (overruling the decision in *Bailey* v *Geddes*, [1937] 3 All ER 671; [1938] 1 KB 156) which establishes that a pedestrian's contributory negligence may be a defence to a claim for damages for injuries sustained on a crossing.

In *M'Kerrell* v *Robertson* [1956] SC (J) 50, a go-chair containing a child was pushed on to a crossing by a woman who at the material time was not herself on the carriageway, and it was held that the woman was a foot passenger on the carriageway within the meaning of this regulation; in *Crank* v *Brooks*, [1980] RTR 441, it was held that a person on foot pushing a bicycle across a crossing was a foot passenger within the meaning of this regulation.

Street refuge or central reservation The provision that the parts of a crossing divided by a street refuge or central reservation are to be treated as separate crossings is in conformity with the decision in *Wilkinson* v *Chetham-Strode*, [1940] 2 All ER 643; [1940] 2 KB 310.

Prohibition against the waiting of vehicles and pedestrians on zebra crossings

9. (1) The driver of a vehicle shall not cause the vehicle or any part thereof to stop within the limits of a zebra crossing unless either he is prevented from proceeding by circumstances beyond his control or it is necessary for him to stop in order to avoid an accident.

(2) No foot passenger shall remain on the carriageway within the limits of a zebra crossing longer than is necessary for the purpose of passing over the crossing with reasonable despatch.

NOTES
Limits of a zebra crossing See the note "Limits of an uncontrolled crossing" to reg 8.

Prohibition against overtaking at zebra crossings
10.   The driver of a vehicle while it or any part of it is in a zebra controlled area and it is proceeding towards the limits of an uncontrolled zebra crossing in relation to which that area is indicated (which vehicle is in this and the next succeeding Regulation referred to as "the approaching vehicle") shall not cause the vehicle, or any part of it—

   (*a*) to pass ahead of the foremost part of another moving motor vehicle, being a vehicle proceeding in the same direction wholly or partly within that area, or

   (*b*) subject to the next succeeding Regulation, to pass ahead of the foremost part of a stationary vehicle on the same side of the crossing as the approaching vehicle, which stationary vehicle is stopped for the purpose of complying with Regulation 8.

For the purposes of this Regulation—

   (i)   the reference to another moving motor vehicle is, in a case where only one other motor vehicle is proceeding in the same direction in a zebra controlled area, a reference to that vehicle, and, in a case where more than one other motor vehicle is so proceeding, a reference to such one of those vehicles as is nearest to the limits of the crossing;

   (ii) the reference to a stationary vehicle is, in a case where only one other vehicle is stopped for the purpose of complying with Regulation 8, a reference to that vehicle and, in a case where more than one other vehicle is stopped for the purpose of complying with that Regulation, a reference to such one of those vehicles as is nearest to the limits of the crossing.

NOTES
Para (b): "which stationary vehicle is stopped . . . for complying with Regulation 8"   As to the meaning of these words, see *Connor* v *Paterson*, [1977] 3 All ER 516.

11.   (1) For the purposes of this Regulation, in the case of an uncontrolled zebra crossing, which is on a road, being a one-way street, and on which there is a street refuge or central reservation, the parts of the crossing which are situated on each side of the street refuge or central reservation as the case may be shall each be treated as a separate crossing.

(2) Nothing in paragraph (*b*) of the last preceding Regulation shall apply so as to prevent the approaching vehicle from passing ahead of the foremost part of a stationary vehicle within the meaning of that paragraph, if the stationary vehicle is stopped for the purpose of complying with Regulation 8 in relation to an uncontrolled zebra crossing which by virtue of this Regulation is treated as a separate crossing from the uncontrolled zebra crossing towards the limits of which the approaching vehicle is proceeding.

Prohibition on stopping in areas adjacent to zebra crossings
12.   (1) For the purposes of this Regulation and the next two following Regulations, the expression "vehicle" shall not include a pedal bicycle not having a sidecar attached thereto, whether additional means of propulsion by mechanical power are attached to the bicycle or not.

(2) Save as provided in Regulations 14 and 15, the driver of a vehicle shall not cause the vehicle or any part thereof to stop in a zebra controlled area.

13.   (1) The provisions of this Regulation shall cease to have effect as from the 30th November 1973.

(2) Save as provided in Regulation 14 the driver of a vehicle shall not cause the vehicle or any part thereof to stop on the carriageway between

   (*a*) an uncontrolled zebra crossing, the approach to which is indicated by a pattern of studs in accordance with the provisions specified in Regulation 2 (3), and (*b*) the line of studs in that pattern situated furthest from the crossing, on the side of the road on which the pattern of studs is placed or, if the road is a one-way street, on either side of the road.

NOTES
Vehicle   See reg 12 (1).

14.   A vehicle shall not by Regulation 12 or 13 be prevented from stopping in any length of road on any side thereof—
   (*a*)   if the driver has stopped for the purpose of complying with Regulation 8 or Regulation 10 (*b*);
   (*b*)   if the driver is prevented from proceeding by circumstances beyond his control or it is necessary for him to stop in order to avoid an accident; or
   (*c*)   for so long as may be necessary to enable the vehicle, if it cannot be used for such purpose without stopping in that length of road, to be used for fire brigade, ambulance or police purposes or in connection with any building operation, demolition or excavation, the removal of any obstruction to traffic, the maintenance, improvement or reconstruction of that length of road, or the laying, erection, alteration, repair or cleaning in or near to that length of road of any traffic sign or sewer or of any main, pipe or apparatus for the supply of gas, water or electricity, or of any telegraph or telephone wires, cables, posts or supports.

NOTES
Vehicle   See reg 12 (1).

15.   A vehicle shall not by Regulation 12 be prevented from stopping in a zebra controlled area—
   (*a*)   if the vehicle is stopped for the purpose of making a left or right turn;
   (*b*)   if the vehicle is a public service vehicle, being a stage carriage or an express carriage being used otherwise than on an excursion or tour within the meaning of section 159(1) of the Transport Act 1968, and the vehicle is waiting, after having proceeded past the zebra crossing in relation to which the zebra controlled area is indicated, for the purpose of enabling persons to board or alight from the vehicle.

NOTES
Section 159 (1) of the Transport Act 1968   Repealed by the Transport Act 1985, s 139 (3), Sch 8. The expressions "stage carriage" and "express carriage" are no longer used in relation to public service vehicles; see instead the definitions of "local service" and "London local service" in the 1985 Act, ss 2, 34 respectively. "Excursion or tour" is defined in s 137 (1) of that Act.

SCHEDULE 1

NOTES
This Schedule specifies the regulations revoked by reg 2 (1), *viz*, the Pedestrian Crossings Regulations 1954, SI 1954/370, and the amending SI 1958/305 and 310, 1959/2296, 1960/13, 1966/476, 492 and 519, and 1968/1196 (of which SI 1958/310, 1960/13 and 1966/519 applied only in relation to Scotland).

SCHEDULE 2   Regulation 4
MANNER OF INDICATING PRESENCE AND LIMITS OF ZEBRA CROSSINGS

PART I
Studs and Marks

1.   (1) Every crossing and its limits shall be indicated by two lines of studs placed across the carriageway in accordance with the following provisions of this paragraph.
   (2) Each line formed by the outside edges of the studs shall be so separated from the other line so formed that no point on one line shall be less than 2·4 metres nor more than 5 metres or such greater distance (not being more than 10·1 metres) as the appropriate Secretary of State may authorise in writing in the case of any particular crossing from the nearest point on the other line:

Provided that the preceding provisions of this sub-paragraph shall be regarded as having been complied with in the case of any crossing which for the most part complies with those provisions notwithstanding that those provisions may not be so complied with as respects the distance from one or more points on one line to the nearest point on the other line, so long as the general indication of the lines is not thereby materially impaired.

(3) The studs of which each line is constituted shall be so placed that the distance from the centre of any one stud to the centre of the next stud in the line is not less than 250 millimetres nor more than 715 millimetres, and a distance of not more than 1·3 metres is left between the edge of the carriageway at either end of the line and the centre of the stud nearest thereto:

Provided that the preceding provisions of this sub-paragraph shall be regarded as having been complied with in the case of any line where most of the studs constituting it comply with those provisions notwithstanding that those provisions may not be complied with as respects one or more such studs, so long as a general indication of the line is not thereby materially impaired.

(4) Studs shall not be fitted with reflecting lenses and shall be—

(a) white, silver or light grey in colour;

(b) square or circular in plan, the sides of a square stud not being less than 95 millimetres nor more than 110 millimetres in length and the diameters of a circular stud not being less than 95 millimetres nor more than 110 millimetres, and

(c) so fixed that they do not project more than 16 millimetres above the carriageway at their highest points nor more than 7 millimetres at their edges.

2.   A crossing or its limits shall not be deemed to have ceased to be indicated in accordance with the preceding provisions of this Part of this Schedule by reason only of the discolouration or temporary removal or displacement of one or more studs in any line so long as the general indication of the line is not thereby materially impaired.

3.   Without derogation from the provisions of the preceding paragraphs of this Part of this Schedule, every crossing shall be further indicated in accordance with the following provisions of this Part and of Part II of this Schedule.

4.   (1) The carriageway shall be marked within the limits of every such crossing with a pattern of alternate black and white stripes:

Provided that where the colour of the surface of the carriageway provides a reasonable contrast with the colour of white that surface may itself be utilised for providing strips which would otherwise be required to be black.

(2) Every stripe shall—

(a) extend along the carriageway from one line formed by the inside edges of the studs or from a part of the crossing which is not more than 155 millimetres from that line to the other line so formed or to a part of the crossing which is not more than 155 millimetres from that line; and

(b) be of a width of not less than 500 millimetres or of such smaller width not being less than 380 millimetres as in the case of any particular crossing the appropriate authority may consider necessary having regard to the layout of the carriageway and, in the case of the first stripe at each end of the crossing, not more than 1·3 metres, or in the case of any other stripe, not more than 715 millimetres or of such greater width not being more than 840 millimetres as in the case of any particular crossing the appropriate authority may consider necessary having regard to the layout of the carriageway.

(3) The preceding provisions of this paragraph shall be regarded as having been complied with in the case of any crossing which for the most part complies with those provisions notwithstanding that those provisions may not be complied with as respects one or more stripes and a crossing shall not be deemed to have ceased to be indicated in accordance with those provisions by reason only of the imperfection, discolouration or partial displacement of one or more of the stripes so long as the general appearance of the pattern of stripes is not materially impaired.

PART II
Traffic Signs

1.   The traffic signs which are to be placed at or near a crossing for the purpose of constituting it and indicating it as a zebra crossing shall consist of globes in relation to which the following provisions in this Part of this Schedule are complied with.

2.   (1) At or near each end of every crossing there shall be placed, and in the case of a crossing on which there is a street refuge or central reservation there may be placed on the refuge or reservation, in accordance with the following provisions of this paragraph globes mounted on posts or brackets.

(2) Globes shall be—

(a) yellow in colour;

(b) not less than 275 millimetres nor more than 335 millimetres in diameter; and

(c) so mounted that the height of the lowest part of the globe is not less than 2·1 metres nor more than 3·1 metres above the surface of the ground in the immediate vicinity.

(3) Globes shall be illuminated by a flashing light, or where the appropriate Secretary of State so authorises in writing in the case of any particular crossing, by a constant light.

(4) Where globes are mounted on or attached to posts specially provided for the purpose,

every such post shall, in so far as it extends above ground level, be coloured black and white in alternate horozontal bands, the lowest band visible to approaching traffic being coloured black and not less than 275 millimetres nor more than 1 metre in width and each other band being not less than 275 millimetres not more than 335 millimetres in width:

Provided that nothing in this sub-paragraph shall apply to any container fixed on any such post which encloses the apparatus for providing the illumination of a globe.

3. A crossing shall not be deemed to have ceased to be indicated in accordance with the preceding provisions of this Part of this Schedule by reason only of—

    (a) the imperfection, discolouration or disfiguroment of any of the globes, posts or brackets; or

    (b) the failure of the illumination of any of the globes:

    Provided that this sub-paragraph shall not apply unless at least one globe is illuminated in accordance with the provisions of sub-paragraph (3) of the last preceding paragraph.

SCHEDULE 3   Regulation 5
MANNER OF INDICATING ZEBRA CONTROLLED AREA AND PROVISIONS AS TO PLACING OF GIVE-WAY LINE

PART I
Traffic Signs

1. Subject to the provisions of Regulation 5 (3), the traffic signs which are to be placed on a road in the vicinity of a zebra crossing for the purpose of constituting a zebra controlled area lying on both sides of the limits of the crossing or on only one side of such limits and indicating the presence and limits of the crossing or on only one side of such limits and indicating the presence and limits of such an area shall consist of a pattern of lines of the size and type shown in the diagram in Part II of this Schedule and so placed as hereinafter provided.

2. A pattern of lines shall, subject as hereinafter provided, consist of:—

    (a) a transverse white broken line (hereinafter referred to as a "give-way line") placed in the carriageway 1 metre from and parallel to the nearer line of studs indicating the limits of the crossing and shall extend across the carriageway in the manner indicated in the said diagram; and

    (b) two or more longitudinal white broken lines (hereinafter referred to as "zig-zag lines") placed on the carriageway or, where the road is a dual-carriageway road, on each part of the carriageway, each zig-zag line containing not less that 8 nor more than 18 marks and extending away from the crossing at a point 150 millimetres from the nearest part of the give-way line on the same side of the crossing to a point 150 millimetres from the nearest part of a terminal line of the size and type shown in the said diagram (hereinafter referred to as a "terminal line").

3. Where the appropriate authority is satisfied in relation to a particular area of carriageway in the vicinity of a zebra crossing that by reason of the layout of, or character of, the roads in the vicinity of the crossing it would be impracticable to lay the pattern of lines as shown in the diagram in Part II of this Schedule and in accordance with the preceding paragraph any of the following variations as respects the pattern shall be permitted—

    (a) the number of marks contained in each zig-zag line may be reduced from 8 to not less than 2;

    (b) a mark contained in a zig-zag line may be varied in length so as to extend for a distance not less than 1 metre and less than 2 metres, but where such a variation is made as respects a mark each other mark in each zig-zag line shall be of the same or substantially the same length as that mark, so however that the number of marks in each zig-zag line shall not be more than 8 nor less than 2.

4. The angle of the give-way line (if any) in relation to and its distance from the nearer line of studs indicating the limits of a crossing may be varied, if the appropriate authority is satisfied that such variation is necessary having regard to the angle of the crossing in relation to the edge of the carriageway at the place where the crossing is situated.

5. Where by reason of Regulation 5 (3) an area of carriageway in the vicinity of a zebra crossing is not constituted a zebra controlled area by the placing of a pattern of lines as provided in the foregoing provisions of this Schedule, a give-way line shall nevertheless be placed on the carriage-way as previously provided in this Schedule unless the appropriate authority is satisfied that by reason of the position of that crossing it is impracticable so to place the line.

6. Each mark contained in a give-way line or in a zig-zag line and each terminal line may be illuminated by the use of reflecting material.

7. A zebra controlled area or its limits shall not be deemed to have ceased to be indicated in accordance with the provisions of this Schedule by reason only of the imperfection, discolouration or partial displacement of either a terminal line or one or more of the marks comprised in a give-way line or a zig-zag line, so long as the general indication of any such line is not thereby materially impaired.

NOTES
Pattern of lines   In addition, a sign of the type shown in diagram 544 in Part I of Schedule 1 to the Traffic Signs Regulations 1981 (*ie* Part I of SI 1981/859, in the title Transport (Part 2B)), indicating that there is a pedestrian crossing ahead, may be erected.

PART II

NOTES
This Part contains a diagram of the pattern of lines mentioned in Part I of this Schedule for indicating a zebra controlled area on one or both sides of a zebra crossing.

THE SPECIAL AND OTHER ROADS (MAPS ETC) REGULATIONS 1971
SI 1971/1706

NOTES
Authority   These regulations were made on 19 October 1971 by the Secretary of State for the Environment and the Secretary of State for Wales under s 17 of the Highways Act 1971 (repealed), ss 284 and 286 of the Highways Act 1959 (repealed), and all other enabling powers. They now have effect under the Highways Act 1980, s 324, Halsbury's Statutes, 4th edn Vol 20, title Highways, Streets and Bridges (3rd edn Vol 50 (1), p 787).
Commencement   1 November 1971; see reg 1 (1).
General   These regulations prescribe the scales of the maps on which the centre lines of special roads and of certain other new highways are indicated and also the manner in which limits of deviation in relation to any such road or highway are shown. See also reg 5.

1. Commencement, citation, interpretation   (1) These Regulations shall come into operation on the 1st November 1971, and may be cited as the Special and Other Roads (Maps etc) Regulations 1971.

(2) In these Regulations:—
"the Act of 1959" means the Highways Act 1959"; and
"the Act of 1971" means the Highways Act 1971.

(3) The Interpretation Act 1889 shall apply for the interpretation of these Regulations as it applies for the interpretation of an Act of Parliament.

NOTES
Highways Act 1959; Highways Act 1971   These are now to be construed as references to the Highways Act 1980, Halsbury's Statutes, 4th edn Vol 20, title Highways, Streets and Bridges (3rd edn Vol 50(1), p 452 *et seq*).
Interpretation Act 1889   Repealed and replaced by the Interpretation Act 1978, printed in the title Statutory Instruments, Vol 1.

2.   Regulations 3 and 4 of these Regulations shall apply, and only apply, in relation to schemes under section 11 of the Act of 1959 and orders under section 7, 9 or 13 of that Act or under section 1 of the Act of 1971 published in draft by the Secretary of State, or made by a local highway authority on or after the coming into operation of these Regulations.

NOTES
Sections 7, 9, 11 and 13 of the Act of 1959; section 1 of the Act of 1971   These are now to be construed as references to schemes under the Highways Act 1980, s 16 and orders under *ibid*, ss 10, 14 and 18, Halsbury's Statutes, 4th edn Vol 20, title Highways, Streets and Bridges (3rd edn Vol 50 (1), pp 481, 472, 478, 483 respectively).

3. Indication of centre lines of special roads and other proposed highways   (1) The centre line of a special road authorised by a scheme under section 11 of the Act of 1959 or of a proposed highway directed by an order under section 7 of that Act to become a trunk road shall be indicated on a map on a scale of not less than six inches to the mile.

(2) The centre line of a new highway to be constructed in pursuance of an order under section 9 or 13 of the Act of 1959 or under section 1 of the Act of 1971 shall be indicated on a map on a scale of not less than 1/2500.

NOTES
Sections 7, 9, 11 and 13 of the Act of 1959; section 1 of the Act of 1971   See the notes to reg 2.

4. Limits of deviation   The limits of deviation in relation to any road or highway referred to in Regulation 3 above or to any part of such road or highway shall be shown either—

(*a*) by broken lines suitably marked on the map on which the centre line of the road or highway, or the relevant part thereof, is indicated, and placed at the appropriate distance on each side of the centre line, or

(*b*) by a statement of the limits of deviation written on or attached to such map, describing the extent of those limits and identifying the road or highway, or the relevant part thereof, to which the particular limits apply.

5. Revocation of provisions of 1962 Regulations   (1) Regulation 1 of the Special Roads and Trunk Roads (Procedure) Regulations 1962 (which prescribes the scale of the map on which the centre line of a special road is to be indicated) is hereby revoked in relation to schemes under section 11 of the Act of 1959 to which Regulation 3 above applies.

(2) (*Amended reg 4 of SI 1962/1319, p 62 ante.*)

NOTES
Section 11 of the Act of 1959   This must now be construed as a reference to the Highways Act 1980, s 16, Halsbury's Statutes, 4th edn Vol 20, title Highways, Streets and Bridges (3rd edn Vol 50(1), p 481).
Special Roads and Trunk Roads (Procedure) Regulations 1962   SI 1962/1319, p 61 *ante*.

THE STOPPING UP OF ACCESSES TO PREMISES (PROCEDURE) REGULATIONS 1971
SI 1971/1707

NOTES
Authority   These regulations were made on 19 October 1971 by the Secretary of State for the Environment and the Secretary of State for Wales under s 2 of the Highways Act 1971 (repealed) and all other enabling powers. They now have effect under the Highways Act 1980, s 124 (4), Halsbury's Statutes, 4th edn Vol 20, title Highways, Streets and Bridges (3rd edn Vol 50 (1), p 593).
Commencement   1 November 1971; see reg 1 (1).
Interpretation   See reg 1 (2) and (3).
General   There regulations prescribe the procedure to be followed in connection with the making and confirmation of orders under the Highways Act 1980, s 124, for the stopping up of private means of access to premises from a highway where the means of access are likely to cause danger to, or to interfere unreasonably with, traffic on the highway.

1. Commencement, citation, interpretation   (1) These Regulations shall come into operation on the 1st November 1971, and may be cited as the Stopping up of Accesses to Premises (Procedure) Regulations 1971.

(2) In these Regulations, unless the context otherwise requires—
"order" means an order to which these Regulations apply;
"owner", in relation to any premises, means a person, other than a mortgagee not in possession, who is for the time being entitled to dispose of the fee simple in the premises, whether in possession or in reversion, and includes also a person holding or entitled to the rents and profits of the premises under a lease the unexpired term whereof exceeds three years;
"the premises" means the premises to which a private means of access is to be stopped up pursuant to an order, or, where the order relates to means of access to two or more premises, both or all of those premises.

(3) The Interpretation Act 1889 shall apply for the interpretation of these Regulations as it applies for the interpretation of an Act of Parliament.

NOTES
Interpretation Act 1889   Repealed and replaced by the Interpretation Act 1978, printed in the title Statutory Instruments, Vol 1.

2. Application of Regulations   These Regulations apply to orders under section 2 of the Highways Act 1971 and have effect for prescribing the procedure to be followed in connection with the making of such orders by the Secretary of State and with the making of such orders by a local highway authority and their confirmation by that authority or by the Secretary of State.

NOTES
Section 2 of the Highways Act 1971 This must now be construed as a reference to the Highways Act 1980, s 124, Halsbury's Statutes, 4th edn Vol 20, title Highways, Streets and Bridges (3rd edn Vol 50 (1), p 593).

3. Publication and contents of notice When the Secretary of State proposes to make an order, or when a local highway authority have made an order, the Secretary of State or, as the case may be, the local highway authority, shall publish in at least one local newspaper circulating in the area in which the premises are situated a notice which shall—

  (*a*) state the general effect of the order proposed by the Secretary of State or made by the local highway authority;
  (*b*) name a place in the said area where a copy of the said order, as proposed or made, and of any map or plan referred to therein may be inspected free of charge at all reasonable hours during a period specified in the notice, being a period of not less than 28 days from the date of publication of the notice;
  (*c*) state that, within the said period, objections to the said order may be made in writing (the ground of each objection being stated) addressed, in the case of an order proposed to be made by the Secretary of State, to the Secretary of State, and in the case of an order made by a local highway authority, to that authority, at the address specified in the notice.

4. Persons to be served with notice (1) Not later than the day on which the notice under Regulation 3 above is first published, the highway authority publishing the notice shall serve on the owner and the occupier of each of the premises affected by the order—

  (*a*) a copy of the said notice;
  (*b*) a copy of the order as proposed or made, as the case may be;
  (*c*) subject to paragraph (2) below, a copy of any map or plan referred to in the order; and
  (*d*) a statement of the authority's reasons for proposing to make, or for having made, the order so far as it affects the premises of such owner and occupier.

(2) If the order provides for the stopping up of means of access to two or more premises, it shall be sufficient for the highway authority to serve on each owner and occupier a copy of that part of the map or plan referred to in the order which relates to the premises of which he is the owner or occupier.

5. New means of access to be shown on map or plan If it appears to a highway authority, when preparing an order, that a new means of access to any premises is likely to have to be provided by that authority to take the place of a means of access to be stopped up under the order, then that authority shall indicate in the map or plan referred to in the order the proposed route of that new means of access, and shall serve on the owner and occupier of the land which will be required for the provision of that new means of access (if different from the owner and occupier of the premises) a copy of the notice and the other documents referred to in Regulation 4 above.

6. Submission of local highway authority's order for confirmation (1) If any objection to an order made by a local highway authority is received by that authority within the period specified in Regulation 3 above and that objection is not withdrawn, the local highway authority, before proceeding further with the order, shall forward the following documents to the Secretary of State—

  (*a*) the original order as made together with two copies thereof;
  (*b*) three copies of each statement of objections and of any correspondence

which the authority have had with any objector since the receipt by them of his objection;

(c) in a case where the authority desire modifications to be made to the order, three copies of a statement of those modifications and of the authority's reasons therefor;

and shall at the same time notify each objector in writing of the action taken by them under this Regulation.

(2) If in a case where there are no unwithdrawn objections to an order made by a local highway authority the authority desire the order to be confirmed with modifications they shall forward to the Secretary of State the order as made, together with two copies thereof and three copies of a statement of the modifications which the authority desire and of their reasons therefor.

7. Consideration of objections by Secretary of State Before the Secretary of State makes an order or confirms an order made by a local highway authority, he shall, in the case of his own order consider any objections received by him within the period specified in Regulation 3 above and in the case of an order made by a local highway authority, consider any objections transmitted to him by that authority under Regulation 6 above and also any proposals of that authority for modifying the order, and shall in either case, if he has caused a local inquiry to be held in connection with the order, consider the report of the person who held the inquiry.

8. Modifications The Secretary of State may make or confirm an order with modifications, whether in consequence of objections or otherwise but where the modifications will in his opinion make a substantial change in the order as proposed or made, then, before making or confirming the order, he shall take such steps as appear to him to be appropriate for informing any person who appears to him to be likely to be affected by the proposed modifications and for giving such person an opportunity of making representations to him with respect thereto, and shall consider any representations made to him by such person.

9. Service of notice of making by Secretary of State or confirmation of order
The Secretary of State or local highway authority, as the case may be, by whom the notice referred to in paragraph 1 of Schedule 2 to the Highways Act 1959 (as applied by section 16 of the Highways Act 1971) is required to be published, shall serve a copy of that notice and of the order, as made or confirmed, upon the owner and occupier of each of the premises to which the order relates and also upon the owner and occupier of any other land affected by the route of any new means of access to premises shown upon the map or plan referred to in the order in accordance with Regulation 5 above.

NOTES
Paragraph 1 of Schedule 2 to the Highways Act 1959 (as applied by section 16 of the Highways Act 1971) This must now be construed as a reference to the Highways Act 1980, Sch 2, para 1, Halsbury's Statutes, 4th edn Vol 20, title Highways, Streets and Bridges (3rd edn Vol 50 (1), p 814).

THE RAILWAY BRIDGES (LOAD-BEARING STANDARDS) (ENGLAND AND WALES) ORDER 1972 SI 1972/1705

NOTES
Authority This order was made on 8 November 1972 by the Secretary of State for the Environment and the Secretary of State for Wales under s 117 of the Transport Act 1968, Halsbury's Statutes, 4th edn Vol 20, title Highways, Streets and Bridges (3rd edn Vol 15, p 524), as amended by para 1 of Sch 3 to the Transport (London) Act 1969 (repealed), and under all other enabling powers. The 1968 Act, s 117 has now been amended by the London Regional Transport Act 1984, s 67 (2), (3), Sch 4, para 4 (1), to the effect that for any reference to the London Transport Executive in the said s 117 (substituted by the 1969 Act, Sch 3, para 1) there is substituted a reference to London Regional Transport. Accordingly, references to a Board or Boards in the

said s 117 are to be read as, or as including, references to London Regional Transport where London Regional Transport are the authority, or one of the authorities, concerned; see the 1984 Act, Sch 4, para 4(3).
Commencement   11 December 1972.
General   This order lays down the load-bearing standards for bridges which belong to the British Railways Board or the London Transport Executive (now replaced by London Regional Transport; see "Authority", *supra*) and which carry roads in England and Wales over their railways. The standards are laid down for existing bridges (art 3) and for new bridges (*ie* bridges constructed or reconstructed after the commencement of this order) (art 4), with details of the standards given in Sch 1 to the order, and with special provisions applicable in relation to particular existing bridges (listed in Schs 2 and 3). Provision is made (by art 5) for the continuance of the application of a load-bearing standard, notwithstanding a change in the classification of the road. The order also provides for the determination of disputes (art 6).

THE WALKWAYS REGULATIONS 1973
SI 1973/686

NOTES
Authority   These regulations were made on 4 April 1973 by the Secretary for the Environment and the Secretary of State for Wales under s 18 of the Highways Act 1971 (repealed), and all other enabling powers. They now have effect under the Highways Act 1980, s 35 (11), Halsbury's Statutes, 4th edn Vol 20, title Highways, Streets and Bridges (3rd edn Vol 50 (1), p 500).
Commencement   7 May 1973; see reg 1 (1).
Amendment   These regulations are printed as amended by the Walkways (Amendment) Regulations 1974, SI 1974/735.
Interpretation   See reg 1 (2)-(7).
General   These regulations, as amended, make provision with respect to walkways (*ie*, footpaths over, through or under parts of a building) created by agreements under the Highways Act 1980, s 35, entered into by local highway authorities or by district councils (in relation to which, see reg 9). As from 1 April 1986, the said s 35 is amended by the Local Government Act 1985, s 8, Sch 4, Pt I, para 9 to refer to non-metropolitan district councils in place of district councils.

1. Commencement, citation and interpretation   (1) These Regulations shall come into operation on 7th May 1973, and may be cited as the Walkways Regulations 1973.

(2) In these Regulations, except where the context otherwise requires, the following expressions have the meanings hereby respectively assigned to them:—

"building" includes a structure and a proposed building or structure;

"building owner" means in relation to an existing walkway, the person or persons (other than the highway authority) who, at the relevant time, would have been able to enter into the agreement for creating the walkway if the walkway had not previously been created, and in relation to a proposed walkway, the person or persons (other than as aforesaid) who have entered, or propose to enter, into the agreement for creating the walkway;

"direct access to the walkway", in relation to any premises, means that access from the premises to the walkway does not involve the use of any highway which is not a walkway;

"local statutory provision" means a statutory provision contained in a local Act or contained in an instrument of local application made or issued under any Act;

"proposed walkway" means a walkway proposed to be created, whether or not the agreement under section 18 of the Highways Act 1971 in relation thereto has been entered into;

"statutory provision" means a provision, whether of a general or special nature, contained in, or in an instrument made or issued under, an Act, and

"statutory provision affecting highways" means a statutory provision relating to highways or to things done on or in connection with highways;

"supported walkway" means such part of a walkway as is supported by a structure;

"walkway" includes a part of a walkway;

'walkway agreement" means an agreement under section 18 of the Highways Act 1971 and, when used in relation to a walkway, means the agreement under which the walkway was first created or which for the time being makes provision in relation to the walkway for such of the matters referred to in subsection (2) of the said section 18 as may be relevant.

(3) Where a provision of these Regulations—

(*a*) prohibits the taking of specified action on or in relation to a walkway without the consent of the building owner, or

(*b*) empowers the building owner himself to take specified action on or in relation to a walkway,

then in a case where the walkway is one which crosses or abuts on two or more premises and the action in question is action proposed to be taken on or in relation to a part of the walkway which crosses or abuts on some, but not all, of those premises, the provision shall, subject to the provisions of the walkway agreement, have effect so as to enable the consent to be given or the action to be taken, as the case may be, by the person or persons who would, under paragraph (2) of this Regulation, have been the building owner if that part of the walkway had constituted the whole of the walkway, and for this purpose the reference in that provision to the building owner, in connection with the giving of that consent or the taking of that action, shall be construed as a reference to that person or those persons.

(4) Where a walkway agreement provides that some person or persons specified in, or determined in accordance with, that agreement may in connection with the walkway to which it relates take some action, or give a consent, under a provision of these Regulations on behalf of the building owner, then for the purposes of the application of the provision in question to the taking of that action or the giving of that consent the reference in that provision to the building owner shall be construed as including a reference to the person or persons so specified or determined.

(5) Where a walkway is stopped up or the right of the public to use the walkway is otherwise determined, whether under these Regulations or under a provision of the walkway agreement or otherwise howsoever, then the provisions of these Regulations (except Regulation 7) shall cease to apply in relation thereto.

(6) Any reference in these Regulations to any enactment shall be construed as a reference to that enactment as amended by or under any subsequent enactment.

(7) The Interpretation Act 1889 shall apply for the interpretation of these Regulations as it applies for the interpretation of an Act of Parliament.

NOTES

Section 18 of the Highways Act 1971   This must now be construed as a reference to the Highways Act 1980, s 35, Halsbury's Statutes, 4th edn Vol 20, title Highways, Streets and Bridges (3rd edn Vol 50 (1), p 500).

Interpretation Act 1889   Repealed and replaced by the Interpretation Act 1978, printed in the title Statutory Instruments, Vol 1.

2. Certain statutory provisions not to apply to walkways   (1) The enactments specified in Schedule 1 to these Regulations and any local statutory provision affecting highways being a provision similar in effect to an enactment so specified, shall not apply to a walkway or proposed walkway or to anything done on or in connection with a walkway or proposed walkway.

(2) Where any statutory provision affecting highways would operate so as to render ineffective, or to interfere with the effect of, any provision in a walkway agreement for limiting the public right of way over a walkway the subject of that agreement or for imposing conditions with respect to that right, or for reserving rights to the building owner, then, subject to paragraph (3) of this Regulation, that statutory provision shall not apply in relation to that walkway to the extent that it would so operate.

(3) Nothing in paragraph (2) of this Regulation shall affect the operation in relation to a walkway of:—

(*a*) any statutory provision for regulating the conduct or activities of members of the public when on a highway or for prohibiting any particular conduct or activity of members of the public when on a highway, (*b*) any statutory provision relating to vehicles when used on a highway, in the application of such provision to any vehicle lawfully on the walkway,

(*c*) any statutory provision relating to the functions of the justices or the police with respect to highways or to things done or occurring on highways,

(*d*) (without prejudice to the generality of (*a*), (*b*) or (*c*) above) any of the enactments specified in Schedule 2 to these Regulations, to the extent there specified.

3. Modification of statutory provision (1) The enactments specified in Schedule 3 to these Regulations and any local statutory provision affecting highways which is similar in effect to an enactment so specified, shall in their application to a walkway or to anything done on or in connection with a walkway be modified so that the power thereby conferred on the highway authority or the local authority to execute works, or to place or do anything, on or in relation to the walkway, or to authorise some other person to execute works, or to place or do anything, on or in relation to the walkway, shall not be exercisable by such authority without the consent of the building owner, except insofar as the walkway agreement provides for such exercise without that consent.

(2) Section 40 of the Highways Act 1959 (which relates to the power of highway authorities to adopt by agreement) shall not apply in relation to a walkway or proposed walkway except insofar as the walkway agreement so provides.

(3) If in any case a walkway becomes a highway maintainable at the public expense, section 226 of the Highways Act 1959 (which relates to the vesting of highways in the highway authority), and any local statutory provision affecting highways which is similar in effect to the said section 226, shall in their application to the walkway be modified so that the vesting of the walkway, together with the material and scrapings thereof, in the highways authority, shall have effect subject to the terms of the walkway agreement.

NOTES
Sections 40 and 226 of the Highways Act 1959   These must now be construed as references to the Highways Act 1980, ss 38 and 263, Halsbury's Statutes, 4th edn Vol 20, title Highways, Streets and Bridges (3rd edn Vol 50 (1), pp 507,743).

4. Rights of statutory undertakers etc   (1) The rights of statutory undertakers, sewerage authorities and the Post Office to place and maintain apparatus in, under, over, along or across a highway shall, in relation to a supported walkway, be restricted as follows, that is to say—

(*a*) the rights aforesaid to place apparatus in, under, over, along or across the walkway may only be exercised subject to the consent of the highway authority and the building owner, and

(*b*) the rights aforesaid to maintain such apparatus may only be exercised subject to any conditions or restrictions accepted by the person placing apparatus as part of the arrangement under which the consent to place the apparatus was given,

and the statutory provisions applicable to the placing and maintenance of apparatus in exercise of such rights shall have effect subject to the provisions of this paragraph.

(2) Nothing in the foregoing provisions of this Regulation shall affect the rights of statutory undertakers, sewerage authorities or the Post Office to place and maintain apparatus in, under, over, along or across land which does not form part of a highway, or their power to acquire such rights, and the rights and power referred to in this paragraph shall apply in relation to a supported walkway as if it were not a highway.

NOTES
The Post Office   The enabling power under which these regulations have effect (*viz* the Highways Act 1980, s 35; see the introductory notes to these regulations under the head "Authority", p

98, *ante*) has been amended by the Telecommunications Act 1984, s 109 (1), Sch 4, para 76 (2) to replace the references to the Post Office by references to the operators of telecommunications code systems; these regulations have not been specifically amended in the light of this provision.

5. Periodic and temporary closure of walkways   (1) Where provision is made in a walkway agreement for the periodic closure of a walkway to which the agreement relates, then the walkway may be closed at the times specified in the agreement and such closure may be effected by shutting gates or other barriers on, or giving access to, the walkway, or by other appropriate means.

(2) The building owner may close a walkway temporarily where such closure is necessary by reason of work being executed, or to be executed, by him on or in connection with the walkway, or on or in connection with any building supporting or abutting on the walkway, and such closure shall be effected by erecting barriers, or taking other measures, for preventing public use of the walkway.

(3) Except in an emergency, the building owner shall not close a walkway temporarily under paragraph (2) of this Regulation until the expiration of at least 21 days from the date by which—

(*a*) he has given notice of his intention to the highway authority for the walkway, to the owners and occupiers of any other premises having direct access to the walkway and to any of the following who have apparatus in, under, over, along or across the walkway, that is to say, statutory undertakers, sewerage authorities and the Post Office, and

(*b*) he has begun to display a notice of such intention in a prominent position at the ends of so much of the walkway as is to be closed.

(4) Any notice displayed as is mentioned in paragraph (3) of this Regulation shall give particulars of any alternative route which may be available to the public during the continuance of the closure.

(5) Except insofar as any contrary provision is made in any arrangement under which consent was given for the placing of apparatus in, under, over, along or across a supported walkway, the periodic or temporary closure of a walkway under this Regulation shall not affect the powers of statutory undertakers, sewerage authorities or the Post Office to maintain, inspect, repair, renew or remove during the period of the closure, any apparatus of theirs which is situated in, under, over, along or across the walkway.

NOTES
The Post Office   See the note to reg 4.

6. Stopping up of walkway by building owner   (1) A walkway may be stopped up by the building owner under the provisions of this Regulation when it is necessary for him to do so in order to enable any of the following operations to be carried out—

(*a*) any alteration or demolition of a building supporting, or abutting on, the walkway,

(*b*) any development (as defined in the Town and Country Planning Act 1971) affecting the walkway.

(2) Before a walkway is stopped up under this Regulation, the building owner shall give notice of his intention:—

(*a*) to the highway authority for the walkway,

(*b*) to any of the following who have apparatus in, under, over, along or across the walkway, that is to say, statutory undertakers, sewerage authorities and the Post Office, and

(*c*) to the owners and occupiers of any premises having direct access to the walkway,

and shall display a copy of that notice in a prominent position at the ends of so much of the walkway as is to be stopped up.

(3) The notice given to persons having apparatus in the walkway and to the owners and occupiers of the said premises and displayed on the walkway as aforesaid shall contain a statement that any person desiring to object to the stopping up may within a period stated in the notice (being a period of

not less than 21 days from the date of the service and first display of the notice) do so in writing addressed to the highway authority and giving the grounds of the objection.

(4) If the highway authority themselves object to the proposed stopping up, or if they consider that, by reason of the weight of objection received by them within the period specified in paragraph (3) of this Regulation from persons appearing to them to be affected, the proposed stopping up should not take place, then they shall notify the building owner to this effect.

(5) If no notification under paragraph (4) of this Regulation is received by the building owner within 42 days of the completion by him of the procedure specified in paragraph (2) of this Regulation, he may then stop up the walkway as proposed, but in all other cases he shall not proceed with the stopping up until the Secretary of State has consented thereto.

(6) Stopping up of a walkway under this Regulation shall be effected by the erection of barriers or the taking of other measures for preventing public use of the walkway.

NOTES
Town and Country Planning Act 1971   Halsbury's Statutes, 4th edn Vol 46, title Town and Country Planning (3rd edn Vol 41, p 1571 *et seq*). "Development" is defined in s 22 (1) of that Act.
The Post Office   See the note to reg 4.

7. Apparatus of statutory undertakers etc in stopped up walkway   (1) Where a walkway is stopped up under Regulation 6 above, or the public right to use a walkway is terminated under a provision of the walkway agreement, and there is in, under, over, along or across the walkway apparatus of a statutory undertaker, sewerage authority or the Post Office, then, subject to paragraphs (2) to (5) of this Regulation, that undertaker or authority or the Post Office, as the case may be, shall have the same rights in respect of that apparatus as if the walkway had been stopped up pursuant to section 209 of the Town and Country Planning Act 1971 (which provides for the stopping up of highways in order to enable development to be carried out) and as if, in the case of apparatus of a statutory undertaker or sewerage authority, the order under that section authorising the stopping up had provided for the preservation of those rights, and the provisions of paragraphs (2) and (3) of this Regulation shall have effect with a view to regulating the continuance or removal of that apparatus in circumstances and under conditions similar to those which would be applicable if the walkway had been stopped up pursuant to the said section 209.

(2) Where any such apparatus as is referred to in paragraph (1) of this Regulation is apparatus of a statutory undertaker or a sewerage authority—

(a) sections 230 and 231 of the Town and Country Planning Act 1971 (power to extinguish rights of statutory undertakers over land acquired under certain enactments or appropriated by a local authority for planning purposes).

(b) section 232 of that Act (power of statutory undertakers to remove or resite apparatus affected by development), and

(c) sections 237 (2) and (3), 238 and 240 of that Act (compensation), so far as applicable for the purposes of the said sections 230, 231 and 232,

shall apply in relation to such apparatus and to the site of the walkway as they apply in relation to apparatus of statutory undertakers and in relation to land acquired by a Minister, a local authority or statutory undertakers under Part VI of the said Act of 1971, or compulsorily under any other enactment, or appropriated by a local authority for planning purposes, subject however to the modifications set out in Schedule 4 to these Regulations (being modifications similar to those having effect by virtue of section 32 (3) of the Mineral Workings Act 1951 in relation to highways stopped up pursuant to section 209 of the said Act of 1971).

(3) Where any such apparatus as is referred to in paragraph (1) of this Regulation is apparatus of the Post Office, section 220 (1) of the said Act of

1971 (provisions as to telegraphic lines) shall apply in relation to the apparatus and to the site of the walkway as if the walkway had been stopped up pursuant to section 209 of the said Act.

(4) Paragraphs (1), (2) and (3) of this Regulation shall, in relation to apparatus in, under, over, along or across a supported walkway, have effect subject to the terms of any arrangement under which the consent to place the apparatus was given.

(5) Paragraphs (1), (2) and (3) of this Regulation shall not apply in relation to apparatus placed and maintained in a supported walkway by statutory undertakers, sewerage authorities or the Post Office in exercise of rights to place and maintain apparatus in, under, over, along or across land which does not form part of a highway, or in exercise of rights created under a power to acquire such rights, but the stopping up of, or the termination of the public right to use, the walkway shall not prejudice the continuation of, or the taking of action pursuant to, those rights (if still subsisting), or the termination of those rights, in accordance with the relevant statutory provisions or the relevant instruments conferring or creating those rights.

NOTES
The Post Office   See the note to reg 4.
Town and Country Planning Act 1971   Halsbury's Statutes, 4th edn Vol 46, title Town and Country Planning (3rd edn Vol 41, p 1571 *et seq*). Section 220 of that Act has been substituted by the Telecommunications Act 1984, s 109 (1), Sch 4, para 53 (7).
Section 32 (3) of the Mineral Workings Act 1951   Halsbury's Statutes, 4th edn Vol 29, title Mines, Minerals and Quarries (3rd edn Vol 22, p 254).

8. Saving for other provisions   (1) Nothing in these Regulations shall affect the stopping up or diversion of a walkway or the prohibition or restriction of the public use of a walkway under the provisions of any enactment specified in Schedule 5 to these Regulations.

(2) Nothing in these Regulations shall affect the operation in relation to a walkway of any statutory provision for improving, raising, lowering or otherwise altering a highway, or for constructing a new highway, or for providing new means of access to premises, or for acquiring land or rights over land for any such purpose, when such improvement, raising, lowering, alteration, construction or provision consists of or is incidental to the construction or improvement of some other highway which is not, and is not intended to be, a walkway.

(3) Where in pursuance of any such statutory provision as is mentioned in paragraph (2) of this Regulation a new footpath is constructed to take the place of a walkway which is stopped up under an enactment referred to in paragraph (1) of this Regulation, then the highway authority for the former walkway and the building owner may agree to accept the new footpath as a substitute for the former walkway and in that event the new footpath shall itself become a walkway and the agreement relating to the new footpath shall be the walkway agreement for it.

[9. Application of Regulations to walkway agreements to which district councils are parties   (1) Where by virtue of section 188 (6) of the Local Government Act 1972 a walkway agreement is entered into by a district council but the highway authority are not a party to that agreement, then in relation to that agreement and to any walkway or proposed walkway to which that agreement applies these Regulations shall have effect with the following amendments:—

(*a*) In Regulation 1 (2), Regulation 4 (1) (*a*) and Regulation 6 (3) and (4) for the words "the highway authority" substitute the words "the district council";

(*b*) in Regulation 5 (3) (*a*) Regulation 6 (2) (*a*) for the words "the highway authority for the walkway" substitute the words "the district council"; and

(*c*) in Regulation 8 (3) for the words "the highway authority for the former walkway" substitute the words "the district council (after consulting the highway authority for the former walkway)".

(2) Where by virtue of section 188 (6) of the Local Government Act 1972 a walkway agreement is entered into by a district council but the highway authority are also a party to that agreement, then in relation to that agreement and to any walkway or proposed walkway to which that agreement applies these Regulations shall have effect with the following amendments:—

(a) in Regulation 1 (2) and Regulation 4 (1) (a) after the words "the highway authority" insert the words "and the district council";

(b) in Regulation 5 (3) (a) after the words "to the highway authority for the walkway" insert the words "to the district council";

(c) in Regulation 6 (2) (a) after the words "to the highway authority for the walkway" insert the words "and to the district council";

(d) in Regulation 6 (4) for the words "If the highway authority themselves object to the proposed stopping up, or if they consider that" substitute the words "If the highway authority or the district council object to the proposed stopping up, or if the highway authority (after consulting the district council) consider that", and for the word "they", where secondly occurring, substitute the words "the highway authority"; and

(e) in Regulation 8 (3) after the words "the highway authority for the former walkway" insert the words "(after consulting the district council)".

(3) In this Regulation and in the amendments made by this Regulation to the preceding Regulations the expression "the district council", in relation to a walkway or proposed walkway, means the council of the district in which the walkway or proposed walkway is, or (as the case may be) will be, situated.]

NOTES
Amendment   This regulation was added by SI 1974/735.
Section 188 (6) of the Local Government Act 1972   This must now be construed as a reference to the Highways Act 1980, s 35, Halsbury's Statutes, 4th edn Vol 20, title Highways, Streets and Bridges (3rd edn Vol 50 (1) p 500).
District councils   See the introductory notes to these regulations under the head "General", p 98, *ante*.

SCHEDULE 1
ENACTMENTS NOT TO APPLY TO WALKWAYS

NOTES
This Schedule (which is referred to in reg 2 (1)) specifies the following enactments:— Public Health Act 1925, ss 26 and 76; National Parks and Access to the Countryside Act 1949, Part IV (ss 27-57); Highways Act 1959, ss 27-34, 37, 39, 43, 72-75, Part VI (ss 108-115), s 119, Parts VIII and IX (ss 157-213), s 214 (so far as it authorises the compulsory acquisition of land), ss 217 and 218; and Schs 7, 9, 12 and 14-15; Private Street Works Act 1961; Highways (Miscellaneous Provisions) Act 1961, ss 11 and 12; Highways Act 1971, s 44 (2) (a) (so far as it authorises the compulsory acquisition of land for use in connection with the improvement of a highway by the highway authority therefor), and s 76. For any subsequent amendment, modification, repeal or consolidation of these enactments, see Halsbury's Statutes.

SCHEDULE 2
PARTICULAR ENACTMENTS
THE APPLICATION OF WHICH IS NOT AFFECTED BY CERTAIN PROVISIONS OF THE WALKWAY AGREEMENT

NOTES
This Schedule (which is referred to in reg 2 (3) (d) specifies the following enactments:— Highways Act 1835, s 72; Town Police Clauses Act 1847, ss 28 and 29; Public Health Acts Amendment Act 1907, s 31; Public Health Act 1936, s 58; Highways Act 1959, ss 117 and 121, s 124 (so far as it relates to structures not authorised by or under the walkway agreement), s 127 (except para (a)), s 128 (so far as it relates to the deposit of anything not authorised by or under the walkway agreement), s 131 (so far as it relates to any obstruction or projection not authorised by or under the walkway agreement), ss 132, 134 and 140-143, s 144 (but so however that, unless the walkway agreement otherwise provides, the expenses referred to in sub-s (3) shall be borne by the authority executing the works), s 146 (1) and (2) (so far as relating to deposit by or on behalf of the building owner), ss 146 (3)-(5) and 147-150; Highways (Miscellaneous Provisions) Act 1961, ss 8 and 10; Public Health Act 1961, ss 24, 25 and 47; Highways Act 1971, ss 34, 36 and 37; Road Traffic Act 1972, s 31. For any subsequent amendment, modification, repeal or consolidation of these enactments, see Halsbury's Statutes.

SCHEDULE 3
ENACTMENTS TO BE MODIFIED IN THEIR APPLICATION TO WALKWAYS

NOTES
This Schedule (which is referred to in reg 3 (1)) specifies the following enactments:— Public Health Act 1875, s 161; Public Health Acts Amendment Act 1890, ss 40 and 42; Public Health Act 1925, ss 14, 18 and 19; Public Health Act 1936, s 87; Local Government (Miscellaneous Provisions) Act 1953, ss 4-7; Parish Councils Act 1957, Part I; Highways Act 1959, ss 46, 53, 64, 67, 71, 77-82, 85, 86, 89, 100-106, 151, 156, 252, and 257; Highways (Miscellaneous Provisions) Act 1961, ss 5 and 6; Public Health Act 1961, ss 44, 45, 49 and 51; Local Government Act 1966, s 28; Road Traffic Regulation Act 1967, s 63; Countryside Act 1968, ss 27 and 28; Parish Councils and Burial Authorities (Miscellaneous Provisions) Act 1970, s 3; Highways Act 1971, ss 19-23, 25, 28, 31, 32, 38, 39, and 41-43. For any subsequent amendment, modification, repeal or consolidation of these enactments, see Halsbury's Statutes.

SCHEDULE 4

NOTES
This Schedule is referred to in reg 7 (2).

MODIFICATIONS OF CERTAIN PROVISIONS OF THE TOWN AND COUNTRY PLAN-NING ACT 1971 AS RESPECTS APPARATUS OF STATUTORY UNDERTAKERS

1. For the reference in section 230 (1) of the Town and Country Planning Act 1971 to land which has been acquired by a Minister, a local authority or statutory undertakers under Part VI of that Act or compulsorily under any other enactment, or has been appropriated by a local authority for planning purposes, and for the references in that section and in section 232 of that Act to land which has been so acquired or appropriated, substitute references to the site of the walkway and for the reference in the said section 230 (1) to any development with a view to which the land was acquired or appropriated substitute a reference to any development affecting the site of the walkway.

2. For references in sections 230, 231, 232, 237 (2) and (3) and 238 of the said Act of 1971 to the acquiring or appropriating authority substitute references to the person entitled to the possession of the site of the walkway.

3. The references in the said sections 230, 231, 232, 237 (2) and (3) and 238 to statutory undertakers, in relation to apparatus or to rights as respects apparatus, shall include references to sewerage authorities.

4. The references in subsection (4) of the said section 230 and in subsection (2) (*b*) of the said section 231 to a local authority or statutory undertakers shall include references to the person entitled to the possession of the site of the walkway.

SCHEDULE 5
ENACTMENTS RELATING TO THE STOPPING UP OF HIGHWAYS OR THE PROHIB-ITION OR RESTRICTION OF THE PUBLIC USE OF ROADS

NOTES
This Schedule (which is referred to in reg 8 (1)) specifies the following enactments:— Acquisition of Land (Authorisation Procedure) Act 1946, s 3; Highways Act 1959, ss 9 and 13; Road Traffic Regulation Act 1967, ss 1, 6, 9 and 12; Highways Act 1971, s 1; Town and Country Planning Act 1971, ss 209, 210, 211 and 214. For any subsequent amendment, modification, repeal or consolidation of these enactments, see Halsbury's Statutes.

THE BOUNDARY BRIDGES (APPOINTED DAY) ORDER 1973
SI 1973/2147

NOTES
Authority This order was made on 17 December 1973 by the Secretary of State for the Environment and the Secretary of State for Wales under s 6 (1) of the Highways Act 1959, as set out in para 4 of Sch 21 to the Local Government Act 1972 (repealed), and under all other enabling powers. It now has effect under the Highways Act 1980, s 3 (1), Halsbury's Statutes, 4th edn Vol 20, title Highways, Streets and Bridges (3rd edn Vol 50 (1), p 464).
Commencement 1 January 1974.
General This order appointed 1 January 1974 as the date before which councils of adjacent counties should have agreed between themselves which of them should on or after 1 April 1974 be the highway authority for each highway carried by a bridge and the approaches thereto where the Secretary of State was not the highway authority and part of the bridge was situated in one county and part in another.
See also the Cross-Boundary Bridges (Appointed Days) Order 1985, SI 1985/1177, p 126, *post*.

THE LOCAL GOVERNMENT (ROAD TRAFFIC AND HIGHWAYS) (TRANSITIONAL PROVISIONS) ORDER 1974
SI 1974/142

NOTES

Authority This order was made on 30 January 1974 by the Secretary of State for the Environment and the Secretary of State for Wales under s 254 (1) (*a*) and (2) (*a*), (*c*) and (*h*) of the Local Government Act 1972, Halsbury's Statutes, 4th edn Vol 25, title Local Government (3rd edn Vol 42, p 1078), and all other enabling powers.

Commencement 1 April 1974.

General This order made transitional and other provisions consequential on the Local Government Act 1972, in connection with schemes, orders and other instruments made and things done before 1 April 1974 in relation to road traffic and highway matters, in order that the new local authorities created by the Act of 1972 could enforce and otherwise deal with instruments made and things done by the previously existing local authorities. The order — (*a*) deals with schemes and orders made (or having effect) under ss 1, 5, 9, 12, 15, 21, 26, 28, 31, 33, 35-37, 73 and 74 of the Road Traffic Regulation Act 1967 (now repealed and replaced by the Road Traffic Regulation Act 1984; see the destination table to that Act in Halsbury's Statutes, 4th edn Vol 38, title Road Traffic (3rd edn Vol 54 (2), p 1702 *et seq*)), or s 31 of the Road Traffic Act 1972, *ibid*, 4th edn Vol 38, title Road Traffic (3rd edn Vol 42, p 1672); (*b*) provides for procedures begun but not completed before 1 April 1974; (*c*) provides for the division of instruments affecting highways; (*d*) contains general saving provisions with regard to highways; (*e*) deals with private street works; and (*f*) adapts certain agreements made between the Secretary of State and existing local authorities.

Other ancillary provisions in relation to highways, made under s 254 (1) and (2) of the Local Government Act 1972, are contained in art 6 of the Local Authorities (England) (Property, etc) Order 1973, SI 1973/1861, and art 6 of the Local Authorities (Wales) (Property, etc) Order 1973, SI 1973/1863, both in the title Local Government (Part 2).

THE HIGHWAYS (INQUIRIES PROCEDURE) RULES 1976
SI 1976/721

NOTES

Authority These rules were made on 7 May 1976 by the Lord Chancellor under s 11 of the Tribunals and Inquiries Act 1971, Halsbury's Statutes, 4th edn Vol 10, title Constitutional Law (Pt 4).

Commencement 10 June 1976; see r 1 (2).

Interpretation See r 3.

Application See r 2.

General These rules prescribe the procedure to be followed at local inquiries held under para 5 or 9 of Schedule 1 to the Highways Act 1959 (now repealed and replaced by the Highways Act 1980, Sch 1, paras 7 and 14, Halsbury's Statutes, 4th edn Vol 20, title Highways, Streets and Bridges (3rd edn Vol 50 (1), pp 809, 812)), in connection with orders or schemes proposed to be made by the Secretary of State, or orders or schemes made by local highway authorities and submitted to the Secretary of State for confirmation, relating to the construction of trunk or special roads, or to side roads and other works associated with the construction or improvement of trunk, special or classified roads (including the construction of road bridges over, or road tunnels under, navigable watercourses).

PART I
GENERAL

1. Citation and commencement (1) These Rules may be cited as the Highways (Inquiries Procedure) Rules 1976.

(2) These Rules shall come into operation on 10th June 1976 but shall not apply to any local inquiry the date, time and place for the holding of which has been announced by the Secretary of State before that date.

2. Application of Rules (1) Subject to paragraph (2) of this rule, these Rules shall apply—

    (*a*) to local inquiries caused by the Secretary of State to be held under paragraph 5 of Schedule 1 to the Highways Act 1959 in connection with—

        (i) orders proposed to be made by him under section 7, 9, 13 or 20 of the Highways Act 1959 or under section 10 of the Highways Act 1971,

        (ii) orders made by a local highway authority under section 13 of the Highways Act 1959 or under section 1 or 10 of the Highways Act 1971 and submitted to the Secretary of State for confirmation, and (*b*) to local inquiries caused by the Secretary of State to be held under paragraph 9 of Schedule 1 to the Highways Act 1959 in connection with—

    (i) schemes proposed to be made by him under section 11 of the Highways Act 1959,

    (ii) schemes made by a local highway authority under the said section 11 or under section 3 of the Highways (Miscellaneous Provisions) Act 1961 and submitted to the Secretary of State for confirmation.

(2) Part II of these Rules applies to local inquiries in connection with orders or schemes proposed to be made by the Secretary of State, Part III of these Rules applies to local inquiries in connection with orders or schemes made by a local highway authority and submitted to the Secretary of State for confirmation, and Parts I and IV of these Rules apply to all local inquiries referred to in paragraph (1) of this rule.

NOTES

Local inquiries . . . held under paragraph 5 of Schedule 1 to the Highways Act 1959   This is now to be construed as a reference to local inquiries held under the Highways Act 1980, Sch 1, para 7, Halsbury's Statutes, 4th edn Vol 20, title Highways, Streets and Bridges (3rd edn Vol 50 (1), p 809).

Orders . . . under section 7, 9 13 or 20 of the Highways Act 1959 or under section 10 of the Highways Act 1971   This is now to be construed as a reference to orders under the Highways Act 1980, ss 10, 14, 18, 106 or 108, Halsbury's Statutes, 4th edn Vol 20, title Highways, Streets and Bridges (3rd edn Vol 50 (1), pp 472, 478, 483, 571, 573).

Orders . . under section 13 of the Highways Act 1959 or under section 1 or 10 of the Highways Act 1971   This is now to be construed as a reference to orders under the Highways Act 1980, ss 14, 18 or 108 (see the preceding note).

Local inquiries . . . held under paragraph 9 of Schedule 1 to the Highways Act 1959   This is now to be construed as a reference to local inquiries held under the Highways Act 1980, Sch 1, para 14, Halsbury's Statutes, 4th edn Vol 20, title Highways, Streets and Bridges (3rd edn Vol 50 (1), p 812).

Schemes . . . under section 11 of the Highways Act 1959   This is now to be construed as a reference to schemes under the Highways Act 1980, s 16, Halsbury's Statutes, 4th edn Vol 20, title Highways, Streets and Bridges (3rd edn Vol 50 (1), p 481).

Schemes . . . under the said section 11 or under section 3 of the Highways (Miscellaneous Provisions) Act 1961   This is now to be construed as a reference to schemes under the Highways Act 1980, ss 16 or 106, Halsbury's Statutes, 4th edn Vol 20, title Highways, Streets and Bridges (3rd edn Vol 50 (1), pp 481, 571).

3. Interpretation   (1) In these Rules, unless the context otherwise requires—

"appointed person" means the person appointed by the Secretary of State to hold the inquiry;

"highway works" means any works for the construction, improvement or alteration of a highway, or for the provision of means of access to premises or the diversion of a navigable watercourse in connection with the construction, improvement or alteration of a highway, and "the highway works", in relation to an order or scheme, means the highway works authorised by that order or scheme;

"improvement", in relation to a highway, has the same meaning as in the Highways Act 1959;

"inquiry" means a local inquiry to which these Rules apply;

"local authority" means a county council, a district council, the Greater London Council, a London Borough Council, the Common Council of the City of London, a parish council, a community council, a parish meeting or any joint board or joint committee whose constituent authorities are any two or more of the foregoing authorities;

"local highway authority" has the same meaning as in the Highways Act 1959;

"the order or scheme" means, in relation to an inquiry, the order or scheme in connection with which the inquiry is, or is to be, held or, when an inquiry is, or is to be, held in connection with more than one order or scheme, all the orders and schemes;

"the promoting authority"—

    (*a*) in relation to an order or scheme proposed to be made by the Secretary of State, means the Secretary of State,

(b) in relation to an order or scheme made by a local highway authority and submitted to the Secretary of State for confirmation, means that local highway authority,

(c) in relation to a scheme under section 11 of the Highways Act 1959 or under section 3 of the Highways (Miscellaneous Provisions) Act 1961 made by two or more local highway authorities and submitted to the Secretary of State for confirmation, means such one or more of those authorities as may, for the purpose of any particular provision of these Rules, be agreed between the authorities themselves or, in default of such agreement, be determined by the Secretary of State or the appointed person;

"site" means the site of any of the highway works authorised by the order or scheme or the site of any highway to which the order or scheme relates;

"statutory objector" means any person who is mentioned in the following table, who has duly objected to the order or scheme in accordance with the provisions of Schedule 1 to the Highways Act 1959 and whose objection has not been withdrawn or disregarded under section 14 (4), (6) or (8) of the Highways Act 1971—

TABLE

1. Any owner (within the meaning of section 295 of the Highways Act 1959), lessee or occupier of land which is likely to be required for the execution of any of the highway works.

2. Any person who is likely to be entitled to claim compensation under Part I of the Land Compensation Act 1973 in respect of the use of any of the highway works.

3. Any local authority in whose area any of the highway works will be situated or in whose area any highway to which the order or scheme relates is situated.

4. In the case of an order or scheme providing for the construction of a bridge over or tunnel under navigable waters, or for the diversion of a navigable watercourse, any navigation authority or water authority having jurisdiction over the waters affected or the area comprising those waters or that watercourse.

5. In the case of an order which authorises the stopping up of any private means of access to premises, the owner (within the meaning of section 16 of the Highways Act 1959) or the occupier of those premises.

6. In the case of an order which authorises the stopping up or diversion of a highway, any person having apparatus under, in, upon, over, along or across the highway.

(2) Any reference in these Rules to works authorised by an order or scheme is a reference to the works which the order or scheme would authorise if it were made by the Secretary of State in the form in which it was prepared in draft by him, or if it were confirmed by the Secretary of State in the form in which it was made by the local highway authority.

(3) For the purpose of these Rules an order under section 7 of the Highways Act 1959 which provides that a new highway which the Secretary of State proposes to construct on a route described in the order shall become a trunk road shall be regarded as authorising the construction of that highway by him on that route, and an order under the said section 7 which provides that an existing highway shall become a trunk road shall be regarded as authorising such improvement of that highway as the Secretary of State proposes to carry out under Part V of the Highways Act 1959 if that order is made.

(4) Any reference in these Rules to any enactment is a reference to that enactment as amended, extended or applied by or under any other enactment.

(5) The Interpretation Act 1889 shall apply to the interpretation of these Rules as it applies to the interpretation of an Act of Parliament.

NOTES

Highways Act 1959   This is now to be construed as a reference to the Highways Act 1980; for the meaning of "improvement" and "local highway authority", see s 329 (1) of that Act, Halsbury's Statutes, 4th edn Vol 20, title Highways, Streets and Bridges (3rd edn Vol 50 (1), p 791).
Scheme under section 11 of the Highways Act 1959 or under section 3 of the Highways (Miscellaneous Provisions) Act 1961   See the note to r 2.
Schedule 1 to the Highways Act 1959   This is now to be construed as a reference to the Highways Act 1980, Sch 1, Halsbury's Statutes, 4th edn Vol 20, title Highways, Streets and Bridges (3rd edn Vol 50 (1), p 808 *et seq*).
Section 14 (4), (6) or (8) of the Highways Act 1971   This is now to be construed as a reference to the Highways Act 1980, Sch 1, paras 18 (2), 19 (2) or 21, Halsbury's Statutes, 4th edn Vol 20, title Highways, Streets and Bridges (3rd edn Vol 50 (1), pp 813, 814).
Part I of the Land Compensation Act 1973   Halsbury's Statutes, 4th edn Vol 9, title Compulsory Acquisition.
Owner (within the meaning of sections 295 and 16 of the Highways Act 1959)   This is now to be construed as a reference to owner within the meaning of the Highways Act 1980, ss 329 (1) and 21 respectively, Halsbury's Statutes, 4th edn Vol 20, title Highways, Streets and Bridges (3rd edn Vol 50 (1), pp 791, 487).
Order under section 7 of the Highways Act 1959   See the note to r 1.
Interpretation Act 1889   Repealed and replaced by the Interpretation Act 1978, printed in the title Statutory Instruments, Vol 1.

PART II
RULES APPLICABLE TO INQUIRIES IN CONNECTION WITH ORDERS OR SCHEMES PROPOSED TO BE MADE BY THE SECRETARY OF STATE

4. Notice of inquiry   (1) A date, time and place for the holding of the inquiry shall be fixed and may be varied by the Secretary of State, who shall give not less than 42 days' notice in writing of the date, time and place to every statutory objector at the address furnished to the Secretary of State:
   Provided that—
   (i) with the consent in writing of the statutory objectors the Secretary of State may give such lesser period of notice as may be agreed with them and in that event he may specify a date for service of the statement referred to in rule 5 (1) later than the date prescribed in that paragraph;
   (ii) where it becomes necessary or advisable to vary the time or place fixed for the inquiry, the Secretary of State shall give such notice of the variation as may appear to him to be reasonable in the circumstances.
   (2) Not later than 14 days before the date of the inquiry, the Secretary of State shall post a notice of the inquiry in a conspicuous place near to the site or, where more than one site is involved, to each site and also in one or more places where public notices are usually posted in the locality or localities concerned, and shall also publish a notice of the inquiry in one or more newspapers circulating in the locality in which the site or sites are situated or, if more than one locality is concerned, in one or more newspapers circulating in each such locality.

5. Statement to be served before inquiry   (1) As soon as may be after receiving the objections of statutory objectors and in any event (except where the Secretary of State specifies a later date under proviso (i) to rule 4 (1)) not less than 28 days before the date of the inquiry, the Secretary of State shall, unless he has already done so, serve on each statutory objector a written statement of his reasons for proposing to make the order or scheme in the terms of the draft prepared by him.
   (2) Where another government department has expressed in writing to the Secretary of State a view in support of the draft order or scheme and the Secretary of State proposes to rely on such expression of view in his submission at the inquiry, he shall include it in the statement referred to in the last foregoing paragraph and shall send a copy of his statement to the government department concerned.

(3) Where the Secretary of State intends to refer to or put in evidence at the inquiry documents (including maps and plans), his statement shall be accompanied by a list of such documents, together with a notice stating the times and place at which the documents may be inspected by any statutory objector; and the Secretary of State shall afford every statutory objector a reasonable opportunity to inspect and, where practicable, to take copies of the documents.

(4) The Secretary of State shall afford any other person interested a reasonable opportunity to inspect and, where practicable, to take copies of his statement and the other documents referred to in the last foregoing paragraph.

6. Representation of Secretary of State at inquiry   (1) The Secretary of State may be represented at the inquiry by counsel or solicitor or by an officer of his department or other person authorised by the Secretary of State to represent him.

(2) The Secretary of State shall make a representative available at the inquiry to give evidence in elucidation of the statement referred to in rule 5, and such representative shall be subject to cross-examination to the same extent as other witnesses, so, however, that the appointed person shall disallow any question which in his opinion is directed to the merits of government policy.

7. Representation of other government departments at inquiry   (1) Where another government department has expressed in writing to the Secretary of State a view in support of the draft order or scheme and the Secretary of State has included that view in his statement, a representative of the department concerned shall be made available to attend the inquiry.

(2) Such representative shall at the inquiry state the reasons for the view expressed by his department and shall give evidence and be subject to cross-examination to the same extent as other witnesses, so, however, that the appointed person shall disallow any question which in his opinion is directed to the merits of government policy.

8. Other appearances at inquiry   (1) Every statutory objector shall be entitled to appear at the inquiry and any other person may appear at the discretion of the appointed person.

(2) Any person appearing at the inquiry in pursuance of this rule may appear in person or be represented by counsel, solicitor or any other person.

(3) Where there are two or more persons having a similar interest in the matter under inquiry the appointed person may allow one or more persons to appear on behalf of some or all persons so interested.

PART III
RULES APPLICABLE TO INQUIRIES IN CONNECTION WITH ORDERS OR SCHEMES MADE BY LOCAL HIGHWAY AUTHORITIES

9. Notice of inquiry   (1) The Secretary of State shall as soon as may be notify the promoting authority of the substance of each objection received by him from a statutory objector and, so far as practicable, shall also notify the promoting authority of the substance of other objections.

(2) A date, time and place for the holding of the inquiry shall be fixed and may be varied by the Secretary of State who shall give or cause to be given not less than 42 day's notice in writing of such date, time and place to every statutory objector at the address furnished to the Secretary of State, and to the promoting authority:
Provided that—
    (i) with the consent in writing of the statutory objectors and of the promoting authority the Secretary of State may give such lesser period of notice as shall be agreed with the statutory objectors

and the promoting authority, and in that event he may specify a date for service of the statement referred to in rule 10 (1) later than the date prescribed in that paragraph;

(ii) where it becomes necessary or advisable to vary the time or place fixed for the inquiry, the Secretary of State shall give such notice of the variation as may appear to him to be reasonable in the circumstances.

(3)The promoting authority shall—

(a) unless the Secretary of State otherwise directs, not later than 14 days before the date of the inquiry, post a notice of the inquiry in a conspicuous place near to the site or, where more than one site is involved, to each site and also in one or more places where public notices are usually posted in the locality or localities concerned;

(b) if the Secretary of State so directs, publish in one or more newspapers circulating in the locality in which the site or sites are situated or, if more than one locality is concerned, in one or more newspapers circulating in each of those localities, such notices of the inquiry as he may specify.

10. Statement to be served before inquiry   (1) As soon as may be after receiving notification of the substance of the objections of statutory objectors and in any event (except where the Secretary of State specifies a later date under proviso (i) to rule 9 (2)) not later than 28 days before the date of the inquiry, the promoting authority shall, unless it has already done so—

(a) serve on each statutory objector a written statement of its reasons for making the scheme or order, and

(b) supply a copy of the statement to the Secretary of State.

(2) Where a government department has expressed in writing to the promoting authority a view in support of the order or scheme and the promoting authority proposes to rely on such expression of view in its submissions at the inquiry, it shall include it in the statement referred to in the last foregoing paragraph and shall send a copy of that statement to the government department concerned.

(3) Where the promoting authority intends to refer to or put in evidence at the inquiry documents (including maps and plans), the authority's statement shall be accompanied by a list of such documents, together with a notice stating the times and place at which the documents may be inspected by any statutory objector; and the promoting authority shall afford any statutory objector a reasonable opportunity to inspect, and, where practicable, take copies of the documents.

(4) The promoting authority shall afford any other person interested a reasonable opportunity to inspect and, where practicable, to take copies of the authority's statement and the other documents referred to in the last foregoing paragraph.

(5) The promoting authority shall make a representative available at the inquiry to give evidence in elucidation of the statement referred to in paragraph (1) of this rule and such representative shall be subject to cross-examination to the same extent as other witnesses.

11. Representation of government departments at inquiry   (1) Where a government department has expressed in writing to the promoting authority a view in support of the order or scheme and the promoting authority has set out such view in the statement referred to in rule 10 (1), a representative of the government department concerned shall be made available to attend the inquiry.

(2) Such representative shall at the inquiry state the reasons for the view expressed by his department and shall give evidence and be subject to cross-examination to the same extent as other witnesses, so, however, that the appointed person shall disallow any question which in his opinion is directed to the merits of government policy.

12. Other appearances at inquiry   (1) The promoting authority and any statutory objectors shall be entitled to appear at the inquiry, and any other person may appear at the discretion of the appointed person.

(2) The promoting authority may appear by any officer appointed for the purpose by the promoting authority or by counsel or solicitor and any other person may appear on his own behalf or be represented by counsel, solicitor or any other person.

(3) Where there are two or more persons having a similar interest in the matter under inquiry the appointed person may allow one or more persons to appear on behalf of some or all persons so interested.

PART IV
RULES APPLICABLE TO ALL INQUIRIES

13. Procedure at inquiry   (1) Except as otherwise provided in these Rules, the procedure at the inquiry shall be such as the appointed person shall in his discretion determine.

(2) Unless in any particular case the appointed person with the consent of the promoting authority otherwise determines, the promoting authority shall begin and shall have the right of final reply; and the other persons entitled or permitted to appear shall be heard in such order as the appointed person may determine.

(3) The promoting authority and the statutory objectors shall be entitled to call evidence and cross-examine persons giving evidence but any other persons appearing at the inquiry may do so only to the extent permitted by the appointed person.

(4) The appointed person shall not require or permit the giving or production of any evidence, whether written or oral, which would be contrary to the public interest but, save as aforesaid and without prejudice to rules 6 (2), 7 (2) and 11 (2), any evidence may be admitted at the discretion of the appointed person, who may direct that documents tendered in evidence may be inspected by any person entitled or permitted to appear at the inquiry and that facilities be afforded him to take or obtain copies thereof.

(5) The appointed person may allow the promoting authority to alter or add to the reasons contained in the statement served under rule 5 (1) or 10 (1), or any list of documents which accompanied such statement, so far as may be necessary for the purpose of determining the questions in issue between the parties, but shall (if necessary by adjourning the inquiry) give every statutory objector an adequate opportunity to consider any such alterations or additions and may make in his report a recommendation as to the payment of any additional costs occasioned by any such adjournment.

(6) The appointed person shall be entitled (subject to disclosure thereof at the inquiry) to take into account any written representations or statements received by him before the inquiry from any person who, for whatever reason, does not attend the inquiry, in so far as such representations or statements appear to the appointed person to be proper and relevant to the matters in issue.

(7) The appointed person may proceed with the inquiry notwithstanding that any of the statutory objectors does not appear.

(8) The appointed person may from time to time adjourn the inquiry and, if the date, time and place of the adjourned inquiry are announced before the adjournment, no further notice shall be required.

14. Site inspections   (1) The appointed person may make an unaccompanied inspection of the site or sites before or during the inquiry, without giving notice of his intention to any person entitled to appear at the inquiry.

(2) The appointed person may, and shall if so requested by the promoting authority or any statutory objector before or during the inquiry, inspect the site or sites involved after the close of the inquiry and shall, in all cases where

he intends to make such an inspection, announce during the inquiry the date and time at which he proposes to do so.

(3) The promoting authority and the statutory objectors shall be entitled to accompany the appointed person on any inspection after the close of the inquiry but the appointed person shall not be bound to defer his inspection if any person entitled to accompany him is not present at the time appointed.

(4) In a case where the objection of a statutory objector relates to a part only of a site or to one or more, but not all, of the sites involved, his right to request a site inspection and to accompany the appointed person shall apply only to that part or to that site or those sites.

15. Procedure after inquiry   (1) The appointed person shall after the close of the inquiry make a report in writing to the Secretary of State, which shall include the appointed person's findings of fact, his conclusions and his recommendations, if any, or his reasons for not making any recommendations.

(2) Where the Secretary of State—

(*a*) differs from the appointed person on a finding of fact, or

(*b*) after the close of the inquiry takes into consideration any new evidence (including expert opinion on a matter of fact) or any new issue of fact (not being a matter of government policy) which was not raised at the inquiry,

and by reason thereof is disposed to disagree with a recommendation made by the appointed person, he shall not come to a decision which is at variance with any such recommendation without first notifying—

(i) all statutory objectors who appeared at the inquiry, and

(ii) in a case where the promoting authority is a local highway authority, that authority,

of his disagreement, and the reasons for it, and affording to them an opportunity of making representations in writing within 21 days or (if the Secretary of State has taken into consideration any new evidence or any new issue of fact not being a matter of government policy) of asking within 21 days for the reopening of the inquiry.

(3) The Secretary of State may in any case if he thinks fit cause the inquiry to be reopened, and shall cause it to be reopened if asked to do so in accordance with the last foregoing paragraph; and if the inquiry is reopened rule 4 (1) and (2) or 9 (2) and (3), as the case may be, shall apply as they applied to the original inquiry but with a substitution in rule 4 (1) or 9 (2) of "28" for "42".

16. Notification of decision   (1) The Secretary of State shall notify his decision, and his reasons therefor, in writing to the promoting authority (in a case where that authority is a local highway authority), to the statutory objectors and to any other person who, having appeared at the inquiry, has asked to be notifed of the decision; and, where a copy of the appointed person's report is not sent with the notification of the decision, the notification shall be accompanied by a summary of the appointed person's conclusions and of his recommendations or his reasons for not making recommendations.

(2) If any person entitled to be notifed of the Secretary of State's decision under the last foregoing paragraph has not received a copy of the appointed person's report, he shall be supplied with a copy thereof on written application made to the Secretary of State within one month from the date on which he is notified of the decision or the date of the first publication of notice of the making or confirmation of the order or scheme, whichever is the later.

(3) For the purposes of this rule "report" does not include documents, photographs or plans appended to the report but any person entitled to be supplied with a copy of the report under paragraph (2) of this rule may apply to the Secretary of State in writing within six weeks of the notification to him of the decision or the supply to him of the report, whichever is the later, for an opportunity of inspecting such documents, photographs and plans, and the Secretary of State shall afford him an opportunity accordingly.

17. Service of notices by post Notices or documents required or authorised to be served or sent under the provisions of these Rules may be sent by post.

THE REMOVAL AND DISPOSAL OF VEHICLES (LOADING AREAS) (MODIFICATION OF ENACTMENTS) REGULATIONS 1978
SI 1978/889

NOTES
Authority These regulations were made on 19 June 1978 by the Secretary of State for Transport and the Secretary of State for Wales under s 37 (7) of the Local Government (Miscellaneous Provisions) Act 1976 (repealed) and all other enabling powers. The now have effect under the Road Traffic Regulation Act 1984, s 103 (1), Halsbury's Statutes, 4th edn Vol 38, title Road Traffic (3rd edn Vol 54 (2), p 1612).
Commencement 19 July 1978.
General These regulations, as construed in accordance with the Road Traffic Regulation Act 1984, s 144 (1), Sch 10, para 2, apply and adapt ss 99-102 of that Act, Halsbury's Statutes, 4th edn Vol 38, title Road Traffic (3rd edn Vol 54 (2), pp 1605-1610), which relate to the removal, storage and disposal of vehicles left on roads in contravention of a statutory prohibition, so that those provisions may be used in relation to vehicles standing in any part of a goods vehicle loading area while parking on that part is prohibited by virtue of s 61 of the 1984 Act (which provides for the control of parking on areas used for loading or unloading goods vehicles). The adaptations consist mainly of the omission of certain provisions in ss 99-102 of the 1984 Act which are irrelevant in relation to vehicles parked in goods vehicle loading areas and the omission of those provisions which involve the exercise of certain functions by the police. Certain necessary alterations in wording are also provided for. The modifications made by these regulations are fully described against the said ss 99-102 in Halsbury's Statutes, 4th edn Vol 38, title Road Traffic (3rd edn Vol 54 (2), pp 1605-1610), and the text of those sections as modified is set out in Schedule 2 to the regulations.
For the removal and disposal of vehicles under the said ss 99-102, as modified by these regulations, see the Removal and Disposal of Vehicles (Loading Areas) Regulations 1986, SI 1986/184, p 137, *post*.

THE CONTROL OF ROAD-SIDE SALES ORDERS (PROCEDURE) REGULATIONS 1978
SI 1978/932

NOTES
Authority These regulations were made on 4 July 1978 by the Secretary of State for Transport and the Secretary of State for Wales under s 84C (2) to (5) and (6) of the Road Traffic Regulation Act 1967 (repealed), as applied by s 7 (3) of the Local Government (Miscellaneous Provisions) Act 1976, Halsbury's Statutes, 4th edn Vol 20, title Highways, Streets and Bridges (3rd edn Vol 46, p 702), and under all other enabling powers. They now have effect under the Road Traffic Regulation Act 1984, Sch 9, paras 21-24, *ibid*, 4th edn Vol 38, title Road Traffic (3rd edn Vol 54 (2), pp 1675, 1676), as applied by the said s 7 (3) as amended by the 1984 Act, s 146, Sch 13, para 34.
Commencement 2 August 1978.
General These regulations lay down the procedure to be followed by highway authorities in England and Wales in connection with the making by them of orders ("control orders") under s 7 of the Local Government (Miscellaneous Provisions) Act 1976, Halsbury's Statutes, 4th edn Vol 20, title Highways, Streets and Bridges (3rd edn Vol 46, p 701), for controlling road-side sales. Part I of the regulations contains general provisions (concerning, *inter alia*, the interpretation and application of the regulations). Part II prescribes the procedure before a control order is made; it provides for preliminary consultations (reg 4), publication of proposals (reg 5), objections to the order (reg 6), public inquiries (regs 7-9), the consideration of objections (reg 10) and the making of modifications to the proposals (reg 11). Part III (regs 12, 13) contains provisions with respect to the form of the order and its operative date or dates; and Part IV contains provisions as to the manner of making the order (reg 14), as to the giving of notice thereof (reg 15) and as to the service of notices by the Secretary of State (reg 16). Schedules 1 to 3 to the regulations specify the requirements as to the particulars to be included in the notices relating to the orders, as to the display of notices in highways and as to the documents to be made available for inspection.

THE MOTORWAYS TRAFFIC (ENGLAND AND WALES) REGULATIONS 1982
SI 1982/1163

NOTES
Authority These regulations were made on 11 August 1982 by the Secretary of State for Transport and the Secretary of State for Wales under the Road Traffic Regulation Act 1967, s 13 (2) and (3) (repealed), and all other enabling powers, and after consultation with representative

organisations. They now have effect under the Road Traffic Regulation Act 1984, s 17 (2), Halsbury's Statutes, 4th edn Vol 38, title Road Traffic (3rd edn Vol 54 (2), p 1528).
Commencement   15 September 1982; see reg 1.
Amendment   These regulations are printed as amended by the Motorways Traffic (England and Wales) (Amendment) Regulations 1983, SI 1983/374 and the Motorways Traffic (England and Wales) (Amendment) Regulations 1984, SI 1984/1479.
Interpretation   See reg 3 and note thereto.
Penalties   Persons using a road in contravention of these regulations are liable on summary conviction to a fine not exceeding level 4 on the standard scale; see the Road Traffic Regulation Act 1984, ss 17 (4), 98, Sch 7, Halsbury's Statutes, 4th edn Vol 38, title Road Traffic (3rd edn Vol 54 (2), pp 1528, 1604, 1665). For provisions as to disqualification and endorsement of licences, see the 1984 Act, s 98, Sch 7 and for additional provisions as to the prosecution and trial of offences, see the 1984 Act, ss 90 and 112-114, by virtue of *ibid*, s 98, Sch 7.
General   These regulations provide for the regulation of traffic using special roads (described in the regulations as "motorways") in cases where such roads can be used only by traffic of Classes I or II set out in the Highways Act 1980, Sch 4, Halsbury's Statutes, 4th edn Vol 20, title Highways, Streets and Bridges (3rd edn Vol 50 (1), p 816).
By the 1984 Act, s 17 (5) (and see reg 4 of these regulations), the provisions of that section and of these regulations do not apply to any part of a special road until such date as may be declared by a notice published as mentioned in s 1 (4) of the Act to be the date on which it is open for use as a special road; see the Special Roads (Notice of Opening) Regulations 1962, SI 1962/1320, p 64, *ante*.
Instruments relating to speed limits for vehicles on roads, including motorways, are in the title Transport (Part 2B).

1. Commencement and citation   These Regulations shall come into operation on 15th September 1982 and may be cited as the Motorways Traffic (England and Wales) Regulations 1982.

2. Revocation   The Motorways Traffic Regulations 1959 and the Motorways Traffic (England and Wales) (Amendment) Regulations 1971 are hereby revoked.

NOTES
The regulations in question are SI 1959/1147 and 1971/1087.

3. Interpretation   (1) In these Regulations, the following expressions have the meanings hereby respectively assigned to them—
   (*a*) "the Act of 1967" means the Road Traffic Regulation Act 1967;
   (*b*) ["carriageway" means that part of a motorway which—
      (i) is provided for the regular passage of vehicular motor traffic along the motorway; and
      (ii) where a hard shoulder is provided, has the approximate position of its left-hand or near-side edge marked with a traffic sign of the type shown in diagram 1012.1 in Schedule 2 to the Traffic Signs Regulations and General Directions 1981.]
   (*c*) "central reservation" means that part of a motorway which separates the carriageway to be used by vehicles travelling in one direction from the carriageway to be used by vehicles travelling in the opposite direction;
   (*d*) "excluded traffic" means traffic which is not traffic of Classes I or II;
   (*e*) "hard shoulder" means a part of the motorway which is adjacent to and situated on the left hand or near side of the carriageway when facing in the opposite direction in which vehicles may be driven in accordance with Regulation 6, and which is designed to take the weight of a vehicle;
   (*f*) "motorway" means any road or part of a road to which these Regulations apply by virtue of Regulation 4;
   (*g*) "verge" means any part of a motorway which is not a carriageway, a hard shoulder, or a central reservation.

(2) A vehicle shall be treated for the purposes of any provision of these Regulations as being on any part of a motorway specified in that provision if any part of the vehicle (whether it is at rest or not) is on the part of the motorway so specified.

(3) Any provision of these Regulations containing any prohibition or restriction relating to the driving, moving or stopping of a vehicle, or to its remaining at rest, shall be construed as a provision that no person shall use a motorway by driving, moving or stopping the vehicle or by causing or permitting it to be driven or moved, or to stop or remain at rest, in contravention of that prohibition or restriction.

(4) In these Regulations references to numbered classes of traffic are references to the classes of traffic set out in Schedule 4 to the Highways Act 1980.

NOTES
Amendment   The definition of "carriageway" in para (1) (b) of this regulation was substituted by SI 1984/1479.
Other expressions   For the meanings of the expressions "motor vehicle", "trailer", "motor car" and "heavy motor car", see the Road Traffic Regulation Act 1984, s 136, Halsbury's Statutes, 4th edn Vol 38, title Road Traffic (3rd edn Vol 54 (2), p 1638).
Road Traffic Regulation Act 1967   This is now to be construed as a reference to the Road Traffic Regulation Act 1984, Halsbury's Statutes, 4th edn Vol 38, title Road Traffic (3rd edn Vol 54 (2), p 1509 *et seq*).
Traffic Signs Regulations and General Directions 1981   SI 1981/859, in the title Transport (Part 2B).
Highways Act 1980, Sch 4   Halsbury's Statutes, 4th edn Vol 20, title Highways, Streets and Bridges (3rd edn Vol 50 (1), p 816).

4. Application   These Regulations apply to every special road or part of a special road which can only be used by traffic of Classes I or II, but shall not apply to any part of any such road until such date as may be declared in accordance with the provisions of section 1(7) of the Act of 1967 to be the date on which it is open for use as a special road.

NOTES
See the head "General", p 115, *ante*.
Section 1 (7) of the Act of 1967   Repealed; see now the Road Traffic Regulation Act 1984, s 1 (4), (5).

5. Vehicles to be driven on the carriageway only   Subject to the following provisions of these Regulations, no vehicle shall be driven on any part of a motorway which is not a carriageway.

6. Direction of driving   (1) Where there is a traffic sign indicating that there is no entry to a carriageway at a particular place, no vehicle shall be driven or moved onto that carriageway at that place.

(2) Where there is a traffic sign indicating that there is no left or right turn into a carriageway at a particular place, no vehicle shall be so driven or moved as to cause it to turn to the left or (as the case may be) to the right into that carriageway at that place.

(3) Every vehicle on a length of carriageway which is contiguous to a central reservation, shall be driven in such a direction that the central reservation is at all times on the right hand or off side of the vehicle.

(4) Where traffic signs are so placed that there is a length of carriageway (being a length which is not contiguous to a central reservation) which can be entered at one end only by vehicles driven in conformity with paragraph (1) of this Regulation, every vehicle on that length of carriageway shall be driven in such a direction only as to cause it to proceed away from that end of that length of carriageway towards the other end thereof.

(5) Without prejudice to the foregoing provisions of this Regulation, no vehicle which—

   (*a*) is on a length of carriageway on which vehicles are required by any of the foregoing provisions of this Regulation to be driven in one direction only and is proceeding in or facing that direction, or (*b*) is on any other length of carriageway and is proceeding in or facing one direction,

shall be driven or moved so as to cause it to turn and proceed in or face the opposite direction.

7. Restriction on stopping (1) Subject to the following provisions of this Regulation, no vehicle shall stop or remain at rest on a carriageway.

(2) Where it is necessary for a vehicle which is being driven on a carriageway to be stopped while it is on a motorway—

(*a*) by reason of a breakdown or mechanical defect or lack of fuel, oil or water, required for the vehicle; or

(*b*) by reason of any accident, illness or other emergency; or

(*c*) to permit any person carried in or on the vehicle to recover or move any object which has fallen onto a motorway; or

(*d*) to permit any person carried in or on the vehicle to give help which is required by any other person in any of the circumstances specified in the foregoing provisions of this paragraph,

the vehicle shall, as soon and in so far as is reasonably practicable, be driven or moved off the carriageway on to, and may stop and remain at rest on, any hard shoulder which is contiguous to that carriageway.

(3) (*a*) A vehicle which is at rest on a hard shoulder shall so far as is reasonably practicable be allowed to remain at rest on that hard shoulder in such a position only that no part of it or of the load carried thereby shall obstruct or be a cause of danger to vehicles using the carriageway.

(*b*) A vehicle shall not remain at rest on a hard shoulder for longer than is necessary in the circumstances or for the purposes specified in paragraph 2 of this Regulation.

(4) Nothing in the foregoing provisions of this Regulation shall preclude a vehicle from stopping or remaining at rest on a carriageway while is it prevented from proceeding along the carriageway by the presence of any other vehicle or any person or object.

NOTES

Para (2): emergency As to the meaning of "emergency", see *Higgins v Bernard* [1972] 1 All ER 1037.

8. Restriction on reversing No vehicle on a motorway shall be driven or moved backwards except in so far as it is necessary to back the vehicle to enable it to proceed forwards or to be connected to any other vehicle.

9. Restriction on the use of hard shoulders No vehicle shall be driven or stop or remain at rest on any hard shoulder except in accordance with paragraphs (2) and (3) of Regulation 7.

10. Vehicles not to use the central reservation or verge No vehicle shall be driven or moved or stop or remain at rest on a central reservation or verge.

11. Vehicles not to be driven by learner drivers No motor vehicle shall be driven on a motorway by a person who is authorised to drive that vehicle only by virtue of his being the holder of a provisional licence under section 88 (2) of the Road Traffic Act 1972, unless, since the date of coming into force of the said provisional licence that person has passed a test prescribed under section 85 of the Road Traffic Act 1972 sufficient to entitle him under that Act to be granted a licence, other than a provisional licence, authorising him to drive that vehicle on a road.

NOTES
Road Traffic Act 1972, ss 85, 88 (2)   Halsbury's Statutes, 4th edn Vol 38, title Road Traffic (3rd edn Vol 42, pp 1735, 1740).

[12. Restriction on use of right hand or off side lane   This Regulation applies to—
  (*a*) a goods vehicle which has an operating weight exceeding 7.5 tonnes;
  (*b*) a motor vehicle constructed solely for the carriage of passengers and their effects the overall length of which exceeds 12 metres;
  (*c*) a motor vehicle drawing a trailer, and
  (*d*) a motor vehicle other than a motor vehicle constructed solely for the carriage of passengers and their effects which does not fall within sub-paragraphs (*a*), (*b*), or (*c*) and which is a heavy motor car, a motor tractor, a light locomotive or a heavy locomotive.
  (2) Subject to the provisions of paragraph (3) below, no vehicle to which this Regulation applies shall be driven or moved or stop or remain at rest on the right hand or offside lane of a length of carriageway which has three or more traffic lanes at any place where all the lanes are open for use by traffic proceeding in the same direction.
  (3) The prohibition contained in paragraph (2) above shall not apply to a vehicle while it is being driven on any right hand or offside lane such as is mentioned in that paragraph in so far as it is necessary for the vehicle to be driven to enable it to pass another vehicle which is carrying or drawing a load of exceptional width.
  (4) In this Regulation—
"goods vehicle" and "operating weight" have the same meanings as in sections 104(1C) and 104(1B) respectively of the Act of 1967, and
"overall length" has the same meaning as in Regulation 3 (1) of the Motor Vehicles (Construction and Use) Regulations 1978.]

NOTES
Amendment   This regulation was substituted by SI 1983/374.
Sections 104 (1C) and 104 (1B) . . . of the Act of 1967   Repealed; see now the Road Traffic Regulation Act 1984, s 138 (3) and (2) respectively, Halsbury's Statutes, 4th edn Vol 38, title Road Traffic (3rd edn Vol 54 (2), p 1640).
Motor Vehicles (Construction and Use) Regulations 1978, reg 3 (1)   SI 1978/1017, in the title Transport (Part 2B).

13. Restrictions affecting persons on foot on a motorway   No person shall at any time while on foot go or remain on any part of a motorway other than a hard shoulder except in so far as it is necessary for him to do so to reach a hard shoulder or to secure compliance with any of these Regulations or to recover or move any object which has fallen on to a motorway or to give help which is required by any other person in any of the circumstances specified in paragraph (2) on Regulation 7.

14. Restrictions affecting animals carried in vehicles   The person in charge of any animal which is carried by a vehicle using a motorway shall, so far as is practicable, secure that—
  (*a*) the animal shall not be removed from or permitted to leave the vehicle while the vehicle is on a motorway, and
  (*b*) if it escapes from, or is necessary for it to be removed from, or permitted to leave, the vehicle—
    (i) it shall not go or remain on any part of the motorway other than a hard shoulder, and
    (ii) it shall whilst it is not on or in the vehicle be held on a lead or otherwise kept under proper control.

15. Use of motorway by excluded traffic   (1) Excluded traffic is hereby authorised to use a motorway on the occasions or in the emergencies and to the extent specified in the following provisions of this paragraph, that is to say—

(*a*) traffic of Classes III or IV may use a motorway for the maintenance, repair, cleaning or clearance of any part of a motorway or for the erection, laying, placing, maintenance, testing, alteration, repair or removal of any structure, works or apparatus in, on, under or over any part of a motorway;

(*b*) pedestrians may use a motorway—

(i) when it is necessary for them to do so as a result of an accident or emergency or of a vehicle being at rest on a motorway in any of the circumstances specified in paragraph (2) of Regulation 7, or

(ii) in any of the circumstances specified in sub-paragraphs (*b*), (*d*), (*e*) or (*f*) of paragraph (1) of Regulation 6.

(2) The Secretary of State may authorise the use of a motorway by any excluded traffic on occasion or in emergency or for the purpose of enabling such traffic to cross a motorway or to secure access to premises abutting on or adjacent to a motorway.

(3) Where by reason of any emergency the use of any road (not being a motorway) by any excluded traffic is rendered impossible or unsuitable the Chief Officer of Police of the police area in which a motorway or any part of a motorway is situated, or any officer of or above the rank of superintendent authorised in that behalf by that Chief Officer, may—

(*a*) authorise any excluded traffic to use that motorway or that part of a motorway as an alternative road for the period during which the use of the other road by such traffic continues to be impossible or unsuitable, and

(*b*) relax any prohibition or restriction imposed by these Regulations in so far as he considers it necessary to do so in connection with the use of that motorway or that part of a motorway by excluded traffic in pursuance of any such authorisation as aforesaid.

NOTES
Chief Officer of Police; police area   These expressions are defined in the Police Act 1964, s 62, Sch 8, as amended, Halsbury's Statutes, 4th edn Vol 33, title Police (3rd edn Vol 25, pp 370, 380).

16. Exceptions and relaxations   (1) Nothing in the foregoing provisions of these Regulations shall preclude any person from using a motorway otherwise than in accordance with the provisions in any of the following circumstances, that is to say—

(*a*) where he does so in accordance with any direction or permission given by a constable in uniform or with the indication given by a traffic sign;

(*b*) where, in accordance with any permission given by a constable, he does so for the purpose of investigating any accident which has occurred on or near a motorway;

(*c*) where it is necessary for him to do so to avoid or prevent an accident or to obtain or give help required as the result of an accident or emergency, and he does so in such a manner as to cause as little danger or inconvenience as possible to other traffic on a motorway;

(*d*) where he does so in the exercise of his duty as a constable or as a member of a fire brigade or of an ambulance service;

(*e*) where it is necessary for him to do so to carry out in an efficient manner—

(i) the maintenance, repair, cleaning, clearance, alteration or improvement of any part of a motorway, or

(ii) the removal of any vehicle from any part of a motorway, or
(iii) the erection, laying, placing, maintenance, testing, alteration, repair or removal of any structure, works or apparatus in, on, under or over any part of a motorway; or
(f) where it is necessary for him to do so in connection with any inspection, survey, investigation or census which is carried out in accordance with any general or special authority granted by the Secretary of State.

(2) Without prejudice to the foregoing provisions of these Regulations, the Secretary of State may relax any prohibition or restriction imposed by these Regulations.

THE HIGHWAYS (ROAD HUMPS) REGULATIONS 1983
SI 1983/1087

NOTES
Authority   These regulations were made on 18 July 1983 by the Secretary of State for Transport and the Secretary of State for Wales under the Highways Act 1980, ss 90C (1) and 90D (1) and (2), as inserted by the Transport Act 1981, s 32 and Sch 10, Pt I, Halsbury's Statutes, 4th edn Vol 20, title Highways, Streets and Bridges (3rd edn Vol 51, p 999), after consultation with representative organisations.
Commencement   25 August 1983; see reg 1.
Interpretation   See reg 2. As to the meaning of "road hump", see the Highways Act 1980, s 90F (1), as inserted by the Transport Act 1981, s 32 and Sch 10, Pt I, Halsbury's Statutes, 4th edn Vol 20, title Highways, Streets and Bridges (3rd edn Vol 51, p 1000).
General   These regulations prescribe requirements for consultation about proposals for the construction of road humps by the Secretary of State or a local highway authority and for the construction and maintenance of road humps. These regulations do not apply where a road hump is specially authorised by the Secretary of State; see the 1980 Act, s 90D (4) as inserted as mentioned above.

1. Citation and Commencement   These Regulations may be cited as the Highways (Road Humps) Regulations 1983 and shall come into operation on 25th August 1983.

2. Interpretation   (1) In these Regulations—
   "the Act" means the Highways Act 1980;
   "hours of darkness" means the time between half-an-hour after sunset and half-an-hour before sunrise;
   "local bus route" means the route of local service within the meaning of section 2 (2) of the Public Passenger Vehicles Act 1981 not being an excursion or tour within the meaning of that Act;
   "principal road" means a highway which is a road for the time being classified as a principal road by virtue of section 12 of the Act (whether as falling within subsection (1), or as being so classified under subsection (3), of that section);
   "road" has the same meaning as in the Road Traffic Act 1972;
   "traffic sign" has the same meaning as it has in section 54 of the Road Traffic Regulation Act 1967.

(2) For the purpose of these Regulations road humps in a highway shall be deemed to form part of a series where they are spaced not less than 50 metres nor more than 150 metres apart.

(3) For the purposes of these Regulations measurements to or from any point to or from a road hump shall be taken to or from that edge of the hump, as shown in the Schedule, which is nearest to the point and for the purposes of Regulations 4 and 5 and this paragraph—
   (a) measurements to or from a horizontal bend shall be taken to or from that part of the bend which is nearest to the hump;
   (b) measurements to or from a road junction shall be taken to or from the point nearest the hump on an imaginary line drawn across the mouth of the junction; and
   (c) a horizontal bend begins and ends where a vehicle would start and finish the change of direction specified in those Regulations.

(4) A reference in these Regulations to a numbered Regulation is a reference to the Regulation bearing that number in these Regulations and a reference to the Schedule is a reference to the Schedule to these Regulations, except where the context otherwise requires.

(5) In these Regulations references to any enactment shall be construed as references to that enactment as amended by or under any subsequent enactment.

NOTES
Highways Act 1980 Halsbury's Statutes, 4th edn Vol 20, title Highways, Streets and Bridges (3rd edn Vol 50 (1), p 452 *et seq*).
Public Passenger Vehicles Act 1981, s 2 (2) Halsbury's Statutes, 3rd edn Vol 51, p 1318. Section 2 is repealed as from 6 January 1986 by the Transport Act 1985, s 139 (3), Sch 8 (see the Transport Act 1985 (Commencement No 1) Order 1985, SI 1985/1887, in the title Transport (Pt 1)); for the meaning of "local service", see s 2 and as to London local services, see s 34 of that Act.
Road Traffic Act 1972 Halsbury's Statutes, 4th edn Vol 38, title Road Traffic (3rd edn Vol 42, p 1633 *et seq*).
Road Traffic Regulation Act 1967, s 54 Repealed; see now the Road Traffic Regulation Act 1984, s 64, Halsbury's Statutes, 4th edn Vol 38, title Road Traffic (3rd edn Vol 54 (2), p 1577).

3. Consultation about road hump proposals   Where the Secretary of State or a local highway authority proposes to construct a road hump under section 90A or 90B of the Act, he or they shall, as well as consulting the chief officer of police as required by section 90C(1) of the Act, also consult the following persons or bodies:—
  (a) where the proposal relates to a highway outside Greater London, the District Council in whose district the highway is situated;
  (b) where the proposal relates to a highway on which there is a local bus route, the operator or operators of the service or services on that route;
  (c) in all cases, one or more organisations representing persons who use the highway to which the proposal relates, or representing persons who are otherwise likely to be affected by the road hump unless it appears to the authority or the Secretary of State that there are no such organisations.

NOTES
Sections 90A, 90B, 90C (1) of the Act   *Ie* the Highways Act 1980, as inserted by the Transport Act 1981, s 32 and Sch 10, Pt I, Halsbury's Statutes, 4th edn Vol 20, title Highways, Streets and Bridges (3rd edn Vol 51, pp 998, 999).

4. Highways and circumstances in which road humps may be constructed   A road hump shall be constructed only—
  (a) in a highway which is not a special road, a trunk road or a principal road, and
  (b) in any part of such highway—
      (i) where to afford illumination throughout the hours of darkness there is a system of street lighting furnished by at least three lamps lit by electricity and placed not more than 38 metres apart or external lighting specially provided for the hump or a street lamp within 5 metres of the hump, and
      (ii) where on each road affording access for vehicular traffic to the road hump or, in the case of a series of road humps, the first in the series to be met by such traffic, there is a feature of one or more of the following descriptions—
          (a) a horizontal bend or a road junction at which such traffic would change its direction by not less than 70 degrees within an inner kerb radius of not more than 25 metres, or
          (b) a traffic sign facing away from the road hump conveying to vehicular traffic the prohibition specified in diagram 616, 617 or 619 in Part II of Schedule 1 to the Traffic Signs Regulations 1981, or
          (c) the end of a carriageway at the closed end of a cul-de-sac, or
          (d) a traffic sign conveying to vehicular traffic the prohibition

specified in diagram 1002.1 in the said part of the said Schedule to those Regulations,
any such feature being, in the case of (*a*), (*b*) or (*c*) within 30 metres and, in the case of (*d*) within 60 metres of the hump.

NOTES
Traffic Signs Regulations 1981, Sch I, Part II   SI 1981/859, in the title Transport (Part 2B).

5. Nature, dimensions, location and spacing of road humps   (1) A road hump constructed or maintained in a highway shall be so constructed and maintained that—

(*a*) it extends across the whole width of the carriageway of the highway and its cross-section conforms to the pattern and measurements shown in the Schedule, a measurement being deemed to conform if it is, in the case of a vertical measurement, no more than 10 per cent greater or no more than 15 per cent less, and, in the case of a horizontal measurement, no more than 5 per cent, greater or less, than the corresponding measurement so shown;

(*b*) no part of it is within 15 metres of a road junction, or a horizontal bend with an inner kerb radius of less than 50 metres at which vehicular traffic would change its direction by more than 45 degrees;

(*c*) it is at right angles to an imaginary line along the centre of the carriageway of the highway in which it is constructed;

(*d*) it is not within 500 metres of another road hump in that highway unless it forms part of a series with that other road hump; and

(*e*) where it is constructed or maintained in a carriageway with a gradient of more than 10 per cent, it is not within 20 metres of the top of that part of the carriageway which has that gradient and the distance between road humps on the gradient is not greater than 70 metres.

(2) A road hump shall not be constructed or maintained in a highway—

(*a*) within the limits of a pedestrian crossing provided under section 23 of the Road Traffic Regulation Act 1967 or within 50 metres of the limits of any such crossing;

(*b*) on a railway level crossing or within 20 metres of the nearest rail forming part of the railway track at any such crossing;

(*c*) within 20 metres of any point on an imaginary line running at right angles across the carriageway from a bus stop sign, or within 10 metres of a bus stop road marking;

(*d*) under or within 25 metres of a structure over the carriageway of the highway any part of which is 6·5 metres or less above the surface of the carriageway;

(*e*) where it would form part of a series extending over more than a kilometre.

(3) In this Regulation "bus stop sign" means a traffic sign indicating a stopping place for stage or scheduled express carriages prescribed, or treated as if prescribed by the Traffic Signs Regulations 1981 and "bus stop road marking" means a traffic sign indicating to vehicular traffic the limits of such a stopping place so prescribed or treated as if prescribed.

(4) In the foregoing paragraph "scheduled express carriage" has the same meaning as in the Traffic Signs Regulations 1981.

NOTES
Road Traffic Regulation Act 1967, s 23   Repealed; see now the Road Traffic Regulation Act 1984, s 25, Halsbury's Statutes, 4th edn Vol 38, title Road Traffic (3rd edn Vol 54 (2), p 1535).
Traffic Signs Regulations 1981   SI 1981/859, in the title Transport (Part 2B).

6. Placing of traffic signs   Where a road hump or a series of road humps is constructed in a highway the highway authority for the highway shall forthwith cause or permit to be placed in accordance with the Traffic Signs Regulations and General Directions 1981—

(*a*) the traffic sign shown in diagram 557.1, in combination with the traffic sign shown in diagram 557.2, 557.3 or 557.4 in Schedule 1 to those Regulations in such positions as the authority may consider requisite for the purpose of securing that adequate warning of the presence of a road hump or a series of road humps is given to persons using the highway; and

(b) on the road hump or, in the case of a series of road humps, on each hump in the series, the traffic sign shown in diagram 1060 in Schedule 2 to those Regulations.

NOTES
Traffic Signs Regulations and General Directions 1981   SI 1981/859, in the title Transport (Part 2B).

SCHEDULE

NOTES
This schedule consists of a diagram showing a cross section and dimensions of a road hump, being 3·7m in length and 100mm in height, except that 75mm is substituted for 100mm where the point on a highway at which the road hump is constructed or maintained is on a local bus route at the time its construction is completed.

THE CYCLE TRACKS REGULATIONS 1984
SI 1984/1431

NOTES
Authority   These regulations were made on 5 September 1984 by the Secretary of State for Transport and the Secretary of State for Wales under the Cycle Tracks Act 1984, s 3 (4), Halsbury's Statutes, 4th edn Vol 20, title Highways, Streets and Bridges (3rd edn Vol 54 (1), p 638), and all other enabling powers.
Commencement   12 September 1984; see reg 1.
Interpretation   See reg 2. For the meaning of "cycle track", "footpath" and "local highway authority", see (by virtue of the Cycle Tracks Act 1984, s 8 (2)) the Highways Act 1980, s 329 (1), Halsbury's Statutes, 4th edn Vol 20, title Highways, Streets and Bridges (3rd edn Vol 50 (1), p 791), as amended by the 1984 Act, s 1.
General   These regulations prescribe the procedure to be followed in connection with the making of orders under the Cycle Tracks Act 1984, s 3 by local highway authorities converting a footpath, or part of a footpath, to a cycle track, and the confirmation of such orders. The validity of such an order is subject to challenge in the High Court; see the 1984 Act, s 3 (6), (7).

1. Citation and commencement   These Regulations may be cited as the Cycle Tracks Regulations 1984 and shall come into operation on 12th September 1984.

2. Interpretation and application   (1) In these Regulations the following expressions have the meanings hereby respectively assigned to them:—

"the Act" means the Cycle Tracks Act 1984;

"the appointed person" means the person appointed by the Secretary of State to hold an inquiry;

"the authority", in relation to any order, means the local highway authority making or proposing to make the order under the Act;

"local authority" means the council of a district or London borough or the Common Council of the City of London;

"the objection period" means the period specified in the notice required by Regulation 4 of these Regulations within which objections to an order may be made;

"operational land" means, in relation to statutory undertakers—

(a) land which is used for the purpose of carrying on their undertaking; and

(b) land in which an interest is held for that purpose,

not being land which, in respect of its nature and situation, is comparable rather with land in general than with land which is used, or in which interests are held, for the purpose of the carrying on of statutory undertakings;

"order" means, in relation to anything occurring or falling to be done before its making, the order as proposed to be made, and in relation to anything occurring or falling to be done on or after its making, the order as made; and "statutory undertakers" has the same meaning as in section 2 (3) of the Act and "statutory undertakings" shall be construed accordingly.

(2) These Regulations apply to orders made or proposed to be made by a local highway authority under section 3 of the Act.

(3) Regulations 3, 4, 7 and 10 of these Regulations apply to orders made or proposed to be made under section 3 (9) of the Act with the substitution for the expression "footpath" of the expression "cycle track".

NOTES
Cycle Tracks Act 1984   Halsbury's Statutes, 4th edn Vol 20, title Highways, Streets and Bridges (3rd edn Vol 50 (1), p 636 *et seq*).

3. Procedure before making an order   Before making an order the authority shall consult with—

(*a*) one or more organisations representing persons who use the footpath to which the order relates or are likely to be affected by any provisions of the order, unless it appears to the authority that there is no such organisation which can appropriately be consulted;

(*b*) any other local authority, parish council or community council within whose area the said footpath is situated;

(*c*) those statutory undertakers whose operational land is crossed by the said footpath; and

(*d*) the chief officer of police of any police area in which the said footpath is situated.

4. Procedure after making an Order   On making an order the authority shall—

(*a*) publish once at least in a local newspaper circulating in the locality in which the footpath to which the order relates is situated a notice which

   (i) describes the general effect of the order stating that it has been and requires confirmation;

   (ii) names a place in the locality in which the footpath to which the order relates is situated where a copy of the order may be inspected free of charge at all reasonable hours; and

   (iii) specifies the period (not being less than 28 days from the date of the first publication of the notice) during which, and the address to which, objections to the order can be made and states that all objections must be made in writing and must specify the grounds thereof.

(*b*) cause a copy of the said notice to be displayed in a conspicuous position at the ends of so much of the footpath to which the order relates as is affected by the order,

(*c*) cause a copy of the said notice to be displayed in one or more places where public notices are usually displayed in the locality concerned, and

(*d*) send a copy of the said notice to all those consulted under Regulation 3 of these Regulations.

5. Objections   (1) Objections to an order may be made during the objection period.

(2) Any person wishing to object to an order shall send within the objection period, and to the address specified in the notice required by Regulation 4 of these Regulations, a written statement of his objection and of the grounds thereof.

6. Local Inquiries   (1) Where an order is submitted to the Secretary of State for confirmation he shall, subject to paragraph (2) below, cause a local inquiry to be held.

(2) The Secretary of State may, if satisfied that in the circumstances of the case the holding of an inquiry under this Regulation is unnecessary, dispense with such an inquiry.

7. Notice of Inquiry   (1) A date, time and place for the holding of the inquiry shall be fixed and may be varied by the Secretary of State, who shall give not less than 42 days notice in writing of the date, time and place to every objector.
Provided that—
(a) with the consent in writing of the objectors the Secretary of State may give such lesser period of notice as may be agreed with them;
(b) where it becomes necessary or advisable to vary the time or place fixed for the inquiry, the Secretary of State shall give such notice of the variation as may appear to him to be reasonable in the circumstances.
(2) The authority shall—
(a) not later than 21 days before the date of the inquiry, display a copy of the notice of the inquiry in a conspicuous place near to the footpath to which the order relates and also in one or more places where public notices are usually displayed in the locality concerned; and
(b) if the Secretary of State so directs, publish in one or more newspapers circulating in the locality in which the footpath to which the order relates is situated such notices of the inquiry as he may specify.

8. Appointment of Inspectors etc   The Secretary of State may, if he thinks fit, by notice served on the objectors or by the notice announcing the holding of the inquiry, direct that a decision as to whether the order the subject matter of the inquiry should be confirmed and, if so, as to the modifications (if any) subject to which it should be confirmed, may be made by the appointed person instead of by the Secretary of State; and a decision made by the appointed person shall be treated as a decision of the Secretary of State.

9. Considerations of Objections at the Inquiry   (1) Any person interested in the subject matter of a local inquiry may appear at the inquiry either in person or by counsel, solicitor or other representative.
(2) Any person so interested may, whether or not he proposes to appear at the inquiry, send to the appointed person at the address given in the notice referred to in Regulation 4 of these Regulations such written representations as he may wish to make in relation to the subject matter of the inquiry with a view to their consideration by the appointed person at the inquiry.
(3) The appointed person may—
(a) refuse to hear any person, or to consider any objection or representation made by any person, if he is satisfied that the views of that person or the objection or representation are frivolous, and
(b) refuse to hear any person if he is satisfied that the views of that person have already been adequately stated by some other person at the inquiry.

10. Notice of final decision on Orders   (1) As soon as practicable after—
(a) receiving notice of a decision of the Secretary of State to confirm an order in pursuance of his powers under section 3 (3) (a) of the Act, or
(b) a decision to confirm an order is made by the authority in pursuance of its powers under section 3 (3) (b) of the Act,
the authority shall give notice—
(i) describing the general effect of the order as confirmed and stating that it has been confirmed (with or without modification) and the date on which it took effect; and
(ii) naming a place in the locality in which the footpath to which the order relates is situated where a copy of the order as confirmed may be inspected free of charge at all reasonable hours.
(2) A notice under paragraph (1) above shall be given—
(a) by publication in the manner required by Regulation 4 (a) of these Regulations,
(b) by causing a copy of such notice to be displayed in the like manner as the notices required to be displayed under Regulation 4(b) of those Regulations, and

(c) in any case where the order was subject to a local inquiry, by sending a copy to all persons who, having appeared at the inquiry or having submitted written representations in accordance with Regulation 9 (2) of these Regulations, asked to be notified of the decision.

THE BUILDERS' SKIPS (MARKINGS) REGULATIONS 1984
SI 1984/1933

NOTES
Authority These regulations were made on 11 December 1984 by the Secretary of State for Transport and the Secretary of State for Wales under the Highways Act 1980, s 139(4), as amended by the Transport Act 1982, s 65, Halsbury's Statutes, 4th edn Vol 20, title Highways, Streets and Bridges (3rd edn Vol 50 (1), p 608), and all other enabling powers.
Commencement 21 January 1985.
General These regulations require that on and after 1 January 1986 each end of every builders' skip any part of which is placed on any part of a highway except a footway or a verge must be marked with a marking which complies with the specifications about design set out in the diagrams and notes in Sch 1 to the regulations, and the requirements specified in Sch 2. The whole of every marking with which a builders' skip is required by these regulations to be marked must be clean and efficient and clearly visible for a reasonable distance to persons using the highway on which the skip is placed; however, the requirement as to visibility does not apply in respect of a marking, or part of a marking, on any door of a builders' skip whilst that door is required to be open for the purpose of loading or unloading the skip.
Penalties Failure to secure that a skip is marked in accordance with these regulations renders the owner liable to a fine not exceeding the current amount at level 3 on the standard scale; see the Highways Act 1980, s 139(4) as amended, Halsbury's Statutes, 4th edn Vol 20, title Highways, Streets and Bridges (3rd edn Vol 50 (1), p 608). As to a defence, see the 1980 Act, s 139 (6), (7), *ibid*.

THE CROSS-BOUNDARY BRIDGES (APPOINTED DAYS) ORDER 1985
SI 1985/1177

NOTES
Authority This order was made on 28 July 1985 by the Secretary of State for Transport under the Local Government Act 1985, Sch 4, para 54 (1) and (2), Halsbury's Statutes, 4th edn Vol 25, title Local Government, and all other enabling powers.
Commencement 29 August 1985.
General This order appointed 1 October 1985 as, for the purposes of the Local Government Act 1985, Sch 4, para 54 (1), the day before which the councils of districts in the metropolitan counties of Greater Manchester, Merseyside, Tyne and Wear, West Midlands, South Yorkshire and West Yorkshire were to agree which of them was to be the highway authority for a highway for which the Secretary of State was not the highway authority and which was carried by a bridge, part of which was situated in one district and part in another district of the same metropolitan county. The order also appointed 1 October 1985 as, for the purposes of para 54(2) of that Schedule, the day before which the councils of the London boroughs concerned were to agree which of them was to be the highway authority for a highway which immediately before the abolition date (1 April 1986) was a metropolitan road and did not on that date become a trunk road by virtue of an order under para 53 (2) of that Schedule, and which was carried by a bridge, part of which was situated in one borough and part in another.

THE REMOVAL, STORAGE AND DISPOSAL OF VEHICLES (CHARGES)
REGULATIONS 1985
SI 1985/1661

NOTES
Authority These regulations were made on 30 October 1985 by the Home Secretary under the Refuse Disposal (Amenity) Act 1978, ss 4 (5) and (6) and 5 (1), Halsbury's Statutes, 4th edn Vol 35, title Public Health (3rd edn Vol 48, pp 1206, 1207), and the Road Traffic Regulation Act 1984, ss 101 (4) and (5) and 102 (2), *ibid*, 4th edn Vol 38, title Road Traffic (3rd edn Vol 54 (2), pp 1609, 1610) and, in respect of those charges prescribed under the 1984 Act, after consultation with representative organisations.
Commencement 1 December 1985; see reg 1 (1).
General These regulations, which revoke and replace Part IV of the Removal and Disposal of Vehicles Regulations 1968, SI 1968/43, and the amending SI 1974/1809, 1975/1894, 1977/354, 1978/1346, 1980/169, 1981/989 and 1982/1682, and Part IV of the Removal and Disposal of Vehicles (Loading Areas) Regulations 1978, SI 1978/1345, and the amending SI 1981/990 and 1982/1696, prescribe new charges for the removal, storage and disposal of vehicles by the police and local authorities. As to the removal and disposal of vehicles, see further SI 1986/183 and 184, pp 128, 137, *post*.

1.   (1) These Regulations may be cited as the Removal, Storage and Disposal of Vehicles (Charges) Regulations 1985 and shall come into operation on 1st December 1985.

(2) The Regulations specified in Schedule 1 to these Regulations are hereby revoked.

NOTES
For the regulations revoked by these regulations, see the head "General", p 126, *ante*.

2.   (1) The prescribed charges for the purposes of sections 4 (5) and (6) and 5 (1) of the Refuse Disposal (Amenity) Act 1978 and sections 101 (4) and (5) and 102(2) of the Road Traffic Regulation Act 1984 described in column 1 of Schedule 2 to these Regulations shall be of the amounts specified in column 3 of that Schedule instead of the amounts specified in column 2 thereof.

(2) For the purposes of calculating the storage charge prescribed in Schedule 2 to these Regulations each period of 24 hours referred to in column 3 thereof shall be reckoned from noon on the first day after removal during which the place at which the vehicle is stored is open for the claiming of vehicles before noon.

SCHEDULE 1   Regulation 1 (2)
REVOCATIONS

NOTES
This schedule lists the regulations revoked by these regulations, as to which, see the head "General", p 126, *ante*.

SCHEDULE 2   Regulation 2
PRESCRIBED CHARGES FOR REMOVAL, STORAGE AND DISPOSAL OF VEHICLES

Charges for removal, storage or disposal of vehicles	Existing prescribed charge	New prescribed charge
1. Removal from a place on a motorway.	£47	£59
2. Removal from a place not on a motorway but within the City of London or the Metropolitan Police District (except removal by a local authority from a place which is in the area of the council of a district which lies partly within and partly outside the Metropolitan Police District).	£45	£57
3. Removal from a place not on a motorway and not covered by item 2 above.	£43	£55
4. Removal from any part of a loading area in the City of London or the Metropolitan Police District (not being, in the case of a vehicle which is removed by a local authority, a place which is in the area of the council of a district which lies partly within and partly outside the Metropolitan Police District).	£45	£57
5. Removal from any part of a loading area not covered by item 4 above.	£43	£55
6. Storage.	£4 for each period of 24 hours or a part thereof during which the vehicle is in the custody of the authority	£5 for each period of 24 hours or a part thereof during which the vehicle is in the custody of the authority
7. Disposal.	£12	£12

THE CONTROL OF PARKING IN GOODS VEHICLE LOADING AREAS ORDERS (PROCEDURE) (ENGLAND AND WALES) REGULATIONS 1986
SI 1986/181

NOTES
Authority   These regulations were made on 4 February 1986 by the Secretary of State for Transport and the Secretary of State for Wales under the Road Traffic Regulation Act 1984, s 124 and Sch 9, Pt III, Halsbury's Statutes, 4th edn Vol 38, title Road Traffic (3rd edn Vol 54 (2), pp 1630, 1675), and all other enabling powers, after consultation with representative organisations.
Commencement   1 April 1986.
General   These regulations, which revoke and replace the Control of Parking in Goods Vehicle Loading Areas Orders (Procedure) Regulations 1978, SI 1978/1347, lay down the procedure to be followed by the county or metropolitan district council, the council of a London borough or the Common Council of the City of London in connection with the making by them of orders ("control orders") under the Road Traffic Regulation Act 1984, s 61 (1), Halsbury's Statutes, 4th edn Vol 38, title Road Traffic (3rd edn Vol 54 (2), p 1575), for controlling the parking of vehicles in areas used for loading or unloading goods vehicles. Part I of the regulations contains general provisions concerning, *inter alia*, the interpretation and application of the regulations. Part II prescribes the procedure before a control order is made; it provides for preliminary consultation with the local authority (reg 4), publication of proposals (reg 5), objections to the order (reg 6), public inquiries (regs 7-9), the consideration of objections and of the report of any inquiry (reg 10) and the making of modifications to the proposals (reg 11). Part III (regs 12, 13) deals with the form of the order and its operative date or dates. Part IV (regs 14, 15) contains provisions with respect to the making of the order, the publication of notice of its making and the erection of traffic signs to convey information as to the effect of the order. Schedules 1 to 3 to the regulations specify the requirements as to the particulars to be included in the notices relating to the orders, as to the display of notices in or near to the loading areas and as to the documents to be made available for inspection.

THE REMOVAL AND DISPOSAL OF VEHICLES REGULATIONS 1986
SI 1986/183

NOTES
Authority   These regulations were made on 4 February 1986 by the Secretary of State for Transport and the Secretaries of State for Scotland and Wales under the Refuse Disposal (Amenity) Act 1978, ss 3 and 4, Halsbury's Statutes, 4th edn Vol 35, title Public Health (3rd edn Vol 48, pp 1203, 1205), as amended by the Local Government, Planning and Land Act 1980, Sch 3, paras 14 and 15, and the Road Traffic Regulation Act 1984, ss 99 and 101, *ibid*, 4th edn Vol 38, title Road Traffic (3rd edn Vol 54 (2), pp 1605, 1608), and all other enabling powers, after consultation with representative organisations.
Commencement   1 April 1986; see reg 1 (1).
Interpretation   See regs 2 and 11. In connection with the expression "constable", note the provisions of the Police Act 1964, s 19, Halsbury's Statutes, 4th edn Vol 33, title Police (3rd edn Vol 25, p 343), conferring jurisdiction on special constables as well as members of police forces.
General   These regulations revoke the Removal and Disposal of Vehicles Regulations 1968, SI 1968/43. Part IV of SI 1968/43, as amended, had already been revoked and replaced by the Removal, Storage and Disposal of Vehicles (Charges) Regulations 1985, SI 1985/1661, p 126, *ante*, and the remainder of that instrument is now replaced by the present regulations, which make provision for the removal and disposal of vehicles under the Refuse Disposal (Amenity) Act 1978, ss 3 and 4, and the Road Traffic Regulation Act 1984, ss 99 and 101.

For regulations relating to the removal and disposal of vehicles illegally parked in areas used for loading and unloading goods vehicles, see the Removal and Disposal of Vehicles (Loading Areas) Regulations 1986, SI 1986/184, p 137, *post*; and as to charges for the removal, storage and disposal of vehicles, see SI 1985/1661 referred to above.

A stationary vehicle on a highway may constitute an actionable nuisance (see, *eg, Ware v Garston Haulage Co Ltd,* [1943] 2 All ER 558; [1944] 1 KB 30 (CA)), but if something has happened which causes a vehicle to become an obstruction but is not the driver's fault, a nuisance is not created unless the obstruction is allowed unreasonably to continue (*Maitland v Raisbeck & Hewitt (R T & J), Ltd,* [1944] 2 All ER 272; [1944] 1 KB 689 (CA)).

PART I
GENERAL

1. Commencement, citation and revocation   (1) These Regulations shall come into operation on 1st April 1986 and may be cited as the Removal and Disposal of Vehicles Regulations 1986.

(2) The Removal and Disposal of Vehicles Regulations 1968 are hereby revoked.

NOTES
Removal and Disposal of Vehicles Regulations 1968 SI 1968/43.

2. Interpretation   In these Regulations, unless the contrary intention appears, the following expressions have the meanings hereby assigned to them respectively, that is to say:—

"the 1978 Act" means the Refuse Disposal (Amenity) Act 1978;

"the 1984 Act" means the Road Traffic Regulation Act 1984;

"motor vehicle" has the meaning assigned to it in section 11(1) of the 1978 Act;

"road", in England and Wales, means any highway and any other road to which the public has access and, in Scotland, has the meaning assigned to it in section 151 of the Roads (Scotland) Act 1984;

"vehicle", in relation to any matter prescribed by these Regulations for the purposes of any provision in sections 3 and 4 of the 1978 Act, means a motor vehicle, and in relation to any matter prescribed by these Regulations for the purposes of any provision in sections 99 and 101 of the 1984 Act has the meaning assigned to it in section 99 (5) of that Act, and, in relation to any matter prescribed by these Regulations for the purposes of section 99 of the 1984 Act, any reference to a vehicle which has been permitted to remain at rest or which has broken down includes a reference to a vehicle which has been permitted to remain at rest or which has broken down before the coming into force of these Regulations.

NOTES
Refuse Disposal (Amenity) Act 1978   Halsbury's Statutes, 4th edn Vol 35, title Public Health (3rd edn Vol 48, p 1200 *et seq*); for ss 3 and 4 see 3rd edn Vol 48, pp 1203, 1205.
Road Traffic Regulation Act 1984   *Ibid*, 4th edn Vol 38, title Road Traffic (3rd edn Vol 54(2), p 1509 *et seq*); for ss 99 and 101, see 3rd edn Vol 54 (2), pp 1605, 1608.
Roads (Scotland) Act 1984   1984 c 54.

PART II
REMOVAL OF VEHICLES

3. Power of constable to require removal of vehicles from roads   (1) Except as provided by regulation 7 of these Regulations, this regulation applies to a vehicle which—

(a) has broken down, or been permitted to remain at rest, on a road in such a position or in such condition or in such circumstances as to cause obstruction to persons using the road or as to be likely to cause danger to such persons, or

(b) has been permitted to remain at rest or has broken down and remained at rest on a road in contravention of a prohibition or restriction contained in, or having effect under, any of the enactments mentioned in Schedule 1 to these Regulations.

(2) A constable may require the owner, driver or other person in control or in charge of any vehicle to which this regulation applies to move or cause to be moved the vehicle and any such requirement may include a requirement that the vehicle shall be moved from that road to a place which is not on that or any other road, or that the vehicle shall not be moved to any such road or to any such position on a road as may be specified.

(3) A person required to move or cause to be moved a vehicle under this regulations shall comply with such requirement as soon as practicable.

4. Power of constable to remove vehicles   Except as provided by regulation 7 of these Regulations, where a vehicle—

(a) is a vehicle to which regulation 3 of these Regulations applies, or

(b) having broken down on a road or on any land in the open air, appears to a constable to have been abandoned without lawful authority, or

(c) has been permitted to remain at rest on a road or on any land in the open air in such a position or in such condition or in such circumstances as to appear to a constable to have been abandoned without lawful authority,

then, subject to the provisions of sections 99 and 100 of the 1984 Act, a constable may remove or arrange for the removal of the vehicle, and, in the case of a vehicle which is on a road, he may remove it or arrange for its removal from that road to a place which is not on that or any other road, or may move it or arrange for its removal to another position on that or another road.

NOTES
Sections 99 and 100 of the 1984 Act   *Ie*, the Road Traffic Regulation Act 1984, Halsbury's Statutes, Vol 38, title Road Traffic (3rd edn Vol 54 (2), pp 1605, 1607).
Arrange for the removal of the vehicle   In exercising this power, a police constable is under a duty to use reasonable care in the choice of an independent contractor to do the work, but, provided he does so, he is not then vicariously liable for any negligence of the contractor in carrying out the removal, save in those circumstances where a private person would be liable for the acts of an independent contractor; see *Rivers v Cutting* [1982] 3 All ER 69 (CA).

5. Power of local authority to remove certain vehicles   (1) Except as provided by regulation 7 of these Regulations, where a vehicle (other than a motor vehicle which a local authority have a duty to remove under section 3 of the 1978 Act)—
    (*a*) having broken down on a road or on any land in the open air in the area of a local authority, appears to them to have been abandoned without lawful authority, or
    (*b*) has been permitted to remain at rest on a road or on any land in the open air in the area of a local authority in such a position or in such condition or in such circumstances as to appear to them to have been abandoned without lawful authority,
the local authority may, subject to the provisions of sections 99 and 100 of the 1984 Act, remove or arrange for the removal of the vehicle to a place which is not on any road.
    (2) In this regulation "local authority" means, in the case of a vehicle situate at a place—
    (*a*) in England, the council of the district or of the London borough, or the Common Council of the City of London;
    (*b*) in Scotland, the regional or islands or district council; or
    (*c*) in Wales, the council of the district.
within whose area is situate that place.

NOTES
Section 3 of the 1978 Act   *Ie*, the Refuse Disposal (Amenity) Act 1978; see the note to reg 2.
Sections 99 and 100 of the 1984 Act   See the note to reg 4.

6. Method of removing vehicles   Any person removing or moving a vehicle under the last two preceding regulations may do so by towing or driving the vehicle or in such other manner as he may think necessary and may take such measures in relation to the vehicle as he may think necessary to enable him to remove or move it as aforesaid.

7. Exception for Severn Bridge   Regulations 3, 4 and 5 of these Regulations shall not apply in relation to any vehicle while on the central section of the specified carriageways (as defined in section 1 of the Severn Bridge Tolls Act 1965) of a road which crosses the Rivers Severn and Wye.

NOTES
Severn Bridge Tolls Act 1965   1965 c 24.

8. Manner of giving notice to occupier of land before removing a vehicle therefrom   For the purpose of section 99 (3) of the 1984 Act, the manner in which the authority shall give notice to a person who appears to them to be an occupier of land on which there is a vehicle which the authority propose to remove, shall be as follows:—
    (1) the notice shall be given in the form set out in Schedule 2 thereto or a form substantially to the like effect;
    (2) the notice shall be addressed to the person who appears to be the occupier by name or by the description of the "the occupier" of the land (describing it);

(3) the notice shall be given—
 (a) by delivering it to the person who appears to be the occupier;
 (b) by leaving it at his usual or last known place of abode;
 (c) by sending it in a prepaid registered letter, or by the recorded delivery service, and addressed to him at his usual or last known place of abode;
 (d) if the person who appears to be the occupier is an incorporated company or body, by delivering it to the secretary or clerk of the company or body at their registered or principal office, or sending it in a prepaid registered letter, or by the recorded delivery service, addressed to the secretary or clerk of the company or body at that office; or
 (e) by sending it, marked clearly and legibly upon the notice and upon the envelope containing it with the words "Important — This Communication affects your property", to the land in a prepaid registered letter or by the recorded delivery service (providing the notice is not returned to the authority sending it), or be delivering it, so marked, to some person on the land, or by affixing it, so marked, to some object on the land.

NOTES
Section 99 (3) of the 1984 Act   *Ie*, the Road Traffic Regulation Act 1984; see the note to reg 4.

9. Manner and period during which occupier of land may object   (1) For the purpose of section 99(3) of the 1984 Act—
 (a) the manner in which a person who appears to an authority to be an occupier of land on which there is a vehicle which the authority propose to remove may object to a proposal by the authority to remove the vehicle shall be as follows:—
  (i) the objection shall be in writing;
  (ii) the objection shall be sent by post addressed to the authority or left at their office.
 (b) the period during which a person who appears to an authority to be an occupier of land on which there is a vehicle which the authority propose to remove may object shall be 15 days from the day when the notice referred to in the last preceding regulation is served on him.
 (2) For the purpose of section 3 (2) of the 1978 Act the period during which a person who appears to an authority to be an occupier of land on which there is a vehicle which the authority propose to remove may object shall be 15 days from the day when the notice mentioned in that section is given to him.

NOTES
Section 99 (3) of the 1984 Act   See the note to reg 4.
Section 3 (2) of the 1978 Act   See the note to reg 2.

10. Period before which notice must be affixed to a vehicle in certain cases before removing it for destruction   For the purposes of section 3 (5) of the 1978 Act and section 99 (4) of the 1984 Act, the period before the commencement of which a notice must be caused to be affixed to a vehicle by an authority who propose to remove it, before they remove it, being a vehicle which in the opinion of the authority is in such a condition that it ought to be destroyed, shall be seven days.

NOTES
Section 3 (5) of the 1978 Act   See the note to reg 2.
Section 99 (4) of the 1984 Act   See the note to reg 4.

PART III
DISPOSAL OF ABANDONED VEHICLES

11. Interpretation of Part III   In this Part of these Regulations, unless the contrary intention appears, the following expressions have the meaning hereby assigned to them respectively, that is to say—

"description of the place of abandonment", in relation to a vehicle, means a description of the place at which that vehicle appears or appeared to be abandoned which will be sufficient to enable that placed to be identified after the vehicle has been removed therefrom;

"H.P. Information Ltd", means Hire Purchase Information Limited, being a company incorporated under the Companies Act 1948;

"owner", in relation to a vehicle which is the subject of a hiring agreement or hire purchase agreement, includes the person entitled to possession of the vehicle under the agreement;

"G.B. registration mark" means a registration mark issued in relation to a vehicle under the Vehicles (Excise) Act 1971;

"specified information", in relation to a vehicle, means such of the following information as can be or could have been ascertained from an inspection of the vehicle, or has been ascertained from any other source, that is to say—

(*a*) in the case of a vehicle which carried a G.B. registration mark, or a mark indicating registration in a country outside Great Britain, particulars of such mark; and

(*b*) the make of the vehicle.

NOTES
Companies Act 1948   Repealed by the Companies (Consequential Provisions) Act 1985, s 29, Sch 1, Halsbury's Statutes, 4th edn Vol 8, title Companies, and consolidated in the Companies Act 1985, *ibid*.
Vehicles (Excise) Act 1971   *Ibid*, 4th edn Vol 13, title Customs and Excise.

12. Steps to be taken to find the owners of certain vehicles   (1) for the purposes of section 4 (1) (*c*) of the 1978 Act and section 101 (3) (*c*) of the 1984 Act, the steps to be taken by an authority to find a person appearing to them to be the owner of the vehicle in a case to which either of those paragraphs applies shall be such of the following steps as are applicable to the vehicle:—

(*a*) if the vehicle carried a G.B. registration mark—

    (i) the authority shall ascertain from the records maintained by the Secretary of State in connection with any functions exercisable by him by virtue of the Vehicles (Excise) Act 1971 the name and address of the person by whom the vehicle is kept and used;

    (ii) the authority shall, where they have found the name and address of a person who may be the owner of the vehicle from the records maintained by the Secretary of State as aforesaid, send a notice to that person in the manner prescribed by the next following regulation giving the specified information, stating whether the vehicle has been removed from the place at which it appeared to have been abandoned, and if so to what place, stating that if he is the owner of the vehicle they require him to remove the vehicle from their custody on or before a specified date, being the date when the relevant period prescribed by regulation 14 of these Regulations will expire, and stating that unless it is removed by him on or before that date they intend to dispose of it; and

    (iii) the authority shall give the specified information and a description of the place of abandonment to the chief officer of the police force in whose area is the place at which the vehicle appeared to have been abandoned (unless the authority is that officer) and the specified information to H.P. Information Ltd, and shall enquire of each person to whom the information is given whether that person can make any enquiries to find the owner of the vehicle;

(*b*) if the vehicle does not carry a G.B. registration mark but carries a mark indicating registration in Northern Ireland the authority shall give the specified information and a description of the place of abandonment to the chief officer of the police force in whose area is the place at which the vehicle appeared to have been abandoned (unless the authority is that officer) and to the Secretary of State for Transport and the specified information to H.P. Information Ltd, and shall enquire of each person to whom the information is given whether that person can make any enquiries to find the owner of the vehicle;

(c) if the vehicle does not carry a G.B. registration mark but carries a mark indicating registration in the Republic of Ireland, the authority shall give the specified information and a description of the place of abandonment to the Secretary of State for Transport, and to the chief officer of the police force in whose area is the place at which the vehicle appeared to have been abandoned (unless the authority is that officer), and shall enquire of each person to whom the information is given whether that person can make any enquiries to find the owner of the vehicle;

(d) if the vehicle does not carry a G.B. registration mark but carries a mark indicating registration in the Channel Islands, the Isle of Man, or any country not mentioned in the foregoing sub-paragraphs of this paragraph, the authority shall give the specified information and a description of the place of abandonment to the chief officer of the police force in whose area is the place at which the vehicle appeared to have been abandoned (unless the authority is that officer), and the specified information to H.P. Information Ltd, and shall enquire of each person to whom the information is given whether that person can make any enquiries to find the owner of the vehicle;

(e) if the vehicle does not carry a G.B. registration mark or any other registration mark, then—

  (i) if the authority is the chief officer of the police force in whose area is the place at which the vehicle appeared to have been abandoned, that officer shall apply to the local authority in whose area is that place, giving the specified information and enquiring whether that authority has any information as to who is the owner of the vehicle; or

  (ii) if the authority is the local authority in whose area is the place at which the vehicle appeared to have been abandoned, the authority shall apply to the chief officer of the police force in whose area is that place, giving the specified information and enquiring whether that officer has any information as to who is the owner of the vehicle.

    For the purposes of this sub-paragraph "local authority" means—

  (aa) in relation to England, the council of a county, a metropolitan district or a London borough, or the Common Council of the City of London or an authority established under section 10 of the Local Government Act 1985;

  (bb) in relation to Scotland, a regional or islands or district Council; and

  (cc) in relation to Wales, the council of a district.

(2) Nothing in the foregoing provisions of this regulation shall require an authority to take any such step as is therein mentioned if they have found a person who appears to them to be the owner of that vehicle and they have sent him a notice in the manner prescribed by the next following regulation containing the specified information, stating that if he is the owner of that vehicle they require him to remove the vehicle from their custody on or before a specified date, being the date when the relevant period prescribed by regulation 14 of these Regulations will expire, and stating that unless it is removed by him on or before that date they intend to dispose of it.

NOTES
Section 4 (1) (c) of the 1978 Act; section 101 (3) (c) of the 1984 Act See the notes to reg 2.
Vehicles (Excise) Act 1971 See the note to reg 11.
Local Government Act 1985, s 10 Halsbury's Statutes, 4th edn Vol 25, title Local Government.

13. Manner of serving notice on owner requiring removal of vehicle   For the purposes of section 4 (1) (*c*) (ii) of the 1978 Act and section 101 (3) (*c*) (ii) of the 1984 Act, a notice requiring a person who appears to an authority to be the owner of a vehicle to remove the vehicle from their custody shall be served—

(*a*) by delivering it to the person who appears to be the owner;

(*b*) by leaving it at his usual or last known place of abode;

(*c*) by sending it in a prepaid registered letter, or by the recorded delivery service, addressed to him at his usual or last known place of abode; or

(*d*) if the person who appears to be the owner is an incorporated company or body, by delivering it to the secretary or clerk of the company or body at their registered or principal office, or sending it in a prepaid registered letter, or by the recorded delivery service, addressed to the secretary or clerk of the company or body at that office.

NOTES
Section 4 (1) (*c*) (ii) of the 1978 Act; s 101 (3) (*c*) (ii) of the 1984 Act   See the notes to reg 2.

14. Period during which owner may remove vehicle before it can be disposed of   For the purposes of section 4 (1) (*c*) (ii) of the 1978 Act and section 101 (3) (*c*) (ii) of the 1984 Act, the period during which a person on whom the notice referred to in paragraph (1) (*a*) (ii) or (2) of regulation 12 of these Regulations has been served shall be required to remove the vehicle of which he appears to the authority serving the notice to be the owner from their custody shall be, in the case of a first or only notice served by the authority in respect of any vehicle, 21 days from the day when the notice is served on him, and in the case of any subsequent notice served by the authority in respect of that vehicle, 14 days from the day when the notice is served on him.

NOTES
Section 4 (1) (*c*) (ii) of the 1978 Act; s 101 (3) (*c*) (ii) of the 1984 Act   See the notes to reg 2.

15. Information to be given relating to the disposal of a vehicle   (1) For the purpose of section 101 (7) of the 1984 Act, after a vehicle has been disposed of the authority by whom it was disposed of shall give information relating to the disposal of the vehicle—

(*a*) if the vehicle carried a G.B. registration mark, to the Secretary of State for Transport, the chief officer of the police force in whose area is the place at which the vehicle appeared to have been abandoned (unless that officer is that authority), and H.P. Information Ltd;

(*b*) if the vehicle did not carry a G.B. registration mark but carried a mark indicating registration in Northern Ireland, to the chief officer of the police force in whose area is the place at which the vehicle appeared to have been abandoned (unless the authority is that officer), to the Secretary of State for Transport, to the Secretary of State for Northern Ireland, Belfast, Northern Ireland, and to H.P. Information Ltd;

(*c*) if the vehicle did not carry a G.B. registration mark but carried a mark indicating registration in the Republic of Ireland, to the Secretary of State for Transport, to the Commissioners of Customs and Excise, to the chief officer of the police force in whose area is the place at which the vehicle appeared to have been abandoned (unless the authority is that officer), and to H.P. Information Ltd;

(*d*) if the vehicle did not carry a G.B. registration mark but carried a mark indicating registration in the Channel Islands, the Isle of Man or any country not mentioned in the foregoing sub-paragraphs of this paragraph, to the Commissioners of Customs and Excise, and to the chief officer of the police force in whose area is the place at which the vehicle appeared to have been abandoned (unless the authority is that officer);

(*e*) if the vehicle did not carry a G.B. registration mark or any other registration mark, to the chief officer of the police force in whose area is the place at which the vehicle appeared to have been abandoned (unless the authority is that officer) and to the local authority in whose area is that place (unless the authority is that local authority).

For the purposes of this paragraph "local authority" means—

(i) in relation to England, the council of a county, a metropolitan district or a London borough, or the Common Council of the City of London or an authority established under Section 10 of the Local Government Act 1985;

(ii) in relation to Scotland, a regional or islands or district council; and

(iii) in relation to Wales, the council of a district; and

(*f*) in the case of any vehicle, to any person who appears to the authority to have been the owner of the vehicle immediately before it was disposed of.

(2) In this regulation "information relating to the disposal of a vehicle" means—

(*a*) any information which is sufficient to relate the information now being given to any information previously given to the same person in respect of the removal, storage or disposal of the vehicle;

(*b*) such of the specified information as has not been previously given to the same person in respect of the removal, storage or disposal of the vehicle; and

(*c*) information as to whether the vehicle was disposed of by destruction or by sale and if by sale the amount of the proceeds thereof.

NOTES

Section 101 (7) of the 1984 Act   See the note to reg 2.

Local Government Act 1985, s 10   See the note to reg 12.

16. Period during which owner may remove vehicle before it is disposed of   For the purpose of section 4 (5) of the 1978 Act and section 101 (4) of the 1984 Act, the period during which a person who has satisfied an authority that he is the owner of a vehicle which is in their custody shall be permitted to remove it from their custody shall be the period commencing on the day when the authority became satisfied that he was the owner and ending on the expiration of the seventh day after that day, or at the time when the vehicle is disposed of, whichever is the later.

NOTES

Section 4 (5) of the 1978 Act; s 101 (4) of the 1984 Act   See the notes to reg 2.

SCHEDULE 1   Regulation 3

CERTAIN ENACTMENTS BY OR UNDER WHICH ARE IMPOSED PROHIBITIONS OR RESTRICTIONS ON THE WAITING OF VEHICLES ON ROADS

. . .

Section 52 of the Metropolitan Police Act 1839 and section 22 of the local Act of the second and third year of the reign of Queen Victoria, chapter 94 (relating to the prevention of obstruction in streets in London).

Section 21 of the Town Police Clauses Act 1847 (relating to the prevention of obstruction in streets in England and Wales elsewhere than in London).

Section 2 of the Parks Regulation (Amendment) Act 1926 (authorising the making of regulations as to Royal Parks).

Section 22 of the Road Traffic Act 1972 (which makes it an offence to fail to conform to the indications given by certain traffic signs).

Section 1 of the 1984 Act (which authorises the making of orders regulating traffic on roads outside Greater London) . . . .

Section 6 of the 1984 Act (authorising the making of orders regulating traffic on roads in Greater London).

Section 9 of the 1984 Act (authorising the making of experimental traffic orders).

Section 12 of the 1984 Act (relating to experimental traffic schemes in Greater London).

Section 14 of the 1984 Act (which provides for the restriction or prohibition of the use of roads in consequence of the execution of works).

Section 17 of the 1984 Act (authorising the making of regulations with respect to the use of special roads).

Section 25 of the 1984 Act (authorising the making of regulations for crossings for foot passengers).

Sections 35 and 45 to 49 of the 1984 Act (relating to parking places for vehicles).

Section 57 of the 1984 Act (relating to parking places in England and Wales for bicycles and motor cycles).

Sections 66 and 67 of the 1984 Act (which empower the police to place traffic signs relating to local traffic regulations and temporary signs for dealing with traffic congestion and danger).

Any enactment contained in any local Act for the time being in force, and any byelaw having effect under any enactment for the time being in force, being an enactment or byelaw imposing or authorising the imposition of a prohibition or restriction similar to any prohibition or restriction which is or can be imposed by or under any of the above-mentioned enactments.

NOTES

The words omitted where indicated by the insertion of stops apply to Scotland.

Metropolitan Police Act 1839, s 52   Halsbury's Statutes, 4th edn Vol 38, title Road Traffic (3rd edn Vol 28, p 35).

Town Police Clauses Act 1847, s 21   *Ibid*, 4th edn Vol 38, title Road Traffic (3rd edn Vol 28, p 69).

Parks Regulation (Amendment) Act 1926, s 2   *Ibid*, 4th edn Vol 32, title Open Spaces and Historic Buildings (Pt 1) (3rd edn Vol 24, p 41).

Road Traffic Act 1972, s 22   *Ibid*, 4th edn Vol 38, title Road Traffic (3rd edn Vol 42, p 1667).

The 1984 Act   *Ie*, the Road Traffic Regulation Act 1984, *ibid*, 4th edn Vol 38, title Road Traffic (3rd edn Vol 54 (2), p 1509 *et seq*).

SCHEDULE 2   Regulation 8
FORM OF NOTICE TO OCCUPIER OF LAND BEFORE REMOVING ABANDONED VEHICLES

To:

of

The   ....
                    (name of authority)

In pursuance of section 99 (3) of the Road Traffic Regulation Act 1984 the above-named authority hereby give you notice that they propose, in pursuance of the Removal and Disposal of Vehicles Regulations 1986 to remove the vehicle(s) described in column 2 of the Schedule hereto from the land described in column 1 of the Schedule hereto, being land of which you appear to the authority to be the occupier, unless, within 15 days from the day when this notice is served on you, you object in the prescribed manner.

SCHEDULE

Col 1 Description of land where vehicle(s) is/are situated	Col 2 Description of vehicles(s) which appear(s) to have been abandoned on that land:

(Signed)

(Date)

NOTES

1.   This Notice is served under section 99(3) of the Road Traffic Regulation Act 1984. That section applies to "vehicles". A "vehicle" is defined in section 99 (5) of that Act as meaning any vehicle, whether or not it is in a fit state for use on roads, and as including any chassis or body, with or without wheels, appearing to have formed part of such a vehicle, and any load carried by and anything attached to such a vehicle.

2.   Under section 99 (3) of the Road Traffic Regulation Act 1984 an authority are not entitled to remove an abandoned vehicle from occupied land if the occupier objects to the proposal in the prescribed manner and within the prescribed period. The manner and period are prescribed by regulation 9 of the Removal and Disposal of Vehicles Regulations 1986. That regulation requires an objection to be in writing and to be sent by post or addressed to the authority or left at their office; it prescribes 15 days from the day when the authority's notice is served as the period during which the occupier can object.

THE REMOVAL AND DISPOSAL OF VEHICLES (LOADING AREAS) REGULATIONS 1986
SI 1986/184

NOTES
Authority These regulations were made on 4 February 1986 by the Secretary of State for Transport and the Secretary of State for Wales under the Road Traffic Regulation Act 1984, s 103, Halsbury's Statutes, 4th edn Vol 38, title Road Traffic (3rd edn Vol 54 (2), p 1612), and all other enabling powers, and after the required consultation.
Commencement 1 April 1986; see reg 1 (1).
Interpretation See reg 2.
General These regulations revoke the Removal and Disposal of Vehicles (Loading Areas) Regulations 1978, SI 1978/1345. Part IV of SI 1978/1345, as amended, had already been revoked and replaced by the Removal, Storage and Disposal of Vehicles (Charges) Regulations 1985, SI 1985/1661, p 126, *ante*, and the remainder of that instrument is now replaced by the present regulations, which make provision for the removal and disposal of vehicles under the Road Traffic Regulation Act 1984, ss 99 to 102, Halsbury's Statutes, 4th edn Vol 38, title Road Traffic (3rd edn Vol 54 (2), pp 1605-1611) as those sections have been applied by s 103 of that Act in relation to vehicles in any part of a loading area while the parking of such vehicles on that part is prohibited (see SI 1978/889, p 114, *ante*).
For regulations relating to the removal and disposal of vehicles generally, see the Removal and Disposal of Vehicles Regulations 1986, SI 1986/183, p 128, *ante*; and as to charges for the removal, storage and disposal of vehicles, see SI 1985/1661, p 126, *ante*.

PART I
GENERAL

1. Citation, commencement and revocation   (1) These Regulations may be cited as the Removal and Disposal of Vehicles (Loading Areas) Regulations 1986, and shall come into operation on 1st April 1986.
(2) The Removal and Disposal of Vehicles (Loading Areas) Regulations 1978 are hereby revoked.

NOTES
Removal and Disposal of Vehicles (Loading Areas) Regulations 1978   SI 1978/1345.

2. Interpretation   In these Regulations—
"the 1984 Act" means the Road Traffic Regulation Act 1984;
"loading area" has the same meaning as in section 61 of the 1984 Act;
"vehicle" has the same meaning as in section 99 of the 1984 Act.

NOTES
Road Traffic Regulation Act 1984   Halsbury's Statutes, 4th edn Vol 38, title Road Traffic (3rd edn Vol 54 (2), p 1509 *et seq*; for ss 61 and 99, see pp 1575, 1605).

PART II
REMOVAL OF VEHICLES

3. Power to require the removal of vehicles from loading areas   (1) This regulation applies to a vehicle which is in any part of a loading area while the parking of it in that part is prohibited by virtue of section 61 of the 1984 Act.
(2) Subject to paragraph (3) below, an officer of the local authority, duly authorised in writing by that authority, may require the owner, driver or other person in control or in charge of any vehicle to which this regulation applies to move it or cause it to be removed, and any such requirement may include a requirement that the vehicle shall be moved from the part of the loading area where it is to some other part of that loading area, or to a place on a highway, or to some other place which is not on a highway (being a place where the vehicle can be lawfully parked).
(3) When making any requirement under paragraph (2) above an officer of the local authority, if requested so to do by the owner, driver or other person in control or in charge of the vehicle, shall produce evidence of his authorisation.
(4) In this regulation and in regulation 4 below "the local authority" means—
(*a*) in Greater London, the Council of the London borough or, as the case may be, the Common Council of the City,

(b) elsewhere in England, or in Wales, the council of the district in whose area is situated the part of the loading area where the vehicle in question is while parking is prohibited as mentioned in paragraph (1) above.

NOTES
Section 61 of the 1984 Act See the note to reg 2.

4. Power to remove vehicles (1) Where, in the case of a vehicle to which regulation 3 above applies—
(a) the owner, driver or other person in control or in charge of the vehicle refuses or fails to comply with a requirement, made under that regulation by a duly authorised officer of the local authority, to move it or cause it to be moved, or
(b) no person who is in control or in charge of the vehicle and who is capable of moving it or causing it to be moved is present on or in the vicinity of the vehicle,
an officer of the local authority (who need not be the officer who has made any requirement as respects the vehicle under regulation 3 above) may move or arrange for the removal of the vehicle to another part of the loading area, or may remove it or arrange for its removal from the loading area to some other place which is not on a highway.
(2) Any person removing or moving a vehicle under this regulation may do so by towing or driving the vehicle or in such other manner as he may think necessary, and may take such measures in relation to the vehicle as he may think necessary to enable him to remove or move it as aforesaid.

PART III
DISPOSAL OF ABANDONED VEHICLES

5. Disposal of abandoned vehicles The provisions of Part III of the Removal and Disposal of Vehicles Regulations 1986 (Disposal of abandoned vehicles) shall apply in relation to a vehicle which has been removed from a loading area under Part II of these Regulations and which appears to an authority to have been abandoned as they apply in relation to a vehicle which has been removed under Part II of those Regulations.

NOTES
Removal and Disposal of Vehicles Regulations 1986 SI 1986/183, p 128, *ante*.

Hire Purchase

See the title Sale of Goods and Hire-Purchase

Hospitals

See, generally, the title, National Health Service

Medical and supplementary professions	Medicine (Part 1)
Mental nursing homes	Persons Mentally Disordered
Midwives	Medicine (Parts 4 & 5)
Nurses	Medicine (Part 4)
Nursing and residential homes	Public Health (Part 2)
Voluntary hospitals	Medicine (Part 6)

Housing

CHRONOLOGICAL LIST OF INSTRUMENTS

SR & O	Description	Remarks	Page
1925/866	Housing Consolidated Regulations 1925	See Preliminary Note "Loans for acquisition or improvement of housing", p 146, *post*	—
1937/79	Housing Act (Extinguishment of Public Right of Way) Regulations 1937	—	149
1937/80	Housing Act (Overcrowding and Miscellaneous Forms) Regulations 1937	—	150
1939/563	Housing Act (Form of Charging Order) Regulations 1939	—	152
SI			
1962/668	Housing (Management of Houses in Multiple Occupation) Regulations 1962	—	152
1972/228	Housing (Prescribed Forms) Regulations 1972	—	160
1972/1792	Housing (Payments for Well Maintained Houses) Order 1972	—	162
1973/753	Housing (Payments for Well Maintained Houses) Order 1973	—	163
1974/618	Slum Clearance Subsidy Regulations 1974	—	163
1974/1406	Housing Act 1974 (Commencement No 1) Order 1974	—	163
1974/1511	Housing (Prescribed Forms) (Amendment etc) Regulations 1974	Amend 1972/228 (*qv*)	—
1974/1562	Housing Act 1974 (Commencement No 2) Order 1974		
1974/1791	Housing Act 1974 (Commencement No 3) Order 1974	See note "Other commencement orders" to 1974/1406, p 164, *post*	—
1975/374	Housing Act 1974 (Commencement No 4) Order 1975		
1975/500	Housing (Prescribed Forms) (Amendment) Regulations 1975	Amend 1972/228 (*qv*)	—
1975/1108	Slum Clearance (Retention of Buildings) (Compensation Notice) Order 1975	—	164
1975/1113	Housing Act 1974 (Commencement No 5) Order 1975	See note "Other commencement orders" to 1974/1406, p 164, *post*	—
1977/1213	Improvement Grant (Rateable Value Limits) Order 1977	—	164
1977/1821	Housing (Homeless Persons) (Property and Staff) Order 1977	—	164
1978/69	Housing (Homeless Persons) (Appropriate Arrangements) Order 1978	—	165
1978/661	Housing (Homeless Persons) (Appropriate Arrangements) (No 2) Order 1978	See note "Application of order" to 1978/69, p 165, *post*	—
1978/1785	Home Purchase Assistance (Recognised Savings Institutions) Order 1978	—	165
1979/1214	Housing Act 1974 (Commencement No 6) Order 1979	See note "Other commencement orders" to 1974/1406, p 164, *post*	—
1980/1342	Housing (Right to Buy) (Maximum Discount) Order 1980	—	165
1980/1345	Housing (Right to Buy) (Designated Regions) Order 1980	—	166
1980/1375	Housing (Right to Buy) (Designated Rural Areas and Designated Regions) (Wales) Order 1980	See note "Further orders" to 1980/1345, p 166, *post*	—

SI	Description	Remarks	Page
1980/1390	Housing (Right to Buy) (Mortgage Costs) Order 1980	—	166
1980/1406	Housing Act 1980 (Commencement No 1) Order 1980	—	167
1980/1423	Housing (Right to Buy) (Mortgage Limit) Regulations 1980	—	167
1980/1465	Housing (Right to Buy) (Prescribed Forms) (No 2) Regulations 1980	—	170
1980/1466	Housing Act 1980 (Commencement No 2) Order 1980		
1980/1557	Housing Act 1980 (Commencement No 3) Order 1980	See note "Other comm- encement orders" to 1980/1406, p 167, *post*	—
1980/1693	Housing Act 1980 (Commencement No 4) Order 1980		
1980/1706	Housing Act 1980 (Commencement No 5) Order 1980		
1980/1735	Grants by Local Authorities (Appropriate Percentage and Exchequer Contributions) Order 1980	—	170
1980/1781	Housing Act 1980 (Commencement No 6) Order 1980	See note "Other comm- encement orders" to 1980/1406, p 167, *post*	—
1980/1930	Housing (Right to Buy) (Prescribed Forms) (No 2) (Welsh Forms) Regulations 1980	—	172
1981/119	Housing Act 1980 (Commencement No 7) Order 1981	See note "Other comm- encement orders" to 1980/1406, p 167, *post*	—
1981/296	Housing Act 1980 (Commencement No 8) Order 1980		
1981/397	Housing (Right to Buy) (Designated Rural Areas and Designated Regions) (England) Order 1981	See note "Further orders" to 1980/1345, p 166, *post*	—
1981/940	Housing (Right to Buy) (Designated Rural Areas and Designated Regions) (England) (No 2) Order 1981		
1981/1347	Housing (Prescribed Forms) (Amendment) Regulations 1981	Amend 1972/228 (*qv*)	—
1981/1576	Housing (Means of Escape from Fire in Houses in Multiple Occupation) Order 1981	—	172
1981/1712	Grants by Local Authorities (Appropriate Percentage and Exchequer Contributions) (Amendment) Order 1981	Amends 1980/1735 (*qv*)	—
1982/21	Housing (Right to Buy) (Designated Rural Areas and Designated Regions) (England) Order 1982	See note "Further orders" to 1980/1345, p 166, *post*	—
1982/187	Housing (Right to Buy) (Designated Rural Areas and Designated Regions) (England) (No 2) Order 1982		
1982/581	Grants by Local Authorities (Appropriate Percentage and Exchequer Contributions) Order 1982	—	172
1982/828	Registered Housing Associations (Account- ing Requirements) Order 1982	—	173
1982/893	Social Security and Housing Benefits Act 1982 (Commencement No 1) Order 1982	*See title* National Ins- urance (Pt 1)	—
1982/903	Housing Benefits (Subsidy) (No 1) Order 1982	See note "Previous ord- ers" to 1985/440 (*qv*)	—
1982/904	Housing Benefits (Subsidy) (No 2) Order 1982		
1982/905	Housing Benefits (Rate Support Grant) Order 1982	See note "Previous ord- er" to 1984/111 (*qv*)	—
1982/906	Social Security and Housing Benefits Act 1982 (Commencement No 2) Order 1982	—	173
1982/976	Home Purchase Assistance (Recognised Lending Institutions) Order 1982	—	177
1982/1039	Grants by Local Authorities (Grants for Tenants) Order 1982	—	177
1982/1112	Housing (Payments for Well Maintained Houses) Order 1982	—	177
1982/1129	Housing Benefits (Permitted Totals for Local Schemes) Regulations 1982	—	177
1982/1205	Grants by Local Authorities (Repairs) Order 1982	—	178

SI	Description	Remarks	Page
1982/1519	Housing Benefits (Miscellaneous Amendments) Regulations 1982	Amend 1982/1129 (*qv*); revoked by 1985/677 so far as they amended 1982/1124	—
1982/1763	Grants by Local Authorities (Appropriate Percentage and Exchequer Contribution) (No 2) Order 1982	—	180
1982/1895	Grants by Local Authorities (Repairs Grants for Airey Houses) (Eligible Expense Limits) Order 1982	—	180
1983/95	Grants by Local Authorities (Appropriate Percentage and Exchequer Contribution) (Repairs Grants for Airey Houses) Order 1982	—	180
1983/207	Registered Housing Associations (Accounting Requirements for Almshouses) Order 1983	Amends 1982/828 (*qv*)	—
1983/337	Supplementary Benefit (Housing Benefits) (Miscellaneous Consequential Amendments) Regulations 1983	*See title* National Insurance (Pt 4)	—
1983/613	Grants by Local Authorities (Eligible Expense Limits) Order 1983	—	181
1984/110	Housing Benefits (Subsidy) Order 1984	See note "Previous orders" to 1985/440 (*qv*)	—
1984/111	Housing Benefits (Rate Support Grant) Order 1984	—	184
1984/244	Slum Clearance Subsidy (Amendment) Regulations 1984	Amend 1974/618 (*qv*)	—
1984/838	Homes Insulation Grants Order 1984	—	184
1984/1001	Housing Benefits (Subsidy) Amendment Order 1984	Amends 1984/110; see note "Previous orders" to 1985/440 (*qv*)	—
1984/1173	Housing (Right to Buy) (Prescribed Persons) Order 1984	—	184
1984/1174	Housing (Local Authority Contributions towards Mortgage Costs) Order 1984	—	186
1984/1175	Housing (Right to Buy) (Prescribed Forms) Regulations 1984	—	186
1984/1280	Housing (Right to a Shared Ownership Lease) (Repairs Etc Adjustment) Order 1984	—	187
1984/1554	Housing (Right to Buy) (Priority of Charges) Order 1984	—	188
1984/1555	Mortgage Indemnities (Recognised Bodies) Order 1984	—	188
1984/1629	Housing Act 1964 (Appropriate Multiplier) Order 1984	—	188
1984/1700	Grants by Local Authorities (Repairs Grants for Airey Houses) (Eligible Expense Limits) (Variation) Order 1984	Amends 1982/1895 (*qv*)	—
1984/1705	Housing Defects (Expenditure Limit) Order 1984	—	189
1984/1833	Registered Housing Associations (Limited Accounting Requirements) Order 1984	Amends 1982/828 (*qv*)	189
1984/1880	Grants by Local Authorities (Appropriate Percentage and Exchequer Contribution) (Repairs Grants for Airey Houses) (Variation) Order 1984	Amends 1983/95 (*qv*)	—
1985/36	Housing (Right to Buy) (Prescribed Forms) (Welsh Forms) (No 3) Regulations 1985	—	189
1985/440	Housing Benefits (Subsidy) Order 1985	—	190
1985/677	Housing Benefits Regulations 1985	—	190
1985/758	Housing (Right to a Shared Ownership Lease) (Further Advances Limit) Regulations 1985	—	192
1985/937	Home Purchase Assistance (Price-limits) Order 1985	—	194
1985/1100	Housing Benefits (Miscellaneous Amendments) Regulations 1985	Amend 1985/677 (*qv*)	—
1985/1244	Housing Benefits (Increase of Needs Allowances) Regulations 1985		
1985/1445	Housing Benefits Amendment (No 2) Regulations 1985		

SI	Description	Remarks	Page
1985/1978	Mortgage Indemnities (Recognised Bodies) Order 1985	See note "Further order" to 1984/1555 (*qv*)	—
1985/1979	Housing (Right to Buy) (Priority of Charges) Order 1985	See note "Further order" to 1984/1554 (*qv*)	—
1986/84	Housing Benefits Amendment Regulations 1986	Amend 1985/677 (*qv*)	—

INSTRUMENTS NO LONGER IN OPERATION

The following instruments, which were formerly included in this title, are no longer in operation:

SR&O		SI	SI		SI
1925/733	lapsed[1]		1978/1078	superseded by	1979/1014
1925/866[2]			1978/1302	lapsed[8]	
1932/648	spent		1978/1412	,, [1]	
1934/913	,,		1979/234	,, [12]	
Date made			1979/894	,, [5]	
10/10/1941	lapsed[3]		1979/1319	,, [8]	
SI			1979/1586	superseded[14]	
1956/1467	spent[4]		1980/31	lapsed[12]	
1963/779	,,		1980/341	,, [1]	
1967/1225	lapsed[5]		1980/855	superseded[14]	
1967/1268	,, [5]		1980/856	,, [15]	
1967/1365	,, [5]		1980/857	,, [14]	
1967/1399	,, [5]		1980/1062	superseded by	1982/504
1967/1705	,, [5]		1980/1391	revoked by	1984/1175
1967/1943	,, [5]		1980/1555	lapsed[8]	
1968/35	,, [5]		1980/1620	revoked by	1985/36
1968/203	,, [5]		1980/1636	lapsed[5]	
1968/366	,, [5]		1980/1736	superseded by	1983/613
1968/838	,, [5]		1980/1737	revoked by	1982/1205
1969/767	,,		1980/2040	lapsed[5]	
1969/1003	superseded by	1970/1093	1981/253	,, [5]	
1971/467	lapsed[5]		1981/290	,, [1]	
1971/1577	,, [5]		1981/297	,, [8]	
1972/422	,, [1]		1981/331	,, [8]	
1972/953	,, [6]		1981/332	,, [8]	
1972/1193	,, [7]		1981/520	,, [5]	
1972/1203	,, [8]		1981/722	revoked by	1984/1803
1972/1507	,, [5]		1981/723	superseded[16]	
1973/614	,, [8]		1981/781	revoked by	1984/1629
1974/421	,, [8]		1981/979	lapsed[5]	
1974/473	,, [5]		1981/1061	revoked by	1983/82
1974/516	,, [8]		1981/1126	,, ,,	1983/82
1974/594	spent		1981/1150	superseded by	1982/1061
1974/1442	lapsed[9]		1981/1401	lapsed[5]	
1974/1891	,, [7]		1981/1417	,, [8]	
1974/1892	,,		1981/1461	superseded by	1983/613
1975/290	spent		1981/1695	,, ,,	1982/504
1975/314	lapsed[10]		1982/303	lapsed[1]	
1975/909	spent[11]		1982/504	superseded by	1983/285
1975/1114	lapsed[5]		1982/1061	lapsed[8]	
1975/1302	,, [5]		1982/1124	revoked by	1985/677
1975/1303	,, [5]		1982/1317	lapsed[8]	
1975/1441	,, [8]		1982/1520	revoked by	1985/677
1975/1451	,, [5]		1982/1772	superseded by	1982/285
1975/1564	,, [8]		1983/4	revoked by	1984/1718
1975/1565	,, [1]		1983/57	,, ,,	1985/677
1975/2001	,, [7]		1983/82	,, ,,	1983/1646
1975/2110	,, [12]		1983/285	superseded by	1984/838
1976/271	spent[11]		1983/438	revoked by	1985/677
1976/1242	lapsed[8]		1983/664	superseded[17]	
1976/1470	,, [8]		1983/672	lapsed[18]	
1976/1802	,, [12]		1983/912	revoked by	1985/677
1977/1467	,, [8]		1983/1014	,, ,,	1985/677
1977/2066	,, [13]		1983/1239	,, ,,	1984/941
1978/10	,, [5]		1983/1242	,, ,,	1984/1105
1978/34	,, [12]		1983/1646	,, ,,	1984/954
1978/217	,, [8]		1984/103	,, ,,	1985/677

SI		SI	SI			SI
1984/104	revoked by	1985/677	1984/1701	lapsed[1]		
1984/940	,, ,,	1985/677	1984/1718	spent		
1984/941	,, ,,	1985/677	1984/1803	superseded[19]		
1981/954	,, ,,	1985/937	1984/1965	revoked by		1985/677
1984/1105	,, ,,	1985/677	1985/368	,, ,,		1985/677

[1] Lapsed on repeal of enabling powers by the Housing (Consequential Provisions) Act 1985, s 3, Sch 1, Pt I.
[2] Partially revoked by SR & O 1932/648; remainder generally lapsed on repeal of enabling powers by the Housing Act 1969, s 89 (3), Sch 10, the Statute Law (Repeals) Act 1977, and the Housing (Consequential Provisions) Act 1985, s 3, Sch 1, Pt I. Note, however that Pt III of this instrument continues to have effect in relation to the Common Council of the City of London; see the 1985 Act, Sch 4, para 3.
[3] Lapsed on repeal of enabling powers by the Statute Law (Repeals) Act 1981.
[4] Spent on discontinuance of the Housing Equalisation Account by the Housing Finance Act 1972; see Sch 10, para 4.
[5] Lapsed on repeal of enabling powers by the Finance Act 1982, ss 27 (1), 157, Sch 22, Pt V.
[6] Lapsed on repeal of enabling powers by the Housing Act 1974, s 130 (4), Sch 15.
[7] Lapsed on repeal of enabling powers by the Housing (Consequential Provisions) Act 1985, s 3, Sch 1, Pt I (and see Sch 4, para 2(2), (3)).
[8] Lapsed on repeal of enabling powers by the Social Security and Housing Benefits Act 1982, ss 28 (5) (*a*), 48 (6), Sch 5.
[9] Lapsed on repeal of enabling powers by the Social Security and Housing Benefits Act 1982, s 48 (6), Sch 5.
[10] Lapsed on repeal of enabling powers by the Housing Act 1980, ss 77, 152, Sch 10, para 4, Sch 26.
[11] Spent (and enabling powers repealed by the Housing (Consequential Provisions) Act 1985, s 3, Sch 1, Pt I).
[12] Lapsed on repeal of enabling powers by the Housing Act 1980, s 152, Sch 26.
[13] Lapsed on partial repeal of enabling powers by the Housing Act 1980, s 152, Sch 26.
[14] Superseded by the Housing Act 1980 (see ss 109, 120, Sch 13).
[15] Superseded by SI 1980/1736 and the Housing Act 1980, s 107, Sch 12.
[16] Superseded by the Housing Act 1985, s 429 (2).
[17] Superseded by the Housing Associations Act 1985, s 93 (2).
[18] Lapsed on repeal of enabling powers by the Housing and Building Control Act 1984, ss 2 (1), 65, Sch 12, Pt II, subject to a saving in s 2 (4) thereof where the tenant's claim to exercise the right to buy was made before 26/8/84; the said s 2 (4) was subsequently repealed by the Housing (Consequential Provisions) Act 1985, s 3, Sch 1, Pt I but any remaining effect was saved by Sch 4, paras 1 and 2 of that Act.
[19] Superseded by the Housing Associations Act 1985, s 48 (3).

CROSS REFERENCES

Accommodation for persons homeless owing to hostile attack	Civil Defence
Borrowing by local authorities	Local Government (Part 3B); Money, Moneylending and Investments (Parts 4 and 8)
Building regulations	Building and Engineering
Building societies	Building Societies
Children's homes	Infants (Part 2)
Coal mining subsidence	Mines, Minerals and Quarries (Part 1)
Community homes	Infants (Part 2)
Compulsory purchase generally	Compulsory Acquisition
Compensation on compulsory purchase	Compensation
County court proceedings	Courts (Part 5A (ii))
Fumigation of buildings	Public Health (Part 4)
Industrial and provident societies	Friendly Societies and Industrial Assurance
Loans by Public Works Loan Commissioners	Money, Moneylending and Investments (Part 4)
Local authorities generally	Local Government
Local land charges register, registration in	Real Property (Part 2)
New towns	Town and Country Planning
Nursing homes and mental nursing homes	Public Health (Part 2)
Parsonage houses	Ecclesiastical Law
Rent regulation	Landlord and Tenant
Residential care homes	Public Health (Part 2)
Secure tenancies	Landlord and Tenant
Town and country planning	Town and Country Planning
Transfer of housing accommodation to London boroughs	Local Government (Part 1)
Transfer of ministerial functions	Constitutional Law (Part 5)
Voluntary homes	Infants (Part 2)
Statutory instruments generally, their validity, effect and termination	Statutory Instruments, Vol 1

PRELIMINARY NOTE

General

Scope of the title   This title deals with instruments made under the enactments (see *infra*) relating to housing, including instruments relating to housing benefit. Other related instruments which directly or indirectly affect housing are to be found elsewhere in this work. In particular, instruments relating to the transfer of housing accommodation to London boroughs are in the title Local Government (Part 1); instruments relating to rent regulation are in the title Landlord and Tenant; building regulations (taking the place of the building byelaws made by individual local authorities) are in the title Building and Engineering; instruments relating to planning and new towns are in the title Town and Country Planning; and instruments relating to compulsory purchase are dealt with generally in the title Compulsory Acquisition. The title Compensation contains the instruments relating to compensation for land acquired compulsorily; and instruments relating to damage arising from subsidence due to mining operations are dealt with in the title Mines, Minerals and Quarries (Part 1). See also the table of cross-references at p 143, *ante*.

Byelaws are not included in the title as they are not statutory instruments. Local housing authorities have power to make byelaws under the Housing Act 1985, s 23, Halsbury's Statutes, 4th edn Vol 21, title Housing, for the management, use and regulation of houses and lodging-houses provided by themselves. The procedure for making and publishing byelaws is laid down in s 236 of the Local Government Act 1972, Halsbury's Statutes, 4th edn Vol 25, title Local Government (3rd edn Vol 42, p 1063). That section also requires a local authority to furnish a copy of any byelaws made by them to any person paying the appropriate fee.

Statutory background   The current statute law relating to housing is now contained chiefly in the consolidating Housing Acts of 1985 (*ie*, the Housing Act 1985, the Housing Associations Act 1985, the Landlord and Tenant Act 1985 and the Housing (Consequential Provisions) Act 1985, which are all contained in Halsbury's Statutes, 4th edn Vol 21, title Housing, except for the Landlord and Tenant Act 1985, which is in Vol 23, title Landlord and Tenant). Previous housing legislation was repealed by the Housing (Consequential Provisions) Act 1985 and generally replaced by provisions of the aforementioned Acts; however, certain obsolete provisions are not re-enacted and other provisions are not replaced because the Local Government Act 1972, Halsbury's Statutes Vol 25, title Local Government, contains general provisions covering the same or similar grounds. It should be noted that certain of the enactments which are not replaced are saved to a certain extent by the Housing (Consequential Provisions) Act 1985, Sch 4, paras 3 and 4. Instruments made under a provision reproduced in the consolidating Acts now have effect as if made under the corresponding provision of the consolidating Acts (see the Housing (Consequential Provisions) Act 1985, s 2 (2)). Section 2 (4) of that Act provides for construction of references in instruments to a provision reproduced in the consolidating Acts as being, or including, references to the corresponding provision of the consolidating Acts. Instruments which now take effect under the Landlord and Tenant Act 1985 are dealt with in the title Landlord and Tenant; instruments which take effect under the other consolidating Acts are generally dealt with in this title (see below).

Other instruments dealt with in this title have been made under Pts II and III of the Social Security and Housing Benefits Act 1982, Halsbury's Statutes, 4th edn Vol 40, title Social Security (3rd edn Vol 52, p 864 *et seq*), which introduced the housing benefits system in place of the rate rebate, rent rebate and rent allowance schemes under previous Acts; see further below.

Central authority   The Minister of Health was formerly the Minister responsible for the administration of the various enactments relating to housing, but by the Transfer of Functions (Minister of Health and Minister of Local Government and Planning) (No 1) Order 1951, SI 1951/142, his functions under those enactments were, with a few exceptions, transferred to the Minister of Local Government and Planning, who was re-named the Minister of Housing and Local Government by the Minister of Local Government and Planning (Change of Style and Title) Order 1951, SI 1951/1900. In relation to Wales most of the functions of the Minister of Housing and Local Government relating to housing were transferred to the Secretary of State for Wales by the Secretary of State for Wales and Minister of Land and Natural Resources Order 1965, SI 1965/319; and by the Secretary of State for the Environment Order 1970, SI 1970/1681, the Ministry of Housing and Local Government was dissolved, and the functions of the Minister were transferred to the Secretary of State (for the Environment). The instruments referred to in this paragraph are all in the title Constitutional Law (Part 5). The functions of the Secretary of State under the Housing Acts of 1985 are accordingly exercisable by the Secretary of State for the Environment and (in relation to Wales) the Secretary of State for Wales.

Responsibility for the administration of the housing benefits system under the Social Security and Housing Benefits Act 1982 lies with the Secretary of State for Social Services.

Local housing authorities   Local housing authorities for the purposes of the Housing Act 1985 are district councils, London borough councils, the Common Council of the City of London and the Council of the Isles of Scilly; see s 1 of that Act. That definition is applied by the Housing Associations Act 1985, s 104(1) and the Landlord and Tenant Act 1985, s 38.

The Housing Act 1985

Housing the homeless   For instruments relating to the duty imposed on local housing authorities by Pt III of the Act (replacing the Housing (Homeless Persons) Act 1977) to provide, secure or attempt to secure accommodation for homeless persons, see the Housing (Homeless Persons) (Property and Staff) Order 1977, SI 1977/1821, p 164, *post*, and the Housing (Homeless Persons) (Appropriate Arrangements) Order 1978 and (No 2) Order 1978, SI 1978/69 and 661, p 165, *post*.

Secure tenancies   Pt IV of the Act, relating to secure tenancies and rights of secure tenants, and instruments taking effect thereunder, are dealt with in the title Landlord and Tenant.

The right to buy   Pt V of the Act (replacing provisions in the Housing Act 1980) confers on secure tenants the right to buy their houses or flats and to be granted a mortgage for that purpose. A secure tenant claiming to exercise the right to buy must give written notice to the landlord, who must in turn give the tenant notice admitting or denying his right to buy (see ss 122, 124). Likewise a tenant claiming to exercise his right to a mortgage must give written notice to the landlord (see s 134). Forms for these purposes are prescribed by SI 1980/1465, p 170, *post*, 1980/1930, p 172, *post*, 1984/1175, p 186, *post*, and 1985/36, p 189, *post*. A secure tenant claiming to exercise the right to buy is entitled to a discount on the purchase price (see ss 129-131), the maximum discount being prescribed by SI 1980/1342, p 165, *post*. Section 130 provides for the discount to be reduced where a previous discount has been given on certain conveyances etc by public sector landlords and others; see further SI 1984/1173, p 184, *post*. The amount which may be secured by a mortgage is calculated in accordance with s 133 and SI 1980/1423, p 167, *post*.

A secure tenant who has claimed to exercise the right to buy has in certain circumstances the right to be granted a shared ownership lease (see s 143). The terms of such a lease are set out in Sch 8 and SI 1984/1280, p 187, *post*. Where the tenant exercises both the right to a mortgage and the right to be granted a shared ownership lease, the deed by which the mortgage is effected must confer a right to further advances in certain circumstances; see s 151, Sch 9 and SI 1985/758, p 192, *post*. Where a tenant exercises his right to a mortgage or right to further advances, s 178 provides that he may be charged the costs incurred in connection with it; as to the maximum amount chargeable, see SI 1980/1390, p 166, *post*.

A conveyance or grant under this Part must contain a covenant as to repayment of discount on early disposal and the liability under such a covenant is a charge on the dwelling-house (see ss 155, 156). As to priority of charges, see SI 1984/1554 and 1985/1979, p 188, *post*. Section 157 imposes restrictions on the disposal of dwelling-houses in certain rural areas; see further SI 1980/1345 and the instruments noted thereunder, p 166, *post*.

Repair notices and improvement notices Part VI of the Act deals with the giving of repair notices by local housing authorities in respect of unfit houses and houses in disrepair and Pt VII with the giving of improvement notices in respect of dwellings without standard amenities. As to the form of such notices, see SI 1972/228, as amended, p 160, *post*. Where the works required by the notice have been completed, the owner in the case of a repairs notice and the person having control of the dwelling in the case of an improvement notice may apply to the local housing authority for a charging order (see ss 200, 229). As to the form of charging order, see SR&O 1939/563, p 152, *post*.

Slum clearance Pt IX of the Act confers various powers on local housing authorities in respect of slum clearance. As to the forms of notices and orders under this Part, see SI 1972/228, as amended, p 160, *post*. In particular, when declaring a clearance area, the local housing authority may extinguish public rights of way over land acquired for clearance; see further s 294 and SR&O 1937/79, p 149, *post*. Slum clearance subsidy is payable to a local housing authority in respect of losses incurred in connection with slum clearance (see s 312). As to the determination of such losses, see Sch 12 and SI 1974/618, p 163, *post*. Compensation is payable for the appropriation of land in a clearance area by virtue of s 594 and the form of compensation notice is prescribed by SI 1975/1108, p 164, *post*.

Overcrowding Part X deals with the overcrowding of dwellings; as to what constitutes overcrowding, see ss 324-326 and SR&O 1937/80, p 150, *post*, which instrument also prescribes forms and other matters for use in connection with the overcrowding provisions. Other forms are prescribed by SI 1972/228, as amended, p 160, *post*.

Houses in multiple occupation Powers to deal with living conditions in houses in multiple occupation are conferred on local housing authorities by Pt XI of the Act. Forms for use in connection with these provisions are prescribed by SI 1972/228, as amended, p 160, *post*. Sections 365-368 confer powers to make provision as to means of escape from fire in houses in multiple occupation; see further SI 1981/1576, p 172, *post*. A code for the management of houses in multiple occupation which may be applied by local housing authorities to such houses is contained in the Housing (Management of Houses in Multiple Occupation) Regulations 1962, SI 1962/668, p 152, *post*. In addition, local housing authorities may make control orders in respect of houses in multiple occupation and compensation is payable to dispossessed proprietors under s 389 which is calculated in accordance with SI 1984/1629, p 188, *post*.

Loans for acquisition or improvement of housing This is dealt with in Pt XIV of the Act. Under s 442, local authorities are empowered to make agreements with building societies or recognised bodies making relevant advances (as defined in s 444) on the security of a house to indemnify them in the event of default by the mortgagor and under s 443 to make contributions towards costs incurred in connection with legal charges securing relevant advances by a building society or recognised body. Recognised bodies are specified for these purposes by SI 1984/1555 and 1985/1978, p 188, *post*, and the maximum contribution towards costs is fixed by SI 1984/1174, p 186, *post*.

The Secretary of State may make advances to recognised lending institutions (as to which, see s 447 and SI 1982/976, p 177, *post*) enabling them to provide assistance to first-time purchasers providing, *inter alia*, the purchase price is within prescribed limits (see SI 1985/937, p 194, *post*); see s 445. The forms of assistance and qualifying conditions are prescribed by s 446 and include the condition that the purchaser must have been saving for at least two years with a recognised savings institution (as to which, see s 448 and SI 1978/1785, p 165, *post*).

Under s 451, the Public Works Loan Commissioners may lend money for the purpose of constructing or improving houses, or facilitating or encouraging such construction or improvement, to persons entitled to specified interests in land. (Powers to lend money to housing associations for these and other purposes are conferred by the Housing Associations Act 1985, s 67). The rate of interest on such loans is fixed by the Treasury under the National Loans Act 1968, s 5, as substituted, Halsbury's Statutes, 4th edn Vol 30, title Money (Pt 3) (3rd edn Vol 22, p 790). As to such loans, see further the title Money, Moneylending and Investments (Part 4) in this work.

Advances to a resident in a house for its purchase could formerly be made under the Small Dwellings Acquisition Acts 1899-1923. Those Acts were repealed by the Housing (Consequential Provisions) Act 1985 and were not re-enacted, except that the Housing Act 1985, s 456 and Sch 18 contain provisions with respect to advances already made under the 1899-1923 Acts. The rate of interest on such advances is to be calculated by reference to the rate fixed by the Treasury in respect of loans to local authorities for housing purposes; see Sch 18, para 1. Powers comparable with those under the 1899-1923 Acts are conferred on local authorities by the Housing Act 1985, ss 435-441. As to local authority mortgage interest rates, see Sch 16.

The power to issue housing bonds under the Housing Act 1957, s 138 and Sch 8 (repealed by the Housing (Consequential Provisions) Act 1985) is saved by Sch 4, para 3 of the 1985 Act in relation to the Common Council of the City of London and the Housing Consolidated Regulations 1925, SR&O 1925/866, Pt III (listed at p 139, *ante*) continue to have effect in relation to the Common Council only.

Grants for improvement, repair and conversion The following grants are payable by local housing authorities under Pt XV: improvement grants, intermediate grants, special grants and repairs grants. The following instruments make provision in relation to such grants: the Grants by Local Authorities (Appropriate Percentage and Exchequer Contributions) Orders 1980, SI 1980/1735, as amended, 1982, SI 1982/581 and (No 2) Order 1982, SI 1982/1763, pp 170, 172, 180 *post*; the Grants by Local Authorities (Appropriate Percentage and Exchequer Contribution) (Repairs Grants for Airey Houses) Order 1982, SI 1983/95, as amended, p 180, *post*; the Grants by Local Authorities (Grants for Tenants) Order 1982, SI 1982/1039, p 177, *post*; the Grants by Local Authorities (Repairs) Order 1982, SI 1982/1205, p 178, *post*; the Grants by Local Authorities (Repairs Grants for Airey Houses) (Eligible Expense Limits) Order 1982, SI 1982/1895, as amended, p 180, *post*; and the Grants by Local Authorities (Eligible Expense Limits) Order 1983, SI 1983/613, p 181, *post*.

In addition, grants for thermal insulation may be made by local housing authorities; see s 521 and the Homes Insulation Grants Order 1984, SI 1984/838, p 184, *post*.

Defective housing Assistance for owners of defective housing may be provided under Pt XVI (replacing the Housing Defects Act 1984) by means of repurchase or reinstatement grant. The amount of reinstatement grant is determined in accordance with s 543 and SI 1984/1705, p 189, *post*.

Compulsory purchase Compulsory purchase of land under the Act and compensation therefor are dealt with in Pt XVII. Section 579 and Sch 22 make special provision as regards the acquisition of land for clearance and forms for these purposes are prescribed by SI 1972/228, as amended, p 160, *post*. Reference has already been made to compensation for the appropriation of land in a clearance area (see under the head "Slum clearance" p 146, *ante*). Payments may be made under Sch 23 in respect of well-maintained houses purchased at site value or demolished or closed under the Act; see further the Housing (Payments for Well Maintained Houses) Orders 1972, SI 1972/1792, 1973, SI 1973/753 and 1982, SI 1982/1112, pp 162, 163, 177 *post*.

Housing Associations

The expression "housing association" is defined in virtually identical terms in both the Housing Act 1985, s 5 and the Housing Associations Act 1985, s 1. The associations were formerly known as public utility societies, a term defined by s 40 (repealed) of the Housing, Town Planning, etc, Act 1919 as "a society registered under the Industrial and Provident Societies Acts 1893 to 1913 (now replaced by the Industrial and Provident Societies Act 1965), the rules whereof prohibit the issue of any share or loan capital with interest or dividend exceeding the rate for the time being prescribed by the Treasury". For the purposes of that section a rate of five per cent a year as from 15 August 1934 onwards was prescribed by SR&O 1934/913 (spent). The definition of "housing association" in the 1985 Acts referred to above also provides for a rate of interest or dividend being prescribed by the Treasury, but no order prescribing a rate for this purpose has been published in the SI series.

The Housing Associations Act 1985 consolidates certain provisions of the Housing Acts relating to housing associations and supersedes a number of instruments made under those Acts. Instruments which now take effect under the 1985 Act are the Registered Housing Associations (Accounting Requirements) Order 1982, SI 1982/828, as amended, p 173, *post* and the Registered Housing Associations (Limited Accounting Requirements) Order 1984, SI 1984/1833, p 189, *post* (both taking effect under s 24 of the Act, concerning general requirements as to accounts and audit) and the Mortgage Indemnities (Recognised Bodies) Orders 1984 and 1985, SI 1984/1555 and 1985/1978, p 188, *post* (which partly take effect under s 85 of the Act and specify certain bodies and classes or descriptions of bodies for the purposes of s 84, relating to agreements by the Housing Corporation to indemnify certain lenders in the event of default by the mortgagor).

Housing Benefits

The housing benefits system was introduced by the Social Security and Housing Benefits Act 1982, Pts II and III, in place of the rate rebate, rent rebate and rent allowance schemes under previous legislation. As to the commencement of the relevant provisions of the 1982 Act, see SI 1982/906, p 173, *post*.

Under s 28 of the 1982 Act, the Secretary of State (for Social Services) is empowered, with the consent of the Treasury, to make schemes for the grant by rating authorities of rate rebates, by housing authorities of rent rebates and by local authorities of rent allowances. Those schemes are contained in the Housing Benefits Regulations 1985, SI 1985/677, as amended, p 190, *post*. Each year the Secretary of State must review the main and housing elements of any needs allowances specified in the aforementioned regulations and may increase such allowances by such amount as he considers appropriate; see s 29, as amended, and the Housing Benefits (Increase of Needs Allowances) Regulations 1985, SI 1985/1244, noted as an amendment to SI 1985/677, p 190, *post*. Under s 30, the authorities previously referred to may modify the statutory schemes, which, as so modified, are known as local schemes. In relation to a local scheme, the permitted total of rebates or allowances must be calculated in the prescribed manner, as to which see the Housing Benefits (Permitted Totals for Local Schemes) Regulations 1982, SI 1982/1129, as amended, p 177, *post*.

Subsidies are payable each year under s 32 to the authorities referred to above, which subsidies are calculated in accordance with the provisions of the Housing Benefits (Subsidy) Order 1985, SI 1985/440, p 190, *post* and the orders referred to under the note "Previous orders" thereto.

Under s 34, as amended, specified items of expenditure relating to housing benefits are not to count as relevant expenditure for rate support grant purposes; see further the Housing Benefits (Rate Support Grant) Order 1984, SI 1984/111, p 184, *post* and the order referred to under the note "Previous order" thereto.

Amendments to regulations relating to supplementary benefit may be made by virtue of s 36 (2) in consequence of the introduction of the housing benefits system; for relevant instruments, see the title National Insurance (Part 4).

THE HOUSING ACT (EXTINGUISHMENT OF PUBLIC RIGHT OF WAY) REGULATIONS 1937
SR&O 1937/79

NOTES
Authority   These regulations were made on 29 January 1937 by the Minister of Health under s 176 (1) of the Housing Act 1936 and all other enabling powers, for the purposes of s 46 of that Act. The latter section (but not s 176 (1)) was repealed by the Housing Act 1957, but, by virtue of the saving provisions of s 191 (2) of that Act, these regulations continued to have effect for the purposes of s 64 of the Act of 1957 as if made under s 178 (1) thereof. Section 176 (1) of the Act of 1936 was later repealed by the Housing (Financial Provisions) Act 1958. The 1957 Act was repealed by the Housing (Consequential Provisions) Act 1985 and by virtue of s 2 (2) thereof these regulations continue to have effect for the purposes of the Housing Act 1985, s 294 as if made under s 614 thereof.
Commencement   29 January 1937; see reg. 1.
General   The Housing Act 1985, s 294, Halsbury's Statutes, 4th edn Vol 21, title Housing, empowers a local housing authority, with the approval of the Secretary of State (see the Preliminary Note at p 144, *ante*), by order to extinguish any public right of way over any land acquired by them under s 290 of that Act, and requires the order to be published in the prescribed manner. As construed in accordance with the Housing (Consequential Provisions) Act 1985, s 2 (4), these regulations prescribe in reg 4 the form of an order under the section and in regs 5 and 6 the manner of its publication.

1.   These Regulations may be cited as the Housing Act (Extinguishment of Public Right of Way) Regulations, 1937, and shall come into operation forthwith.

2.   The Interpretation Act, 1889, applies to the interpretation of these Regulations as it applies to the interpretation of an Act of Parliament.

NOTES
Interpretation Act 1889   Repealed and replaced by the Interpretation Act 1978, in the title Statutory Instruments, Vol 1.

3.   *(Revoked SR&O 1936/740.)*

4.   An order made by a local authority under Section 46 of the Housing Act, 1936, for the extinguishment of any public right of way over any land which—
   (1) they have purchased or resolved to purchase under Part III of the Housing Act, 1936; or
   (2) is land belonging to the local authority which they have included in a clearance area or which might have been purchased by the authority as being land surrounded by or adjoining a clearance area had it not previously been acquired by them; or
   (3) is land belonging to the local authority and is comprised in a redevelopment plan in respect of which the approval of the Minister of Health has become operative,
shall be in the form set out in the schedule hereto or in a form substantially to the like effect.

NOTES
Section 46 of the Housing Act 1936   This is now to be construed as a reference to the Housing Act 1985, s 294, Halsbury's Statutes, 4th edn Vol 21, title Housing.

Purchased . . . under Part III of the Housing Act 1936   This is now to be construed as a reference to acquisition under the Housing Act 1985, s 290, Halsbury's Statutes, 4th edn Vol 21, title Housing.

Resolved to purchase   Where a local housing authority have resolved to purchase the land an order may be made and approved in advance of the purchase; see the Housing Act 1985, s 294 (2).

Redevelopment plan   Provisions governing such plans were contained in s 56 (repealed) of the Housing Act 1957. General improvement areas were substituted by the Housing Act 1969, Part II (repealed) for the redevelopment areas provided for under ss 55-58 (repealed) of the Act of 1957. As to general improvement areas, see now the Housing Act 1985, ss 253-259, Halsbury's Statutes, 4th edn Vol 21, title Housing. It should be noted, however, that the power to make an order under s 294 of the 1985 Act only extends to land acquired by the local housing authority under s 290 of that Act (land acquired for clearance).

Minister of Health   As to the transfer of that Minister's housing functions, see the Preliminary Note under the head "Central authority", p 144, *ante*.

5. Not less than six weeks before submitting the order for the approval of the Minister of Health the local Authority shall—

    (*a*) publish in one or more local newspapers circulating within their district a notice in the form set out in the schedule hereto describing the public right of way to which the order relates and naming a place at which a copy of the order and of the map referred to therein may be seen at all reasonable hours; and

    (*b*) affix a copy of the same notice in a prominent position at each end of the public right of way to which the order relates.

NOTES

Not less than six weeks   If any objection to the order is made to the Secretary of State before the expiration of six weeks from the publication thereof, he may not approve the order until he has caused a public local inquiry to be held; see the Housing Act 1985, s 294 (3), Halsbury's Statutes, 4th edn Vol 21, title Housing.

Minister of Health   This reference should now be construed as a reference to the Secretary of State; see the Preliminary Note under the head "Central authority", p 144, *ante*.

Publish   The Secretary of State may dispense with publication of the advertisement if there is reasonable cause; see the Housing Act 1985, s 615, Halsbury's Statutes, 4th edn Vol 21, title Housing.

6. Every notice affixed in accordance with the last preceding clause shall be kept exhibited in such a position for a period of not less than six weeks.

SCHEDULE

NOTES

The Schedule sets out the forms of the order extinguishing a public right of way prescribed by reg 4 and the notice of the making of an order extinguishing a public right of way prescribed by reg 5 (*a*).

THE HOUSING ACT (OVERCROWDING AND MISCELLANEOUS FORMS) REGULATIONS 1937
SR&O 1937/80

NOTES

Authority   These regulations were made on 29 January 1937 by the Minister of Health under s 176 (1) of the Housing Act 1936 and all other enabling powers. The regulations were made for the purposes of provisions of the Act of 1936 which (unlike s 176 (1) itself) were repealed by the Housing Act 1957. By virtue, however, of s 191 (2) of the Act of 1957 these regulations continued to have effect for the purposes of the corresponding provisions of that Act as if made under s 178 (1) thereof. Section 176 (1) of the Act of 1936 was later repealed by the Housing (Financial Provisions) Act 1958. The 1957 Act has been repealed by the Housing (Consequential Provisions) Act 1985 and by virtue of s 2 (2) thereof these regulations continue to have effect for the purposes of the corresponding provisions of the Housing Act 1985, Halsbury's Statutes 4th edn Vol 21, title Housing, as if made under ss 326, 614 thereof.

Commencement   29 January 1937; see reg 1.

Interpretation   The expression "dwelling-house" is replaced in the provisions of the Housing Act 1985 by "dwelling", which is defined in s 343 thereof, as is "landlord". As to the meaning of "room", see ss 325 (2), 326 (2). For the definition of "the Act", see reg 2 (i) and the note thereto.

General   As construed in accordance with the Housing (Consequential Provisions) Act 1985, s 2 (4), these regulations prescribe forms and matters relating to the overcrowding provisions contained in Part X of the Housing Act 1985 and two forms of certificates by a local authority for certain purposes of Part IX of the Act.

Penalties   The penalty for an occupier causing or permitting overcrowding is, under the Housing

Act 1985, s 327 (3), Halsbury's Statutes, 4th edn Vol 21, title Housing, a fine not exceeding level 1 on the standard scale and a further fine not exceeding £2 in respect of every day subsequent to the date of conviction on which the offence continues.

1. These Regulations may be cited as the Housing Act (Overcrowding and Miscellaneous Forms) Regulations, 1937, and shall come into operation forthwith.

2. (i) in these Regulations the expression "the Act" means the Housing Act, 1936.

(ii) The Interpretation Act, 1889, applies to the interpretation of these Regulations as it applies to the interpretation of an Act of Parliament.

NOTES
Housing Act 1936   This is now to be construed as a reference to the Housing Act 1985, Halsbury's Statutes, 4th edn Vol 21, title Housing.
Interpretation Act 1889   Repealed and replaced by the Interpretation Act 1978, in the title Statutory Instruments, Vol 1 of this work.

3. (*Revoked SR&O 1936/765.*)

4. For determining for the purposes of Part IV of the Act the number of persons permitted to use a house for sleeping, the floor area of a room shall be ascertained for the purposes of the Fifth Schedule to the Act, in the following manner—

    (i) The area of any part of the floor space over which the vertical height of the room is, by reason of a sloping roof or ceiling, reduced to less than 5 feet shall be excluded from the computation of the floor area of that room.

    (ii) Subject to any exclusion under the foregoing rule, the floor shall be measured so as to include in the computation of the floor area any floor space formed by a bay window extension and any area at floor level which is covered or occupied by fixed cupboards or projecting chimney breasts.

    (iii) All measurements for the purpose of computing the floor area shall be made at the floor level and, subject as aforesaid, shall extend to the back of all projecting skirtings.

NOTES
This regulation implements the Housing Act 1985, s 326 (4).
Part IV of, and Schedule 5 to, the Act   For the meaning of "the Act", see reg 2 (i) and the note thereto. Part IV of, and Schedule 5 to, the Act of 1936 are now replaced by the Housing Act 1985, Part X (ss 324-344); s 326 thereof contains provisions for determining the number of persons permitted to use a house for sleeping.

5. The summary of the provisions of sections 58, 59 and 61 of the Act which, under subsection (1) of section 62 of the Act, is required to be inserted in every rent book or similar document, used in relation to a dwelling-house by or on behalf of the landlord thereof, shall be in the form set out in Part I of the Schedule hereto.

NOTES
This regulation implements the Housing Act 1985, s 332 (1).
Sections 58, 59, 61 and 62 (1) of the Act   For the meaning of "the Act", see reg 2 (i) and the note thereto. The Housing Act 1985, s 332 (1) requires rent books etc to contain a summary of ss 324-331 thereof and a statement of the permitted number of persons in relation to the dwelling.

6. The forms set out in Part II of the schedule hereto, or forms substantially to the like effect, shall be used by a local authority in connection with their powers and duties under the Act in all cases to which those forms are applicable.

NOTES
The Secretary of State may dispense with the service of notices by a local authority where there is reasonable cause for so doing; see the Housing Act 1985, s 615.

SCHEDULE
PART I
NOTES
This part contains the form mentioned in reg 5. As to the summary now required, see the notes to that regulation.

PART II
NOTES
This Part contains the forms to be used by local authorities prescribed by reg 6. The following is a list of the forms with the provision of the Housing Act 1985 to which each is applicable shown in brackets:

Form No	Description
A	Notice before Entry for the Purpose of Measurement of the Rooms of a House (s 337).
B	Notice requiring Statement of Persons sleeping in a House (s 335).
C	Notice that a House is overcrowded (s 331 (2)).
D	Notice to Occupier to Abate Overcrowding (s 338).
E	Licence for Temporary Use of House by Persons in Excess of the Permitted Number (s 330 (3)).
F	Notice revoking Licence to exceed the Permitted Number of Persons (s 330 (4)).
G	Certificate as to Suitable Alternative Accommodation (s 342).
H	Certificate of Availability of Suitable Alternative Accommodation (s 309).
I	Certificate of Fitness of a House (s 310 (3)).

A further form of notice which may be served before entry for the purpose of measuring rooms is contained in the Housing (Prescribed Forms) Regulations 1972, SI 1972/228, p 160, *post*. Form No 1 in Schedule 2 to those regulations may be used for that purpose as well as before entry for certain other purposes.

THE HOUSING ACT (FORM OF CHARGING ORDER) REGULATIONS 1939
SR&O 1939/563

NOTES
Authority   These regulations were made on 16 May 1939 by the Minister of Health under ss 21 (1) and 176 (1) of the Housing Act 1936 and all other enabling powers. Section 21 (1) (but not s 176 (1)) of the Act of 1936 was repealed by the Housing Act 1957, but, by virtue of the saving provisions of s 191 (2) of that Act, these regulations continued to have effect for the purposes of s 15 (1) of the Act of 1957, as if made under s 178 (1) thereof. Section 176 (1) of the Act of 1936 was later repealed by the Housing (Financial Provisions) Act 1958. The 1957 Act was repealed by the Housing (Consequential Provisions) Act 1985 and by virtue of s 2 (2) thereof these regulations continue to have effect for the purposes of the Housing Act 1985, ss 201 (1), 230 (1), Halsbury's Statutes, 4th edn Vol 21, title Housing, as if made under s 614 thereof.
Commencement   16 May 1939.
General   As construed in accordance with the Housing (Consequential Provisions) Act 1985, s 2 (4), these regulations prescribe the form of a charging order granted by a local authority under the Housing Act 1985, ss 200, 229, Halsbury's Statutes, 4th edn Vol 21, title Housing, to an owner or person having control of a dwelling on completion of works. For the effect of charging orders, see the 1985 Act, ss 201, 230. They may be registered as land charges, Class A; see s 2 of the Land Charges Act 1972, Halsbury's Statutes, 4th edn Vol 37, title Real Property (3rd edn Vol 42, p 1593); and for registration procedure, see the Land Charges Rules in the title Real Property (Part 2) in this work.

THE HOUSING (MANAGEMENT OF HOUSES IN MULTIPLE OCCUPATION) REGULATIONS 1962
SI 1962/668

NOTES
Authority   These regulations were made on 29 March 1962 by the Minister of Housing and Local Government under s 13 of the Housing Act 1961 (repealed) and all other enabling powers. They now have effect under the Housing Act 1985, s 369, Halsbury's Statutes, 4th edn Vol 21, title Housing.
Commencement   22 May 1962; see reg 1 (2).
Amendment   These regulations are printed as amended by s 58 (1) and (2) of the Housing Act 1969 (repealed); the amendments made by those provisions are saved by the Housing (Consequential Provisions) Act 1985, Sch 4, para 13.
Interpretation   See reg 2 and the note "Other expressions" thereto.
Penalties, etc   By the Housing Act 1985, s 369 (5), Halsbury's Statutes, 4th edn Vol 21, title Housing, if any person knowingly contravenes or without reasonable excuse fails to comply with

any regulation under that section as applied under the Act in relation to any house he is liable on summary conviction to a fine not exceeding level 3 on the standard scale.

As to power of entry for ascertaining whether these regulations have been contravened, see the Housing Act 1985, s 395 (2).

General As construed in accordance with the Housing (Consequential Provisions) Act 1985, s 2 (4), these regulations provide a code of management which a local housing authority may apply, by order under the Housing Act 1985, s 370, Halsbury's Statutes, 4th edn Vol 21, title Housing, to any house which is occupied by persons who do not form a single household and which is in an unsatisfactory condition in consequence of defective management. In the case of a building which comprises separate dwellings *(eg, a tenement building or a block of flats)* the regulations may be applied, in the circumstances mentioned in s 374 of the Act, to the building as a whole instead of to individual dwellings therein.

So much of these regulations as imposes duties on persons who live in a house to which the regulations apply also applies to persons who live in a house as respects which a control order is in force; see the Housing Act 1985, s 382 (5), Halsbury's Statutes, 4th edn Vol 21, title Housing.

Under the 1985 Act, s 372 the local housing authority may require the doing of work to make good defects in the condition of a house which are due to neglect to comply with the requirements imposed by these regulations.

An order under the 1985 Act, s 370 is a local land charge (s 370 (5)). As to registration, see the Local Land Charges Rules 1977, SI 1977/985, in the title Real Property (Part 2) in this work.

For forms which are to be used under the 1985 Act, ss 370, 372, see Forms Nos 35 and 36 in the Housing (Prescribed Forms) Regulations 1972, SI 1972/228, p 160, *post.*

PART I
PRELIMINARY

1. Application, citation and commencement (1) These regulations apply to any house [which is occupied by persons who do not form a single household], and to any such building as is mentioned in section 21 (1) of the Act, being a house, or, as the case may be, a building, in respect of which an order under section 12 of the Act is for the time being in force.

(2) These regulations may be cited as the Housing (Management of Houses in Multiple Occupation) Regulations 1962, and shall come into operation on 22nd May, 1962.

NOTES
Amendment The words printed between square brackets in para (1) of this regulation have been substituted by virtue of s 58 (1) and (2) of the Housing Act 1969 (repealed); the amendment is saved by the Housing (Consequential Provisions) Act 1985, Sch 4, para 13.
Sections 21 (1) and 12 of the Act *Ie,* the Housing Act 1961, as stated in the recital of powers at the head of these regulations. These must now be construed as references to the Housing Act 1985, s 374 (1) and s 370 respectively.

2. Interpretation (1) In these regulations the following expressions have the meanings hereinafter assigned to them, namely—

"management order" means an order under section 12 of the Act applying the regulations to a house and "the relevant management order", in a reference to a house or part of a house, means the management order in force with respect to that house;

"manager", in relation to a house, means the person who is an owner or a lessee of the house and who, directly or through an agent or trustee, receives rents or other payments from persons who are tenants of parts of the house, or who are lodgers; and, where those rents or other payments are received through another person as his agent or trustee, includes that other person;

"rents" means rents or other payments from tenants of parts of a house, or from lodgers therein, and "the rents", in relation to a person who is an owner or lessee of a house or an agent or trustee through whom rents are received, means such rents or other payments as are received by, or through, that person; and

"staircase" includes a landing.

(2) In these regulations—
(*a*) references to a house include references to a building comprising separate dwellings which satisfies the conditions in paragraph (*a*) or paragraph (*b*) of section 21 (1) of the Act;
(*b*) references to a lessee of a house include references to any under-lessee,

tenant, or person having an estate or interest in the house under an agreement for a lease, underlease or tenancy, and to any person who retains possession of the house by virtue of the Rent Acts and not as being entitled to any tenancy; and

(*c*) references to a person having an estate or interest in a house include references to a person who retains possession of the house by virtue of the Rent Acts as aforesaid.

(3) Any requirement of these regulations (howsoever expressed) with respect to repair shall be construed as requiring a standard of repair that is reasonable in all the circumstances, and in determining the appropriate standard of repair for a room in, or for any part of, a house regard shall be had to the age, character and prospective life of the house.

(4) The Interpretation Act 1889 shall apply to the interpretation of these regulations as it applies to the interpretation of an Act of Parliament.

NOTES
Other expressions The expression "local authority" used in these regulations is not used in the relevant provisions of the Housing Act 1985, which instead refer to "local housing authority". That expression is defined in s 1 of the Act as meaning a district council, a London borough Council, the Common Council of the City of London or the Council of the Isles of Scilly. The expression "house" is defined in s 399 of the Act and "owner" in s 398; as to "lessee" and "person having an estate or interest" see further s 398.
Sections 21 (1) (a) or (b) and 12 of the Act *Ie*, the Housing Act 1961, as stated in the recital of powers at the head of these regulations. These must now be construed as references to the Housing Act 1985, ss 374 (1) (*a*) or (*b*) and 370 respectively; it should be noted that, by virtue of s 374 (1) (*c*), the provisions of the Act for remedying inadequate management also apply to a tenement block in which all or any of the flats are without one or more of the standard amenities as they apply to a house in multiple occupation.
Rent Acts It is thought that this refers to the Rent and Mortgage Interest Restrictions Acts 1920 to 1939; all the Acts cited collectively by that title were repealed and replaced by the Rent Act 1968, which was itself repealed and replaced by the Rent Act 1977. See also the definition of "lessee" in the Housing Act 1985, s 398.
Interpretation Act 1889 Repealed and replaced by the Interpretation Act 1978, in the title Statutory Instruments, Vol 1 in this work.

PART II
DUTIES OF MANAGEMENT

3. General (1) When a management order is made as respects any house it shall be the duty of a person who is manager of the house by virtue of being an owner or lessee thereof who receives the rents,—

(*a*) if he does not live in the house, to make such arrangements (including arrangements for adequate supervision of the house) as may be necessary to enable him, directly or through an agent authorised in that behalf, to discharge effectively his obligations under the following regulations;

(*b*) in any case, to inform any person who is his agent or trustee, and through whom he receives the rents, that the order has been made and that these regulations accordingly apply to the house and impose obligations on that person.

(2) Where a person who is manager of a house by virtue of being an agent or trustee through whom rents are received is aware that some action is required to discharge an obligation of the manager under the following regulations, he shall, unless he discharges that obligation himself, take such steps as may be necessary to bring the need for action promptly to the attention of the owner or lessee of the house who receives the rents through him; and where he receives from the local authority a material complaint with respect to management of the house of which he is manager as aforesaid, such a person shall, if required by the authority so to do,—

(*a*) transmit that complaint to the said owner or lessee, and

(*b*) provide the local authority with the name and address of the person to whom the complaint is accordingly transmitted;

but this paragraph shall not be taken as exempting a person who is a manager of a house by virtue of being an agent or trustee through whom rents are received from the obligations imposed on managers by the following regulations or from liability for failure without reasonable excuse to comply with them.

(3) Nothing in the following regulations shall be taken to require or authorise anything to be done in connection with water supply, drainage, or the supply of gas or electricity otherwise than in accordance with any enactment relating thereto, or to oblige the manager of a house to take, in a matter connected therewith, any action which is the responsibility of a local authority or statutory undertaker, other than such action as may be necessary to bring the matter promptly to the attention of the local authority or statutory undertaker concerned.

For this purpose "enactment" includes an enactment in any local Act and an order, rule, regulation, byelaw or scheme made under or by virtue of any Act, including any order or scheme confirmed by Parliament.

NOTES
Local authority   See the note "Other expressions" to reg 2, *ante.*

4. Water supply and drainage   (1) The manager shall ensure that all means of water supply and drainage in the house (including the curtilage, if any) are in and are maintained in proper state of repair, a clean condition and good order, and shall, in particular, ensure—

(*a*) that any tank, cistern or similar receptacle, provided for the storage of water for drinking or other domestic purposes is effectively covered, and that all such receptacles and the water stored in them are kept in a clean and proper condition;

(*b*) that any water fitting which is so placed, whether inside or outside the house, as to render it liable to damage by frost shall (unless it is an overflow pipe) be reasonably protected against such damage.

For this purpose "water fitting" includes any pipe (other than a main), tap, cock, valve, ferrule, meter, cistern, bath, watercloset, soil pan or other similar apparatus used in connection with the supply or use of water.

(2) The manager shall not unreasonably cause a supply of water to any tenant or lodger in the house to be interrupted.

5. Supply of gas and electricity and installations for lighting and heating   (1) The manager shall ensure that the installations in the house—

(*a*) for the supply of gas and electricity,

(*b*) for lighting, and

(*c*) for space heating or heating water,

serving any part of the house in common use, are in and are maintained in repair and proper working order, and that installations for lighting in places to which this regulation applies are readily available for use by tenants and lodgers to such extent and at such times as those persons may reasonably require.

(2) The last foregoing paragraph shall extend to installations for lighting on staircases and at entrances to the house which are used by tenants or lodgers, whether in common or otherwise, except any staircase which is comprised in a part of the house let to a tenant or lodger as his living accommodation and which either does not open directly on to a part of the house in common use or is separated from such part by a door.

(3) The manager shall not unreasonably cause a supply of gas or electricity to any tenant or lodger in the house to be interrupted.

6. Rooms and installations in common use   (1) The manager shall ensure that the following rooms and installations in the house (including the curtilage, if any) are in and are maintained in a proper state of repair (including, where appropriate, reasonable decorative repair), a clean condition and good order:—

(*a*) all rooms in common use, not being parts of the house to which the next following regulation relates;

(*b*) such of the following installations as are in common use, namely, sanitary conveniences, baths, sinks, washbasins and installations for cooking or for storing food;

(*c*) in the case of any room in common use being a kitchen, bathroom, lavatory or washhouse, such installations therein (if any) as are not subject to any of the foregoing provisions of these regulations.

(2) Nothing in this regulation shall oblige the manager to repair, keep in repair or maintain anything which a tenant or lodger is entitled to remove from the house.

7. Other parts of the house in common use   (1) The manager shall ensure that such of the following parts of the house as are in and are maintained in a proper state of repair (including reasonable decorative repair), a clean condition and good order and are kept reasonably free from obstructions:—

(*a*) staircases, passageways and corridors;

(*b*) halls and lobbies;

(*c*) entrances to the house, including entrance doors, porches and entrance steps;

(*d*) balconies.

(2) The last foregoing paragraph shall extend to any staircase, passageway or corridor which gives access to the living accommodation of a tenant or lodger in the house and which, though not itself in common use, opens directly on to a part of the house in common use from which it is not separated by a door.

(3) The manager's duties under this regulation shall, without prejudice to the generality thereof, include the duty to ensure (in places to which the regulation applies) that all handrails and banisters are kept in good order and repair, that any missing handrails and (in so far as considerations of safety may require) banisters are replaced, and that such additional handrails and banisters as are necessary for the safety of tenants or lodgers living in the house are provided.

8. Accommodation let to tenants or lodgers   (1) The following provisions of this regulation shall have effect with respect to the repair and maintenance of premises (being a room or set of rooms in a part of any house to which the regulations apply) which are let to a tenant or lodger as his living accommodation, and to the repair and maintenance of the installations therein, but shall be without prejudice to other provisions of these regulations in so far as they may extend to such premises or installations.

(2) It shall be the duty of the manager, when he lets any premises as aforesaid, to ensure at the commencement of the letting—

(*a*) that the premises are, internally, in a reasonable state of structural repair, and in a clean condition; and

(*b*) that the installations therein for the supply, and for making use of the supply, of water, gas and electricity, and for sanitation (including installations therein for space heating or heating water) are in a reasonable state of repair and proper working order.

(3) With respect to premises which on the date of the making of the relevant management order are let to a tenant or lodger as his living accommodation, it shall be the duty of the manager, subject to the provisions of paragraph (5) of this regulation, to take within a reasonable time thereafter such steps (if any) as may be necessary—

(*a*) to put the premises, internally, in a reasonable state of structural repair; and

(*b*) to put in a reasonable state of repair and proper working order the installations in the premises—

(i) for the supply of water, gas and electricity, and for sanitation (including basins, sinks, baths and sanitary conveniences but not, except as aforesaid, fixtures, fittings and appliances for making use of the supply of water, gas or electricity), and

(ii) for space heating or heating water.

(4) While premises to which this regulation applies are occupied by a tenant or lodger as his living accommodation it shall be the duty of the manager, subject to the provisions of the next following paragraph, to ensure that the installations falling within sub-paragraph (*b*) of the last foregoing paragraph are kept in repair and proper working order:

Provided that the manager shall not be required by this paragraph to carry out any repair the need for which arises in consequence of use of the premises otherwise than in a tenant-like manner by the person to whom they are let.

(5) Nothing in this regulation shall oblige the manager to repair, keep in repair or maintain anything which a tenant or lodger is entitled to remove from the premises.

9. Windows and ventilation   The manager shall ensure that all windows and other means of ventilation in any part of the house occupied or used (whether in common or otherwise) by tenants or lodgers, are in and are maintained in good order and repair:

Provided that, save in so far as may be necessary for the proper discharge of any other of his duties under these regulations, the manager shall not be required to carry out, in a part of the house which is for the time being let to a tenant or lodger as his living accommodation, any repair to a window or other means of ventilation the need for which arises after the date of the relevant management order in consequence of use of that part otherwise than in a tenant-like manner by the person to whom it is let.

10. Means of escape from fire   The manager shall ensure that all means of escape from fire in the house (including any escape apparatus) are in and are maintained in proper repair and good order and kept free from obstruction, and that there are displayed in the house with respect to such means of escape as aforesaid (other than any exit in ordinary use) such notices as the local authority may, if they think fit, reasonably require.

11. Miscellaneous parts of the premises   (1) The manager shall ensure that every outbuilding, yard, area and forecourt, which belongs to the house and is in common use, is in and is maintained in a proper state of repair, a clean condition and good order, and that any garden in common use belonging to the house is kept in a tidy condition.

(2) The manager shall ensure that boundary walls, fences and railings (including basement area railings), in so far as they belong to the house, are kept and maintained in reasonable repair so as not to constitute a danger to persons living on the premises.

(3) If any part of the house is subject to a closing order, or not in use, the manager shall ensure that such part, including any passage and staircase directly giving access to it, is kept reasonably clean and free from refuse and litter.

NOTES
Part of the house is subject to a closing order   A closing order relating to part of a building may be made under the Housing Act 1985, s 266, Halsbury's Statutes, 4th edn Vol 21, title Housing. The relevant form of order is Form No 13 in the Housing (Prescribed Forms) Regulations 1972, SI 1972/228, p 160, *post*.

12. Disposal of refuse and litter   The manager shall ensure that refuse and litter are not allowed to accumulate in, or in the curtilage of, the house save where properly stored pending disposal, and to that end he shall in particular,—

(*a*) provide, and maintain the provision of, suitable refuse and litter bins or other suitable receptacles on a scale adequate to the requirements of tenants and lodgers in the house, except in so far as such provision is made by the local authority, and

(b) make such supplementary arrangements for the disposal of refuse and litter from the house as may be necessary having regard to any existing service provided by the local authority.

NOTES
Local authority   See the note "Other expressions" to reg 2, *ante.*

13. General safety of occupants   The manager shall ensure that such precautions are taken as are reasonably required, having regard to structural conditions in the house and to the number of persons living there, to protect tenants and lodgers and members of their households from injury as a result of those conditions; and in particular he shall (without prejudice to any of his foregoing obligations) ensure as respects any roof or balcony which is not in all respects safe, either that reasonable measures are taken to prevent access thereto, or that it is made safe, and that such safeguards as may be necessary are provided against the danger of accidents resulting from the presence on staircases and landings of windows the sills of which are at or near floor level.

PART III
ANCILLARY PROVISIONS

14. Manager's duty to display certain documents for information   (1) The manager of a house to which the regulations apply shall cause to be displayed in a suitable position in the house so as to be readily accessible to the occupants—

(a) a notice containing the name and address of the person (or of each person) who is manager of the house, describing him as manager and, where appropriate, as agent or trustee for the receipt of rents;

(b) a copy of the relevant management order and a copy of these regulations; and

(c) if the local authority so require, such notice as the authority may provide for indicating briefly the main provisions of the regulations relating to management of the house and the provisions of the Act as respects failure to comply with them;

and he shall take all reasonable steps to ensure that the documents which are displayed in accordance with this regulation remain so displayed (with any requisite amendments) while the relevant management order is in force.

(2) The manager shall make such amendments to the foregoing documents as may from time to time be required, and, in the case of amendments of these regulations and of the notice referred to in sub-paragraph (c) of the last foregoing paragraph, as are brought to his attention by the local authority.

NOTES
Local authority   See the note "Other expressions" to reg 2, *ante.*

15. Manager's duty to inform local authority about occupancy of the house
The manager of a house to which the regulations apply shall, when required by the local authority so to do, provide the authority with such of the following particulars as they may require (and in such time and manner as they may reasonably specify) with respect to occupancy of the house, or, where part only of the house is occupied by tenants or lodgers, with respect to occupancy of that part:—

(a) the number of individuals and households accommodated;

(b) the number of individuals in each household;

(c) the purpose for which each room in the house, or in the relevant part of the house, is being used.

NOTES
Local authority   See the note "Other expressions" to reg 2, *ante.*

16. Duties of occupants   With a view to ensuring that the manager can effectively carry out the duties with which he is charged by these regulations, it shall be a general obligation of tenants and lodgers and members of their households, accommodated in the house, to take reasonable care not to hinder or frustrate the due performance of those duties, and, in particular every such person, in so far as he is able, shall—

(*a*) allow the manager, at all reasonable times, to enter any room or other place comprised in that person's tenancy or lodging, for purposes connected with the carrying out by the manager of his duties;

(*b*) provide the manager, at his request, with all such information as he may reasonably require for the purpose of his duties;

(*c*) comply with any reasonable arrangements made by the manager for the storage and disposal of refuse and litter; and

(*d*) take reasonable care to avoid causing damage to anything which the manager is obliged by these regulations to keep in repair.

17. Register of managers   (1) The local authority shall maintain a register of the names and addresses of persons who are for the time being managers of houses to which the regulations apply, and shall include therein such particulars as they reasonably believe to be correct relating to the capacity in which such persons are managers, that is to say whether as owners or lessees receiving rents, or as agents or trustees through whom rents are received.

(2) As soon as may be after making or amending an entry in the register in reliance on information obtained otherwise than from the person to whom such entry relates the local authority shall take reasonable steps to bring the entry or amendment to the notice of the said person.

(3) The local authority shall, at the request of a person who appears to them to have an interest or prospective interest in a house, to be resident therein, or to be otherwise sufficiently concerned therewith, disclose to him the contents of any entry in the register relating to that house.

NOTES
Local authority   See the note "Other expressions" to reg 2, *ante*.

18. Provision of information by persons with an estate or interest in a house   (1) When a management order is made in respect of a house, an owner or lessee of the house who receives the rents shall, on being served with a copy of the order and warned in writing (whether by means of a note appended to the copy of the order or otherwise) of the requirements of this paragraph, provide the local authority with the following information—

(*a*) his name and address,

(*b*) particulars of his estate or interest in the house,

(*c*) particulars sufficient to show what parts of the house are let to tenants, or lodgers, from whom he is in receipt of rents, and

(*d*) the name and address of any agent or trustee through whom he receives such rents.

(2) Without prejudice to any other requirement of this regulation, a person who has an estate or interest in a house or any part of a house to which the regulations apply shall, at the request of the local authority, provide the authority with such of the following items of information as they may require, namely:—

(*a*) any of those mentioned in the last foregoing paragraph;

(*b*) the name and address of any other person known to him to be manager of the house, with particulars showing how he knows that such person is manager;

(*c*) if he is a person who receives the rents through another person as his agent or trustee, whether, and in what respects, such other person is authorised to act in matters connected with the management of the house apart from the receipt of rents.

(3) An owner or lessee of a house to which the regulations apply shall, if at any time he appoints a person to receive the rents as his agent or trustee, forthwith give the local authority notice of the fact together with the name and address of the person appointed.

(4) A person who acquires or ceases to hold an estate or interest in a house to which the regulations apply shall, if he thereby becomes or ceases to be manager of the house, forthwith give the local authority notice of the fact together with particulars of the estate or interest which he has acquired or ceased to hold, and, where he has sold or transferred the estate or interest to some other person, the name and address of that person.

(5) The information called for by or under this regulation shall, except in so far as the local authority may in any particular case otherwise allow, be provided to the authority in writing; and any information requested by the local authority under paragraph (2) of this regulation shall be given to them within such time, if any, as they may reasonably specify.

NOTES
On being served with a copy of the order   This copy is to be served under the Housing Act 1985, s 370 (3), Halsbury's Statutes, 4th edn Vol 21, title Housing.
Local authority   See the note "Other expressions" to reg 2, *ante*.

19. Procedural arrangements with managers   To assist the efficient management of houses in accordance with these regulations a local authority may, by agreement with a person who is manager of any house in respect of which they have made a management order, make arrangements as to the manner in which business relating to management of the house shall normally be conducted between the authority and that person, and, where there is more than one person who is manager of the house, such arrangements may provide for any business as aforesaid to be conducted with one such person in the first instance; but arrangements made in pursuance of this regulation shall be without prejudice to any of the local authority's powers in relation to houses to which these regulations apply.

NOTES
Local authority   See the note "Other expressions" to reg 2, *ante*.

THE HOUSING (PRESCRIBED FORMS) REGULATIONS 1972 SI 1972/228

NOTES
Authority   These regulations were made on 21 February 1972 by the Secretary of State for the Environment and the Secretary of State for Wales under s 178 of the Housing Act 1957, as extended by para 2 of Schedule 2 to the Land Compensation Act 1961, s 28 (2) of the Housing Act 1961, ss 44 (4) and 91 (5) of the Housing Act 1964, and s 91 (3) of the Housing Act 1969, and all other enabling powers. The 1957 Act was repealed by the Housing (Consequential Provisions) Act 1985 and by virtue of s 2 (2) thereof these regulations continue to have effect as if made under the Housing Act 1985, s 614, Halsbury's Statutes, 4th edn Vol 21, title Housing.
Commencement   1 May 1972.
Amendment   These regulations have been amended by the Housing (Prescribed Forms) (Amendment etc) Regulations 1974, SI 1974/1511, the Housing (Prescribed Forms) (Amendment) Regulations 1975, SI 1975/500 and the Housing (Prescribed Forms) (Amendment) Regulations 1981, SI 1981/1347.
General   These regulations revoke the Housing (Prescribed Forms) Regulations 1966, SI 1966/253, and, as construed in accordance with the Housing (Consequential Provisions) Act 1985, s 2 (4), prescribe new forms of orders, notices, advertisements, etc, required to be used under certain provisions of the Housing Act 1985 and the Land Compensation Act 1961 (as amended). Forms for other purposes of the Housing Act 1985 are prescribed by SR&O 1937/79 and 80, pp 149, 150 *ante*, SR&O 1939/563, p 152, *ante*, SI 1980/1465 and 1930, pp 170, 172, *post*, SI 1984/1175, p 186, *post* and SI 1985/36, p 189, *post*. It should be noted that forms etc referring to an enactment repealed by the Housing (Consequential Provisions) Act 1985 are generally to be construed as referring to the consolidating Acts; see Sch 4, para 16 thereof.
   By virtue of the 1985 Act, s 615, the Secretary of State may dispense with the publication of advertisements or the service of notices required to be published or served by a local authority if he is satisfied that there is reasonable cause. Appended to certain of the forms are notes setting out, *inter alia*, the right of persons served to object or appeal. These notes are material parts of the form, and if omitted the local authority may be restrained from enforcing the order of which the form gives notice; see *Rayner v Stepney Corpn* [1911] 2 Ch 312.

A list of the forms prescribed by these regulations is set out below. Unless otherwise indicated, the provisions indicated against the title of each form are the relevant provisions of the Housing Act 1985. It should be noted that the provisions of the Housing Acts 1957 and 1961 relating to clearance areas and the provisions of the Housing Act 1964 relating to compulsory improvement of dwellings were repealed by the Housing Act 1974 and accordingly there is no provision of the 1985 Act to be indicated against the titles of Forms 15-23, 28-31, 43-47 and 52-62.

The description of the forms has, where necessary, been amended to take account of the repeal of certain Housing Acts and their replacement by the Housing Act 1985.

Forms 2C, 4A, 4B, 4C and 4D have been added, and Forms 4, 34, 38 and 63 substituted, by SI 1981/1347; Form 66 has been added by SI 1974/1511, and Forms 67-70 by SI 1975/500; Form 1 has been amended by the said SI 1975/300; and the Notes to Forms 17, 19, 26 and 33 by SI 1974/1511.

Form 1	Notice before entry for the purpose of inspection, etc (ss 54, 197, 222, 260, 319, 340, 395, 600).
Form 2A	Notice requiring execution of works to unfit house (s 189).
Form 2B	Notice requiring execution of works of repair (s 190).
Form 2C	Notice requiring execution of works of repair upon a representation made by an occupying tenant (s 190).
Form 3	Closing order in respect of a house which is a listed building etc (ss 265, 304).
Form 4	Notice to abate overcrowding in house in multiple occupation (ss 358 (1), 359 (2) (a)).
Form 4A	Notice to abate overcrowding by new resident in house in multiple occupation (ss 358 (1), 359 (2) (b)).
Form 4B	Notice of intention to serve an overcrowding notice in respect of a house in multiple occupation (s 358 (2)).
Form 4C	Revocation or variation of an overcrowding notice in respect of a house in multiple occupation (s 363).
Form 4D	Notice requiring information in connection with premises in respect of which an overcrowding notice under [sections 358 and 359 of the Housing Act 1985] is in force (s 364).
Form 5	Order declaring expenses of execution of works to be payable by instalments (Sch 10, para 5).
Form 6	Notice of time and place for consideration of condition of house liable to be made subject to demolition or closing order (s 264).
Form 7	Order for demolition of a house (s 265).
Form 8	Notice of intention to cleanse building to which a demolition order or clearance order applies (s 273).
Form 9	Notice to proceed with demolition after a building has been cleansed (s 273).
Form 10	Notice to occupier to quit house after demolition order has become operative (s 270).
Form 11	Notice of determination by local authority to purchase house in lieu of making a demolition order (s 300).
Form 12	Notice of time and place for consideration of condition of part of a building liable to be made subject to closing order (ss 264, 266).
Form 13	Closing order in respect of part of a building (s 266).
Form 14	Closing order in lieu of demolition order in respect of a house (s 265).
Form 15	Clearance order.
Form 16	Clearance order providing for postponement of demolition.
Form 17	Personal notice of the making of a clearance order for demolition of buildings.
Form 18	Advertisement of the making of a clearance order for demolition of buildings.
Form 19	Personal notice of the making of a clearance order for demolition of houses but postponing demolition.
Form 20	Advertisement of the making of a clearance order for demolition of houses but postponing demolition.
Form 21	Advertisement and personal notice of clearance order which has been confirmed.
Form 22	Notice to occupier to quit building after clearance order has become operative.
Form 23	Notice requiring demolition of house the demolition of which has been postponed under a clearance order.
Form 24	Compulsory purchase order in respect of land comprised in a clearance area and land surrounded by or adjoining the area (s 290, Sch 22, para 2).
Form 25	Advertisement of the making of a compulsory purchase order in respect of land comprised in a clearance area and land surrounded by or adjoining the area (Sch 22, para 3 (2)).
Form 26	Personal notice of the making of a compulsory purchase order in respect of land comprised in a clearance area and land surrounded by or adjoining the area (Sch 22, para 3 (3)).
Form 27	Advertisement and personal notice of compulsory purchase order which has been confirmed in respect of land comprised in a clearance area and land surrounded by or adjoining the area (Sch 22, para 6).
Form 28	Compulsory purchase order in respect of land cleared of buildings in accordance with a clearance order.
Form 29	Advertisement of a compulsory purchase order in respect of land cleared of buildings in accordance with a clearance order.
Form 30	Personal notice of the making of a compulsory purchase order in respect of land which has been cleared of buildings in accordance with a clearance order.

Form 31   Advertisement and personal notice of compulsory purchase order which has been confirmed in respect of land cleared of buildings in accordance with a clearance order.
Form 32   Declaration of unfitness order (Land Compensation Act 1961, Sch 2, para 2, as substituted by the Housing (Consequential Provisions) Act 1985, Sch 2, para 4).
Form 33   Notice of the making of a declaration of unfitness order (Land Compensation Act 1961, Sch 2, para 2, as substituted by the Housing (Consequential Provisions) Act 1985, Sch 2, para 4).
Form 34   Notice requiring the provision of necessary means of escape from fire in a house in multiple occupation where part of the house is not used for human habitation (s 366 (1) (*b*)).
Form 35   Order applying management regulations to premises in multiple occupation (s 370).
Form 36   Notice requiring execution of works to make good neglect of proper standards of management (s 372 (1)).
Form 37   Notice requiring execution of works to render premises reasonably suitable for occupation by the persons or households occupying them (s 352 (1)).
Form 38   Notice requiring the provision of necessary means of escape from fire in a house in multiple occupation (s 366 (1) (*a*)).
Form 39   Notice of intention to give a direction to prevent or reduce overcrowding in a house in multiple occupation (s 354 (3)).
Form 40   Direction to prevent or reduce overcrowding in a house in multiple occupation (s 354 (1) (*b*)).
Form 41   Revocation or variation of a direction to prevent or reduce overcrowding in a house in multiple occupation (s 357).
Form 42   Notice requiring information in connection with a house in respect of which a direction under section [354 of the Housing Act 1985] is in force (s 356).
Form 43   Order excluding buildings from a clearance area and modifying or revoking a clearance order.
Form 44   Advertisement of making of an order excluding buildings from a clearance area and modifying or revoking a clearance order.
Form 45   Personal notice of making of an order excluding buildings from a clearance area and modifying or revoking a clearance order.
Form 46   Advertisement and personal notice of confirmation of an order excluding buildings from a clearance area and modifying or revoking a clearance order.
Form 47   Notice of re-imposition of obligations under a clearance order.
Form 48   Closing order substituted for demolition order in respect of a house (s 275).
Form 49   Notice of information as to service of notice requiring works (ss 352 (3), 372 (4)).
Form 50   Control order (s 379).
Form 51   Notice of the effect of, and grounds for making, a control order (s 379 (4)).
Form 52   Preliminary notice of local authority's proposals for improvement of dwelling in an improvement area declared under section 13 of the Housing Act 1964.
Form 53   Notification of representations made in respect of dwelling not in an improvement area declared under section 13 of the Housing Act 1964.
Form 54   Preliminary notice of local authority's proposals for improvement of dwelling not in an improvement area declared under section 13 of the Housing Act 1964.
Form 55   Preliminary notice of local authority's proposals for improvement of dwellings in a tenement block.
Form 56   Immediate improvement notice in respect of dwelling in an improvement area declared under section 13 of the Housing Act 1964.
Form 57   Immediate improvement notice in respect of dwelling not in an improvement area declared under section 13 of the Housing Act 1964.
Form 58   Immediate improvement notice in respect of tenement block.
Form 59   Suspended improvement notice.
Form 60   Final improvement notice on change of occupation or receipt of the tenant's consent.
Form 61   Final improvement notice served after expiration of five years from declaration of improvement area irrespective of change of occupation or receipt of tenant's consent.
Form 62   Notification of the tenant's appeal to the County Court.
Form 63   Closing order in respect of part of a house in multiple occupation (s 368 (4)).
Form 64   Notice specifying works carried out in house while subject to control order for the purpose of recovering capital expenditure incurred (Sch 13, Pt IV, para 26).
Form 65   Notice of balances proposed to be paid under [Schedule 13, Pt IV, para 25 (1) to the Housing Act 1985] (Sch 13, Pt IV, para 25 (2)).
Form 66   Notification of local authority's decision as to the state of maintenance of a house or dwelling for the purposes of payments for good maintenance. (Sch 23, para 7).
Form 67   Rehabilitation order (Sch 11, Pt II, para 9).
Form 68   Advertisement of making of a rehabilitation order (Sch 11, Pt II, para 10 (2)).
Form 69   Personal notice of making of rehabilitation order (Sch 11, Pt II, para 10 (3)).
Form 70   Advertisement and personal notice of confirmation of a rehabilitation order (Sch 11, Pt II, para 12).

THE HOUSING (PAYMENTS FOR WELL MAINTAINED HOUSES) ORDER) 1972
SI 1972/1792

NOTES
Authority   This order was made on 3 November 1972 by the Secretary of State for the Environ-

ment under para 1 (1) of Part I of Sch 2 to the Housing Act 1957, as that Part had effect by virtue of s 66 of the Housing Act 1969, and all other enabling powers. The 1957 and 1969 Acts were repealed by the Housing (Consequential Provisions) Act 1985 and by virtue of s 2 (2) thereof this order continues to have effect as if made under the Housing Act 1985, Sch 23, para 4 (1), Halsbury's Statutes, 4th edn Vol 21, title Housing.
Commencement 30 November 1972.
Modification This order has been modified by the Housing (Payments for Well Maintained Houses) Order 1973, SI 1973/753, *infra,* and by the Housing (Payments for Well Maintained Houses) Order 1982, SI 1982/1112, p 177, *post.*
General Payments in respect of well maintained houses which are subject to demolition or closing orders, have been purchased under the Housing Act 1985, s 192 or s 300, or are subject to clearance may be made by local housing authorities under the 1985 Act, Sch 23, paras 1-3, Halsbury's Statutes, 4th edn Vol 21, title Housing. Under Sch 23, para 4 (1), the amount of the payment is an amount equal to the rateable value of the house multiplied by four or such other multiplier as may be prescribed by order of the Secretary of State, but subject to the limit that the amount must not exceed the amount, if any, by which the full value of the house exceeds its site value. As construed in accordance with the Housing (Consequential Provisions) Act 1985, s 2 (4), this order provides that, in relation to any payment made after the coming into operation of this order, where the relevant order in consequence of which the right to the payment arises becomes operative on or after 17 October 1972, the multiplier is to be eight instead of four.

THE HOUSING (PAYMENTS FOR WELL MAINTAINED HOUSES) ORDER 1973
SI 1973/753

NOTES
Authority This is as noted to SI 1972/1792, p 162, *ante,* except that this order was made on 13 March 1973.
Commencement 19 April 1973.
Modification this order has been modified by the Housing (Payments for Well Maintained Houses) Order 1982, SI 1982/1112, p 177, *post.*
General As construed in accordance with the Housing (Consequential Provisions) Act 1985, s 2 (4), this order prescribes a multiplier of 3⅛ to be used in calculating by reference to the rateable value of a house the amount of a well maintained payment under the Housing Act 1985, Sch 23, para 1, 2 or 3, Halsbury's Statutes, 4th edn Vol 21, title Housing, which falls to be made by an authority after the order came into operation, where relevant action is taken by them on or after 1 April 1973. In such a case it replaces the multiplier of 8 which was prescribed by the Housing (Payments for Well Maintained Houses) Order 1972, SI 1972/1792, p 162, *ante.*

THE SLUM CLEARANCE SUBSIDY REGULATIONS 1974
SI 1974/618

NOTES
Authority These regulations were made on 29 March 1974 by the Secretary of State for the Environment and the Secretary of State for Wales, with the concurrence of the Treasury , under s 11 (3)−(6), (8) and (10) of the Housing Finance Act 1972, and all other enabling powers. The 1972 Act was repealed by the Housing (Consequential Provisions) Act 1985 and by virtue of s 2 (2) thereof these regulations now have effect as if made under the Housing Act 1985, s 313, Sch 12, Halsbury's Statutes, 4th edn Vol 21, title Housing.
Commencement 31 March 1974.
Amendment These regulations have been amended by the Slum Clearance Subsidy (Amendment) Regulations 1984, SI 1984/244.
General The Housing Act 1985, s 312, Halsbury's Statutes, 4th edn Vol 21, title Housing, provides for the payment of slum clearance subsidy to a local housing authority for any year in which the authority incur a loss in connection with the exercise of their slum clearance functions. The amount of slum clearance subsidy is to be 75 per cent of the loss. As construed in accordance with the Housing (Consequential Provisions) Act 1985, s 2 (4), these regulations prescribe the method of determining whether a local housing authority have incurred a loss in carrying out their slum clearance functions and of determining the amount of any such loss.

THE HOUSING ACT 1974 (COMMENCEMENT No 1) ORDER 1974
SI 1974/1406

NOTES
Authority This order was made on 19 August 1974 by the Secretary of State under s 131 (3) of the Housing Act 1974, Halsbury's Statutes, 4th edn Vol 21, title Housing, and all other enabling powers.

General This order brought into operation on 20 August 1974 certain provisions of the Housing Act 1974; the provisions specified, if not already repealed, were all subsequently repealed by the Housing (Consequential Provisions) Act 1985, with the exception of s 131 (part) and Sch 13, paras 38-45 (except para 40 (6)). It also brought a further provision, now repealed, into force on 31 August 1974.

Other commencement orders Further provisions of the Housing Act 1974 were brought into operation by SI 1974/1562 and 1791, 1975/374 and 1113 and 1979/1214, all listed at p 139, *ante*. Most of the provisions brought into force by these orders, if not already repealed, have been repealed by the Housing (Consequential Provisions) Act 1985, with the exception of s 11 (brought into force by SI 1974/1562) and s 120 (brought into force by SI 1974/1791).

THE SLUM CLEARANCE (RETENTION OF BUILDINGS) (COMPENSATION NOTICE) ORDER 1975
SI 1975/1108

NOTES
Authority This order was made on 1 July 1975 by the Secretary of State for the Environment and the Secretary of State for Wales under s 115 (11) of the Housing Act 1974, and all other enabling powers. The said s 115 was repealed by the Housing (Consequential Provisions) Act 1985 and by virtue of s 2 (2) thereof it is thought that this order now has effect as if made under the Housing Act 1985, s 614, Halsbury's Statutes, 4th edn Vol 21, title Housing.
Commencement 5 August 1975.
General This order, as construed in accordance with the Housing (Consequential Provisions) Act 1985, s 2 (4), prescribes the form of notice to be served by local housing authorities under the Housing Act 1985, s 594 (4) where compensation is payable under s 594 (1)-(3) of that Act.

THE IMPROVEMENT GRANT (RATEABLE VALUE LIMITS) ORDER 1977
SI 1977/1213

NOTES
Authority This order was made on 21 July 1977 by the Secretary of State for the Environment and the Secretary of State for Wales, with the consent of the Treasury, under ss 62 (3) and 128 (2) of the Housing Act 1974, and all other enabling powers. Those provisions of the 1974 Act were repealed by the Housing (Consequential Provisions) Act 1985 and by virtue of s 2 (2) thereof this order now has effect as if made under the Housing Act 1985, s 469 (4), Halsbury's Statutes, 4th edn Vol 21, title Housing.
Commencement 15 August 1977.
General This order (which revokes and replaces the Improvement Grant (Rateable Value Limits) Order 1976, SI 1976/526), as construed in accordance with the Housing (Consequential Provisions) Act 1985, s 2 (4), specifies limits of rateable value for the purposes of the Housing Act 1985, s 469, Halsbury's Statutes, 4th edn Vol 21, title Housing, (which sets a rateable value limit on improvement grants for dwellings for owner-occupation). The limits specified are as follows— (*a*) in relation to dwellings falling within s 469 (1) (*a*) which are in Greater London, a limit of £400, and in relation to dwellings elsewhere, a limit of £225; (*b*) in relation to houses converted as mentioned in s 469 (1) (*b*) which are in Greater London, a limit of £600, and in relation to such houses elsewhere, a limit of £350.

THE HOUSING (HOMELESS PERSONS) (PROPERTY AND STAFF) ORDER 1977
SI 1977/1821

NOTES
Authority This order was made on 7 November 1977 by the Secretary of State for the Environment and the Secretary of State for Wales under s 14 of the Housing (Homeless Persons) Act 1977, and all other enabling powers. The 1977 Act was repealed by the Housing (Consequential Provisions) Act 1985 and s 14 thereof was not re-enacted in the Housing Act 1985 (except s 14 (4) which is replaced by the Housing (Consequential Provisions) Act 1985, Sch 4, para 7 (2)). However, by virtue of the Housing (Consequential Provisions) Act 1985, Sch 4, para 7 (1), the repeal of the said s 14 does not affect the operation of any order previously made under that section.
Commencement 8 December 1977.
General This order provided for the transfer (from councils of non-metropolitan counties to the councils of districts) of property held for the purposes of s 21 (1) (*b*) (repealed) of the National Assistance Act 1948 (which section concerned the provision of temporary accommodation for persons in urgent need thereof) and related liabilities, contracts, etc. The order also provided for the transfer, with specified exceptions, of staff employed on 30 November 1977 in

the discharge of functions under that provision or employed by agreement (after that date) in the discharge of similar functions of district councils under the Housing (Homeless Persons) Act 1977. Staff were to be transferred under schemes made by county councils or in accordance with general principles of transfer, and provison was made for the protection of their interests. The order provided for the transfer of both staff and property to take place on 1 April 1978.

THE HOUSING (HOMELESS PERSONS) (APPROPRIATE ARRANGEMENTS) ORDER 1978
SI 1978/69

NOTES
Authority This order was made on 20 January 1978 by the Secretary of State for the Environment and the Secretary of State for Wales, under s 5 (8), (9) (*a*) and (10) of the Housing (Homeless Persons) Act 1977, and all other enabling powers. The 1977 Act was repealed by the Housing (Consequential Provisions) Act 1985 and by virtue of s 2 (2) thereof this order now has effect as if made under the Housing Act 1985, s 67 (4)-(6), Halsbury's Statutes, 4th edn Vol 21, title Housing.
Commencement 21 January 1978.
General This order, as construed in accordance with the Housing (Consequential Provisions) Act 1985, s 2 (4), sets out the "appropriate arrangements" for the purposes of the Housing Act 1985, s 67, Halsbury's Statutes, 4th edn Vol 21, title Housing (which section specifies circumstances in which a local housing authority may transfer responsibility for a homeless person to another local housing authority). In accordance with the order any question falling to be determined under the said s 67 (*ie,* any question as to whether the circumstances which may result in a transfer of responsibility exist in a particular case) which has not been determined by agreement between the authorities concerned, is to be determined either by a person agreed upon by the two authorities or in default by an "appointed person". The "appointed person" is selected from a panel of persons who may be appointed which must be drawn up by the Association of District Councils, the Association of Metropolitan Authorities and the London Boroughs Association. He is appointed by the Chairman or Chairmen of the association or associations representing the parties in dispute.
Application of order The arrangements set out in this order are arrangements agreed between the associations named above and apply in cases involving only English or Welsh housing authorities. The Housing (Homeless Persons) (Appropriate Arrangements) (No 2) Order 1978, SI 1978/661 (also made under s 5 (8), (9) (*a*) and (10) of the Housing (Homeless Persons) Act 1977 and now having effect under the Housing Act 1985, s 67 (4) (see "Authority", *supra*)) sets out analogous arrangements, agreed by the Convention of Scottish Local Authorities, which are to be followed where only Scottish housing authorities are involved or where an English or Welsh authority are in dispute with a Scottish authority.

THE HOME PURCHASE ASSISTANCE (RECOGNISED SAVINGS INSTITUTIONS) ORDER 1978
SI 1978/1785

NOTES
Authority This order was made on 4 December 1978 by the Secretary of State for the Environment and the Secretaries of State for Scotland and Wales, with the consent of the Treasury, under s 2 (1) and (7) of the Home Purchase Assistance and Housing Corporation Guarantee Act 1978 and all other enabling powers. The 1978 Act was repealed by the Housing (Consequential Provisions) Act 1985 and by virtue of s 2 (2) thereof this order now has effect as if made under the Housing Act 1985, s 448 (2), Halsbury's Statutes, 4th edn Vol 21, title Housing.
Commencement 5 December 1978.
General A condition for receiving assistance under the Housing Act 1985, s 446, Halsbury's Statutes, 4th edn Vol 21, title Housing, is that the purchaser shall have been saving for at least two years with a recognised saving institution. Such institutions are those specified in s 448 (1) of the Act, and this order, as construed in accordance with the Housing (Consequential Provisions) Act 1985, s 2 (4), adds the following institutions to those so specified—The Clydebank Municipal Bank Limited; Cumnock Municipal Bank Limited; Cunninghame District Municipal Bank Limited; Kilsyth and Cumbernauld District Municipal Bank Limited; Motherwell District Municipal Bank Limited; The Stockton-on-Tees Municipal Savings Bank Limited; Strathkelvin District Municipal Bank Limited; and West Lothian District Municipal Bank Limited.

THE HOUSING (RIGHT TO BUY) (MAXIMUM DISCOUNT) ORDER 1980
SI 1980/1342

NOTES
Authority This order was made on 4 September 1980 by the Secretary of State for the Environment and the Secretary of State for Wales under the Housing Act 1980, ss 7 (4) and 151 (1), and all other enabling powers. The said s 7 (4) was repealed by the Housing (Consequential Provisions) Act 1985 and by virtue of s 2 (2) thereof this order now has effect as if made under

the Housing Act 1985, s 131 (2), Halsbury's Statutes, 4th edn Vol 21, title Housing.
Commencement   3 October 1980.
General   This order, as construed in accordance with the Housing (Consequential Provisions) Act 1985, s 2 (4), prescribes £25,000 as the maximum discount by which the price payable for a dwelling-house on a conveyance or grant under the Housing Act 1985, Part V, Halsbury's Statutes, 4th edn Vol 21, title Housing, may be reduced under s 131 thereof.

THE HOUSING (RIGHT TO BUY) (DESIGNATED REGIONS) ORDER 1980 SI 1980/1345

NOTES
Authority   This order was made on 5 September 1980 by the Secretary of State for the Environment under the Housing Act 1980, ss 19 (12) and 151 (1) and (3), and all other enabling powers. The said s 19 was repealed by the Housing (Consequential Provisions) Act 1985 and by virtue of s 2 (2) thereof this order now has effect as if made under the Housing Act 1985, s 157 (3) (*a*), Halsbury's Statutes, 4th edn Vol 21, title Housing.
Commencement   3 October 1980.
General   The Housing Act 1985, s 157 (1), (2) provides that where in pursuance of Part V of that Act, Halsbury's Statutes, 4th edn Vol 21, title Housing, a conveyance or grant is executed by a local authority, the Development Board for Rural Wales or a housing association, of a dwelling-house situated in a National Park, an area of outstanding natural beauty or a rural area designated by order of the Secretary of State, the conveyance or grant may contain a covenant limiting the freedom of the tenant and his successors in title to dispose of the dwelling-house without the consent of the landlord. Under s 157 (3), such consent is not to be withheld where the disposal is made to a person who has, throughout the three years immediately preceding the application for consent, had either his only or principal home or his place of work in a region designated by order of the Secretary of State which, or part of which is comprised in the National Park or area.

This order, as construed in accordance with the Housing (Consequential Provisions) Act 1985, s 2 (4), designates for the purposes or s 157 (3) in respect of dwelling-houses in National Parks or areas of outstanding natural beauty situated in England a region comprising the Park or area in which the dwelling-house is situated and, so far as not situated in the Park or area, the county in which it is situated. Special provision is made for dwelling-houses situated in the Wye Valley Area of Outstanding Natural Beauty and in the Isles of Scilly.
Further orders   The following orders, which were all made under the Housing Act 1980, ss 19 (1), (12) and 151 (1), (3) and now have effect as if made under the Housing Act 1985, s 157 (1) (*c*), (3) (*a*), designate specified rural areas for the purposes of the Housing Act 1985, s 157 (1) (see "General", *supra*) and specified regions for the purposes of s 157 (3) thereof (see "General", *supra*): (i) the Housing (Right to Buy) (Designated Rural Areas and Designated Regions) (Wales) Order 1980, SI 1980/1375, designating rural areas in Wales and in respect of dwelling-houses in National Parks, areas of outstanding natural beauty or rural areas so designated, situated in Wales, a region comprising the Park or area in which the dwelling-house is situated, and, so far as not situated in that Park or area, the county in which it is situated; (ii) the Housing (Right to Buy) (Designated Rural Areas and Designated Regions) (England) Order 1981, SI 1981/397, designating eighteen rural areas in England and in respect of dwelling-houses in those areas regions comprising the areas in which the dwelling-house is situated and, so far as not situated in that area, the county in which it is situated; (iii) the Housing (Right to Buy) (Designated Rural Areas and Designated Regions) (England) (No 2) Order 1981, SI 1981/940, designating the District of Mid Devon with specified exceptions as a rural area and the County of Devon as the designated region in respect of any dwelling-house situated in that rural area; (iv) the Housing (Right to Buy) (Designated Rural Areas and Designated Regions) (England) Order 1982, SI 1982/21, designating the district of North Norfolk, with specified exceptions, as a rural area and the county of Norfolk as the designated region in respect of any dwelling-house situated in that rural area; and (v) the Housing (Right to Buy) (Designated Rural Areas and Designated Regions) (England) (No 2) Order 1982, SI 1982/187, designating the District of Teignbridge, with specified exceptions, as a rural area and the County of Devon as the designated region in respect of any dwelling-house situated in that rural area.

THE HOUSING (RIGHT TO BUY) (MORTGAGE COSTS) ORDER 1980 SI 1980/1390

NOTES
Authority   This order was made on 15 September 1980 by the Secretary of State for the Environment and the Secretary of State for Wales under the Housing Act 1980, ss 21 (2) and 151 (1), and all other enabling powers. The said s 21 was repealed by the Housing (Consequential Provisions) Act 1985 and by virtue of s 2 (2) thereof this order now has effect as if made under the Housing Act 1985, s 178 (2), Halsbury's Statutes, 4th edn Vol 21, title Housing.
Commencement   3 October 1980.
General   This order, as construed in accordance with the Housing (Consequential Provisions) Act 1985, s 2 (4), specifies £50 as the maximum amount chargeable by the landlord or the Housing Corporation in respect of the costs incurred by it in connection with the tenant's exercise of his right to a mortgage.

THE HOUSING ACT 1980 (COMMENCEMENT No 1) ORDER 1980
SI 1980/1406

NOTES

Authority This order was made on 17 September 1980 by the Secretary of State under the Housing Act 1980, ss 151 (1) and 153 (4), Halsbury's Statutes, 4th edn Vol 23, title Landlord and Tenant, and all other enabling powers.

General This order brought into force on 1 October 1980 one section of the Housing Act 1980 which is now repealed by the Housing (Consequential Provisions) Act 1985 and on 3 October 1980 certain other sections of the 1980 Act. The sections brought into force on 3 October 1980 which have not now been repealed, either by the 1985 Act or by previous Acts, are ss 81-86, 88, 89, 141 (and Sch 21 (part)), 143, 148 and 152 (and Schs 25 and 26 (part)), Halsbury's Statutes, 4th edn Vol 23, title Landlord and Tenant.

Other commencement orders Further provisions of the Housing Act 1980 were brought into force on various dates in 1980 and 1981 by the following orders: the Housing Act 1980 (Commencement No 2) Order 1980, SI 1980/1466, the Housing Act 1980 (Commencement No 3) Order 1980, SI 1980/1557, the Housing Act 1980 (Commencement No 4) Order 1980, SI 1980/1693, the Housing Act 1980 (Commencement No 5) Order 1980, SI 1980/1706, the Housing Act 1980 (Commencement No 6) Order 1980, SI 1980/1781, the Housing Act 1980 (Commencement No 7) Order 1981, SI 1981/119 and the Housing Act 1980 (Commencement No 8) Order 1981, SI 1981/296. It should be noted that a number of the provisions brought into force by these orders have now been repealed, either by the Housing (Consequential Provisions) Act 1985 or by previous Acts; in particular, all the provisions brought into force by SI 1980/1693 have now been repealed. In addition, the Rent Rebates and Rent Allowances (England and Wales) (Appointed Day) Order 1981, SI 1981/297, which appointed a day for the purposes of a section of the 1980 Act which is now repealed, has now lapsed.

For the unrepealed provisions of the 1980 Act, see Halsbury's Statutes, 4th edn Vol 1, title Agriculture (Pt 3) and Vol 23, title Landlord and Tenant (Pts 1 and 2); and as to the sections of that Act which have not as yet been brought into force, see the note to s 153 thereof.

THE HOUSING (RIGHT TO BUY) (MORTGAGE LIMIT) REGULATIONS 1980
SI 1980/1423

NOTES

Authority These regulations were made on 23 September 1980 by the Secretary of State for the Environment and the Secretary of State for Wales under the Housing Act 1980, ss 9 (4) and 151 (1), and all other enabling powers. The said s 9 has been repealed by the Housing (Consequential Provisions) Act 1985 and by virtue of s 2 (2) thereof these regulations now have effect as if made under the Housing Act 1985, s 133 (3), Halsbury's Statutes, 4th edn Vol 21, title Housing.

Commencement 3 October 1980; see reg 1 (1).

General These regulations, as construed in accordance with the Housing (Consequental Provisions) Act 1985, s 2 (4), provide for the calculation of the tenant's available annual income and specify the appropriate factor by which it must be multiplied to arrive at the limit which applies under the Housing Act 1985, s 133 to a mortgage for a tenant buying his home under the Act who has a right to a mortgage.

1. Citation etc. (1) These regulations may be cited as the Housing (Right to Buy) (Mortgage Limit) Regulations 1980 and shall come into operation on 3rd October 1980.

(2) In these regulations—

"admissable source" means a source of income of the tenant which is to be taken into account for the purposes of these regulations; and

"tenant" means a person to whom the right to a mortgage belongs.

2. Available annual income The amount to be taken into account as the tenant's available annual income under section 9 of the Housing Act 1980 (which deals with the amount to be secured by mortgage) is to be calculated by taking the amount which in accordance with regulations 3 to 6 is to be taken into account as his annual income and deducting from it in accordance with regulation 7 sums related to his commitments.

NOTES

Housing Act 1980, s 9 Repealed and consolidated in the Housing Act 1985, s 133, Halsbury's Statutes, 4th edn Vol 21, title Housing.

3. Income from employment (1) This regulation applies to income from an employment.

(2) The amount to be taken into account as income to which this regulation applies is the tenant's current annual pay, namely his current pay expressed as an annual amount or, where that amount does not fairly represent his current annual pay, such amount as does.

(3) In this regulation—

"employment" includes a part-time employment and an office but does not include a casual or temporary employment; and

"pay" includes any commission, bonus, allowance (but not an expense allowance) tip, gratuity or other payment made to the tenant in connection with his employment but does not include any benefit in kind; and references to pay are references to it before any statutory or other deduction has been made.

4. Income from a business   (1) This regulation applies to income from a business carried on by the tenant (whether or not with any other person).

(2) The amount to be taken into account as the tenant's annual income from the business is an amount which, having regard to the latest available information fairly represents the current annual net profit of the business or, if the tenant shares the net profit with any other person, his share of the net profit.

(3) In this regulation "business" includes any trade, profession or vocation.

5. Other income   (1) This regulation applies to income from a source to which regulations 3 and 4 do not apply.

(2) No account shall be taken of state benefits other than benefits under—

(a) sections 36 and 37 of the National Insurance Act 1965 (graduated retirement benefits);

(b) sections 8, 15 and 16 of the Social Security Pensions Act 1975 (widower's retirement pensions, widow's and widower's invalidity pensions); and

(c) the following provisions of the Social Security Act 1975 to the extent that they relate to any benefit by way of pension or other periodical payments—

sections 15, 16 and 36 (invalidity benefits);

sections 24 to 26 (widow's benefits);

sections 28, 29, 39 and 40 (retirement pensions);

section 57 (1) (disability benefits);

sections 67 (1), 69, 70, 71 (1) and 72 (1) (industrial death benefits); and

section 76 (industrial disease benefits).

(3) The amount to be taken into account as the tenant's annual income from a source to which this regulation applies, which is not excluded from account by paragraph (2), is an amount which before any statutory or other deduction represents the tenant's current income from that source expressed as an annual amount.

(4) In this regulation "state benefits" means any benefits under the Family Income Supplements Act 1970, the Social Security Act 1975 to 1980, the Child Benefit Act 1975 and the Supplementary Benefits Act 1976.

NOTES

National Insurance Act 1965, ss 36, 37   Repealed but continued in force by the Social Security (Graduated Retirement Benefit) (No 2) Regulations 1978, SI 1978/393; see Halsbury's Statutes, 4th edn Vol 40, title Social Security (3rd edn Vol 23, pp 296, 298).

Social Security Pensions Act 1975, ss 8, 15, 16   *Ibid,* 4th edn Vol 40, title Social Security (3rd edn Vol 45, pp 1392, 1397, 1398).

Social Security Act 1975, ss 15, 16, 24-26, 28, 29, 36, 39, 40, 57 (1), 67 (1), 69, 70, 71 (1), 72 (1), 76   *Ibid,* 4th edn Vol 40, title Social Security (3rd edn Vol 45, p 1094 *et seq*).

Family Income Supplements Act 1970   *Ibid,* 4th edn Vol 40, title Social Security (3rd edn Vol 40, p 1079 *et seq*).

Social Security Acts 1975 to 1980   *Ie,* the Social Security Act 1975, the Social Security Pensions Act 1975, the Social Security (Miscellaneous Provisions) Act 1977, the Social Security Act 1979, the Social Security Act 1980 and the Social Security (No 2) Act 1980; see the Social Security (No 2) Act 1980, s 8 (1), Halsbury's Statutes, 4th edn Vol 40, title Social Security (3rd edn Vol 50 (2), p 1767).

Child Benefit Act 1975   *Ibid,* 4th edn Vol 40, title Social Security (3rd edn Vol 45, p 1481 *et seq*).

Supplementary Benefits Act 1976   *Ibid*, 4th edn Vol 40, title Social Security (3rd edn Vol 46, p 1046 *et seq*).

6. Income from more than one source   If the tenant has income from more than one admissable source, the amount to be taken into account as his annual income shall be the total amount of his annual income from all admissable sources determined in accordance with the provisions of these regulations.

7. Deductions for commitments   (1) Sums related to the tenant's commitments are to be deducted from the amount to be taken into account as his annual income if he is liable to make:
   (*a*) any maintenance payments; or
   (*b*) any payments under a credit agreement; or
   (*c*) any payments under a court order;
and the payments are likely to continue for more than 18 months.
   (2) The sums which are to be deducted are sums equal in total to the total of the annual amounts currently payable, for which the conditions in paragraph (1) are satisfied.
   (3) In this regulation—
"credit agreement" means a loan agreement, hire purchase agreement or other agreement for credit; and
"maintenance payment" means any payment by the tenant for the maintenance of a dependent child under the age of 16 or for the maintenance of his spouse or former spouse.

8. Estimates   The landlord, or, if the landlord is a housing association, the Housing Corporation, may accept any estimate made for the purposes of regulations 3 to 7.

9. Joint tenants   Where the right to a mortgage belongs to more than one tenant, the preceding provisions of these regulations shall be applied separately to determine the amount of each tenant's available annual income.

10. Multipliers   (1) This regulation specifies the appropriate factor to be applied as a multiplier of the tenant's available annual income to arrive at the limit imposed by section 9 of the Housing Act 1980.
   (2) If the tenant's income is the principal income, the appropriate factor in relation to his available annual income is the multiplier shown in the following Table corresponding to his age on the date of service of the notice under section 5 of the Housing Act 1980 claiming to exercise the right to buy.

TABLE

Tenant's age on the date of service of the notice	*Multiplier*
Under 60 . .	2·5
60 and over but under 65 . .	2·0
65 and over	1·0

   (3) If the tenant's income is not the principal income, the appropriate factor in relation to his available annual income is 1.
   (4) Subject to paragraph (5), a tenant's income is the principal income for the purposes of this regulation if he is the only tenant with income or there is more than one tenant with income and the tenants require the landlord or,

if the landlord is a housing association, the Housing Corporation, to treat his income as the principal income.

(5) The income of only one tenant shall be treated as the principal income for the purposes of this regulation.

NOTES
Housing Act 1980, ss 5, 9   Repealed and consolidated in the Housing Act 1985, ss 122, 133, Halsbury's Statutes, 4th edn Vol 21, title Housing.

THE HOUSING (RIGHT TO BUY) (PRESCRIBED FORMS) (No 2) REGULATIONS 1980
SI 1980/1465

NOTES
Authority   These regulations were made on 2 October 1980 by the Secretary of State for the Environment and the Secretary of State for Wales under the Housing Act 1980, ss 22 (1) and 151 (1), and all other enabling powers. The said s 22 was repealed and s 151 (1) partially repealed by the Housing (Consequential Provisions) Act 1985 and by virtue of s 2 (2) thereof these regulations now have effect as if made under the Housing Act 1985, s 176 (1), Halsbury's Statutes, 4th edn Vol 21, title Housing.
Commencement   10 October 1980.
General   These regulations, as construed in accordance with the Housing (Consequential Provisions) Act 1985, s 2 (4), prescribe the form of notice to be used by a secure tenant who is exercising the right to buy under the Housing Act 1985, Part V, Halsbury's Statutes, 4th edn Vol 21, title Housing, for the purpose of claiming the right to a mortgage under s 134 of the Act.

THE GRANTS BY LOCAL AUTHORITIES (APPROPRIATE PERCENTAGE AND EXCHEQUER CONTRIBUTIONS) ORDER 1980
SI 1980/1735

NOTES
Authority   This order was made on 13 November 1980 with the consent of the Treasury by the Secretary of State for the Environment and the Secretary of State for Wales under the Housing Act 1974, ss 59, 78 (4) and (5) and 128 (1) and (1A), and all other enabling powers. Those sections have now been repealed by the Housing (Consequential Provisions) Act 1985 and by virtue of s 2 (2) thereof this order now has effect as if made under the Housing Act 1985, ss 509 and 517, Halsbury's Statutes, 4th edn Vol 21, title Housing.
Commencement   15 December 1980; see art 1.
Amendment   The order is printed as amended by the Grants by Local Authorities (Appropriate Percentage and Exchequer Contributions) (Amendment) Order 1981, SI 1981/1712, in relation to applications for grant approved after 31 December 1981.
General   This order, as construed in accordance with the Housing (Consequential Provisions) Act 1985, s 2 (4), prescribes the "appropriate percentage" of the cost of the works to be carried out for the purpose of determining the amount of a grant under the Housing Act 1985, Part XV, in relation to grants approved on or after 15 December 1980. The percentage is to be different in different descriptions of cases. The order also specifies the percentages of grants which may be contributed by the Secretary of State.

In relation to applications for intermediate grants or repairs grants made on or before 31 December 1982 and approved after 12 April 1982, see the Grants by Local Authorities (Appropriate Percentage and Exchequer Contributions) Order 1982, SI 1982/581, p 172, *post*; and in relation to applications for such grants made on or before 31 March 1984 and approved after 31 December 1982, see the Grants by Local Authorities (Appropriate Percentage and Exchequer Contributions) (No 2) Order 1982, SI 1982/1763, p 180, *post*. See also the Grants by Local Authorities (Appropriate Percentage and Exchequer Contribution) (Repairs Grants for Airey Houses) Order 1982, SI 1983/95, as amended, p 180, *post*.

Citation and commencement

1.   This order may be cited as the Grants by Local Authorities (Appropriate Percentage and Exchequer Contributions) Order 1980, and shall come into operation on 15th December 1980.

Appropriate percentage for determining the amount or the maximum amount of grant

2.   The appropriate percentage in relation to an application for a grant approved after 14th December 1980 shall be the percentage applicable to that application in accordance with the following provisions of this order.

3. (1) Subject to article 6, the appropriate percentage in relation to an application for a grant to which paragraph (2) or (3) applies is 75 per cent.

(2) This paragraph applies to an application for a grant where one or more of the following conditions is satisfied:

(*a*) on the date on which the application is approved the premises in respect of which it is made are in a housing action area;

(*b*) the application is in respect of a dwelling or a house in multiple occupation which is, or which forms part of, or which in the case of a dwelling is to be provided by the conversion of, a house in relation to which the local authority have served a notice under section 9 (1) or 16 of the Housing Act 1957 and the relevant works consist of or include works which if executed would contribute towards rendering the house fit for human habitation;

(*c*) (i) the dwelling to which the application relates lacks, or is to be provided by the conversion of a dwelling which lacks, one or more of the standard amenities, and

(ii) the relevant works consist of or include the provision of a standard amenity which is lacking, and

(iii) the local authority are satisfied that the standard amenity which is to be provided, or, where more than one such amenity is to be provided, each of them, has been lacking for a period of not less than 12 months ending on the date on which the application was made;

(*d*) the application is in respect of a dwelling which is or is to be provided by the conversion of a dwelling which is in need of works of repair of a substantial and structural character, and the relevant works consist of or include such works.

[(*e*) the application is for an improvement grant in respect of the provision or improvement of a dwelling for a disabled occupant and the relevant works consist of or include works needed to meet a requirement arising from the particular disability from which he suffers;

(*f*) the application is for an intermediate grant and the relevant works consist of or include the provision for a disabled occupant of any standard amenity where an existing amenity of the same description is not or will not be readily accessible to the disabled occupant by reason of his disability.]

(3) This paragraph applies to an application for a special grant where either of the following conditions is satisfied:

(*a*) the relevant works consist of or include the provision of any of the standard amenities and the local authority consider such provision is necessary to make the house in multiple occupation reasonably suitable for occupation by the number of individuals or households for the time being occupying it;

(*b*) the house is not provided with such means of escape from fire as the local authority consider necessary and the relevant works consist of or include the provision of such means of escape.

NOTES

Amendment Article 3 (2) (*e*), (*f*) of this order were inserted by SI 1981/1712 in relation to an application for grant approved after 31 December 1981.

Housing Act 1957, s 9 (1) or 16 Repealed and consolidated in the Housing Act 1985, ss 189 (1), (2), 264, 268 (1) and 275 (2), Halsbury's Statutes, 4th edn Vol 21, title Housing.

4. In relation to an application for a grant to which article 3 does not apply but where on the date on which the application is approved, the premises in respect of which the application is made are in a general improvement area, the appropriate percentage is 65 per cent.

5. Subject to article 6, in relation to an application for a grant to which neither article 3 nor 4 applies, the appropriate percentage is 50 per cent.

6. In relation to an application for a grant, where it appears to the local authority that the applicant would not without undue hardship be able to finance so much of the cost of the relevant works as is not met by the grant,—
  (*a*) if apart from this article the appropriate percentage would be 75 per cent, it shall instead be 90 per cent.; and
  (*b*) if apart from this article the appropriate percentage would be 50 per cent, it shall instead be 65 per cent.

Contributions by the Secretary of State

7. With respect to applications for grants approved after 14th December 1980 the percentages specified in subsection (3) of section 78 of the Housing Act 1974 are varied in the following descriptions of cases:—
  (*a*) in paragraph (*a*), by the substitution of 75 per cent. where the premises are in a general improvement area;
  (*b*) in paragraph (*b*), by the substitution of 90 per cent. in respect of cases in which in accordance with this order the appropriate percentage is 75 per cent. or 90 per cent.

NOTES
Housing Act 1974, s 78 (3)   Repealed and consolidated in the Housing Act 1985, s 516 (3), Halsbury's Statutes, 4th edn Vol 21, title Housing.

THE HOUSING (RIGHT TO BUY) (PRESCRIBED FORMS) (No 2) (WELSH FORMS) REGULATIONS 1980
SI 1980/1930

NOTES
Authority   These regulations were made on 26 November 1980 by the Secretary of State for Wales under the Housing Act 1980, ss 22 (1) and 151 (1), as extended by the Welsh Language Act 1967, s 2 (2) and (3), and all other enabling powers. The said s 22 was repealed and s 151 (1) partially repealed by the Housing (Consequential Provisions) Act 1985 and by virtue of s 2 (2) thereof these regulations now have effect as if made under the Housing Act 1985, s 176 (1), as so extended, Halsbury's Statutes, 4th edn Vol 21, title Housing.
Commencement   30 January 1981.
General   These regulations, as construed in accordance with the Housing (Consequential Provisions) Act 1985, s 2 (4), prescribe a version in Welsh of the form of notice for use by a secure tenant claiming to exercise his right to a mortgage under the right to buy provisions of the Housing Act 1985, Part V, Halsbury's Statutes, 4th edn Vol 21, title Housing. The form may be used only in relation to a house or flat situated in Wales.

THE HOUSING (MEANS OF ESCAPE FROM FIRE IN HOUSES IN MULTIPLE OCCUPATION) ORDER 1981
SI 1981/1576

NOTES
Authority   This order was made on 2 November 1981 by the Secretary of State for the Environment and the Secretary of State for Wales under the Housing Act 1980, s 147 and Sch 24, para 1, and all other enabling powers. Those provisions were repealed by the Housing (Consequential Provisions) Act 1985 and by virtue of s 2 (2) thereof this order now has effect as if made under the Housing Act 1985, s 365 (2), Halsbury's Statutes, 4th edn Vol 21, title Housing.
Commencement   3 December 1981.
General   This order, as construed in accordance with the Housing (Consequential Provisions) Act 1985, s 2 (4), provides that the exercise by local authorities of their powers under the Housing Act 1985, ss 366 and 368, Halsbury's Statutes, 4th edn Vol 21, title Housing, to require houses in multiple occupation to be provided with means of escape from fire is to be mandatory where the house in multiple occupation is of at least three storeys, exluding any storey lying wholly or mainly below the floor area of the principal entrance to the house, with a combined floor area in excess of 500 square metres.

THE GRANTS BY LOCAL AUTHORITIES (APPROPRIATE PERCENTAGE AND EXCHEQUER CONTRIBUTIONS) ORDER 1982
SI 1982/581

NOTES
Authority   This is as noted to SI 1980/1735, p 170, *ante,* except that this order was made on 21 April 1982.

Commencement   22 April 1982.
General   The order, as construed in accordance with the Housing (Consequential Provisions) Act 1985, s 2 (4), further prescribes the "appropriate percentage" of the cost of the works to be carried out for the purpose of determining the amount of a grant under the Housing Act 1985, Part XV. In the case of applications for intermediate grants and repairs grants made on or before 31 December 1982 and approved after 12 April 1982, the appropriate percentage is to be 90 per cent. The order also further specifies the percentages of grants which may be contributed by the Secretary of State; where the application for the grant was made on or before 31 December 1982 and was approved after 12 April 1982, he may contribute 95 per cent towards the expenses of a local authority in making repairs grants and 90 per cent in the case of intermediate grants

See further the Grants by Local Authorities (Appropriate Percentage and Exchequer Contributions) Order 1980, SI 1980/1735, as amended, p 170, *ante,* and the Grants by Local Authorities (Appropriate Percentage and Exchequer Contributions) (No 2) Order 1982, SI 1982/1763, p 180, *post.*

THE REGISTERED HOUSING ASSOCIATIONS (ACCOUNTING REQUIREMENTS) ORDER 1982
SI 1982/828

NOTES
Authority   This order was made on 17 June 1982 by the Secretary of State for the Environment and the Secretaries of State for Wales and Scotland under the Housing Act 1980, ss 124 (1) and 151, and all other enabling powers. The said s 124 was repealed by the Housing (Consequential Provisions) Act 1985 and by virtue of s 2 (2) thereof this order now has effect as if it was made under the Housing Associations Act 1985, s 24, Halsbury's Statutes, 4th edn Vol 21, title Housing.
Commencement   1 September 1982.
Amendment   This order has been amended by the Registered Housing Associations (Accounting Requirements for Almshouses) Order 1983, SI 1983/207, listed at p 141, *ante,* and the Registered Housing Associations (Limited Accounting Requirements) Order 1984, SI 1984/1833, p 189, *post.*
General   This order, as construed in accordance with the Housing (Consequential Provisions) Act 1985, s 2 (4), lays down accounting requirements for housing associations registered with the Housing Corporation to ensure that their accounts are prepared in the requisite form and give a true and fair view of their state of affairs, so far as their housing activities are concerned. The order also lays down the method by which an association is to consitute its Grant Redemption Fund under the Housing Associations Act 1985, s 53, Halsbury's Statutes, 4th edn Vol 21, title Housing, and show that Fund in its accounts.

The requirements laid down by this order are modified by SI 1983/207 referred to above in relation to almshouses, and by SI 1984/1833, p 189, *post,* in consequence of the introduction by that order of alternative accounting requirements for qualifying housing associations.
Penalties   If the provisions of the Housing Associations Act 1985, s 24 (4) (furnishing of accounts and auditor's report) or the accounts furnished under that provision do not comply with the accounting requirements laid down by this order, as amended, or by SI 1984/1833, p 189, *post,* every responsible person (as defined in s 27 (1)), and the association itself, is liable on summary conviction to a fine not exceeding level 3 on the standard scale; see the Housing Associations Act 1985, s 27 (2), Halsbury's Statutes, 4th edn Vol 21, title Housing.

THE SOCIAL SECURITY AND HOUSING BENEFITS ACT 1982 (COMMENCEMENT No 2) ORDER 1982
SI 1982/906

NOTES
Authority   This order was made on 1 July 1982 by the Secretary of State for Social Services under the Social Security and Housing Benefits Act 1982, s 48 (3) and (4), Halsbury's Statutes, 4th edn Vol 40, title Social Security (3rd edn Vol 52, p 876), and all other enabling powers.
General   This order brings into force on specified dates in 1982 and 1983 those provisions of the Social Security and Housing Benefits Act 1982 concerned with housing benefits and related matters; see also the Social Security and Housing Benefits Act 1982 (Commencement No 1) Order 1982, SI 1982/893, in the title National Insurance (Pt 1).

1. Citation and interpretation   (1) This order may be cited as the Social Security and Housing Benefits Act 1982 (Commencement No 2) Order 1982.

(2) In this order "the Act" means the Social Security and Housing Benefits Act 1982.

2. Appointed days   (1) The day appointed for the coming into operation—
   (*a*) of the provisions of the Act specified in column 1 of the Schedule 1 to this order shall be 19th July 1982;

(*b*) of the provisions of the Act specified in column 1 of Schedule 2 to this order shall be 22nd November 1982;

(*c*) of the provisions of the Act specified in column 1 of Schedule 3 to this order shall be 1st April 1983;

(*d*) of the provisions of the Act specified in column 1 of Schedule 4 to this order shall be 4th April 1983.

and of section 28 (1) to (4) of the Act shall be in accordance with the following paragraphs of this article.

(2) The provisions of section 28 (1) to (4) of the Act shall come into operation as follows—

(*a*) on 22nd November in so far as they relate to rate rebate or rent rebate; and in their application to a person and his partner where that person fulfils the following condition—

    (i) he or his partner is a tenant of a housing authority and that if he is a joint tenant he is a joint tenant only with his partner,

    (ii) he is entitled to qualifying supplementary benefit,

    (iii) his dwelling is occupied as a home only by himself or persons who are members of his assessment unit,

    (iv) the amount of qualifying supplementary benefit to which he is entitled exceeds his housing requirements, and

    (v) he is not a person to whom section 8 (1) or 9 of the Supplementary Benefits Act 1976 (persons affected by or returning to work after a trade dispute) applies;

(*b*) On 1st April 1983 to the extent that they are not then in operation in so far as they relate to rate rebate and in their application to a person, and his partner, where that person is not a tenant of a housing authority;

(*c*) on 4th April 1983 for all other purposes.

(3) In paragraph (2) of this Article—

(*a*) "assessment unit" means an assessment unit, being a claimant, partner and any dependant of his, within the meaning of regulation 2 of the Supplementary Benefit (Requirements) Regulations 1980 ("Requirements Regulations");

(*b*) the reference to a person's "housing requirements" is to housing requirements assessed under the following provisions of the Requirements Regulations as though they applied to that person—

    (i) regulation 15.

    (ii) regulation 19 (*a*),

    (iii) regulation 19 (*b*) in so far as it relates to sewerage and allied environmental services in Scotland,

    (iv) regulation 19 (*e*),

    (v) regulation 19 (*g*) in so far as it relates to the provisions set out in heads (ii) to (iv) above;

(*c*) "partner" means a member of a married couple, being a man and woman who are married to each other and are members of the same household, or of an unmarried couple, being a man and woman who are not married to each other but are living together as husband and wife as members of the same household;

(*d*) "qualifying supplementary benefit" means supplementary pension or allowance under section 1 of the Supplementary Benefits Act 1976 which is payable to a person who for the purposes of the Requirements Regulations is responsible for housing expenditure except any such pension or allowance which is payable in accordance with section 4 of the Supplementary Benefits Act 1976 for the period to which regulation 5 (3) (*a*) of the Supplementary Benefit (Urgent Cases) Regulations 1981 (first 14 days) applies.

NOTES
Supplementary Benefits Act 1976, ss 1, 4, 8 (1) and 9 Halsbury's Statutes, 4th edn Vol 40, title Social Security (3rd edn Vol 46, pp 1048, 1049, 1052).
Supplementary Benefit (Requirements) Regulations 1980 SI 1980/1299; revoked and replaced by the Supplementary Benefit (Requirements) Regulations 1983, SI 1983/1399, as amended, in

the title National Insurance (Pt 4) in this work. The corresponding provisions of the 1983 Reg-
ulations are regs 2 and 18 (reg 15 of the 1980 Regulations is not replaced).
Supplementary Benefit (Urgent Cases) Regulations 1981   SI 1981/1529, as amended, in the title
National Insurance (Pt 4) in this work.

3. Transitional provision and savings   (1) Where by virtue of Article 2 (1)
(*c*) or (2) of this order an enactment mentioned in paragraphs 5, 6, 19, 27,
28 or 35 (2) of Schedule 4 to the Act is to be amended with effect from
respectively the 1st or 4th April 1983 by the substitution, for a reference to
any subsidy or scheme under an enactment repealed or to be repealed by or
under the Act, of a reference to the corresponding subsidy or scheme under
the Act, any reference in the enactment to be so amended to that subsidy or
scheme shall be treated until that date as including a reference to any corresponding subsidy payable under the Act or any scheme in force under the Act.

(2) Payment of any subsidy under any enactment repealed with effect from
4th April 1983 by section 32 (7) of the Act and Article 2 (1) (*d*) of this order
may be made after that date, but only in respect of a period ending before
that date, as though the enactment had not been repealed.

SCHEDULE 1   Article 2 (1) (*a*)
Provisions of the Act for which 19th July 1982 is appointed as the day of coming into operation.

Provision of the Act 1	Subject matter 2
Section 32 (1)-(6)	Subsidies to authorities
Section 33	Administration of subsidies
Section 34	Rate fund contributions and rate support grant
Section 35	Interpretation
Section 36 (1)-(3)	Other supplementary provisions
The following paragraph of Schedule 4, and section 48 (5) so far as it relates to that paragraph— paragraph 35 (1)	Amendment of section 54 of the Local Government, Planning and Land Act 1980 (rate support grant)

NOTES
Local Government, Planning and Land Act 1980, s 54   Halsbury's Statutes, 4th edn Vol 25, title
Local Government (3rd edn Vol 50 (2), p 1349).

SCHEDULE 2   Article 2 (1) (*b*)
Provisions of the Act for which 22nd November 1982 is appointed as the day of coming into
operation.

Provision of the Act 1	Subject matter 2
Section 29	Up-rating of needs allowances

SCHEDULE 3   Article 2 (1) (*c*)
Provisions of the Act for which 1st April 1983 is appointed as the day of coming into operation.

Provision of the Act 1	Subject matter 2
Section 30	Local schemes for housing benefits
Section 31	Publicity for housing benefits schemes
The following paragraphs of Schedule 4 and section 48 (5) so far as it relates to those paragraphs— Paragraphs 19, 27 and 28	Amendments to legislation consequential upon or connected with housing benefits.

SCHEDULE 4   Article 2 (1) (*d*)
Provisions of the Act for which 4th April 1983 is appointed as the day of coming into operation.

Provision of the Act 1	Subject matter 2
Section 28 (5)	Repeal of legislation
Section 32 (7)	Repeal of legislation
Section 36 (4)	Other supplementary provision
The following paragraphs of Schedule 4, and section 48 (5) so far as it relates to those paragraphs—	
Paragraphs 5, 6 22, 29, 35 (2) and (3), 36	Amendments to legislation consequential upon or connected with housing benefits
The following repeals in Schedule 5, and section 48 (6) so far as it relates to those repeals—	
The repeal of entries in section 1 (2) and of sections 1 (3), 5, 6 and 11, Part II of and Schedules 2 and 3 to the Housing (Financial Provisions) Scotland Act 1972	Repeal of legislation consequential upon or connected with housing benefits
The repeal of entries in section 1 (2) and words in section 104 (1) and in paragraph 1 of Schedule 1, of section 17 (2) and Part II of and Schedules 3 and 4 to the Housing Finance Act 1972	
The repeal of the Furnished Lettings (Rent Allowances) Act 1973	
The repeal of sections 112 to 115 of and paragraph 23 of Schedule 12 to the Local Government (Scotland) Act 1973	
The repeal of sections 8 (1) and (4), 11-14 and of words in section 8 (3) of the Local Government Act 1974	
The repeal of sections 11 and 12 of and paragraphs 4 to 6 of Schedule 3 to the Rent Act 1974	
The repeal of words in section 1 (1) and in section 16 (1), and of sections 3, 12 of and paragraphs 3 to 5 and 8 (3) of Schedule 5 to the Housing Rents and Subsidies Act 1975	
The repeal of paragraphs 6 and 8 of Schedule 3 to the Housing Rents and Subsidies (Scotland) Act 1975	
The repeal of section 12 (3) of and paragraphs 26-28 and 32 of Schedule 7 to the Supplementary Benefits Act 1976	
The repeal of sections 19 and 20, of words in section of, and 22 of Part III of Schedule 5 to the Development of Rural Wales Act 1976	
The repeal of section 32 of and Schedule 7 to the Rent (Agriculture) Act 1976	
The repeal of paragraphs 52-54, 56-57 of Schedule 23 to the Rent Act 1977	
The repeal of sections 12 and 13 of and paragraphs 8-10 and 34-36 of Schedule 2 to the Housing (Financial Provisions) (Scotland) Act 1978	
The repeal of sections 117-119 of and Schedule 15 to the Housing Act 1980	
The repeal of sections 78-79 of the Tenants' Rights Etc. (Scotland) Act 1980	
The repeal of section 45 and of, and relating to, 54 (6) (c) of the Local Government, Planning and Land Act 1980	

HOME PURCHASE ASSISTANCE (RECOGNISED LENDING INSTITUTIONS) ORDER 1982
SI 1982/976

NOTES

Authority This order was made on 15 July 1982 by the Secretary of State, with the consent of the Treasury, under the Home Purchase Assistance and Housing Corporation Guarantee Act 1978, s 2 (1) and (7), and all other enabling powers. The 1978 Act was repealed by the Housing (Consequential Provisions) Act 1985 and by virtue of s 2 (2) thereof this order now has effect as if made under the Housing Act 1985, s 447 (2), Halsbury's Statutes, 4th edn Vol 21, title Housing.

Commencement 18 August 1982.

General A condition for receiving assistance under the Housing Act 1985, s 445, Halsbury's Statutes, 4th edn Vol 21, title Housing, is that the purchaser must have obtained finance for the purchase of the property, and improvements, if any, by means of a secured loan from a recognised lending institution. Such institutions are those specified in s 447 (1) of the Act, and this order, as construed in accordance with the Housing (Consequential Provisions) Act 1985, s 2 (4), adds National Westminster Home Loans Limited to those so specified.

THE GRANTS BY LOCAL AUTHORITIES (GRANTS FOR TENANTS) ORDER 1982
SI 1982/1039

NOTES

Authority This order was made on 23 July 1982 by the Secretary of State for the Environment and the Secretary of State for Wales under the Housing Act 1980, ss 106 (1) and 151, and all other enabling powers. The said s 106 was repealed by the Housing (Consequential Provisions) Act 1985 and by virtue of s 2 (2) thereof this order now has effect as if made under the Housing Act 1985, s 463 (3) (*d*), Halsbury's Statutes, 4th edn Vol 21, title Housing.

Commencement 26 August 1982.

General Under the Housing Act 1985, s 463 (1) a local housing authority may only entertain an application for a grant under Part XV of that Act, Halsbury's Statutes, 4th edn Vol 21, title Housing, from a person who has or proposes to acquire an owner's interest in the land or who is a tenant of the dwelling who has one of the types of tenancy specified in s 463 (3). The Secretary of State may extend that provision to other tenancies which satisfy such conditions as he may prescribe. This order, as construed in accordance with the Housing (Consequential Provisions) Act 1985, s 2 (4), prescribes the following conditions: (i) the tenancy shall be the tenancy of an agricultural holding; and (ii) if the tenancy is for a term of years, less than five years shall remain unexpired at the date of the application.

THE HOUSING (PAYMENTS FOR WELL MAINTAINED HOUSES) ORDER 1982
SI 1982/1112

NOTES

Authority This order was made on 1 July 1982 by the Secretary of State for the Environment and the Secretary of State for Wales under the Housing Act 1957, Sch 2, Pt I, para 1 (1), as that Part had effect by virtue of the Housing Act 1969, s 66, and all other enabling powers. The 1957 and 1969 Acts were repealed by the Housing (Consequential Provisions) Act 1985 and by virtue of s 2 (2) thereof this order continues to have effect as if made under the Housing Act 1985, Sch 23, para 4 (1), Halsbury's Statutes, 4th edn Vol 21, title Housing.

Commencement 6 August 1982.

General This order, as construed in accordance with the Housing (Consequential Provisions) Act 1985, s 2 (4), prescribes a multiplier of 14 to be used in calculating by reference to the rateable value of a house the amount of a well maintained payment under the Housing Act 1985, Sch 23, para 1, 2 or 3, Halsbury's Statutes, 4th edn Vol 21, title Housing, where the order in respect of which the payment is to be made is itself made on or after 6 July 1982 and the payment falls to be made after this order came into operation. In such a case it replaces the multiplier of 3⅛ which was prescribed by the Housing (Payments for Well Maintained Houses) Order 1973, SI 1973/753, p 163, *ante.*

THE HOUSING BENEFITS (PERMITTED TOTALS FOR LOCAL SCHEMES) REGULATIONS 1982
SI 1982/1129

NOTES

Authority These regulations were made on 3 August 1982 by the Secretary of State for Social Services, with the consent of the Treasury, under the Social Security and Housing Benefits Act 1982, s 30 (6), Halsbury's Statutes, 4th edn Vol 40, title Social Security (3rd edn Vol 52, p 870), and all other enabling powers.

Commencement   1 April 1983; see reg 1 (1).
Amendment   These regulations are printed as amended by the Housing Benefits (Miscellaneous Amendments) Regulations 1982, SI 1982/1519.
Construction   See reg 1 (2).
General   These regulations set out the basis for calculating the permitted total of rebates or allowances for authorities granting rate rebates, rent rebates or rent allowances under local modifications of the statutory schemes for granting such rebates or allowances, as to which, see the Housing Benefits Regulations 1985, SI 1985/677, as amended, p 190, *post*. Under the Social Security and Housing Benefits Act 1982, s 30 (4), Halsbury's Statutes, 4th edn Vol 40, title Social Security (3rd edn Vol 52, p 870), such modifications must be so framed as to secure that, in the authority's estimate, the total of the rebates or allowances to be granted under the local scheme in any year will not exceed the amount calculated in the manner prescribed by these regulations.

1. Citation, commencement and interpretation   (1) These regulations may be cited as the Housing Benefits (Permitted Totals for Local Schemes) Regulations 1982 and shall come into operation on 1st April 1983.

(2) In these regulations—

"benefit" means rate rebate, rent rebate or rent allowance, as the circumstances may require;

"certificated case benefits" means the amount of benefit that would have been granted by an authority in certificated cases within the meaning of the Housing Benefits Regulations if the local scheme had not been in force;

. . .

"Housing Benefits Regulations" means the Housing Benefits Regulations 1982;

"standard case benefits" means the amount of benefit, other than certificated case benefits, that would have been granted by an authority under the Housing Benefits Regulations if:

(i) the local scheme had not been in force,

(ii) regulation 4 of those regulations did not permit any modification of the statutory scheme, and

(iii) regulation 22 of those regulations (additional amount of benefit in exceptional circumstances) were omitted.

NOTES
Amendment   The definition in reg 1 (2) indicated by dots was omitted by SI 1982/1519.
Housing Benefits Regulations 1982   SI 1982/1124; these regulations, as amended, are revoked and replaced by the Housing Benefits Regulations 1985, SI 1985/677, as amended, p 190, *post*.

2. Permitted totals of benefits   For the purposes of section 30 of the Social Security and Housing Benefits Act 1982 the permitted total of benefits for any year shall be, in relation to an authority's local scheme, [the aggregate of 100% of certificated case benefits for that year and 110% of standard case benefits for that year].

NOTES
Amendment   The words in square brackets in this regulation were substituted by SI 1982/1519.
Social Security and Housing Benefits Act 1982, s 30   Halsbury's Statutes, 4th edn Vol 40, title Social Security (3rd edn Vol 52, p 869).

THE GRANTS BY LOCAL AUTHORITIES (REPAIRS) ORDER 1982 SI 1982/1205

NOTES
Authority   This order was made on 20 August 1982 by the Secretary of State for the Environment and the Secretary of State for Wales, with the consent of the Treasury, under the Housing Act 1974, ss 63 (2), 71 (2) (*b*), (3A) and (3B) and 128, and all other enabling powers. Those sections were repealed by the Housing (Consequential Provisions) Act 1985 and by virtue of s 2 (2) thereof this order now has effect as if made under the Housing Act 1985, ss 471 (5), 491 (2) (*b*) and 492, Halsbury's Statutes, 4th edn Vol 21, title Housing.
Commencement   29 September 1982.
General   This order (which revokes and replaces the Grants by Local Authorities (Repairs) Order 1980, SI 1980/1737), as construed in accordance with the Housing (Consequential Provisions) Act 1985, s 2 (4), prescribes, for the purposes of the Housing Act 1985, s 471 (2), a higher

percentage for the repairs element of an improvement grant in certain cases and enables repairs grants to be made for the replacement of lead water pipes. It also defines the meaning of "old dwelling" for the purposes of the 1985 Act, s 492 (1) and specifies the rateable value limits for repairs grants under s 492 (2).

1. Citation, commencement and interpretation   (1) This order may be cited as the Grants by Local Authorities (Repairs) Order 1982 and shall come into operation on 29th September 1982.

(2) In this order "the Act" means the Housing Act 1974.

NOTES

Housing Act 1974   This is now to be construed as a reference to the Housing Act 1985, Halsbury's Statutes, 4th edn Vol 21, title Housing.

2. Repairs element of improvement grant   For the purposes of section 63 (2) of the Act, 70 per cent. is hereby prescribed as the percentage of the estimated expense allowable for works of repair and replacement where the dwelling is, or is to be provided by the conversion of a dwelling which is, in need of works of repair of a substantial and structural character.

NOTES

Section 63 (2) of the Act   *Ie,* the Housing Act 1974. This is now to be construed as a reference to the Housing Act 1985, s 471 (2), Halsbury's Statutes, 4th edn Vol 21, title Housing.

3. Requirements for repairs grant   The requirements prescribed for the purposes of section 71 (2) (*b*) of the Act are that the relevant works shall consist of the replacement of the whole or part of a pipe which is made of lead and which connects, or forms part of a pipe which connects, the tap in the dwelling mainly used for supplying drinking water directly or indirectly to the main, by such a pipe not made of lead.

NOTES

Section 71 (2) (*b*) of the Act   *Ie,* the Housing Act 1974. This is now to be construed as a reference to the Housing Act 1985, s 491 (2) (*b*), Halsbury's Statutes, 4th edn Vol 21, title Housing.

4. Meaning of old dwelling   For the purposes of section 71 (3A) (*a*) of the Act, the expression "old dwelling" means a dwelling which is, or forms part of, a building which was erected before:—

(*a*) 3rd October 1961, if the relevant works satisfy the requirements prescribed by article 3 above; or

(*b*) 1st January 1919, in any other case.

NOTES

Section 71 (3A) (*a*) of the Act   *Ie,* the Housing Act 1974. This is now to be construed as a reference to the Housing Act 1985, s 492 (1), Halsbury's Statutes, 4th edn Vol 21, title Housing.

5. Rateable value limits for repairs grants   For the purposes of section 71 (3A) (*b*) of the Act the following rateable value limits are hereby specified:—

(*a*) in relation to dwellings in Greater London, £400;
and

(*b*) in relation to dwellings elsewhere, £225.

NOTES

Section 71 (3A) (*b*) of the Act   *Ie,* the Housing Act 1974. This is now to be construed as a reference to the Housing Act 1985, s 492 (2), Halsbury's Statutes, 4th edn Vol 21, title Housing.

6. Revocation of previous order   The Grants by Local Authorities (Repairs) Order 1980 is hereby revoked.

NOTES

Grants by Local Authorities (Repairs) Order 1980   SI 1980/1737.

THE GRANTS BY LOCAL AUTHORITIES (APPROPRIATE PERCENTAGE AND EXCHEQUER CONTRIBUTION) (NO 2) ORDER 1982
SI 1982/1763

NOTES
Authority This is as noted to SI 1980/1735, p 170, *ante*, except that this order was made on 7 December 1982.
Commencement 31 December 1982.
General This order, as construed in accordance with the Housing (Consequential Provisions) Act 1985, s 2 (4), further prescribes the "appropriate percentage" of the cost of the works to be carried out for the purpose of determining the amount of a grant under the Housing Act 1985, Part XV. In the case of applications for intermediate grants and repairs grants made on or before 31 March 1984 and approved after 31 December 1982, the appropriate percentage is to be 90 per cent. The order also further specifies the percentages of grants which may be contributed by the Secretary of State; where the application for the grant was made on or before 31 March 1984 and approved after 31 December 1982, he may contribute 95 per cent of the expenses of a local authority in making repairs grants and 90 per cent in the case of intermediate grants.
   See further the Grants by Local Authorities (Appropriate Percentage and Exchequer Contributions) Orders 1980 and 1982, SI 1980/1735 and 1982/581, pp 170, 172, *ante*.

THE GRANTS BY LOCAL AUTHORITIES (REPAIRS GRANTS FOR AIREY HOUSES) (ELIGIBLE EXPENSE LIMITS) ORDER 1982
SI 1982/1895

NOTES
Authority This order was made on 22 December 1982 by the Secretary of State for the Environment and the Secretary of State for Wales under the Housing Act 1974, ss 72 (3) and (3A) and 128, and all other enabling powers. Those sections have been repealed by the Housing (Consequential Provisions) Act 1985, Halsbury's Statutes, 4th edn Vol 21, title Housing.
Commencement 14 February 1983.
Amendment This order has been varied by the Grants by Local Authorities (Repairs Grants for Airey Houses) (Eligible Expense Limits) (Variation) Order 1984, SI 1984/1700.
General This order prescribed limits on the amount of the estimated expense of the works to be carried out which was eligible to be taken into account when an application for a repairs grant for a house or flat built by the Airey Duo-Slab 2 system was approved. The eligible expense limits prescribed were £14,000 for dwellings in Greater London and £10,500 elsewhere.
   This order has been varied by SI 1984/1700 referred to above so that it has ceased to have effect except in relation to applications for repairs grants approved before 1 December 1984 and such applications made before that date but not approved before then. In relation to applications made but not approved before that date, the prescribed eligible expense limit is varied to £14,000 in all cases. Financial assistance may now be available for certain owners of Airey houses and flats by virtue of the Housing Act 1985, Part XVI, Halsbury's Statutes, 4th edn Vol 21, title Housing.
   Eligible expense limits for other cases are prescribed by the Grants by Local Authorities (Eligible Expense Limits) Order 1983, SI 1983/613, p 181, *post*.

THE GRANTS BY LOCAL AUTHORITIES (APPROPRIATE PERCENTAGE AND EXCHEQUER CONTRIBUTION) (REPAIRS GRANTS FOR AIREY HOUSES) ORDER 1982
SI 1983/95

NOTES
Authority This order was made on 1 February 1983 by the Secretary of State for the Environment and the Secretary of State for Wales, with the consent of the Treasury, under the Housing Act 1974, ss 59, 78 (4) and (5) and 128, and all other enabling powers. Those sections have now been repealed by the Housing (Consequential Provisions) Act 1985, Halsbury's Statutes, 4th edn Vol 21, title Housing.
Commencement 14 February 1983.
Amendment This order has been varied by the Grants by Local Authorities (Appropriate Percentage and Exchequer Contribution) (Repairs Grants for Airey Houses) (Variation) Order 1984, SI 1984/1880.
General This order further prescribed the "appropriate percentage" of the cost of the works to be carried out for the purpose of determining the amount of grant under the Housing Act 1985, Part XV; in the case of an application for a repairs grant relating to a house or flat built by the Airey Duo-Slab 2 system approved after 13 February 1983, the appropriate percentage was to be 90 per cent. The order also specified the percentage of grants which might be contributed by the Secretary of State in relation to applications for repairs grants made in respect of Airey houses or flats and approved after 13 February 1983, as 100 per cent of the expenses of a local authority.

By virtue of SI 1984/1880, referred to above, this order has ceased to have effect except in relation to applications for repairs grants approved before 1 December 1984 and applications for such grants made before that date and not approved before then. In relation to applications made before 1 December 1984 and not approved before that date, the appropriate percentage for contributions by the Secretary of State is varied to 90 per cent. Financial assistance may now be available for certain owners of Airey houses and flats by virtue of the Housing Act 1985, Part XVI, Halsbury's Statutes, 4th edn Vol 21, title Housing.

THE GRANTS BY LOCAL AUTHORITIES (ELIGIBLE EXPENSE LIMITS) ORDER 1983
SI 1983/613

NOTES
Authority This order was made on 19 April 1983 by the Secretary of State for the Environment and the Secretary of State for Wales under the Housing Act 1974, ss 58 (2) and (3), 64 (3) and (4), 68 (3A) and (3B), 70A, 72 (3) and (3A) and 128, and all other enabling powers. Those sections were repealed by the Housing (Consequential Provisions) Act 1985 and by virtue of s 2 (2) thereof this order now has effect as if made under the Housing Act 1985, ss 472, 481, 489 and 497, Halsbury's Statutes, 4th edn Vol 21, title Housing.
Commencement 20 May 1983; see art 1 (1).
Amendment This order has been partially superseded by the Housing Act 1985, s 508 (1), Halsbury's Statutes, 4th edn Vol 21, title Housing.
General This order (which supersedes the Grants by Local Authorities (Eligible Expense Limits) Order 1980, SI 1980/1736, as amended), as construed in accordance with the Housing (Consequential Provisions) Act 1985, s 2 (4), increases the limits on the amount of the estimated expense of the works to be carried out which is eligible to be taken into account when an application for a grant under the Housing Act 1985, Part XV, is approved.
Eligible expense limits for other cases are prescribed by the Grants by Local Authorities (Repairs Grants for Airey Houses) (Eligible Expense Limits) Order 1982, SI 1982/1895, as amended, p 180, *ante*.

1. Citation, commencement and interpretation (1) This order may be cited as the Grants by Local Authorities (Eligible Expense Limits) Order 1983 and shall come into operation on 20th May 1983.
(2) In this order—
"the Act" means the Housing Act 1974, and
"listed building" means a building which is for the time being included in a list compiled or approved by the Secretary of State under section 54 of the Town and Country Planning Act 1971, and a reference to a grade is to the grade indicated in respect of a building in such a list.
(3) In this order a reference to a dwelling which is a listed building includes a reference to a dwelling which is in or which is to be provided by the conversion of a listed building.

NOTES
Housing Act 1974 This is now to be construed as a reference to the Housing Act 1985, Halsbury's Statutes, 4th edn Vol 21, title Housing.
Town and Country Planning Act 1971, s 54 *Ibid,* 4th edn Vol 46, title Town and Country Planning (3rd edn Vol 41, p 1651).

2. Standard amenities *(Superseded by the Housing Act 1985, s 508 (1)).*

3. Improvement grants (1) There are hereby specified—
  (*a*) for the purposes of section 64 (3) (*a*) of the Act, the amounts ascertained from Table 1, and
  (*b*) for the purposes of section 64 (3) (*b*) of the Act, the amounts ascertained from Table 2 in relation to the descriptions of dwellings set out in those Tables.
(2) In the Tables—
"category A" applies to any dwelling which on the date on which the application for the grant is approved is covered by one or more of the following descriptions:—
  (*a*) it is in a housing action area;

(*b*) it is or forms part of a house in relation to which the local authority have served a notice under section 9 (1) or 16 of the Housing Act 1957 and the relevant works consist of or include works which if executed would contribute towards rendering the house fit for human habitation;

(*c*)   (i) it lacks, or is to be provided by the conversion of a dwelling which lacks, one or more of the standard amenities, and

(ii) the relevant works consist of or include the provision of a standard amenity which is lacking, and

(iii) the local authority are satisfied that the standard amenity which is to be provided, or, where more than one such amenity is to be provided, each of them, has been lacking for a period of not less than 12 months, ending on the date on which the application was made;

(*d*) it is in need of works of a substantial and structural character, and the relevant works consist of or include such works;

(*e*) it is a dwelling for a disabled occupant and the relevant works consist of or include works needed to meet a requirement arising from the particular disability from which he suffers; and

"category B" applies to any dwelling other than one to which category A applies.

(3) In paragraph 2 a reference to a dwelling includes a reference to a dwelling which is to be provided by the conversion of a dwelling.

TABLE 1

Specified amounts for the purposes of section 64 (3) (*a*) of the Housing Act 1974

	Dwellings in Greater London		Dwellings elsewhere	
	Category A £	Category B £	Category A £	Category B £
PART 1 Dwellings which are not listed buildings	13,800	9,000	10,200	6,600
PART 2 Dwellings which are listed buildings of the following grades:—				
Grade I	15,540	10,740	11,940	8,340
Grade II*	14,840	10,040	11,240	7,640
Grade II (Unstarred)	14,320	9,520	10,720	7,120

TABLE 2

Specified amounts for the purposes of section 64 (3) (*b*) of the Housing Act 1974

	Dwellings in Greater London		Dwellings elsewhere	
	Category A £	Category B £	Category A £	Category B £
PART 1 Dwellings which are not listed buildings	16,000	10,400	11,800	7,700
PART 2 Dwellings which are listed buildings of the following grades:—				
Grade I	17,700	12,180	13,500	9,420
Grade II*	17,000	11,480	12,800	8,720
Grade II (Unstarred)	16,490	10,970	12,290	8,210

NOTES
Housing Act 1974, s 64 (3) (a), (b) This is now to be construed as a reference to the Housing
Act 1985, s 472 (2) (a), (b), Halsbury's Statutes, 4th edn Vol 21, title Housing.
Housing Act 1957, s 9 (1) or 16 This is now to be construed as a reference to the Housing Act
1985, s 190 or 264 (1), Halsbury's Statutes, 4th edn Vol 21, title Housing.

4. Intermediate grants (1) The amounts of—
    (a) £4,200 in respect of dwellings in Greater London, and
    (b) £3,000 in respect of dwellings elsewhere
are hereby prescribed for the purposes of section 68 (3A) (a) of the Act.
    (2) The amounts of—
    (a) £420 in respect of dwellings in Greater London, and
    (b) £300 in respect of dwellings elsewhere
are hereby prescribed for the purposes of section 68 (3A) (b) of the Act as
the amount to be multiplied by the number of standard amenities to be
provided.
    (3) The amounts of—
    (a) £1,680 in respect of dwellings in Greater London, and
    (b) £1,200 in respect of dwellings elsewhere
are hereby prescribed for the purposes of section 68 (3A) (b) of the Act as
the maximum to which the amount prescribed by paragraph (2), multiplied
by the number of standard amenities to be provided, is subject.

NOTES
Section 68 (3A) (a), (b) of the Act *Ie,* the Housing Act 1974. This is now to be construed as a
reference to the Housing Act 1985, s 481 (2), (3), Halsbury's Statutes, 4th edn Vol 21, title
Housing.

5. Special grants (1) The amounts of—
    (a) £10,800 in respect of houses in multiple occupation in Greater London,
        and
    (b) £8,100 in respect of houses in multiple occupation elsewhere
are hereby prescribed for the purposes of section 70A (3) of the Act as the
maximum amount of the contributory element as regards the provision of
means of escape from fire.
    (2) The amounts of—
    (a) £4,200 in respect of houses in multiple occupation in Greater London,
        and
    (b) £3,000 in respect of houses in multiple occupation elsewhere
are hereby prescribed for the purposes of section 70A (4) of the Act as the
maximum amount of the contributory element as regards works of repair and
replacement.

NOTES
Section 70A (3) and (4) of the Act *Ie,* the Housing Act 1974. This is now to be construed as a
reference to the Housing Act 1985, s 489 (3) and (4), Halsbury's Statutes, 4th edn Vol 21, title
Housing.

6. Repairs grants (1) The amounts mentioned in paragraph (2) are hereby
prescribed as the limits of eligible expense for the purposes of section 72 (3)
of the Act in relation to the descriptions of dwellings set out in that paragraph.
    (2) The prescribed amounts are:—
    (a) in respect of a dwelling which is not a listed building, £6,600 where the
        dwelling is in Greater London and £4,800 where it is elsewhere;
    (b) in respect of a dwelling which is a Grade I listed building, £7,480 where
        the building is in Greater London and £5,680 where it is elsewhere;
    (c) in respect of a dwelling which is a Grade II* listed building, £7,130
        where the building is in Greater London and £5,330 where it is
        elsewhere; and

(*d*) in respect of a dwelling which is a Grade II (Unstarred) listed building, £6,860 where the building is in Greater London and £5,060 where it is elsewhere.

NOTES
Section 72 (3) of the Act   *Ie,* the Housing Act 1974. This is now to be construed as a reference to the Housing Act 1985, s 497 (1), Halsbury's Statutes, 4th edn Vol 21, title Housing.

THE HOUSING BENEFITS (RATE SUPPORT GRANT) ORDER 1984
SI 1984/111

NOTES
Authority   This order was made on 8 February 1984 by the Secretary of State for Social Services, with the consent of the Treasury, under the Social Security and Housing Benefits Act 1982, s 34 (2), Halsbury's Statutes, 4th edn Vol 40, title Social Security (3rd edn Vol 52, p 873), and the Social Security Act 1975, s 166 (2), *ibid,* 4th edn Vol 40, title Social Security (3rd edn Vol 45, p 1261), as applied by the 1982 Act, s 45 (1), and all other enabling powers.
Commencement   1 April 1984.
General   This order provides that certain items are not to count as relevant expenditure for the purposes of rate support grant for the year beginning 1 April 1984 and each subsequent year. Those items are a local authority's rate fund contribution towards the amount of rent rebates under the statutory rent rebate scheme and the amount of rent allowances granted by a local authority under the statutory rent allowance scheme.
Previous order   The items which were not to count as relevant expenditure for the initial year ending on 31 March 1983 and the year beginning 1 April 1983 were prescribed by the Housing Benefits (Rate Support Grant) Order 1982, SI 1982/905, listed at p 140, *ante.*

THE HOMES INSULATION GRANTS ORDER 1984
SI 1984/838

NOTES
Authority   This order was made on 19 June 1984 by the Secretary of State for the Environment and the Secretaries of State for Wales and Scotland, with the approval of the Treasury, under the Homes Insulation Act 1978, s 1 (4), (5) (*b*) and (9), and all other enabling powers. The 1978 Act was repealed by the Housing (Consequential Provisions) Act 1985 and by virtue of s 2 (2) thereof this order now has effect as if made under the Housing Act 1985, s 521, Halsbury's Statutes, 4th edn Vol 21, title Housing.
Commencement   20 July 1984.
General   This order (which supersedes the Homes Insulation Grants Order 1983, SI 1983/285), as construed in accordance with the Housing (Consequential Provisions) Act 1985, s 2 (4), prescribes the maximum percentages of the cost of works and the money sums payable as grant under the Homes Insulation Scheme 1984, made under the Homes Insulation Act 1978 and now taking effect under the Housing Act 1985, s 521, and requiring local housing authorities to make grants towards the cost of works undertaken to improve the thermal insulation of dwellings in their district. In the case of applications on the ground of special need, the percentage and amount are 90% or £95, whichever is the less, and in all other cases, 66% or £69, whichever is the less.

THE HOUSING (RIGHT TO BUY) (PRESCRIBED PERSONS) ORDER 1984
SI 1984/1173

NOTES
Authority   This order was made on 1 August 1984 by the Secretary of State for the Environment and the Secretary of State for Wales under the Housing Act 1980, s 151 (3) and Sch 1A, paras 9 (2) and 10 (2), and all other enabling powers. The said Sch 1A has been repealed by the Housing (Consequential Provisions) Act 1985 and by virtue of s 2 (2) thereof this order now has effect as if made under the Housing Act 1985, s 130 (2) and Sch 4, para 8 (1), Halsbury's Statutes, 4th edn Vol 21, title Housing.
Commencement   26 August 1984.
General   This order, as construed in accordance with the Housing (Consequential Provisions) Act 1985, s 2 (4), prescribes certain additional persons who are to be treated as public sector landlords for the purposes of the Housing Act 1985, s 130 (2) and Sch 4, para 8, and also prescribes the circumstances in which they are to be so treated.

1.   (1) This order may be cited as the Housing (Right to Buy) (Prescribed Persons) Order 1984 and shall come into operation on 26th August 1984.

(2) In this order "Schedule 1A" means Schedule 1A to the Housing Act 1980.

NOTES
Housing Act 1980, Sch 1A   This is now to be construed as a reference to the Housing Act 1985, s 130 and Sch 4, Halsbury's Statutes, 4th edn Vol 21, title Housing

2.   The persons listed in the Schedule to this order and any predecessor of any of those persons are hereby prescribed for the purposes of paragraphs 9 (2) and 10 (2) of Schedule 1A.

NOTES
Schedule 1A, paras 9 (2) and 10 (2)   *Ie*, to the Housing Act 1980. This is now to be construed as a reference to the Housing Act 1985, s 130 (2) and Sch 4, para 8, Halsbury's Statutes, 4th edn Vol 21, title Housing.

3.   (1) Subject to paragraph (2) below, all circumstances are prescribed for the purposes of paragraphs 9 (2) and 10 (2) of Schedule 1A.

(2) The prescribed circumstances for the purposes of paragraph 9 (2) of Schedule 1A do not include the following circumstances—

(*a*) if the interest of the landlord belongs to a Minister of the Crown or government department, any case where the dwelling-house is let to a person appointed under section 3 (1) of the Prison Act 1952; and

(*b*) if the interest of the landlord belongs to the Trinity House, any case where the dwelling-house is held otherwise than in connection with its functions as a general light-house authority within the meaning of section 634 of the Merchant Shipping Act 1894.

NOTES
Schedule 1A, paras 9 (2) and 10 (2)   See the note to art 2.
Prison Act 1952, s 3 (1)   Halsbury's Statutes, 4th edn Vol 34, title Prisons (3rd edn Vol 25, p 829).
Merchant Shipping Act 1894, s 634   *Ibid*, 4th edn Vol 39, title Shipping and Navigation (3rd edn Vol 31, p 361).

SCHEDULE   Article 2.

An area board established by section 1 (2) of the Electricity Act 1947.
A community council.
An education and library board established under the Education and Libraries (Northern Ireland) Order 1972
A fire authority for the purposes of the Fire Services Acts 1947 to 1959.
A government department.
An internal drainage board within the meaning of section 6 of the Land Drainage Act 1976.
A Minister of the Crown.
A parish council and the trustees of a parish without a parish council.
A passenger transport executive established under Part II of the Transport Act 1968.
A police authority.
A water authority established in accordance with section 2 of the Water Act 1973 and a water authority in Scotland as constituted under section 148 of the Local Government (Scotland) Act 1973.
The Agricultural and Food Research Council.
The British Airports Authority.
The British Broadcasting Corporation.
The British Gas Corporation.
The British Railways Board.
The British Steel Corporation.
The British Waterways Board.
The Central Electricity Generating Board.
The Civil Aviation Authority.
The Commissioners of Northern Lighthouses.
The Countryside Commission for Scotland.
The Electricity Council.
The Fire Authority for Northern Ireland established under the Fire Services (Northern Ireland) Order 1973.
The Highlands and Islands Development Board.
The Lake District Special Planning Board.

London Regional Transport.
The Medical Research Council.
The National Bus Company.
The National Coal Board.
The National Library of Wales.
The National Museum of Wales.
The Natural Environment Research Council.
The Nature Conservancy Council.
The North of Scotland Hydro-Electric Board.
The Northern Ireland Electricity Service established under the Electricity Supply (Northern Ireland) Order 1972.
The Northern Ireland Transport Holding Company established under the Transport Act (Northern Ireland) 1967.
The Peak Park Joint Planning Board.
The Police Authority for Northern Ireland.
The Post Office.
The Science and Engineering Research Council.
The Scottish Sports Council.
The South of Scotland Electricity Board.
The Sports Council.
The Sports Council for Wales
The Trinity House.
The United Kingdom Atomic Energy Authority.
The Welsh Development Agency.

NOTES
Electricity Act 1947, s 1 (2)   Halsbury's Statutes, 4th edn Vol 15, title Electricity.
Education and Libraries (Northern Ireland) Order 1972   SI 1972/1263 (NI 12).
Fire Services Act 1947 to 1959   Halsbury's Statutes, 4th edn Vol 18, title Fire Services (3rd edn Vol 13, p 696, *et seq*).
Land Drainage Act 1976, s 6   *Ibid*, 4th edn Vol 22, title Land Drainage (3rd edn Vol 46, p 815).
Transport Act 1968, Pt II   *Ibid*, 4th edn Vol 38, title Road Traffic (3rd edn Vol 28, p 668 *et seq*).
Water Act 1973, s 2   *Ibid*, 4th edn Vol 49, title Water (3rd edn Vol 43, p 1823).
Local Government (Scotland) Act 1973, s 148   1973 c 65.
Fire Services (Northern Ireland) Order 1973   SI 1973/601 (NI 9).
Electricity Supply (Northern Ireland) Order 1972   SI 1972/1072 (NI 9).
Transport Act (Northern Ireland) 1967   1967 c 37 (NI).

THE HOUSING (LOCAL AUTHORITY CONTRIBUTIONS TOWARDS MORTGAGE COSTS) ORDER 1984
SI 1984/1174

NOTES
Authority   This order was made on 1 August 1984 by the Secretary of State for the Environment and the Secretary of State for Wales under the Housing and Building Control Act 1984, s 21 (1) and all other enabling powers. The said s 21 has been repealed by the Housing (Consequential Provisions) Act 1985 and by virtue of s 2 (2) thereof this order now has effect as if made under the Housing Act 1985, s 443 (2), Halsbury's Statutes, 4th edn Vol 21, title Housing.
Commencement   26 August 1984.
General   This order, as construed in accordance with the Housing (Consequential Provisions) Act 1985, s 2 (4), fixes at £200 the maximum contribution that a local authority may make towards costs incurred by a person in connection with obtaining a mortgage in certain circumstances under the Housing Act 1985, s 443.

THE HOUSING (RIGHT TO BUY) (PRESCRIBED FORMS) REGULATIONS 1984
SI 1984/1175

NOTES
Authority   These regulations were made on 1 August 1984 by the Secretary of State for the Environment and the Secretary of State for Wales under the Housing Act 1980, ss 22 (1) and 151 (3), and all other enabling powers. The said s 22 (1) was repealed by the Housing (Consequential Provisions) Act 1985 and by virtue of s 2 (2) thereof these regulations now have effect as if made under the Housing Act 1985, s 176 (1), Halsbury's Statutes, 4th edn Vol 21, title Housing.
Commencement   26 August 1984.
General   These regulations (which revoke and replace the Housing (Right to Buy) (Prescribed Forms) (No 1) Regulations 1980, SI 1980/1391), as construed in accordance with the Housing (Consequential Provisions) Act 1985, s 2 (4), prescribe the forms of notice for use in connection

with the right to buy under the Housing Act 1985, ss 122 (1), 124 (1), Halsbury's Statutes, 4th edn Vol 21, title Housing, and the particulars to be contained in them. The forms are: (i) the form of notice to be used by a secure tenant to claim the right to buy (Form RTB1); and (ii) the form of notice to be used by a landlord to accept or reject the tenant's claim (Form RTB2). A notice claiming the right to buy served by a secure tenant before 1 November 1984 is not invalidated by these regulations if it is in the form required by SI 1980/1391 referred to above or in a substantially similar form.

THE HOUSING (RIGHT TO A SHARED OWNERSHIP LEASE) (REPAIRS ETC ADJUSTMENT) ORDER 1984
SI 1984/1280

NOTES
Authority This order was made on 10 August 1984 by the Secretary of State for the Environment and the Secretary of State for Wales under the Housing and Building Control Act 1984, Sch 3, paras 5 (2) and (5) and 10 (2) (*a*), and all other enabling powers. The said Sch 3 was repealed by the Housing (Consequential Provisions) Act 1985 and by virtue of s 2 (2) thereof this order now has effect as if made under the Housing Act 1985, Sch 8, para 4 (3), (4), Halsbury's Statutes, 4th edn Vol 21, title Housing.
Commencement 26 August 1984; see art 1.
General This order, as construed in accordance with the Housing (Consequential Provisions) Act 1985, s 2 (4), requires an adjustment to be made in certain circumstances to the rent payable, or the charge for repairs, maintenance or insurance made, under a shared ownership lease granted under the Housing Act 1985, Part V, Halsbury's Statutes, 4th edn Vol 21, title Housing. The adjustment is required in relation to periods when the tenant's stake in the dwelling is less than 100%.

1. This order may be cited as the Housing (Right to a Shared Ownership Lease) (Repairs Etc. Adjustment) Order 1984 and shall come into operation on 26th August 1984.

2. A shared ownership lease granted in pursuance of Part I of the Housing and Building Control Act 1984 shall provide for an adjustment to be made in accordance with the following provisions of this order for any period when the tenant's total share is less than 100 per cent.

NOTES
Housing and Building Control Act 1984, Pt I This is now to be construed as a reference to the Housing Act 1985, Pt V, Halsbury's Statutes, 4th edn Vol 21, title Housing.

3. If the dwelling-house is a house or (whether or not it is a house) the landlord is a housing association, the rent payable under the lease as determined under paragraph 5 (1) of Schedule 3 to the Housing and Building Control Act 1984 shall be adjusted by reducing it by 25 per cent.

NOTES
Housing and Building Control Act 1984, Sch 3, para 5 (1) This is now to be construed as a reference to the Housing Act 1985, Sch 8, para 4 (1), Halsbury's Statutes, 4th edn Vol 21, title Housing.

4. If the dwelling-house is a flat and the landlord is not a housing association, any amount payable by the tenant under the lease which is payable, directly or indirectly, for repairs, maintenance or insurance shall be adjusted by reducing it by the amount determined by the formula—

$$A = \frac{M(100-S)}{100}$$

where—
A is the amount of the reduction;
M is the amount which under the lease would otherwise be payable by the tenant, directly or indirectly, for repairs, maintenance or insurance; and
S is the tenant's total share expressed as a percentage.

THE HOUSING (RIGHT TO BUY) (PRIORITY OF CHARGES) ORDER 1984
SI 1984/1554

NOTES

Authority This order was made on 28 September 1984 by the Secretary of State for the Environment and the Secretary of State for Wales, with the consent of the Treasury, under the Housing Act 1980, s 8 (5), and all other enabling powers. The said s 8 has been repealed by the Housing (Consequential Provisions) Act 1985 and by virtue of s 2 (2) thereof this order now has effect under the Housing Act 1985, s 156 (4), Halsbury's Statutes, 4th edn Vol 21, title Housing.
Commencement 20 October 1984.
General Under the Housing Act 1985, s 156 (1), (2), Halsbury's Statutes, 4th edn Vol 21, title Housing, the liability to repay discount following the exercise of the right to buy is secured by a charge on the dwelling, which charge has priority in certain circumstances after certain legal charges, including charges securing amounts advanced by an approved lending institution. Such institutions are listed in s 156 (4) and the Secretary of State is empowered to specify additional bodies or classes or descriptions of bodies as such institutions. As construed in accordance with the Housing (Consequential Provisions) Act 1985, s 2 (4), this order specifies certain bodies for these purposes and for the purposes of the Housing Act 1985, s 36 (4), Halsbury's Statutes, 4th edn Vol 21, title Housing (disposal of land held for housing purposes by local authorities) and of the Housing Associations Act 1985, Sch 2, para 2, *ibid*, 4th edn Vol 21, title Housing (disposal of houses by a housing association). The bodies are: National Westminster Home Loans Limited, the Bank of England, the Post Office and recognised banks and licensed institutions within the meaning of the Banking Act 1979, Halsbury's Statutes, 4th edn Vol 4, title Banking, other than any bank or institution falling within the Home Purchase Assistance and Housing Corporation Guarantee Act 1978, Schedule, para 7 (now repealed and replaced by the Housing Act 1985, s 622 (see para (*b*) of the definition of "bank"), Halsbury's Statutes, 4th edn Vol 21, title Housing.
Further order The Housing (Right to Buy) (Priority of Charges) Order 1985, SI 1985/1979, listed at p 142, *ante*, which came into operation on 6 January 1986 and specifies for the above purposes National Home Loans Corporation plc, Lombard Home Loans Limited and London and Manchester (Mortgages) Limited.

THE MORTGAGE INDEMNITIES (RECOGNISED BODIES) ORDER 1984
SI 1984/1555

NOTES

Authority This order was made on 28 September 1984 by the Secretary of State for the Environment and the Secretary of State for Wales, with the consent of the Treasury, under the Housing and Building Control Act 1984, s 20 (5), and all other enabling powers. The said s 20 was repealed by the Housing (Consequential Provisions) Act 1985 and by virtue of s 2 (2) thereof this order now has effect as if made under the Housing Act 1985, s 444 (1) and the Housing Associations Act 1985, s 85 (2), both in Halsbury's Statutes, 4th edn Vol 21, title Housing.
Commencement 20 October 1984.
General Local authorities and the Housing Corporation may, under the Housing Act 1985, s 442 and the Housing Associations Act 1985, s 84 respectively (both in Halsbury's Statutes, 4th edn Vol 21, title Housing), with the approval of the Secretary of State, enter into agreements with recognised bodies providing for indemnities where such bodies make advances secured by way of mortgage on dwellings bought from public sector landlords. This order, as construed in accordance with the Housing (Consequential Provisions) Act 1985, s 2 (4), specifies the following bodies and classes or descriptions of bodies as recognised bodies for these purposes: National Westminster Home Loans Limited, the Bank of England, the Post Office, insurance companies to which the Insurance Companies Act 1982, Pt II, Halsbury's Statutes, 4th edn Vol 22, title Insurance (Pt 2) (3rd edn Vol 52, p 303 *et seq*) applies, Trustee Savings Banks within the meaning of the Trustee Savings Banks Act 1981, *ibid*, 4th edn Vol 39, title Savings Banks (3rd edn Vol 51, p 1481 *et seq*), recognised banks and licensed institutions within the meaning of the Banking Act 1979, *ibid*, 4th edn Vol 4, title Banking, and friendly societies and branches thereof which are registered within the meaning of the Friendly Societies Act 1974, *ibid*, 4th edn Vol 19, title Friendly Societies and Industrial Assurance (3rd edn Vol 44, p 279, *et seq*).
Further order The Mortgage Indemnities (Recognised Bodies) Order 1985, SI 1985/1978, listed at p 142, *ante*, which came into operation on 6 January 1986 and specifies for the above purposes National Home Loans Corporation plc and Lombard Home Loans Limited.

THE HOUSING ACT 1964 (APPROPRIATE MULTIPLIER) ORDER 1984
SI 1984/1629

NOTES

Authority This order was made on 18 October by the Secretary of State for the Environment and the Secretary of State for Wales under the Housing Act 1964, s 78 (5D), and all other enabling powers. The said s 78 was repealed by the Housing (Consequential Provisions) Act

1985 and by virtue of s 2 (2) thereof this order now has effect as if made under the Housing Act 1985, Sch 13, Pt II, para 13, Halsbury's Statutes, 4th edn Vol 21, title Housing.
Commencement   25 December 1984.
General   This order (which revokes and replaces the Housing Act 1964 (Appropriate Multiplier) Regulations 1981, SI 1981/781), as construed in accordance with the Housing (Consequential Provisions) Act 1985, s 2 (4), increases from 2⅓ to 3⅓ the appropriate multiplier which is to be used in calculating the amount of compensation to which a dispossessed proprietor is entitled under the Housing Act 1985, s 389, Halsbury's Statutes, 4th edn Vol 21, title Housing, in respect of the period during which a control order under Part XI of that Act is in force.

THE HOUSING DEFECTS (EXPENDITURE LIMIT) ORDER 1984
SI 1984/1705

NOTES
Authority   This order was made on 30 October 1984 by the Secretary of State for the Environment and the Secretaries of State for Scotland and Wales, under the Housing Defects Act 1984, Sch 1, para 2, and all other enabling powers. That Act was repealed by the Housing (Consequential Provisions) Act 1985 and by virtue of s 2 (2) thereof this order now has effect as if made under the Housing Act 1985, s 543 (4), Halsbury's Statutes, 4th edn Vol 21, title Housing.
Commencement   1 December 1984.
General   This order as construed in accordance with the Housing (Consequential Provisions) Act 1984, s 2 (4), specifies £14,000 as the expenditure limit for the purposes of ascertaining the amount of reinstatement grant payable under the Housing Act 1985, ss 541, 543, Halsbury's Statutes, 4th edn Vol 21, title Housing.

THE REGISTERED HOUSING ASSOCIATIONS (LIMITED ACCOUNTING REQUIREMENTS) ORDER 1984
SI 1984/1833

NOTES
Authority   This is as noted to SI 1982/828, p 173, *ante*, except that this order was made on 22 November 1984.
Commencement   1 January 1985.
General   This order allows qualifying housing associations (defined in art 2) to prepare their accounts for accounting periods commencing on or after 1 January 1985 in an alternative form. They may either comply with the requirements of this order or those of the Registered Housing Associations (Accounting Requirements) Order 1982, SI 1982/828, as modified by SI 1983/207, p 173, *ante*. The order permits a qualifying association to prepare one revenue account and one additional financial statement and to observe the requirements in Sch 1 to the 1982 Order, concerning the disclosure of information, as modified by this order.

THE HOUSING (RIGHT TO BUY) (PRESCRIBED FORMS) (WELSH FORMS) (NO 3) REGULATIONS 1985
SI 1985/36

NOTES
Authority   These regulations were made on 10 January 1985 by the Secretary of State for Wales under the Housing Act 1980, ss 22 (1) and 151 (1) as extended by the Welsh Language Act 1967, s 2 (2) and (3), and all other enabling powers. The said s 22 was repealed, and the said s 151 (1) partially repealed, by the Housing (Consequential Provisions) Act 1985 and by virtue of s 2 (2) thereof these regulations now have effect as if made under the Housing Act 1985, s 176 (1), as so extended, Halsbury's Statutes, 4th edn Vol 21, title Housing.
Commencement   4 February 1985.
General   These regulations (which revoke and replace the Housing (Right to Buy) (Prescribed Forms) (No 1) (Welsh Forms) Regulations 1980, SI 1980/1620), as construed in accordance with the Housing (Consequential Provisions) Act 1985, s 2 (4), prescribe Welsh versions of (*a*) the form of Notice to be used by a secure tenant claiming to exercise the right to buy under the Housing Act 1985, Part V, Halsbury's Statutes, 4th edn Vol 21, title Housing, and (*b*) the forms of Notices to be used by the landlord to admit or, as the case may be, deny the tenant's right to buy. They also prescribe the particulars to be contained in the forms. A notice claiming the right to buy served by a secure tenant before 1 March 1985 is not invalidated by these regulations if it is in the form required by SI 1980/1620 referred to above or in a substantially similar form. The forms may be used only in relation to a house or flat situated in Wales.

THE HOUSING BENEFITS (SUBSIDY) ORDER 1985
SI 1985/440

NOTES
Authority This order was made on 19 March 1985 by the Secretary of State for Social Services, with the consent of the Treasury, under the Social Security and Housing Benefits Act 1982, s 32 (2), Halsbury's Statutes, 4th edn Vol 40, title Social Security (3rd edn Vol 52, p 871), and all other enabling powers. The said s 32 (2) has been amended, with effect from 1 April 1985, by the Social Security Act 1985, s 22.
Commencement 1 April 1985.
General This order sets out the manner in which the subsidy payable under the Social Security and Housing Benefits Act 1982, s 32, Halsbury's Statutes, 4th edn Vol 40, title Social Security (3rd edn Vol 52, p 870), to authorities who grant rate rebates, rent rebates or rent allowances under that Act is to be calculated in respect of the year beginning 1 April 1985. It sets out the basis on which the subsidy in respect of rebates and allowances is to be calculated and the basis of calculating the amount of subsidy in respect of administrative costs.
Previous orders Corresponding orders in respect of previous years were: the Housing Benefits (Subsidy) (No 1) Order 1982, SI 1982/903 (in respect of the initial year ending 31 March 1983); the Housing Benefits (Subsidy) (No 2) Order 1982, SI 1982/904 (in respect of the financial year beginning 1 April 1983); the Housing Benefits (Subsidy) Order 1984, SI 1984/110, as amended by SI 1984/1001 (in respect of the financial year beginning 1 April 1984), all listed at pp 140, 141, *ante*.

THE HOUSING BENEFITS REGULATIONS 1985
SI 1985/677

NOTES
Authority These regulations were made on 29 April 1985 by the Secretary of State for Social Services, with the consent of the Treasury, under the Social Security and Housing Benefits Act 1982, s 28 (1), Halsbury's Statutes, 4th edn Vol 40, title Social Security (3rd edn Vol 52, p 865), and the Social Security Act 1975, s 166 (2) and (3), *ibid*, 4th edn Vol 40, title Social Security (3rd edn Vol 45, pp 1261, 1262), as applied by the 1982 Act, s 45 (1), and all other enabling powers.
Commencement Partly on 21 May 1985; fully on 1 August 1985.
General These regulations revoke and replace with one change the Housing Benefits Regulations 1982, SI 1982/1124, and the amending SI 1982/1519 (insofar as they amended 1982/1124), 1983/57 and 1014, 1984/103, 104, 940, 941, 1105, 1728 (insofar as they amended 1982/1124) and 1965 and 1985/368. The Housing Benefits (Transitional) Regulations 1982, SI 1982/1520, and the amending SI 1982/1520 and 1983/438 and 912 are revoked without replacement. The regulations deal with eligibility for housing benefit (Pt II), the amount of benefit, (Pt III), the benefit period (Pt IV), claims and changes of circumstances (Pt V), payment of benefit (Pt VI), recovery of overpayments (Pt VII) and the determination of questions (Pt VIII). The only change of substance from the 1982 Regulations made by these regulations concerns the minimum interval between payments of rent allowance (see reg 50).
Amendment These regulations have been amended by the Housing Benefits (Miscellaneous Amendments) Regulations 1985, SI 1985/1100, the Housing Benefits (Increase of Needs Allowances) Regulations 1985, SI 1985/1244, the Housing Benefits Amendment (No 2) Regulations 1985, SI 1985/1445 and the Housing Benefits Amendment Regulations 1986, SI 1986/84.
  Reasons of space preclude the printing of these regulations in full in this volume, but an outline of their scope is given by the arrangement of the regulations, *infra*. Where a provision of the regulations has been subsequently amended, the number of the amending instrument is given in brackets following the relevant provision.

ARRANGEMENT OF REGULATIONS
PART I
GENERAL

PART III
AMOUNT OF HOUSING BENEFIT

PART IV
BENEFIT PERIOD

PART V
CLAIMS AND CHANGES OF CIRCUMSTANCES

PART VI
PAYMENT

PART VII
RECOVERY OF OVERPAYMENTS

PART VIII
DETERMINATIONS AND REPRESENTATIONS

PART IX
REVOCATIONS

SCHEDULE 3: Deductions in respect of charges for fuel and services and in respect of rent for the purpose of computing eligible rent (*amended by SI 1985/1100*)
SCHEDULE 4: Areas of high rent
SCHEDULE 5: Constitution of review boards
SCHEDULE 6: Revocations

THE HOUSING (RIGHT TO A SHARED OWNERSHIP LEASE) (FURTHER ADVANCES LIMIT) REGULATIONS 1985
SI 1985/758

NOTES
Authority These regulations were made on 14 May 1985 by the Secretary of State for the Environment and the Secretary of State for Wales under the Housing and Building Control Act 1984, s 16 (6), and all other enabling powers. The said s 16 was repealed by the Housing (Consequential Provisions) Act 1985 and by virtue of s 2 (2) thereof these regulations now have effect as if made under the Housing Act 1985, Sch 9, para 4, Halsbury's Statutes, 4th edn Vol 21, title Housing.
Commencement 19 June 1985; see reg 1 (1).
Construction See regs 1 (2), 3 (3), 4 (3), 5 (4), 7 (3).
General These regulations, as construed in accordance with the Housing (Consequential Provisions) Act 1985, s 2 (4), lay down the method of calculating the available annual income of a tenant under a shared ownership lease and specify the appropriate factors by which such income must be multiplied to arrive at the limit on the amount of any further advance to finance the acquisition of any additional share in his dwelling under the Housing Act 1985, Sch 9, Halsbury's Statutes, Vol 21, title Housing.

1. Citation, commencement and interpretation (1) These regulations may be cited as the Housing (Right to a Shared Ownership Lease) (Further Advances Limit) Regulations 1985 and shall come into operation on 19th June 1985.
(2) In these regulations—
"admissible source" means a source of income of the tenant which is to be taken into account for the purposes of these regulations; and
"tenant" means a person to whom the right to a further advance belongs.

2. Available annual income The amount to be taken into account as the tenant's available annual income under section 16 of the Housing and Building Control Act 1984 (which deals with the right to further advances) is to be calculated by taking the amount which in accordance with regulations 3 to 6 is to be taken into account as his annual income and deducting from it in accordance with regulation 7 sums related to his commitments.

NOTES
Housing and Building Control Act 1984, s 16 This is now to be construed as a reference to the Housing Act 1985, Sch 9, Halsbury's Statutes, 4th edn Vol 21, title Housing.

3. Income from employment (1) This regulation applies to income from an employment.
(2) The amount to be taken into account as income to which this regulation applies is the tenant's current annual pay, namely his current pay expressed as an annual amount or, where that amount does not fairly represent his current annual pay, such amount as does.
(3) In this regulation—
"employment" includes a part-time employment and an office but does not include a casual or temporary employment; and
"pay" includes any commission, bonus, allowance (but not an expense allowance), tip, gratuity or other payment made to the tenant in connection with his employment but does not include any benefit in kind; and references to pay are references to it before any statutory or other deductions has been made.

4. Income from a business (1) This regulation applies to income from a business carried on by the tenant (whether or not with any other person).

(2) The amount to be taken into account as the tenant's annual income from the business is an amount which, having regard to the latest available information, fairly represents the current annual net profit of the business or, if the tenant shares the net profit with any other person, his share of the net profit.

(3) In this regulation "business" includes any trade, profession or vocation.

5. Other income (1) This regulation applies to income from a source to which regulations 3 and 4 do not apply.

(2) No account shall be taken under this regulation of state benefits other than benefits under—

(*a*) sections 36 and 37 of the National Insurance Act 1965 (graduated retirement benefits);

(*b*) sections 8, 15, and 16 of the Social Security Pensions Act 1975 (widower's retirement pensions, widow's and widower's invalidity pensions); and

(*c*) the following provisions of the Social Security Act 1975 to the extent that they relate to any benefit by way of pension or other periodical payments—

sections 15, 16 and 36 (invalidity and severe disablement benefits);
sections 24 to 26 (widow's benefits);
sections 28, 29, 39 and 40 (retirement pensions);
section 57 (1) (disability benefits);
sections 67 (1), 69, 70, 71 (1) and 72 (1) (industrial death benefits); and
section 76 (industrial disease benefits).

(3) The amount to be taken into account as the tenant's annual income from a source to which this regulation applies, which is not excluded from account by paragraph (2), is an amount which before any statutory or other deduction represents the tenant's current income from that source expressed as an annual amount.

(4) In this regulation "state benefits" means any benefits under the Family Income Supplements Act 1970, the Social Security Acts 1975 to 1984, the Child Benefit Act 1975 and the Supplementary Benefits Act 1976.

NOTES
National Insurance Act 1965, ss 36, 37 Repealed but continued in force by the Social Security (Graduated Retirement Benefit) (No 2) Regulations 1978, SI 1978/393; see Halsbury's Statutes, 4th edn Vol 40, title Social Security (3rd edn Vol 23, pp 296, 298).
Social Security Pensions Act 1975, ss 8, 15, 16 *Ibid*, 4th edn Vol 40, title Social Security (3rd edn Vol 45, pp 1392, 1397, 1398).
Social Security Act 1975, ss 15, 16, 24-26, 28, 29, 36, 39, 40, 57 (1), 67 (1), 69, 70, 71 (1), 72 (1), 76 *Ibid*, 4th edn Vol 40, title Social Security (3rd edn Vol 45, p 1094 *et seq*).
Family Income Supplements Act 1970 *Ibid*, 4th edn Vol 40, title Social Security (3rd edn Vol 40, p 1079 *et seq*).
Social Security Acts 1975 to 1984 *Ie* the Social Security Act 1975, the Social Security Pensions Act 1975, the Social Security (Miscellaneous Provisions) Act 1977, the Social Security Act 1979, the Social Security Act 1980, the Social Security (No 2) Act 1980, the Social Security Act 1981, the Social Security and Housing Benefits Act 1982 and the Health and Social Security Act 1984; see the 1984 Act, s 29 (2), Halsbury's Statutes, 4th edn Vol 40, title Social Security (3rd edn Vol 54 (1), p 1107).
Child Benefit Act 1975 *Ibid*, 4th edn Vol 40, title Social Security (3rd edn Vol 45, p 1481 *et seq*).
Supplementary Benefits Act 1976 *Ibid*, 4th edn Vol 40, title Social Security (3rd edn Vol 46, p 1046 *et seq*).

6. Income from more than one source If the tenant has income from more than one admissible source, the amount to be taken into account as his annual income shall be the total amount of his annual income from all admissible sources determined in accordance with the provisions of these regulations.

7. Deductions for commitments (1) Sums related to the tenant's commitments are to be deducted from the amount to be taken into account as his annual income if he is liable to make—

(*a*) any maintenance payments; or

(*b*) any payments under a credit agreement; or
(*c*) any payments under a court order;
and the payments are likely to continue for more than 18 months.

(2) The sums which are to be deducted are sums equal in total to the total of the annual amounts currently payable for which the conditions in paragraph (1) are satisfied.

(3) In this regulation—

"credit agreement" means a loan agreement, hire purchase agreement or other agreement for credit; and

"maintenance payment" means any payment by the tenant for the maintenance of a dependent child under the age of 16 or for the maintenance of his spouse or former spouse.

8. Estimates   The landlord, or, if the landlord is a housing association, the Housing Corporation, may accept any estimate made for the purposes of regulations 3 to 7.

9. Joint tenants   Where the right to a further advance belongs to more than one tenant, the preceding provisions of these regulations shall be applied separately to determine the amount of each tenant's available annual income.

10. Multipliers   (1) This regulation specifies the appropriate factor to be applied as a multiplier of the tenant's available annual income to arrive at the limit imposed by section 16 of the Housing and Building Control Act 1984.

(2) If the tenant's income is the principal income, the appropriate factor in relation to his available income is the multiplier shown in the following Table corresponding to his age on the date of service of the notice claiming to exercise his right to acquire an additional share.

TABLE

Tenant's age on the date of service of the notice	Multiplier
Under 60	2.5
60 and over but under 65	2.0
65 and over	1.0

(3) If the tenant's income is not the principal income, the appropriate factor in relation to his available annual income is 1.

(4) Subject to paragraph (5), a tenant's income is the principal income for the purposes of this regulation if he is the only tenant with income or there is more than one tenant with income and the tenants require the landlord, or, if the landlord is a housing association, the Housing Corporation, to treat his income as the principal income.

(5) The income of only one tenant shall be treated as the principal income for the purposes of this regulation.

NOTES
Housing and Building Control Act 1984, s 16   See the note to reg 2.

**THE HOME PURCHASE ASSISTANCE (PRICE-LIMITS) ORDER 1985
SI 1985/937**

NOTES
Authority   This order was made on 18 June 1985 by the Secretary of State for the Environment and the Secretaries of State for Wales and Scotland under the Home Purchase Assistance and Housing Corporation Guarantee Act 1978, ss 1 (2) and 2 (7), and all other enabling powers. That Act was repealed by the Housing (Consequential Provisions) Act 1985 and by virtue of s 2 (2) thereof this order now has effect as if made under the Housing Act 1985, ss 445, Halsbury's Statutes, 4th edn Vol 21, title Housing.
Commencement   20 July 1985; see art 1.

General   This order (which revokes and replaces the Home Purchase Assistance (Price-limits) Order 1984, SI 1984/954), as construed in accordance with the Housing (Consequential Provisions) Act 1985, s 2 (4), prescribes limits for different parts of Great Britain within which the purchase price of the property must fall to be eligible for assistance under the Housing Act 1985, s 445, Halsbury's Statutes, 4th edn Vol 21, title Housing.

1. Citation and commencement   This order may be cited as the Home Purchase Assistance (Price-limits) Order 1985 and shall come into operation on 20th July 1985

2. Prescribed price-limits   The amounts mentioned in column 2 of the Schedule to this order are hereby prescribed as the price-limits in respect of house property situated in the parts of Great Britain mentioned in respect thereof in column 1.

3. Revocation   The Home Purchase Assistance (Price-limits) Order 1984 is hereby revoked.

NOTES
Home Purchase Assistance (Price-limits) Order 1984   SI 1984/954.

SCHEDULE

Column 1	Column 2
The counties of Cleveland, Cumbria, Durham, Northumberland and Tyne and Wear	£21,500
The counties of Humberside, North Yorkshire, South Yorkshire and West Yorkshire	£20,400
The counties of Derbyshire, Leicestershire, Lincolnshire, Northamptonshire and Nottinghamshire	£22,100
The counties of Cambridgeshire, Norfolk and Suffolk	£26,000
Greater London	£38,000
The counties of Bedfordshire, Berkshire, Buckinghamshire, East Sussex, Essex, Hampshire, Hertfordshire, Isle of Wight, Kent, Oxfordshire, Surrey and West Sussex	£33,500
The counties of Avon, Cornwall, Devon, Dorset, Gloucestershire, Somerset and Wiltshire and the Isles of Scilly	£28,200
The counties of Hereford and Worcester, Shropshire, Staffordshire, Warwickshire and West Midlands	£21,900
The counties of Cheshire, Greater Manchester, Lancashire and Merseyside	£21,700
Wales	£22,700
Scotland	£26,000

Husband and Wife

ARRANGEMENT

(NB—There is no Chronological List of Instruments covering all the instruments allocated to this title, because the names of the Parts clearly indicate which particular instruments fall within the scope of each. Reference should, therefore, be made to the lists which appear at the head of each Part)

CROSS REFERENCES

Adoption of children — Infants (Part 1)

Attachment of earnings orders, magistrates' courts — Magistrates (Part 1)

Child benefit — National Insurance (Part 3)

Children, generally — Infants

Commonwealth divorce jurisdiction — Conflict of Laws

County courts, fees — Courts (Part 5A (iii))

Education of children — Education

Foreign marriages, consular fees — Constitutional Law (Part 8)

Infants, marriage consents — Infants (Part 4)

Law Reform (Married Women and Tortfeasors) Act 1935, appointed day — Tort (this is a note between the titles Tithe and Town and Country Planning)

Legal advice — Solicitors (Part 1A)

Legal aid — Courts (Part 8)

Marriage forms — Registration concerning the Individual

Marriage registration, generally — Registration concerning the Individual

Married women, national insurance — National Insurance (Part 1)

Maternity benefit — National Insurance (Part 1)

Matrimonial causes, Commonwealth jurisdiction — Conflict of Laws

Matrimonial homes, Land Registry forms, etc — Real Property (Part 1)

Matrimonial homes, registration of land charge — Real Property (Part 2)

Paternity, blood tests — Evidence (Part 1); Magistrates Courts (Parts 3 and 5)

Rules of court (RSC; CCR) — Magistrates

Summary jurisdiction, generally — Registration concerning the Individual

Superintendent registrar, duties — Registration concerning the Individual

Supreme Court, fees — Courts (Part 3C)

Statutory instruments generally, their validity, effect and termination — Statutory Instruments, Vol 1

PART 1
Marriage

CHRONOLOGICAL LIST OF INSTRUMENTS

SI	Description	Remarks	Page
1970/1539	Foreign Marriage Order 1970	—	207
1970/1780	Marriage (Registrar General's Licence) Regulations 1970	—	210
1971/1216	Marriage (Authorised Persons) (Amend-ment) Regulations 1971	Amend 1952/1869 (*qv*)	—
1974/573	Marriage (Authorised Persons) (Amend-ment) Regulations 1974		
1984/413	Marriage Act 1983 (Commencement) Order 1984	Brought the Marriage Act 1983 into force on 1 May 1984	—

INTRODUCTORY NOTE
The instruments relating to marriage can conveniently be discussed in two categories, namely, (i) those which relate to marriages in England (and, in certain cases, other parts of the United Kingdom), and (ii) those which relate to marriages abroad.

Marriages in England   The law relating to marriages in England is contained mainly in the Marriage Acts 1949 to 1983. The first Act in that series, namely, the Marriage Act 1949, Halsbury's Statutes, 4th edn Vol 27, title Matrimonial Law (Pt 1) and Vol 37, title Registration concerning the Individual, consolidated, with minor modifications, most of the previously existing enactments as to the solemnisation and registration of marriages. Certain matters under the Acts are left to be dealt with by subordinate legislation; of the relevant statutory instruments, those containing general provisions are included in this Part of the title, and those concerned only with the registration of marriages are in the title Registration concerning the Individual. The main purpose of subordinate legislation as respects marriages in England is to ensure that adequate publicity is provided for intended marriages and that all marriages are registered.

A marriage in England may be solemnised (i) after publication of banns, (ii) by special licence, (iii) by common licence, (iv) after the issue of a superintendent registrar's certificate (or certificate and licence), (v) by licence of the Registrar General, or (vi) after the issue of a naval officer's certificate. Apart from provisions in respect of naval marriages (see p 200, *post*), there is no subordinate legislation in this title appertaining to banns, special licences or common licences; for the law as to such marriages, see generally, 14 Halsbury's Laws (4th Edn), paras 1006 *et seq*.

Marriage on the authority of a superintendent registrar   In addition to marriage in a register office, marriages may be solemnised elsewhere on the authority of a superintendent registrar's certificate, either with or without his licence; see s 26 of the Marriage Act 1949, as amended, Halsbury's Statutes, 4th edn Vol 27, title Matrimonial Law (Pt 1) (3rd edn Vol 17, p 66). The Marriage Act 1983, Halsbury's Statutes, 4th edn Vol 27, title Matrimonial Law (Pt 1) (3rd edn Vol 43, p 679 *et seq*), enables the marriage of a housebound or detained person to be solemnized on the authority of the certificate of a superintendent register issued under the Marriage Act 1949, Part III, Halsbury's Statutes, 4th edn Vol 27, title Matrimonial Law (Pt 1) (3rd edn Vol 17, p 66 *et seq*), at the place where that person is for the time being. The 1983 Act was brought into force on 1 May 1984 by the Marriage Act 1983 (Commencement) Order 1984, SI 1984/413, listed, *ante*, made under s 12 (5) of the Act. The general duties of a superintendent registrar are prescribed by the Registration of Births, Deaths and Marriages Regulations 1968, SI 1968/2049 (as amended), in the title Registration concerning the Individual. The manner and form of registration of marriages solemnised in the presence of a registrar are governed by Part XI of those regulations. See also under "Marriage forms", *infra*.

Marriages in registered buildings   A registered building is a place of worship (other than of the Church of England) duly registered for the solemnisation of marriages. A registrar of marriages may be requested to attend a marriage in a registered building, in which case he will register the marriage in his own register; otherwise the marriage will be registered in the register kept by the authorised person for the building, and may be solemnised either by the authorised person or the minister. Sections 41 to 44 of the Marriage Act 1949, Halsbury's Statutes, 4th edn Vol 27, title Matrimonial Law (Pt 1) (3rd edn Vol 17, p 78 *et seq*) relate to marriages in registered buildings; see also s 6 of the Sharing of Church Buildings Act 1969, Halsbury's Statutes, 4th edn Vol 14, title Ecclesiastical Law (Pt 5 (*a*)). Matters of detail in regard to the appointment and duties of authorised persons and the registration of marriages by them are prescribed by the Marriage (Authorised Persons) Regulations 1952, SI 1952/1869, as amended, p 203 *post.*

Marriage on the authority of Registrar General elsewhere than in registered buildings The Marriage (Registrar General's Licence) Act 1970, Halsbury's Statutes, 4th edn Vol 27, title Matrimonial Law (Pt 1) (3rd edn Vol 17, p 784 *et seq*), allows a marriage, other than a marriage according to the rites of the Church of England or the Church in Wales, to be solemnised on the authority of a licence of the Registrar General elsewhere than in a registered building or the office of a superintendent registrar if one of the parties is seriously ill and not expected to recover and cannot be moved to a place where the marriage could lawfully be solemnised under the Marriage Act 1949. The Marriage (Registrar General's Licence) Regulations 1970, SI 1970/ 1780, p 210, *post,* provide for the manner in which such a marriage is to be registered and prescribe necessary forms.

Naval marriages Where a marriage is to be solemnised in England, Scotland or Northern Ireland, and one of the parties is an officer, seaman or marine borne on the books of one of Her Majesty's ships, banns of marriage may be published on board that ship; moreover the captain or officer commanding the ship is authorised to issue a certificate for marriage equivalent to a superintendent registrar's certificate. Naval marriages are governed by the provisions of ss 14 and 39 of the Marriage Act 1949, Halsbury's Statutes, 4th edn Vol 27, title Matrimonial Law (Pt 1) (3rd edn Vol 17, pp 57, 77), and the Order in Council as to naval marriages dated 21 December 1908, SR & O 1908/1316, p 203, *post.*

Recognition of certificates, etc, issued in HM dominions abroad Where a marriage is to be contracted or solemnised in the United Kingdom, and one of the parties is a British subject resident in any of Her Majesty's dominions outside the United Kingdon to which the Marriage of British Subjects (Facilities) Act 1915, Halsbury's Statutes, 4th edn Vol 27, title Matrimonial Law (Pt 1) (3rd edn Vol 17, p 35 *et seq*), has been applied, a certificate of the publication of banns or of notice of marriage, issued according to the law of the territory in which he is resident, is deemed to be of the same effect as a certificate for marriage issued by a superintendent registrar in England or a registrar in Scotland or Northern Ireland. The territories to which the Act applies are set out at p 202 *post* under the heading "Marriages within the Commonwealth".

Marriage forms The Registration of Births, Deaths and Marriages Regulations 1968, SI 1968/2049, as amended, in the title Registration concerning the Individual, prescribe, *inter alia,* (i) the notice to be given to a superintendent registrar when a marriage is to be solemnised on the authority of his certificate, or his certificate and licence; (ii) the form of a superintendent registrar's certificate, and certificate and licence; (iii) instructions for the solemnisation of marriage in a registered building without the presence of a registrar; and (iv) the form of entry of marriage in a marriage register book (for all marriages within s 26 of the Act of 1949). Some few marriage forms are also prescribed by instruments in this title; see in particular the Marriage (Authorised Persons) Regulations 1952, SI 1952/1869, p 203, *post,* and the Marriage (Registrar General's Licence) Regulations 1970, SI 1970/1780, p 210, *post.*

Minors A marriage between persons either of whom is under the age of sixteen years is void, and in general the consent of both parents (or guardians) is required in the case of a marriage where one of the parties is under the age of eighteen; see ss 2 and 3 of the Marriage Act 1949 and s 1 (1) and (2) of the Family Law Reform Act 1969, Halsbury's Statutes, 4th edn Vol 6, title Children. Under the said s 3 consent may in certain circumstances be dispensed with by the Registrar General or by a court. The Magistrates' Courts (Guardianship of Minors) Rules 1974, SI 1974/706, in the title Infants (Part 4), regulate applications to magistrates' courts; as to applications for relief to the High Court and the County Court, see, respectively, RSC Order 90, r 8, in the current Supreme Court Practice; and CCR Order 46, r 9, in the current County Court Practice.

Validation of marriages   The Provisional Order (Marriages) Act 1905, Halsbury's Statutes, 4th edn Vol 27, title Matrimonial Law (Pt 1) (3rd edn Vol 17, p 30 *et seq*), provides that a Secretary of State may, in the case of a marriage solemnised in England which appears to be invalid or of doubtful validity, make a provisional order for the purpose of removing the invalidity or doubt. Orders made under this power (which has been extended by the Marriages Validity (Provisional Orders) Act 1924, Halsbury's Statutes, 4th edn Vol 27, title Matrimonial Law (Pt 1) (3rd edn Vol 17, p 39 *et seq*) are now subject to the Statutory Orders (Special Procedure) Act 1945, Halsbury's Statutes, 4th edn Vol 41, title Statutes (3rd edn Vol 32, p 658 *et seq*), by virtue of the Statutory Orders (Special Procedure) (Substitution) Order 1949, SI 1949/2393, as amended, printed in the title Statutory Instruments, Vol 1, of this work. They may be printed in the SR & O/SI series and must be notified in the *London Gazette,* but are not included in the government annual volumes.

Marriages abroad   The instruments relating to marriages abroad and printed in this Part of the title are made under the Foreign Marriage Act 1892 and the Foreign Marriage Act 1947, Halsbury's Statutes, 4th edn Vol 27, title Matrimonial Law (Pt 1) (3rd edn Vol 17, pp 16, 42). Orders applying the Marriage of British Subjects (Facilities) Act 1915, Halsbury's Statute, 4th edn Vol 27, title Matrimonial Law (Pt 1) (3rd edn Vol 17, p 35 *et seq*), to Her Majesty's dominions are listed at p 202, *post.*

Marriages on foreign territory   Machinery exists for according automatic recognition to marriages validly contracted abroad. The Foreign Marriage Act 1892, Halsbury's Statutes, 4th edn Vol 27, title Matrimonial Law (Pt 1) (3rd edn Vol 17, p 16 *et seq*), provides that where one at least of the parties to a marriage abroad is a British subject, the marriage may be solemnised by a marriage officer in accordance with the Act and shall have the same validity as if it had been lawfully solemnised in the United Kingdom. Section 11 of the Act governs the appointment of marriage officers who are authorised to solemnise and register foreign marriages. As to solemnisation, see further the Foreign Marriage Order 1970, SI 1970/1539, p 207, *post.* Chaplains to Her Majesty's naval, military or air forces serving in foreign territory, and any other person authorised by the commanding officer of any part of such forces, may solemnise marriages under the Act where one of the parties is serving in those forces, or is employed in one of certain other prescribed capacities; see s 22 of the Act of 1892 and the Foreign Marriage (Armed Forces) Order 1964, SI 1964/1000, as amended, p 204, *post.* By art 6 of the last mentioned order, provisions of the laws of New Zealand and Australia corresponding to s 22 of the Act are recognised as having effect as part of the law of the United Kingdom in relation to forces raised in those Dominions.

Where a marriage has been solemnised according to the local law of a foreign country and one at least of the parties is a British subject, the marriage certificate may be authenticated by the signature of the British consul and the marriage may be registered in the United Kingdom; see art 7 of the Foreign Marriage Order 1970 SI 1970/1539, p 208, *post.* Nothing in the Act of 1892, however, affects the validity of a marriage solemnised in accordance with the local law of a country, whether the marriage is subsequently registered or not; see ss 18 and 23.

Marriages within the Commonwealth   Where a marriage between British subjects is intended to be solemnised or contracted in any part of Her Majesty's dominions, or any protectorate, to which the Marriage of British Subjects (Facilities) Act 1915, Halsbury's Statutes, 4th edn Vol 27, title Matrimonial Law (Pt 1) (3rd edn Vol 17, p 35 *et seq*), has been applied by Order in Council under that Act, and one of the parties to the marriage is resident in the United Kingdom, a superintendent registrar in England, or a registrar in Scotland or Northern Ireland, may issue a "certificate of marriage" as if both parties to the marriage were resident in England, Scotland or Northern Ireland as the case may be. The Act contains reciprocal provisions applying to marriages in the United Kingdom. The following table shows the territories to which the Act has been applied. Constitutional and jurisdictional changes affecting the territories concerned are noted in the title Dominions and Dependencies (Part 1) under the heading "Jurisdictional Charges".

TABLE OF TERRITORIES

Territory	Order	Operative Date
Bahamas	1917/1242	16 November 1917
Barbados	1917/1242	16 November 1917
Basutoland (now Lesotho)	1917/1242	16 November 1917
Bechuanaland (now Botswana)	1917/1243	16 November 1917
Bermudas	1917/210	6 February 1917
British Honduras (now Belize)	1917/210	6 February 1917
Ceylon and its Dependencies (now Sri Lanka)	1918/249	12 February 1918
Cyprus	1925/1324	16 December 1925
Dominica	1916/555 as amended by 1939/1896	28 July 1916
Fiji	1918/1285	27 September 1918
Gambia		
Colony	1916/555	28 July 1916
Protectorate	1916/556	28 July 1916
Gibraltar	1917/1242	16 November 1917
Gilbert and Ellice Islands Colony (now Kiribati and Tuvalu)	1917/747	17 July 1917
Gold Coast Colony (now part of Ghana)	1916/555	28 July 1916
Grenada	1917/1242	16 November 1917
Guernsey, Bailiwick of	1927/1084	3 November 1927
Hong Kong	1916/555	28 July 1916
Isle of Man	1925/1032	12 October 1925
Jamaica	1917/747	17 July 1917
Jersey	1930/229	28 March 1930
Kenya	1916/556	28 July 1916
Labuan (now part of Malaysia)	1916/555	28 July 1916
Leeward Islands	1916/555	28 July 1916
Malacca (now part of Malaysia)	1916/555	28 July 1916
Mauritius	1916/555	28 July 1916
New Zealand	1920/2081	13 October 1920
Newfoundland	1916/632	18 August 1916
Nigeria Colony and Protectorate (now part of Nigeria)	1920/826	26 April 1920
Northern Rhodesia Protectorate (now Zambia)	1919/473	28 March 1919
Nyasaland Protectorate (now Malawi)	1917/748	7 July 1917
Pacific Protectorate	1917/749	17 July 1917
Penang (now part of Malaysia)	1916/555	28 July 1916
St Lucia	1916/862	16 November 1916
St Vincent	1916/555	28 July 1916
Seychelles	1916/862	16 November 1916
Sierra Leone		
Colony	1916/862	16 November 1916
Protectorate	1916/822	16 November 1916
Singapore	1916/555	28 July 1916
Southern Rhodesia (now Zimbabwe*)	1918/1066	15 August 1918
Straits Settlements. *See* Labuan, Malacca, Penang and Singapore		
Swaziland Protectorate (now Swaziland)	1917/1243	16 November 1917
Trinidad and Tobago	1916/555	28 July 1916
Uganda Protectorate (now part of Uganda)	1916/556	28 July 1916
Victoria	1916/632	18 August 1916
Zanzibar Protectorate (now part of Tanzania)	1917/748	7 July 1917

*By virtue of the Zimbabwe (Independence and Membership of the Commonwealth) (Consequential Provisions) Order 1980, SI 1980/701 (in the title Dominions and Dependencies (Pt 1)), SR & O 1918/1066 has effect as if the reference to Southern Rhodesia were a reference to Zimbabwe.

ORDER IN COUNCIL AS TO NAVAL MARRIAGES
SR & O 1908/1316

NOTES
Authority This Order in Council was made on 21 December 1908 under s 3 of the Naval Marriages Act 1908. That Act was repealed, so far as it related to marriages solemised in England, by s 79 of, and Schedule 5 to, the Marriage Act 1949, Halsbury's Statutes, 4th edn Vol 27, title Matrimonial Law (Pt 1) (3rd edn Vol 17, pp 97, 103), but by virtue of the saving provisions of s 79 (2) this order continues to have effect as if made under ss 14 (2) and 39 (2) thereof
Commencement 1 January 1909
General Under ss 4 and 5 of the Naval Marriages Act 1908 and ss 14 and 39 of the Marriage Act 1949, banns may be published and marriage certificates may be issued on board Her Majesty's ships for the purpose of a marriage to be solemnised in the United Kingdom. This order, the main provisions of which are summarised below, prescribes certain matters chiefly in connection with the publication of banns, and notice of intended marriage in regard to naval marriages.
Summary A Banns of Marriage Book is to be provided on every ship and banns are to be published from that book, which is to be signed by the chaplain or other person who has published the banns. Any officer, seaman or marine borne on the books of any of Her Majesty's ships at sea may be described in banns as "of Her Majesty's ship —" without the addition of any parish or chapelry, and that description is sufficient for the purposes of any declaration to be made at the time of giving notice of the intended marriage. Notice of the intended marriage is to be given to the commanding officer of the ship on one of the four forms (Forms A, B, C and D) prescribed in the schedule to the order (the forms differ according to whether the marriage is to be solemnised in England, Scotland or Northern Ireland).

Where any enactment requires a registrar to file a notice of marriage, to keep it with his official records and to enter a copy of it in a Marriage Notice Book, the commanding officer must comply with such enactment as if he were a registrar, and attest with his signature the entry in his Marriage Notice Book. Where a marriage is to be solemnised otherwise than after the publication of banns, the commanding officer must cause a notice of the marriage to be displayed in some conspicuous part of the ship for a period of (*a*) twenty-one successive days after it has been entered in the Marriage Notice Book (if the marriage is intended to be solemnised in England or in the office of the registrar in Northern Ireland), or (*b*) seven consecutive days after entry in the Marriage Notice Book (if the marriage is to be solemnised in Scotland).

When an officer, seaman or marine has given notice of marriage in accordance with this order, it is sufficient for the other party, in giving notice to a registrar, to describe him as borne on the books of one of Her Majesty's ships together with the name of the ship, without stating his dwelling place, length of residence, district, parish or county.

The same provisions as to perjury apply to notices and declarations given or made under this order as would apply were the notices or declaration given or made to a registrar or other person in accordance with any other enactment.

THE MARRIAGE (AUTHORISED PERSONS) REGULATIONS 1952
SI 1952/1869

NOTES
Authority These regulations were made on 21 October 1952 by the Registrar General, with the approval of the Minister of Health, under s 74 of the Marriage Act 1949, Halsbury's Statutes, 4th edn Vol 27, title Matrimonial Law (Pt 1) (3rd edn Vol 17, p 92), and all other enabling powers.
Commencement 1 December 1952.
Amendment These regulations have been amended by the London Authorities (Miscellaneous Health Provisions) Order 1965, SI 1965/528 (in the title Public Health (Part 8)) (which in regs 10 and 13) (1) for references to a metropolitan borough substituted references to a London borough); by the Marriage (Authorised Persons) (Amendment) Regulations 1971, SI 1971/1216 (relating to registration in the case of a party whose previous marriage was annulled on the ground that it was voidable); and by the Marriage (Authorised Persons) (Amendment) Regulations 1974, SI 1974/573 (which in regs 10 and 13 (1) for references to an administrative county and a county borough substituted references to a non-metropolitan county and a metropolitan district).
Interpretation In the summary printed below, as in the regulations themselves, "the Act" means the Marriage Act 1949, Halsbury's Statutes, 4th edn Vol 27, title Matrimonial Law (Pt 1) (3rd edn Vol 17, p 44 *et seq*); "authorised person" means a person certified under s 43 of the Act by the trustees or governing body of a registered building as having been authorised to act as such; "registered building" means a building registered under Part III of the Act; "trustees or governing body", in relation to Roman Catholic registered buildings, includes a bishop or vicar general of the diocese, and in relation to chapels registered for marriages under s 70 of the Act means the Admiralty (now the Secretary of State (for Defence)) or any person authorised by them, in the case of a naval chapel, and a Secretary of State or any person authorised by him, in the case of any other chapel; and "superintendent registrar" means a superintendent registrar of births, deaths and marriages. The expression "Registrar General" is defined in s 78 (1) of the Act to mean the Registrar General of Births, Deaths and Marriages in England (now called the Registrar General for England and Wales: see s 1 of the Registration Service Act 1953, Halsbury's Statutes, 4th edn Vol 37, title Registration concerning the Individual (3rd edn Vol 27, p 1055)).
General See the Introductory Note under the head "Marriages in registered buildings", p 199, *ante*.

Offences   Any authorised person who refuses or fails to comply with these regulations is guilty of an offence under the Marriage Act 1949 and is liable to penalties; see s 77 of that Act, Halsbury's Statutes, 4th edn Vol 27, title Matrimonial Law (Pt 1) (3rd edn Vol 17, p 95).

Summary   These regulations (which revoke and replace SR & O 1899/78 and 1909/1332 and regulations dated 19 February 1918 (not printed in the SR & O series)) contain provisions as to the appointment of persons authorised in pursuance of the Act to attend marriages solemnised in a registered building without the presence of a registrar, as to the manner of safeguarding marriage register books in a registered building, and as to the duties of authorised persons in connection with the solemnisation and registration of such marriages.

Appointment of authorised persons   The name and address of a person authorised by the trustees or governing body of a registered building to attend marriages in that building must, in pursuance of s 43 (1) of the Act, be certified by them (in the form scheduled to the regulations or in a substantially similar form) within one day from the date when he is authorised. Where an authorised person for a registered building ceases to be authorised to be present at the solemnisation of marriages in the building, the trustees or governing body of the building must thereupon inform the Registrar General of the fact and must state whether they intend to certify, in place of that person, some other person to act as authorised person; and where, when the vacancy occurs, there is no other authorised person for the building, the trustees or governing body must further inform the Registrar General what provision is being made for the solemnisation and registration of marriages in the building and, if necessary, for the preparation and delivery of the certified copies under s 57 of the Act, while there is no authorised person.

Custody of register books   The marriage register books for a registered building must be kept in the custody of the authorised person for that building or, where there are two or more authorised persons, such one of them as is notified to the Registrar General by the trustees or governing body or, in default of an authorised person, the trustees or governing body until another authorised person is appointed. The marriage register books and forms for certified copies must, when not actually in use, be kept locked up in a strong fire-resisting receptacle in the registered building or in some other place approved by the Registrar General. If the registration of the building is cancelled, or if the trustees or governing body decide that marriages shall no longer be solemnised without the presence of a registrar, or the Registrar General attaches a condition to that effect, the books must be sent to the Registrar General in order that they may be closed and deposited in appropriate custody.

Production, scrutiny and disposal of certificates, etc   Before permitting the solemnisation of a marriage in his presence, an authorised person must require the production of every document on the authority of which the marriage is to be solemnised and must by scrutiny of the documents satisfy himself that the marriage may be lawfully solemnised. The authorised person must make a note upon every certificate or licence delivered to him of the number of the entry in the marriage register books in which the marriage has been registered and must preserve every such certificate or certificate and licence in the fire-resisting receptacle required to be provided for the registered building until the end of the quarter, when it must be delivered to the superintendent registrar with the corresponding certified copy of the marriage entry for transmission to the Registrar General.

Registration of marriages   Immediately after the solemnisation of a marriage under s 44 of the Act, in the presence of an authorised person, the authorised person must, in some part of the registered building and in the presence of the parties and two witnesses to the marriage, register the marriage in the prescribed form (*ie*, Form 23 in Schedule 1 to the Registration of Births, Deaths and Marriages Regulations 1968, SI 1968/2049, in the title Registration concerning the Individual) in each of the duplicate register books provided for the building. Detailed instructions are given as to the making of entries and the signing of the register, and also as to the inscribing of new register books and the cancelling of blank spaces. An entry is complete when the authorised person has signed it and appended to his signature his official description. Every entry, and every certified copy of an entry given under s 57 or s 63 of the Act, must be in ink of durable quality. There are also provisions as to the correction by authorised persons of erroneous entries. An authorised person must not correct an error discovered after completion of the entry without first reporting to the Registrar General and he must comply with any instructions which the Registrar General may give for the purpose of verifying the facts and ascertaining the parties or witnesses who will be available to witness a correction. He must not register any marriage to which he is a party or witness.

THE FOREIGN MARRIAGE (ARMED FORCES) ORDER 1964
SI 1964/1000

NOTES

Authority   This Order in Council was made on 3 July 1964 under ss 18 (2) and (3), 21 and 22 of the Foreign Marriage Act 1892, Halsbury's Statutes, 4th edn Vol 27, title Matrimonial Law (Pt 1) (3rd edn Vol 17, pp 24, 27), as amended by s 2, 3, 4 (2) and 6 of the Foreign Marriage Act 1947, *ibid*, 4th edn Vol 27, title Matrimonial Law (Pt 1) (3rd edn Vol 17, p 43), and all other enabling powers.

Commencement   1 October 1964; see art 9 (2).

Amendment   This order is printed as amended by the Foreign Marriage (Armed Forces) (Amendment) Order 1965, SI 1965/137 (made under s 3 of the Foreign Marriage Act 1947, Halsbury's Statutes, 4th edn Vol 27, title Matrimonial Law (Pt 1) (3rd edn Vol 17, p 43).

General   Section 22 (1) of the Foreign Marriage Act 1892, as amended, provides that marriages celebrated by a service chaplain in any foreign territory (defined in s 22 (2) of the Act) shall be as valid as if celebrated in the United Kingdom as long as one of the parties is a member of the naval, military or air forces of Her Majesty. This order (i) prescribed the persons to whom (in addition to members of the armed forces) s 22 (1) is applicable, (ii) prescribes conditions which must be complied with, (iii) makes provision as to registration of such marriages, and (iv) recognises provisions of the laws of New Zealand and Australia similar to s 22 of the Act of 1892 as having effect as part of the law of the United Kingdom in relation to forces raised in those dominions.

As to marriages solemnised abroad under the Act of 1892, as amended, otherwise than under s 22 thereof, see the Foreign Marriage Order 1970, SI 1970/1539, p 207, *post*.

1. The persons to whom (in addition to members of the naval, military or air forces of Her Majesty) section 22 (1) of the Foreign Marriage Act 1892 (as re-enacted by the Foreign Marriage Act 1947) (in this Order hereafter referred to as "the said section 22 (1)") shall apply shall be persons employed in any of the capacities specified in Article 2 of this Order in the territory where the the marriage is solemnised; in the prescribed conditions for the purposes of the said subsection shall in all cases be those specified in Article 3 of this Order.

NOTES
Section 22 (1) of the Foreign Marriage Act 1892, as re-enacted   Halsbury's Statutes, 4th edn Vol 27, title Matrimonial Law (Pt 1) (3rd edn Vol 17, p 26).
Foreign Marriage Act 1947   Halsbury's Statutes, 4th edn Vol 27, title Matrimonial Law (Pt 1) (3rd edn Vol 17, p 42 *et seq*).

2.   The capacities referred to in Article 1 of this Order are those of female persons employed—
- (*a*) with the medical or dental branches of the Royal Navy as officers;
- (*b*) as members of the Women's Royal Naval Service;
- (*c*) as members of Queen Alexandra's Royal Naval Nursing Service or any reserve thereof;
- (*d*) as a member of a Voluntary Aid Detachment under the Ministry of Defence.

3.   The prescribed conditions referred to in Article 1 of this Order are:—
- (*a*) that before a marriage is solemnised under the said section 22 (1), there shall be produced to the Chaplain or other person authorised pursuant to the said section 22 (1) a certificate signed or purporting to be signed by or on behalf of the Commander in the territory in which that party to the marriage is serving or employed such certificate to state that the Commander has no objection to the marriage; Provided that if both parties to the marriage shall be persons to whom the said section 22 (1) applies certificates in respect of both such persons shall be produced as hereinbefore provided;
- (*b*) that the certificate referred to in paragraph (*a*) of this Article shall contain the full names, addresses, rank, (where appropriate), and marital status of the parties to the marriage and the capacity in which the person signing or purporting to be signing the same does so;
- (*c*) that the marriage shall be solemnised in the presence of not less than two witnesses in addition to the parties and the person solemnising the marriage.

NOTES
Said section 22 (1)   *Ie*, s 22 (1) of the Foreign Marriage Act 1892, as re-enacted, Halsbury's Statutes, 4th edn Vol 27, title Matrimonial Law (Pt 1) (3rd edn Vol 17, p 26).
Commander in the territory   For meaning, see art 4.

4.   For the purpose of this Order the expression "the Commander in the Territory" means:—
- (*a*) where a party to the marriage is a member of the naval forces, or a person employed in any of the capacities specified in Article 2 of this Order, the officer commanding the naval forces of Her Majesty in the territory;

(*b*) where a party to the marriage is a member of the military forces, the officer commanding the military forces of Her Majesty in the territory;

(*c*) where a party to the marriage is a member of the air forces, the officer commanding the air forces of Her Majesty in the territory.

5. Where a marriage has been solemnised under section 22 of the Foreign Marriage Act 1892, whether before or after the date of this Order, the same shall be registered (if not registered at the date of this Order) in the manner provided for in the Service Departments Register Order 1959.

NOTES
Date of this Order 3 July 1964.
Service Departments Register Order 1959 SI 1959/406, in the title Registration concerning the Individual.
Section 22 of the Foreign Marriage Act 1892 Halsbury's Statutes, 4th edn Vol 27, title Matrimonial Law (Pt 1) (3rd edn Vol 17, p 26).

6. The provisions set forth in Schedule 1 to this Order, being laws in force in New Zealand and Australia respectively and which make provisions appearing to be similar to the provisions of section 22 of the Foreign Marriage Act 1892 as originally enacted or as re-enacted by section 2 of the Foreign Marriage Act 1947, shall have effect as part of the law of the United Kingdom in relation respectively to forces raised in these Dominions.

NOTES
Section 22 of the Foreign Marriage Act 1892 For the section as originally enacted, see the notes to s 1 of the Foreign Marriage Act 1947, Halsbury's Statutes, 4th edn Vol 27, title Matrimonial Law (Pt 1) (3rd edn Vol 17, p 43).

7. The Orders specified in column 1 of Schedule 2 to this Order are hereby revoked to the extent respectively specified in column 3 of that Schedule.

8. (1) The Interpretation Act 1889 shall apply for the interpretation of this Order as it applies for the interpretation of an Act of Parliament and as if this Order were an Act of Parliament.

(2) Section 38 of the Interpretation Act 1889 shall apply in relation to the Orders or provisions of Orders hereby revoked as if this Order was an Act of Parliament and those Orders and provisions of Orders were enactments repealed by an Act of Parliament.

NOTES
Interpretation Act 1889 Repealed and replaced by the Interpretation Act 1978, printed in the title Statutory Instruments, Vol 1, of this work.

9. (1) This Order may be cited as the Foreign Marriage (Armed Forces) Order 1964.

(2) This Order shall come into force on 1st October 1964.

[SCHEDULE 1   Article 6

NEW ZEALAND Section 44 of the Marriage Act 1955 reads as follows—
"A service marriage solemnised out of New Zealand by any member of the forces who is a chaplain or who is duly authorised in that behalf shall be deemed to have been and to be as valid as if it had been solemnised in New Zealand in accordance with the provisions of this Act."
AUSTRALIA Sections 71 and 73 of the Marriage Act 1961 read as follows—
"71. (1) Subject to this Part, a marriage between parties of whom one at least is a member of the Defence Force may be solemnised in an overseas country by or in the presence of a chaplain.
(2) The Governor General may, by Proclamation, declare that a part of the Queen's Dominions that has been occupied by a state at war with the Commonwealth and in which facilities for marriage in accordance with the local law have not, in the opinion of the Governor General, been adequately restored shall be deemed to be an overseas country for the purposes of this section."
"73. A marriage solemnised under this Part, being a marriage which, if it had been solemnised in Australia in accordance with Division 2 of Part IV of this Act, would have been a valid marriage, is valid throughout the Commonwealth and all the Territories of the Commonwealth."]

NOTES
The text of this Schedule is that substituted for the original text by SI 1965/137.

SCHEDULE 2

NOTES
This Schedule lists the orders and provisions revoked by art 7, *viz,* the Foreign Marriages (Egypt, Iran and Iraq) Order in Council 1944, SR & O 1944/1130; arts 2, 3 and 4 of, and Schedules 1, 2 and 3 to, the Foreign Marriage Order in Council 1947, SR & O 1947/2875; the Foreign Marriage Order 1957, SI 1957/860; the Foreign Marriage (Amendment) Order 1959, SI 1959/538; and the Foreign Marriages (Egypt, Iran and Iraq) Amendment Order 1959, SI 1959/297. (The remaining provisions of SR & O 1947/2875 were revoked by SI 1964/926 (now revoked).)

THE FOREIGN MARRIAGE ORDER 1970
SI 1970/1539

NOTES
Authority This Order in Council was made on 19 October 1970 under ss 18 and 21 of the Foreign Marriage Act 1892 (as amended by ss 4 (2) and 6 of the Foreign Marriage Act 1947), Halsbury's Statutes, 4th edn Vol 27, title Matrimonial Law (Pt 1) (3rd edn Vol 17, pp 24, 25), and all other enabling powers.
Commencement 1 January 1971; see art 1.
Interpretation See art 2.
General This order contains regulations as to marriages, between parties of whom one at least is a British subject, solemnised abroad by marriage officers under the Foreign Marriage Act 1892; as to marriage officers for these purposes, see s 11 of the Act, Halsbury's Statutes, 4th edn Vol 27, title Matrimonial Law (Pt 1) (3rd edn Vol 17, p 21). As to marriages celebrated abroad by service chaplains under s 22 of the Act, see SI 1964/1000, p 204, *ante.*
As to fees payable to marriage officers for services under the Act and this order, see the Consular Fees Order 1983, SI 1983/1518, and the Consular Fees Regulations 1981, SI 1981/476 (in the title Constitutional Law (Part 8)).

1. This Order may be cited as the Foreign Marriage Order 1970. It shall come into operation on 1st January 1971.

2. (1) Unless otherwise provided in this Order, expressions used in this Order shall have the same meaning as in the Foreign Marriage Act 1892.

(2) The Interpretation Act 1889 shall apply for the interpretation of this Order as it applies for the interpretation of an Act of Parliament.

NOTES
Foreign Marriage Act 1892 Halsbury's Statutes, 4th edn Vol 27, title Matrimonial Law (Pt 1) (3rd edn Vol 17, p 16 *et seq*). For definitions of expressions used in the Act, see in particular s 24.
Interpretation Act 1889 Repealed and replaced by the Interpretation Act 1978, printed in the title Statutory Instruments, Vol 1 of this work.

3. (1) Before a marriage is solemnised in a foreign country under the Foreign Marriage Acts 1892 to 1947, the marriage officer must be satisfied:
   (*a*) that at least one of the parties is a British subject; and
   (*b*) that the authorities of that country will not object to the solemnisation of the marriage; and
   (*c*) that insufficient facilities exist for the marriage of the parties under the law of that country; and
   (*d*) that the parties will be regarded as validly married by the law of the country to which each party belongs.
(2) If a marriage officer, by reason of anything in this Article, refuses to solemnise or allow to be solemnised in his presence the marriage of any person requiring such marriage to be solemnised, that person shall have the same right to appeal to the Secretary of State as is given by section 5 of the Foreign Marriage Act 1892.

NOTES
British subject For provisions now governing British nationality, see, in particular the British Nationality Act 1981, Part I, Halsbury's Statutes, 4th edn Vol 31, title Nationality and Immigration (3rd edn Vol 51, p 9 *et seq*).
Foreign Marriage Acts 1892 to 1947 For the Acts within this collective title, see s 7 of the Foreign Marriage Act 1947 and the note thereto, Halsbury's Statutes, 4th edn Vol 27, title Matrimonial Law (Pt 1) (3rd edn Vol 17, p 44).
Section 5 of the Foreign Marriage Act 1892 Halsbury's Statutes, 4th edn Vol 27, title Matrimonial Law (Pt 1) (3rd edn Vol 17, p 18).

4.   (1) In special cases, where the Secretary of State is satisfied that for some good cause the requirements of the Foreign Marriage Act 1892 as to residence and notice for a marriage intended to be solemnised under the Act cannot be complied with, and he is satisfied that the intended marriage is not clandestine and that adequate public notice of the intended marriage has been given in the place or places where each of the parties resided not less than fifteen days next preceding the giving of such notice, he may authorise the marriage officer to dispense with those requirements.

(2) In cases falling under paragraph (1) of this Article, the oath under section 7 of the Foreign Marriage Act 1892 shall omit the matter specified in subsection (*b*) of that section.

NOTES
Foreign Marriage Act 1892   Halsbury's Statutes, 4th edn Vol 27, title Matrimonial Law (Pt 1) (3rd edn Vol 17, p 16 *et seq*).

5.   For the purpose of marriages to be solemnised by or before a consular officer who is a marriage officer, every place within the curtilage or precincts of the building which is for the time being used for the purpose of his office shall be part of the official house of such marriage officer, and every place to which the public have ordinary access in such official house shall be deemed to be part of the office of such marriage officer.

6.   When a certified copy of an entry in a marriage register kept under section 9 of the Foreign Marriage Act 1892, relating to a party shown to be from Scotland or Northern Ireland is received by the Registrar General, he shall send a copy of that entry to the Registrar General for Scotland or Northern Ireland, as the case may require.

NOTES
Section 9 of the Foreign Marriage Act 1892   Halsbury's Statutes, 4th edn Vol 27, title Matrimonial Law (Pt 1) (3rd edn Vol 17, p 20).

7.   (1) Where a marriage between parties, of whom one at least is a British subject, has been duly solemnised or has taken place in a foreign country in accordance with the local law of the country, either party to the marriage, being a British subject, may produce to the consul of Her Majesty's Government in the United Kingdom for the district in which the marriage has been solemnised or has taken place (or in the absence of such officer to the appropriate consul of any other Government who, by arrangement with Her Majesty's Government in the United Kingdom, have undertaken consular representation in that district on behalf of Her Majesty's Government in the United Kingdom) a certified copy of the entry in the marriage register duly authenticated by the appropriate authority in that country or a marriage certificate issued by the appropriate authority of the country, accompanied by a translation into English, and may request him to accept the certificate as a certificate of marriage issued in accordance with the local law and to certify the translation; and the consul, on payment of the appropriate fee, shall, if he is satisfied that the certificate has been duly issued by the appropriate authority and that the translation is a true one, transmit the said certificate and translation, together with his own certificate regarding the accuracy of the translation, to the Registrar General or, in the case of any certificate relating to a party shown to be from Scotland or Northern Ireland, to the Registrar General for Scotland or Northern Ireland as the case may require.

(2) Any person shall be entitled to have from the appropriate Registrar General a certified copy of any document received by that Registrar General as aforesaid, on payment of fees in respect of the provisions of the copy and any necessary search for the document. The fees shall be the fees which are for time being charged by the appropriate Registrar General for the provision of a certified copy of, and any necessary search for, an entry in the records

in his custody of marriages performed in England and Wales, Scotland or Northern Ireland, as the case may be.

(3) Any copy of any foreign marriage certificate issued by the appropriate Registrar General under the provisions of paragraph (2) of this Article shall, without further proof, be received in evidence to the like extent as if it were a certificate duly issued by the authorities of the foreign country in which the marriage was celebrated.

NOTES
British subject See the note to art 3.

8. The forms in the Schedule to this Order shall be used in all cases to which they are applicable.

9. (1) The Foreign Marriage Order 1964 and the Foreign Marriage (Amendment) Order are hereby revoked.

(2) Section 38 of the Interpretation Act 1889 shall apply in relation to the said Orders as if the present Order were an Act of Parliament and as if the said Orders were enactments repealed by an Act of Parliament.

NOTES
Foreign Marriage Order 1964 SI 1964/926.
Foreign Marriage (Amendment) Order 1967 SI 1967/1143.
Section 38 of the Interpretation Act 1889 This is now to be construed as a reference to ss 16 (1) and 17 (2) (*a*) of the Interpretation Act 1978, printed in the title Statutory Instruments, Vol 1, of this work.

SCHEDULE   Art 8

FORMS
NO 1 — NOTICE OF MARRIAGE
(*Section 2 of the Foreign Marriage Act* 1892)

To [Her Majesty's Consul-General *or* Consul *or* Vice-Consul] at
 I hereby give you notice that a marriage is intended to be had within three calendar months from the date thereof between me and the other party herein named and described (that is to say):

Name and Surname	Condition	Profession	Age	Residence	Length of Residence
A.B.					
C.D.					

                    Witness my hand, this   day of
                          (Signed) A.B., *or*
                               C.D.

No 2 — FORM OF OATH
(*Section 7 of the Foreign Marriage Act* 1892)
 I, A.B. of ...., make oath and say as follows:

1. A marriage is proposed to be solemnised between me and C.D.

2. I believe that there is not any impediment in kindred or alliance, or other lawful hindrance to the above marriage.

3. Both I and C.D. have for three weeks immediately preceding this date had our usual residence [to be omitted in within the district of [*here insert the official title of the marriage officer, and the place where he* cases falling under *is appointed to reside*], that is to say, I at.., and C.D. Article 4 of this at ....   Order]

4. [I am not under the age of 18 years] [*or as the case may be*, I am under the age of 18 years and the widow/er of E.F. who died on the   day of   ] [*or*, I am under the age of 18 years and the consent of G.H. and I.J., whose consent is required by law to my marriage, is given as shown by the writing under their/his/her hand now shown to me and marked   ] [*or*, I am under the age of 18 years and there is no person whose consent to my marriage is required [*or*, I am under the age of 18 years and the necessity of obtaining the consent of the persons whose consent to my marriage is required by law has been dispensed with].

5. [C.D. is not under the age of 18 years] [*or, as the case may be,* C.D. is under the age of 18 years and the widow/er of K.L. who died on the   day of   ] [*or,* C.D. is under the age of 18 years and the consent of M.N. and O.P., whose consent is required by law to his/her marriage, is given as shown by the writing under their/his/her hand now shown to me and marked [   ] [*or,* C.D. is under the age of 18 years and there is no person whose consent to his/her marriage is required] [*or* C.D. is under the age of 18 years and the necessity of obtaining the consent of the persons whose consent to his/her marriage is required by law has been dispensed with].

6. I make the foregoing statements solemnly and deliberately, conscientiously believing the same to be true, well knowing that if any person knowingly and wilfully makes a false oath or signs a false notice under the Foreign Marriage Act 1892, for the purpose of procuring a marriage, he may be guilty of an offence under section 3 of the Perjury Act 1911; and well knowing also that any person who, being married or single, shall marry any other person during the life of the husband or wife or either party as the case may be, may be guilty of an offence under section 57 of the Offences against the Person Act 1861.

Sworn at ....
this........................... day 19
Before me, XY H.M. Consul (*or as the case may be*)   A.B.
at ....
X.Y. (Official seal)

NO 3 — CERTIFICATE OF COPY OF MARRIAGE REGISTER
(*s 10 (1) of the Foreign Marriage Act 1892*)

I, ..., Her Majesty's Consul [*or as the case may be*], residing at ...., hereby certify that this is a true copy of the entries of marriages registered in this office, from the entry of the marriage of A.B. and C.D. number *one*, to the entry of the marriage of E.F. and G.H., number *two*.

Witness my hand seal this   day of   19   .
(Signature and official seal of marriage officer).

THE MARRIAGE (REGISTRAR GENERAL'S LICENCE) REGULATIONS 1970
SI 1970/1780

NOTES
Authority   These regulations were made on 30 November 1970 by the Registrar General, with the approval of the Secretary of State for Social Services, under ss 55 and 74 of the Marriage Act 1949, Halsbury's Statutes, 4th edn Vol 27, title Matrimonial Law (Pt 1) (3rd edn Vol 27, pp 1008, 1018), s 18 of the Marriage (Registrar General's Licence) Act 1970, *ibid*, 4th edn Vol 27, title Matrimonial Law (Pt 1) (3rd edn Vol 40, p 739), and all other enabling powers.
Commencement   1 January 1971.
General   These regulations prescribe the form of notice to be given for a marriage by Registrar General's licence pursuant to the Marriage (Registrar General's Licence) Act 1970 and the form of licence. They also amend regs 67 (2) and 69 of the Registration of Births, Deaths and Marriages Regulations 1968, SI 1968/2049 (in the title Registration concerning the Individual), so as to provide for the manner in which such a marriage is to be registered.
    As to the Marriage (Registrar General's Licence) Act 1970, Halsbury's Statutes, 4th edn Vol 27, title Matrimonial Law (Pt 1) (3rd edn Vol 40, p 784 *et seq*), and marriages allowed in accordance with that Act, see the Introductory Note under the head "Marriage on the authority of Registrar General elsewhere than in registered buildings", p 200, *ante*.

PART 2
Matrimonial Causes

CHRONOLOGICAL LIST OF INSTRUMENTS

SR & O	Description	Remarks	Page
1945/1276	Matrimonial Causes (War Marriages) (Aden, Cyprus and Tanganyika Territory) Order 1945		
1946/683	Matrimonial Causes (War Marriages) (Malta) Order 1946		
1946/896	Matrimonial Causes (War Marriages) (Fiji, Jamaica and Kenya) Order 1946		
1946/2019	Matrimonial Causes (War Marriages) (Australia and South Africa) Order 1946		
SI 1948/111	Matrimonial Causes (War Marriages) (New Zealand) Order 1948	See Introductory Note under the head "War marriages", p 214 *post*	—
1948/864	Matrimonial Causes (War Marriages) (British Guiana) Order 1948		
1948/1331	Matrimonial Causes (War Marriages) (Seychelles) Order 1948		
1948/2073	Matrimonial Causes (War Marriages) (Mauritius) Order 1948		
1949/1050	Matrimonial Causes (War Marriages) (Leeward Islands) Order 1949		
1950/672	Matrimonial Causes (War Marriages) (Appointed Day) Order 1950	Appointed 1 June 1950 for the purposes of the Matrimonial Causes (War Marriages) Act 1944.	—
1958/2080	Matrimonial Causes (Property and Maintenance) Act (Commencement) Order 1958	Made under s 9 (2) of Matrimonial Causes (Property and Maintenance) Act 1958; brought the Act into operation on 1 January 1959	—
1965/1974	Matrimonial Causes Act 1965 (Commencement) Order 1965	Made under s 46 (3) of the Act of 1965; brought the Act into force on 1 January 1966 (this Act is now largely repealed by the Matrimonial Causes Act 1973)	—
1968/228	Matrimonial Causes Act 1967 (Commencement) Order 1968	Made under s 11 (2) of the Act of 1967; brought the Act into force on 11 April 1968 (this Act is prospectively repealed by the Matrimonial and Family Proceedings Act 1984, s 46 (3), Sch 3)	—
Date made 20 July 1972	Matrimonial Causes (Decree Absolute) General Order 1972	—	216
SI 1973/1972	Matrimonial Causes Act 1973 (Commencement) Order 1973	Made under s 55 (2) of the Act of 1973; brought the Act into operation on 1 January 1974	—
Date made 15 March 1973	Matrimonial Causes (Decree Absolute) General Order 1973	Amends Order dated 20 July 1972 (*qv*)	—
SI 1977/344	Matrimonial Causes Rules 1977	—	216
1977/559	Domestic Violence and Matrimonial Proceedings Act 1976 (Commencement) Order 1977	Made under s 5 (2) of the Act of 1976; brought the Act into force on 1 June 1977	—
1978/527	Matrimonial Causes (Amendment) Rules 1978	Amend 1977/344 (*qv*)	—
1979/399	Matrimonial Causes (Costs) Rules 1979	—	276

SI	Description	Remarks	Page
1979/400	Matrimonial Causes (Amendment) Rules 1979	Amend 1977/344 *(qv)*	—
1980/819	Matrimonial Causes Fees Order 1980	—	286
1980/977	Matrimonial Causes (Amendment) Rules 1980	Amend 1977/344 *(qv)*	—
1980/1484	Matrimonial Causes (Amendment No 2) Rules 1980	Amend 1977/344 *(qv)*	—
1980/1582	Magistrates' Courts (Matrimonial Proceedings) Rules 1980	—	290
1981/5	Matrimonial Causes (Amendment) Rules 1981	Amend 1977/344 *(qv)*	—
1981/1099	Matrimonial Causes (Amendment No 2) Rules 1981	Amend 1977/344 *(qv)*	—
1981/1275	Matrimonial Homes and Property Act 1981 (Commencement No 1) Order 1981	Brought the Matrimonial Homes and Property Act 1981, ss 7, 8, 9, 10 (1), (3), into force on 1 October 1981; made under s 9 of the Act	—
1981/1515	Matrimonial Causes Fees (Amendment) Order 1981	Amends 1980/819 *(qv)*	—
1982/1708	Matrimonial Causes Fees (Amendment) Order 1982	Amends 1980/819 *(qv)*	—
1982/1853	Matrimonial Causes (Amendment) Rules 1982	Amend 1977/344 *(qv)*	—
1983/50	Matrimonial Homes and Property Act 1981 (Commencement No 2) Order 1983	Brought the provisions of the Matrimonial Homes and Property Act 1981 not brought into force by 1981/1275 into force on 14 February 1983; made under s 9 of the Act	—
1983/713	Civil Courts Order 1983	See title Courts (Part 5A (i))	—
1983/1686	Matrimonial Causes Fees (Amendment) Order 1983	Amends 1980/819 *(qv)*	—
1984/1511	Matrimonial Causes (Amendment) Rules 1984	Amend 1977/344 *(qv)*	—
1984/1589	Matrimonial and Family Proceedings Act 1984 (Commencement No 1) Order 1984	Brought the Matrimonial and Family Proceedings Act 1984, s 44, Sch 1, paras 2, 4, 9-13, 22, 23 *(c)* (in part), 27, Sch 3 (in part) into force on 12 October 1984; made under s 47 (2) of the Act	—
1985/144	Matrimonial Causes (Amendment) Rules 1985	Amend 1977/344 *(qv)*	—
1985/1315	Matrimonial Causes (Amendment No 2) Rules 1985	Amend 1977/344 *(qv)*	—
1985/1316	Matrimonial and Family Proceedings Act 1984 (Commencement No 2) Order 1985	Brought the Matrimonial and Family Proceedings Act 1984, Pt III, Sch 1, paras 1 *(a)*, 5, 8, 15 into force on 16 September 1985; made under s 47 (2) of the Act	—

INSTRUMENTS NO LONGER IN OPERATION

The following instruments, which were formerly included in this Part of the title, are no longer in operation:

SI		SI	SI		SI
1960/2223	lapsed[1]		1980/1217	revoked by	1983/713[3]
1967/1790	,,[2]		1982/1769	,, ,,	1983/713[3]
1978/1759	revoked by	1983/713[3]	1983/659	,, ,,	1983/713[3]
1980/790	,, ,,	1983/713[3]			

[1]Lapsed on repeal of the Matrimonial Proceedings (Magistrates' Courts) Act 1960 by the Domestic Proceedings and Magistrates' Courts Act 1978, s 89 (2) *(b)*, Sch 3.
[2]Lapsed on repeal of the Matrimonial Homes Act 1967 by the Matrimonial Homes Act 1983, s 12, Sch 3 and the County Courts Act 1984, s 148 (3), Sch 4.
[3]In the title Courts (Pt 5A (i))

INTRODUCTORY NOTE

Jurisdiction The High Court has jurisdiction in matrimonial causes and matters by virtue of the Supreme Court Act 1981, s 26, Halsbury's Statutes, 4th edn Vol 11, title Courts, this jurisdiction being assigned to the Family Division (formerly the Probate, Divorce and Admiralty Division) (see the Supreme Court Act 1981, Sch 1, para 3, *ibid*, 4th edn Vol 11, title Courts). In regard to declarations of legitimacy and validity of marriage, the jurisdiction of the High Court rests on s 45 of the Matrimonial Causes Act 1973, Halsbury's Statutes, 4th edn Vol 27, title Matrimonial Law (Pt 3) (3rd edn Vol 43, p 594) together with s 26 of the 1981 Act, and is also assigned to the Family Division (see Sch 1, para 3 of the Act of 1981). The Matrimonial Causes Act 1967, s 10, Halsbury's Statutes, 4th edn Vol 27, title Matrimonial Law (Pt 3) (3rd edn Vol 17, p 230), as amended by the Supreme Court Act 1981, Sch 5, defines "matrimonial cause" as "an action for divorce, nullity of marriage, judicial separation, or jactitation of marriage or an application under section 3 of the Matrimonial Causes Act 1973". The said s 10 is, however, prospectively repealed by the Matrimonial and Family Proceedings Act 1984, s 43 (6), Sch 3, *ibid*, 4th edn Vol 27, title Matrimonial Law (Pt 3) (3rd edn Vol 54 (1), pp 805, 812) as from a day to be appointed. As from a day to be appointed, "matrimonial cause" is defined in the 1984 Act, s 32 as an action for divorce, nullity of marriage, judicial separation or jactitation of marriage only.

By virtue of s 1 (1) of the said Act of 1967, Halsbury's Statutes, 4th edn Vol 27, title Matrimonial Law (Pt 3) (3rd edn Vol 17, p 225) (prospectively repealed by the Matrimonial and Family Proceedings Act 1984, s 43 (6), Sch 3, as from a day to be appointed) (the 1967 Act having been brought into force on 11 April 1968 by SI 1968/228, listed at p 211, *ante*), any county court which the Lord Chancellor by order designates as a divorce county court has jurisdiction to hear and determine any undefended matrimonial cause, although it may try such a cause only if it is also designated as a court of trial; and, by sub-s (3) of the same section, every matrimonial cause must be commenced in a divorce county court. For a list of divorce county courts and courts of trial, see the Civil Courts Order 1983, SI 1983/713, in the title Courts (Pt 5A (i)) which replaced the Divorce County Courts Order 1978, SI 1978/1759. The powers of the divorce county courts as such also extend to the exercise of ancillary powers relating to financial provision and in relation to children; see s 2 of the Act of 1967, Halsbury's Statutes, 4th edn Vol 27, title Matrimonial Law (Pt 3) (3rd edn Vol 17, p 226) (prospectively repealed by the Matrimonial and Family Proceedings Act 1984, s 43 (6), Sch 3, as from a day to be appointed). As from a day to be appointed, the said ss 1 and 2 are replaced by the 1984 Act, ss 33 and 34. In addition, county courts have jurisdiction in the following proceedings subject, in certain cases, to the power of removal into the High Court:—declarations as to legitimation under s 45 of the Matrimonial Causes Act 1973; proceedings under the Guardianship of Minors Act 1971 and the Guardianship Act 1973; disputes as to the property of husband and wife under s 17 of the Married Women's Property Act 1882, Halsbury's Statutes, 4th edn Vol 27, title Matrimonial Law (Pt 2) (3rd edn Vol 17, p 120); and proceedings as to rights of occupation of a matrimonial home or, in certain circumstances, for the transfer from one spouse to another of the tenancy of the matrimonial home (see the Matrimonial Homes Act 1983, ss 1 (9), 7, Sch 1, Halsbury's Statutes, 4th edn Vol 27, title Matrimonial Law (Pt 2) (3rd edn Vol 53, pp 659, 669, 673).

The jurisdiction of magistrates' courts in matrimonial proceedings rests primarily on the Domestic Proceedings and Magistrates' Courts Act 1978, Part I, Halsbury's Statutes, 4th edn Vol 27, title Matrimonial Law (Pt 3) (3rd edn Vol 48, p 734 *et seq*) which was brought into force on 1 November 1979 and 1 February 1981 by SI 1979/731 and 1980/1478, in the title Magistrates; as to procedure, see the Magistrates' Courts (Matrimonial Proceedings) Rules 1980, SI 1980/1582, p 290, *post* (which instrument now has effect under the Magistates' Courts Act 1980, s 144, Halsbury's Statutes, 4th edn Vol 27, title Magistrates (3rd edn Vol 50 (2), p 1565)). Magistrates' courts also have powers (*eg*, as to custody and maintenance) under the Guardianship of Minors Act 1971, Halsbury's Statutes, 4th edn Vol 6, title Children; see the Magistrates' Courts (Guardianship of Minors) Rules 1974, SI 1974/706, in the title Infants (Part 4) in this work.

Procedure   Section 50 of the Matrimonial Causes Act 1973, Halsbury's Statutes, 4th edn Vol 27, title Matrimonial Law (Pt 3) (3rd edn Vol 43, p 600) (prospectively repealed by the Matrimonial and Family Proceedings Act 1984, s 46 (3), Sch 3, *ibid*, 4th edn Vol 27, title Matrimonial Law (Pt 3) (3rd edn Vol 54 (1), pp 805, 812) and replaced by s 40 thereof, as from a day to be appointed), empowers the authority specified in sub-s (1) thereof to make rules of court for the purposes of that Act and the other enactments specified in the said subs-s (1). The powers extend to both High Court and county court proceedings except where the jurisdiction of county courts is general and not confined to divorce county courts, in which case rules are made for High Court proceedings only. Rules of court made under these powers may apply, with or without modification, any rules of court made under the Supreme Court Act 1981, ss 84, 85, Halsbury's Statutes, 4th edn Vol 11, title Courts, the County Courts Act 1984, s 75, *ibid*, 4th edn Vol 11, title County Courts, or any other enactment; and they may provide for the enforcement in the High Court of orders made in a divorce county court. The rules currently in force under s 50 of the Act of 1973 are the Matrimonial Causes Rules 1977, SI 1977/344, as amended, p 216, *post*, and the Matrimonial Causes (Costs) Rules 1979, SI 1979/399, p 276 *post*. By r 3 of the Matrimonial Causes Rules 1977, subject to the provisions of those rules and of any enactment, the County Court Rules 1981 (SI 1981/1687) and the Rules of the Supreme Court 1965 (SI 1965/1776) (for which see, respectively, the County Court Practice and the Supreme Court Practice) are to apply (with the necessary modifications) to the commencement of matrimonial proceedings in, and to the practice and procedure in such proceedings pending in, a divorce county court and the High Court respectively. The practice is further regulated by directions issued by the President of the Family Division or the Senior Registrar with the concurrence of the Lord Chancellor (see r 131 of the Rules of 1977, p 273, *post*).

Appeals to the Court of Appeal are governed by the practice of that Court, and by RSC Ord 59.

By virtue of the Matrimonial Causes (Decree Absolute) General Order 1972, p 216, *post*, the normal period after which a decree nisi of divorce or nullity of marriage can be made absolute is now six weeks.

Fees   The fees to be taken in matrimonial proceedings in the High Court and divorce county courts are prescribed by the Matrimonial Causes Fees Order 1980, SI 1980/819, made under the Matrimonial Causes Act 1973, s 51, Halsbury's Statutes, 4th edn Vol 27, title Matrimonial Law (Pt 3) (3rd edn Vol 43, p 602), which is prospectively repealed by the Matrimonial and Family Proceedings Act 1984, s 46 (3), Sch 3, *ibid*, 4th edn Vol 27, title Matrimonial Law (Pt 3) (3rd edn Vol 54 (1), pp 805, 812) and replaced by s 41 thereof as from a day to be appointed; and also under the Public Offices Fees Act 1879, ss 2, 3, Halsbury's Statutes, 4th edn Vol 30, title Money (Pt 1) (3rd edn Vol 22, p 855), p 286 *post*.

War marriages   Section 1 of the Matrimonial Causes (War Marriages) Act 1944, gave the High Court temporary jurisdiction to entertain in certain circumstances petitions for divorce or nullity notwithstanding that the parties were domiciled elsewhere than in the United Kingdom. This jurisdiction applied in relation to certain marriages solemnised on or after 3 September 1939 and before 1 June 1950 (this date having been fixed by SI 1950/672, listed at p 211, *ante*), and divorce and nullity proceedings were to be commenced not later than five years after the latter date; thus, proceedings may no longer be instituted under the Act, and the said s 1 has been repealed by the Statute Law (Repeals) Act 1975.

By s 4 (1) (*c*) of the Act of 1944, Halsbury's Statutes, 4th edn Vol 27, title Matrimonial Law (Pt 3) (3rd edn Vol 17, p 153) decrees or orders made by a court having jurisdiction in any of Her Majesty's dominions, or protected states, outside the United Kingdom will be recognised by all British courts (other than Dominion courts) if made under a law which has been declared by Order in Council to correspond substantially to the provisions of the Act. Laws, or ordinances, made by the legislatures of the territories set out in the following table have been so declared and are accordingly recognised by British courts. (Constitutional and jurisdictional changes affecting the territories concerned are noted in the title Dominions and Dependencies (Part 1) under the heading "Jurisdictional Changes".)

TABLE OF TERRITORIES

Territory	Declaratory Order	Commonwealth Legislation
Aden	1945/1276	Divorce (War Marriage) Ordinance 1945
Australia	1946/2019	Matrimonial Causes Act 1945: Part II
British Guiana	1948/864	Matrimonial Causes (War Marriages) Ordinance 1947
Cyprus	1945/1276	Matrimonial Causes (War Marriages) Law 1945
Fiji	1946/896	Matrimonial Causes (War Marriages) Ordinance 1945
Jamaica	1946/896	Divorce (War Marriages) Law 1945
Kenya	1946/896	Matrimonial Causes (War Marriages) Ordinance 1945
Leeward Islands	1949/1050	Matrimonial Causes (War Marriages) Act 1948
Mauritius	1948/2073	Divorce (War Marriages) Ordinance 1945
New Zealand	1948/111	Matrimonial Causes (War Marriages) Act 1947: Part I
Seychelles	1948/1331	Divorce (War Marriages) Ordinance 1948
South Africa*	1946/2019	Matrimonial Causes Jurisdiction Act 1945
Tanganyika Territory ..	1945/1276	Matrimonial Causes (War Marriages) Ordinance 1945

By proviso (i) to s 4 (1), the effect of the Act of 1944 may be modified by Order in Council in its application to the courts of any of Her Majesty's dominions (other than a self-governing dominion), and the Matrimonial Causes (War Marriages) (Malta) Order 1946, SR&O 1946/683, provided that the courts of Malta (now an independent country within the Commonwealth) should not be required to recognise the validity of any decree or order made under a law mentioned in s 4 (1) of the Act of 1944, if they would not have recognised the decree or order if the parties had been domiciled, at the time when the decree or order was made, within the juridiction of the court by which it was made.

Colonial divorce jurisdiction   The Indian and Colonial Divorce Jurisdiction Act 1926 conferred jurisdiction in divorce on Indian courts where the parties were British subjects domiciled in England or Scotland, and the like jurisdiction was conferred on the courts of any of Her Majesty's dominions (other than a self-governing dominion) to which the Act had been extended by Order in Council. Owing to constitutional changes, the jurisdiction conferred by the Act on Indian courts ceased to apply except in regard to proceedings commenced before 15 August 1947 (see s 17 (1) of the Indian Independence Act 1947, Halsbury's Statutes, 4th edn Vol 7, title Commonwealth and Other Territories (Pt 1 (b)). As to orders made for the purpose of extending the Act to colonies, and rules regulating the exercise of divorce jurisdiction in such territories, see the Preliminary Note to the title Conflict of Laws, under the head "Divorce Jurisdiction within the Commonwealth". The Colonial and

---

*As to the continued recognition under s 4 of the Matrimonial Causes (War Marriages) Act 1944 of matrimonial decrees and orders made in South Africa before 31 May 1962 (*ie*, when that country became a republic outside the Commonwealth), see the South Africa Act 1962, Sch 3, para 9, Halsbury's Statutes, 4th edn Vol 7, title Commonwealth and Other Territories (Pt 3 (d)).

Other Territories (Divorce Jurisdiction) Act 1950, Halsbury's Statutes, 4th edn Vol 27, title Matrimonial Law (Pt 4) (3rd edn Vol 6, p 378), extended the Act of 1926 to persons domiciled in Northern Ireland. For the extension of jurisdiction of colonial courts under the Matrimonial Causes (War Marriages) Act 1944, see the head "War marriages", p 214, *ante*.

THE MATRIMONIAL CAUSES (DECREE ABSOLUTE) GENERAL ORDER 1972

NOTES
Authority   This order was made on 20 July 1972 by the High Court of Justice (and signed for and on behalf of the Court by the Lord Chancellor and the President of the Family Division) under ss 5(7) and 10 of the Matrimonial Causes Act 1965. The order now has effect as if made under ss 1 (5) and 15 of the Matrimonial Causes Act 1973, Halsbury's Statutes, 4th edn Vol 27, title Matrimonial Law (Pt 3) (3rd edn Vol 43, pp 542, 558).
Commencement   1 September 1972; see art 1.
Amendment   This order is printed as amended by the Matrimonial Causes (Decree Absolute) General Order 1973, dated 15 March 1973.
General   This order (which is not published in the SI series) supersedes the Matrimonial Causes (Decree Absolute) General Order 1946, SR & O 1946/1305, as amended by the Matrimonial Causes (Decree Absolute) General Order 1957 (dated 12 February 1957). Its effect is to reduce from three months to six weeks the normal period after which a decree nisi of divorce or nullity of marriage can be made absolute. See also *Practice Direction*, [1972] 3 All ER 416.
   The procedure for filing a notice of application to make absolute a decree nisi is prescribed by r 65 of the Matrimonial Causes Rules 1977, SI 1977/344, as amended, p 242, *post*.

1.   (1) This Order may be cited as the Matrimonial Causes (Decree Absolute) General Order 1972 and shall come into operation on 1st September 1972.
   (2) In this Order a decree means a decree of divorce or nullity of marriage.

2.   [(1) Subject to paragraph (2)] in relation to any decree nisi granted after the coming into operation of this Order the period of six months specified in section 5 (7) of the Matrimonial Causes Act 1965 shall be reduced to six weeks and accordingly the decree shall not be made absolute until the expiration of six weeks from its grant unless the court by special order fixes a shorter period.
   [(2) Where the period of six weeks mentioned in paragraph (1) would expire on a day on which the office registry of the court in which the cause is proceeding is closed, the period shall be extended until the end of the first day thereafter on which the office or registry is open.]

NOTES
Amendment   The words in square brackets in para (1) and the whole of para (2) were inserted by the order dated 15 March 1973.
Section 5 (7) of the Matrimonial Causes Act 1965   Repealed. Now replaced by s 1 (5) of the Matrimonial Causes Act 1973, Halsbury's Statutes, 4th edn Vol 27, title Matrimonial Law (Pt 1) (3rd edn Vol 43, p 542).

THE MATRIMONIAL CAUSES RULES 1977
SI 1977/344

ARRANGEMENT OF RULES

PRELIMINARY

NOTES
Authority   These rules were made on 28 February 1977 under s 50 of the Matrimonial Causes
Act 1973, Halsbury's Statutes, 4th edn Vol 27, title Matrimonial Law (Pt 3) (3rd edn Vol 43, p
539), by the authority having power to make rules of court for the purposes mentioned in that
section. The said s 50 is prospectively repealed by the Matrimonial and Family Proceedings Act
1984, s 46 (3), Sch 3, *ibid*, 4th edn Vol 27, title Matrimonial Law (Pt 3) (3rd edn Vol 54 (1),
pp 805, 812), as from a day to be appointed and from that date the rules will take effect under
the 1984 Act, ss 33 (2), 40, 42 (2), (5), if still in force at the commencement of those sections.
Commencement   1 April 1977; see r 1.
Amendment   These rules are printed as amended by the Matrimonial Causes (Amendment)
Rules 1978, SI 1978/527, the Matrimonial Causes (Amendment) Rules 1979, SI 1979/400, the
Matrimonial Causes (Amendment) Rules 1980, SI 1980/977, the Matrimonial Causes (Amend-
ment No 2) Rules 1980, SI 1980/1484, the Matrimonial Causes (Amendment) Rules 1981, SI
1981/5, the Matrimonial Causes (Amendment No 2) Rules 1981, SI 1981/1099, the Matrimonial
Causes (Amendment) Rules 1982, SI 1982/1853, the Matrimonial Causes (Amendment) Rules
1984, SI 1984/1511, the Matrimonial Causes (Amendment) Rules 1985, SI 1985/144 and the
Matrimonial Causes (Amendment No 2) Rules 1985, SI 1985/1315.
Interpretation   See r 2 and note thereto.
General   These rules consolidate with minor amendments the Matrimonial Causes Rules 1973
SI 1973/2016, as amended by SI 1974/2168, 1975/1359 and 1976/607 and 2166. See further,
generally, the Introductory Note under the head "Procedure", p 214, *ante*.
Costs   Provision for the costs in matrimonial proceedings is made by the Matrimonial Causes
(Costs) Rules 1979, SI 1979/399, p 276, *post*, which (by r 2 (2) thereof) are to be construed as
one with these rules.
Fees   The fees to be taken in matrimonial proceedings in the High Court and divorce county
courts are prescribed by the Matrimonial Causes Fees Order 1980, SI 1980/819, as amended, p
286, *post*.

PRELIMINARY

1. Citation and commencement   These Rules may be cited as the Matrimonial
Cause Rules 1977 and shall come into operation on 1st April 1977.

2. Interpretation   (1) The Interpretation Act 1889 shall apply to the interpretation of these Rules as it applies to the interpretation of an Act of Parliament.
    (2) In these Rules, unless the context other requires—
    "the Act of 1882" means the Married Women's Property Act 1882;
    "the Act of 1967", means the Matrimonial Causes Act 1967;
    "the Act of 1973" means the Matrimonial Causes Act 1973;
    ["the Act of 1984" means the Matrimonial and Family Proceedings Act
      1984;]
    "ancillary relief" means—
      (*a*) an avoidance of disposition order,
      (*b*) a financial provision order,
      (*c*) an order for maintenance pending suit,
      (*d*) a property adjustment order, or
      (*e*) a variation order;
    "avoidance of disposition order" means an order under section 37 (2) (*b*)
      or (*c*) of the Act of 1973;
    "cause" means a matrimonial cause as defined by section 10 (1) of the Act
      of 1967;

["consent order" means an order under section 33A of the Act of 1973;]

"court" means a judge or the registrar;

"court of trial" means a divorce county court designated by the Lord Chancellor as a court of trial pursuant to section 1 (1) of the Act of 1967 and, in relation to matrimonial proceedings pending in a divorce county court, the divorce registry shall be treated as a court of trial having its place of sitting at the Royal Courts of Justice;

"defended cause" means a cause not being an undefended cause;

"directions for trial" means directions for trial given under rule 33;

"district registry" means any district registry having a divorce county court within its district;

"divorce county court" means a county court so designated by the Lord Chancellor pursuant to section 1 (1) of the Act of 1967;

"divorce registry" means the principal registry of the Family Division;

"divorce town", in relation to any matrimonial proceedings, means a place at which sittings of the High Court are authorised to be held outside the Royal Courts of Justice for the hearing of those proceedings or proceeding of the class to which they belong;

"financial provision order" means any of the orders mentioned in section 21 (1) of the Act of 1973 except an order under section 27 (6) of that Act;

"financial relief" has the same meaning as in section 37 of the Act of 1973;

"matrimonial proceedings" means any proceedings with respect to which rules may be made under section 50 of the Act of 1973;

"notice of intention to defend" has the meaning assigned to it by rule 15;

"person named" includes a person described as "passing under the name of A.B.";

"the President" means the President of the Family Division or, in the case of his incapacity through illness or otherwise or of a vacancy in the office of President, the senior puisne judge of that Division;

"registrar", in relation to proceedings pending in a divorce county court, the divorce registry of a district registry, means the registrar or one of the registrars of that county court or registry, as the case may be;

"registry for the divorce town" shall be construed in accordance with rule 44 (4);

"Royal Courts of Justice", in relation to matrimonial proceedings pending in a divorce county court, means such place, being the Royal Courts of Justice or elsewhere, as may be specified in directions given by the Lord Chancellor pursuant to section 4 (2) (*a*) of the Act of 1967;

["senior registrar" means the senior registrar of the Family Division or, in his absence from the divorce registry, the senior of the registrars in attendance at the registry;]

"special procedure list" has the meaning assigned to it by rule 33 (3);

"undefended cause" means—

. . .

   (i) a cause in which no answer has been filed or any answer filed has been struck out, or

  (ii) a cause which is proceeding only on the respondent's answer and in which no reply or answer to the respondent's answer has been filed or any such reply or answer has been struck out, or

 (iii) a cause to which rule 18 (4) applies and in which no notice has been given under that rule or any notice so given has been withdrawn, [or

 (iv) a cause in which an answer has been filed claiming relief but in which no pleading has been filed opposing the grant of a decree on the petition or answer or any pleading or part of a pleading opposing the grant of such relief has been struck out] [or

  (v) any cause not within (i) to (iv) above in which a decree has been pronounced.]

"variation order" means an order under section 31 of the Act of 1973;

"welfare" has the same meaning as in section 41 of the Act of 1973.

(3) Unless the context otherwise requires, a cause begun by petition shall be treated as pending for the purposes of these Rules notwithstanding that a final decree or order has been made on the petition.

(4) Unless the context otherwise requires, a rule referred to by number means the rule so numbered in these Rules.

(5) In these Rules a form referred to by number means the form so numbered in Appendix 1 to these Rules, or a form substantially to the like effect, with such variations as the circumstances of the particular case may require.

(6) In these Rules any reference to an Order and rule is—

(a) if prefixed by the letters "CCR", a reference to that Order and rule in the County Court Rules 1936, and

(b) if prefixed by the letters "RSC", a reference to that Order and rule in the Rules of the Supreme Court 1965.

(7) Unless the context otherwise requires, any reference in these Rules to any rule or enactment shall be construed as a reference to that rule or enactment as amended, extended or applied by any other rule or enactment.

NOTES
Amendment   In para (2) the definition of "the Act of 1984" was added and the definition of "Senior registrar" was substituted by the Matrimonial Causes (Amendment No 2) Rules 1985, SI 1985/1315. The definition of "consent order" was added by the Matrimonial Causes (Amendment) Rules 1984, SI 1984/1511. The first words printed between square brackets in the definition of "undefended cause" were inserted by the Matrimonial Causes (Amendment) Rules 1978, SI 1978/527, and the second words printed between square brackets in that definition were inserted by the Matrimonial Causes (Amendment No 2) Rules 1981, SI 1981/1099. The words omitted where indicated in the definition of "undefended cause" were revoked by the Matrimonial Causes (Amendment) Rules 1985, SI 1985/144,
Matrimonial cause   As to this term see the Introductory Note at p 213 *ante*.
Divorce county court; court of trial   For the county courts currently designated as divorce county courts and courts of trial, see the Civil Courts Order 1983, SI 1983/713, in the title Courts (Part 5A (i)).
County Court Rules 1936   These rules were revoked and replaced by the County Court Rules 1981, SI 1981/1687, printed in the County Court Practice; see also the title Courts (Part 5A (ii)) in the present work.
Rules of the Supreme Court 1965   SI 1965/1776, printed in the Supreme Court Practice; see also the title Courts (Part 3B) in the present work.
Interpretation Act 1889   Repealed and replaced by the Interpretation Act 1978, printed in the title Statutory Instruments, Vol 1, of this work.
Married Womens Property Act 1882   Halsbury's Statutes, 4th edn Vol 27, title Matrimonial Law (Pt 2) (3rd edn Vol 17, p 116 *et seq*).
Matrimonial Causes Act 1967, ss 1 (1), 4 (2) (a) and 10 (1)   Halsbury's Statutes, 4th edn Vol 27, title Matrimonial Law (Pt 3) (3rd edn Vol 17, pp 225, 227, 230). This whole Act is prospectively repealed by the Matrimonial and Family Proceedings Act 1984, s 46 (3) and Sch 3, *ibid*, 4th edn Vol 27, title Matrimonial Law (Pt 3) (3rd edn Vol 54 (1), pp 805, 812) as from a day to be appointed, and replaced by provisions of that Act.
Matrimonial Causes Act 1973, ss 3, 21 (1), 27 (6), 31, 33A, 37, 41 and 50   Halsbury's Statutes, 4th edn Vol 27, title Matrimonial Law (Pt 3) (3rd edn: for ss 21 (1), 27 (6), 31, 37, 41 and 50 see Vol 43, pp 562, 571, 576, 584, 588, 60 (s 50 is prospectively repealed by the Matrimonial and Family Proceedings Act 1984, s 46 (3) and Sch 3, Halsbury's Statutes, 4th edn Vol 27, title Matrimonial Law (Pt 3) (3rd edn Vol 54 (1), pp 805, 812) and replaced by s 40 thereof as from a day to be appointed); s 3 was substituted by the Matrimonial and Family Proceedings Act 1984, s 1, Halsbury's Statutes, 4th edn Vol 27, title Matrimonial Law (Pt 3) (3rd edn Vol 54 (1), p 762), and s 33A was inserted by s 7 of that Act, *ibid*, 4th edn Vol 27, title Matrimonial Law (Pt 3) (3rd edn Vol 54 (1), p 771).
Matrimonial and Family Proceedings Act 1984   Halsbury's Statutes, 4th edn Vol 27, title Matrimonial Law (Pt 3) (3rd edn Vol 54 (1), p 756 *et seq*).

3. Application of other rules   (1) Subject to the provisions of these Rules and of any enactment, the County Court Rules 1936 and the Rules of the Supreme Court 1965 shall apply, with the necessary modifications, to the commencement of matrimonial proceedings in, and to the practice and procedure in matrimonial proceedings pending in, a divorce county court and the High Court respectively.

(2) For the purpose of paragraph (1) any provision of these Rules authorising or requiring anything to be done in matrimonial proceedings shall be treated as if it were, in the case of proceedings pending in a divorce county court, a

provision of the County Court Rules 1936 and, in the case of proceedings pending in the High Court, a provision of the Rules of the Supreme Court 1965.

NOTES
County Court Rules 1936   See the note to r 2.
Rules of the Supreme Court 1965   See the note r 2.

4. County court proceedings in divorce registry   (1) Subject to the provisions of these Rules, matrimonial proceedings pending at any time in the divorce registry which, if they had been begun in a divorce county court, would be pending at that time in such a court shall be treated, for the purposes of these Rules and of any provision of the County Court Rules 1936 and the County Courts Act 1959, as pending in a divorce county court and not in the High Court.

In this paragraph "matrimonial proceedings" includes proceedings for the exercise of any power under Part II or III of the Act of 1973 if, but only if, the power is exercisable in connection with any petition, decree or order pending in or made by, or treated as pending in or made by, a divorce county court.

(2) Unless the context otherwise requires, any reference to a divorce county court in any provision of these Rules or of the County Court Rules 1936 as applied by these Rules, which related to the commencement or prosecution of proceedings in a divorce county court, or the transfer of proceedings to or from such a court, includes a reference to the divorce registry.

NOTES
County Court Rules   See the note to r 2.
County Courts Act 1959   Halsbury's Statutes, 4th edn Vol 11, title County Courts. This Act is largely repealed by the County Courts Act 1984, s 148 (3), Sch 4, Halsbury's Statutes, 4th edn Vol 11, title County Courts, and replaced by provisions of that Act.

COMMENCEMENT ETC OF PROCEEDINGS

5, 6.   *(Revoked by the Matrimonial Causes (Amendment) Rules 1985, SI 1985/144).*

7. Discontinuance of cause before service of petition   Before a petition is served on any person, the petitioner may file a notice of discontinuance and the cause shall thereupon stand dismissed.

8. Cause to be begun by petition   (1) Every cause . . . shall be begun by petition.

(2) Where a petition for divorce, nullity or judicial separation discloses that there is a minor child of the family who is under 16 or who is over that age and is receiving instruction at an educational establishment or undergoing training for a trade or profession, the petition shall be accompanied by a statement signed by the petitioner personally containing the information required by Form 4, to which shall be attached a copy of any medical report mentioned therein.

NOTES
Amendment   The words omitted where indicated in para (1) of this rule were revoked by the Matrimonial Causes (Amendment) Rules 1985, SI 1985/144.

9. Contents of petition   Unless otherwise directed, every petition shall contain the information required by Appendix 2 to these Rules.

NOTES
See further as to standard form of petition, accompanying documents and other related matters, *Practice Direction,* [1977] 1 All ER 845.

10. Petitioner relying on section 11 or 12 of the Civil Evidence Act 1968   A petitioner who, in reliance on section 11 or 12 of the Civil Evidence Act 1968, intends to adduce evidence that a person—

(*a*)   was convicted of an offence by or before a court in the United Kingdom or by a court-martial there or elsewhere, or (*b*) was found guilty of adultery in matrimonial proceedings or was adjudged to be the father of a child in affiliation proceedings before a court in the United Kingdom.

must include in his petition a statement of his intention with particulars of—
  (i)   the conviction, finding or adjudication and the date thereof,
  (ii) the court or court-martial which made the conviction, finding or adjudication and, in the case of a finding or adjudication, the proceedings in which it was made, and
  (iii) the issue in the proceedings to which the conviction, finding or adjudication is relevant.

NOTES
Sections 11 and 12 of the Civil Evidence Act 1968   Halsbury's Statutes, 4th edn Vol 17, title Evidence.

11. Signing of petition   Every petition shall be signed by counsel if settled by him or, if not, by the petitioner's solicitor in his own name or the name of his firm, or by the petitioner if he sues in person.

12. Presentation of petition   (1) A petition, other than a petition under rule 109 or 110, may be presented to any divorce county court.

(2) Unless otherwise directed on an application made *ex parte*, a certificate of the marriage to which the cause related shall be filed with the petition.

(3) Where a solicitor is acting for a petitioner for divorce or judicial separation, a certificate in Form 3 shall be filed with the petition, unless otherwise directed on a application made *ex parte*.

(4) Where there is before a divorce county court or the High Court a petition which has not been dismissed or otherwise disposed of by a final order, another petition by the same petitioner in respect of the same marriage shall not be presented without leave granted on an application made in the pending proceedings:

Provided that no such leave shall be required where it is opposed, after the expiration of the period of [one year] from the date of the marriage, to present a petition for divorce alleging such of the facts mentioned in section 1 (2) of the Act of 1973 as were alleged in a petition for judicial separation presented before the expiration of that period.

(5) The petition shall be presented by filing it, together with any statement and report required by rule 8 (2), in the court office, with as many copies of the petition as there are persons to be served and a copy of the statement and report required by rule 8 (2) for service on the respondent.

(6) CCR Order 6, rule 4 (2) (which, as applied by rule 5 of that Order, deals with the filing and service of petitions), shall not apply but on the filing of the petition the registrar shall—
  (*a*) enter the cause in the books of the court, and
  (*b*) annex to every copy of the petition for service a notice in Form 5 with Form 6 attached and shall also annex to the copy petition for service on a respondent the copy of any statement and report filed pursuant to paragraph (5) of this rule.

NOTES
Amendment   The words "one year" printed between square brackets in para (4) of this rule were substituted by the Matrimonial Causes (Amendment) Rules 1985, SI 1985//144.
Another petition   The filing of a second petition without leave while the first petition is still on the file is an irregularity which can be cured by the court granting leave retrospectively; see *Cooper v Cooper*, [1964] 3 All ER 167 (followed in *Ricci v Ricci* (1972), 116 Sol Jo 59).

13. Parties   (1) Subject to paragraph (2), where a petition alleges that the respondent has committed adultery, the person with whom the adultery is alleged to have been committed shall be made a co-respondent in the cause unless—
  (*a*) that person is not named in the petition and, if the adultery is relied

on for the purpose of section 1 (2) (*a*) of the Act of 1973, the petition contains a statement that his or her identity is not known to the petitioner, or

(*b*) the court otherwise directs.

(2) Where a petition alleges that the respondent has been guilty of rape upon a person named, then, notwithstanding anything in paragraph (1), that person shall not be made a co-respondent in the cause unless the court so directs.

(3) Where a petition alleges that the respondent has been guilty of an improper association (other than adultery) with a person named, the court may direct that the person named be made a co-respondent in the cause, and for that purpose the registrar may give notice to the petitioner and to any other party who had given notice of intention to defend of a date and time when the court will consider giving such a direction.

(4) An application for directions under paragraph (1) may be made *ex parte* if no notice of intention to defend has been given.

(5) Paragraphs (1) and (3) of this rule do not apply where the person named has died before the filing of the petition.

SERVICE OF PETITION, ETC

14. Service of petition   (1) Subject to the provisions of this rule and rules 113 and 117, a copy of every petition shall be served personally or by post on every respondent or co-respondent.

(2) Service may be effected—

(*a*) where the party to be served is a person under disability within the meaning of rule 112, through the petitioner, and

(*b*) in any other case, through the court or, if the petitioner so requests, through the petitioner.

(3) Personal service shall in no case be effected by the petitioner himself.

(4) A copy of any petition which is to be served through the court shall be served by post by an officer of the court or, if on a request by the petitioner the registrar so directs, by a bailiff delivering a copy of the petition to the party personally.

(5) For the purposes of the foregoing paragraphs, a copy of a petition shall be deemed to be duly served if—

(*a*) an acknowledgment of service in Form 6 is signed by the party to be served or by a solicitor on his behalf and is returned to the court office, and

(*b*) where the form purports to be signed by the respondent, his signature is proved at the hearing.

(6) Where a copy of a petition has been sent to a party and no acknowledgment of service has been returned to the court office, the registrar, if satisfied by affidavit or otherwise that the party has nevertheless received the document, may direct that the document shall be deemed to have been duly served on him.

(7) Where a copy of a petition has been served on a party personally and no acknowledgment of service has been returned to the court office, service shall be proved by filing an affidavit of service (or, in the case of service by bailiff, an indorsement of service under CCR Order 8, Rule 2 (*c*) (i)) showing, in the case of a respondent, the server's means of knowledge of the identity of the party served.

(8) Where an acknowledgment of service is returned to the court office, the registrar shall send a photographic copy thereof to the petitioner.

(9) An application for leave to substitute some other mode of service for the modes of service prescribed by paragraph (1), or to substitute notice of the proceedings by advertisement or otherwise, shall be made *ex parte* by lodging an affidavit setting out the grounds on which the application is made; and the form of any advertisement shall be settled by the registrar:

Provided that no orders giving leave to substitute notice of the proceedings by advertisement shall be made unless it appears to the registrar that there is a reasonable probability that the advertisement will come to the knowledge of the person concerned.

(10) CCR Order 8, Rule 6 (4), shall apply in relation to service by bailiff under this rule as it applies to service of a summons by bailiff in accordance with Rule 8 of that Order.

(11) Where in the opinion of the registrar it is impracticable to serve a party in accordance with any of the foregoing paragraphs or it is otherwise necessary or expedient to dispense with service of a copy of a petition on the respondent or on any other person, the registrar may make an order dispensing with such service.

An application for an order under this paragraph shall, if no notice of intention to defend has been given, be made in the first instance *ex parte* by lodging an affidavit setting out the grounds of the application, but the registrar may, if he thinks fit, require the attendance of the petitioner on the application.

NOTES

Advertisement   As to the circumstances in which an advertisement will be ordered, see *Practice Direction*, [1975] 3 All ER 432.

Dispense with service   As to the circumstances in which the registrar may make an order dispensing with service of a copy of a petition on the respondent or any other person, see *Weighman v Weighman*, [1947] 2 All ER 852; *Paolantonio v Paolantonio*, [1950] 2 All ER 404; *Spalenkova v Spalenkova*, [1954] P 141, [1953] 2 All ER 880; *N v N*, [1957] 1 All ER 536; *Whitehead v Whitehead (otherwise Vasbor)*, [1963] P 117 at 138, 139, [1962] 3 All ER 800 at 811, 812; *Purse v Purse*, [1981] 2 All ER 465.

15. Notice of intention to defend   (1) In these Rules any reference to a notice of intention to defend is a reference to an acknowledgment of service in Form 6 containing a statement to the effect that the person by whom or on whose behalf it is signed intends to defend the proceedings to which the acknowledgment relates, and any reference to giving notice of intention to defend is a reference to returning such a notice to the court office.

(2) In relation to any person on whom there is served a document requiring or authorising an acknowledgment of service to be returned to the court office, references in these Rules to the time limited for giving notice of intention to defend are references to eight days after service of the document, inclusive of the day of service, or such other time as may be fixed.

. . .

[(3)] Subject to [paragraph (2)], a person may give notice of intention to defend notwithstanding that he has already returned to the court office an acknowledgment of service not constituting such a notice.

NOTES

Amendment   The words omitted where indicated in this rule were revoked and the words "(3)" and "paragraph (2)" printed between square brackets were substituted by the Matrimonial Causes (Amendment No 2) Rules 1985, SI 1985/1315.

16. Consent to the grant of a decree   (1) Where, before the hearing of a petition alleging two years' separation coupled with the respondent's consent to a decree being granted, the respondent wishes to indicate to the court that he consents to the grant of a decree, he must do so by giving the registrar a notice to that effect signed by the respondent personally.

For the purposes of this paragraph an acknowledgment of service containing a statement that the respondent consents to the grant of a decree shall be treated as such a notice if the acknowledgment is signed—

(*a*) in the case of a respondent acting in person, by the respondent, or

(*b*) in the case of a respondent represented by a solicitor, by the respondent as well as by the solicitor.

(2) A respondent to a petition which alleges any such fact as is mentioned in paragraph (1) may give notice to the court either that he does not consent to a decree being granted or that he withdraws any consent which he has already given.

Where any such notice is given and none of the other facts mentioned in section 1 (2) of the Act of 1973 is alleged, the proceedings on the petition shall be stayed and the registrar shall thereupon give notice of the stay to all parties.

PLEADINGS AND AMENDMENT

17. Supplemental petition and amendment of petition   (1) A supplemental petition may be filed only with leave.

(2) A petition may be amended without leave before it is served but only with leave after it has been served.

(3) Subject to paragraph (4), an application for leave under this rule—

(*a*) may, if every opposite party consents in writing to the supplemental petition being filed or the petition being amended, be made *ex parte* by lodging in the court office the supplemental petition or a copy of the petition as proposed to be amended, and

(*b*) shall, in any other case, be made on notice (or in the High Court by summons), to be served, unless otherwise directed, on every opposite party.

(4) The registrar may, if he thinks fit, require an application for leave to be supported by an affidavit.

(5) An order granting leave shall—

(*a*) where any party has given notice of intention to defend, fix the time within which his answer must be filed or amended;

(*b*) where the order is made after directions for trial have been given, provide for a stay of the hearing until after the directions have been renewed.

(6) An amendment authorised to be made under this rule shall be made by filing a copy of the amended petition.

(7) Rules 11 and 13 shall apply to a supplemental or amended petition as they apply to the original petition.

(8) Unless otherwise directed, a copy of a supplemental or amended petition, together with a copy of the order (if any) made under this rule shall be served on every respondent and co-respondent named in the original petition or in the supplemental or amended petition.

(9) The petitioner shall file the documents required by paragraph (8) to be served on any person and thereupon, unless otherwise directed, rules 12 (6) (except sub paragraph (*a*)) and 14 shall apply in relation to that person as they apply in relation to a person required to be served with an original petition.

NOTES

Amendment of petition   There is no special practice to prohibit an amendment to a petition to allege acts which occurred before the petition was filed and of which evidence was previously available; see *Nelson v Nelson and Slinger*, [1958] 2 All ER 744 (CA). Where the desired amendment is fundamental and going to the relief sought, the proper course is to obtain a stay of the petition and leave to file a fresh petition (*Bainbridge v Bainbridge*, [1962] 2 All ER 267).

18. Filing of answer to petition   (1) Subject to paragraph (2) and to rules 16, 20 and 49, a respondent or co-respondent who—

(*a*) wishes to defend the petition or to dispute any of the facts alleged in it,

(*b*) being the respondent wishes to make in the proceedings any charge against the petitioner in respect of which the respondent prays for relief, or

(*c*) being the respondent to a petition to which section 5 (1) of the Act of 1973 applies, wishes to oppose the grant of a decree on the ground mentioned in that subsection,

shall, within 21 days after the expiration of the time limited for giving notice of intention to defend, file an answer to the petition.

(2) An answer may be filed . . . notwithstanding . . . that the person filing the answer has not given notice of intention to defend.

(3) Any reference in these Rules to a person who has given notice of intention to defend shall be construed as including a reference to a person who has filed an answer without giving notice of intention to defend.

(4) Where in a cause in which relief is sought under section 12 (*d*) of the Act of 1973 the respondent files an answer containing no more than a simple denial of the facts stated in the petition, he shall, if he intends to rebut the charges in the petition, give the registrar notice to that effect when filing his answer.

(5) On the filing of an answer the registrar shall order the cause to be transferred to the High Court, unless in a case to which paragraph (4) applies the respondent has not given such a notice as is mentioned in that paragraph.

NOTES
Amendment   The words omitted where indicated in para (2) of this rule were revoked by the Matrimonial Causes (Amendment No 2) Rules 1985, SI 1985/1315.

19. Filing of reply and subsequent pleadings   (1) A petitioner may file a reply to an answer within 14 days after he has received a copy of the answer pursuant to rule 23.

(2) If the petitioner does not file a reply to an answer, he shall, unless the answer prays for a decree, be deemed, on making a request for directions for trial, to have denied every material allegation of fact made in the answer.

(3) No pleading subsequent to a reply shall be filed without leave.

20. Filing of pleadings after directions for trial   No pleading shall be filed without leave after directions for trial have been given.

NOTES
Leave   See *Huxford v Huxford*, [1972] 1 All ER 330 (leave to file answer out of time granted to wife respondent to petition on adultery); and *Collins v Collins*, [1972] 2 All ER 658 (wife respondent to petition on 5 years' separation refused leave to file answer out of time on basis that no stigma attached to decree granted on such ground).

21. Contents of answer and subsequent pleadings   (1) Where an answer, reply or subsequent pleading contains more than a simple denial of the facts stated in the petition, answer or reply, as the case may be, the pleading shall set out with sufficient particularity the facts relied on but not the evidence by which they are to be proved and, if the pleading is filed by the husband or wife, it shall, in relation to those facts, contain the information required in the case of a petition by paragraph 1 (*k*) of Appendix 2.

(2) Unless otherwise directed, an answer by a husband or wife who disputes any statement required by paragraphs 1 (*f*), (*g*) and (*h*) of Appendix 2 to be included in the petition shall contain full particulars of the facts relied on.

(3) Paragraph 5 (*a*) of Appendix 2 shall, where appropriate, apply, with the necessary modifications, to a respondent's answer as it applies to a petition:

Provided that it shall not be necessary to include in the answer any claim for costs against the petitioner.

(4) Where an answer to any petition contains a prayer for relief, it shall contain the information required by paragraph 1 (*j*) of Appendix 2 in the case of the petition in so far as it has not been given by the petitioner.

(5) Rule 10 shall apply, with the necessary modifications, to a pleading other than a petition as it applies to a petition.

(6) Where a party's pleading includes such a statement as is mentioned in rule 10, then if the opposite party—
  (*a*) denies the conviction, finding or adjudication to which the statement relates, or
  (*b*) alleges that the conviction, finding or adjudication was erroneous, or
  (*c*) denies that the conviction, finding or adjudication is relevant to any issue in the proceedings,
he must make the denial or allegation in his pleading.

(7) Rule 11 shall apply, with the necessary modifications, to a pleading other than a petition as it applies to a petition.

NOTES
Denial A bare denial of desertion is not a proper plea and the party must plead the facts on which he relies (*Slater v Slater*, [1952] 1 All ER 1343). In cases of allegation of cruelty under the old law it was generally sufficient to deny the allegation without setting out the respondent's version of events; see *Finch v Finch*, [1960] 2 All ER 52. See also *Haque v Haque*, [1977] 3 All ER 667 (answer containing bare denial of allegations in petition not incorrect; form of answer at option of respondent).

22. Allegation against third person in pleading (1) Rules 13 and 14 shall apply, with the necessary modifications, to a pleading other than a petition as they apply to a petition, so however that for the references in those rules to a co-respondent there shall be substituted references to a party cited.

(2) Rule 18 shall apply, with the necessary modifications, to a party cited as it applies to a co-respondent.

23. Service of pleadings A party who files an answer, reply or subsequent pleading shall at the same time file a copy for service on every opposite party and thereupon the registrar shall annex to every copy for service on a party cited in the pleading a notice in Form 5 with Form 6 attached and shall send a copy to every other opposite party.

24. Supplemental answer and amendment of pleadings Rule 17 shall apply, with the necessary modifications, to the filing of a supplemental answer, and the amendment of a pleading or other document not being a petition, as it applies to the filing of a supplemental petition and the amendment of a petition.

25. Service and amendment of pleadings in Long Vacation RSC Order 3, rule 3, RSC Order 18, rule 5, and RSC Order 20, rule 6 (which restrict the service and amendment of pleadings in the Long Vacation), shall not apply to any matrimonial proceedings pending in the High Court.

26. Particulars (1) A party on whom a pleading has been served may in writing request the party whose pleading it is to give particulars of any allegation or other matter pleaded and, if that party fails to give the particulars within a reasonable time, the party requiring them may apply for an order that the particulars be given.

(2) The request or order in pursuance of which particulars are given shall be incorporated with the particulars, each item of the particulars following immediately after the corresponding item of the request or order.

(3) A party giving particulars, whether in pursuance of an order or otherwise, shall at the same time file a copy of them.

NOTES
As to particulars, see *Hartopp v Hartopp and Cowley (Earl)* (1902), 71 LJP 78 (CA) (adultery); *Hubbock v Hubbock*, [1942] 2 All ER 412 (CA) (condonation); *MacLulich v MacLulich*, [1920] P 439 (CA) (desertion); *Wise* (otherwise *Blakely*) *v Wise*, [1944] P 56; 1 All ER 446 (impotence). See, further, 13 Halsbury's Laws (4th edn), paras 747-752.

27. Re-transfer of cause to divorce county court (1) [Subject to paragraph, (3), where] a cause begun by petition has been transferred to the High Court under rule 18 (5) and subsequently becomes undefended, the court shall order it to be re-transferred to a divorce county court, unless (because of the proximity of the probable date of trial or otherwise) the court thinks it desirable that the cause should be heard and determined in the High Court.

(2) Nothing in paragraph (1) shall require a cause to be transferred at the time when it becomes undefended if in the opinion of the court the question whether it is desirable to retain it in the High Court cannot conveniently be considered until later.

[(3) A cause which has been transferred to the High Court under rule 18 (5) and which has become undefended by reason of the grant of a decree shall, unless the judge otherwise directs, thereafter be re-transferred to the divorce county court to which the petition was presented.]

NOTES
Amendment   The words "Subject to paragraph (3), where" printed between square brackets in para (1) of this rule were substituted, and para (3) was added by the Matrimonial Causes (Amendment No 2) Rules 1981, SI 1981/1099.

PREPARATIONS FOR TRIAL

28. Discovery of documents in defended cause   (1) RSC Order 24 (which deals with the discovery and inspection of documents) shall apply to a defended cause begun by petition as it applies to an action begun by writ, with the following modifications:—

  (*a*) rule 1 (2), the second paragraph of rule 2 (1), rule 2 (2) to (4), rules 4 (2) and 6, and in rule 16 (1) the words from "including" to the end, shall be omitted,

  (*b*) in rule 2 (7) for the words "the summons for directions is taken out" there shall be substituted the words "directions for trial are given".

(2) For the purposes of RSC Order 24, rule 2 (1), as applied by paragraph (1) of this rule, pleadings shall be deemed to be closed at the expiration of 14 days after the service of the reply or, if there is no reply, at the expiration of 14 days after service of the answer, and are deemed to be closed then notwithstanding that any request or order for particulars previously made has not been complied with.

(3) The petitioner and any party who has filed an answer shall be entitled to have a copy of any list of documents served on any other party under RSC Order 24 as applied by paragraph (1) of this rule, and such copy shall, on request, be supplied to him free of charge by the party who served the list.

In this paragraph "list of documents" includes an affidavit verifying the list.

29. Discovery by interrogatories in defended cause   (1) RSC Order 26 (which deals with discovery by interrogatories) shall apply to a defended cause begun by petition as it applies to a cause within the meaning of that Order, but with the omission of—

  (*a*) in rule 1 (2), the words "or the notice under Order 25, rule 7",

  (*b*) rule 2, and

  (*c*) in rule 6 (1), the words from "including" to the end.

(2) A copy of the proposed interrogatories shall be filed when the summons for an order under RSC Order 26, rule 1, is issued.

NOTES
As to interrogatories with respect to adultery, see *Nast v Nast and Walker*, [1972] 1 All ER 1171 (CA). Interrogatories will not be allowed unless necessary for disposing fairly of the case or for saving costs (*Ramsey v Ramsey*, [1957] 1 WLR 542; *Hulbert v Hulbert*, [1957] 2 All ER 226 (CA)).

30. Medical examination in proceedings for nullity   (1) In proceedings for nullity on the ground of incapacity to consummate the marriage the petitioner shall, subject to paragraph (2), apply to the registrar to determine whether medical inspectors should be appointed to examine the parties.

(2) An application under paragraph (1) shall not be made in an undefended cause—

  (*a*) if the husband is the petitioner, or

  (*b*) if the wife is the petitioner and—

    (i) it appears from the petition that she was either a widow or divorced at the time of marriage in question, or

    (ii) it appears from the petition or otherwise that she has borne a child, or

    (iii) a statement by the wife that she is not a virgin is filed,

unless, in any such case, the petitioner is alleging his or her own incapacity.

(3) References in paragraphs (1) and (2) to the petitioner shall, where the cause is proceeding only on the respondent's answer or where the allegation of incapacity is made only in the respondent's answer, be construed as references to the respondent.

(4) An application under paragraph (1) by the petitioner shall be made—

(*a*) where the respondent has not given notice of intention to defend, after the time limited for giving the notice has expired;

(*b*) where the respondent has given notice of intention to defend, after the expiration of the time allowed for filing his answer or, if he has filed an answer, after it has been filed;

and an application under paragraph (1) by the respondent shall be made after he has filed an answer.

(5) Where the party required to make an application under paragraph (1) fails to do so within a reasonable time, the other party may, if he is prosecuting or defending the cause, make an application under that paragraph.

(6) In proceedings for nullity on the ground that the marriage has not been consummated owing to the wilful refusal of the respondent, either party may apply to the registrar for the appointment of medical inspectors to examine the parties.

(7) If the respondent has not given notice of intention to defend, an application by the petitioner under paragraph (1) or (6) may be made *ex parte.*

(8) If the registrar hearing an application under paragraph (1) or (6) considers it expedient to do so, he shall appoint a medical inspector or, if he thinks it necessary, two medical inspectors to examine the parties and report to the court the result of the examination.

(9) At the hearing of any such proceedings as are referred to in paragraph (1) the court may, if it thinks fit, appoint a medical inspector or two medical inspectors to examine any party who has not been examined or to examine further any party who has been examined.

(10) The party on whose application an order under paragraph (8) is made or who has the conduct of proceedings in which an order under paragraph (9) has been made for the examination of the other party, shall serve on the other party notice of the time and place appointed for his or her examination.

NOTES

The court may . . . appoint a medical inspector   This power carries with it the usual power to adjourn the case if necessary (see *S v S (otherwise W)*, [1962] 2 All ER 816 (CA) at p 824).

31. Conduct of medical examination   (1) Every medical examination under rule 30 shall be held at the consulting room of the medical inspector or, as the case may be, of one of the medical inspectors appointed to conduct the examination:

Provided that the registrar may, on the application of a party, direct that the examination of that party shall be held at the court office or at such other place as the registrar thinks convenient.

(2) Every party presenting himself for examination shall sign, in the presence of the inspector or inspectors, a statement that he is the person referred to as the petitioner or respondent, as the case may be, in the order for the examination, and at the conclusion of the examination the inspector or inspectors shall certify on the statement that it was signed in his or their presence by the person who has been examined.

(3) Every report made in pursuance of rule 30 shall be filed and either party shall be entitled to be supplied with a copy on payment of the prescribed fee.

(4) In an undefended cause it shall not be necessary for the inspector or inspectors to attend and give evidence at the trial unless so directed.

(5) In a defended cause, if the report made in pursuance of rule 30 is accepted by both parties, notice to that effect shall be given by the parties to the registrar and to the inspector or inspectors not less than seven clear days before the date fixed for the trial; and where such notice is given, it shall not be necessary for the inspector or inspectors to attend and give evidence at the trial.

(6) Where pursuant to paragraph (4) or (5) the evidence of the inspector or inspectors is not given at the trial, his or their report shall be treated as

information furnished to the court by a court expert and be given such weight as the court thinks fit.

32. Order for transfer of cause   (1) The court may order that a cause pending in a divorce county court be transferred to the High Court, where, having regard to all the circumstances including the difficulty or importance of the cause or of any issue arising therein, the court thinks it desirable that the cause should be heard and determined in the High Court.

(2) The court may order that any cause pending in a divorce county court shall be transferred to another divorce county court.

(3) Where a cause has been transferred to the High Court, the registrar of the registry in which it is proceeding or a judge may order that the cause be transferred to another registry.

(4) An order under any of the foregoing paragraphs may be made by the judge or registrar, as the case may be, of his own motion or on the application of a party, but before making an order of his own motion the judge or registrar shall give the parties an opportunity of being heard on the question of transfer and for that purpose the registrar may give the parties notice of a date, time and place at which the question will be considered.

33. Directions for trial   (1) On the written request of the petitioner or of any party who is defending a cause begun by petition, the registrar shall give directions for the trial of the cause if he is satisfied—

(*a*) that a copy of the petition (including any supplemental or amended petition) and any subsequent pleading has been duly served on every party required to be served and, where that party is a person under disability, that any affidavit required by rule 113 (2) has been filed;

(*b*) if no notice of intention to defend has been given by any party entitled to give it, that the time limited for giving such notice has expired;

(*c*) if notice of intention to defend has been given by any party, that the time allowed him for filing an answer has expired;

(*d*) if an answer has been filed, that the time allowed for filing any subsequent pleading has expired;

(*e*) in proceedings for nullity—

(i)   that any application required by rule 30 (1) has been made, and

(ii) where an order for the examination of the parties has been made on an application under rule 30, that the notice required by paragraph (10) of that rule has been served and that the report of the inspector or inspectors has been filed.

(2) Subject to paragraph (3), where the cause is pending in a divorce county court other than the divorce registry and is to be tried at that court, the registrar shall, if he considers it practicable to do so, give directions for trial by fixing the date, place and, as nearly as may be, the time of the trial and giving notice therof to every party to the cause.

(3) Where the cause is an undefended cause for divorce or judicial separation and, in a case to which section 1 (2) (*d*) of the Act of 1973 applies, the respondent has given the registrar a notice under rule 16 (1) that he consents to the grant of a decree, then, unless otherwise directed,—

(i)   there shall be filed with the request for directions for trial an affidavit by the petitioner containing the information required by Form 7 (*a*), 7 (*b*), 7 (*c*), 7 (*d*) or 7 (*e*) (whichever is appropriate), as near as may be in the order there set out, together with any corroborative evidence on which the petitioner intends to rely; and

(ii) the registrar shall give directions for trial by entering the cause in a list to be known as the special procedure list.

In the case of an undefended cause proceeding on the respondent's answer, this paragraph shall have effect as if for the references to the petitioner and the respondent there were substituted references to the respondent and the petitioner respectively.

(4) In any other case the registrar shall give directions for trial by setting the cause down for trial and giving notice that he has done so to every party to the cause. [Provided that, in the case of a defended cause the registrar may treat the request for directions for trial as a summons for directions under RSC Order 25, and in that event he shall give the parties notice of a date, time and place at which the request will be considered and that Order shall apply, with the necessary modifications, as if the cause and any application made therein for ancillary relief or for an order relating to a child were an action to which rule 1 of the Order applies.]

NOTES
Amendment   The proviso to para (4) was added by SI 1978/527.

34. Determination of place of trial   (1) Directions for trial, except where given under rule 33 (3), shall determine the place of trial.

(2) In the case of an undefended cause to which rule 33 (3) does not apply, the request for directions shall state—

(*a*) the place of trial desired,

(*b*) the place where the witnesses whom it is proposed to call at the trial reside,

(*c*) an estimate of the probable length of trial, and

(*d*) any other fact which may be relevant for determining the place of trial.

(3) In the case of a defended cause, the party intending to make a request for directions shall, not less than eight days before making his request, give notice of the place of trial desired to every other party who has given notice of intention to defend and, if the party intending to make the request is the respondent, to the petitioner.

The notice shall state the number of witnesses to be called on behalf of the party giving the notice and the places where he and his witnesses reside.

(4) If any party to whom notice is given under paragraph (3) does not consent to the place of trial specified in the notice, he may, within eight days after receiving it, apply to the registrar to direct trial at some other place; and if he does consent to the place so specified, he shall within that period send to the party by whom the notice was given a statement signed by his solicitor (or by him, if he is acting in person) indicating that the notice has been received and specifying the number of witnesses to be called on his behalf and the places where he and his witnesses reside.

(5) Where no application for trial at some other place is made under paragraph (4) within the period specified in that paragraph, the party making the request for directions shall state in his request—

(*a*) the place of trial desired;

(*b*) the number of witnesses to be called on his behalf and the places where he and his witnesses reside;

(*c*) if it be the case, that no statement has been received from any party (naming him) to whom notice was given under paragraph (3); and

(*d*) an estimate of the probable length of the trial;

and shall file with the request any statement sent to him by any other party in accordance with paragraph (4).

(6) If circumstances arise tending to show that the estimate of the probable length of the trial given under paragraph (2) (*c*) or (5) (*d*) or made on an application under paragraph (4) is inaccurate, a further estimate shall be filed.

(7) In determining the place of trial the registrar shall have regard to all the circumstances of the case so far as it is possible for him to do so on the basis of the information available to him, including the convenience of the parties and their witnesses, the costs likely to be incurred, the date on which the trial can take place, the estimated length of the trial and the respective facilities for trial at the Royal Courts of Justice and elsewhere.

(8) Directions determining the place of trial of any cause may be varied by the registrar of the court or registry in which the cause is proceeding on the application of any party to the cause.

35. Directions as to allegations under section 1 (2) (b) of Act of 1973   (1) Where in a defended cause the petitioner alleges that the respondent has behaved in such a way that the petitioner cannot reasonably be expected to live with the respondent, the registrar may, of his own motion on giving directions for trial or on the application of any party made at any time before the trial, order or authorise the party who has made the request for or obtained such directions to file a schedule of the allegations and counter allegations made in the pleadings or particulars.

(2) Where such an order is made or authority given, the allegations and counter-allegations shall, unless otherwise directed, be listed concisely in chronological order, each counter-allegation being set out against the allegation to which it relates, and the party filing the schedule shall serve a copy of it on any other party to the cause who has filed a pleading.

36. Stay under Domicile and Matrimonial Proceedings Act 1973   (1) An application to the court by the petitioner or respondent in proceedings for divorce for an order under paragraph 8 of Schedule 1 to the Domicile and Matrimonial Proceedings Act 1973 (in this rule referred to as "Schedule 1") shall be made to the registrar, who may determine the application or refer the application, or any question arising thereon, to a judge for his decision as if the application were an application for ancillary relief.

(2) An application for an order under paragraph 9 of Schedule 1 shall be made to the judge.

(3) Where, on giving directions for trial, it appears to the registrar from any information given pursuant to paragraph 1 (*j*) of Appendix 2 or rule 21 (4) or paragraph (4) of this rule that any proceedings which are in respect of the marriage in question or which are capable of affecting its validity or subsistence are continuing in any country outside England and Wales and he considers that the question whether the proceedings on the petition should be stayed under paragraph 9 of Schedule 1 ought to be determined by the court, he shall fix a date and time for the consideration of that question by a judge and give notice thereof to all parties.

In this paragraph "proceedings continuing in any country outside England and Wales" has the same meaning as in paragraph 1 (*j*) of Appendix 2.

(4) Any party who makes a request for directions for trial in matrimonial proceedings within the meaning of paragraph 2 of Schedule 1 shall, if there has been a change in the information given pursuant to paragraph 1 (*j*) of Appendix 2 and rule 21 (4), file a statement giving particulars of the change.

(5) An application by a party to the proceedings for an order under paragraph 10 of Schedule 1 may be made to the registrar, and he may determine the application or may refer the application, or any question arising thereon, to a judge as if the application were an application for ancillary relief.

NOTES
Schedule 1 to the Domicile and Matrimonial Proceedings Act 1973   Halsbury's Statutes, 4th edn Vol 27, title Matrimonial Law (Pt 3) (3rd edn Vol 43, p 628).

EVIDENCE

37. Evidence generally   (1) Subject to the provisions of rules 39, 40 and 48 and of the Civil Evidence Act 1968 and any other enactment, any fact required to be proved by the evidence of witnesses at the trial of a cause begun by petition shall be proved by the examination of the witnesses orally and in open court.

(2) Nothing in rules 39 and 40 shall affect the power of the judge at the trial to refuse to admit any evidence if in the interest of justice he thinks fit to do so.

NOTES
Civil Evidence Act 1968   Halsbury's Statutes, 4th edn Vol 17, title Evidence.

38. Taking of affidavit in county court proceedings   In relation to matrimonial proceedings pending or treated as pending in a divorce county court, section 87 (1) of the County Courts Act 1959 shall have effect as if after paragraph (*c*) there were inserted the following words—
> "or
>   (*d*) a registrar of the divorce registry; or
>   (*e*) any officer of the divorce registry authorised by the President under section 2 of the Commissioners for Oaths Act 1889; or
>   (*f*) any clerk in the Central Office of the Royal Courts of Justice authorised to take affidavits for the purpose of proceedings in the Supreme Court.

NOTES
Section 87 (1) of the County Courts Act 1959   Repealed by the County Courts Act 1984, s 148 (3), Sch 4, Halsbury's Statutes, 4th edn Vol 11, title County Courts, and replaced by s 58 (1) of that Act, *ibid.*
Section 2 of the Commissioners for Oaths Act 1889   Halsbury's Statutes, 4th edn Vol 17, title Evidence.

39. Evidence by affidavit, etc   (1) The court may order—
    (*a*) that the affidavit of any witness may be read at the trial on such conditions as the court thinks reasonable;
    (*b*) that the evidence of any particular fact shall be given at the trial in such manner as may be specified in the order and in particular—
        (i)   by statement on oath of information or belief, or
        (ii) by the production of documents or entries in books, or
        (iii) by copies of documents or entries in books, or
        (iv) in the case of a fact which is or was a matter of common knowledge either generally or in a particular district, by the production of a specified newspaper containing a statement of that fact; and
    (*c*) that not more than a specified number of expert witnesses may be called.
    (2) An application to the registrar for an order under paragraph (1) shall—
    (*a*) if no notice of intention to defend has been given, or
    (*b*) if the petitioner and every party who has given notice of intention to defend consents to the order sought, or
    (*c*) if the cause is undefended and directions for trial have been given, be made *ex parte* by filing an affidavit stating the grounds on which the application is made.
    (3) Where an application is made before the trial for an order that the affidavit of a witness may be read at the trial or that evidence of a particular fact may be given at the trial by affidavit, the proposed affidavit or a draft thereof shall be submitted with the application; and where the affidavit is sworn before the hearing of the application and sufficiently states the grounds on which the application is made, no other affidavit shall be required under paragraph (2).
    (4) The court may, on the application of any party to a cause begun by petition, make an order under CCR Order 20, rule 18, or (if the cause is pending in the High Court) under RSC Order 39, rule 1, for the examination on oath of any person, and CCR Order 20, rule 18, or (if the cause is pending in the High Court) RSC Order 38, rule 9, and Order 39, rules 1 to 14, (which regulate the procedure where evidence is to be taken by deposition) shall have effect accordingly with the appropriate modifications.
    (5) On any application made—
    (*a*) in a divorce county court, by originating application or in accordance with CCR Order 13, rule 1 (which deals with applications in the course of proceedings), or
    (*b*) in the High Court, by originating summons, summons, notice or motion, evidence may be given by affidavit unless these Rules otherwise provide or the court otherwise directs, but the court may, on the application of any party, order the attendance for cross-examination of the person making any such affidavit; and where, after such an order has been made, that person

does not attend, his affidavit shall not be used as evidence without the leave of the court.

(6) CCR Order 20, rule 19 (6) (which enables the opposite party by notice to require the attendance of a deponent), shall not apply to an affidavit made in matrimonial proceedings.

NOTES
As to medical evidence upon affidavit in insanity cases, see *Practice Note*, [1956] 2 All ER 833; and see *Usher v Usher (by her guardian)* and *Abley v Abley (by her guardian)*, [1956] 2 All ER 762. Proof of original entry in register of births by the production of a photograph certified by the superintendent registrar or registrar of births and deaths may be allowed in case of undue expense or inconvenience of travel to inspect the register (*Practice Note*, [1956] 3 All ER 745).

40. Evidence of marriage outside England and Wales (1) The celebration of a marriage outside England and Wales and its validity under the law of the country where it was celebrated may, in any matrimonial proceedings in which the existence and validity of the marriage is not disputed, be proved by the evidence of one of the parties to the marriage and the production of a document purporting to be—
  (*a*) a marriage certificate or similar document issued under the law in force in that country; or
  (*b*) a certified copy of an entry in a register of marriages kept under the law in force in that country.

(2) Where a document produced by virtue of paragraph (1) is not in English it shall, unless otherwise directed, be accompanied by a translation certified by a notary public or authenticated by affidavit.

(3) This rule shall not be construed as precluding the proof of a marriage in accordance with the Evidence (Foreign, Dominion and Colonial Documents) Act 1933 or in any other manner authorised apart from this rule.

NOTES
Evidence (Foreign, Dominion and Colonial Documents) Act 1933 Halsbury's Statutes, 4th edn Vol 17, title Evidence.

41. Issue of witness summons or subpoena (1) A witness summons in a cause pending in a divorce county court may be issued in that court or in the court of trial at which the cause is to be tried.

(2) A writ of subpoena in a cause pending in the High Court may issue out of—
  (*a*) the registry in which the cause is proceeding, or
  (*b*) if the cause is to be tried at the Royal Courts of Justice, the divorce registry, or
  (*c*) if the cause is to be tried at a divorce town, the registry for that town.

42. Hearsay and expert evidence in High Court (1) RSC Order 38, rules 7, 21 (1) and 36 shall not apply in relation to an undefended cause in the High Court.

(2) RSC Order 38, rule 21, shall have effect in relation to a defended cause in the High Court as if—
  (*a*) for the reference in pargraph (4) to Order 38, rule 3, there were substituted a reference to rule 39 of these Rules; and
  (*b*) paragraph (5) were omitted.

TRIAL ETC.

43. Mode and place of trial (1) Unless otherwise directed and subject to rule 48, every cause and any issue arising therein shall be tried by a judge without a jury.

(2) Any cause begun by petition (except one entered in the special procedure list) which is pending in a divorce county court may be tried at any court of trial.

(3) Any cause begun by petition which is pending in the High Court may be tried at the Royal Courts of Justice or at any divorce town.

(4) A judge or the district registrar of the registry for the divorce town at which any cause has been set down for trial may, where it appears to him that the cause cannot conveniently be tried at that town, change the place of trial to some other divorce town.

The power conferred by this paragraph may be exercised by the judge or district registrar of his own motion or on the application of a party, but before acting of his own motion the judge or district registrar shall give the parties an opportunity of being heard on the question of change, and for that purpose the district registrar may give the parties notice of a date, time and place at which the question will be considered.

44. Transmission of file etc. on setting down cause   (1) Where a cause pending in a divorce county court is set down for trial at another divorce county court, the registrar of the court in which the cause is pending shall send the file of the cause to the registrar of the court of trial.

(2) As soon as practicable after a cause pending in a divorce county court has been set down for trial, the registrar of the court of trial shall fix the date, place and, as nearly as may be, the time of the trial and give notice thereof to every party to the cause.

(3) On setting down for trial a cause pending in the High Court, the registrar of the registry in which the cause is proceeding shall—

- (*a*) if the cause is to be tried at the Royal Courts of Justice and is not proceeding in the divorce registry, and
- (*b*) if the cause is to be tried at a divorce town and is not proceeding in the registry for that town, send the file of the cause to that registry.

(4) In these Rules any reference to the registry for the divorce town at which a cause is to be tried shall, in relation to a divorce town in which there is no district registry, be construed as a reference to such district registry as the Lord Chancellor may designate for the purpose or, if the divorce town is not situated within the district of any district registry, as a reference to the divorce registry.

45. Trial of issue   Where directions are given for the separate trial of any issue and those directions have been complied with, the registrar shall—

- (*a*) if the issue arises on an application for ancillary relief or in proceedings for the exercise of any power under Part III of the Act of 1973, proceed as if the issue were a question referred to a judge on an application for ancillary relief and rule 82 shall apply accordingly;
- (*b*) in any other case, set the issue down for trial and thereupon rule 44 shall apply as if the issue were a cause.

46. Lists at divorce towns and exercise of registrar's jurisdiction   (1) The registrar of the registry for each divorce town shall prepare and keep up to date a list of the causes which are for the time being set down for trial at that divorce town.

(2) Causes shall be entered in each of the lists in the order in which they were set down for trial and for the purpose of this paragraph—

- (*a*) a cause proceeding in another registry shall, subject to subparagraph (*b*), be treated as having been set down for trial when the file of the cause is received in the registry for the divorce town at which it is to be tried;
- (*b*) a cause remitted for trial from another divorce town shall be treated as having been set down for trial at the end of the day on which it was originally set down for trial.

(3) The district registrar of the registry for the divorce town at which a cause has been set down for trial or, in the case of a cause set down for trial at the Royal Courts of Justice, a registrar of the divorce registry may, if it appears to him to be desirable having regard to the proximity of the date of the trial or otherwise, exercise in the cause any jurisdiction of the registrar of the registry in which the cause is proceeding.

[(4) RSC Order 34, rule 5 (3), shall apply, with the necessary modifications, to a defended cause as it applies to an action begun by writ.]

NOTES
Amendment Paragraph (4) was added by SI 1978/527.

47. Further provisions as to date of trial Except with the consent of the parties or by leave of a judge, no cause, whether defended or undefended, shall be tried until after the expiration of 10 days from the date on which the directions for trial were given:

Provided that nothing in this rule shall apply to a cause entered in the special procedure list.

48. Disposal of causes in special procedure list (1) As soon as practicable after a cause has been entered in the special procedure list, the registrar shall consider the evidence filed by the petitioner and—
 (*a*) if he is satisfied that the petitioner has sufficiently proved the contents of the petition and is entitled to a decree . . ., the registrar shall make and file a certificate to that effect;
 (*b*) if he is not so satisfied he may either give the petitioner an opportunity of filing further evidence or remove the cause from the special procedure list whereupon rule 33 (3) shall cease to apply.

(2) On the filing of a certificate under paragraph (1) a day shall be fixed for the pronouncement of a decree by a judge in open court at a court of trial and the registrar shall send to each party notice of the day and place so fixed and a copy of the certificate but [subject to paragraph (2A)] it shall not be necessary for any party to appear on that occasion.

[(2A) Where the registrar makes a certificate under paragraph (1) and the petition contains a prayer for costs, the registrar may—
 (*a*) if satisfied that the petitioner is entitled to such costs, include in his certificate a statement to that effect;
 (*b*) if not so satisfied, refer the prayer to the judge who pronounces the decree and give to any party who objects to paying such costs notice that, if he wishes to proceed with his objection, he must attend before the judge on the day fixed pursuant to paragraph (2).]

(3) Within 14 days after the pronouncement of a decree in accordance with a certificate under paragraph (1), any person may inspect the certificate and the evidence filed under rule 33 (3) and may bespeak copies on payment of the prescribed fee.

(4) Where there are children of the family to whom section 41 of the Act of 1973 applies and . . . no application by the respondent for custody of or access to the children is pending, then, unless in the circumstances of the particular case the court thinks is inappropriate to do so, the registrar shall after filing his certificate under paragraph (1), fix an appointment for consideration by a judge in chambers of the arrangements for the children and send notice of the appointment to the petitioner and the respondent.

Unless otherwise directed, nothing in this paragraph shall apply to an undefended cause which is proceeding on the respondent's answer.

NOTES
Amendment The words omitted where indicated by dots in paras (1) (*a*) and (4) were deleted, and para (2A) and the words in square brackets in para (2) were inserted by SI 1978/527.
The registrar shall consider the evidence filed by the petitioner As to the correct approach to special procedure divorces, see *R v Nottingham County Court, ex parte Byers*, [1985] 1 All ER 735.

49. Right to be hear on ancillary questions (1) A respondent may, without filing an answer, be heard on—
 (*a*) any question of custody of, or access to, any child of the family,
 (*b*) any question whether any such child should be committed to the care of a local authority under section 43 of the Act of 1973,

(c) any question whether a supervision order should be made as respects any such child under section 44 of that Act, and

(d) any question of ancillary relief.

(2) A respondent, co-respondent or party cited may, without filing an answer, be heard on any question as to costs, but the court may at any time order any party objecting to a claim for costs to file and serve on the party making the claim a written statement setting out the reasons for his objection.

(3) A party shall be entitled to be heard on any question pursuant to paragraph (1) or (2) whether or not he has returned to the court office an acknowledgement of service stating his wish to be heard on that question.

(4) In proceedings after a decree nisi of divorce or a decree of judicial separation no order the effect of which would be to make a co-respondent or party cited liable for costs which are not directly referable to the decree shall be made unless the co-respondent or party cited is a party to such proceedings or has been given notice of the intention to apply for such an order.

50. Respondent's statement as to arrangements for children   (1) A respondent on whom there is served a statement in accordance with rule 8 (2) may file in the court office a written statement of his views on the present and proposed arrangements for the children, and on receipt of such a statement from the respondent the registrar shall send a copy to the petitioner.

(2) Any such statement of the respondent's views shall, if practicable, be filed within the time limited for giving notice of intention to defend and in any event before the judge makes an order under section 41 of the Act of 1973.

51. Order as to arrangements for children to be drawn up   Any order made pursuant to section 41 (1) or (4) of the Act of 1973 shall be drawn up.

52. Restoration of matters adjourned etc. at the hearing   (1) Where at the trial of a cause any application is adjourned by the judge for hearing in chambers, it may be restored—

(a) in the High Court, by notice without a summons, or

(b) in a divorce county court, on notice under CCR Order 13, rule 1 (which deals with applications in the course of proceedings),

(c) in the High Court or a divorce county court, by notice given by the registrar when in his opinion the matter ought to be further considered,

and the notice shall state the place and time for the hearing of the restored application and be served on every party concerned.

(2) Where in proceedings for divorce, nullity of marriage or judicial separation the judge has not made an order pursuant to section 41 (1) of the Act of 1973, paragraph (1) shall, unless the judge otherwise directs, apply as if an application with respect to the arrangements for the care and upbringing of any such child had been adjourned for hearing in chambers.

53. Shorthand note etc. of proceedings at trial   (1) Official shorthand writers shall be appointed by the Lord Chancellor for the purpose of trials of causes in the High Court:

Provided that if at any divorce town no shorthand writer has been appointed under this paragraph or the person so appointed is not available, a shorthand writer may be appointed by the judge hearing causes at that town.

(2) Unless the judge otherwise directs, a shorthand note shall be taken of the proceedings at the trial in open court of every cause pending in the High Court.

(3) A shorthand note may be taken of any other proceedings before a judge if directions for the taking of such a note are given by or on behalf of the Lord Chancellor.

(4) The shorthand writer shall sign the note and certify it to be a correct shorthand note of the proceedings and shall retain the note unless he is directed by the registrar to forward it to him.

(5) On being so directed the shorthand writer shall furnish the registrar with a transcript of the whole or such part as may be directed of the shorthand note.

(6) Any party, any person who has intervened in a cause or the Queen's Proctor shall be entitled to require from the shorthand writer a transcript of the shorthand note, and the shorthand writer shall, at the request of any person so entitled, supply that person with a transcript of the whole or any part of the note on payment of the shorthand writer's charges at such rate as may be fixed by the Minister for the Civil Service.

(7) Except as aforesaid, the shorthand writer shall not, without the permission of the court, furnish the shorthand note or a transcript of the whole or any part thereof to anyone.

(8) In these Rules references to a shorthand note include references to a record of the proceedings made by mechanical means and in relation to such a record references to the shorthand writer shall be effect as if they were references to the person responsible for transcribing the record.

NOTES
As to shorthand notes of county court matrimonial causes, see *Practice Direction,* [1973] 3 All ER 224.

54. Application for re-hearing   (1) An application for re-hearing of a cause tried by a judge alone (whether in the High Court or a divorce county court), where no error of the court at the hearing is alleged, shall be made to a judge.

(2) Unless otherwise directed, the application shall be made to the judge by whom the cause was tried and shall be heard in open court.

(3) The application shall be made—
(*a*) in the High Court, by a notice to attend before the judge on a day specified in the notice, and
(*b*) in the county court, on notice in accordance with CCR Order 13, rule 1 (which deals with applications in the course of proceedings),
and the notice shall state the grounds of the application.

(4) Unless otherwise directed, the notice must be issued within six weeks after the judgment and served on every other party to the cause not less than 14 days before the day fixed for the hearing of the application.

(5) The applicant shall file a certificate that the notice has been duly served on each person required to be served therewith.

(6) The application shall be supported by an affidavit setting out the allegations on which the applicant relies or exhibiting a copy of any pleading which he proposes to file if the application is granted, and a copy of the affidavit shall be served on every other party to the cause.

(7) Not less than seven days before the application is heard the applicant shall file of a transcript of so much as is relevant of any official shorthand note of the proceedings at the trial.

(8) Any other application for re-hearing shall be made by way of appeal to the Court of Appeal.

(9) This rule shall apply, with the necessary modifications, to a cause disposed of under rule 48 as it applies to a cause tried by a judge alone.

NOTES
Error of the court An allegation, express or by implication, that the trial judge came to a wrong conclusion on the material before him is an "error of the court" (*Peek v Peek,* [1947] 2 All ER 297, as where it is alleged that the judge believed the wrong set of witnesses (*Petty v Petty,* [1943] 2 All ER 511; *Prince v Prince,* [1951] P 71; [1950] 2 All ER 375 (CA); or that he wrongly refused an adjournment (*Woodman v Woodman,* [1967] 1 All ER 410). The question whether the case was defended or undefended is irrelevant in determining whether an "error of the court" is alleged or not (*Peek v Peek, supra*).
   No "error of the court" is alleged where a re-hearing is sought because a party was misled into not defending (*Pratt v Pratt,* [1966] 3 All ER 272); or because he failed to defend through ignorance or lack of advice (*Nash v Nash,* [1967] 1 All ER 535); or because the party had not been served with the proceedings (*Manners v Manners,* [1936] 1 All ER 41); or where a re-hearing of a suit previously undefended is sought on grounds of public policy (*Winter v Winter,* [1942] 2 All ER 390); or on the ground that the petitioner failed to make proper disclosure of his own adultery (*Alhadeff v Alhadeff,* [1951] WN 367); or on the ground that fresh adultery has been

discovered (*Wells-King v Wells-King,* |1955| 1 All ER 585); or when the judge has drawn an inference from undisputed evidence which was justifiable on the material before him, although subsequently proved to be incorrect (*Prince v Prince, supra*).

The judge has no power to order a re-hearing where the decree absolute has already been pronounced in circumstances of procedural irregularity (*Edwards v Edwards,* [1951] 1 All ER 63.

DECREES AND ORDERS

55. Decrees and orders   Every decree, every order made in open court and every other order which is required to be drawn up shall be drawn up—
- (*a*) in the case of a decree or order made at a divorce county court, by the registrar of that court;
- (*b*) in the case of a decree or order made at the Royal Courts of Justice, by a registrar of the divorce registry;
- (*c*) in the case of a decree or order made at a divorce town, by the registrar of the registry for that town.

(2) CCR Order 24, rule 5 (which deals with the preparation of a decree), shall not apply to a decree made in a cause pending in a divorce county court.

(3) The registrar to whom the file of a cause has been sent under rule 44 shall, as soon as practicable after the cause has been tried, return the file to the registrar from whom he received it, together with any documentary evidence produced during the trial which has not been ordered to be returned to the party who produced it and the decree or order pronounced or made in the cause.

56. Application for rescission of decree   (1) An application by a respondent under section 10 (1) of the Act of 1973 for the rescission of a decree of divorce shall be made to a judge and shall be heard in open court.

(2) Paragraphs (3) and (5) of rule 54 shall apply to an application under this rule as they apply to an application under that rule.

(3) Unless otherwise directed, the notice of the application shall be served on the petitioner not less than 14 days before the day fixed for the hearing of the application.

(4) The application shall be supported by an affidavit setting out the allegations on which the applicant relies and a copy of the affidavit shall be served on the petitioner.

57. Application under section 10 (2) of Act of 1973   (1) An application by the respondent to a petition for divorce for the court to consider the financial position of the respondent after the divorce shall be made by notice in Form 12.

(2) Where a petitioner is served with a notice in Form 12, then, unless he has already filed an affidavit under rule 73 (2), he shall, within 14 days after the service of the notice, file an affidavit in answer to the application containing full particulars of his property and income, and if he does not do so, the court may order him to file an affidavit containing such particulars.

(3) Within 14 days after service of any affidavit under paragraph (2) or within such other time as the court may fix, the respondent shall file an affidavit in reply containing full particulars of his property and income unless already given in an affidavit filed by him under rule 73 (3).

(4) The powers of the court on the hearing of the application may be exercised by the registrar.

(5) Where the court has granted a decree nisi on the basis of a finding that the petitioner was entitled to rely in support of his petition on the fact of two years' or five years' separation and has made no such findings as to any other fact mentioned in section 1 (2) of the Act of 1973, the registrar by whom an application under section 10(2) is to be heard shall fix an appointment for the hearing, and rules 77 (3) to (7), 80 and 81 shall apply to the application as if it were an application for ancillary relief.

(6) At any time before the hearing of the application is concluded (and

without prejudice to any right of appeal), the registrar may, and if so requested by either party shall, refer the application, or any question arising thereon, to a judge.

(7) A statement of any of the matters mentioned in subsection (3) of section 10 of the Act of 1973 with respect to which the court is satisfied, or, where the court has proceeded under subsection (4) of the said section, a statement that the conditions for which that subsection provides have been fulfilled, shall be entered in the court minutes.

58. Copies of decrees and orders   (1) A copy of every decree shall be sent by the registrar to every party to the cause.

(2) A sealed or other copy of a decree or order made in open court shall be issued to any person requiring it on payment of the prescribed fee.

59. Service of order   (1) Where an order made in matrimonial proceedings has been drawn up, the registrar [of the court where the order is made] shall, unless otherwise directed, send a copy of the order to every party affected by it.

(2) Where a party against whom the order is made is acting by a solicitor, a copy may, if the registrar thinks fit, be sent to that party as if he were acting in person, as well as to his solicitor.

(3) It shall not be necessary for the person in whose favour the order was made to prove that a copy of the order has reached any other party to whom it is required to be sent.

(4) This rule is without prejudice to RSC Order 45, rule 7 (which deals with the service of an order to do or abstain from doing an act), CCR Order 25, rule 68 (which deals with orders enforceable by attachment), and any other rule or enactment for the purposes of which an order is required to be served in a particular way.

NOTES
Amendment   The words "of the court where the order is made" printed between square brackets in para (1) of this rule were inserted by the Matrimonial Causes (Amendment) Rules 1984, SI 1984/1511.

60.   (*Revoked by the Matrimonial Causes (Amendment) Rules 1980, SI 1980/ 977*).

61. Intervention to show cause by Queen's Proctor   (1) If the Queen's Proctor wishes to show cause against a decree nisi being made absolute, he shall give notice to that effect to the registrar and to the party in whose favour it was pronounced, and, if the cause is pending in a divorce county court, the registrar shall thereupon order it to be transferred to the High Court.

(2) Within 21 days after giving notice under paragraph (1) the Queen's Proctor shall file his plea setting out the grounds on which he desires to show cause, together with a copy for service on the party in whose favour the decree was pronounced and every other party affected by the decree.

(3) The registrar shall serve a copy of the plea on each of the persons mentioned in paragraph (2).

(4) Subject to the following provisions of this rule, these Rules shall apply to all subsequent pleadings and proceedings in respect of the plea as if it were a petition by which a cause is begun.

(5) If no answer to the plea is filed within the time limited or, if an answer is filed and struck out or not proceeded with, the Queen's Proctor may apply forthwith by motion for an order rescinding the decree and dismissing the petition.

(6) Rule 33 shall apply to proceedings in respect of a plea by the Queen's Proctor as it applies to the trial of a cause, so however that if all the charges in the plea are denied in the answer the application for directions shall be

made by the Queen's Proctor and in any other case it shall be made by the party in whose favour the decree nisi has been pronounced.

NOTES
Contested interventions by the Queen's Proctor under this rule, or by any other person under r 62, should be heard in open court; see *Biggs v Biggs and Wheatley*, [1977] 1 All ER 20.

62. Intervention to show cause by person other than Queen's Proctor   (1) If any person other than the Queen's Proctor wishes to show cause under section 9 of the Act of 1973 against a decree nisi being made absolute, he shall file an affidavit stating the facts on which he relies and a copy shall be served on the party in whose favour the decree was pronounced.

(2) A party on whom a copy of an affidavit has been served under paragraph (1) may, within 14 days after service, file an affidavit in answer and, if he does so, a copy thereof shall be served on the person showing cause.

(3) The person showing cause may file an affidavit in reply within 14 days after service of the affidavit in answer and, if he does so, a copy shall be served on each party who was served with a copy of his original affidavit.

(4) No affidavit after an affidavit in reply shall be filed without leave.

(5) Any person who files an affidavit under paragraph (1), (2) or (3) shall at the same time file a copy for service on each person required to be served therewith and the registrar shall thereupon serve the copy on that person.

(6) A person showing cause shall apply to the judge for directions within 14 days after expiry of the time allowed for filing an affidavit in reply or, where no affidavit in answer has been filed, within 14 days after expiry of the time allowed for filing such an affidavit.

(7) If the person showing cause does not apply under paragraph (6) within the time limited, the person in whose favour the decree was pronounced may do so.

(8) If directions are given for the trial of an intervention in a cause pending in a divorce county court, the registrar shall thereupon order the cause to be transferred to the High Court.

63. Intervention to show cause to be tried in London   The trial of any intervention under rule 61 or 62, whether the cause is proceeding in the divorce registry or a district registry, shall take place at the Royal Courts of Justice, unless the President otherwise directs.

64. Rescission of decree nisi by consent   [(1) Where a reconciliation has been effected between the petitioner and the respondent—
   (*a*) after a decree nisi has been pronounced but before it has been made absolute, or
   (*b*) after the pronouncement of a decree of judicial separation,
either party may apply for an order rescinding the decree by consent.]

(2) Where the cause is pending in a divorce county court, the application shall be made on notice to the other spouse and to any other party against whom costs have been awarded or who is otherwise affected by the decree, and where the cause is pending in the High Court, a copy of the summons by which the application is made shall be served on every such person.

(3) The application shall be made to a judge and may be heard in chambers.

NOTES
Amendment   Para (1) of this rule was substituted by the Matrimonial Causes (Amendment) Rules 1979, SI 1979/400.

65. Decree absolute on lodging notice   (1) Subject to rule 66 (1), an application by a spouse to make absolute a decree nisi pronounced in his favour may be made by lodging with the registrar a notice in Form 8.

(2) On the lodging of such a notice, the registrar shall search the court minutes and if he is satisfied—

[(*a*) that no application for rescission of the decree or for re-hearing of the cause and no appeal against the decree or the dismissal of an application for re-hearing of the cause is pending;
(*b*) that no order has been made by a judge extending the time for making an application for re-hearing of the cause or by the Court of Appeal extending the time for appealing against the decree or the dismissal of an application for re-hearing of the cause or, if any such order has been made, that the time so extended has expired;]
(*c*) that no application for such an order as is mentioned in sub-paragraph (*b*) is pending;
(*d*) that no intervention under rule 61 or 62 is pending;
(*e*) that the judge has made an order under section 41 (1) of the Act of 1973;
(*f*) where a certificate has been granted under section 12 of the Administration of Justice Act 1969 in respect of the decree—
   (i) that no application for leave to appeal directly to the House of Lords is pending;
   (ii) that no extension of the time to apply for leave to appeal directly to the House of Lords has been granted or, if any such extension has been granted, that the time so extended has expired; and
   (iii) that the time for any appeal to the Court of Appeal has expired; and
(*g*) that the provisions of section 10 (2) to (4) of the Act of 1973 do not apply or have been complied with,
the registrar shall make the decree absolute:

[Provided that if the notice is lodged more than 12 months after the decree nisi there shall be lodged with the notice an explanation in writing:—
(*a*) giving reasons for the delay;
(*b*) stating whether the parties have lived with each other since the decree nisi and, if so, between what dates; and
(*c*) stating whether the applicant being the wife has, or being the husband has reason to believe that his wife has, given birth to any child since the decree nisi and, if so, stating the relevant facts and whether or not it is alleged that the child is or may be a child of the family;
and the registrar may require the applicant to file an affidavit verifying the said explanation and may make such order on the application as he thinks fit or refer the application to a judge, but shall refer the application to a judge where it appears that there is or may be a child of the family born since decree nisi and no order has been made under section 41 (1) of the Act of 1973 in respect of that child.]

NOTES
Amendment   The words printed between square brackets in para (2) of this rule were substituted by the Matrimonial Causes (Amendment No 2) Rules 1985, SI 1985/1315, and the proviso to para (2) was substituted by the Matrimonial Causes (Amendment) Rules 1984, SI 1984/1511.
File an affidavit   In *Court v Court*, [1982] 2 All ER 531 it was held that the court might accept oral evidence from the applicant instead of an affidavit.
Cohabitation since the decree nisi   As to the effect of cohabitation after grant of decree nisi, see *Court v Court, supra* and *Savage v Savage*, [1982] 3 All ER 49.
Period prescribed for making the decree absolute   See the Matrimonial Causes (Decree Absolute) General Order 1972 (as amended), p 216, *ante*.
Section 12 of the Administration of Justice Act 1969   Halsbury's Statutes, 4th edn Vol 11, title Courts.

66. Decree absolute on application   (1) In the following cases an application for a decree nisi to be made absolute shall be made to a judge, that is to say—
(*a*) where, within six weeks after a decree nisi has been pronounced, the Queen's Proctor gives to the registrar and to the party in whose favour the decree was pronounced a notice that he requires more time to decide whether to show cause against the decree being made absolute and the notice has not been withdrawn, or

(*b*) where there are other circumstances which ought to be brought to the attention of the court before the decree nisi is made absolute.

Unless otherwise directed, the summons by which application is made (or, where the cause is pending in a divorce county court, notice of the application) shall be served on every party to the cause (other than the applicant) and, in a case to which sub-paragraph (*a*) applies, on the Queen's Proctor.

(2) An application by a spouse for a decree nisi pronounced against him to be made absolute may be made to a judge or the registrar, and the summons by which the application is made (or, where the cause is pending in a divorce county court, notice of the application) shall be served on the other spouse not less than four clear days before the day on which the application is heard.

(3) An order granting an application under this rule shall not take effect until the registrar has searched the court minutes and is satisfied as to the matters mentioned in rule 65 (2).

NOTES
Failure to serve a summons under para (2) of this rule renders a decree absolute voidable and not void; see *Batchelor v Batchelor,* [1983] 3 All ER 618.

67. Indorsement and certificate of decree absolute   (1) Where a decree nisi is made absolute, the registrar shall make an indorsement to that effect on the decree, stating the precise time at which it was made absolute.

(2) On a decree nisi being made absolute, the registrar shall—
(*a*) send to the petitioner and the respondent a certificate in Form 9 or 10, whichever is appropriate, authenticated by the seal of the divorce county court or registry from which it is issued, and
(*b*) if the cause is proceeding in a district registry or a divorce county court other than the divorce registry, send to the divorce registry an index card relating to the cause.

(3) A central index of decrees absolute shall be kept at the divorce registry and any person shall be entitled to require a search to be made therein, and to be furnished with a certificate of the result of the search, on payment of the prescribed fee.

(4) A certificate in Form 9 or 10 that a decree nisi has been made absolute shall be issued to any person requiring it on payment of the prescribed fee.

ANCILLARY RELIEF

68. Application by petitioner or respondent for ancillary relief   (1) Any application by a petitioner or by a respondent who files an answer claiming relief, for—
(*a*) an order for maintenance pending suit,
(*b*) a financial provision order,
(*c*) a property adjustment order,
shall be made in the petition or answer, as the case may be.

(2) Notwithstanding anything in paragraph (1), an application for ancillary relief which should have been made in the petition or answer may be made subsequently—
(*a*) by leave of the court, either by notice in Form 11 or at the trial, or
(*b*) where the parties are agreed upon the terms of the proposed order, without leave by notice in Form 11.

(3) An application by a petitioner or respondent for ancillary relief, not being an application which is required to be made in the petition or answer, shall be made by notice in Form 11.

NOTES
Leave of the court   Leave should not be refused where the applicant appears to have reasonable prospects of obtaining the relief claimed; see *Chaterjee v Chaterjee,* [1976] 1 All ER 719; also leave is required even though the form of relief claimed was not available at the date of the petition; see *Mckay v Chapman,* [1978] 2 All ER 548.

69. Application by guardian etc. for ancillary relief in respect of children Any of the following persons, namely—

(*a*) the guardian of any child of the family,

(*b*) any person who has the custody or the care and control of a child of the family under an order of the High Court or a divorce county court,

(*c*) a local authority to whom the care of a child of the family has been committed by an order made under section 43 of the Act of 1973,

(*d*) any person who has obtained leave to intervene in the cause for the purpose of applying for the custody of a child of the family,

(*e*) the Official Solicitor if appointed the guardian *ad litem* of a child of the family under rule 115, . . .

(*f*) any other person in whose care a child of the family is and who has obtained leave to intervene in the cause for the purpose of applying for ancillary relief in respect of that child. [and

(*g*) a child of the family who has been given leave to intervene in the cause for the purpose of applying for ancillary relief,]

may apply for an order for ancillary relief as respects that child by notice in Form 11.

NOTES
Amendment The words omitted where indicated in this rule were revoked and the words printed between squared brackets were inserted by the Matrimonial Causes (Amendment) Rules 1985, SI 1985/144.
Guardian ad litem As to appointment, see 24 Halsbury's Laws (4th edn) para 666.
Official Solicitor As to the duties of the Official Solicitor, see 10 Halsbury's Laws (4th edn) para 950.

70. Application in Form 11 or 12 Where an application for ancillary relief is made by notice in Form 11 or an application under rule 57 is made by notice in Form 12, the notice shall be filed—

(*a*) if the cause is pending in a divorce county court, in that court, or

(*b*) if the cause is pending in the High Court, in the registry in which it is proceeding,

and within four days after filing the notice the applicant shall serve a copy on the respondent to the application.

71. Application for ancillary relief after order of magistrates' court Where an application for ancillary relief is made while there is in force an order of a magistrates' court for maintenance of a spouse or child, the applicant shall file a copy of the order on or before the hearing of the application.

72. Children to be separately represented on certain applications. (1) Where an application is made to the High Court or a divorce county court for an order for a variation of settlement, the court shall, unless it is satisfied that the proposed variation does not adversely affect the rights or interests of any children concerned, direct that the children be separately represented on the application, either by a solicitor or by a solicitor and counsel, and may appoint the Official Solicitor or other fit person to be guardian *ad litem* of the children for the purpose of the application.

(2) On any other application for ancillary relief the court may give such a direction or make such appointment as it is empowered to give or make by paragraph (1).

(3) Before a person other than the Official Solicitor is appointed guardian *ad litem* under this rule there shall be filed a certificate by the solicitor acting for the children that the person proposed as guardian has no interest in the matter adverse to that of the children and that he is a proper person to be such guardian.

NOTES
Guardian ad litem: Official Solicitor See the notes to r 69.

73. General provisions as to evidence etc. on application for ancillary relief   (1) A petitioner or respondent who has applied for ancillary relief in his petition or answer and who intends to proceed with the application before a registrar shall, subject to rule 83, file a notice in Form 13 and within four days after doing so serve a copy on the other spouse.

[(2) Where an application is made for ancillary relief, not being an application to which rule 75 or rule 76A applies, the notice in Form 11 or 13, as the case may be, shall, unless otherwise directed, be supported by an affidavit by the applicant containing full particulars of his property and income, and stating the facts relied on in support of the application.

(3) Within 14 days after service of an affidavit under paragraph (2) or within such other time as the court may fix, the respondent to the application shall file an affidavit in answer containing full particulars of his property and income.]

NOTES
Amendment   Paras (2) and (3) of this rule were substituted by the Matrimonial Causes (Amendment No 2) Rules 1985, SI 1985/1315; para (2) had been previously amended by the Matrimonial Causes (Amendment No 2) Rules 1980, SI 1980/1484, and the Matrimonial Causes (Amendment) Rules 1984, SI 1984/1511; para (3) had been previously substituted by the Matrimonial Causes (Amendment) Rules 1984, SI 1984/1511.
File an affidavit   As to the standard form prepared by the registrars of the Divorce Registry see *Practice Direction*, [1973] 1 All ER 192.

74. Evidence on application for property adjustment or avoidance of disposition order . . .
[(1) Where an application is made for a property adjustment order or an avoidance of disposition order] the affidavit in support shall contain, so far as known to the applicant, full particulars—
   (*a*) in the case of an application for a transfer or settlement of property—
      (i) of the property in respect of which the application is made,
      (ii) of the property to which the party against whom the application is made is entitled either in possession or reversion;
   (*b*) in the case of an application for an order for a variation of settlement—
      (i) of all settlements, whether ante-nuptial or post-nuptial, made on the spouses, and
      (ii) of the funds brought into settlement by each spouse;
   (*c*) in the case of an application for an avoidance of disposition order—
      (i) of the property to which the disposition relates,
      (ii) of the persons in whose favour the disposition is alleged to have been made, and in the case of a disposition alleged to have been made by way of settlement, of the trustees and the beneficiaries of the settlement.
[[(2)] Where an application for a property adjustment order or an avoidance of disposition order relates to land, the notice in Form 11 or 13 shall identify the land and—
   (*a*) state whether the title to the land is registered or unregistered and, if registered, the Land Registry title number; and
   (*b*) give particulars, so far as known to the applicant, of any mortgage of the land or any interest therein.
[(3)] A copy of Form 11 or 13, as the case may be, together with a copy of the supporting affidavit, shall be served on the following persons as well as on the respondent to the application, that is to say—
   (*a*) in the case of an application for an order for a variation of settlement order, the trustees of the settlement and the settlor if living;
   (*b*) in the case of an application for an avoidance of disposition order, the person in whose favour the disposition is alleged to have been made;
and such other persons, if any, as the registrar may direct.
[(4)] In the case of an application to which paragraph (3) refers, a copy of Form 11 or 13, as the case may be, shall be served on any mortgagee of whom

particulars are given pursuant to that paragraph; any person so served may apply to the court in writing, within 14 days after service, for a copy of the applicant's affidavit.

[(5)] Any person who—

(a) is served with an affidavit pursuant to paragraph (4); or
(b) receives an affidavit following an application made in accordance with paragraph (5);

may, within 14 days after service or receipt, as the case may be, file an affidavit in answer.]

NOTES
Amendment   The words omitted where indicated in this rule were revoked and the first words printed between square brackets were substituted by the Matrimonial Causes (Amendment No 2) Rules 1985, SI 1985/1315. These rules also provided for the renumbering of paras (3)-(6) (which were themselves substituted by the Matrimonial Causes (Amendment) Rules 1984, SI 1984/1511 as paras (2)-(5).

75. Evidence on application for variation order   [On or after the filing of a notice in Form 11 in respect of an application for a variation order, the registrar may order the applicant to file an affidavit setting out full particulars of his property and income and the grounds on which the application is made [and rule 73 (3) shall apply to a respondent served with such an affidavit].]

NOTES
Amendment   This rule was substituted by the Matrimonial Causes (Amendment) Rules 1984, SI 1984/1511, and the words "and rule 73 (3) shall apply to a respondent served with such an affidavit" were subsequently inserted by the Matrimonial Causes (Amendment No 2) Rules 1985, SI 1985/1315.

76. Service of affidavit in answer or reply   (1) A person who files an affidavit for use on an application under rule 73, 74 or 75 shall at the same time serve a copy on the opposite party and, where the affidavit contains an allegation of adultery or of an improper association with a named person, then, unless otherwise directed, it shall be indorsed with a notice in Form 14 and a copy of the affidavit or of such part thereof as the court may direct, indorsed as aforesaid, shall be served on that person by the person who files the affidavit, and the person against whom the allegation is made shall be entitled to intervene in the proceedings by applying for directions under rule 77 (6) within eight days of service of the affidavit on him, inclusive of the day of service.

(2) Rule 49 (4) shall apply to a person served with an affidavit under paragraph (1) of this rule as it applies to a co-respondent.

[76A. [Information on application for consent order for financial relief]   (1) Subject to paragraphs (2) and (3) there shall be lodged with every application for a consent order under any of sections 23, 24, 24A or 27 of the Act of 1973 minutes of the order in the terms sought, indorsed with a statement signed by the respondent to the application signifying his agreement, and a statement of information which may be made in more than one document and shall include—

(a) the duration of the marriage, the age of each party and of any minor or dependent child of the family;
(b) an estimate in summary form of the approximate amount or value of the capital resources and net income of each party and of any minor child of the family;
(c) what arrangements are intended for the accommodation of each of the parties and any minor child of the family;
(d) whether either party has remarried or has any present intention to marry or to cohabit with another person;

(*e*) where the terms of the order provide for the transfer of property, a statement confirming that any mortgagee of that property has been served with notice of the application and that no objection to such a transfer has been made by the mortgagee within 14 days from such service; and

(*f*) any other especially significant matters.

(2) Where an application is made for a consent order varying an order for periodical payments paragraph (1) shall be sufficiently complied with if the statement of information required to be lodged with the application includes only the information in respect of net income mentioned in paragraph (1) (*b*), and an application for a consent order for interim periodical payments pending the determination of an application for ancillary relief may be made in like manner.

(3) Where the parties attend the hearing of an application for financial relief the court may dispense with the lodging of minutes of the order and a statement of information in accordance with paragraph (1) and give directions for—

(*a*) the order to be drawn, and

(*b*) the information which would otherwise be required to be given in such a statement to be given,

in such a manner as it sees fit.]

NOTES
Amendment   This rule was substituted by the Matrimonial Causes (Amendment No 2) Rules 1985, SI 1985/1315, having been previously inserted, together with the heading, by the Matrimonial Causes (Amendment) Rules 1984, SI 1984/1511.

77. Investigation by registrar of application for ancillary relief   (1) On or after the filing of a notice in Form 11 or 13 an appointment shall be fixed for the hearing of the application by the registrar.

(2) An application for an avoidance of disposition order shall, if practicable, be heard at the same time as any related application for financial relief.

(3) Notice of the appointment, unless given in Form 11 or 13 (as the case may be), shall be given by the registrar to every party to the application.

(4) Any party to an application for ancillary relief may by letter require any other party to give further information concerning any matter contained in any affidavit filed by or on behalf of that other party or any other relevant matter, or to furnish a list of relevant documents or to allow inspection of any such document, and may, in default of compliance by such other party, apply to the registrar for directions.

(5) At the hearing of an application for ancillary relief the registrar shall, subject to rules 78, 79 80 and 81, investigate the allegations made in support of and in answer to the application, and may take evidence orally and may [at any stage of the proceedings, whether before or during the hearing,] order the attendance of any person for the purpose of being examined or cross-examined, and . . . order the discovery and production of any document or require further affidavits.

(6) The registrar may at any stage of the proceedings give directions as to the filing and service of pleadings and as to the further conduct of the proceedings.

(7) Where any party to such an application intends on the day appointed for the hearing to apply only for directions, he shall file and serve on every other party a notice to that effect.

NOTES
Amendment   The words "at any stage of the proceedings, whether before or during the hearing," printed between square brackets in para (5) of this rule were inserted and the words omitted where indicated in that paragraph were revoked by the Matrimonial Causes (Amendment) Rules 1980, SI 1980/977.

78. Order on application for ancillary relief (1) Subject to rule 79, the registrar shall, after completing his investigation under rule 77, make such order as he thinks just.

(2) Pending the final determination of the application, the registrar may make an interim order upon such terms as he thinks just.

79. Reference of application to judge The registrar may at any time refer an application for ancillary relief, or any question arising thereon, to a judge for his decision.

80. Transfer of application for ancillary relief: general provisions. (1) If the court considers that an application for ancillary relief pending in a divorce county court gives rise to a contested issue of conduct of a nature which is likely materially to affect the question whether any, or what, order should be made therein and for that reason the application should be transferred to the High Court, the court shall, subject to paragraph (5) of this rule, make an order for transfer accordingly and, where an application is transferred to the High Court under this paragraph, it shall be heard by a judge of that Court.

(2) Where an application for ancillary relief is pending in a divorce county court and the parties to the proceedings consent to the making of an order for the transfer of the application to the High Court, an application for that purpose may be made to a judge or the registrar who shall, subject to paragraph (5) of this rule, order the transfer unless he is of opinion that it would not be justified.

(3) Without prejudice to paragraphs (1) and (2) of this rule, the court in which an application for ancillary relief is pending may, if it is a divorce county court, order the transfer of the application to the High Court or, if it is the High Court, order the transfer of the application of a divorce county court, where the transfer appears to the court to be desirable.

(4) The judge before hearing and the registrar before investigating under rule 77 an application for ancillary relief pending in a divorce county court shall consider whether the case is one in which the court should exercise its powers under paragraph (1) or (3) of this rule.

(5) In considering whether an application should be transferred from a divorce county court to the High Court or from the High Court to a divorce county court, the court shall have regard to all relevant considerations, including the nature and value of the property involved, the relief sought and the financial limits for the time being relating to the jurisdiction of county courts in other matters.

(6) Where a decree nisi has been pronounced in the cause, the court shall, before making an order for the transfer of the application to the High Court, consider whether it would be more convenient to transfer the cause to the High Court under rule 32.

(7) Where pursuant to the provisions of this rule an application for ancillary relief or the cause is transferred to the High Court, the court may, on making the order for transfer, give directions as to the further conduct of the proceedings.

(8) Where an application for ancillary relief is pending in a divorce county court, the court may order that the application be transferred to another divorce county court.

(9) Where an application for ancillary relief is pending in the High Court, the registrar of the registry in which the application is proceeding or a judge may order that the application be transferred to another registry.

(10) An order under paragraph (1), (3), (8) or (9) may be made by the court of its own motion or on the application of a party, but before making an order of its own motion the court shall give the parties an opportunity of being heard on the question of transfer and for that purpose the registrar may give the parties notice of a date, time and place at which the question will be considered.

81. Transfer to High Court for purpose of expedition   Without prejudice to the last foregoing rule, a judge or the registrar may, on the application of a party or of his own motion, order that an application for ancillary relief pending in a divorce county court shall be transferred to the High Court if he is of opinion that the transfer is desirable for the purpose of expediting the hearing of the application; but where a transfer is ordered under this rule, the costs of the application for ancillary relief shall be on the county court scale unless the judge or registrar who hears the application considers that a transfer would have been justified otherwise than for expediting the hearing and for that reason directs that the costs incurred after the transfer of the application shall be on the High Court scale.

82. Arrangements for hearing of application etc. by judge   (1) Where an application for ancillary relief or any question arising thereon has been referred or adjourned to a judge, the registrar shall fix a date and time for the hearing of the application or the consideration of the question and give notice thereof to all parties.

(2) The hearing or consideration shall, unless otherwise directed, take place in chambers.

(3) Where the application is proceeding in a divorce county court which is not a court of trial or is pending in the High Court and proceeding in a district registry which is not in a divorce town, the hearing or consideration shall take place at such court of trial or divorce town as in the opinion of the registrar is the nearest or most convenient.

For the purposes of this paragraph the Royal Courts of Justice shall be treated as a divorce town.

83. Request for periodical payments order at same rate as order for maintenance pending suit   (1) Where at or after the date of a decree nisi of divorce or nullity of marriage an order for maintenance pending suit is in force, the party in whose favour the order was made may, if he has made an application for an order for periodical payments for himself in his petition or answer, as the case may be, request the registrar in writing to make such an order (in this rule referred to as a "corresponding order") providing for payments at the same rate as those provided for by the order for maintenance pending suit.

(2) Where such a request is made, the registrar shall serve on the other spouse a notice in Form 15 requiring him, if he objects to the making of a corresponding order, to give notice to that effect to the registrar and to the applicant within 14 days after service of the notice in Form 15.

(3) If the other spouse does not give notice of objection within the time aforesaid, the registrar may make a corresponding order without further notice to that spouse and without requiring the attendance of the applicant or his solicitor, and shall in that case serve a copy of the order on the applicant as well as on the other spouse.

84. Application for order under section 37 (2) (a) of Act of 1973   (1) An application under section 37 (2) (*a*) of the Act of 1973 for an order restraining any person from attempting to defeat a claim for financial provision or other-wise for protecting the claim [may be made to the registrar].

(2) [Rules 79 and 82] shall apply, with the necessary modifications, to the application as if it were an application for ancillary relief.

NOTES
Amendment   The words in square brackets were substituted by SI 1978/527.

85. Exclusion of sections 99 and 101 of County Courts Act 1959   (1) Section 99 of the County Courts Act 1959 (satisfaction of money judgments) shall not apply to an order made on an application for ancillary relief in proceedings pending in a divorce county court.

(2) Section 101 of the County Courts Act 1959 (register of judgments and

orders) shall not apply to any decree or order made in proceedings pending in a divorce county court.

NOTES
Sections 99 and 101 of the County Courts Act 1959   Repealed, except for s 99 (3), by the County Courts Act 1984, s 148 (3), Sch 4, Halsbury's Statutes, 4th edn Vol 11, title County Courts, and replaced by ss 71, 73 of that Act, *ibid*. Section 99 (3) is prospectively repealed by the Administration of Justice Act 1982, s 75, Sch 9, Pt I, Halsbury's Statutes, 4th edn Vol 11, title Courts, as from a day to be appointed.

ENFORCEMENT OF ORDERS

86. Enforcement of order for payment of money, etc   (1) Before any process is issued for the enforcement of an order made in matrimonial proceedings for the payment of money to any person, an affidavit shall be filed verifying the amount due under the order and showing how that amount is arrived at.

In a case to which CCR Order 25, rule 13A (which deals with the execution of a High Court judgment in the county court), applies, the information required to be given in an affidavit under this paragraph may be given in the affidavit filed pursuant to that rule.

(2) Except with the leave of the registrar, no writ of *fieri facias* or warrant of execution shall be issued to enforce payment of any sum due under an order for ancillary relief or an order made under the provisions of section 27 of the Act of 1973 where an application for a variation order is pending.

(3) For the purposes of RSC Order 46, rule 6 (which deals with the issue of a writ of execution), the divorce registry shall be the appropriate office for the issue of a writ of execution to enforce an order made in matrimonial proceedings in the High Court which are proceeding in that registry.

(4) Where a warrant of execution has been issued to enforce an order made in matrimonial proceedings pending in the divorce registry which are treated as pending in a divorce county court, the goods and chattels against which the warrant has been issued shall, wherever they are situate, be treated for the purposes of section 138 of the County Courts Act 1959 as being out of the jurisdiction of the divorce registry.

(5) The Attachment of Earnings Act 1971 and Part VII of CCR Order 25 (which deals with attachment of earnings) shall apply to the enforcement of an order made in matrimonial proceedings in the divorce registry which are treated as pending in a divorce county court as if the order were an order made by such a court.

(6) Where an application under CCR Order 25, rule 2 (which deals with the oral examination of a judgment debtor), relates to an order made by a divorce county court—

(*a*) the application shall be made to such divorce county court as in the opinion of the applicant is nearest to the place where the debtor resides or carries on business, and

(*b*) there shall be filed with the application the affidavit required by paragraph (1) of this rule and, except where the application is made to the court in which the order sought to be enforced was made, a copy of the order shall be exhibited to the affidavit;

and accordingly paragraph (2) of the said rule 2 shall not apply.

NOTES
Section 138 of the County Courts Act 1959   Repealed by the County Courts Act 1984, s 148 (3), Sch 4, Halsbury's Statutes, 4th edn Vol 11, title County Courts, and replaced by s 103 of that Act, *ibid*.
Attachment of Earnings Act 1971   Halsbury's Statutes, 4th edn Vol 22, title Judgments and Execution (3rd edn Vol 41, p 791).

87. Judgment summonses: general provisions   (1) In this rule and in rules 88 and 89, unless the context otherwise requires—

"order" means an order made in matrimonial proceedings for the payment of money;

"judgment creditor" means a person entitled to enforce an order under section 5 of the Debtors Act 1869;

"debtor" means a person liable under an order;

"judgment summons" means a summons under the said section 5 requiring a debtor to appear and be examined on oath as to his means.

(2) An application for the issue of a judgment summons may be made—

(*a*) in the case of an order of the High Court, to the divorce registry, a district registry or a divorce county court, whichever in the opinion of the judgment creditor is most convenient,

(*b*) in the case of an order of a divorce county court, to whichever divorce county court is in the opinion of the judgment creditor most convenient,

having regard (in either case) to the place where the debtor resides or carries on business and irrespective of the court or registry in which the order was made.

(3) The application shall be made by filing a request in Form 16 together with the affidavit required by rule 86 (1) and, except where the application is made to the registry or divorce county court in which the order was made, a copy of the order shall be exhibited to the affidavit.

(4) A judgment summons shall not be issued without the leave of a judge if the debtor is in default under an order of commitment made on a previous judgment summons in respect of the same order.

(5) Every judgment summons shall be in Form 17 and shall be served on the debtor personally not less than 10 clear days before the hearing and at the time of service there shall be paid or tendered to the debtor a sum reasonably sufficient to cover his expenses in travelling to and from the court at which he is summoned to appear.

(6) CCR Order 25, rule 41 (which deals with the issue of successive judgment summonses), shall apply to a judgment summons, whether issued in the High Court or a divorce county court, as if for the words "within the district" in paragraph (2) of that rule there were substituted the words "at the address stated in Form 16".

(7) Where the order was made in a different registry or divorce county court from that in which the judgment summons is issued, the registrar of the first-mentioned registry or court shall, if so requested by the registrar of the registry or court in which the summons is issued, send him the file of the matrimonial proceedings for the purpose of the hearing of the summons.

(8) On the hearing of the judgment summons the judge may—

(*a*) where the order is for lump sum provision or costs, or

(*b*) where the order is for maintenance pending suit or other periodical payments and it appears to him that the order would have been varied or suspended if the debtor had made an application for that purpose,

make a new order for payment of the amount due under the original order, together with the costs of the judgment summons, either at a specified time or by instalments.

(9) If the judge makes an order of commitment, he may direct its execution to be suspended on terms that the debtor pays to the judgment creditor the amount due, together with the costs of the judgment summons, either at a specified time or by instalments, in addition to any sums accruing due under the original order.

(10) All payments under a new order or an order of commitment shall be made to the judgment creditor unless the judge otherwise directs.

(11) Where an order of commitment is suspended on such terms as are mentioned in paragraph (9)—

(*a*) all payments thereafter made under the said order shall be deemed to be made, first, in or towards the discharge of any sums from time to time accruing due under the original order and, secondly, in or towards the discharge of the debt in respect of which the judgment summons was issued and the costs of the summons;

(*b*) CCR Order 25, rule 54 (4) and (5) (which deal with an application for a further suspension), shall apply to the said order, whether it was made in the High Court or a divorce county court; and

(*c*) the said order shall not be issued until the judgment creditor has filed an affidavit of default on the part of the debtor.

NOTES
Section 5 of the Debtors Act 1869 Halsbury's Statutes, 4th edn Vol 4, title Bankruptcy and Insolvency.

88. Special provisions as to judgment summonses in the High Court   (1) RSC Order 38, rule 2 (3) (which enables evidence to be given by affidavit in certain cases), shall apply to a judgment summons issued in the High Court as if it were an originating summons.

(2) Witnesses may be summoned to prove the means of the debtor in the same manner as witnesses are summoned to give evidence on the hearing of a cause, and writs of subpoena may for that purpose be issued out of the registry in which the judgment summons is issued.

(3) Where the debtor appears at the hearing, the travelling expenses paid to him may, if the judge so directs, be allowed as expenses of a witness, but if the debtor appears at the hearing and no order of commitment is made, the judge may allow to the debtor, by way of set-off or otherwise, his proper costs, including compensation for loss of time, as upon an attendance by a defendant at a trial in court.

(4) Where a new order or an order of commitment is made, the registrar of the registry in which the judgment summons was issued shall send notice of the order to the debtor and, if the original order was made in another registry, to the registrar of that registry.

(5) An order of commitment shall be directed to the tipstaff, for execution by him, or to the registrar of the county court within the district of which the debtor is to be found, for execution by a deputy tipstaff.

(6) Unless the judge otherwise directs, the judgment creditor's costs of and incidental to the judgment summons shall be fixed without taxation in accordance with the following provisions—

(*a*) Subject to sub-paragraph (*c*), where the amount in respect of which the judgment summons is issued is paid before the hearing, there may be allowed—
 (i)   the court fees paid by the judgment creditor,
 (ii) any travelling expenses paid to the judgment debtor,
 (iii) the fee paid to the commissioner on the affidavit filed under rule 86 (1), and
 (iv) if the judgment creditor is represented by a solicitor, £3 in respect of the solicitor's charges.

(*b*) Where an order is made on the hearing and the judgment creditor is awarded costs, there may be allowed—
 (i)   the court fees paid by the judgment creditor,
 (ii) subject to paragraph (3), any travelling expenses paid to the judgment debtor,
 (iii) the fees paid to the commissioner on any necessary affidavit,
 (iv) if the judgment creditor is represented by a solicitor without counsel, £8 in respect of the solicitor's charges, and
 (v)   if the judgment creditor is represented by solicitor and counsel, £6 in respect of the solicitor's charges and £9 in respect of counsel's fees.

(*c*) Where the amount in respect of which the judgment summons is issued is paid too late to prevent the attendance of the judgment creditor or, as the case may be, his solicitor or counsel, at the hearing, the sums specified in sub-paragraph (*b*) may, if the judge so orders, be allowed instead of the sums specified in sub-paragraph (*a*).

(*d*) Where the costs of and incidental to a judgment summons are directed to be taxed, RSC Order 62 (which deals generally with the costs of proceedings in the High Court) shall have effect in relation to those costs with such modifications as may be necessary.

NOTES
Order; judgment creditor; debtor; judgment summons   See the definitions in r 87 (1).

89. Special provisions as to judgment summonses in divorce county courts   (1) CCR Order 25, rules 33, 37, 38, 39, 40 (4), 48, 49 (2), 54 (1) and (3) and 55 (which deal with the issue of a judgment summons in a county court and the subsequent procedure), shall not apply to a judgment summons issued in a divorce county court.

(2) CCR Order 25, rule 49 (1) (which relates to a judgment summons heard in a county court on the order of another court), shall apply to such a summons as if for the words "any court other than a county court" there were substituted the words "any other court".

(3) CCR Order 25, rule 54 (2) (which relates to the suspension of an order of commitment), shall apply to such a summons subject to rule 87 (9) and (10) of these Rules.

NOTES
Judgment summons: order   For definitions, see r 87 (1).

90. Committal and injunction   (1) Notwithstanding anything in RSC Order 52, rule 4 (1) (which requires an application for an order of committal to be made by motion), but subject to rule 6 of that Order (which, except in certain cases, requires such an application to be heard in open court), an application for an order of committal in matrimonial proceedings pending in the High Court shall be made by summons.

(2) Where no judge is conveniently available to hear the application, then, without prejudice to CCR Order 25, rule 70 (3) (which in certain circumstances gives jurisdiction to a county court registrar), an application for—
(*a*) the discharge of any person committed, or
(*b*) the discharge by consent of an injunction granted by a judge,
may be made to the registrar who may, if satisfied of the urgency of the matter and that it is expedient to do so, make any order on the application which a judge could have made.

(3) Where an order or warrant for the committal of any person to prison has been made or issued in matrimonial proceedings pending in the divorce registry which are treated as pending in a divorce county court, that person shall, wherever he may be, be treated for the purposes of section 161 of the County Courts Act 1959 as being out of the jurisdiction of the divorce registry; but if the committal is for failure to comply with the terms of an injunction, the order or warrant may, if a judge so directs, be executed by the tipstaff within any county court district.

(4) For the purposes of section 157 of the County Courts Act 1959 in its application to the hearing of matrimonial proceedings at the Royal Courts of Justice, the tipstaff shall be deemed to be an officer of the court.

NOTES
As to committal, see further 13 Halsbury's Laws (4th edn), paras 1205, 1206.
Sections 157 and 161 of the County Courts Act 1959   Repealed by the County Courts Act 1984, s 148 (3), Sch 4, Halsbury's Statutes, 4th edn Vol 11, title County Courts, and replaced by ss 118, 122 of that Act, *ibid*.

91. [Transfer] of county court order [to] High Court   [(1) Any person who desires the transfer to the High Court of any order made by a divorce county court in matrimonial proceedings except an order for periodical payments or for the recovery of arrears of periodical payments shall apply to the court *ex parte* by affidavit stating the amount which remains due under the order, and on the filing of the application the transfer shall have effect.]

(2) Where an order is so [transferred], it shall have the same force and effect and the same proceedings may be taken on it as if it were an order of the High Court.

NOTES
Amendment The words printed between square brackets in this rule and in the heading to this rule were inserted and substituted by the Matrimonial Causes (Amendment No 2) Rules 1985, SI 1985/1315.

APPLICATIONS RELATING TO CHILDREN

92. Custody, care and supervision of children (1) Subject to paragraph (2), an application for an order relating to the custody or education of a child, or for an order committing him to the care of a local authority under section 43 of the Act of 1973 or providing for his supervision under section 44 of that Act, shall be made to a judge.

[[(2) An application—
(*a*) which is unopposed or for an order in terms agreed between the parties; or]
(*b*) [for] access to a child where the other party consents to give access and the only question for determination is the extent to which access is to be given
. . .
may be made to the registrar who may make such order on the application as he see fit or may refer the application or a question arising thereon to a judge for his decision.]

(3) Without prejudice to the right of any other person entitled to apply for an order as respects a child, a guardian or step-parent of any child of the family and any other person who, by virtue of an order of a court, has the custody or control of such a child or his care or supervision in pursuance of section 43 or 44 of the Act of 1973 may, without obtaining leave to intervene in the cause, apply by summons or (where the cause is proceeding in a divorce county court) by notice under CCR Order 13, rule 1 (which deals with applications in the course of proceedings), for such an order as is mentioned in paragraph (1).

(4) On any application to a judge relating to the custody, care and control of, or access to, a child—
(*a*) neither the applicant nor the respondent shall be entitled to be heard in support of or, as the case may be, in opposition to the application unless he is available at the hearing to give oral evidence or the judge otherwise directs;
(*b*) the judge may refuse to admit any affidavit by any person (other than the applicant or respondent) who is or is proposed to be responsible for the child's care and upbringing or with whom the child is living or is proposed to live unless that person is available at the hearing to give oral evidence;
(*c*) a witness summons or writ of subpoena to compel the attendance of any such person as is mentioned in sub-paragraph (*b*) may issue in accordance with rule 41 without (in the case of a writ of subpoena) the production of the note from a judge or registrar mentioned in RSC Order 32, rule 7;
(*d*) no witness summons or writ of subpoena shall be issued to compel the attendance of any other witness except with the production of such a note and accordingly in any such case RSC Order 32, rule 7, shall apply, with such modifications as may be appropriate, to a witness summons as it applies to a writ of subpoena.

(5) Where an affidavit filed for use in proceedings relating to a child contains an allegation of adultery or of an improper association with a named person, then, unless otherwise directed, it shall be indorsed with a notice in Form 14 and a copy of the affidavit, or of such part thereof as the court may direct, indorsed as aforesaid, shall be served on that person by the person who files

the affidavit, and the person against whom the allegation is made shall be entitled to intervene in the proceedings by applying for directions under paragraph (7) within eight days of service of the affidavit on him, inclusive of the day of service.

(6) Rule 49 (4) shall apply to a person served with an affidavit under paragraph (5) of this rule as it applies to a co-respondent.

(7) The court may at any stage of the proceedings give directions as to the filing and service of pleadings and as to the further conduct of the proceedings [and may restore for hearing any application under paragraph (1) or (2) which it has adjourned].

(8) Unless otherwise directed, any order giving a parent custody or care and control of a child shall provide that no step (other than the institution of proceedings in any court) be taken by that parent which would result in the child being known by a new surname before he or she attains the age of 18 years or, being a female, marries below that age, except with the leave of a judge or the consent in writing of the other parent.

NOTES
Amendment   Para (2) of this rule was substituted, and the words "and may restore for hearing any application under paragraph (1) or (2) which it has adjourned" printed between square brackets in para (7) were inserted by the Matrimonial Causes (Amendment) Rules 1984, SI 1984/1511. The words omitted where indicated in para (2) were revoked and the words "An application — (*a*) which is unopposed or for an order in terms agreed between the parties; or" and the word "for" also in that paragraph were inserted by the Matrimonial Causes (Amendment No 2) Rules 1985, SI 1985/1315.

93. Further provisions as to orders under sections 43 and 44 of Act of 1973   (1) Before an order is made committing a child to the care of a local authority under section 43 of the Act of 1973, the registrar shall fix a date, time and place for the hearing of any representations by the local authority and shall send notice in Form 18 to the authority not less than 14 days before the date so fixed.

(2) If the local authority wish to represent that, in the event of an order being made under section 43, the court should make a financial provision order in favour of the child, the authority shall, within seven days after receipt of the notice, file an affidavit setting out such facts relevant to the property and income of the person against whom the financial provision order is sought as are known to the authority and shall at the same time serve a copy of the affidavit on that person.

(3) A person on whom a copy of the local authority's affidavit is served under paragraph (2), may, within four days after service, file an affidavit in answer and, if he does so, he shall at the same time serve a copy of the affidavit on the local authority.

(4) An application by a local authority or by an officer appointed under section 44 of the Act of 1973 for the variation or discharge of an order made under section 43 or 44 of that Act or for directions as to the exercise of the powers of the authority or officer under the order may, in case of urgency or where the application is unlikely to be opposed, be made by letter addressed to the court and the authority or officer shall, if practicable, notify any interested party of the intention to make the application.

(5) In proceedings under section 43 or 44 a local authority may be represented by their director of social services or other officer employed by them for the purposes of their social services functions under the Local Authority Social Services Act 1970.

NOTES
Local Authority Social Services Act 1970   Halsbury's Statutes, 4th edn Vol 25, title Local Government (3rd edn Vol 40, p 991 *et seq*).

94. Removal of child out of England and Wales   (1) In any cause begun by petition the petitioner or the respondent may apply at any time for an order prohibiting the removal of any child of the family under 18 out of England

and Wales without the leave of the court except on such terms as may be specified in the order.

Unless otherwise directed, an application under this paragraph may be made *ex parte*.

(2) Unless otherwise directed, any order relating to the custody or care and control of a child shall provide for the child not to be removed out of England and Wales without the leave of the court except on such terms as may be specified in the order.

(3) Subject to rule 97 (2), an application for leave to remove a child out of England and Wales shall be made to a judge except in the following cases when it may be made to the registrar, namely—

(*a*) where the application is unopposed, or

(*b*) where the application is for the temporary removal of the child [unless it is opposed on the ground that the child may not be duly returned]

[and the registrar may make such order on the application as he thinks fit or may refer the application or any question arising thereon to a judge for his decision].

NOTES

As to invoking Home Office assistance to prevent unauthorised removal from England and Wales of a minor subject to an order under this rule, see *Practice Note*, [1963] 3 All ER 66, and *Practice Direction*, [1973] 3 All ER 194.

Amendment   In para (3) the first group of words in square brackets were substituted, and the second group added, by SI 1978/527.

95. Reference to court welfare officer   (1) A judge or the registrar may at any time refer to a court welfare officer for investigation and report any matter arising in matrimonial proceedings which concerns the welfare of a child.

(2) Without prejudice to paragraph (1), any party to an application to which rule 92 applies may, before the application is heard, request the registrar to call for a report from a court welfare officer on any matter arising on the application, and if the registrar is satisfied that the other parties to the application consent and that sufficient information is available to enable the officer to carry out the investigation, the registrar may refer the matter to a court welfare officer for investigation and report before the hearing.

(3) Where a reference is made under this rule—

(*a*) the court welfare officer may inspect the court file;

(*b*) after completing his investigation, the officer shall file his report and the registrar shall thereupon notify the parties that they may inspect it and may bespeak copies on payment of the prescribed fee;

[(*c*) the officer may at any stage apply to the Registrar for directions as to the further conduct of the application or other proceedings relating to the matter referred to him; and]

[(*d*)] the registrar shall give notice to the officer of the date of hearing of the application or other proceeding.

NOTES

Amendment   In para (3) the words printed between square brackets were inserted and the original para (*c*) was changed to para (*d*) by the Matrimonial Causes (Amendment) Rules 1984, SI 1984/1511.

Report from court welfare officer   As to the seeking of such a report, see *Practice Direction*, [1972] 2 All ER 352.

96. Notice of other proceedings relating to children   If, while a cause is pending, proceedings relating to any child of the family are begun in the High Court, a county court or a magistrates' court, a concise statement of the nature of the proceedings shall forthwith be filed by the person beginning the proceedings or, if he is not a party to the cause, by the petitioner.

97. Transfer of proceedings relating to children   (1) Rules 80 and 81 shall, so far as applicable, apply to proceedings for the exercise of any power under

Part III of the Act of 1973 as they apply to an application for ancillary relief with the following modifications—

    (*a*) for the words "The judge before hearing and the registrar before investigating under rule 77 an application for ancillary relief" in paragraph (4) of rule 80 there shall be substituted the words "The court before hearing an application";

    (*b*) paragraph (5) of rule 80 shall be omitted.

    (2) Where it appears to the court that an application pending in a divorce county court for leave to remove a child permanently out of England and Wales is contested, or that any such proceedings pending in a divorce county court as are mentioned in paragraph (1) of this rule relate to a child who is a ward of court, the court shall order that the proceedings be transferred to the High Court:

    Provided that, if a decree nisi has been pronounced in the cause, the court shall, before ordering a transfer as aforesaid, consider whether it would be more convenient to transfer the cause to the High Court under rule 32.

    (3) where in any cause it appears to the court that an application pending in a divorce county court for a declaration under section 42 (3) of the Act of 1973 is contested, the court shall make an order that the cause be transferred to the High Court.

OTHER APPLICATIONS

[98. Application in case of failure to provide reasonable maintenance (1) Every application under section 27 of the Act of 1973 shall be made by originating application in Form 19.

    (2) The application may be made to any divorce county court and there shall be filed with the application an affidavit by the applicant and also a copy of the application and of the affidavit for service on the respondent.

    (3) The affidavit shall state—

    (*a*) the same particulars regarding the marriage, the court's jurisdiction, the children and the previous proceedings as are required in the case of a petition by sub-paragraphs (*a*), (*c*), (*d*), (*f*) and (*i*) of paragraph 1 of Appendix 2;

    (*b*) particulars of the respondent's failure to provide reasonable maintenance for the applicant, or, as the case may be, of the respondent's failure to provide, or to make a proper contribution towards, reasonable maintenance for the children of the family; and

    (*c*) full particulars of the applicant's property and income and of the respondent's property and income, so far as may be known to the applicant.

    (4) CCR Order 6, rule 4 (2) (*c*) (ii) and (*d*) (which deal with the service of an originating application), shall not apply but there shall be annexed to the copy of the application for service a copy of the affidavit referred to in paragraph (2) and a notice in Form 20 with Form 6.

    (5) Subject to paragraph (6), the respondent shall, within 14 days after the time allowed for sending the acknowledgement of service, file an affidavit stating—

    (*a*) whether the alleged failure to provide, or to make a proper contribution towards, reasonable maintenance is admitted or denied, and, if denied, the grounds on which he relies;

    (*b*) any allegation which he wishes to make against the applicant; and

    (*c*) full particulars of his property and income, unless otherwise directed.

    (6) Where the respondent challenges the jurisdiction of the court to hear the application he shall, within 14 days after the time allowed for sending the acknowledgment of service, file an affidavit setting out the grounds of the challenge; and the obligation to file an affidavit under paragraph (5) shall not arise until 14 days after the question of jurisdiction has been determined and the court has decided that the necessary jurisdiction exists.

    (7) Where the respondent's affidavit contains an allegation of adultery or of an improper association with a person named, the provisions of rule 76

(which deal with service on, and intervention by, a named person) shall apply.

(8) If the respondent does not file an affidavit in accordance with paragraph (5), the court may order him to file an affidavit containing full particulars of his property and income, and the registrar shall serve a copy of any such affidavit on the applicant.

(9) Within 14 days after being served with a copy of any affidavit filed by the respondent, the applicant may file a further affidavit as to means and as to any fact in the respondent's affidavit which is disputed, and in that case the registrar shall serve a copy on the respondent.

No further affidavit shall be filed without leave.]

NOTES
Amendment   this rule was substituted by the Matrimonial Causes (Amendment) Rules 1981, SI 1981/5.

[99. Investigation, etc. of applications under rule 98   Rules 77 to 82 (regarding the investigation of any application for ancillary relief, the making of an interim order, the reference of the application to the judge, the transfer of the application and the arrangements for the application to be heard) shall apply, with such modifications as may be appropriate, to an application for an order under section 27 of the Act of 1973 as if the application were an application for ancillary relief.]

NOTES
Amendment   This rule was substituted by the Matrimonial Causes (Amendment) Rules 1981, SI 1981/5.

100. Application for alteration of maintenance agreement during lifetime of parties (1) An application under section 35 of the Act of 1973 for the alteration of a maintenance agreement shall be made by originating application containing, unless otherwise directed, the information required by Form 21.

(2) The application may be filed in any divorce county court and may be heard and determined by the registrar.

(3) There shall be filed with the application an affidavit by the applicant exhibiting a copy of the agreement and verifying the statements in the application and also a copy of the application and of the affidavit for service on the respondent.

(4) CCR Order 6, rule 4 (2) (*c*) (ii) and (*d*) (which deal with the service of an originating application), shall not apply but there shall be annexed to the copy of the application for service a copy of the affidavit referred to in paragraph (2) and a notice in Form 20 with Form 6 attached.

(5) The respondent shall, within 14 days after the time limited for giving notice of intention to defend, file an affidavit in answer to the application containing full particulars of his property and income and, if he does not do so, the court may order him to file an affidavit containing such particulars.

(6) A respondent who files an affidavit under paragraph (5) shall at the same time file a copy which the registrar shall serve on the applicant.

101. Application for alteration of maintenance agreement after death of one party   (1) An application to the High Court under section 36 of the Act of 1973 for the alteration of a maintenance agreement after the death of one of the parties shall be made by originating summons in Form 22.

(2) The summons may be issued out of the divorce registry or any district registry.

(3) There shall be filed in support of the summons an affidavit by the applicant exhibiting a copy of the agreement and an official copy of the grant of representation to the deceased's estate and of every testamentary document admitted to proof and stating—

(*a*) whether the deceased died domiciled in England and Wales;
(*b*) the place and date of the marriage between the parties to the agreement and the name and status of the wife before the marriage;

(*c*) the name of every child of the family and of any other child for whom the agreement makes financial arrangements, and—
  (i) the date of birth of each such child who is still living (or, if it be the case, that he has attained 18), and the place where and the person with whom any such minor child is residing,
  (ii) the date of death of any such child who has died since the agreement was made;
(*d*) whether there have been in any court any, and if so what, previous proceedings with reference to the agreement or to the marriage or to the children of the family or to any other children for whom the agreement makes financial arrangements, and the date and effect of any order or decree made in such proceedings;
(*e*) whether there have been in any court any proceedings by the applicant against the deceased's estate under the Inheritance (Provision for Family and Dependants) Act 1975 or any Act repealed by that Act and the date and effect of any order made in such proceedings;
(*f*) in the case of an application by the surviving party, the applicant's means;
(*g*) in the case of an application by the personal representatives of the deceased, the surviving party's means, so far as they are known to the applicants, and the information mentioned in sub-paragraph (*a*), (*b*) and (*c*) of rule 102 (3);
(*h*) the facts alleged by the applicant as justifying an alteration in the agreement and the nature of the alteration sought;
(*i*) if the application is made after the end of the period of six months from the date from which representation in regard to the deceased's estate was first taken out, the grounds on which the court's permission to entertain the application is sought.

(4) There shall be lodged in the court office a copy of the summons and of the affidavit for service on every respondent.

(5) The registrar shall annex to every copy of the summons for service a copy of the affidavit in support and an acknowledgment of service in Form 6.

NOTES
Inheritance (Provisions for Family and Dependants) Act 1975   Halsbury's Statutes, 4th edn Vol 17, title Executors and Administrators.

102. Further proceedings on application under rule 101   (1) Without prejudice to his powers under RSC Order 15 (which deals with parties and other matters), the registrar may at any stage of the proceedings direct that any person be added as a respondent to an application under the last foregoing rule.

(2) RSC Order 15, rule 13 (which enables the court to make representation orders in certain cases), shall apply to the proceedings as if they were mentioned in paragraph (1) of the said rule 13.

(3) A respondent who is a personal representative of the deceased shall, within 14 days after the time limited for giving notice of intention to defend, file an affidavit in answer to the application stating—
(*a*) full particulars of the value of the deceased's estate for probate, after providing for the discharge of the funeral, testamentary and administration expenses, debts and liabilities payable thereout, including the amount of the estate duty and interest thereon;
(*b*) the person or classes of persons beneficially interested in the estate (giving the names and addresses of all living beneficiaries) and the value of their interests so far as ascertained, and
(*c*) if such be the case, that any living beneficiary (naming him) is a minor or a patient within the meaning of rule 112.

(4) If a respondent who is a personal representative of the deceased does not file an affidavit stating the matters mentioned in paragraph (3), the registrar may order him to do so.

(5) A respondent who is not a personal representative of the deceased may, within 14 days after the time limited for giving notice of intention to defend, file an affidavit in answer to the application.

(6) Every respondent who files an affidavit in answer to the application shall at the same time lodge a copy, which the registrar shall serve on the applicant.

103. Application of other rules to proceedings under section 35 or 36 of Act of 1973   (1) The following rules shall apply, with the necessary modifications, to an application under section 35 or 36 of the Act of 1973 as if it were an application for ancillary relief—

(*a*) in the case of an application under either section, rules 76 77 (4) to (7), 78 and 79;

(*b*) in the case of an application under section 35, rules 80 to 82; and

(*c*) in the case of an application under section 36, rules 80 (9) and (10) and 82 (1) and (2).

(2) Subject to paragraph (1) and to the provisions of rules 100 to 102, these Rules shall, so far as applicable, apply with the necessary modifications to an application under section 35 or section 36 (as the case may be) of the Act of 1973, as if the application were a cause, the originating application or summons a petition, and the applicant the petitioner.

104. Proceedings in High Court under section 17 of Act of 1882   (1) An application to the High Court under section 17 of the Act of 1882 shall be made by originating summons in Form 23, which may be issued out of the divorce registry or a district registry, and at the same time the application shall, unless otherwise directed, file an affidavit in support of the summons and shall lodge in the court office a copy of the summons and of the affidavit for service on the respondent and on any mortgagee mentioned therein pursuant to paragraph (3).

(2) The jurisdiction of a judge of the High Court under the said section 17 may be exercised by a registrar.

(3) Where the application concerns the title to or possession of land, the originating summons . . . shall—

(*a*) state, whether the title to the land is registered or unregistered, and, if registered, the Land Registry title number; and

(*b*) give particulars, so far as known to the applicant, of any mortgage of the land or any interest therein.

(4) The registrar shall annex to the copy of the originating summons for service on the respondent a copy of the affidavit in support and an acknowledgment of service in Form 6.

(5) Where particulars of a mortgage are given pursuant to paragraph (3), the registrar shall serve on the mortgagee a copy of the originating summons . . . and any person so served [may apply to the court in writing, within 14 days after service, for a copy of the affidavit in support, within 14 days of receiving such an affidavit may file an affidavit in answer and] shall be entitled to be heard on the application.

(6) No appearance need be entered to the originating summons.

(7) If the respondent intends to contest the application, he shall within 14 days after the time limited for giving notice to defend, file an affidavit in answer to the application setting out the grounds on which he relies and lodge in the court office a copy of the affidavit for service by the registrar on the applicant.

(8) If the respondent fails to file an affidavit under paragraph (7), the registrar may by order specify a time within which the respondent must, if he wishes to defend, file an affidavit, and may, on or after making such an order, direct that the respondent shall be debarred from defending the application unless an affidavit is filed within that time.

(9) The registrar may grant an injunction in proceedings under the said section 17 if, but only so far as, the injunction is ancillary or incidental to any relief sought in those proceedings.

(10) Without prejudice to paragraph (7) of this rule, RSC Order 28, rule 7 (which enables a counterclaim to be made in an action begun by originating summons), shall apply, with the necessary modifications, to a respondent to an originating summons under this rule as it applies to a defendent who has entered an appearance to an originating summons.

(11) Rules 77 (4) to (7), 78, 79 and 82 shall apply, with the necessary modifications, to an application under section 17 of the Act of 1882 as they apply to an application for ancillary relief.

(12) Subject to the provisions of this rule, these Rules shall, so far as applicable, apply, with the necessary modifications, to an application under section 17 of the Act of 1882 as if the application were a cause, the originating summons a petition, and the applicant the petitioner.

NOTES
Amendment   The words omitted where indicated in paras (3) and (5) of this rule were revoked, and the words printed between square brackets in para (5) were substituted by the Matrimonial Causes (Amendment) Rules 1984, SI 1984/1511.

105. Transfer of proceedings under section 17 of Act of 1882, etc.   (1) The court in which an application under section 17 of the Act of 1882 or section 36 of the Act of 1973 is pending may, if it is a county court, order the transfer of the application to the High Court or, if it is the High Court, order the transfer of the application to a divorce county court, where the transfer appears to the court to be desirable.

(2) In considering whether an application should be transferred under paragraph (1) from a county court to the High Court or from the High Court to a divorce county court, the court shall have regard to all relevant considerations, including the nature and value of the property involved, and, in the case of an application under section 36 of the Act of 1973, the limits for the time being of the jurisdiction of county courts under section 22 of the Inheritance (Provision for Family and Dependants) Act 1975.

(3) Rule 80 (10) shall apply to an order under paragraph (1) of this rule as it applies to an order under paragraph (3) of that rule.

NOTES
Section 22 of the Inheritance (Provision for Family and Dependants) Act 1975   Repealed by the Administration of Justice Act 1982, s 75, Sch 9, Part I, Halsbury's Statutes, 4th edn Vol 11, title Courts. As to the county court limit, see now the County Courts Act 1984, s 147, *ibid*, 4th edn Vol 11, title County Courts.

106. Exercise in divorce registry of county court jurisdiction under section 17 of Act of 1882, etc.   (1) Where any proceedings for divorce, nullity or judicial separation pending in the divorce registry are treated as pending in a divorce county court, an application under section 17 of the Act of 1882 by one of the parties to the marriage may be made to the divorce registry as if it were a county court.

(2) In relation to proceedings begun in the divorce registry under paragraph (1) of this rule or transferred from the High Court to the divorce registry under rule 105 (1).

   (*a*) section 4 of the Act of 1967 and the rules made thereunder shall have effect, with the necessary modifications, as they have effect in relation to proceedings begun in or transferred to the divorce registry under that section;

   (*b*) CCR Order 2, rule 13 (which relates to venue), and CCR Order 46, rule 11 (2) (which deals with reference to the registrar), shall not apply, and a registrar may exercise the jurisdiction conferred on a circuit judge by the said section 17 subject to the right of appeal conferred by CCR Order 37, rule 5.

107. [Proceedings under sections 1 and 9 of and Schedule 1 to the Matrimonial Homes Act 1983   (1) Subject to paragraph (2) below the jurisdiction of the High Court under sections 1 and 9 of the Matrimonial Homes Act 1983 may be exercised in chambers and the provisions of rule 104 (except paragraph (2)) shall apply, with the necessary modifications, to proceedings under those sections as they apply to an application under section 17 of the Act of 1882.

(2) Where a cause begun in accordance with rule 8 (1) is pending in the High Court an application under the said section 1 or section 9 by one of the parties shall be made as an application in that cause in accordance with rule 122 (1) (*b*).

(3). An application for an order under the said section 1 or section 9 (except, subject to paragraph (4) below, an order to oust the respondent from the dwelling house to which the application relates) may be heard and determined by a registrar.

(4) Where the applicant asks for an order under the said section 1 or section 9 terminating the respondent's rights of occupation and it appears to the registrar, on the ex parte application of the applicant, that the respondent is not in occupation of the dwelling house to which the application relates and his whereabouts cannot after reasonable inquiries be ascertained, the registrar may dispense with service of the summons on the respondent and hear and determine the application.

(5) The jurisdiction of the court under Schedule 1 to the said Act of 1983 may be exercised by a registrar.

(6) Where an application is made for an order under the said Schedule 1, notice of the application (or, in the High Court, the summons by which the application is made) shall be served on—

(*a*) the spouse entitled as mentioned in paragraph 1 of that Schedule to occupy the dwelling house to which the application relates, and

(*b*) the landlord of the dwelling house,

and any person so served shall be entitled to be heard on the application.

(7) Any court in which an application for an order under the said Schedule is pending may, if it is a divorce county court, order the transfer of the application to the High Court or another divorce county court or, if it is the High Court, order the transfer of the application to a divorce county court, where the transfer appears to the court to be desirable and, unless the court otherwise directs, a transfer of the cause in which the decree is sought or granted shall include a transfer of the application.]

NOTES
Amendment   This rule was substituted by the Matrimonial Causes (Amendment) Rules 1984, SI 1984/1511.
Sections 1 and 9 of and Schedule 1 to the Matrimonial Homes Act 1983   Halsbury's Statutes, 4th edn Vol 27, title Matrimonial Law (Pt 2) (3rd edn Vol 53, pp 658, 671, 673).

108. Proceedings in respect of polygamous marriage   (1) The provisions of this rule shall have effect where a petition, originating application or originating summons asks for matrimonial relief within the meaning of section 47 (2) of the Act of 1973 in respect of a marriage entered into under a law which permits polygamy (in this rule referred to as a polygamous marriage).

(2) The petition, orginating application or originating summons—

(*a*) shall state that the marriage in question is polygamous;

(*b*) shall state where or not there is, to the knowledge of the petitioner or applicant, any living spouse or his or hers additional to the respondent or, as the case may be, any living spouse of the respondent additional to the petitioner or applicant (in this rule referred to as an additional spouse); and

(*c*) if there is any additional spouse, shall give his or her full name and address and the date and place of his or her marriage to the petitioner or applicant or, as the case may be, to the respondent, or state, so far as may be applicable, that such information is unknown to the petitioner or applicant.

(3) Without prejudice to its powers under RSC Order 15 (which deals with parties) or CCR Order 15 (which deals with amendment), the court may order that any additional spouse be added as a party to the proceedings or be given notice of the proceedings or of any application in the proceedings for any such order as is mentioned in section 47 (2) (*d*) of the Act of 1973.

(4) Any order under paragraph (3) may be made at any stage of the proceedings and either on the application of any party or by the court of its own motion and, where an additional spouse is mentioned in a petition or an acknowledgement of service of a petition, the petitioner shall, on making any application in the proceedings or, if no previous application has been made in the proceedings, on making a request for directions for trial, ask for directions as to whether an order should be made under paragraph (3).

(5) Any person to whom notice is given pursuant to an order under paragraph (3) shall be entitled, without filing an answer or affidavit, to be heard in the proceedings or on the application to which the notice relates.

109. Application for declaration affecting matrimonial status   (1) Where, apart from costs, the only relief sought in any proceedings is a declaration with respect to a person's matrimonial status, the proceedings shall be begun by petition.

(2) The petition shall state—

(*a*) the names of the parties and the residential address of each of them at the date of presentation of the petition;

(*b*) the place and date of any ceremony of marriage to which the application relates;

(*c*) whether there have been any previous proceedings in any court in England and Wales or elsewhere between the parties with reference to the marriage or the ceremony of marriage to which the application relates or with respect to the matrimonial status of either of them, and, if so, the nature of the proceedings;

(*d*) all other material facts alleged by the petitioner to justify the making of the declaration and the grounds on which he alleges that the court has jurisdiction to make it;

and shall conclude with a prayer setting out the declaration sought and any claim for costs.

(3) Nothing in the foregoing provisions shall be construed—

(*a*) as conferring any jurisdiction to make a declaration in circumstances in which the court could not otherwise make it, or

(*b*) as affecting the power of the court to refuse to make a declaration notwithstanding that it has jurisdiction to make it.

(4) Where the petition is under section 45 of the Act of 1973 for a declaration as to the validity of a marriage, paragraphs (2) to (7) of rule 110 shall apply to the petition as they apply to a petition under that rule.

110. Application under section 45 of Act of 1973 for a declaration of legitimacy or legitimation   (1) A petition by which proceedings in the High Court are begun under section 45 of the Act of 1973 for a declaration of legitimacy or legitimation shall, in addition to stating the grounds on which the petitioner relies, set out the date and place of birth of the petitioner and the maiden name of his mother, and, if the petitioner is known by a name other than that which appears in the certificate of his birth, that fact shall be stated in the petition and in any decree made thereon.

(2) The petition shall be supported by an affidavit by the petitioner verifying the petition and giving particulars of every person whose interest may be affected by the proceedings and his relationship to the petitioner:

Provided that if the petitioner is under 16, the affidavit shall, unless otherwise directed, be made by his next friend.

(3) An affidavit for the purposes of paragraph (2) may contain statements of information or belief with the sources and grounds thereof.

(4) On filing the petition the petitioner shall issue and serve on the Attorney-General a summons for directions as to the person, other than the Attorney-General, who are to be made respondents to the petition.

(5) It shall not be necessary to serve the petition on the Attorney-General otherwise than by delivering a copy of it to him in accordance with sub-section (6) of the said section 45.

(6) The Attorney-General may file an answer to the petition within 21 days after directions have been given under paragraph (4) and no directions for trial shall be given until that period has expired.

(7) A respondent who files an answer shall at the same time lodge in the divorce registry as many copies of the answer as there are other parties to the proceedings and the registrar shall send one of the copies to each of those parties.

111. General provisions as to proceedings under rule 109 or 110　(1) Proceedings to which rule 109 or 110 relates shall be begun in the divorce registry.

(2) Where the proceedings are proceedings for a declaration as to the validity or subsistence of a marriage of the petitioner, paragraph 1 (*j*) of Appendix 2 shall apply to the petition as if it were a petition for divorce.

(3) Unless a judge otherwise directs, the trial of the proceedings shall take place at the Royal Courts of Justice.

(4) Subject to rules 109 and 110 and paragraphs (2) and (3) of this rule, these Rules shall, so far as applicable, apply, with the necessary modifications, to the proceedings as if they were a cause.

[111A. Application for leave under section 13 of the Act of 1984　(1) An application for leave to apply for an order for financial relief under Part III of the Act of 1984 shall be made *ex parte* by originating summons issued in Form 25 out of the divorce registry and shall be supported by an affidavit by the applicant stating the facts relied on in support of the application with particular reference to the matters set out in section 16 (2) of that Act.

(2) The affidavit in support shall give particulars of the judicial or other proceedings by means of which the marriage to which the application relates was dissolved or annulled or by which the parties to the marriage were legally separated and shall state, so far as is known to the applicant:—

(*a*) the names of the parties to the marriage and the date and place of the marriage;

(*b*) the occupation and residence of each of the parties to the marriage;

(*c*) whether there are any living children of the family and, if so, the number of such children and the full names (including surname) of each and his date of birth or, if it be the case, that he is over 18;

(*d*) whether either party to the marriage has remarried;

(*e*) an estimate in summary form of the approximate amount or value of the capital resources and net income of each party and of any minor child of the family;

(*f*) the grounds on which it is alleged that the court has jurisdiction to entertain an application for an order for financial relief under Part II of the said Act of 1984.

(3) The registrar shall fix a date and time for the hearing of the application by a judge in chambers and give notice thereof to the applicant.]

NOTES
Amendment　This rule was inserted by the Matrimonial Causes (Amendment No 2) Rules 1985, SI 1985/1315.

[111B. Application for an order for financial relief or an avoidance of transaction order under Part III of the Act of 1984　(1) An application for an order for financial relief under Part III of the Act of 1984 shall be made by originating summons issued in Form 26 out of the divorce registry and at the same time the applicant, unless otherwise directed, shall file an affidavit in support of the summons giving full particulars of his property and income.

(2) The applicant shall serve a sealed copy of the originating summons on the respondent and shall annex thereto a copy of the affidavit in support, if one has been filed, and a notice of proceedings and acknowledgement of service in Form 28, and rule 15 shall apply to such an acknowledgement of service as if the references in paragraph (1) of that rule to Form 6 and in paragraph (2) of that rule to eight days were, respectively, references to Form 28 and 31 days.

(3) Rules 72, 74, 75, 76A, 77(4), (6) and (7), and 82 (1) and (2) shall apply, with the necessary modifications, to an application for an order for financial relief under this rule as they apply to an application for ancillary relief made by notice in Form 11 and the court may order the attendance of any person for the purpose of being examined or cross-examined and the discovery and production of any document.

(4) An application for an interim order for maintenance under section 14 or an avoidance of transaction order under section 23 of the Act of 1984 may be made, unless the court otherwise directs, in the originating summons under paragraph (1) or by summons in accordance with rule 122 (1) and an application for an order under section 23 shall be supported by an affidavit, which may be the affidavit filed under paragraph (1), stating the facts relied on.

(5) If the respondent intends to contest the application he shall, within 28 days after the time limited for giving notice to defend, file an affidavit in answer to the application setting out the grounds on which he relies and shall serve a copy on the applicant.

(6) In respect of any application for an avoidance of transaction order the court may give such a direction or make such appointment as it is empowered to give or make by paragraph (3) and rule 74 shall apply, with the necessary modifications, to an application for an avoidance of transaction order as it applies to an application for an avoidance of disposition order.

(7) Where the originating summons contains an application for an order under section 22 of the Act of 1984 the applicant shall serve a copy on the landlord of the dwelling house and he shall be entitled to be heard on the application.

(8) An application for an order for financial relief under Part III of the Act of 1984 or for an avoidance of transaction order shall be determined by a judge.]

NOTES
Amendment   This rule was inserted by the Matrimonial Causes (Amendment No 2) Rules 1985, SI 1985/1315.

[111C. Application for an order under section 24 of the Act of 1984 preventing a transaction   (1) An application under section 24 of the Act of 1984 for an order preventing a transaction shall be made by originating summons issued in Form 27 out of the divorce registry and shall be supported by an affidavit by the applicant stating the facts relied on in support of the application.

(2) The applicant shall serve a sealed copy of the originating summons on the respondent and shall annex thereto a copy of the affidavit in support and a notice of proceedings and acknowledgement of service in Form 28, and rule 15 shall apply to such an acknowledgement of service as if the references in paragraph (1) of that rule to Form 6 and in paragraph (2) of that rule to eight days were, respectively, references to Form 28 and 31 days.

(3) If the respondent intends to contest the application he shall, within 28 days after the time limited for giving notice to defend, file an affidavit in answer to the application setting out the grounds on which he relies and shall serve a copy on the applicant.

(4) The application shall be determined by a judge.

(5) Rule 82 (save paragraph (3)) shall apply, with the necessary modifications, to the application as if it were an application for ancillary relief.]

NOTES
Amendment   This rule was inserted by the Matrimonial Causes (Amendment No 2) Rules 1985, SI 1985/1315.

DISABILITY

112. Person under disability must sue by next friend, etc.   (1) In this rule—
"patient" means a person who, by reason of mental disorder within the meaning of the Mental Health Act 1959, is incapable of managing and administering his property and affairs;
"person under disability" means a person who is a minor or a patient;
"Part VIII" means Part VIII of the Mental Health Act 1959.

(2) A person under disability may begin and prosecute any matrimonial proceedings by his next friend and may defend any such proceedings by his guardian *ad litem* and, except as otherwise provided by this rule, it shall not be necessary for a guardian *ad litem* to be appointed by the court.

(3) No person's name shall be used in any proceedings as next friend of a person under disability unless he is the Official Solicitor or the documents mentioned in paragraph (8) have been filed.

(4) Where a person is authorised under Part VIII to conduct legal proceedings in the name of a patient or on his behalf, that person shall, subject to paragraph (3), be entitled to be next friend or guardian *ad litem* of the patient in any matrimonial proceedings to which his authority extends.

(5) Where a person entitled to defend any matrimonial proceedings is a patient and there is no person authorised under Part VIII to defend the proceedings in his name or on his behalf, then—

(a) the Official Solicitor shall, if he consents, be the patient's guardian *ad litem*, but at any stage of the proceedings an application may be made on not less than four days' notice to the Official Solicitor, for the appointment of some other person as guardian;

(b) in any other case, an application may be made on behalf of the patient for the appointment of a guardian *ad litem*;

and there shall be filed in support of any application under this paragraph the documents mentioned in paragraph (8).

(6) Where a petition, answer, originating application or originating summons has been served on a person whom there is reasonable ground for believing to be a person under disability and no notice of intention to defend has been given, or answer or affidavit in answer filed, on his behalf, the party at whose instance the document was served shall, before taking any further step in the proceedings, apply to a registrar for directions as to whether a guardian *ad litem* should be appointed to act for that person in the cause, and on any such application the registrar may, if he considers it necessary in order to protect the interests of the person served, order that some proper person be appointed his guardian *ad litem*.

(7) No notice of intention to defend shall be given, or answer or affidavit in answer filed, by or on behalf of a person under disability unless the person giving the notice or filing the answer or affidavit—

(a) is the Official Solicitor or, in a case to which paragraph (5) applies, is the Official Solicitor or has been appointed by the court to be guardian *ad litem*; or

(b) in any other case, has filed the documents mentioned in paragraph (8).

(8) The documents referred to in paragraphs (3), (5) and (7) are—

(a) a written consent to act by the proposed next friend or guardian *ad litem*;

(b) where the person under disability is a patient and the proposed next friend or guardian *ad litem* is authorised under Part VIII to conduct the proceedings in his name or on his behalf, an office copy, sealed with the seal of the Court of Protection, of the order or other authorisation made or given under Part VIII; and

(c) except where the proposed next friend or guardian *ad litem* is authorised as mentioned in sub-paragraph (*b*), a certificate by the solicitor acting for the person under disability—

(i) that he knows or believes that the person to whom the certificate relates is a minor or patient stating (in the case of a patient) the grounds of his knowledge or belief, and where the person under disability is a patient, that there is no person authorised as aforesaid, and

(ii) that the person named in the certificate as next friend or guardian *ad litem* has no interest in the cause or matter in question adverse to that of the person under disability and that he is a proper person to be next friend or guardian.

NOTES
Guardian ad litem; Official Solicitor   See the note to r 69.
Mental Health Act 1959   Halsbury's Statutes, 4th edn Vol 28, title Mental Health (3rd edn Vol 25, p 42 *et seq*). Part VIII was repealed by the Mental Health Act 1983, s 148, Sch 6, Halsbury's Statutes, 4th edn Vol 28, title Mental Health (3rd edn Vol 53, pp 1168, 1188) and replaced by ss 93-113 of that Act, *ibid*, 4th edn Vol 28, title Mental Health (3rd edn Vol 53, p 1128 *et seq*). "Mental disorder" is defined in the Mental Health Act 1983, s 1 (2), Halsbury's Statutes, 4th edn Vol 28, title Mental Health (3rd edn Vol 53, p 1038).

113. Service on person under disability   (1) Where a document to which rule 14 applies is required to be served on a person under disability within the meaning of the last foregoing rule, it shall be served—

(*a*) in the case of a minor who is not also a patient, on his father or guardian or, if he has no father or guardian, on the person with whom he resides or in whose care he is;

(*b*) in the case of a patient—

(i) on the person (if any) who is authorised under Part VIII of the Mental Health Act 1959 to conduct in the name of the patient or on his behalf the proceedings in connection with which the document is to be served, or

(ii) if there is no person so authorised, on the Official Solicitor if he has consented under rule 112 (5) to be the guardian *ad litem* of the patient, or

(iii) in any other case, on the person with whom the patient resides or in whose care he is:

Provided that the court may order that a document which has been, or is to be, served on the person under disability or on a person other than one mentioned in sub-paragraph (*a*) or (*b*) shall be deemed to be duly served on the person under disability.

(2) Where a document is served in accordance with paragraph (1), it shall be indorsed with a notice in Form 24; and after service has been effected the person at whose instance the document was served shall, unless the Official Solicitor is the guardian *ad litem* of the person under disability or the court otherwise directs, file an affidavit by the person on whom the document was served stating whether the contents of the document were, or its purport was, communicated to the person under disability and, if not, the reasons for not doing so.

NOTES
Part VIII of the Mental Health Act 1959   Repealed by the Mental Health Act 1983, s 148, Sch 6, Halsbury's Statutes, 4th edn Vol 28, title Mental Health (3rd edn Vol 53, pp 1168, 1188) and replaced by ss 93-113 of that Act, *ibid*, 4th edn Vol 28, title Mental Health (3rd edn Vol 53, p 1128 *et seq*).

114. Petition for nullity on ground of insanity, etc.   (1) Where a petition for nullity has been presented on the ground that at the time of the marriage the respondent was suffering from mental disorder within the meaning of the Mental Health Act 1959 of such a kind or to such an extent as to be unfitted for marriage, then, whether or not the respondent gives notice of intention to defend, the petitioner shall not proceed with the cause without the leave of the registrar.

(2) The registrar by whom an application for leave is heard may make it a condition of granting leave that some proper person be appointed to act as guardian *ad litem* of the respondent.

NOTES
Guardian ad litem   See the note to r 69.
Mental disorder within the meaning of the Mental Health Act 1959   "Mental disorder" is now defined in the Mental Health Act 1983, s 1 (2), Halsbury's Statutes, 4th edn Vol 28, title Mental Health (3rd edn Vol 53, p 1038).

115. Separate representation of children   (1) Without prejudice to rule 72, if in any matrimonial proceedings it appears to the court that any child ought to be separately represented, the court may appoint—
(*a*) the Official Solicitor, or
(*b*) some other proper person,
(provided, in either case, that he consents) to be the guardian *ad litem* of the child, with authority to take part in the proceedings on the child's behalf.
(2) An order under paragraph (1) may be made by the court of its own motion or on the application of a party to the proceedings or of the proposed guardian *ad litem*.
(3) The court may at any time direct that an application be made by a party for an order under paragraph (1) and may stay the proceedings until the application has been made.
(4) Unless otherwise directed, on making an application for an order under paragraph (1) the applicant shall—
(*a*) unless he is the proposed guardian *ad litem*, file a written consent by the proposed guardian to act as such;
(*b*) unless the proposed guardian *ad litem* is the Official Solicitor, file a certificate by a solicitor that the proposed guardian has no interest in the proceedings adverse to that of the child and that he is a proper person to be guardian.
(5) Unless otherwise directed, a person appointed under this rule or rule 72 to be the guardian *ad litem* of a child in any matrimonial proceedings shall be treated as a party for the purpose of any provision of these Rules requiring a document to be served on or notice to be given to a party to the proceedings.

NOTES
As the the representation of a child whose paternity or whose status as a child of the family is in issue, see *Practice Direction*, [1965] 1 All ER 905.
Official Solicitor; guardian ad litem   See the notes to r 69.

PROCEDURE: GENERAL

116. Security for costs   CCR Order 3, rule 1 (which requires a person bringing proceedings to give security for costs if he is not resident in England or Wales), shall not apply to matrimonial proceedings in a county court.

117. Service out of England and Wales   (1) Any document in matrimonial proceedings may be served out of England and Wales without leave either in the manner prescribed by these Rules or—
(*a*) where the proceedings are pending in the High Court, in accordance with RSC Order 11, rules 5 and 6 (which relate to the service of a writ abroad); or
(*b*) where the proceedings are pending in a divorce county court, in accordance with CCR Order 8, rules 46 to 48 (which relate to the service of process abroad).
(2) Where the document is served in accordance with RSC Order 11, rules 5 and 6, those rules and rule 8 of the said Order 11 (which deals with the expenses incurred by the Secretary of State) shall have effect in relation to service of the document as they have in relation to service of notice of a writ, except that the official certificate of service referred to in paragraph (5) of the said rule 5 shall, if the document was served personally, show the server's means of knowledge of the identity of the person served.

(3) Where the document is served in accordance with CCR Order 8, rules 46 to 48, those rules shall have effect subject to the following modifications:—

(*a*) paragraph (5) of the said rule 46 (which in certain circumstances requires the document to be annexed to a notice of process) shall not apply;

(*b*) the document need not be served personally on the person required to be served so long as it is served in accordance with the law of the country in which service is effected;

(*c*) the official certificate or declaration with regard to service referred to in paragraph (6) of the said rule 48 shall, if the document was served personally, show the server's means of knowledge of the identity of the person served; and

(*d*) in paragraph (7) of the said rule 48 (which deals with the method of service through the court) the words "or in the manner in which default summonses are required to be served" shall be omitted.

(4) Where a petition is to be served on a person out of England and Wales, then—

(*a*) the time within which that person must give notice of intention to defend shall be determined having regard to the practice adopted under RSC Order 11, rule 4 (4) (which requires an order for leave to serve a writ out of the jurisdiction to limit the time for appearance), and the notice in Form 5 shall be amended accordingly;

(*b*) if the petition is to be served otherwise than in accordance with RSC Order 11, rules 5 and 6, or CCR Order 8, rules 46 to 48, and there is reasonable ground for believing that the person to be served does not understand English, the petition shall be accompanied by a translation, approved by the registrar, of the notice in Form 5, in the official language of the country in which service is to be effected or, if there is more than one official language of that country, in any one of these languages which is appropriate to the place where service is to be effected:

Provided that this sub-paragraph shall not apply in relation to a document which is to be served in a country in which the official language, or one of the official languages, is English.

(5) Where a document specifying the date of hearing of any proceedings is to be served out of England and Wales, the date shall be fixed having regard to the time which would be limited under paragraph (4) (*a*) for giving notice of intention to defend if the document were a petition.

118. Service by post   Where a document is required by these rules to be sent to any person, it shall, unless otherwise directed, be sent by post—

(*a*) if a solicitor is acting for him, to the solicitor's address;

(*b*) if he is acting in person, to the address for service given by him or, if he has not given an address for service, his last known address, but if in the opinion of the registrar the document would be unlikely to reach him if sent to that address, the registrar may dispense with sending the document to him.

119. Service of documents where no special mode of service prescribed   Unless otherwise directed, service of any document in matrimonial proceedings shall, if no other mode of service is prescribed or ordered, be effected—

(*a*) if a solicitor is acting for the person to be served, by leaving the document at, or sending it by post to, the solicitor's address;

(*b*) if the person to be served is acting in person, by delivering the document to him or by leaving it at, or sending it by post to, the address for service given by him or, if he has not given an address for service, his last known address:

Provided that where, in a case to which sub-paragraph (*b*) applies, it appears to the registrar that it is impracticable to deliver the document to the person to be served and that, if the document were left at, or sent by post to, the address specified in that sub-paragraph, it would be unlikely to reach him, the registrar may dispense with service of the document.

120. Service by bailiff in proceedings in divorce registry   Where, in any proceedings pending in the divorce registry which are treated as pending in a divorce county court, a document is to be served by bailiff, it shall be sent for service to the registrar of the county court within the district of which the document is to be served.

121. Proof of service by officer of court, etc.   (1) Where a petition is sent to any person by an officer of the court, he shall [record] the date of posting and the address written on the letter and shall sign the [record] and add the name of the court or registry to which he is attached.

(2) Without prejudice to section 186 of the County Courts Act 1959, [a record] made pursuant to paragraph (1) shall be evidence of the facts stated therein.

(3) Where the court has authorised notice by advertisement to be substituted for service and the advertisement has been inserted by some person other than the registrar, that person shall file copies of the newspapers containing the advertisement.

NOTES
Amendment   The words printed between square brackets in paras (1) and (2) of this rule were substituted by the Matrimonial Causes (Amendment) Rules 1984, SI 1984/1511.
Section 186 of the County Courts Act 1959   Repealed by the County Courts Act 1984, s 148 (3), Sch 4, Halsbury's Statutes, 4th edn Vol 11, title County Courts, and replaced by ss 133 (1) and (2) and 147 (1) of that Act.

122. Mode of making applications   (1) Except where these Rules, or any rules applied by these Rules, otherwise provide, every application in matrimonial proceedings—
  (*a*) shall be made to a registrar;
  (*b*) shall, if the proceedings are pending in the High Court, be made by summons or, if the proceedings are pending in a divorce county court, be made in accordance with CCR Order 13, rule 1 (which deals with applications in the course of proceedings).
(2) For the purposes of paragraph (1), CCR Order 13, rule 1, shall have effect as if for the period of one clear day mentioned in paragraph (1) (*b*) (i) of that rule (which prescribes the length of notice to be given) there were substituted a period of two clear days.

NOTES
See also, as to applications for injunctions, *Practice Direction*, [1972] 2 All ER 1360.

123. Place of hearing of application by judge   (1) Any application in a cause which is to be heard by a judge otherwise than at the trial may, except where these Rules otherwise provide or the court otherwise directs, be heard—
  (*a*) if the cause is pending in the High Court—
       (i) at the Royal Courts of Justice, or
       (ii) in the case of an application in a cause proceeding in a district registry, at the divorce town in which that registry is situated or, if it is not situated in a divorce town, then at the appropriate divorce town, or
       (iii) in the case of an application in a cause which has been set down for trial at a divorce town, at that town;
  (*b*) if the cause is pending in a divorce county court—
       (i) at that court if it is a court of trial and otherwise at the appropriate court of trial, or
       (ii) in the case of an application in a cause which has been set down for trial at a court of trial, at that court.

(2) In this rule "application" includes an appeal from an order or decision made or given by the registrar and "appropriate divorce town" and "appropriate court of trial" mean such divorce town or court of trial as in the opinion of the registrar is the nearest or most convenient.

124. Appeal from registrar in county court proceedings   (1) CCR Order 13, rule 1 (1) (*h*) (which enables the judge to vary or rescind an order made by the registrar in the course of proceedings), and CCR Order 37, rule 5 (which gives a right of appeal to the judge from a judgment or final decision of the registrar), shall not apply to an order or decision made or given by the registrar in matrimonial proceedings pending in a divorce county court, but any party may appeal from such an order or decision to a judge on notice filed within five days after the order or decision was made or given and served not less than two clear days before the day fixed for hearing of the appeal, which shall be heard in chambers unless the judge otherwise orders.

(2) Except so far as may be otherwise ordered, an appeal under paragraph (1) shall not operate as a stay of proceedings on the order or decision appealed against.

125. No notice of intention to proceed after year's delay   RSC Order 3, rule 6 (which requires a party to give notice of intention to proceed after a year's delay), shall not apply to any matrimonial proceedings pending in the High Court.

126. Filing of documents at place of hearing, etc.   Where the file of any matrimonial proceedings has been sent from one divorce county court or registry to another for the purpose of a hearing or for some other purpose, any document needed for that purpose and required to be filed shall be filed in the other court or registry.

127. Mode of giving notice   Unless otherwise directed, any notice which is required by these Rules to be given to any person shall be in writing and, if it is to be given by the registrar, shall be given by post.

128. Removal of proceedings to High Court under section 115 of County Courts Act 1959   (1) The power of the High court or a judge thereof under section 115 of the County Courts Act 1959 to order the removal into the High Court, otherwise than by order of certiorari, of matrimonial proceedings pending in a divorce county court may be exercised by a registrar of the divorce registry or by the registrar of any district registry having that county court within its district, except where a judge of the county court has refused to order the transfer of the proceedings to the High Court.

(2) Proceedings for the exercise of the power shall be begun by originating summons.

No appearance need be entered to the summons.

(3) Rule 129 (3) shall have effect in relation to an order for the removal of matrimonial proceedings into the High Court as if it were an order for the transfer of the proceedings to the High Court.

(4) Where by virtue of any provision of these Rules a county court has power to order that any proceedings pending in the court be transferred to the High Court, the High Court shall have power, exercisable in the like circumstances, to order the removal of the proceedings into the High Court, and the foregoing paragraphs of this rule shall apply as if the power conferred by this paragraph were conferred by the said section 115.

NOTES
Section 115 of the County Courts Act 1959   Repealed by the Supreme Court Act 1981, s 152 (4), Sch 7, Halsbury's Statutes, 4th edn Vol 11, title Courts.

129. Procedure on transfer of cause or application   (1) Where any cause or application is ordered to be transferred from one court or registry to another, the registrar of the first-mentioned court or registry shall, unless otherwise directed, give notice of the transfer to the parties and send a copy of the notice and the file of the proceedings to the registrar of the other court or registry.

(2) Any provision in these Rules, or in any order made or notice given pursuant to these Rules, for the transfer of proceedings between a divorce county court and the High Court shall, in relation to proceedings which, after the transfer, are to continue in the divorce registry, be construed—

    (*a*) in the case of a transfer from the High Court to a divorce county court, as a provision for the proceedings to be treated as pending in a divorce court, and

    (*b*) in the case of a transfer from a divorce county court to the High Court, as a provision for the proceedings no longer to be treated as pending in a divorce county court.

(3) Proceedings transferred from a divorce county court to the High Court pursuant to any provision in these Rules shall, unless the order of transfer otherwise directs, proceed in the registry nearest to the divorce county court from which they are transferred, but nothing in this paragraph shall prejudice any power under these Rules to order the transfer of the proceedings to a different registry.

MISCELLANEOUS

130. Inspection etc. of documents retained in court   (1) A party to any matrimonial proceedings or his solicitor or the Queen's Proctor or a person appointed under rule 72 or 115 to be the guardian *ad litem* of a child in any matrimonial proceedings may have a search made for, and may inspect and bespeak a copy of, any document filed or lodged in the court office in those proceedings.

(2) Except as provided by rules 48 (3) and 95 (3) and paragraph (1) of this rule, no document filed or lodged in the court office than a decree or order made in open court, shall be open to inspection by any person without the leave of the registrar, [or of the Lord Chancellor given with the concurrence of the President,] and no copy of any such document, or of an extract from any such document, shall be taken by, or issued to, any person without such leave.

NOTES

Amendment   The words "or of the Lord Chancellor given with the concurrence of the President," printed between square brackets in para (2) of this rule were inserted by the Matrimonial Causes (Amendment No 2) Rules 1985, SI 1985/1315.

131. Practice to be observed in district registries and divorce county courts   (1) The President and the senior registrar may, with the concurrence of the Lord Chancellor, issue directions for the purpose of securing in the district registries and the divorce county courts due observance of statutory requirements and uniformity of practice in matrimonial proceedings.

(2) RSC Order 63, rule 11 (which requires the practice of the Central Office to be followed in the district registries), shall not apply to matrimonial proceedings.

132. Revocations and savings   The rules specified in the Schedule to these Rules are hereby revoked, so, however, that—

    (*a*) the provisions of those rules specified in column 1 of the Schedule to the Matrimonial Causes Rules 1973 and in force immediately before 11th January 1974 shall continue to apply to such extent as may be necessary for giving effect to the transitional provisions and savings in the Act of 1973;

(b) the definition of "the Act of 1965", rules 101 (3) (e), 103 and 105 and Form 23 in the Matrimonial Causes Rules 1973 as in force immediately before 1st April 1976, shall continue to apply to proceedings under section 26 of the Matrimonial Causes Act 1965 or section 36 of the Act of 1973 relating to the estate of a person who died before that date.

NOTES
Matrimonial Causes Rules 1973 SI 1973/2016.
Section 26 of the Matrimonial Causes Act 1965 Repealed by the Inheritance (Provision for Family and Dependants) Act 1975, s 26 (2), Schedule, Halsbury's Statutes, 4th edn Vol 17, title Executors and Administrators.

SCHEDULE

NOTES
This Schedule specifies the rules revoked by r 132, *viz.*, the Matrimonial Causes Rules 1973, SI 1973/2016, and the amending SI 1974/2168, 1975/1359, and 1976/607 and 2166.

APPENDIX 1

NOTES
This Appendix contains the forms listed below; the relevant rules are specified against each form. The forms (of which Form 1 has been revoked by SI 1985/144, Form 5 has been amended by SI 1978/527, 1980/977 and 1984/1511, Form 6 has been amended by SI 1978/527 and 1980/977, Form 7 has been amended by SI 1985/1315, Forms 9 and 10 have been amended by SI 1984/1511, Form 11 has been amended by SI 1984/1511, 1985/144 and 1985/1315, Forms 19 and 20 have been respectively substituted and amended by SI 1981/5, and Forms 25, 26, 27 and 28 have been added by SI 1985/1315) are not reproduced in this work but will be found printed in Rayden on Divorce (14th Edn), p 3560 *et seq*. The prescribed forms are:-

Form
Form 1.   (*Revoked*).
Form 2.   General Heading of Proceedings.
Form 3.   Certificate with Regard to Reconciliation (r 12 (3)).
Form 4.   Statement as to Arrangements for Children (r 8 (2)).
Form 5.   Notice of Proceedings (r 12 (6)).
Form 6.   Acknowledgement of Service (r 14 (5)).
Form 7(a).   Affidavit by Petitioner in Support of Petition under Section 1 (2) (a) of Matrimonial Causes Act 1973 (r 33 (3)).
Form 7(b).   Affidavit by Petitioner in Support of Petition under Section 1 (2) (b) of Matrimonial Causes Act 1973 (r 33 (3)).
Form 7(c).   Affidavit by Petitioner in Support of Petition under Section 1 (2) (c) of Matrimonial Causes Act 1973 (r 33 (3)).
Form 7(d).   Affidavit by Petitioner in Support of Petition under Section 1 (2) (d) of Matrimonial Causes Act 1973 (r 33 (3)).
Form 7(e).   Affidavit by Petitioner in Support of Petition under Section 1 (2) (e) of Matrimonial Causes Act 1973 (r 33 (3)).
Form 8.   Notice of Application for Decree Nisi to be Made Absolute (r 65 (1)).
Form 9.   Certificate of Making Decree Nisi Absolute (Divorce) (r 67 (2)).
Form 10.   Certificate of Making Decree Nisi Absolute (Nullity) (r 67 (2)).
Form 11.   Notice of Application for Ancillary Relief (r 68 (2), (3)).
Form 12.   Notice of Application under Rule 57 (r 57).
Form 13.   Notice of Intention to Proceed with Application for Ancillary Relief Made in Petition or Answer (r 73 (1)).
Form 14.   Notice of Allegation in Proceedings for Ancillary Relief (rr 76 and 92 (5)).
Form 15.   Notice of Request for Periodical Payments Order at Same Rate as Order for Maintenance Pending Suit (r 83 (2)).
Form 16.   Request for Issue of Judgment Summons (r 87 (3)).
Form 17.   Judgment Summons (r 87 (5)).
Form 18.   Notice of Appointment to Hear Representations before Child is Committed to Care of Local Authority (r 93 (1)).
Form 19.   Originating Application on Ground of Failure to Provide Reasonable Maintenance (r 98 (1)).
Form 20.   Notice of Application under Rule 98 or 100 (rr 98 (3) and 100 (4)).
Form 21.   Originating Application for Alteration of Maintenance Agreement During Parties' Lifetime (r 100 (1)).
Form 22.   Originating Summons for Alteration of Maintenance Agreement after Death of One of the Parties (r 101 (1)).
Form 23.   Originating Summons under Section 17 of the Married Women's Property Act 1882 [or Section 1 of the Matrimonial Homes Act 1967] (r 104 (1)).
Form 24.   Notice to be Indorsed on Document Served in Accordance with Rule 113 (1) (r 113 (2)).
Form 25.   Ex Parte Originating Summons under Section 13 of the Matrimonial and Family Proceedings Act 1984 (r 111A (1)).
Form 26.   Originating Summons under Section 12 of the Matrimonial and Family Proceedings Act 1984 (r 111B (1)).

Form 27.   Originating Summons under Section 24 of the Matrimonial and Family Proceedings
            Act 1984 (r 111 c (1)).
Form 28.   Notice of Proceedings and Acknowledgement of Service (rr 111B (2) and 111C (2)).

APPENDIX 2

CONTENTS OF PETITION

(Unless otherwise directed under rule 9.)

1. Every petition other than a petition for jactitation of marriage or under rule 109 or 110
shall state:—
   (a) the names of the parties to the marriage and the date and place of the marriage;
   (b) the last address at which the parties to the marriage have lived together as husband and wife;
   (c) where it is alleged that the court has jurisdiction based on domicile—
     (i) the country in which the petitioner is domiciled, and
     (ii) if that country is not England and Wales, the country in which the respondent is
      domiciled;
   (d) where it is alleged that the court has jurisdiction based on habitual residence—
     (i) the country in which the petitioner has been habitually resident throughout the period
      of one year ending with the date of the presentation of the petition, or
     (ii) if the petitioner has not been habitually resident in England and Wales, the country
      in which the respondent has been habitually resident during that period,
    with details in either case, including the addresses of the places of residence at each place;
   (e) the occupation and residence of the petitioner and the respondent;
   (f) whether there are any living children of the family and, if so—
     (i) the number of such children and the full names (including surname) of each and his
      date of birth or (if it be the case) that he is over 18, and
     (ii) in the case of each minor child over the age of 16, whether he is receiving instruction
      at an educational establishment or undergoing training for a trade, profession or
      vocation;
   (g) whether (to the knowledge of the petitioner in the case of a husband's petition) [any other
    child now living] has been born to the wife during the marriage and, if so, the full names
    (including surname) of the child and his date of birth, or if it be the case, that he is over 18;
   (h) if it be the case, that there is a dispute whether a living child is a child of the family;
   (i) whether or not there are or have been any other proceedings in any court in England and
    Wales or elsewhere with reference to the marriage or to any children of the family or
    between the petitioner and the respondent with reference to any property of either or
    both of them and, if so—
     (i) the nature of the proceedings,
     (ii) the date and effect of any decree or order, and
     (iii) in the case of proceedings with reference to the marriage, whether there has been
      any resumption of cohabitation since the making of the decree or order;
   (j) whether there are any proceedings continuing in any country outside England and Wales
    which relate to the marriage or are capable of affecting its validity or subsistence and, if so—
     (i) particulars of the proceedings, including the court in or tribunal or authority before
      which they were begun,
     (ii) the date when they were begun,
     (iii) the names of the parties,
     (iv) the date or expected date of any trial in the proceedings, and
     (v) such other facts as may be relevant to the question whether the proceedings on the
      petition should be stayed under Schedule 1 to the Domicile and Matrimonial Proceed-
      ings Act 1973;
    and such proceedings shall include any which are not instituted in a court of law in that
    country, if they are instituted before a tribunal or other authority having power under
    the law having effect there to determine questions of status, and shall be treated as
    continuing if they have been begun and have not been finally disposed of;
   (k) [where the fact on which the petition is based is five years separation,] whether any, and
    if so what, agreement or arrangement has been made or is proposed to be made between
    the parties for the support of the respondent or, as the case may be, the petitioner or any
    child of the family;
   (l) in the case of a petition for divorce, that the marriage has broken down irretrievably;
   (m) the fact alleged by the petitioner for the purposes of section 1 (2) of the Act of 1973 or,
    where the petition is not for divorce or judicial separation, the ground on which relief is
    sought, together in any case with brief particulars of the individual facts relied on but not
    the evidence by which they are to be proved;
   (n) any further or other information required by such of the following paragraphs and by rule
    108 as may be applicable.
2. A petition for a decree of nullity under section 12 (e) or (f) of the Act of 1973 shall state
whether the petitioner was at the time of the marriage ignorant of the facts alleged.
3. A petition for a decree of presumption of death and dissolution of marriage shall state:—
   (a) the last place at which the parties to the marriage cohabited;
   (b) the circumstances in which the parties ceased to cohabit;
   (c) the date when and the place where the respondent was last seen or heard of; and
   (d) the steps which have been taken to trace the respondent.
4. A petition for jactitation of marriage shall state:—

(*a*) the residence and domicile of the petitioner and respondent at the date of the institution of the cause;

(*b*) the dates, times and places of the alleged boastings and assertions;

(*c*) that the alleged boastings and assertions are false and that the petitioner has not acquiesced therein.

5. Every petition shall conclude with:—

(*a*) a prayer setting out particulars of the relief claimed, including any claim for custody of a child of the family and any application for a declaration under section 42 (3) of the Act of 1973, any claim for costs and any application for ancillary relief which it is intended to claim;

(*b*) the names and addresses of the persons who are to be served with the petition, indicating if any of them is a person under disability;

[(*c*) the petitioner's address for service, which, where the petitioner sues by a solicitor, shall be the solicitor's name or firm and address. Where the petitioner, although suing in person, is receiving legal advice from a solicitor, the solicitor's name or firm and address may be given as the address for service if he agrees. In any other case, the petitioner's address for service shall be the address of any place in England or Wales at or to which documents for the petitioner may be delivered or sent.]

NOTES

Amendment The words "any other child now living" printed between square brackets in para 1 (*g*) of the Appendix were substituted, and the words "where the fact on which the petition is based is five years separation," printed between square brackets in para 1 (*k*) were inserted by the Matrimonial Causes (Amendment) Rules 1980, SI 1980/977. Para 5 (*c*) of this Appendix was substituted by the Matrimonial Causes (Amendment) Rules 1979, SI 1979/400.

Schedule 1 to the Domicile and Matrimonial Proceedings Act 1973 Halsbury's Statutes, 4th edn Vol 27, title Matrimonial Law (Pt 1) (3rd edn Vol 43, p 628).

MATRIMONIAL CAUSES (COSTS) RULES 1979
SI 1979/399

NOTES

Authority These rules were made on 28 March 1979 by the Supreme Court Rule Committee under the Matrimonial Causes Act 1973, s 50, Halsbury's Statutes, 4th edn Vol 27, title Matrimonial Law (Pt 3) (3rd edn Vol 43, p 600), which is prospectively repealed by the Matrimonial and Family Proceedings Act 1984, s 46 (3), Sch 3, *ibid*, 4th edn Vol 27, title Matrimonial Law (Pt 3) (3rd edn Vol 54 (1), pp 805, 812), as from a day to be appointed, and replaced by s 40 thereof.

Commencement 24 April 1979; see r 1.

Interpretation See r 2 and note thereto.

General These rules revoke and replace the Matrimonial Causes (Costs) Rules 1977, SI 1977/345, and the Matrimonial Causes (Costs) (Amendment) Rules 1978, SI 1978/922. They introduce a new composite scale ("the matrimonial scale") for the taxation of costs of matrimonial proceedings in the High Court, in a divorce county court or in both.

1. Citation and commencement   (1) These Rules may be cited as the Matrimonial Causes (Costs) Rules 1979 and, subject to paragraph (2), shall come into operation on 24th April 1979.

(2) These Rules shall apply to all bills of costs in respect of matrimonial proceedings lodged on or after 24th April 1979, save that for the period of two months thereafter a party entitled to require any costs to be taxed may prepare and lodge a bill in the form required before 24th April 1979 and shall be entitled to have a bill so lodged taxed as if these Rules had not been made.

2. Interpretation   (1) In these Rules, unless the context otherwise requires—

"the Act of 1974" means the Legal Aid Act 1974;

"ancillary application" means an application for one or more of the following forms of relief:—

(*a*) ancillary relief,

(*b*) an injunction,

(*c*) an order under section 37 (2) (*a*) of the Act of 1973 restraining any person from attempting to defeat a claim for financial relief or otherwise for protecting the claim, or

(*d*) an order relating to the custody or education of a child or an order committing him to the care of the local authority under section 43 of the Act of 1973 or providing for his supervision under section 44 of that Act, except where the order is made at or immediately after the trial of a cause or on a children appointment;

"children appointment" means an appointment fixed under rule 48 (4) of the principal rules, whether or not any such order as is mentioned in paragraph (*d*) above is made on the appointment;

"matrimonial proceedings" means any proceedings with respect to which rules may be made under section 50 of the Act of 1973;

"principal rules" means the Matrimonial Causes Rules 1977;

"the matrimonial scale" means the scale of costs set out in the Appendix to these Rules.

(2) These Rules shall be construed as one with the principal rules.

NOTES
Legal Aid Act 1974   Halsbury's statutes, 4th edn Vol 24, title Legal Aid (3rd edn Vol 44, pp 126, 1035).
Matrimonial Causes Rules 1977   SI 1977/344, p 216 *ante*.
Other expressions   Reference should also be made (by virtue of para (2)) to r 2 (2) of the Matrimonial Causes Rules 1977, SI 1977/344, p 216, *ante*, for the meaning of "the Act of 1973" (which refers to the Matrimonial Causes Act 1973, Halsbury's Statutes, 4th edn Vol 27, title Matrimonial Law (Pt 3) (3rd edn Vol 43, p 539 *et seq*)), "ancillary relief", "cause", "divorce county court", "matrimonial proceedings", "President", "registrar" and certain other expressions which occur in these rules. As respects the meaning of "registrar" see further r 3 (3) of these rules.
The letters "CCR" in these rules referred originally to the County Court Rules 1936 but the 1936 rules were revoked and replaced by the County Court Rules 1981, SI 1981/1687, printed in the County Court Practice; see also the title Courts (Part 5A (ii)) in the present work. The letters "RSC" refer to the Rules of the Supreme Court 1965, SI 1965/1776, printed in the Supreme Court Practice; see also the title Courts (Part 3B) in the present work.

3. Powers of registrars and others to tax costs   (1) Without prejudice to a taxing master's powers, under RSC Order 62, rule 12 (1), to tax the costs of or arising out of any cause or matter in the Supreme Court, including matrimonial proceedings, the costs of matrimonial proceedings may be taxed as follows:—

(*a*) a registrar of the divorce registry may tax the costs of any matrimonial proceedings in that registry which are treated as pending in a divorce county court, and, subject to paragraph (2) of this rule, any matrimonial proceedings in the High Court;

(*b*) a senior executive officer of the divorce registry, authorised in that behalf by the President, may tax the costs of any proceedings within the scope of that authority that a registrar of the divorce registry may tax under sub-paragraph (*a*);

(*c*) the registrar of a district registry may tax the costs of any matrimonial proceedings in the High Court which are proceeding in that registry;

(*d*) a registrar of a divorce county court may tax the costs of any matrimonial proceedings in that county court;

(*e*) a clerk of a divorce county court who is nominated by the Lord Chancellor for the purpose of this rule may tax the costs of any matrimonial proceedings in that county court if the amount of the bill of costs does not exceed £200;

Provided that—

(i) a clerk shall not have power to tax a solicitor's bill of costs in pursuance of an order under the Solicitors Act 1974 and

(ii) a party to the proceedings may, before the taxation begins, object to the bill or to any part of it being taxed by the clerk and, where any such objection is made, that bill or part shall be taxed by the registrar.

(2) Where the costs of or arising out of any matrimonial proceedings in a district registry are to be taxed, and the taxation thereof is within the powers of the registrar of that registry, those costs shall be taxed by him unless the Court otherwise directs.

(3) Unless the context otherwise requires, any reference in these Rules (except rule 10) or the principal rules, or in any rules applied by the principal rules, to "the registrar" in relation to the taxation or assessment of any costs

shall, where the costs are to be or have been taxed or assessed by a senior executive officer of the divorce registry or a clerk of a divorce county court in exercise of the powers conferred by (*b*) or (*e*) of paragraph (1), be construed as a reference to that officer or clerk.

NOTES
Solicitors Act 1974   Halsbury's Statutes, 4th edn Vol 41, title Solicitors (3rd edn Vol 44, p 1478 *et seq*).

4. Time for beginning proceedings for taxation   A party who is entitled to require the costs of any matrimonial proceedings to be taxed must begin proceedings for the taxation of those costs not later than three months after the judgment, final decree or order in the proceedings:

Provided that where a notice in Form 11 or 13 has been filed within three months after the judgment, final decree or order, the proceedings for taxation may be begun at any time within three months after the making of any order on the application to which the notice relates.

5. Procedure for taxation   (1) Where a party (in this rule called "the applicant") is entitled to require taxation of the costs of any matrimonial proceedings, he must within the time (if any) specified in rule 4 of these Rules, lodge his bill of costs, together with all necessary vouchers and papers and a copy of the bill for every party who is liable to pay the costs.

(2) The registrar shall send to every such party a copy of the bill together with a notice requiring him to inform the registrar, within 14 days after receipt of the notice, if he wishes to be heard on the taxation.

(3) If a party to whom notice has been given under paragraph (2) informs the registrar within the time limited that he wishes to be heard on the taxation, the registrar shall fix an appointment for the taxation and give not less than seven days' notice of the appointment to the applicant and that party.

(4) If no party to whom notice has been given under paragraph (2) informs the registrar within the time limited that he wishes to be heard on the taxation, the registrar, unless he directs otherwise, shall send to the applicant a notice specifying the amount which the registrar proposes to allow in respect of the bill and requiring him to inform the registrar, within 14 days after receipt of the notice, if he wishes to be heard on the taxation.

(5) If the applicant informs the registrar within the time limited that he wishes to be heard on the taxation, the registrar shall fix an appointment for the taxation and give seven days' notice of thé appointment to the applicant.

(6) The foregoing provisions of this rule shall apply to the taxation of a bill which is to be paid out of the legal aid fund under the Act of 1974 subject to the modification that, if the bill is not also to be taxed as between party and party, paragraph (2) shall not apply and paragraph (4) shall apply as if the words preceding "the registrar, unless he otherwise directs" were omitted.

(7) This rule shall not apply to the taxation of a solicitor's bill to his own client.

(8) In relation to matrimonial proceedings CCR Order 47, rule 38 (which deals with taxation between party and party), shall have effect as if paragraph (1) of this rule were substituted for paragraph (1) of that rule.

(9) Paragraphs (1), (2) and (3) of CCR Order 47, rule 40 (which deals with taxation between solicitor and client) shall not apply to the taxation of a bill to which this rule applies.

6. Scale of costs   (1) The taxation of the costs of matrimonial proceedings shall be in accordance with the matrimonial scale and the provisions of this rule.

(2) On a taxation of the costs of matrimonial proceedings in the High Court the amounts to be allowed shall be in accordance with *column* 1 of the matrimonial scale.

(3) On a taxation of the costs of matrimonial proceedings in a divorce county court the amounts to be allowed shall be in accordance with *column* 2 of the matrimonial scale, subject to paragraph (4) of this rule.

(4) On a taxation, whether as between party and party or on the common fund basis, of the costs of a cause for divorce or judicial separation which has proceeded throughout in a divorce county court, the amount to be allowed in respect of any item of costs opposite which a sum appears in *column* 3 of the matrimonial scale shall not be more or less than that sum unless the registrar, taking into consideration the factors mentioned in CCR Order 47, rule 16, is satisfied that, in the circumstances of the particular case, a higher or, as the case may be, a lower figure than the average for that item in a cause under the same provision of the Act of 1973 is justified.

(5) Except where the judge has otherwise directed and subject to paragraph (4), the registrar may, if he thinks fit, allow on taxation of the costs of matrimonial proceedings in a divorce county court such larger sums than those appearing in *column* 2 of the matrimonial scale as he thinks fit.

(6) Where, in respect of proceedings in a divorce county court, allowances are claimed under item 10 (*a*) of the matrimonial scale in more than one section of a bill of costs, the amounts to be allowed shall not, in total exceed the figure appearing in *column* 2, save where a larger sum is allowed in accordance with paragraph (5).

(7) Disbursements for which no allowance is made in the matrimonial scale shall be taxed and allowed, or disallowed, according to the principles applicable to the taxation of costs generally, contained in RSC Order 62, rules 28, 29 and 31.

7. Litigants in person   (1) Where in any matrimonial proceedings in a divorce county court any costs of a litigant in person are ordered to be paid by any other party to the proceedings or in any other way, then, unless the court otherwise orders, those costs shall be assessed by the registrar without taxation and in determining for the purposes of CCR Order 47, rule 2, the sum which would have been allowed if the work and disbursements to which the costs relate had been done or made by a solicitor on behalf of the litigant in person it shall be assumed that the solicitor would have elected that the costs be fixed under rule 8 of these Rules.

(2) An application for an assessment of costs under this rule shall be made within the time provided by rule 4 for beginning proceedings for a taxation.

8. Fixed costs   (1) In this rule—
"assisted person" means a person in respect of whom a certificate is in force under Part I of the Act of 1974 entitling him to legal aid in a cause or, as the case may be, an ancillary application from its commencement.

(2) Where in an undefended cause for divorce or judicial separation the petitioner is granted a decree with costs, whether as between party and party or not, the costs shall, if his solicitor so elects, be fixed in accordance with the provisions of this rule instead of being taxed:

Provided that where the petitioner is an assisted person for whom counsel has acted, the costs shall not be fixed unless counsel elects that the sums payable to him under section 10 (1) of the Act of 1974 shall be as provided by paragraph (4) (*b*).

(3) Where costs are fixed there shall be allowed as between party and party such of the following items as are applicable:

(*a*) in respect of solicitors' charges—
    (i) if counsel was briefed at the hearing,   £73.75,
    (ii) if counsel was not briefed at the hearing,   £84.75,
    (iii) if the case was dealt with in the special procedure list,   £60.50,
    (iv) where an order has been made for substituted service
        or to dispense with service,   £9.25,
    (vi) for any statement as to the arrangements for the
        children filed under rule 8 (2) of the principal rules,   £2.25,
(*b*) in respect of counsel's fees—
    (i) for settling the petition,   £5,

(ii) for giving written advice on evidence,   £3.75,
(iii) with brief on hearing,   £11,
    and where there is no local Bar in the court town or
    within 25 miles thereof, a further sum of   £ 4.50,
    and
(iv) on conference   £ 2.75;
(*c*) in respect of other disbursements, such amounts as would have been allowed if the costs had been taxed, not exceeding (i) in respect of inquiry agents' fees the sum of £27.50 and (ii) in respect of travelling expenses, or the alternative of agency correspondence, the sum of £3.25.

(4) If a petitioner whose costs are to be fixed is an assisted person, then, notwithstanding that the costs have been ordered to be taxed for the purposes of Schedule 2 to the Act of 1974—

(*a*) the sums payable under section 10 (1) of that Act to the solicitor acting for him shall be such of the fixed amounts specified in paragraph 3 (*a*) and (*c*) as are applicable, together with a further sum of £7.75;
(*b*) the sums payable under the said section 10 (1) to counsel acting for the assisted person shall be such of the fixed amounts specified in paragraph (3) (*b*) as are applicable.

(5) A petitioner's solicitor who elects to have his costs fixed under paragraph (2) shall give notice to that effect to the registrar, within the time specified in rule 4 of these Rules, stating the sums which he claims should be allowed, and he shall at the same time lodge all necessary papers and vouchers including, in a case to which the proviso to paragraph (2) applies, counsel's election under that proviso.

(6) Where the petitioner is allowed the costs of a children appointment, whether as between party and party or not, those costs shall, if the petitioner's solicitor so elects and no counsel's fee is claimed, be fixed at the sum of £6.50 together with such of the sums mentioned in paragraph 3 (*c*) as may be appropriate.

Paragraphs (4) (*a*) (except the words "together with a further sum of £7.75") and (5) shall apply, with the necessary modifications, in relation to the costs mentioned in this paragraph as they apply in relation to the costs mentioned in paragraph (2).

(7) Where an ancillary application is granted with costs, whether as between party and party or not, in the circumstances mentioned in any of the following items, then, unless the registrar otherwise directs, the costs shall, if the applicant's solicitor so elects, be fixed at the sum mentioned in that item instead of being taxed:—

(*a*) in respect of solicitor's charges—
    (i) where a consent order for ancillary relief has been made, £11;
    (ii) where any other consent order has been made and no affidavit has been filed by either party, £11;
    (iii) where an order has been made after a hearing at which the respondent has not appeared, £16.50;
    (iv) where an order has been made after a hearing at which the respondent has appeared, £27.50, or, if counsel is allowed, £24.25;
(*b*) in respect of counsel's fees where counsel is allowed—
    (i) in the circumstances mentioned in item (*a*) (ii) or (iii), £11;
    (ii) in the circumstances mentioned in item (*a*) (iv), £11, with brief and, in addition, £2.75 for any conference;
(*c*) in respect of other disbursements—
    (i) such of the items mentioned in paragraph (3) (*c*) as are appropriate;
    (ii) such amount as the Law Society certifies to be reasonable for conveying or transferring property pursuant to the order made on the application.

The proviso to paragraph (2), paragraph (4) (except the words "together with a further sum of £7.75") and paragraph (5) shall apply, with the necessary modifications, in relation to the costs mentioned in this paragraph as they apply in relation to the costs mentioned in paragraph (2).

(8) Except as provided in paragraphs (6) and (7), nothing in this rule shall apply to the costs of an ancillary application or a children appointment and accordingly the costs of any such application or appointment may be taxed notwithstanding anything done under paragraph (2).

(9) In addition to the amount of costs allowed under the foregoing paragraphs in respect of the supply of goods or services on which value added tax is chargeable there may be allowed as a disbursement a sum equivalent to value added tax at the appropriate rate on that amount.

9. Payment of costs   (1) Where in any matrimonial proceedings, the costs payable by a party are required to be taxed, they shall be payable within such time as may be specified in an order for payment made on or after the signature of the taxing officer's certificate of the result of the taxation and, unless otherwise directed, the time so specified shall be seven days after the making of the order.

(2) Where costs are to be assessed under rule 7 of these Rules, or are fixed under rule 8 of these Rules, instead of being taxed, paragraph (1) of this rule shall have effect as if for the reference to the taxing officer's certificate of the result of the taxation there were substituted a reference to the registrar's certificate of the amount of assessed or fixed costs allowed.

(3) Section 99 (3) of the County Courts Act 1959 shall not apply to costs payable under an order made in proceedings pending in a divorce county court.

NOTES
County Courts Act 1959, s 99 (3)   Halsbury's Statutes, 4th edn Vol 11, title County Courts (this provision is prospectively repealed by the Administration of Justice Act 1982, s 77, Sch 9, Pt I, *ibid*, 4th edn Vol 11, title Courts, as from a day to be appointed, and replaced by Pt VI thereof).

10. Personal liability of solicitor for costs   Paragraphs (1) to (6) of RSC Order 62, rule 8 (which deals with the personal liability of a solicitor for costs), shall apply to proceedings in a divorce county court as they apply to proceedings in the High Court, subject to the following modifications:—
- (*a*) "the Court" shall have the same meaning as in the County Court Rules 1936; and
- (*b*) "taxing officer" shall mean the registrar.

NOTES
County Court Rules 1936   These rules were revoked and replaced by the County Court Rules 1981, SI 1981/1687, printed in the County Court Practice; see also the title Courts (Part 5A (ii)) in the present work.

11. Modified application of the Rules of the Supreme Court   (1) RSC Order 62, rules 21 (3), 22, 23 and 24, shall not apply to the taxation of costs of matrimonial proceedings.

(2) The scale of costs contained in Appendix 2 to RSC Order 62 shall not apply to the taxation of costs of matrimonial proceedings and references to items and amounts in that scale made in RSC Order 62, rule 32 (2) and in paragraph 7 of Part VII of Appendix 2, shall be construed as references to items and amounts in the matrimonial scale.

12. Modified application of the county court rules   (1) For the purposes of CCR Order 47, rules 29 and 31, a witness or party who has attended the hearing of an ancillary application, or a party who has attended for medical examination under rule 30 of the principal rules, shall be treated as having attended the hearing of an action or matter.

(2) CCR Order 47, rules 17, 19, 21 (1), 23 and 29 (2) shall apply to matrimonial proceedings in a divorce county court as they apply to an action or matter in which the costs are on scale 2, 3 or 4.

13. County court proceedings in divorce registry   Paragraphs 1 to 4 of Schedule 2 to the Act of 1974 and section 74 (3) of the Solicitors Act 1974 shall apply to matrimonial proceedings in the divorce registry which are treated as pending in a divorce county court.

NOTES
Solicitors Act 1974, s 74 (3)   Halsbury's Statutes, 4th edn Vol 41, title Solicitors (3rd edn Vol 44, p 1548).

14. Savings   Where part of any matrimonial proceeding has taken place in the High Court, whether before or after the coming into operation of these Rules, nothing in these Rules or in section 76 of the County Courts Act 1959 shall authorise the costs of that part of the proceedings to be awarded or taxed on any of the county court scales.

NOTES
County Courts Act 1959, s 76   Repealed by the County Courts Act 1984, s 148 (3), Sch 4, Halsbury's Statutes, 4th edn Vol 11, title County Courts, and replaced by s 45 of that Act, *ibid*.

15. Revocation   The following Rules are hereby revoked—
    The Matrimonial Causes (Costs) Rules 1977 and
    The Matrimonial Causes (Costs) (Amendments) Rules 1978.

NOTES
Matrimonial Causes (Costs) Rules 1977   SI 1977/345.
Matrimonial Causes (Costs) (Amendments) Rules 1978   SI 1978/922.

APPENDIX
MATRIMONIAL SCALE
PART I
PREPARATION OF DOCUMENTS

ITEM	*Column 1*	*Column 2*	*Column 3*
1. Institution of proceedings:			
Preparing, presenting or issuing, filing and service of any petition, originating summons or originating application, notice of originating motion or other document instituting proceedings	£4—£14	£2.25—£8.75	£7.25
2. Interlocutory proceedings and proceedings in chambers:			
Preparing, issuing, filing and service of any summons or application, or notice of application or notice of motion (other than an originating motion), notice of interlocutory appeal or any writ or warrant of execution (including renewing)	£2—£14	£1.25—£3	
3. Other documents:			
Preparing (including where necessary filing, serving or delivering) any document not otherwise provided for, including:			
(*a*) Any document to obtain an order for substituted service or giving leave to serve out of the jurisdiction			
(*b*) Pleadings (other than pleadings instituting proceedings), particulars of pleadings, requests for such particulars, interrogatories, affidavits and lists of documents, notice to produce, admit			

	Column 1	Column 2	Column 3
or inspect documents, and amendments to any documents			
(c) Any other affidavit			
(d) Any brief to counsel or case to counsel to advise in writing or in conference			
(e) Any instructions to counsel to settle any document, except where an allowance for the preparation of that document is recoverable under items 1, 2 or 3			
for first 5 A4 pages	£3 per page or propor- tionately	£1.50 per page or propor- tionately	
for each A4 page thereafter	£1 (or prop- ortionately)	75p (or prop- ortionately)	

Note: Items 1, 2 and 3 include engrossing and one copy for service. Any additional copies required are to be charged under item 4. Items 3 (*d*) and (*e*) each include the company for counsel.

	Column 1	Column 2	Column 3
4. *Copy documents:*			
(a) Typed top copy			
A5 (quarto)	20p per page	20p per page	
A4 (foolscap)	35p per page	35p per page	
A3 (brief)	50p per page	50p per page	
(b) Photographic, printed and carbon copies			
A5 and A4	15p per page	15p per page	
A3	30p per page	30p per page	

PART II
COUNSEL'S FEES

ITEM

5. *Counsel's fees in connection with proceedings in a divorce county court:*

	Column 1	Column 2	Column 3
(a) With brief on trial of cause or matter or on hearing of ancillary application .	—	£5.50—£30	
With brief on trial of cause or matter			£11
(b) For each day or part of day on which trial of cause or matter or hearing of ancillary application is continued after the first day	—	£3—£15	
(c) With any other brief (including a brief on a children appointment)	—	£3—£8	
(d) Where there is no local Bar in the court town or within 25 miles thereof, if in the opinion of the registrar the maximum fee allowable with the brief is insufficient, a further fee may be allowed, not exceeding for each day on which the trial or hearing takes place .	—	£4.50	
(e) On conference in chambers or elsewhere for each half hour or part thereof	—	£2.75	

	Column 1	Column 2	Column 3
and for leading counsel for each half hour or part thereof	—	£4	
(*f*) For settling any document	—	£3—£8	
For settling a petition			£5
(*g*) For advising in writing	—	£3—£8	£3.75

Note: 1. Fees to counsel are not to be allowed unless the payment of them is vouched by the signature of counsel.

Note: 2. For the purpose of item 5 (*d*) there shall be deemed to be a local Bar only in such places as may from time to time be specified in a certificate of the General Council of the Bar published in their Annual Statement. Item 5 (*d*) is not to be allowed in any court within 25 miles of Charing Cross.

PART III
ATTENDANCES

ITEM

6. Interlocutory attendances:

Attending the hearing of any summons or other application (including attending for directions only) at court or in chambers or elsewhere, attending to obtain appointment to examine witnesses and attending on such appointment.

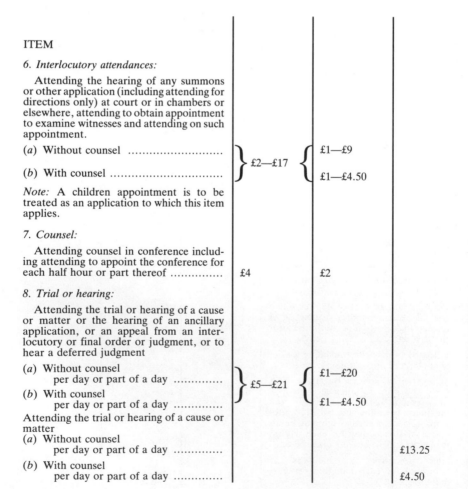

	Column 1	Column 2	Column 3
(*a*) Without counsel		£1—£9	
(*b*) With counsel		£1—£4.50	

(Column 1 bracket: £2—£17)

Note: A children appointment is to be treated as an application to which this item applies.

7. Counsel:

Attending counsel in conference including attending to appoint the conference for each half hour or part thereof ....

	Column 1	Column 2	Column 3
	£4	£2	

8. Trial or hearing:

Attending the trial or hearing of a cause or matter or the hearing of an ancillary application, or an appeal from an interlocutory or final order or judgment, or to hear a deferred judgment

	Column 1	Column 2	Column 3
(*a*) Without counsel per day or part of a day		£1—£20	
(*b*) With counsel per day or part of a day		£1—£4.50	

(Column 1 bracket: £5—£21)

Attending the trial or hearing of a cause or matter

	Column 1	Column 2	Column 3
(*a*) Without counsel per day or part of a day			£13.25
(*b*) With counsel per day or part of a day			£4.50

	Column 1	Column 2	Column 3
9. *Accountant General:*			
Attendances at his office or at the Bank of England for any necessary purpose, including the preparation of any relevant document or certificate	Discretionary	—	—

PART IV
PREPARATION FOR TRIAL

ITEM

	Column 1	Column 2	Column 3
10. (a) *Instructions for trial or hearing* of any cause or matter, whatever the mode of trial or hearing, or for the hearing of any appeal	Discretionary	Such sum as is fair and reasonable in all the circumstances not exceeding £57.25	Special procedure cases, £47.25; other cases, £53
(b) *Instructions for hearing* of an ancillary application	Discretionary	Discretionary	

Note to item 10.
This item is intended to cover:—
(a) The doing of any work not otherwise provided for and which was properly done in preparing for a trial, hearing, appeal or ancillary application, or before a settlement of the matters in dispute, including—
(i) *The client:* taking instructions to sue, defend, counter-claim, appeal or oppose etc; attending upon and corresponding with client;
(ii) *Witnesses:* interviewing and corresponding with witnesses and potential witnesses, taking and preparing proofs of evidence and, where appropriate, arranging attendance at Court, including issue of subpoena or witness summons;
(iii) *Expert evidence:* obtaining and considering reports or advice from experts and plans, photographs and models; where appropriate arranging their attendance at Court, including issue of subpoena or witness summons;
(iv) *Inspections:* inspecting any property or place material to the proceedings;
(v) *Searches and inquiries:* making searches in the Public Record Office and elsewhere for relevant documents, searches in the Companies Registry and similar matters;
(vi) *Other parties:* attending upon and corresponding with other parties or their solicitors;
(vii) *Discovery:* perusing, considering or collating documents for affidavit or list of documents; attending to inspect or produce for inspection any documents required to be produced or inspected by order of the court or otherwise;

	Column 1	Column 2	Column 3
(viii) *Documents:* consideration of pleadings, affidavits, cases and instructions to and advice from counsel, any law involved and any other relevant documents, including collating; (ix) *Negotiations:* work done in connection with negotiations with a view to settlement; (x) *Agency:* correspondence with and attendance upon or other work done by London or other agents; (xi) *Notices:* preparation and service of miscellaneous notices, including notices to witnesses to attend court.			
(*b*)The general care and conduct of the proceedings.			

Note: The sums sought under each subparagraph (i) to (xi) of paragraph (*a*) should be shown separately against each item followed by the total of all items under paragraph (*a*); the sum charged under paragraph (*b*) should be shown separately; and the total of the items under (*a*) and (*b*) should then follow.

PART V
TAXATION OF COSTS

ITEM

		Column 1	Column 2	Column 3
11.	(*a*) *Taxation:* Preparing bill of costs and copies and attending to lodge; attending taxation; vouching and completing bill; paying taxing fee and lodging for certificate or order ..	Discretionary	Discretionary	
	(*b*) *Review:* Preparing and delivering objections to decision of taxing officer on taxation, or answers to objections, including copies for service and lodging, considering opponent's answers or objections, as the case may be, attending hearing of review	Discretionary	Discretionary	

MATRIMONIAL CAUSES FEES ORDER 1980
SI 1980/819

NOTES
Authority   This order was made on 12 June 1980 by the Lord Chancellor and the Treasury under the Matrimonial Causes Act 1973, s 51, Halsbury's Statutes, 4th edn Vol 27, title Matrimonial Law (Pt 3) (3rd edn Vol 43, p 602), which is prospectively repealed by the Matrimonial and Family Proceedings Act 1984, s 46 (3), Sch 3, *ibid*, 4th edn Vol 27, title Matrimonial Law (Pt 3) (3rd edn Vol 54 (1), pp 805, 812), as from a day to be appointed, and replaced by s 41 thereof; and also under the Public Offices Fees Act 1879, ss 2, 3, Halsbury's Statutes, 4th edn Vol 30, title Money (Pt 1) (3rd edn Vol 22, p 855).
Commencement   7 July 1980; see art 1.
Amendment   This order is printed as amended by the Matrimonial Causes Fees (Amendment) Order 1981, SI 1981/1515, the Matrimonial Causes Fees (Amendment) Order 1982, SI 1982/1708, and the Matrimonial Causes Fees (Amendment) Order 1983, SI 1983/1686.

General   This order revokes the Matrimonial Causes Fees Order 1975, SI 1975/1346, and sets out in separate schedules the fees to be taken: (*a*) in all matrimonial proceedings; (*b*) in matrimonial proceedings pending in divorce county courts; and (*c*) in matrimonial proceedings pending in the High Court.

1.   This Order may be cited as the Matrimonial Causes Fees Order 1980 and shall come into operation on 7th July 1980.

2.   In this Order—
  (*a*) A rule referred to by number only means the rule so numbered in the Matrimonial Causes Rules 1977, and a form referred to by number only means the form so numbered in Appendix 1 to those Rules;
  (*b*) expressions used in the Matrimonial Causes Rules 1977 have the same meaning as in those Rules;
  (*c*) references to County Court Orders Rules and Forms are to Orders and Rules in the County Court Rules 1936 and to the Forms in the Appendix thereto.

NOTES
Matrimonial Causes Rules 1977   SI 1977/344, p 216 *ante*.
County Court Rules 1936   Revoked and replaced by the County Court Rules 1981, SI 1981/1687, printed in the County Court Practice; see also the title Courts (Part 5A (ii)) in the present work.

3.   (1) Subject to Article 4, fees shall be taken as follows:—
  (*a*) the fees specified in Schedule 1 to this Order shall be taken in all matrimonial proceedings, whether in the High Court or a divorce county court;
  (*b*) the fees specified in Schedule 2 shall be taken in matrimonial proceedings pending in a divorce county court (including matrimonial proceedings in the divorce registry which are treated as pending in a divorce county court and not in the High Court);
  (*c*) the fees specified in Schedule 3 shall be taken in matrimonial proceedings pending in the High Court.
  (2) Any fees made payable by this Order shall be taken in cash.

4.   No fee shall be payable under this Order where the person who would otherwise be liable to pay it is in receipt of—
  (*a*) legal advice and assistance under section 1 of the Legal Aid Act 1974 in connection with the proceeding; or
  (*b*) a supplementary pension or an allowance under Part I of the Supplementary Benefits Act 1976; or
  [(*c*) a family income supplement under section 1 of the Family Income Supplements Act 1970,
unless he is also in receipt of legal aid under Part I of the Legal Aid Act 1974 in connection with the same proceeding.]

NOTES
Amendment   The words printed between square brackets in this article were substituted by the Matrimonial Causes Fees (Amendment) Order 1981, SI 1981/1515.
Legal Aid Act 1974, Part I   Halsbury's Statutes, 4th edn Vol 24, title Legal Aid (3rd edn Vol 44, p 1036 *et seq*).
Supplementary Benefits Act 1976, Part I   Halsbury's Statutes, 4th edn Vol 40, title Social Security (3rd edn Vol 46, p 1048 *et seq*).
Family Income Supplements Act 1970, s 1   *Ibid,* 4th edn Vol 40, title Social Security (3rd edn Vol 40, p 1080).

5.   Where it appears to the Lord Chancellor that the payment of any fee prescribed by this Order would, owing to the exceptional circumstances of the particular case, involve undue hardship he may reduce or remit the fee in that case.

6.   The Matrimonial Causes Fees Order 1975 is hereby revoked save as to any fee due or payable before the commencement of this Order.

NOTES
Matrimonial Causes Fees Order 1975   SI 1975/1346.

SCHEDULE 1

FEES TO BE TAKEN IN ALL MATRIMONIAL PROCEEDINGS

Fee

1. **Commencement of Proceedings**
    (i) On filing an originating application or on sealing an originating summons   £10
    (ii) On presenting any petition other than a second petition presented with leave granted under rule 12 (4) ....   [£40]

2. **Applications for Ancillary Relief**
    On filing a notice in Form 11 or 13 except where the terms of any agreement as to the order which the court is to be asked to make are set out in the notice .   [£12]

3. **Searches**
    On making a search in the central index of decrees absolute kept at the Divorce Registry £2

4. **Copies of Documents**
    For a copy of any document, or for examining a plain copy and marking it as an office copy, per page:
    (*a*) Typewritten 50p
    (*b*) Carbon or photographic 25p

Note
This fee is payable whether or not the copy is issued as an office copy.

5. ...

6. **Taxation**
    (i) On the taxation of costs or expenses ....   For every £1
    No fee is payable where costs are allowed without taxation. The Registrar   or part thereof
    may in any case before taxation require a deposit of the amount of fees   allowed 5p
    which would be payable if the bill or the expenses were allowed by him
    at the full amount thereof.
    (ii) On the withdrawal of a bill of costs which has been lodged for taxation, such fee (not exceeding the amount which would have been payable under Fee No. 6 (i) if the bill had been allowed in full) as may be reasonable having regard to the amount of work done in the court office.

7. **Registration of Maintenance Orders**
    On an application for a maintenance order to be—
    (*a*) registered under the Maintenance Orders Act 1950 or the Maintenance Orders Act 1958 ....   £2
    (*b*) sent abroad for enforcement under Maintenance Orders (Reciprocal Enforcement) Act 1972 ....   £10

NOTES
Amendment   The figures "£40" and "£12" printed between square brackets in this Schedule were substituted by the Matrimonial Causes Fees (Amendment) Order 1982, SI 1982/1708, and the words omitted where indicated were revoked by the Matrimonial Causes Fees (Amendment) Order 1981, SI 1981/1515.
Maintenance Orders Act 1950   For procedure for registration see s 17 of that Act, Halsbury's Statutes, 4th edn Vol 27, title Matrimonial Law (Pt 3) (3rd edn Vol 17, p 283).
Maintenance Orders Act 1958   For registration of orders see s 2 of that Act, Halsbury's Statutes, 4th edn Vol 27, title Matrimonial Law (Pt 3) (3rd edn Vol 17, p 295).
Maintenance Orders (Reciprocal Enforcement) Act 1972   For application for order to be sent abroad for enforcement see s 2 of that Act, *ibid*, 4th edn Vol 27, title Matrimonial Law (Pt 3) (3rd edn Vol 42, p 718).

SCHEDULE 2

FEES TO BE TAKEN IN MATRIMONIAL PROCEEDINGS PENDING IN DIVORCE COUNTY COURTS

Fee

1. **Service**
    On a request for service by bailiff of any document except—   [£5]
    (*a*) an order in County Court Form 179
    (*b*) an interpleader summons under an execution
    (*c*) an order made under section 23 of the Attachment of Earnings Act 1971.
    [(*d*) an order made under County Court Order 25, Rule 3 (4)]
    This fee is payable in respect of each person to be

served, but in respect of a document not requiring
personal service only one fee is payable in respect of
two or more persons to be served at the same address.
This fee is not payable where service is to be effected
by post pursuant to County Court Order 8, Rule 8 (2).

Fee

2.   Enforcement
On an application for enforcement of a judgment or
order—
(i)   by the issue of a warrant of execution against
goods except a warrant to enforce payment of a
court fee or an order for payment of a fine ....

For every £1 or part thereof the
amount for which the warrant is-
sues 15p. Minimum fee, [£5]
Maximum fee, [£30]

(ii) (*a*) By an application for an order for the attendance of a judgment debtor or any other person under County Court Order 25, [Rule 3 or
4] ....   [£6]
. . . .

(iii) By entering garnishee proceedings ....   [£10]

Notes
(1)   Garnishee proceedings under County Court Order 27 may not be taken in the Divorce Registry
. . .

(iv) By an application for an order charging the land
or securities of a judgment debtor £5
(v)   By the issue of a judgment summons ....   [£10]
. . .

3.   Sale
(i)   For removing or taking steps to remove goods
to a place of deposit ....   The reasonable expenses thereof

Note
This fee includes the reasonable expenses of feeding and caring for any animals.
(ii) For advertising a sale by public auction pursuant
to section 132 of the County Courts Act 1959 .   The reasonable expenses thereof.
(iii) For the appraisement of goods ....   5p in the £1 of the appraised value.
(iv) For the sale of goods (including advertisements,
catalogues, sale and commission and delivery of
goods) ....

15p in the £1 on the amount
realised by the sale or such other
sum as the registrar may consider
to be justified in the circumstances.

(v)   Where no sale takes place by reason of an execution being withdrawn, satisfied or stopped .....

(*a*) 10p in the £1 on the value of
the goods seized, the value to
be the appraised value where
the goods have been appraised
or such other sum as the registrar may consider to be justified in the circumstances, and
in addition;
(*b*) any sum payable under Fee 3
(i), (ii) or (iii).

NOTES
Amendment   The second, fifth, and seventh amendments printed between square brackets in
this Schedule were made and the words omitted where indicated were revoked by the Matrimonial
Causes Fees (Amendment) Order 1982, SI 1982/1708. All other amendments to this Schedule
were made by the Matrimonial Causes Fees (Amendment) Order 1983, SI 1983/1686.
Attachment of Earnings Act 1971, s 23   Halsbury's Statutes, 4th edn Vol 22, title Judgments
and Execution (3rd edn Vol 41, p 813).
County Courts Act 1959, s 132   Repealed by the County Courts Act 1984, s 148 (3), Sch 4,
Halsbury's Statutes, 4th edn Vol 11, title County Courts, and replaced by s 97 of that Act, *ibid*.

SCHEDULE 3

FEES TO BE TAKEN IN MATRIMONIAL PROCEEDINGS
PENDING IN THE HIGH COURT

Fee
1.   Examination
On the examination of a witness before trial £5

2.	Enforcement	Fee
	(i) On sealing a writ of execution	[£6]
	(ii) On an application to examine a judgment debtor before an officer of the court	[£6]
	(iii) On the issue of a judgment summons	[£10]
	. . .	
	(v) On an application for a garnishee order *nisi*, a charging order *nisi* or for the appointment of a receiver by way of equitable execution	[£10]
	(vi) On issuing a certified copy of a judgment or order for the purposes of Part II of the Administration of Justice Act 1920 or the Foreign Judgments (Reciprocal Enforcement) Act 1933	£10

3.	Registration of Maintenance Orders	
	On an application to transmit a maintenance order abroad under the Maintenance Orders (Facilities for Enforcement) Act 1920	£10

NOTES
Amendment   The first and fourth amendments printed between square brackets in this Schedule were made and the words omitted where indicated were revoked by the Matrimonial Causes Fees (Amendment) Order 1982, SI 1982/1708. All other amendments to this Schedule were made by the Matrimonial Causes Fees (Amendment) Order 1983, SI 1983/1686.
Administration of Justice Act 1920, Part II   Halsbury's Statutes, 4th edn Vol 22, title Judgments and Execution (3rd edn Vol 6, p 353 *et seq*).
Foreign Judgments (Reciprocal Enforcement) Act 1933   Halsbury's Statutes, 4th edn Vol 22, title Judgments and Execution (3rd edn Vol 6, p 365 *et seq*).
Maintenance Orders (Facilities for Enforcement) Act 1920   Halsbury's Statutes, 4th edn Vol 27, title Matrimonial Law (Pt 3) (3rd edn Vol 17, p 272 *et seq*). This Act is prospectively repealed by the Maintenance Orders (Reciprocal Enforcement) Act 1972, s 22 (2) (*a*), *ibid*, 4th edn Vol 27, title Matrimonial Law (Pt 3) (3rd edn Vol 42, p 738, as from a day to be appointed.

MAGISTRATES' COURTS (MATRIMONIAL PROCEEDINGS) RULES 1980
SI 1980/1582

NOTES
Authority   These rules were made on 17 October 1980 by the Lord Chancellor under the Justices of the Peace Act 1949, s 15, which has now been repealed. The rules now have effect as if made under the Magistrates' Courts Act 1980, s 144, Halsbury's Statutes, 4th edn Vol 27, title Magistrates (3rd edn Vol 50 (2), p 1565).
Commencement   1 February 1981; see r 1 (1).
Interpretation   See r 2.
General   These rules, which revoke and replace the Magistrates' Courts (Matrimonial Proceedings) Rules 1960, SI 1960/2229, prescribe the forms of applications, orders and notices in connection with matrimonial proceedings in magistrates' courts, specify respondents for certain applications and additional courts to have jurisdiction in certain cases, and provide for transfer of applications between courts.

1. Citation, commencement and revocation   (1) These Rules may be cited as the Magistrates' Courts (Matrimonial Proceedings) Rules 1980 and shall come into operation on 1st February 1981.

(2) Subject to rule 2 (4) below, the Magistrates' Courts (Matrimonial Proceedings) Rules 1960 are revoked.

NOTES
Magistrates' Courts (Matrimonial Proceedings) Rules 1960   SI 1960/2229.

2. Interpretation and application   (1) In these Rules "the Act" means the Domestic Proceedings and Magistrates' Courts Act 1978.

(2) Expressions used in these Rules have the meaning which they bear in the Act.

(3) Any reference in these Rules to a form is a reference to a form in the Schedule to these Rules and includes a reference to a form to the like effect with such variations as the circumstances may require.

(4) These Rules shall not apply in relation to any such application or order as is referred to in paragraph 1 or 2 of Schedule 1 to the Domestic Proceedings and Magistrates' Courts Act 1978 (transitional provisions); and, accordingly,

the Magistrates' Courts (Matrimonial Proceedings) Rules 1960 shall continue
to apply in relation to any such application or order but with the following
modification, that is to say, on any complaint made by virtue of paragraph 2
(*d*) of the said Schedule 1 for the variation or revocation of a provision
requiring access to a child to be given to a grandparent rule 7 of the said
Rules of 1960 shall be construed as applying to the complaint as it applies to
a complaint made by virtue of section 8 of the Matrimonial Proceedings
(Magistrates' Courts) Act 1960 and as if paragraph (5) of that rule included
a reference to that grandparent.

NOTES
Domestic Proceedings and Magistrates' Courts Act 1978 Halsbury's Statutes, 4th edn Vol 6,
title Children, Vol 27, title Matrimonial Law (Pt 3) (3rd edn Vol 48, pp 2, 730, 818, 880).
Magistrates' Courts (Matrimonial Proceedings) Rules 1960 SI 1960/2229.
Matrimonial Proceedings (Magistrates' Courts) Act 1960, s 8 Repealed by the Domestic Proceed-
ings and Magistrates' Courts Act 1978, s 89 (2) (*b*), Sch 3, Halsbury's Statutes, 4th edn Vol 27,
title Matrimonial Law (Pt 3) (3rd edn Vol 48, pp 799, 812), and replaced by ss 20, 21 of that
Act, *ibid*, 4th edn Vol 27, title Matrimonial Law (Pt 3) (3rd edn Vol 48, pp 768, 771).

3. Application for order under section 2 (orders for financial provision) (1)
An application for an order under section 2 of the Act shall be in writing and
shall state the ground or grounds on which the application is made; Form 1
may be used for this purpose.

(2) Where the ground or one of the grounds so stated is the ground mentioned in paragraph (*c*) in section 1 of the Act (that the respondent has
behaved in such a way that the applicant cannot reasonably be expected to
live with the respondent) the application shall indicate briefly the circumstances alleged to support that ground.

(3) A summons issued in respect of such an application shall be in Form 2.

**4. Application for order under section 6 (orders for payments agreed by the
parties)** (1) An application for an order under section 6 of the Act shall be
in writing and shall state the type or types of financial provision applied for,
the amount of any payment to be made thereunder and, in the case of periodical payments, the term for which the payments are to be made; Form 3 may
be used for this purpose:

Provided that a magistrates' court may proceed on an application made
orally where it is made by virtue of section 6 (4) of the Act.

(2) A summons issued in respect of such an application shall be in Form 4.

(3) For the purposes of subsection (8) of the said section 6 evidence of the
consent of the respondent to the making of the order and of the financial
resources of the respondent shall be by way of a written statement in Form
5 signed by the respondent in the presence of one of the following persons:—

(*a*) in England and Wales—
    any justice of the peace, justices' clerk, or solicitor;
(*b*) in Scotland—
    any justice of the peace, sheriff or solicitor;
(*c*) in Northern Ireland—
    any justice of the peace or solicitor;
(*d*) outside the United Kingdom—
    (i) any person for the time being authorised by law in the place where
      the document is executed to administer an oath for any judicial
      or other legal purpose;
    (ii) a British consular officer;
    (iii) a notary public; or
    (iv) if the person executing the document is serving in any of the
      regular armed forces of the Crown, an officer holding a commission
      in any of those forces.

(4) For the purposes of the said subsection (8) a written statement purporting to be signed and witnessed in accordance with paragraph (3) above shall
be admissible as evidence without further proof of the signature of the respon-

dent and shall be deemed to have been so signed and witnessed on the date and at the place specified in the document, unless the contrary is proved.

5. Application for order under section 7 (orders for payments where parties are living apart by agreement)   (1) An application for an order under section 7 of the Act shall be in writing in Form 6.

(2) A summons issued in respect of such an application shall be in Form 7.

(3) Where, under subsection (4) of the said section 7, a magistrates' court decides to treat such an application as if it were an application for an order under section 2 of the Act, the court shall indicate orally which of grounds (*a*) and (*b*) in that subsection it considers applicable and a memorandum of the decision and the grounds therefor shall be entered in the court's register.

(4) Where a magistrates' court decides as aforesaid and the respondent is not then present or represented in court, or the respondent or his representative does not then agree to the continuance of the hearing, the court shall adjourn the hearing and the clerk of the court shall serve notice of the decision and the grounds therefor on the respondent. Any such notice shall be in Form 8.

6. Respondents to application for order under section 14 (3), 20 or 21   (1) The following persons (not being the applicant) shall be made respondents on an application for the variation or revocation of an order under section 14 (3), 20 or 21 of the Act, that is to say:—

(*a*) in the case of the variation or revocation of an order made under section 2 (1), 6, 7 or 11 (2) (*a*) the parties to the marriage in question;

(*b*) in the case of the variation or revocation of an order made under section 11 (3) (*a*) requiring payments to be made to or for the benefit of a child to a person who is not a party to the marriage in question and who has the legal custody of the child—

(i) that person;

(ii) the parties to the marriage in question;

(*c*) in the case of the variation or revocation of an order made under section 11 (4) requiring payments to be made to a local authority or to a child in respect of whom the care has been committed to a local authority—

(i) that local authority;

(ii) the parties to the marriage in question;

(*d*) in the case of the variation or revocation of an order made under section 14 (1) requiring access to a child to be given to a grandparent—

(i) the person who has the legal custody of the child;

(ii) the grandparent concerned;

(*e*) in the case of the variation or revocation of an order made under section 19 the parties to the marriage in question and also—

(i) if the order requires payments to be made for the benefit of a child who has his home with a person who is not a party to the marriage in question, that person;

(ii) if the order gives the legal custody of a child to a person who is not a party to the marriage in question, that person;

(*f*) in the case of the variation or revocation of any order referred to in sub-paragraphs (*a*) to (*e*) above requiring payments to be made to or for the benefit of a child who is 16 years of age or over, that child, in addition to the persons who are to be made respondents by virtue of those sub-paragraphs;

(*g*) in the case of the variation or revocation of an order made under section 8 in respect of a child of the family—

(i) the parties to the marriage in question;

(ii) any person who is a parent of the child but not a party to the marriage in question;

    (iii) if the order gives the legal custody of the child to a person who is not a party to the marriage in question or parent of the child, that person,
           and also, if the child is required by an order made under section 9 to be under the supervision of a local authority or a probation. officer, the local authority or, as the case may be, the probation officer;

  (*h*) in the case of the variation or revocation of an order made under section 9 requiring a child to be under the supervision of a local authority or a probation officer—
    (i) the parties to the marriage in question;
    (ii) any person who is a parent of the child but not a party to the marriage in question;
    (iii) the local authority or, as the case may be, the probation officer;
    (iv) if, by virtue of an order made under section 8, a person who is not a party to the marriage in question or parent of the child has the legal custody of the child, that person,

  (*i*) in the case of the revocation of an order made under section 10 committing the care of a child to a local authority—
    (i) the parties to the marriage in question;
    (ii) any person who is a parent of the child but not a party to the marriage in question;
    (iii) the local authority.

(2) References in paragraph (1) above to the parent of a child include the father of an illegitimate child if, but only if, he has been adjudged by a court to be the father of that child.

7. Notice to local authority with regard to child   Where a magistrates' court is required, under section 10 (3) (*a*) of the Act, to notify a local authority of the courts' intention to make an order committing the care of a child to a local authority, the court shall cause notice in Form 9 to be delivered or sent by post to that authority.

8. Notice to parties to the marriage of court's powers to make provision with regard to children   In a case where the powers of the court under section 8, 9, 10 or 11 of the Act to make provision with regard to any child of the family of the parties are or may be exercisable, the clerk of the court shall—
  (*a*) upon the making of an application under section 1, 6, 7 or 21 of the Act, cause a notice in Form 10 to be given to the applicant;
  (*b*) upon the issue of a summons after the making of such an application as aforesaid, cause a similar notice to be served on the respondent with the summons.

9. Notice to parent of child (other than a party to the marriage) of court's powers to make provision with regard to children   (1) In the case of an application for an order under section 2, 6, 7, 14 or 21 of the Act where—
  (*a*) there is a child of the family of the parties to the marriage in question who is not a child of both parties to the marriage; and
  (*b*) the court is required, under section 12 (2) of the Act, to take steps with a view to giving notice of the application, and of the time and place appointed for the hearing, to any person who, though not one of the parties to the marriage in question, is a parent of that child,
the court may exercise its powers under sections 8 to 10 of the Act in relation to that child if at the hearing a written statement signed by the clerk of the court that the steps required by paragraph (2) below have been taken with a view giving notice to the parent as aforesaid has been submitted to the court.

    (2) Subject to paragraph (3) below, the steps required by this rule are the following:—

(*a*) before the summons is issued on the application the applicant shall be required to say whether or not there is a child of the family who is not a child of both the parties to the marriage in question and in respect of whom a notice is required to be given to his parent or parents under section 12 (2) of the Act, and, if there is, to give the name and address of the parent or parents so far as this information is known to, or can in the opinion of the clerk conveniently be obtained by the applicant;

(*b*) at least 10 days before the hearing at which the court proposes to make an order on the application the clerk shall cause a notice to be sent to any parent referred to in sub-paragraph (*a*) above whose name and address are known to the clerk, whether from information given by the applicant in accordance with that sub-paragraph or otherwise.

(3) A notice sent in accordance with sub-paragraph (*b*) of paragraph (2) above to a parent who is not a party to the proceedings shall be in Form 11.

(4) Where, after notice has been sent to a parent in accordance with sub-paragraph (*b*) of paragraph (2) above, the hearing at which the court proposes to exercise the said powers is adjourned, the court may exercise the said powers at the adjourned hearing if it is satisfied that reasonable steps have been taken to give the parent adequate notice of the time and place thereof.

10. Notice to respondent of court's powers with regard to family protection orders   Where a summons is issued on an application for an order under section 16 or 17 (1) of the Act, a notice in Form 12 indicating the powers conferred on a court by sections 16 and 18 (1) shall be served on the respondent with the summons.

11. Jurisdication in proceedings for order under section 2, 6, 7 or 16   In the case of an application for an order under section 2, 6, 7 or 16 of the Act a magistrates' court shall, subject to section 11 of the Administration of Justice Act 1964 and any determination of the committee of magistrates thereunder, have jurisdiction to hear the application if the applicant and the respondent last ordinarily resided together as man and wife within the commission area for which the court is appointed, as well as any such court as has jurisdiction by virtue of section 30 (1) of the Act.

NOTES
Administration of Justice Act 1964, s 11   Halsbury's Statutes, 4th edn Vol 26, title London (3rd edn Vol 20, p 663).

12. Transfer of proceedings for order under section 2, 6, 7 or 16   (1) Where an application is made to a magistrates' court for an order under section 2, 6, 7 or 16 of the Act and a summons has been issued in consequence thereof, then, on an application in that behalf made by the respondent in accordance with paragraph (2) below, a justice of the peace acting for the same place as that court may, if it appears that the case could be more conveniently heard in another magistrates' court having jurisdiction to hear it by virtue of rule 11 above, determine that the proceedings shall be removed into that other court.

(2) An application under paragraph (1) above may be made orally or in writing by or on behalf of the respondent and, unless the respondent applies in person, there shall be lodged with the clerk of the court in which the proceedings were begun a statutory declaration by the respondent which shall state—

(*a*) the grounds upon which the application is made;

(*b*) the address of the respondent to which notices may be sent;

(*c*) a summary of the evidence which the respondent proposes to adduce in the proceedings, including the names, addresses and the occupation, if known, of any witnesses to be called by the respondent;

(*d*) the occupation of the respondent and, if known, of the applicant in the proceedings.

(3) The justice adjudicating on an application under paragraph (1) above shall, unless he determines that the application shall be refused forthwith, afford to the person who applied for the order an opportunity of making representations, either orally or in writing, thereon.

(4) Where a justice determines under paragraph (1) above that proceedings shall be removed into another magistrates' court, he shall cause the clerk of the court in which the proceedings were begun to send to the clerk of that other court the complaint, a copy of the summons and any other relevant documents; and, on receipt thereof in that other court, the complaint shall be deemed to have been made in, and the summons to have been issued by, that other court, and any justice acting for the same place as that other court may appoint a time and place for the hearing of the proceedings which, upon notice thereof being sent to the parties to the proceedings, shall be deemed to have been the time and place appointed in the summons.

13. Consideration of applications for family protection orders   (1) Where an application has been made to a magistrates' court for an order under section 16 of the Act and the applicant makes a statement to the clerk of the court, either orally or in writing, to the effect that there is imminent danger of physical injury to the applicant or a child of the family, the clerk shall take such steps as may be necessary to ensure that the court considers as soon as practicable whether or not to exercise its power to make an expedited order under section 16 (2) and (6) of that Act.

(2) On an application to a magistrates' court for an order under section 16 (3) of the Act, the date fixed for the hearing of the application shall be as soon as practicable and in any event not later than 14 days after the date on which the summons is issued.

14. Form of court orders   (1) An order under section 2, 6, 7, 8, 9, 10 or 11 of the Act shall be in Form 13.

(2) An order under section 16 of the Act shall be in Form 14.

(3) A power of arrest attached under section 18 (1) of the Act to an order under section 16 shall be in Form 15.

(4) A warrant of arrest under section 18 (4) of the Act shall be in Form 16.

15. Entries in court's registers   (1) Where a clerk of a magistrates' court receives notice of any direction made by the High Court or a county court under section 28 of the Act by virtue of which an order made by the magistrates' court under Part I of the Act ceases to have effect, particulars thereof shall be entered in the court's register.

(2) Where the hearing of an application under section 1 of the Act is adjourned after the court has decided that it is satisifed of any ground mentioned in that section and the parties to the proceedings agree to the resumption of the hearing in accordance with section 31 by a court which includes justices who were not sitting when the hearing began, particulars of the agreement shall be entered in the court's register.

16. Substitution of new supervisor for child   (1) Where an order made under section 9 of the Act by a magistrates' court provides for a child to be under the supervision of a local authority or a probation officer appointed for or assigned to a petty sessions area, and the court is of the opinion, upon representations made to it orally or in writing by or on behalf of that local authority or, as the case may be, by or on behalf of a probation officer appointed for or assigned to that area that the child is or will be resident in the area of another local authority or, as the case may be, in another petty sessions area, the court may vary the order by substituting the other local authority or, as the case may be, by substituting a probation officer appointed for or assigned to the other petty sessions area.

(2) Where a magistrates' court varies an order made under section 9 of the Act in accordance with this rule, the court shall cause a notice in Form 17 to be sent—
(a) to the person who has the legal custody of the child; and
(b) to the local authority or, as the case may be, the clerk to the justices
for the petty sessions area substituted by the order under this rule,
and shall cause the local authority or probation officer by or on whose behalf the representations were made to be informed that the order has been so varied.

17. Copy of extract from register to be sent to grandparent applying under section 14 (1)   Where at any time while an order made under section 8 (2) of the Act regarding the legal custody of a child is in force, an application is made to a magistrates' court under section 14 (1) by a grandparent of the child for an order requiring access to the child to be given to that grandparent, the clerk of the court shall send to that grandparent a certified copy of an extract from the court's register containing the particulars of the order made under section 8 (2).

18. Notification of orders made under section 13 or 17 (1)   (1) Where a magistrates' court makes an order under section 13 (1) of the Act regarding a dispute between two persons who have a parental right or duty jointly by virtue of an order made by another magistrates' court under section 8 (2) or makes an order under section 13 (2) varying or revoking any such order under section 13 (1), the clerk of the court shall send a copy thereof to the clerk of the court which made the order under section 8 (2).
(2) Where a magistrates' court makes an order under section 17 (1) of the Act varying or revoking an order made by another magistrates' court under section 16 for the protection of a party to a marriage or a child of the family, the clerk of the court shall send a copy thereof to the clerk of the court which made the order under section 16.

19. Notification of certain family protection orders   (1) Where a magistrates' court makes an expedited order under section 16 (2) and (6) of the Act (hereinafter referred to as an "expedited order"), the clerk of the court shall serve notice of the making of the order on the respondent by causing a copy of the order to be delivered to the respondent personally:
Provided that if a justice of the peace is satisfied by evidence on oath that prompt personal service on the respondent is impracticable he may allow service to be effected—
(a) by leaving a copy of the order for him with some person at his last known or usual place of abode; or
(b) by sending a copy of the order by post in a letter addressed to him at his last known or usual place of abode.
(2) (a) Where a magistrates' court makes an order under section 16 of the Act to which a power of arrest is attached, the clerk of the court shall cause a copy of the order to be sent to the officer for the time being in charge of any police station for the address at which the person who applied for the order resides.
(b) Where a magistrates' court makes an order under section 17 (1) of the Act varying or revoking any order under the said section 16 to which a power of arrest is attached, the clerk of the court shall cause a copy of the order under section 17 (1) to be sent to the officer for the time being in charge of the police station to which a copy of the order under section 16 was sent in pursuance of sub-paragraph (a) above and, if the person who applied for the order under section 16 has since changed address, any police station for the new address.

(3) In the case of an expedited order a copy thereof shalls not be sent to the police in pursuance of paragraph 2 (*a*) above until notice of the making of the order has been served on the respondent in accordance with paragraph (1) above and the clerk of the court shall, before sending it to the police, enter on it an endorsement in Form 18 indicating that it has been so served and the date on which the order takes effect.

(4) Where a copy of an expedited order is sent to the police in pursuance of paragraph (2) (*a*) above, a copy of the order and its endorsement shall also be sent to the person who applied for the order.

(5) Where, by virtue of section 16 (8) (*b*) of the Act, an expedited order to which a power of arrest is attached expires on the date of the commencement of the hearing by a magistrates' court of an application for an order under section 16 of that Act, the clerk of the court shall cause notice of the expiry to be sent to the officer for the time being in charge of the police station to which a copy of the order was sent in pursuance of paragraph (2) (*a*) above.

20. Service of documents (1) Subject to the provisions of rule 19 (1) above, service on any person of a document under these Rules may be effected—
  (*a*) by delivering it to him; or
  (*b*) by leaving it for him with some person at his last known or usual place of abode; or
  (*c*) by sending it to him by post in a letter addressed to him at his last known or usual place of abode or at an address given by him for that purpose.

(2) In the case of a notice sent by post for the purposes of rule 12 (4) above the notice shall be sent in a registered letter or by recorded delivery service.

SCHEDULE

NOTES
This Schedule contains the forms listed below. The forms are not reproduced in this work but will be found printed in Rayden on Divorce (14th edn), pp 3761-3774. The prescribed forms are:

FORM
  1. Complaint for order under section 2.
  2. Summons on complaint for order under section 2.
  3. Complaint for order under section 6.
  4. Summons on complaint for order under section 6.
  5. Consent to order under section 6.
  6. Complaint for order under section 7.
  7. Summons on complaint for order under section 7.
  8. Notice of decision to treat application for order under section 7 as application for order under section 2.
  9. Notice to local authority of intention to commit to them the care of a child.
 10. Notice to parties to the marriage of court's powers to make provision with regard to children.
 11. Notice to parent of child (other than a party to the marriage) of court's power to make provision with regard to children.
 12. Notice to respondent of court's powers with regard to family protection orders.
 13. Orders under sections 2, 6, 7, 8, 9, 10 or 11.
 14. Family protection order.
 15. Power of arrest attached to family protection order.
 16. Warrant of arrest for breach of family protection order.
 17. Notice of appointment of new supervisor for child.
 18. Endorsement of expedited family protection order.

PART 3
Maintenance Orders

CHRONOLOGICAL LIST OF INSTRUMENTS

SI	Description	Remarks	Page
1977/1890	Magistrates' Courts (Maintenance Orders Act 1958) (Amendment) Rules 1977	Amend 1959/3 (*qv*)	—
1978/279	Recovery Abroad of Maintenance (Convention Countries) Order 1978	Amends 1975/423 (*qv*)	—
1979/115	Reciprocal Enforcement of Maintenance Orders (Designation of Reciprocating Countries) Order 1979	Amends 1974/556 (*qv*)	332
1979/116	Maintenance Orders (Facilities for Enforcement) (Revocation) Order 1979	See note "Further revocation" to 1974/557, p 322 *post*	—
1979/170	Magistrates' Courts (Reciprocal Enforcement of Maintenance Orders) (Amendment) Rules 1979	Amend 1974/668 (*qv*)	—
1979/1314	Recovery of Maintenance (United States of America) Order 1979	—	332
1979/1317	Reciprocal Enforcement of Maintenance Orders (Hague Convention Countries) Order 1979	—	334
1979/1561	Magistrates' Courts (Recovery Abroad of Maintenance) (Amendment) Rules 1979	Modify 1975/488 (*qv*)	—
1980/108	Magistrates' Courts (Reciprocal Enforcement of Maintenance Orders) (Hague Convention Countries) Rules 1980	—	335
1980/558	Attachment of Earnings (Employer's Deduction) Order 1980	—	335
1980/1584	Magistrates' Courts (Recovery Abroad of Maintenance) (Amendment) Rules 1980	Amend 1975/488 (*qv*)	—
1980/1895	Magistrates' Courts (Maintenance Orders Act 1950) (Amendment) Rules 1980	Amend 1950/2035 (*qv*)	—
1980/1896	Magistrates' Courts (Maintenance Orders Act 1958) (Amendment) Rules 1980	Amend 1959/3 (*qv*)	—
1980/1981	Administration of Justice Act 1977 (Commencement No 7) Order 1980	Brought the Administration of Justice Act 1977, s 3, Sch 3 (so far as not already in force) (relating to enforcement of maintenance orders) into force on 1 January 1981; made under s 32 (6) of the Act	—
1981/606	Recovery Abroad of Maintenance (United States of America) Order 1981	Amends 1979/1314 (*qv*)	—
1981/837	Reciprocal Enforcement of Maintenance Orders (Hague Convention Countries) (Variation) Order 1981	Amends 1979/1317 (*qv*)	—
1981/1545	Reciprocal Enforcement of Maintenance Orders (Hague Convention Countries) (Variation) (No 2) Order 1981	Amends 1979/1317 (*qv*)	—
1981/1674	Reciprocal Enforcement of Maintenance Orders (Hague Convention Countries) (Variation) (No 3) Order 1981	Amends 1979/1317 (*qv*)	—
1982/1530	Recovery Abroad of Maintenance (Convention Countries) Order 1982	Amends 1975/423 (*qv*)	—
1983/885	Reciprocal Enforcement of Maintenance Orders (Hague Convention Countries) (Variation) Order 1983	Amends 1979/1317 (*qv*)	—
1983/1124	Maintenance Orders (Facilities for Enforcement) (Revocation) Order 1983	See note "Further revocation" to 1974/557, p 322, *post*	—
1983/1125	Reciprocal Enforcement of Maintenance Orders (Designation of Reciprocating Countries) Order 1983	Amends 1974/556 (*qv*)	336
1983/1148	Magistrates' Courts (Reciprocal Enforcement of Maintenance Orders) (Amendment) Rules 1983	Amend 1974/668 (*qv*)	—
1983/1523	Reciprocal Enforcement of Maintenance Orders (Hague Convention Countries) (Variation) (No 2) Order 1983	Amends 1979/1317 (*qv*)	—
1984/1824	Recovery of Maintenance (United States of America) (Variation) Order 1984	Amends 1979/1314 (*qv*)	—

INTRODUCTORY NOTE

This Part of the title is concerned with instruments relating to: (*a*) the reciprocal enforcement of maintenance orders under the Maintenance Orders (Reciprocal Enforcement) Act 1972, Halsbury's Statutes, 4th edn Vol 27, title Matrimonial Law (Pt 3) (3rd edn Vol 42, p 714) and certain earlier Acts, in particular, the Maintenance Orders (Facilities for Enforcement) Act 1920, Halsbury's Statutes, 4th edn Vol 27, title Matrimonial Law (Pt 3) (3rd edn Vol 17, p 272) (prospectively repealed by the Maintenance Orders (Reciprocal Enforcement) Act 1972, s 22 (2) (*a*), as from a day to be appointed; see *infra*), and the Maintenance Orders Act 1950, Halsbury's Statutes, 4th edn Vol 6, title Children, Vol 27, title Matrimonial Law (Pt 3) (3rd edn Vol 17, pp 235, 280, 594); and (*b*) enforcement facilities under the Maintenance Orders Act 1958, *ibid*, 4th edn Vol 27, title Matrimonial Law (Pt 3) (3rd edn Vol 17, p 293 *et seq*). These enactments and subordinate legislation are briefly considered in the following paragraphs of this Note; but when s 22 (2) (*a*) of the Maintenance Orders (Reciprocal Enforcement) Act 1972 is brought into force (*ie* on a day to be appointed by order under s 49 (2) thereof) the Maintenance Orders (Facilities for Enforcement) Act 1920 will be repealed, and already the new provisions set out in Part I of the 1972 Act govern the reciprocal enforcement of maintenance orders as between the United Kingdom and any country designated a "reciprocating country" by Order in Council under s 1 of the Act. The whole of the Act (except the said s 22 (2)) is now in force by virtue of SI 1974/517 and 1975/377 (listed at p 298, *ante*).

Reciprocal arrangements under the Acts of 1920 and 1972   The Maintenance Orders (Facilities for Enforcement) Act 1920 provides for the registration and enforcement in England and Northern Ireland of maintenance orders made before or after the passing of the Act (16 August 1920) in any part of Her Majesty's dominions outside the United Kingdom to which the Act extends, and *vice versa*; and by virtue of the Maintenance Orders (Facilities for Enforcement) Order 1959, SI 1959/377, p 318, *post*, the Act extends to the countries and territories specified in Schedule 1 to that Order. Many more countries and territories were formerly specified in that Schedule, but they have since been designated as reciprocating countries for the purposes of Part I of the Maintenance Orders (Reciprocal Enforcement) Act 1972, Halsbury's Statutes, 4th edn Vol 27, title Matrimonial Law (Pt 3) (3rd edn Vol 42, p 717 *et seq*) (see SI 1974/556, 1975/2187, 1979/115 and 1983/1125, pp 319, 331, 332, 336, *post*) and in relation to them the said Order of 1959 has been revoked and the Schedule amended accordingly; see the Maintenance Orders (Facilities for Enforcement) (Revocation) Order 1974, SI 1974/557, p 322, *post*, and the orders (SI 1975/2188, 1979/116 and 1983/1124) noted thereto.

All the countries and territories (with the exception of the Union of South Africa) which so far have been designated as reciprocating countries are countries or territories within the Commonwealth. Any country or territory outside the United Kingdom may, however, be so designated if Her Majesty is satisfied that in the event of the benefits conferred by Part I of the Act of 1972 being applied to, or to particular classes of, maintenance orders made by the courts of that country or territory, similar benefits will in that country or territory be applied to, or to those classes of, maintenance orders made by the courts in the United Kingdom; see s 1 (1) of the Act of 1972.

However, as from 1 March 1980, the Reciprocal Enforcement of Maintenance Orders (Hague Convention Countries) Order 1979, 1979/1317, as amended, p 334, *post*, made provision for the application of Part I of the 1972 Act to States party to the 1973 Hague Convention on the Recognition and Enforcement of Decisions Relating to Maintenance Obligations in the same way as it applies in relation to reciprocating countries, subject to certain exceptions, adaptations and modifications.

For rules making provision, in relation to magistrates' courts, for the various matters which are to be prescribed under Part I of the Act of 1972, see SI 1974/668, p 322, *post* and SI 1980/108, p 335 *post*.

Reciprocal enforcement of claims for recovery of maintenance: convention countries   Part II (ss 25-39) of the Maintenance Orders (Reciprocal Enforcement) Act 1972, Halsbury's Statutes, 4th edn Vol 27, title Matrimonial Law (Pt 3) (3rd edn Vol 42, p 740 *et seq*), made provision with a view to the accession of the United Kingdom to the United Nations Convention on the Recovery Abroad of Maintenance done at New York on 20 June 1956 (Cmnd. 4485). The object of the Convention is to enable a claimant in one convention country to claim maintenance from a person in another in accordance with the laws of that other country. Section 26 of the Act enables a person in the United Kingdom to apply to a convention country for maintenance against a person subject to the jurisdiction of that country; and ss 27-30 relate to an application by a person in a convention country for maintenance against a person in the United Kingdom. Enforcement is dealt with in s 33, and variation and revocation of registered orders by ss 34 and 35. The Part includes provisions relating to the admissibility of evidence given in a convention country and to obtaining or asking for evidence by letters of request.

Under s 25 of the Act it may be declared by Order in Council that any country or territory specified in the order, being a country or territory outside the United Kingdom to which the Convention extends, is a convention country for the purposes of Part II of the Act. For the countries which have been so specified, see the Recovery Abroad of Maintenance (Convention Countries) Order 1975, SI 1975/423 (as amended), p 327, *post*; and for rules making provision, in relation to magistrates' courts, for the various matters which are to be prescribed under Part II of the Act, see SI 1975/488, p 328, *post*.

Reciprocal arrangements under the Act of 1950   While the Act of 1920 made provision for the enforcement of English maintenance orders in Her Majesty's dominions outside the United Kingdom, it in no way assisted the enforcement of English maintenance orders in Scotland and Northern Ireland (or *vice versa*). The Maintenance Orders Act 1950, Halsbury's Statutes, 4th edn Vol 6, title Children, Vol 27, title Matrimonial Law (Pt 3) (3rd edn Vol 17, pp 235, 280, 594), provides the necessary machinery. Under this Act, maintenance orders, to which s 16 thereof applies, made by superior or inferior courts in one part of the United Kingdom may be registered in, and enforced by, courts in another part of the United Kingdom. Machinery for registration and enforcement is provided by Part II of the Act of 1950.

The procedure as respects applications for the registration in the Court of Session or in the Supreme Court of Judicature of Northern Ireland of maintenance orders made in the High Court in England, or for registering in the latter court orders made in the former courts, is prescribed by RSC Order 104, rr 4 and 5, in the Supreme Court Practice (see also the title Courts (Part 3B) in this work). Maintenance orders are enforceable in magistrates' courts in England if made by like courts in Scotland or Northern Ireland or by the sheriff court in Scotland; registration procedure is prescribed by the Maintenance Orders Act 1950 (Summary Jurisdiction) Rules 1950, SI 1950/2035, p 304, *post*. Those rules also prescribe the manner of making application for the registration of an English maintenance order in Scotland or Northern Ireland, and the procedure to be followed when an order is varied or discharged. Parallel provisions have been made by the appropriate authorities in Scotland and Northern Ireland, but such provisions are outside the scope of this work.

Enforcement, etc of orders under the Act of 1958   The Maintenance Orders Act 1958, Halsbury's Statutes, 4th edn Vol 27, title Matrimonial Law (Pt 3) (3rd edn Vol 17, p 293 *et seq*) which came into force on 16 February 1959 (see SI 1958/2111, listed at p 298 *ante*), makes provision for the registration, enforcement and variation in magistrates' courts of maintenance orders (defined in s 1 (1A), as inserted by the Administration of Justice Act 1970, s 27 (3)) made by the High Court or county courts and for the registration and enforcement of magistrates' court maintenance orders in the High Court (Part I of the Act); and the Attachment of Earnings Act 1971, Halsbury's Statutes, 4th edn Vol 22, title Judgments and Execution (3rd edn Vol 41, p 791 *et seq*) (containing in amended form provisions formerly in Part II of the Act of 1958) enables the earnings of defaulters under maintenance orders to be attached by means of "attachment of earnings orders". Maintenance orders registered under Part II of the Maintenance Orders Act 1950 (as to which see above), as well (it is thought) as those registered in or confirmed by a court in England or Wales under the Maintenance Orders (Facilities for Enforcement) Act 1920 (see p 300, *ante*), do not come within the scope of Part I of the Act of 1958. Such orders registered or confirmed in England or Wales, and those registered in a magistrates' court under Part I of the Maintenance Orders (Reciprocal Enforcement) Act 1972, Halsbury's Statutes, 4th edn Vol 27, title Matrimonial Law (Pt 3) (3rd edn Vol 42, p 717 *et seq*), may be the subject of attachment of earnings orders under the Attachment of Earnings Act 1971; see paras 9 and 10 of Schedule 1 to that Act, and para 11 (added by the Act of 1972). The procedure to be followed in magistrates' courts in connection with the matters dealt with by the Acts of 1958 and 1971 is prescribed, respectively, by the Magistrates' Courts (Maintenance Orders Act 1958) Rules 1959, SI 1959/3, p 310, *post*, and the Magistrates' Courts (Attachment of Earnings) Rules 1971, SI 1971/809, in the title Magistrates. For procedure in the High Court, see RSC Order 104, rr 7-19, in the Supreme Court Practice, and for that in the county courts, see CCR Order 46, r 17, in the County Court Practice; as to the Supreme Court Rules and the County Court Rules, see also the title Courts (Parts 3B and 5A (ii)) in this work.

THE MAINTENANCE ORDERS (FACILITIES FOR ENFORCEMENT) RULES 1922
SR & O 1922/1355

NOTES
Authority   These rules were made on 18 October 1922 by the Lord Chancellor under the Maintenance Orders (Facilities for Enforcement) Act 1920, Halsbury's Statutes, 4th edn Vol 27, title Matrimonial Law (Pt 3) (3rd edn Vol 17, p 272) and subsequently had effect as if contained in rules made under the Justices of the Peace Act 1949, s 15. The relevant provisions of s 15 of the 1949 Act were repealed by the Magistrates' Courts Act 1980, s 154 (3), Sch 9, and by virtue of s 145 (5) the rules now have effect as if made under s 144 of that Act, Halsbury's Statutes, 4th edn Vol 27, title Magistrates (3rd edn Vol 50 (2), p 1565; for s 154 (3), Sch 9, see pp 1575, 1604). As to the repeal of the Act of 1920 by the Maintenance Orders (Reciprocal Enforcement) Act 1972, see the Introductory Note at p 300, *ante*.
Commencement   18 October 1922; *ie* date when made.
Amendment   These rules are printed as amended by the Maintenance Orders (Facilities for Enforcement) (Amendment) Rules 1970, SI 1970/762.
Interpretation   References in these rules to "the Act" are to the Maintenance Orders (Facilities for Enforcement) Act 1920, Halsbury's Statutes, 4th edn Vol 27, title Matrimonial Law (Pt 3) (3rd edn Vol 17, p 272) (prospectively repealed by the Maintenance Orders (Reciprocal Enforcement) Act 1972, s 22 (2) (*a*), *ibid*, 4th edn Vol 27, title Matrimonial Law (Pt 3) (3rd edn Vol 42, p 738), as from a day to be appointed). For the meaning of "maintenance order", see s 10 of that Act.
General   These rules prescribe the procedure for courts of summary jurisdiction (magistrates' courts) in England in relation to the registration and enforcement of maintenance orders (including provisional orders) made by courts in any part of Her Majesty's dominions outside the United Kingdom to which the Act of 1920 extends; see further the Introductory Note at p 300, *ante*.

1.   The copy of an Order made by a Court outside the United Kingdom and received by the Secretary of State under section 1 of the Maintenance Orders (Facilities for Enforcement) Act, 1920, shall, unless the Order was made by a Court of Superior Jurisdiction, be sent, (*a*) if the defendant is alleged to be living within a division assigned to one of the Metropolitan Police Courts, to the Chief Clerk of that Court, or, if the Secretary of State so directs, to the Chief Clerk of Bow Street Police Court;

(*b*) if he is alleged to be living in any district for which a Stipendiary Magistrate is specially appointed, to the Clerk to that Magistrate;

(*c*) if he is alleged to be living within the City of London, to the Chief Clerk at the Mansion House Justice Room; and

(*d*) if he is alleged to be living elsewhere, to the Clerk to the Justices acting for the Petty Sessional Division or the Borough within which he is living.

NOTES
Metropolitan police courts   Now magistrates' courts for the Inner London Area; see para 2 of Schedule 3 to the Administration of Justice Act 1964, Halsbury's Statutes, 4th edn Vol 26, title London (3rd edn Vol 20, p 683).
Section 1 of the Maintenance Orders (Facilities for Enforcement) Act 1920   Halsbury's Statutes, 4th edn Vol 27, title Matrimonial Law (Pt 3) (3rd edn Vol 17, p 272).

2.   The copy of a Provisional Order made by a Court outside the United Kingdom and received by the Secretary of State under section 4 of the Act shall be sent to a Court of Summary Jurisdiction in the manner provided by the foregoing Rule, with the accompanying documents and a requisition for the issue of a summons.

3.   The Clerk to whom any Order is sent in accordance with the above Rules shall enter it in his register on the date on which he receives it in the same manner as though the Order had been made at his Court, distinguishing it from the other entries in such manner as he may find most convenient, so as to show that it is entered in pursuance of the Act.

4.   When an Order provisionally made outside the United Kingdom has been confirmed, with or without modification, under section 4 of the Act, by a Court of Summary Jurisdiction, or the Court has decided not to confirm it, the Clerk of the Court shall send notice thereof to the Court from which it issued, and also to the Secretary of State.

5.   When an Order has been registered in a Court of Summary Jurisdiction under section 1 of the Act, or a Provisional Order has been confirmed by a Court of Summary Jurisdiction under section 4, that Court shall, unless satisfied that it is undesirable to do so, direct that all payments due thereunder shall be made through an officer of the Court, or such other person as it may specify for the purpose. Such direction may be given without any complaint or application, the provisions of Rule 46 of the Summary Jurisdiction Rules, 1915, notwithstanding.

NOTES
Summary Jurisdiction Rules 1915   SR & O 1915/200 (now revoked). For the equivalent provision to r 46 of those rules see now the Magistrates' Courts Act 1980, s 60, Halsbury's Statutes, 4th edn Vol 27, title Magistrates (3rd edn Vol 50 (2), p 1492).

6.   The person through whom the payments are directed to be made shall collect the monies due under the Order in the same manner as though it were an Affiliation Order, and may take proceedings in his own name for enforcing payment, and shall send the monies, when so collected, to the Court from which the Order originally issued [or to such other person or authority as that court or the Secretary of State may from time to time direct].

Provided that if the Court from which the Order originally issued is in Malta or in a Colony not possessing responsible Government or in a British Protectorate other than Northern or Southern Rhodesia, the monies so collected shall be paid to the Crown Agents for the Colonies for transmission to the person to whom they are due.

NOTES
Amendment   The words printed between square brackets were inserted by SI 1970/762.
Crown Agents for the Colonies   Now the Crown Agents, a statutory body constituted under the
Crown Agents Act 1979, Halsbury's Statutes, 4th edn Vol 10, title Constitutional Law (Pt 5).

7.   When a Provisional Order made under section 3 of the Act has been
remitted under sub-section (4) of that section to a Court of Summary Jurisdiction for the purpose of taking further evidence, notice specifying the further
evidence required and the time and place fixed for taking it shall be sent by
the Clerk of the Court to the person on whose application the Provisional
Order was made.

8.   These Rules may be cited as the Maintenance Orders (Facilities for Enforcement) Rules, 1922.

THE MAINTENANCE ORDERS ACT 1950 (SUMMARY JURISDICTION) RULES 1950
SI 1950/2035

NOTES
Authority   These rules were made on 15 December 1950 by the Lord Chancellor under s 29
(repealed) of the Summary Jurisdiction Act 1879, as extended and adapted by ss 5 (repealed),
25 (1), (3), 28 (1) and 30 (2) (repealed) of the Maintenance Orders Act 1950, and under all
other enabling powers. The rules subsequently had effect as if contained in rules made under s
15 of the Justices of the Peace Act 1949, the relevant provisions of which were repealed by the
Magistrates' Courts Act 1980, s 154 (3), Sch 9, and by virtue of s 145 (5), the rules now have
effect as if made under s 144 of that Act, Halsbury's Statutes, 4th edn Vol 27, title Magistrates
(3rd edn Vol 50 (2), p 1565; for s 154 (3), Sch 9, see pp 1575, 1604).
Commencement   1 January 1951; see r 17.
Amendment   These rules are printed as amended by the Magistrates' Courts (Maintenance
Orders Act 1950) (Amendment) Rules 1980, SI 1980/1895.
Interpretation   See r 16 (1). "The Act" means the Maintenance Orders Act 1950 and "the Act
of 1958" means the Maintenance Orders Act 1958.
General   These rules are concerned with: (*a*) the transfer of wife maintenance proceedings (see
r 1 and the note thereto); and (*b*) procedure in relation to enforcement of maintenance orders
made by courts of summary jurisdiction in England and also in relation to enforcement of
maintenance orders made by courts in Scotland or Northern Ireland.

PART I
TRANSFER OF WIFE MAINTENANCE PROCEEDINGS

1.   (1) Where proceedings under section 4 of the Summary Jurisdiction (Married Women) Act, 1895, are begun against a defendant residing in Scotland
or Northern Ireland in a court having jurisdiction by virtue of subsection (1)
of section 1 of the Maintenance Orders Act, 1950, then, upon an application
in that behalf made by the defendant in accordance with paragraph (2) of
this Rule, a justice acting for the same place as that court may, if it appears
that the case could be more conveniently heard in a court of summary jurisdiction having jurisdiction in the place where the parties last ordinarily resided
together as man and wife, determine that the proceedings shall be removed
into the last-mentioned court.

(2) An application under the foregoing paragraph may be made orally or
in writing by or on behalf of the defendant and, unless the defendant applies
in person, there shall be lodged with the clerk of the court in which the
proceedings under the said section 4 have been begun a statutory declaration
by the defendant which shall state the grounds upon which the application is
made and the address of the defendant to which notices may be sent.

(3) The justice adjudicating on an application made under paragraph (1)
of this Rule shall, unless he determines that the application shall be refused
forthwith, afford to the complainant an opportunity of making representations,
either orally or in writing, thereon.

(4) Where a justice determines under paragraph (1) of this Rule that the proceedings under the said section 4 shall be removed into another court of summary jurisdiction, he shall cause the clerk of the court in which the said proceedings have been begun to send to the clerk of that other court the complaint, a copy of the summons and any other relevant documents; and, on receipt thereof in that other court, the complaint shall be deemed to have been made in, and the summons to have been issued by, that other court, and any justice acting for the same place as that other court may appoint a time and place for the hearing of the proceedings which, upon notice thereof being sent by registered post to the complainant and defendant, shall be deemed to have been the time and place appointed in the summons.

NOTES
The 1895 Act, s 4, and the 1950 Act, s 1, were repealed by the Matrimonial Proceedings (Magistrates' Courts) Act 1960, and replaced by provisions thereof. This rule was continued in force by virtue of the proviso to s 18 (1) of the 1960 Act (repealed). The 1960 Act was itself repealed by the Domestic Proceedings and Magistrates' Courts Act 1978; as to provisions concerning jurisdiction and procedure, see s 30 (3) thereof, Halsbury's Statutes, 4th edn Vol 27, title Matrimonial Law (Pt 3) (3rd edn Vol 48, p 781). *Quaere* whether this rule continues in force for the purposes of the said s 30 (3); see the 1978 Act, s 89 (1), Sch 1, para 2, *ibid*, 4th edn Vol 27, title Matrimonial Law (Pt 3) (3rd edn Vol 48, pp 799, 800).

PART II
PROCEDURE UNDER PART II OF THE ACT IN RELATION TO MAINTENANCE ORDERS MADE BY COURTS OF SUMMARY JURISDICTION IN ENGLAND

2. (1) An application for the registration in a court in Scotland or Northern Ireland under Part II of the Act of a maintenance order made by a court of summary jurisdiction in England may be made, either orally or in writing by or on behalf of the person entitled to the payments thereunder, to a justice acting for the same place as the court which made the order; and, unless the applicant appears in person, there shall be lodged with the clerk of the court which made the order a statutory declaration by the applicant which shall contain the particulars specified in paragraph (2) of this Rule.

(2) A statutory declaration lodged under the foregoing paragraph shall state—
  (*a*) the address of the person liable to make the payments under the order;
  (*b*) the reason why it is convenient that the order should be enforced in Scotland or Northern Ireland, as the case may be;
  (*c*) unless a certificate of arrears is lodged under section 20 of the Act, the amount of any arrears due under the order;
  (*d*) that the order is not already registered under Part II of the Act.

(3) If it appears to the justice dealing with an application made as aforesaid that the person liable to make the payments under the order resides in Scotland or Northern Ireland, and that it is convenient that the order should be enforceable there, he shall cause the clerk of the court which made the order to send to the sheriff-clerk of the sheriff court in Scotland, or as the case may be, to the clerk of the court of summary jurisdiction in Northern Ireland, having jurisdiction in the place in which the person liable to make the payments under the order appears to be—
  (*a*) a certified copy of the order;
  (*b*) the certificate of arrears or statutory declaration (if any);
  (*c*) if no statutory declaration has been lodged, written notice of the address of the person liable to make the payments under the order.

(4) A memorandum of any proceedings taken under the foregoing provisions of this Rule for the registration of a maintenance order in a court in Scotland or Northern Ireland shall be entered in the register . . . ; and on the receipt by the clerk of the court which made the order (who shall be the prescribed officer of that court for the purposes of subsection (4) of section 17 of the Act) of notice under the said subsection (4) of section 17 of the Act) of notice

under the said subsection (4) of the registration of the order he shall cause particulars of the notice to be registered in his court by means of a memorandum entered and signed by him in the register . . .

NOTES
Amendment   The words omitted where indicated in para (4) of this rule were revoked by the Magistrates' Courts (Maintenance Orders Act 1950) (Amendment) Rules 1980, SI 1980/1895.

3.   (1) An application to a court of summary jurisdiction in England under subsection (5) of section 22 of the Act to adduce evidence in connection with a maintenance order made by that court and registered in a court in Scotland or Northern Ireland may be made orally by or on behalf of the applicant and the proceedings may be *ex parte*.
   (2) The court in which application is made under the last foregoing paragraph shall cause a transcript or summary of any evidence taken therein to be sent to the clerk of the court in which the order is registered.
   (3) The clerk of the court of summary jurisdiction in England by which a maintenance order registered in a court in Scotland or Northern Ireland was made shall be the prescribed officer to whom any transcript or summary of evidence adduced in the court in Scotland or Northern Ireland under the said subsection (5) shall be sent.

4.   (1) Where a maintenance order made by a court of summary jurisdiction in England and registered in a court in Scotland or Northern Ireland is varied under subsection (1) of section 22 of the Act by the court in which it is registered, the clerk of the court which made the order shall be the prescribed officer to whom, under subsection (1) of section 23 of the Act, notice of the variation shall be given; and on receipt of such notice he shall cause particulars of the same to be registered in his court by means of a memorandum entered and signed by him in the register . . .

   (2) Where a maintenance order made by a court of summary jurisdiction in England and registered in a court in Scotland or Northern Ireland is discharged or varied by the court which made it, the clerk of that court shall give notice of the discharge or variation to the clerk of the court in which the order is registered by sending to him a certified copy of the order discharging or varying the maintenance order.

NOTES
Amendment   The words omitted where indicated in para (1) of this rule were revoked by the Magistrates' Courts (Maintenance Orders Act 1950) (Amendment) Rules 1980, SI 1980/1895.

5.   (1) An application under subsection (2) of section 24 of the Act for the cancellation of the registration of a maintenance order made by a court of summary jurisdiction in England and registered in a court in Scotland or Northern Ireland may be made, either orally or in writing by or on behalf of the person liable to make the payments thereunder, to a justice acting for the same place as the court which made the order; and, unless the applicant appears in person, there shall be lodged with the clerk of the court which made the order a statutory declaration by the applicant stating the facts upon which he relies in support of the application.
   (2) If it appears to the justice dealing with an application made as aforesaid that the person liable to make the payments under the order has ceased to reside in Scotland or Northern Ireland, as the case may be, he shall cause the clerk of the court which made the order to send notice to that effect to the clerk of the court in which the order is registered.

6.   On the cancellation under section 24 of the Act of the registration in a court in Scotland or Northern Ireland of a maintenance order made by a court of summary jurisdiction in England, the clerk of the last-mentioned court shall be the prescribed officer to whom, under subsection (3) of the said section 24, notice of the cancellation shall be given; and on receipt of such notice he shall cause particulars of the same to be registered in his court by means of a memorandum entered and signed by him in the register . . .

NOTES
Amendment   The words omitted where indicated in this rule were revoked by the Magistrates' Courts (Maintenance Orders Act 1950) (Amendment) Rules 1980, SI 1980/1895.

PART III
PROCEDURE IN COURTS OF SUMMARY JURISDICTION IN ENGLAND UNDER PART II OF THE ACT IN RELATION TO MAINTENANCE ORDERS MADE BY COURTS IN SCOTLAND OR NORTHERN IRELAND

7.   The clerk of the court of summary jurisdiction in England specified in paragraph (*b*) of subsection (3) of section 17 of the Act shall be the prescribed officer for the purpose of subsection (2) of the said section 17, and on receiving, in pursuance of that section, a certified copy of a maintenance order made by a court in Scotland or Northern Ireland he shall cause the order to be registered in his court by means of a memorandum entered and signed by him in the register . . ., and shall send written notice to the clerk of the court by which the order was made that it has been duly registered.

NOTES
Amendment   The words omitted where indicated in this rule were revoked by the Magistrates' Courts (Maintenance Orders Act 1950) (Amendment) Rules 1980, SI 1980/1895.

8.   An application for the variation under subsection (1) of section 22 of the Act of the rate of the payments under a maintenance order registered under Part II of the Act in a court of summary jurisdiction in England shall be made by way of complaint in accordance with the Summary Jurisdiction Acts, and thereupon a summons may be issued directed to any person whom the justice to whom the complaint is made may consider proper to answer the same.

NOTES
Summary Jurisdiction Acts   The provisions of these Acts are now largely repealed; for replacing provisions, see, in particular, the Magistrates' Courts Act 1980, Halsbury's Statutes, 4th edn Vol 27, title Magistrates (3rd edn Vol 50 (2), p 1433 *et seq*), and the Magistrates Courts Rules 1981, SI 1981/552, as amended, in the title Magistrates in this work.

9.   (1) An application to a court of summary jurisdiction in England under subsection (5) of section 22 of the Act to adduce evidence in connection with a maintenance order registered therein under Part II of the Act may be made orally by or on behalf of the applicant and the proceedings may be *ex parte*.

(2) The court in which application is made under the last foregoing paragraph shall cause a transcript or summary of any evidence taken therein to be sent to the clerk of the court in Scotland or Northern Ireland by which the order was made.

(3) The clerk of the court of summary jurisdiction in England in which a maintenance order is registered under Part II of the Act shall be the prescribed officer to whom any transcript or summary of evidence adduced under the said subsection (5) in the court in Scotland or Northern Ireland by which the order was made shall be sent.

[**9A.**   (1) An application to a magistrates' court under section 21 (2) of the Act to adduce evidence in connection with a maintenance order made by the Court of Session and registered in the magistrates' court under Part I of the Act of 1958 by virtue of section 1 (2) of the Act of 1958 may be made orally by or on behalf of the applicant and the proceedings may be *ex parte*.

(2) The court in which application is made under paragraph (1) above shall cause a transcript or summary of any evidence taken therein to be sent to the Deputy Principal Clerk of Session.]

NOTES
Amendment   This rule was added by the Magistrates' Courts (Maintenance Orders Act 1950) (Amendment) Rules 1980, SI 1980/1895.

10.   (1) Where a maintenance order registered under Part II of the Act in a court of summary jurisdiction in England is varied under subsection (1) of section 22 of the Act by that court, the clerk of the court shall
[(*a*)   give notice of the variation to the clerk of the court in Scotland or Northern Ireland by which the order was made; and
　(*b*)   if the order is registered in the High Court under Part I of the Act of 1958 by virtue of section 1 (2) of the Act of 1958, give notice of the variation to the appropriate officer of the High Court,
by sending to the clerk of the court and, where necessary, the appropriate officer of the High Court, a certified copy of the order of variation.]
(2) Where a maintenance order registered under Part II of the Act in a court of summary jurisdiction in England is discharged or varied by any other court, the clerk of the court in which it is registered shall be the prescribed officer to whom under [section 23 (1)] of the Act notice of the discharge or variation shall be given; and on receipt of a certified copy of an order discharging or varying the registered order, he shall cause particulars of the same to be registered in his court by means of a memorandum entered and signed by him in the register . . .

NOTES
Amendment   The words printed between square brackets in paras (1) and (2) of this rule were substituted and the words omitted where indicated were revoked by the Magistrates' Courts (Maintenance Orders Act 1950) (Amendment) Rules 1980, SI 1980/1895.

11.   (1) An application under subsection (1) of section 24 of the Act for the cancellation of the registration of a maintenance order registered under Part II of the Act in a court of summary jurisdiction in England shall be made to the clerk of that court by lodging with him a written application in that behalf (which shall state the date of the registration of the order) together with a copy of the order the registration of which it is sought to cancel.
(2) Where, in pursuance of an application made as aforesaid, the clerk cancels the registration of the maintenance order he shall send written notice of the cancellation to the clerk of the court by which the order was made [and, where the order is registered in the High Court under Part I of the Act of 1958 by virtue of section 1 (2) of the Act of 1958, to the appropriate officer of the High Court].

NOTES
Amendment   The words printed between square brackets in para (2) of this rule were added by the Magistrates' Courts (Maintenance Orders Act 1950) (Amendment) Rules 1980, SI 1980/1895.

12.   Where a maintenance order is registered under Part II of the Act in a court of summary jurisdiction in England, the clerk of that court shall be the prescribed officer to whom notice shall be sent under subsection (2) of section 24 of the Act that the person liable to make the payments under the order has ceased to reside in England; and on receipt of such notice the clerk shall cancel the registration of the order and shall send written notice of the cancellation to the clerk of the court by which the order was made [and, where the order is registered in the High Court under Part I of the Act of 1958 by virtue of section 1 (2) of the Act of 1958, to the appropriate officer of the High Court].

NOTES
Amendment   The words printed between square brackets at the end of this rule were added by the Magistrates' Courts (Maintenance Orders Act 1950) (Amendment) Rules 1980, SI 1980/1895.

[**12A.** Where the clerk of a magistrates' court in which a maintenance order is registered under Part I of the Act of 1958 receives a notice of cancellation under section 24 (3) of the Act from the appropriate officer of the High Court, he shall—

(*a*) cause the particulars of such notice to be entered in the register; and

(*b*) cancel the registration under the said Part I; and

(*c*) give notice of the cancellation to the appropriate officer of the court in Scotland or Northern Ireland, as the case may be, which made the order, that is to say either—

  (i) the Deputy Principal Clerk of Session, in the case of the Court of Session; or

  (ii) the Chief Registrar of the Queen's Bench Division (Matrimonial), in the case of the High Court of Justice in Northern Ireland.]

NOTES
Amendment This rule was added by the Magistrates' Courts (Maintenance Orders Act 1950) (Amendment) Rules 1980, SI 1980/1895.

PART IV

FORMS

13. (1) A notice under subsection (4) of section 19 of the Act that the payments under a maintenance order [made by a sheriff court in Scotland or a court of summary jurisdiction in Northern Ireland have] become payable through or to any officer or person shall be in the form number 1 in the Schedule to these Rules, or any form to the like effect, and shall be sent by registered post by the clerk of that court to the person liable to make the payments under the order at his last known address.

(2) A notice under the said subsection (4) that the payments under a maintenance order made by a court of summary jurisdiction in England have, on its registration under Part II of the Act in a court in Scotland or Northern Ireland, ceased to be payable through or to any officer or person shall be in the form number 2 in the Schedule to these Rules, or any form to the like effect, and shall be sent by registered post by the clerk of the first-mentioned court to the person liable to make the payments under the order at his last known address.

NOTES
Amendment The words printed between square brackets in para (1) of this rule were substituted by the Magistrates' Courts (Maintenance Orders Act 1950) (Amendment) Rules 1980, SI 1980/1895.

14. A certificate lodged under subsection (1) of section 20 of the Act as to the amount of any arrears due under a maintenance order made by an court of summary jurisdiction in England shall be in the form number 3 in the Schedule to these Rules, or any form to the like effect.

15. A notice under subsection (5) of section 24 of the Act of the cancellation of the registration under Part II of the Act of a maintenance order in a court of summary jurisdiction in England shall be in the form number 4 in the Schedule to these Rules, or any form to the like effect, and shall be sent by registered post by the clerk of that court to the person liable to make the payments under the order at his last known address.

PART V

INTERPRETATION AND COMMENCEMENT

16. (1) In Parts II to V of these Rules, unless the context otherwise requires, the following expressions have the meanings hereby respectively assigned to them—

"maintenance order" has the same meaning as in Part II of the Act;

"the Act" means the Maintenance Orders Act, 1950;

["the Act of 1958" means the Maintenance Orders Act 1958;

"appropriate officer of the High Court" means the Senior Registrar of the Principal Registry of the Family Division of the High Court or the district registrar of the relevant district registry;

"register" means the register kept in accordance with rule 54 of the Magistrates' Courts Rules 1968;]

and other expressions used in these Rules have the meanings assigned to them in section 28 of the Act.

(2) References in Part III of these Rules to the clerk of the court by which the order was made shall be construed, in relation to a maintenance order made by a county court in Northern Ireland, as references to the Clerk of the Crown and Peace for the appropriate county in Northern Ireland.

(3) The Interpretation Act, 1889, shall apply to the interpretation of these Rules as it applies to the interpretation of an Act of Parliament.

NOTES
Amendment The definitions of "the Act of 1958", "appropriate officer of the High Court" and "register" printed between square brackets in para (1) of this rule were substituted by the Magistrates' Courts (Maintenance Orders Act 1950) (Amendment) Rules 1980, SI 1980/1895.
Maintenance order See the Maintenance Orders Act 1950, s 16, Halsbury's Statutes, 4th edn Vol 27, title Matrimonial Law (Pt 3) (3rd edn Vol 17, p 280).
Maintenance Orders Act 1950 Halsbury's Statutes, 4th edn Vol 6, title Children, Vol 27, title Matrimonial Law (Pt 3) (3rd edn Vol 17, pp 235, 280, 594)
Maintenance Orders Act 1958 *Ibid,* 4th edn Vol 27, title Matrimonial Law (Pt 3) (3rd edn Vol 17, p 293 *et seq*).
Magistrates' Courts Rules 1968 SI 1968/1920, revoked and replaced by the Magistrates' Courts Rules 1981, SI 1981/552, in the title Magistrates in this work; for the provision equivalent to r 54 of the 1968 rules see now r 66 of the 1981 rules.
Interpretation Act 1889 Repealed and replaced by the Interpretation Act 1978, in the title Statutory Instruments, Vol 1 of this work.

17. These Rules may be cited as the Maintenance Orders Act, 1950 (Summary Jurisdiction) Rules, 1950, and shall come into operation on the first day of January, 1951.

SCHEDULE
NOTES
This Schedule sets out the four forms prescribed by rr 13 to 15. They are—
Form 1   Notice to person liable to make payments that sums payable under a maintenance order registered in a court of summary jurisdiction in England have become payable through collecting officer.
Form 2   Notice to person liable to make payments that sums payable under a maintenance order made by a court of summary jurisdiction in England have ceased to be payable to or through any officer or person.
Form 3   Certificate of arrears.
Form 4   Notice of cancellation of registration of maintenance order in magistrates' court.
Amendment   Form 4 was substituted by the Magistrates' Courts (Maintenance Orders Act 1950) (Amendment) Rules 1980, SI 1980/1895.

**THE MAGISTRATES' COURTS (MAINTENANCE ORDERS ACT 1958) RULES 1959
SI 1959/3**

NOTES
These rules were made on 1 January 1959 by the Lord Chancellor under s 15 of the Justices of the Peace Act 1949, as extended by s 122 of the Magistrates' Courts Act 1952. The relevant provisions of s 15 of the 1949 Act and s 122 of the 1952 Act were repealed by the Magistrates'

Courts Act 1980, s 154 (3), Sch 9, and the rules now have effect as if made under s 144 of that Act, Halsbury's Statutes, 4th edn Vol 27, title Magistrates (3rd edn Vol 50 (2), p 1565; for s 154 (3), Sch 9, see pp 1575, 1604).
Commencement   16 February 1959; see r 26.
Amendment   These rules are printed as amended by the Magistrates' Courts (Attachment of Earnings) Rules 1971, SI 1971/809, in the title Magistrates, the Magistrates' Courts (Maintenance Orders Act 1958) (Amendment) Rules 1977, SI 1977/1890, and the Magistrates' Courts (Maintenance Orders Act 1958) (Amendment) Rules 1980, SI 1980/1896, the latter two instruments being listed, *ante*.
Interpretation   See generally r 25. References in these rules to "the Act" are to the Maintenance Orders Act 1958, Halsbury's Statutes, 4th edn Vol 27, title Matrimonial Law (Pt 3) (3rd edn Vol 17, p 293 *et seq*); see r 25 (4).
General   See the Introductory Note under the head "Enforcement, etc, of orders under the Act of 1958", p 301, *ante*. Provisions formerly contained in Part II of these rules relating to the attachment of earnings are revoked and replaced by the Magistrates' Courts (Attachment of Earnings) Rules 1971, SI 1971/809, in the title Magistrates.

PART I
PROCEDURE UNDER PART I OF THE ACT

1. Applications for registration under section 2 (3) of the Act   An application for the registration in the High Court of a magistrates' court order need not be in writing or an oath.

2. Manner in which magistrates' court is to be satisfied as to various matters
(1) On an application for the registration in the High Court of a magistrates' court order, the court shall be satisfied in the manner provided by paragraph (4) of this Rule as to the amount due and unpaid under the order at the time the application was made.
(2) Where such an application as aforesaid is granted, the court shall be satisfied in the manner provided by paragraph (4) of this Rule that no process for the enforcement of the order issued before the grant of the application remains in force.
(3) Where the court receives a notice given under section five of the Act (which relates to the cancellation of registration), the court shall be satisfied in the manner provided by paragraph (4) of this Rule that no process for the enforcement of the order issued before the giving of the notice remains in force and that no proceedings for the variation of the order are pending in a magistrates' court.
(4) For the purpose of satisfying the court as to the matters referred to in this Rule—
  (*a*) if the person through or to whom payments are ordered to be made is the clerk of a magistrates' court, there shall be produced a certificate in that behalf purporting to be signed by the clerk in the form numbered 1, 2 or 3, as the case may be, in the Schedule to these Rules;
  (*b*) in any other case, there shall be produced a document purporting to be a statutory declaration in that behalf in the form numbered 4, 5 or 6, as the case may be, in the Schedule to these Rules.

[2A. Receipt by magistrates' court of notice of registration in the High Court of order previously registered in magistrates' court   Where a magistrates' court receives from the High Court notice of the registration in the High Court of an order made by a sheriff court in Scotland or a court of summary jurisdiction in Northern Ireland and previously registered in that magistrates' court in accordance with section 17 (4) of the Act of 1950, the clerk of the court shall cause the particulars of such notice to be entered in the register.]

NOTES
Amendment   This rule was added by the Magistrates' Courts (Maintenance Orders Act 1958) (Amendment) Rules 1980, SI 1980/1896.

3. Copy of magistrates' court order sent to the High Court for registration
Where an application for the registration of a magistrates' court order is granted and the court is satisfied that no process issued for the enforcement

of the order before the grant of the application remains in force, the court shall, in accordance with paragraph (*c*) of subsection (4) of section two of the Act, cause the clerk to send a copy of the order, certified to be a true copy thereof in the form numbered 7 in the Schedule to these Rules [to the appropriate officer of the High Court.]

NOTES
Amendment   The words "to the appropriate officer of the High Court" printed between square brackets at the end of this rule were substituted by the Magistrates' Courts (Maintenance Orders Act 1958) (Amendment) Rules 1980, SI 1980/1896.
Appropriate officer of the High Court   See r 25 (4).

4. Registration of High Court or county court order in a magistrates' court
Where a clerk of a magistrates' court in accordance with paragraph (*b*) of subsection (2) of section two of the Act receives from an officer of the High Court or the registrar of a county court a certified copy of a High Court or county court order, he shall cause the order to be registered in his court by means of a memorandum entered and signed by him in the register and shall send written notice to that officer of the High Court or the registrar of the county court, as the case may be, that it has been duly registered.

[4A. Registration in magistrates' court of order made in Court of Session or High Court in Northern Ireland
Where a clerk of a magistrates' court, in pursuance of section 2 (2) (*b*) of the Act, receives from the appropriate officer of the original court in Scotland or Northern Ireland a certified copy of an order made by the Court of Session or the High Court in Northern Ireland, he shall cause the order to be registered in his court by means of a memorandum entered and signed by him in the register and shall send written notice to the appropriate officer of the High Court and to the appropriate officer of the original court that the order has been duly registered.]

NOTES
Amendment   This rule was added by the Magistrates' Courts (Maintenance Orders Act 1958) (Amendment) Rules 1980, SI 1980/1896.
Appropriate officer   See r 25 (4).

5. Notices as respects payments through a clerk of a magistrates' court   (1)
A notice under subsection (4) of section nineteen of the Maintenance Orders Act, 1950, as applied by subsection (6) of section two of the Act, that the payments under a High Court or county court order [or an order made by the Court of Session or the High Court in Northern Ireland] have, on its registration in a magistrates' court, become payable through the clerk of a magistrates' court shall be given by the clerk of the court of registration in the form numbered 8 in the Schedule to these Rules.

(2) A notice under the said subsection (4), as so applied, that the payments under a magistrates' court order [or an order made by a Sheriff Court in Scotland or a court of summary jurisdiction in Northern Ireland and registered in a magistrates' court under Part II of the Act of 1950] have, on its registration in the High Court, ceased to be payable to a clerk to a magistrates' court shall be given by the clerk of the [administering] court and shall be in the form numbered 9 in the Schedule to these Rules and, where payments have been payable through a clerk other than the clerk of the [administering] court, he shall send a copy of the said notice to that other clerk.

(3) A notice under subsection (5) of section five of the Act that the registration in a magistrates' court of a High Court or county court order [or an order made by the Court of Session or the High Court in Northern Ireland] has been cancelled and that payments thereunder have ceased to be payable through a clerk of a magistrates' court shall be given by the clerk of the court of registration and shall be in the form numbered 10 in the Schedule to these Rules and, where payments have been payable through a clerk other than the clerk of the court of registration, he shall send a copy of the said notice to that other clerk.

(4) A notice given in accordance with the preceding provisions of this Rule shall be delivered to the person liable to make payments under the order to which the notice relates or sent by post to that person at his last known address.

NOTES
Amendment   The amendments printed between square brackets in this rule were made by the Magistrates' Courts (Maintenance Orders Act 1958) (Amendment) Rules 1980, SI 1980/1896.

6. Remission to the original court of application for variation of registered maintenance order   An order under subsection (4) of section four of the Act remitting an application for the variation of a High Court or county court order registered in a magistrates' court to the original court shall be in the form numbered 11 in the Schedule to these Rules.

7. Notice of variation, remission, discharge or cancellation of registration by a magistrates' court of a registered order   (1) Where a High Court or county court order registered in a magistrates' court is, under subsection (2) of section four of the Act, varied by a magistrates' court, the clerk of the last-mentioned court shall give notice of the variation to the High Court or county court, as the case may be.

(2) Where an application for the variation of a High Court or county court order registered in a magistrates' court is, under subsection (4) of section four of the Act, remitted to the original court a by a magistrates' court, the clerk of the last-mentioned court shall give notice of the remission to the High Court or county court, as the case may be.

(3) Where the registration of a High Court or county court order in a magistrates' court is, under subsection (4) of section five of the Act, cancelled by the court of registration, the clerk of the last-mentioned court shall give notice of cancellation to the High Court or county court, as the case may be, stating, if such be the case, that the cancellation is in consequence of a notice given under subsection (1) of the said section five.

[(3A) Where the registration in a magistrates' court of an order made in the Court of Session or the High Court in Northern Ireland is cancelled under section 5 (4) of the Act by that magistrates' court, the clerk of that magistrates' court shall give notice of the cancellation to the appropriate officer of the original court and to the appropriate officer of the High Court (where the order is registered by virtue of Part II of the Act of 1950).

(3B) Where the registration in a magistrates' court of an order under Part II of the Act of 1950 is cancelled by that magistrates' court by virtue of section 5 (4) of the Act the clerk of the court shall give notice of the cancellation to the appropriate officer of the original court and to the appropriate officer of the High Court (where the order is registered under Part I of the Act).]

(4) Where a magistrates' court order registered in the High Court is varied or discharged by a magistrates' court, the clerk of the last-mentioned court shall give notice of the variation or discharge, as the case may be, to the High Court.

(5) Notice under the preceding provisions of this Rule shall be given by sending to the appropriate officer of the High Court or the registrar of the county court, as the case may be, a copy of the order of variation, remission, cancellation or discharge, as the case may be, certified to be a true copy thereof by the clerk of the magistrates' court and marked, in the case of a High Court maintenance order, with the title and cause number, if any, and in the case of a county court maintenance order, with the plaint or application number.

(6) For the purposes of the preceding paragraph the appropriate officer of the High Court shall be—
(a) in relation to a High Court order registered in a magistrates' court, the officer to whom notice of registration was given under Rule 4 of these Rules;

(*b*) in relation to a magistrates' court order registered in the High Court, the officer to whom a copy of the order was sent under Rule 3 of these Rules.

(7) Where a magistrates' court order registered in the High Court is discharged by a magistrates' court and it appears to the last-mentioned court that no arrears remain to be recovered, notice under subsection (3) of section five of the Act shall be given by an endorsement in the form numbered 12 in the Schedule to these Rules on the certified copy of the order of discharge referred to in paragraph (5) of this Rule.

NOTES
Amendment   Paras (3A) and (3B) of this rule were added by the Magistrates' Courts (Maintenance Orders Act 1958) (Amendment) Rules 1980, SI 1980/1896.
Appropriate officer   See r 25 (4).

8. Notices received from the High Court or a county court or from a person entitled to payments   [Subject to rule 8A below], where any notice is received—
   (*a*) of the registration in the High Court of a magistrates' court order;
   (*b*) of the discharge or variation by the High Coiurt or a county court of a High Court or county court order registered in a magistrates' court;
   [(*bb*)of the discharge or variation by the Court of Session or High Court in Northern Ireland of an order made by such court and registered in a magistrates' court;]
   (*c*) under subsection (1) or (2) of section five of the Act (which relates to the cancellation of registration);
the clerk of the magistrates' court shall cause particulars of the notice to be registered in his court by means of a memorandum entered and signed by him in the register and, in the case of a notice under subsection (1) or (2) of section five of the Act, shall cause the person in possession of any warrant of commitment, issued but not executed, for the enforcement of the order to be informed of the giving of the notice.

NOTES
Amendment   The words printed between square brackets in this rule were inserted by the Magistrates' Courts (Maintenance Orders Act 1958) (Amendment) Rules 1980, SI 1980/1896.

[8A. Notice of cancellation of registration in High Court under Part I of the Act   Where any notice is received by a court that the registration of an order in the High Court has been cancelled under section 5 (4) of the Act, the clerk of the court shall cause the particulars of the notice to be entered in the register.]

NOTES
Amendment   This rule was added by the Magistrates' Courts (Maintenance Orders Act 1958) (Amendment) Rules 1980, SI 1980/1896.

9. Jurisdiction as respects complaints for variation of High Court maintenance orders   Rule 34 of the Magistrates' Courts Rules, 1952 (which relates to jurisdiction to hear certain complaints), shall apply to a complaint for the variation of a [High Court or county court order] registered in a magistrates' court as if the order were an affiliation order made by the court of registration and as if in paragraph (4) of the said Rule for the words "shall cause" there were substituted the words "may cause".

NOTES
Amendment   The words printed between square brackets were substituted by SI 1977/1890.
Magistrates' Courts Rules 1952   SI 1952/2190 (revoked). See now the Magistrates' Courts Rules 1981, SI 1981/552, in the title Magistrates; for the equivalent provision to r 34 of the 1952 rules see r 41 of the 1981 rules.

PART II

10-20 (*Revoked and replaced by the Magistrates' Courts (Attachment of Earnings) Rules 1971, SI 1971/809, in the title Magistrates*).

PART III
MISCELLANEOUS AND SUPPLEMENTAL

21. Administering court to be informed of proceedings in foreign court   Where any decision is reached, or warrant of distress or commitment is issued, in pursuance of a complaint or application relating to a maintenance order or the enforcement of a maintenance order (including an application under section twelve of the Act, which relates to the determination whether payments are earnings), being a complaint or application heard by a magistrates' court other than the administering court—
  (*a*) the clerk of the first-mentioned court shall forthwith send by post to the clerk of the administering court an extract from the register containing a minute or memorandum of the decision or of the issue of the warrant as the case may be;
  (*b*) on receipt of the extract the last-mentioned clerk shall enter the minute or memorandum in his register.

NOTES
Section 12 of the Act   Repealed. *Cf* now s 16 of the Attachment of Earnings Act 1971, Halsbury's Statutes, 4th edn Vol 22, title Judgments and Execution (3rd edn Vol 41, p 807).

22. Review of committals, etc   (1) Where for the purpose of enforcing a maintenance order a magistrates' court has exercised its power under subsection (2) of section sixty-five of the Magistrates' Courts Act, 1952, or subsection (3) or (5) of section eighteen of the Act to postpone the issue of a warrant of commitment and under the terms of the postponement the warrant falls to be issued, the clerk of the court shall give notice to the defendant in the form numbered 15 in the Schedule to these Rules and shall attach to the said notice a copy of the form numbered 16 in the said Schedule.
    (2) An application under subsection (1) of the said section eighteen requesting that the warrant shall not be issued shall be in the form numbered 16 in the Schedule to these Rules and shall be delivered to the clerk of the court or sent to him by post.
    (3) For the purposes of subsection (2) of the said section eighteen the period for the receipt by the clerk of an application under subsection (1) of the said section shall be the period of eight days beginning with the day on which the clerk sends to the defendant the notice referred to in paragraph (1) of this Rule.
    (4) An application under subsection (4) of the said section eighteen requesting that a warrant of commitment which has been executed shall be cancelled shall be in the form numbered 17 in the Schedule to these Rules.
    (5) Where an application by a defendant under subsection (1) or (4) of the said section eighteen is considered by the court the clerk of the court shall give notice of the decision of the court, if the person in question is not present—
  (*a*) to the person in whose favour the maintenance order in question was made; and
  (*b*) except where an application under subsection (1) of the said section eighteen is dismissed, to the defendant.
    (6) Where on considering an application by a defendant under subsection (4) of the said section eighteen the court—
  (*a*) makes an order under paragraph (*b*) of subsection (5) of the said section for the cancellation of the warrant of commitment; or
  (*b*) remits under subsection (6) of the said section the whole or any part of the sum in respect of which the warrant was issued;
the clerk of the court shall forthwith give written notice of the decision to the person in charge of the prison or other place in which the defendant is detained.

NOTES
Section 65 (2) of the Magistrates' Courts Act 1952   Repealed by the Magistrates' Courts Act 1980, s 154, Sch 9, Halsbury's Statutes, 4th edn Vol 27, title Magistrates (3rd edn Vol 50 (2), pp 1575, 1604), and replaced by s 77 of that Act, *ibid*, 4th edn Vol 27, title Magistrates (3rd edn Vol 50 (2), p 1510).

23. Warrants of commitment   (1) A warrant of commitment for the enforcement of a maintenance order, being an affiliation order or an order enforceable as an affiliation order, issued in pursuance of a complaint under section seventy-four of the Magistrates' Courts Act, 1952, as amended by section sixteen of the Act, shall be in the form numbered 18 in the Schedule to these Rules:

Provided that where the issue of the warrant has been postponed under section sixty-four of the Magistrates' Courts Act, 1952, or under section eighteen of the Act the warrant shall be in the form numbered 19 in the Schedule to these Rules.

(2) (*Revoked by SI 1971/809*).

NOTES
Sections 65 and 74 of the Magistrates' Courts Act 1952   Repealed by the Magistrates' Courts Act 1980, s 154, Sch 9, Halsbury's Statutes, 4th edn Vol 27, title Magistrates (3rd edn Vol 50 (2), pp 1575, 1604), and replaced by ss 77, 93 of that Act, *ibid*, 4th edn Vol 27, title Magistrates (3rd edn Vol 50 (2), pp 1510, 1523).

24. Revocations   (1) The forms of warrants of commitment numbered 20 and 21 in the Schedule to the Bastardy (Forms) Order, 1915, shall be omitted therefrom and the form numbered 88 in the Schedule to the Magistrates' Courts (Forms) Rules, 1952, shall cease to apply to a warrant of commitment the issue of which has been postponed under section sixty-five of the Magistrates' Courts Act, 1952, or under section eighteen of the Act, being a warrant of commitment for the enforcement of a maintenance order.

(2) The forms numbered 23, 24 and 25 in the Schedule to the Bastardy (Forms) Order, 1915 (which relate to the attachment of pension or income), shall be omitted therefrom.

(3) The following provisions of the Magistrates' Courts Rules, 1952, are hereby revoked, that is to say—

(*a*) paragraph (8) of Rule 34 (which relates to the giving of information as respects certain proceedings in a foreign court); and

(*b*) Rule 36 (which relates to the attachment of income or pension).

NOTES
Bastardy (Forms) Order 1915   SR & O 1915/208, in the title Infants (Part 4).
Magistrates' Courts (Forms) Rules 1952   SI 1952/2191 (revoked); see now the Magistrates' Courts (Forms) Rules 1981, SI 1981/553, in the title Magistrates.
Magistrates' Courts Rules 1952   SI 1952/2190 (revoked); see now the Magistrates' Courts Rules 1981, SI 1981/552, in the title Magistrates.
Section 65 of the Magistrates' Courts Act 1952   Repealed by the Magistrates' Courts Act 1980, s 154, Sch 9, Halsbury's Statutes, 4th edn Vol 27, title Magistrates (3rd edn Vol 50 (2), pp 1575, 1604), and replaced by s 77 of that Act, *ibid*, 4th edn Vol 27, title Magistrates (3rd Vol 50 (2), p 1510).

25. Interpretation   (1) Subsection (3) of section one of the Act shall apply to the interpretation of Part I of these Rules as it applies to the interpretation of Part I of the Act.

(2) Section twenty-one of the Act shall apply to the interpretation of these Rules as it applies to the interpretation of the Act.

(3) The Interpretation Act, 1889, shall apply to the interpretation of these Rules as it applies to the interpretation of an Act of Parliament.

[(4) In these rules—

"the Act" means the Maintenance Orders Act 1958;

"the Act of 1950" means the Maintenance Orders Act 1950;

"appropriate officer of the High Court" means the Senior Registrar of the Principal Registry of the Family Division of the High Court or such district registrar as may be specified by the applicant;

"appropriate officer of the original court" means—
(i) the Sheriff-clerk, in the case of a sheriff court in Scotland;
(ii) the clerk of petty sessions, in the case of a magistrates' court in Northern Ireland;
(iii) the Deputy Principal Clerk of Session, in the case of the Court of Session;
(iv) the Chief Registrar of the Queen's Bench Division (Matrimonial), in the case of the High Court of Justice in Northern Ireland.]

(5) Any reference in these Rules to the administering court in relation to a maintenance order or a related attachment of earnings order is a reference to the magistrates' court—
(a) which made the maintenance order;
(b) in which the maintenance order is registered under the Act, under Part II of the Maintenance Orders Act, 1950, or under the Maintenance Orders (Facilities for Enforcement) Act, 1920; or
(c) by which the maintenance order was confirmed under the Maintenance Orders (Facilities for Enforcement) Act, 1920.

(6) Any reference in these Rules to the register is a reference to the register kept in accordance with Rule 54 of the Magistrates' Courts Rules, 1952.

(7) Any reference in these Rules to a form in the Schedule to these Rules shall include a reference to a form to the like effect with such variations as the circumstances may require.

NOTES
Amendment Para (4) of this rule was substituted by the Magistrates' Courts (Maintenance Orders Act 1958) (Amendment) Rules 1980, SI 1980/1896.
Magistrates' Courts Rules 1952 SI 1952/2190 (revoked). The register referred to is now kept in accordance with the Magistrates' Courts Rules 1981, SI 1981/552, r 66, in the title Magistrates.
Interpretation Act 1889 Repealed and replaced by the Interpretation Act 1978, in the title Statutory Instruments, Vol 1 of this work.
Maintenance Orders Act 1958 Halsbury's Statutes, 4th edn Vol 27, title Matrimonial Law (Pt 3) (3rd edn Vol 17, p 293 *et seq*).
Maintenance Orders Act 1950 *Ibid*, 4th edn Vol 6, title Children, Vol 27, title Matrimonial Law (Pt 3) (3rd edn Vol 17, pp 235, 280, 594).
Maintenance Orders (Facilities for Enforcement) Act 1920 Halsbury's Statutes, 4th edn Vol 27, title Matrimonial Law (Pt 3) (3rd edn Vol 17, p 272). This Act is prospectively repealed by the Maintenance Orders (Reciprocal Enforcement) Act 1972, s 22 (2) (a), *ibid*, 4th edn Vol 27, title Matrimonial Law (Pt 3) (3rd edn Vol 42, p 738) as from a day to be appointed.

26. Citation and commencement These Rules may be cited as the Magistrates' Courts (Maintenance Orders Act, 1958) Rules, 1959, and shall come into operation on the sixteenth day of February, 1959.

SCHEDULE

NOTES
This Schedule contains the forms described below; the relevant rules are specified against each form. The forms are not reproduced in this work but will be found in Stone's Justices' Manual.

Form 1	Certificate of clerk of magistrates' court as to amount due and unpaid (r 2 (4) (a)).
Form 2	Certificate of clerk of magistrates' court that no process for enforcement remains in force (r 2 (4) (a)).
Form 3	Certificate of clerk of magistrates' court that no process for enforcement remains in force and no proceedings for variation are pending (r 2 (4) (a)).
Form 4	Declaration as to the amount due and unpaid (r 2 (4) (b)).
Form 5	Declaration that no process of enforcement remains in force (r 2 (4) (b)).
Form 6	Declaration that no process for enforcement remains in force and no proceedings for variation are pending (r 2 (4) (b)).
Form 7	Certificate of clerk of magistrates' court that copy of maintenance order is a true copy sent for registration (r 3).
Form 8	Notice that payments have become payable through the clerk of a magistrates' court (r 5 (1)).
Form 9	Notice that payments have ceased to be payable through the clerk of the magistrates' court (r 5 (2)).
Form 10	Notice of cancellation of registration (r 5 (3)).
Form 11	Order remitting to the original court application for variation of registered maintenance order (r 6).
Form 12	Endorsement that no arrears remain to be recoverable (r 7 (7)).
Form 13	*(Revoked by SI 1971/809.)*

Form 14   *(Revoked by SI 1971/809.)*
Form 15   Notice that warrant of commitment falls to be issued (r 22 (1)).
Form 16   Application requesting that warrant should not be issued (r 22 (1), (2)).
Form 17   Application requesting that warrant should be cancelled (r 22 (4)).
Form 18   Warrant of commitment for the enforcement of affiliation order or order enforceable
           as an affiliation order for use in case of immediate issue (r 23 (1)).
Form 19   Warrant of commitment for enforcement of affiliation order or order enforceable
           as an affiliation order for use where issue has been postponed (r 23 (1)).
Form 20   *(Revoked by SI 1971/809.)*

NOTES
Amendment   Forms 3, 6, 8, 9, 10 were substituted by the Magistrates' Courts (Maintenance Orders Act 1958) (Amendment) Rules 1980, SI 1980/1896.

THE MAINTENANCE ORDERS (FACILITIES FOR ENFORCEMENT) ORDER 1959
SI 1959/377

NOTES
Authority   This Order in Council was made on 11 March 1959 under s 12 of the Maintenance Orders (Facilities for Enforcement) Act 1920, Halsbury's Statutes, 4th edn Vol 27, title Matrimonial Law (Pt 3) (3rd edn Vol 17, p 279) and s 19 of the Maintenance Orders Act 1958, *ibid*, 4th edn Vol 27, title Matrimonial Law (Pt 3) (3rd edn Vol 17, p 315), and all other enabling powers. Section 12 of the Act of 1920 and s 19 of the Act of 1958 are repealed, as from a day to be appointed, by the Maintenance Orders (Reciprocal Enforcement) Act 1972; see further the Introductory Note at p 300, *ante*.
Commencement   11 March 1959; *ie*, date when made.
Partial revocation   See the Maintenance Orders (Facilities for Enforcement) (Revocation) Order 1974, SI 1974/557, p 322, *post*, and SI 1975/2188, 1979/116 and 1983/1124 which are noted thereto. The orders make consequential amendments in Schedule 1 hereto.
General   See the Introductory Note under the head "Reciprocal arrangements under the Acts of 1920 and 1972", p 300, *ante*.

1.   The Maintenance Orders (Facilities for Enforcement) Act, 1920, shall extend to the countries and territories specified in the First Schedule hereto.

NOTES
Maintenance Orders (Facilities for Enforcement) Act 1920   Halsbury's Statutes, 4th edn Vol 27, title Matrimonial Law (Pt 3) (3rd edn Vol 17, p 272). This Act is prospectively repealed by the Maintenance Orders (Reciprocal Enforcement) Act 1972, s 22 (2) (*a*), *ibid*, 4th edn Vol 27, title Matrimonial Law (Pt 3) (3rd edn Vol 42, p 738), as from a day to be appointed.

2.   The Orders extending the Maintenance Orders (Facilities for Enforcement) Act, 1920, to the territories mentioned in Part 1 of the Second Schedule hereto and the Orders specified in Part 2 of the Second Schedule hereto are hereby revoked.

3.   (1) This Order may be cited as the Maintenance Orders (Facilities for Enforcement) Order, 1959.
    (2) The Interpretation Act, 1889, shall apply for the purposes of interpreting this Order as it applies for the purpose of interpreting an Act of Parliament.

NOTES
Interpretation Act 1889   Repealed and replaced by the Interpretation Act 1978, in the title Statutory Instruments, Vol 1 of this work.

FIRST SCHEDULE

Aden Colony.
. . .
Australia.
. . .
  Territory of Cocos (Keeling) Islands,
  Territory of Christmas Island
    (Indian Ocean).
Bahamas.
. . .
Basutoland.
Bechuanaland Protectorate.
. . .
British Guiana.
British Honduras.

British Solomon Islands Protectorate.
Brunei.
Cayman Islands.
Ceylon.
Cyprus.
. . .
Dominica.
Federation of Malaya.
. . .
Gambia Colony.
. . .
Gilbert and Ellice Islands.
Grenada.
Bailiwick of Guernsey.

Jamaica.
Jersey.

. . .

Leeward Islands.
  Antigua.
  Montserrat.
  St Christopher and Nevis. . .
  Virgin Islands.

. . .

Mauritius.

. . .

Newfoundland and Prince Edward
  Island.
Nigeria, excluding the Cameroons.

. . .

North Borneo.
Northern Rhodesia Protectorate.

. . .

Nyasaland Protectorate.

. . .

St Lucia.
St Vincent.
Sarawak.

. . .

Seychelles.
Sierra Leone.
Sierra Leone Protectorate.

. . .

Somaliland Protectorate.

. . .

Swaziland Protectorate.

. . .

Trinidad and Tobago.

. . .

Uganda Protectorate.

. . .

Yukon Territory.
Zanzibar Protectorate.

NOTES
Many of the countries and territories listed above have been affected by subsequent constitutional and jurisdictional changes and certain of them have been renamed; see the title Dominions and Dependencies (Part 1).
Amendment   This Schedule is printed as amended (*a*) by SI 1974/557, 1975/2188, 1979/116 and 1983/1124 (see p 322, *post*); and (*b*) by s 4 (4) of the Pakistan Act 1973 (which deleted Pakistan).

SECOND SCHEDULE

NOTES
This Schedule, which consists of two parts, specified the Orders in Council revoked by art 2.
  The revoked orders specified in Part 1 are (the territories concerned being shown in each case in brackets):—SR & O 1921/962 (Dominica, Grenada, Leeward Islands and Mauritius); 1921/1136 (Malta and Straits Settlements); 1921/1244 (Nyasaland and Somaliland Protectorates); 1921/1395 (St. Vincent, Nigeria and Cyprus); 1921/1396 (Nigeria and the Northern Territories of the Gold Coast); 1921/1640 (Isle of Man); 1921/1641 (Ashanti, Ceylon, Hong Kong, Gibraltar and St Lucia); 1921/1642 (Southern Rhodesia and the Uganda Protectorate); 1921/1935 (Gold Coast, Gambia and Trinidad and Tobago); 1922/128 (Basutoland and Falkland Islands); 1922/127 (British India); 1922/129 (Northern Rhodesia, Bechuanaland, Swaziland and Zanzibar Protectorates); 1922/130 (Queensland); 1922/468 (Western Australia and Tasmania); 1922/721 (New Zealand); 1922/722 (Bermuda and Gilbert and Ellice Islands); 1922/1207 (Fiji and Seychelles); 1922/1208 (British Solomon Islands Protectorate); 1923/474 (Barbados, British Guiana, Kenya and Sierra Leone); 1923/475 (Kenya and Sierra Leone Protectorates); 1923/476 (Northern Territory of Australia); 1923/477 (South Australia); 1923/1285 (Bahamas, British Honduras, St Helena and Norfolk Island); 1923/1286 (South Africa); 1924/82 (New South Wales); 1924/760 (Papua); 1924/1222 (Jamaica); 1926/558 (Federated Malay States, Perak, Selangor, Negri Sembilan and Pahang); 1926/586 (Victoria); 1927/659 (Australia); 1936/81 (Cayman Islands); 1939/522 (Aden); 1940/201 (Malay Protected States, Brunei, Johore, Kedah, Kelanton, Perlis and Trengganu); 1940/661 (Sarawak); 1946/1908 (Saskatchewan, British Columbia and Manitoba); 1947/1170 (Alberta).
  The revoked orders specified in Part 2 are (the territories concerned being shown in each case in brackets):— SI 1948/2579 (North Borneo); 1949/602 (Ontario); 1951/146 (Yukon Territory); 1951/429 (Nova Scotia); 1952/154 (Newfoundland and Prince Edward Island); 1952/454 (New Brunswick); 1952/1220 (Northwest Territories); 1953/1215 (Jersey); 1955/1395 (Guernsey).

THE RECIPROCAL ENFORCEMENT OF MAINTENANCE ORDERS (DESIGNATION OF RECIPROCATING COUNTRIES) ORDER 1974
SI 1974/556

NOTES
Authority   This Order in Council was made on 26 March 1974 under ss 1 and 24 of the Maintenance Orders (Reciprocal Enforcement) Act 1972, Halsbury's Statutes, 4th edn Vol 27, title Matrimonial Law (Pt 3) (3rd edn Vol 42, pp 717, 739).
Commencement   8 May 1974; see art 1.
Amendment   This order is printed as amended by the Reciprocal Enforcement of Maintenance Orders (Designation of Reciprocating Countries) Order 1979, SI 1979/115, p 332, *post*, and the Reciprocal Enforcement of Maintenance Orders (Designation of Reciprocating Countries) Order 1983, SI 1983/1125, p 336, *post*.
General   Part I of the Maintenance Orders (Reciprocal Enforcement) Act 1972 makes fresh provision for the reciprocal enforcement of maintenance orders made in the United Kingdom or in countries and territories outside the United Kingdom; see further the Introductory Note

at p 300, *ante*. Section 1 of the Act enables any country to be designated as a reciprocating country for the purposes of the said Part I; and this order so designates the countries or territories set out in the Schedule.

For further orders designating other countries for the purposes of Part I, see SI 1975/2187, 1979/115 and 1983/1125 pp 331, 332, 336, *post*. Part I of the Act is also applied to States party to the 1973 Hague Convention on the Recognition and Enforcement of Decisions Relating to Maintenance Obligations by SI 1979/1317, p 334, *post*.

1. This Order may be cited as the Reciprocal Enforcement of Maintenance Orders (Designation of Reciprocating Countries) Order 1974 and shall come into operation on 8th May 1974.

2. (1) In this Order—
"the Act of 1972" means the Maintenance Orders (Reciprocal Enforcement) Act 1972;
"the Act of 1920" means the Maintenance Orders (Facilities for Enforcement) Act 1920;
"column (1)" and "column (2)" mean respectively columns (1) and (2) of the Schedule to this Order.
(2) The Interpretation Act 1889 shall apply for the interpretation of this Order as it applies for the interpretation of an Act of Parliament.

NOTES
Maintenance Orders (Reciprocal Enforcement) Act 1972   Halsbury's Statutes, 4th edn Vol 27, title Matrimonial Law (Pt 3) (3rd edn Vol 42, p 714).
Maintenance Orders (Facilities for Enforcement) Act 1920   Halsbury's Statutes, 4th edn Vol 27, title Matrimonial Law (Pt 3) (3rd edn Vol 17, p 272. This Act is prospectively repealed by the Maintenance Orders (Reciprocal Enforcement) Act 1972, s 22 (2) (*a*), *ibid*, 4th edn Vol 27, title Matrimonial Law (Pt 3) (3rd edn Vol 42, p 738), as from a day to be appointed.
Interpretation Act 1889   Repealed and replaced by the Interpretation Act 1978, in the title Statutory Instruments, Vol 1 of this work.

3. Each of the countries and territories specified in column (1) is hereby designated as a reciprocating country for the purposes of Part I of the Act of 1972 as regards maintenance of the description specified in respect of that country or territory in column (2).

4. (1) Sections 5, 12 to 15, 17, 18 and 21 of the Act of 1972 shall apply in relation to a maintenance order transmitted under section 2 or 3 of the Act of 1920 to one of the countries and territories specified in column (1), being an order of the description specified in respect of that country or territory in column (2) to which immediately before the coming into operation of this Order the Act of 1920 applied, as they apply in relation to a maintenance order sent to that country or territory in puruance of section 2 of the Act of 1972 or made by virtue of section 3 or 4 of the Act of 1972 and confirmed by a competent court in that country or territory.

(2) Sections 8 to 21 of the Act of 1972 shall apply in relation to a maintenance order made in one of the countries and territories specified in column (1), being an order of the description specified in respect of that country or territory in column (2) to which immediately before the coming into operation of this Order the Act of 1920 applied and not being an order which immediately before that date is registered in the High Court or the High Court of Justice in Northern Ireland under section 1 of the Act of 1920, as they apply in relation to a registered order.

(3) A maintenance order made by a court in one of the countries and territories specified in column (1) being an order of the description specified in respect of that country or territory in column (2) which has been confirmed by a court in England, Wales or Northern Ireland under section 4 of the Act of 1920 and is in force immediately before the coming into operation of this Order, shall be registered under section 7 (5) of the Act of 1972 in like manner as if it had been confirmed by that court in England, Wales or Northern Ireland under subsection (2) of that section.

(4) Any proceedings brought under or by virtue of any provision of the Act of 1920 in a court in England, Wales or Northern Ireland which are pending immediately before the coming into operation of this Order, being proceedings affecting a person resident in one of the countries and territories specified in column (1), shall be continued as if they had been brought under or by virtue of the corresponding provision of the Act of 1972.

SCHEDULE   Article 3
COUNTRIES AND TERRITORIES DESIGNATED AS
RECIPROCATING COUNTRIES

(1) Country or territory	(2) Description of maintenance orders to which designation extends
Australian Capital Territory	Maintenance orders other than— . . . (b) orders obtained by or in favour of a public authority
British Columbia	Maintenance orders generally
Gibraltar	Maintenance orders generally
Manitoba	Maintenance orders [generally]
New South Wales	Maintenance orders other than— . . . (b) orders obtained by or in favour of a public authority
New Zealand	[Maintenance orders generally]
Northern Territory of Australia	Maintenance orders other than— . . . (b) orders obtained by or in favour of a public authority
Nova Scotia	Maintenance orders other than— (a) maintenance orders of the description contained in [paragraph (b) of the definition of "Maintenance order" in section 21 (1) of the Act of 1972 (orders for the payment of birth and funeral expenses of child), and] (b) orders obtained by or in favour of a public authority
Ontario	Maintenance orders other than— . . . (b) maintenance orders of the description contained in the said paragraph (b), and
Queensland	Maintenance orders other than— . . . (b) orders obtained by or in favour of a public authority
South Australia	Maintenance orders other than— . . . (b) orders obtained by or in favour of a public authority
Tasmania	Maintenance orders other than . . . (b) orders obtained by or in favour of a public authority
Victoria	Maintenance orders other than— . . . (b) orders obtained by or in favour of a public authority

NOTES
This Schedule is printed as amended by SI 1979/115 and 1983/1125.

THE MAINTENANCE ORDERS (FACILITIES FOR ENFORCEMENT) (REVOCATION) ORDER 1974
SI 1974/557

NOTES
Authority   This Order in Council was made on 26 March 1974 under s 19 of the Maintenance Orders Act 1958, Halsbury's Statutes, 4th edn Vol 27, title Matrimonial Law (Pt 3) (3rd edn Vol 17, p 315) (repealed, as from a day to be appointed, by the Maintenance Orders (Reciprocal Enforcement) Act 1972).
Commencement   8 May 1974.
General   This order revoked the Maintenance Orders (Facilities for Enforcement) Order 1959, SI 1959/377, p 318, *ante*, insofar as it extended the Maintenance Orders (Facilities for Enforcement) Act 1920 to the Australian Territories and States (except Western Australia), British Columbia, Gibraltar, Manitoba, New Zealand, Nova Scotia and Ontario. Those countries and territories are now designated as reciprocating countries for the purposes of Part I of the Maintenance Orders (Reciprocal Enforcement) Act 1972 by the Reciprocal Enforcement of Maintenance Orders (Designation of Reciprocating Countries) Order 1974, SI 1974/556, p 319, *ante*.
    Further revocation   The Maintenance Orders (Facilities for Enforcement) (Revocation) Order 1975, SI 1975/2188 (made under the like enabling power), similarly revoked SI 1959/377 insofar as it extended the Act of 1920 to Barbados, Bermuda, Ghana, India, Kenya Colony, Kenya Protectorate, Malta, New Brunswick, Northwest Territories of Canada and the Republic of South Africa. Those countries are now designated as reciprocating countries for the purposes of Part I of the Maintenance Orders (Reciprocal Enforcement) Act 1972 by the Reciprocal Enforcement of Maintenance Orders (Designation of Reciprocating Countries) Order 1975, SI 1975/2187, p 331, *post*.
    Likewise the Maintenance Orders (Facilities for Enforcement) (Revocation) Order 1979, SI 1979/116, revoked SI 1959/377 insofar as it extended the Act of 1920 to Alberta, Fiji, Hong Kong, Norfolk Island, Saskatchewan, Singapore, Turks and Caicos Islands and Western Australia. Those countries are now designated as reciprocating countries for the purposes of Part I of the Act of 1972 by SI 1979/115, p 332, *post*.
    In addition the Maintenance Orders (Facilities for Enforcement) (Revocation) Order 1983, SI 1983/1124, revoked SI 1959/377 insofar as it extended the Act of 1920 to Anguilla, the Falkland Islands and Dependencies, the Isle of Man, Papua, St Helena and Zimbabwe. Those countries and territories are designated as reciprocating countries for the purposes of Part I of the Act of 1972 by SI 1983/1125, p 336, *post*.

THE MAGISTRATES' COURTS (RECIPROCAL ENFORCEMENT OF MAINTENANCE ORDERS) RULES 1974
SI 1974/668

NOTES
Authority   These rules were made on 4 April 1974 by the Lord Chancellor under s 15 of the Justices of the Peace Act 1949, as extended by s 122 of the Magistrates' Courts Act 1952, and ss 2 (3) and (4), 3 (5) (*b*) and (*c*), 5 (4) and (9) (*a*), 6 (2) and (3), 7 (2) and (5), 8 (5) and (6), 9 (5) and (10), 10 (1)-(5) and (7), 11 (1) (*b*), 14 (1), 16 (1), 18 (1) and 23 (3) of the Maintenance Orders (Reciprocal Enforcement) Act 1972, Halsbury's Statutes, 4th edn Vol 27, title Matrimonial Law (Pt 3) (3rd edn Vol 42, p 718 *et seq*). The relevant provisions of s 15 of the 1949 Act and s 122 of the 1952 Act were repealed by the Magistrates' Courts Act 1980, s 154 (3), Sch 9, and the rules now have effect as if made under s 144 of that Act, Halsbury's Statutes, 4th edn Vol 27, title Magistrates (3rd edn Vol 50 (2), p 1565; for s 154 (3), Sch 9, see pp 1575, 1604).
Commencement   8 May 1974; see r 1.
Amendment   These rules are printed as amended by the Magistrates' Courts (Reciprocal Enforcement of Maintenance Orders) (Amendment) Rules 1975, SI 1975/2236, the Magistrates' Courts (Reciprocal Enforcement of Maintenance Orders) (Amendment) Rules 1979, SI 1979/170, and the Magistrates' Courts (Reciprocal Enforcement of Maintenance Orders) (Amendment) Rules 1983, SI 1983/1148.
Interpretation   See r 2.
General   These rules make provision, in relation to magistrates' courts, for the various matters which are to be prescribed under Part I of the Maintenance Orders (Reciprocal Enforcement) Act 1972.

1.   These Rules may be cited as the Magistrates' Courts (Reciprocal Enforcement of Maintenance Orders) Rules 1974 and shall come into operation on 8th May 1974.

2.   (1) In these Rules, unless the context otherwise requires—
    "the Act" means the Maintenance Orders (Reciprocal Enforcement) Act 1972; and

"his register", in relation to a justices' clerk, means the register kept by that clerk in pursuance of rule 54 of the Magistrates' Courts Rules 1968.

(2) The Interpretation Act 1889 shall apply for the interpretation of these Rules as it applies for the interpretation of an Act of Parliament.

NOTES

Magistrates' Courts Rules 1968 SI 1968/1920; revoked and replaced by the Magistrates' Courts Rules 1981, SI 1981/552, in the title Magistrates.

Maintenance Orders (Reciprocal Enforcement) Act 1972 Halsbury's Statutes, 4th edn Vol 27, title Matrimonial Law (Pt 3) (3rd edn Vol 42, p 714).

Interpretation Act 1889 Repealed and replaced by the Interpretation Act 1978, in the title Statutory Instruments, Vol 1 of this work.

3. The officer of any court, by or in relation to whom anything is to be done in pursuance of any provision of Part I of the Act shall, where that court is a magistrates' court, be the justices' clerk.

4. (1) An application under section 2 of the Act (transmission of maintenance order made in the United Kingdom for enforcement in reciprocating country) may, where the court which made the maintenance order to which the application relates is a magistrates' court, be made in writing by or on behalf of the payee under the order.

(2) Any application made in pursuance of paragraph (1) above shall—

(*a*) specify the date on which the order was made;

(*b*) contain such particulars as are known to the applicant of the whereabouts of the payer;

(*c*) specify any matters likely to assist in the identification of the payer;

(*d*) where possible, be accompanied by a recent photograph of the payer.

(3) In this rule, "the payer" means the payer under the order to which the application relates.

5. A document setting out or summarising any evidence, required by section 3 (5) (*b*), 5 (4) or 9 (5) of the Act (provisional orders) to be authenticated shall be authenticated by a certificate, signed by one of the justices before whom that evidence was given, that the document is the original document containing or recording or, as the case may be, summarising that evidence or a true copy of that document.

6. (1) Subject to paragraph (2) below, any documents required by section 5 (4) or 9 (5) of the Act to be sent to a court in a reciprocating country shall be sent to that court by post.

(2) Where the court to which the documents are to be sent is in a country specified in Schedule 1 to these Rules, such documents shall be sent to the Secretary of State for transmission to that court.

7. (1) For the purposes of compliance with section 5 (9) of the Act (revocation by United Kingdom court of provisional order) there shall be served on the person on whose application the maintenance order was made a notice which shall—

(*a*) set out the evidence received or taken, as the case may be, in pursuance of that subsection;

(*b*) inform that person that it appears to the court that the maintenance order ought not to have been made; and

(*c*) inform that person that if he wishes to make representations with respect to the evidence set out in the notice he may do so orally or in writing and that if he wishes to adduce further evidence he should notify the clerk of the magistrates' court which made the maintenance order.

(2) Where a justices' clerk receives notification that the person on whose application the maintenance order was made wishes to adduce further evidence, he shall fix a date for the hearing of such evidence and shall send that person written notice of the date fixed.

8. (1) Where a certified copy of an order, not being a provisional order, is received by a justices' clerk who is required under any provision of Part I of the Act to register the order, he shall cause the order to be registered in his court by means of a minute or memorandum entered and signed by him in his register.

(2) Where any magistrates' court makes or confirms an order which is required under section 7 (5) or 9 (10) of the Act to be registered, the justices' clerk shall enter and sign a minute or memorandum thereof in his register.

(3) Every minute or memorandum entered in pursuance of paragraph (1) or (2) above shall specify the section of the Act under which the order in question is registered.

9. (1) Payment of sums due under a registered order shall, while the order is registered in a magistrates' court, be made to the clerk of the registering court during such hours and at such place as that clerk may direct; and a justices' clerk to whom payments are made under this rule shall send those payments by post to the court which made the order or to such other person or authority as that court or the Secretary of State may from time to time direct:

Provided that if the court which made the order is in one of the countries or territories specified in Schedule 2 to these Rules the justices' clerk shall [unless the Secretary of State otherwise directs] send any such sums to the Crown Agents for Overseas Governments and Administrations for transmission to the person to whom they are due.

(2) Where it appears to a justices' clerk to whom payments under any maintenance order are made by virtue of paragraph (1) above that any sums payable under the order are in arrear he may and, if such sums are in arrear to an amount equal to four times the sum payable weekly under the order, he shall, whether the person for whose benefit the payment should have been made requests him to do so or not, proceed in his own name for the recovery of those sums, unless it appears to him that it is unreasonable in the circumstances to do so.

NOTES
Amendment   The words printed between square brackets in the proviso to para (1) were inserted by SI 1979/170.

10. (1) Subject to paragraph (2) below, where a request is made by or on behalf of a court in a reciprocating country for the taking in England and Wales of the evidence of a person residing therein, the following magistrates' courts shall have power under section 14 (1) of the Act (obtaining of evidence needed for purpose of certain proceedings) to take that evidence, that is to say—
  (*a*) where the maintenance order to which the proceedings in the court in the reciprocating country relate was made by a magistrates' court, the court which made the order;
  (*b*) where the maintenance order to which those proceedings relate is registered in a magistrates' court, the court in which the order is registered;
  (*c*) a magistrates' court which has received such a request from the Secretary of State.

(2) The power conferred by paragraph (1) above may, with the agreement of a court having that power, be exercised by any other magistrates' court which, because the person whose evidence is to be taken resides within its jurisdiction or for any other reason, the first-mentioned court considers could more conveniently take the evidence; but nothing in this paragraph shall derogate from the power of any court specified in paragraph (1) above.

(3) Subject to paragraph (4) below, where the evidence of any person is to be taken by a magistrates' court under the foregoing provisions of this rule—
  (*a*) the evidence shall be taken in the same manner as if that person were a witness in proceedings on a complaint;
  (*b*) any oral evidence so taken shall be put into writing and read to the

person who gave it, who shall be required to sign the document; and
(c) the justices by whom the evidence of any person is so taken shall certify
at the foot of any document setting out the evidence of, or produced
in evidence by, that person that such evidence was taken, or document
received in evidence, as the case may be, by them.

(4) Where such a request as is mentioned in paragraph (1) above includes
a request that the evidence be taken in a particular manner, the magistrates'
court by which the evidence is taken shall, so far as circumstances permit,
comply with that request.

(5) Any document such as is mentioned in paragraph (3) (c) above shall
be sent—
(a) where the request for the taking of the evidence was made by or on
behalf of a court in a country specified in Schedule 1 to these Rules,
to the Secretary of State for transmission to that court;
(b) in any other case, to the court in the reciprocating country by or on
behalf of which the request was made.

11. Any request under section 14 (5) of the Act for the taking or providing
of evidence by a court in a reciprocating country shall, where made by a
magistrates' court, be communicated in writing to the court in question.

12. (1) Where a magistrates' court makes an order, not being a provisional
order, varying a maintenance order to which section 5 of the Act (variation
and revocation of maintenance order made in the United Kingdom) applies,
the justices' clerk shall send written notice of the making of the order to the
Secretary of State; and where the order is made by virtue of paragraph (a)
or (b) of subsection (3) of that section, he shall send such written notice to
the court in a reciprocating country which would, if the order had been a
provisional order, have had power to confirm the order.

(2) Where a magistrates' court revokes a maintenance order to which section 5 of the Act applies, the justices' clerk shall send a written notice of the
revocation to the Secretary of State and to the court in a reciprocating country
which has power to confirm that maintenance order, or by which the order
has been confirmed, or in which the order is registered for enforcement, as
the case may be.

(3) Where under section 9 of the Act (variation and revocation of maintenance order registered in United Kingdom court) a magistrates' court makes
an order, not being a provisional order, varying or revoking a registered
order, the justices' clerk shall send written notice of the making of the order
to the court in a reciprocating country which made the registered order.

(4) Where under section 7 (2) of the Act (confirmation by United Kingdom
court of provisional maintenance order made in reciprocating country) a magistrates' court confirms an order to which section 7 of the Act applies, the
justices' clerk shall send written notice of the confirmation to the court in a
reciprocating country which made the order.

13. (1) Where a justices' clerk—
(a) registers under section 6 (3) of the Act (registration in United Kingdom
court of maintenance order made in reciprocating country) an order
to which section 6 of the Act applies; or
(b) registers under section 7 (5) of the Act an order which has been confirmed in pursuance of section 7 (2) of the Act,
he shall send written notice to the Secretary of State that the order has been
duly registered.
(2) (*Renumbered to stand as r* 14 (1) (*see post*) by SI 1975/2336.)
(3) Where a justices' clerk registers a maintenance order under section 10
(4) of the Act, he shall send written notice to the Secretary of State . . . that
the order has been duly registered.

NOTES
Amendment   The words omitted in para (3) were deleted by SI 1975/2236.

[**14.** (1) Where a justices' clerk cancels the registration of a maintenance order under section 10 (1) of the Act (cancellation of registration and transfer of order) he shall send written notice of the cancellation to the payer under the order.

(2) Where a justices' clerk registers a maintenance order under section 6 (3), 7 (5), 9 (10), 10 (4), 10 (5) or 23 (3) of the Act, he shall send to the payer under the order written notice stating—

(*a*) that the order has been duly registered;

(*b*) that sums due under the order should be paid to the justices' clerk; and

(*c*) the hours during which and the place at which such payments should be made.]

NOTES

Para (2) was inserted by SI 1975/2236, which also renumbered as para 14 (1) the paragraph formerly numbered 13 (2).

SCHEDULE 1   Rules 6 (2) and 10 (5)

RECIPROCATING COUNTRIES TO WHICH DOCUMENTS ARE TRANSMITTED VIA THE SECRETARY OF STATE

British Columbia
New Zealand
Nova Scotia
Ontario
[Ghana
India
Kenya
New Brunswick
Northwest Territories of Canada
The Republic of South Africa]
[Alberta
Saskatchewan
Turks and Caicos Islands
United Republic of Tanzania (except Zanzibar)]
[Papua New Guinea
Zimbabwe]

NOTES

Amendment   The countries and territories printed between the first set of square brackets were inserted by SI 1975/2236, those between the second set by SI 1979/170, and those between the third set by SI 1983/1148.

SCHEDULE 2   Rule 9 (1)

COUNTRIES AND TERRITORIES IN WHICH SUMS ARE PAYABLE THROUGH CROWN AGENTS FOR OVERSEAS GOVERNMENTS AND ADMINISTRATIONS
Gibraltar
[Barbados
Bermuda
Ghana
Kenya]
[Fiji
Hong Kong
Singapore
Turks and Caicos Islands
United Republic of Tanzania (except Zanzibar)]
[Anguilla
Falkland Islands and Dependencies
St Helena]

NOTES

Amendment   The countries and territories printed between the first set of square brackets were inserted by SI 1975/2236, those between the second set by SI 1979/170, and those between the third set by SI 1983/1148.

THE RECIPROCAL ENFORCEMENT OF MAINTENANCE ORDERS (REPUBLIC OF IRELAND) ORDER 1974
SI 1974/2140

NOTES

Authority This Order in Council was made on 18 December 1974 under s 40 of the Maintenance Orders (Reciprocal Enforcement) Act 1972, Halsbury's Statutes, 4th edn Vol 27, title Matrimonial Law (Pt 3) (3rd edn Vol 42, p 753).

Commencement 1 April 1975.

General This order applies the provisions of Part I of the Maintenance Orders (Reciprocal Enforcement) Act 1972 to the Republic of Ireland subject to exceptions, adaptations and modifications (set out in Schedule 1). Schedule 2 to the order sets out the said Part I as so applied.

The principal modifications effected by the order are:— (*a*) in England and Wales and Northern Ireland, a provisional maintenance order may be confirmed by the court which made it and it does not require confirmation by a court in the Republic of Ireland; (*b*) a maintenance order made by a court in the Republic of Ireland may not be varied or revoked by a court in the United Kingdom and only a United Kingdom court may vary or revoke a maintenance order made in the United Kingdom; (*c*) registration of a maintenance order made in the Republic of Ireland may be refused on certain grounds (*eg*, if such registration is contrary to public policy or is irreconcilable with a judgment given in the United Kingdom in proceedings between the same parties) and all orders which are registered are orders requiring no confirmation.

THE MAGISTRATES' COURTS (RECIPROCAL ENFORCEMENT OF MAINTENANCE ORDERS) (REPUBLIC OF IRELAND) RULES 1975
SI 1975/286

NOTES

Authority These rules were made on 27 February 1975 by the Lord Chancellor under s 15 of the Justices of the Peace Act 1949, as extended by s 122 of the Magistrates' Courts Act 1952, and ss 2 (3) and (4), 3 (5) (*b*) and (*c*), (6A) and (6C), 5 (2), 6 (2), (3), (6) and (9), 8 (5) and (6), 9 (3), 10 (1)-(5) and (7), 14 (1), 16 (1) and 18 (1) of the Maintenance Orders (Reciprocal Enforcement) Act 1972, Halsbury's Statutes, 4th edn Vol 27, title Matrimonial Law (Pt 3) (3rd edn Vol 42, p 718 *et seq*), as extended by art 3 of the Reciprocal Enforcement of Maintenance Orders (Republic of Ireland) Order 1974, SI 1974/2140 (*supra*). The relevant provisions of s 15 of the 1949 Act and s 122 of the 1952 Act were repealed by the Magistrates' Courts Act 1980, s 154 (3), Sch 9, and the rules now have effect as if made under s 144 of that Act, Halsbury's Statutes, 4th edn Vol 27, title Magistrates (3rd edn Vol 50 (2), p 1565; for s 154 (3), Sch 9, see pp 1575, 1604).

Commencement 1 April 1975.

General These rules make provision, in relation to magistrates' courts, for the various matters which are to be prescribed under Part I of the Maintenance Orders (Reciprocal Enforcement) Act 1972 as set out in the Reciprocal Enforcement of Maintenance Orders (Republic of Ireland) Order 1974, SI 1974/2140 (see *supra*). The rules are similar to the Magistrates' Courts (Reciprocal Enforcement Maintenance Orders) Rules 1974, SI 1974/668, p 322 *ante*, with modifications consequent upon those made to the Act by the order of 1974.

The text of the rules is set out in Stone's Justices' Manual.

THE RECOVERY ABROAD OF MAINTENANCE (CONVENTION COUNTRIES) ORDER 1975
SI 1975/423

NOTES

Authority This Order in Council was made on 18 March 1975 under s 25 of the Maintenance Orders (Reciprocal Enforcement) Act 1972, Halsbury's Statutes, 4th edn Vol 27, title Matrimonial Law (Pt 3) (3rd edn Vol 42, p 740).

Commencement 12 April 1975.

Amendment This order has been amended by the Recovery Abroad of Maintenance (Convention Countries) Order 1978, SI 1978/279 (which added Switzerland to the countries specified in the Schedule hereto) and also by the Recovery Abroad of Maintenance (Convention Countries) Order 1982, SI 1982/1530 (which added Suriname to the countries specified in the Schedule), both listed, *ante*.

General This order declares that the countries and territories specified in the Schedule (which lists the countries and territories to which the United Nations Convention on the Recovery Abroad of Maintenance, done at New York on 20 June 1956, extends) are convention countries for the purposes of Part II of the Maintenance Orders (Reciprocal Enforcement) Act 1972, Halsbury's Statutes, 4th edn Vol 27, title Matrimonial Law (Pt 3) (3rd edn Vol 42, p 740, *et seq*). The Schedule (as amended) reads as follows:—

CONVENTION COUNTRIES

Algeria	Holy See
Austria	Hungary
Barbados	Israel
Begium	Italy
Brazil	Luxembourg
Central African Republic	Monaco
Chile	Morocco
Czechosolovakia	Netherlands (Kingdom in Europe and
Denmark	Netherlands Antilles)
Ecuador	Niger
Finland	Norway
France (including the overseas depart-	Pakistan
ments of Guadeloupe, Guiana,	Philippines
Martinique and Reunion)	Poland
Comoro Archipelago	Portugal
French Polynesia	Spain
French Territory of the Afars and	Sri Lanka
Issas	[Suriname]
New Caledonia and Dependencies	Sweden
St Pierre and Miquelon	[Switzerland]
Germany, Federal Republic of, and	Tunisia
Berlin (West)	Turkey
Greece	Upper Volta
Guatemala	Yugoslavia
Haiti	

THE MAGISTRATES' COURTS (RECOVERY ABROAD OF MAINTENANCE) RULES 1975
SI 1975/488

NOTES
Authority   These rules were made on 21 March 1975 by the Lord Chancellor under s 15 of the Justices of the Peace Act 1949, as extended by s 122 of the Magistrates' Courts Act 1952, and ss 27 (8)-(10), 31 (1)-(3), (6) and (8), 33 (4) and (5), 35 (4) and 38 (2) of the Maintenance Orders (Reciprocal Enforcement) Act 1972, Halsbury's Statutes, 4th edn Vol 27, title Matrimonial Law (Pt 3) (3rd edn Vol 42, p 742 *et seq*). The relevant provisions of s 15 of the 1949 Act and s 122 of the 1952 Act were repealed by the Magistrates' Courts Act 1980, s 154 (3), Sch 9, and the rules now have effect as if made under s 144 of that Act, Halsbury's Statutes, 4th edn Vol 27, title Magistrates (3rd edn Vol 50 (2), p 1565; for s 154 (3), Sch 9, see pp 1575, 1604).
Commencement   12 April 1975; see r 1.
Amendment   These rules are printed as amended by the Magistrates' Courts (Recovery of Maintenance) (Amendment) Rules 1980, SI 1980/1584.
Modification   By virtue of the Magistrates' Courts (Recovery Abroad of Maintenance) (Amendment) Rules 1979, SI 1979/1561, the provisions of these rules apply in relation to an American State for the time being specified in the Recovery of Maintenance (United States of America) Order 1979, SI 1979/1314, p 332 *post*, as they apply in relation to a Convention country, subject to the insertion of r 5A, *infra*.
General   These rules make provision, in relation to magistrates' courts, for the various matters which are to be prescribed under Part II of the Maintenance Orders (Reciprocal Enforcement) Act 1972, Halsbury's Statutes, 4th edn Vol 27, title Matrimonial Law (Pt 3) (3rd edn Vol 42, p 740 *et seq*).

1.   These Rules may be cited as the Magistrates' Courts (Recovery Abroad of Maintenance) Rules 1975 and shall come into operation on 12th April 1975.

2.   (1) In these Rules, unless the context otherwise requires—
"the Act" means the Maintenance Orders (Reciprocal Enforcement) Act 1972; and
"his register", in relation to a justices' clerk, means the register kept by that clerk in pursuance of rule 54 of the Magistrates' Courts Rules 1968.
(2) The Interpretation Act 1889 shall apply to the interpretation of these Rules as it applies to the interpretation of an Act of Parliament.

NOTES
Magistrates' Court Rules 1968   SI 1968/1920; revoked and replaced by the Magistrates' Courts Rules 1981, SI 1981/552, in the title Magistrates.
Maintenance Orders (Reciprocal Enforcement) Act 1972   Halsbury's Statutes, 4th edn Vol 27, title Matrimonial Law (Pt 3) (3rd edn Vol 42, p 714).
Interpretation Act 1889   Repealed and replaced by the Interpretation Act 1978, in the title Statutory Instruments, Vol 1 of this work.

3. The officer of any court, by or in relation to whom anything is to be done in pursuance of any provision of Part II of the Act, shall, where that court is a magistrates' court, be the justices' clerk.

4. Where a magistrates' court dismisses a complaint under section 27 of the Act (application for recovery of maintenance), or a complaint by a person in a convention country for the variation of a registered order, the justices' clerk shall send written notice of the court's decision to the Secretary of State and any such notice shall include a statement of the justices' reasons for their decision.

5. (1) Where a magistrates' court makes an order which is required under section 27 (8) of the Act to be registered, the justices' clerk shall enter and sign a minute or memorandum of the order in his register.

(2) Where a justices' clerk in pursuance of section 32 (2) or (3) of the Act (transfer of orders), receives a certified copy of an order, he shall cause the order to be registered in his court by means of a minute or memorandum entered and signed by him in his register.

(3) Every minute or memorandum entered in pursuance of paragraph (1) or (2) above shall specify the section and subsection of the Act under which the order in question is registered.

[**5A.** Where an application under section 26 (1) or (2) of the Act or a certificate under section 26 (3A) of the Act is required to be registered in a magistrates' court in pursuance of the Recovery of Maintenance (United States of America) Order 1979, the justices' clerk shall enter and sign a minute or memorandum of the application or certificate in his register.]

NOTES
Modification   This rule is relevant only in relation to an American State for the time being specified in the Recovery of Maintenance (United States of America) Order 1979, SI 1979/1314, p 332 *post*, and was inserted solely in that respect by the Magistrates' Courts (Recovery Abroad of Maintenance) (Amendment) Rules 1979, SI 1979/1561.

6. (1) Where a justices' clerk registers an order in pursuance of section 27 (8) or 32 (2) or (3) of the Act, he shall send written notice to the Secretary of State that the order has been duly registered.

(2) Where a justices' clerk is required by section 32 (6) of the Act to give notice of the registration of an order he shall do so by sending written notice to the officer specified in that subsection that the order has been duly registered.

7. (1) Payment of sums due under a registered order shall, while the order is registered in a magistrates' court, be made to the clerk of the registering court during such hours and at such place as that clerk may direct; and a justices' clerk to whom payments are made under this rule shall send those payments by post to such person or authority as the Secretary of State may from time to time direct.

(2) Where it appears to a justices' clerk to whom payments under a registered order are made by virtue of paragraph (1) above that any sums payable under the order are in arrear he may and, if such sums are in arrear to an amount equal

   [(*a*) in the case of payments to be made monthly or less frequently, to twice the sum payable periodically; or

   (*b*) in any other case, to four times the sum payable periodically],

he shall, whether the person for whose benefit the payment should have been made requests him to do so or not, proceed in his own name for the recovery of those sums, unless it appears to him that it is unreasonable in the circumstances to do so.

NOTES
Amendment   The words printed between square brackets in para (2) of this rule were substituted for the words "to four times the sum payable weekly under the order" by the Magistrates' Courts (Recovery Abroad of Maintenance) (Amendment) Rules 1980, SI 1980/1584, but the substitution will not have effect in relation to any order as is referred to in the Domestic Proceedings and Magistrates' Courts Act 1978, Sch 1, para 3, Halsbury's Statutes, 4th edn Vol 27, title Matrimonial Law (Pt 3) (3rd edn Vol 48, p 801), as amended.

8.   (1) Notice under section 35 (4) of the Act (variation of orders by magistrates' courts) of the making of a complaint for the variation or revocation of a registered order and of the time and place appointed for the hearing of the complaint shall be in the form specified in the Schedule to these Rules and shall be sent by post by the justices' clerk to the Secretary of State for onward transmission to the appropriate authority in the convention country in which the defendant is residing.

(2) The time appointed for the hearing of the said complaint shall be not less than six weeks later than the date on which the said notice is sent to the Secretary of State.

9.   (1) Where a magistrates' court receives from the Secretary of State a request under section 38 (1) of the Act (taking evidence at request of court in convention country) to take the evidence of any person, that evidence shall be taken in accordance with the provisions of this rule.

(2) Subject to paragraph (3) below—
(*a*) the evidence shall be taken in the same manner as if the person concerned were a witness in proceedings on a complaint;
(*b*) any oral evidence so taken shall be put into writing and read to the person who gave it, who shall be required to sign the document; and
(*c*) the justices by whom the evidence of any person is so taken shall certify at the foot of any document setting out the evidence of, or produced in evidence by, that person that such evidence was taken, or document received in evidence, as the case may be, by them.

(3) Where the request referred to in section 38 (1) of the Act includes a request that the evidence be taken in a particular manner, the court by which the evidence is taken shall, so far as circumstances permit, comply with that request.

10.   (1) Where a justices' clerk receives from the Secretary of State a request under section 38 (1) of the Act to take the evidence of any person, that evidence shall be taken in accordance with the provisions of this rule.

(2) Subject to paragraph (3) below—
(*a*) the person whose evidence is to be taken shall be examined on oath by or before the justices' clerk;
(*b*) any oral evidence shall be put into writing and read to that person who shall be required to sign the document; and
(*c*) the justices' clerk shall certify at the foot of any document setting out the evidence of, or produced in evidence by, that person that such evidence was taken, or document received in evidence, as the case may be, by him.

(3) Where the request referred to in section 38 (1) of the Act includes a request that the evidence be taken in a particular manner the justices' clerk by whom the evidence is taken shall, so far as circumstances permit, comply with that request.

(4) For the purposes of this rule a justices' clerk shall have the like power to administer oaths as has a single justice of the peace.

11.   Any document such as is mentioned in paragraph (2) (*c*) of rule 9 or 10 of these Rules shall be sent to the Secretary of State for onward transmission to the appropriate authority in the convention country in which the request referred to in section 38 (1) of the Act originated.

SCHEDULE

NOTES
This Schedule sets out the form of notice under s 35 (4) of the Maintenance Orders (Reciprocal Enforcement) Act 1972, Halsbury's Statutes, 4th edn Vol 27, title Matrimonial Law (Pt 3) (3rd edn Vol 42, p 749), which is referred to in 1 8 (1). The form, which is not reproduced in this work, is printed in Stone's Justices' Manual.

THE RECIPROCAL ENFORCEMENT OF MAINTENANCE ORDERS (DESIGNATION OF RECIPROCATING COUNTRIES) ORDER 1975
SI 1975/2187

NOTES
Authority This Order in Council was made on 19 December 1975 under ss 1 and 24 of the Maintenance Orders (Reciprocal Enforcement) Act 1972, Halsbury's Statutes, 4th edn Vol 27, title Matrimonial Law (Pt 3) (3rd edn Vol 42, pp 717, 739).
Commencement 28 January 1976.
General This order designates as reciprocating countries or territories for the purposes of Part I of the Maintenance Orders (Reciprocal Enforcement) Act 1972, Halsbury's Statutes, 4th edn Vol 27, title Matrimonial Law (Pt 3) (3rd edn Vol 42, p 717 *et seq*), the countries or territories designated in the Schedule hereto. For further orders so designating other countries and territories, see SI 1974/556, p 319 *ante*, SI 1979/115, p 332, *post* and SI 1983/1125, p 336 *post*. The order also contains transitional provisions in respect of maintenance orders and proceedings to which the Maintenance Orders (Facilities for Enforcement) Act 1920 had applied: the provisions are identical to those contained in the said SI 1974/556.
  The Schedule to this order is in the following terms:

COUNTRIES AND TERRITORIES DESIGNATED AS RECIPROCATING COUNTRIES

(1) Country or territory	(2) Description of maintenance orders to which designation extends
Barbados	Maintenance orders generally.
Bermuda	Maintenance orders generally.
Ghana	Maintenance orders other than— (a) affiliation orders, and (b) maintenance orders of the description contained in paragraph (b) of the definition of "maintenance order" in the said section 21 (1).
India	Maintenance orders other than— (a) affiliation orders, and (b) maintenance orders of the description contained in paragraph (b) of the definition of "maintenance order" in the said section 21 (1); and (c) orders obtained by or in favour of a public authority.
Kenya	Maintenance orders other than— (a) affiliation orders, and (b) maintenance orders of the description contained in paragraph (b) of the definition of "maintenance order" in the said section 21 (1).
Malta	Maintenance orders generally.
New Brunswick	Maintenance orders other than— (a) affiliation orders, and (b) maintenance orders of the description contained in paragraph (b) of the definition of "maintenance order" in the said section 21 (1); and (c) orders obtained by or in favour of a public authority.
Northwest Territories of Canada	Maintenance orders other than— (a) affiliation orders; (b) maintenance orders of the description contained in paragraph (b) of the definition of "maintenance order" in the said section 21 (1); and (c) orders obtained by or in favour of a public authority.
The Republic of South Africa	Maintenance orders other than— (a) affiliation orders, and (b) maintenance orders of the description contained in paragraph (b) of the definition of "maintenance order" in the said section 21 (1).

  The references to "the said section 21 (1)" above are to s 21 (1) of the Maintenance Orders (Reciprocal Enforcement) Act 1972, Halsbury's Statutes, 4th edn Vol 27, title Matrimonial Law (Pt 3) (3rd edn Vol 42, p 737).

THE RECIPROCAL ENFORCEMENT OF MAINTENANCE ORDERS (DESIGNATION OF RECIPROCATING COUNTRIES) ORDER 1979
SI 1979/115

NOTES

Authority This Order in Council was made on 6 February 1979 under ss 1, 24 and 45 (1) of the Maintenance Orders (Reciprocal Enforcement) Act 1972, Halsbury's Statutes, 4th edn Vol 27, title Matrimonial Law (Pt 3) (3rd edn Vol 42, pp 717, 739, 756).

Commencement 1 April 1979.

General This order (which amends SI 1974/556, p 319, *ante*) designates as reciprocating countries or territories for the purposes of Part I of the Maintenance Orders (Reciprocal Enforcement) Act 1972, Halsbury's Statutes, 4th edn Vol 27, title Matrimonial Law (Pt 3) (3rd edn Vol 42, p 717 *et seq*), the countries and territories designated in the Schedule hereto. (For other orders so designating countries and territories, see SI 1974/556 (p 319, *ante*), SI 1975/2187 (p 331, *ante*) and SI 1983/1125, p 336 *post*). This order also contains transitional provisions in respect of maintenance orders and proceedings to which the Maintenance Orders (Facilities for Enforcement) Act 1920 had applied: the provisions are identical to those contained in the said SI 1974/556.

The Schedule to this order is in the following terms:

COUNTRIES AND TERRITORIES DESIGNATED AS RECIPROCATING COUNTRIES

(1) Country or territory	(2) Description of maintenance orders to which designation extends
Alberta	Maintenance orders other than— (*a*) provisional affiliation orders; (*b*) maintenance orders of the description contained in paragraph (*b*) of the definition of "maintenance order" in section 21 (1) of the Act of 1972; (*c*) orders obtained by or in favour of a public authority.
Fiji	Maintenance orders generally.
Hong Kong	Maintenance orders generally.
Norfolk Island	Maintenance orders other than orders obtained by or in favour of a public authority.
Saskatchewan	Maintenance orders other than— (*a*) provisional affiliation orders; and (*b*) maintenance orders of the description contained in the said paragraph (*b*).
Singapore	Maintenance orders generally.
Turks and Caicos Islands	Maintenance orders other than— (*a*) affiliation orders; (*b*) maintenance orders of the description contained in the said paragraph (*b*); and (*c*) orders obtained by or in favour of a public authority.
United Republic of Tanzania (except Zanzibar)	Maintenance orders other than— (*a*) affiliation orders; (*b*) maintenance orders of the description contained in paragraph (*b*); and (*c*) orders obtained by or in favour of a public authority.
Western Australia	Maintenance orders other than orders obtained by or in favour of a public authority

RECOVERY OF MAINTENANCE (UNITED STATES OF AMERICA) ORDER 1979
SI 1979/1314

NOTES

Authority This Order in Council was made on 19 October 1979 under the Maintenance Orders (Reciprocal Enforcement) Act 1972, s 40, Halsbury's Statutes, 4th edn Vol 27, title Matrimonial Law (Pt 3) (3rd edn Vol 42, p 753).

Commencement 1 January 1980; see art 1.

Amendment This Order in Council is printed as amended by the Recovery Abroad of Maintenance (United States of America) Order 1981, SI 1981/606, and the Recovery of Maintenance (United States of America) (Variation) Order 1984, SI 1984/1824, which add further American States to the list contained in Sch 1 to the order.

General   This Order in Council applies the Maintenance Orders (Reciprocal Enforcement) Act 1972, Part II, Halsbury's Statutes, 4th edn Vol 27, title Matrimonial Law (Pt 3) (3rd edn Vol 42, p 740 *et seq*), to specified American States, subject to a modification requiring registration in the court (in the Maintenance Orders (Reciprocal Enforcement) Act 1972 register) of an application for recovery of maintenance and a certificate signed by a magistrate (or sheriff) to the effect that the application sets forth facts from which the duty to maintain and the foreign court's jurisdiction may be determined.

By virtue of the Magistrates' Courts (Recovery Abroad of Maintenance (Amendment) Rules 1979, SI 1979/1561, American States specified in Sch 1 to this instrument are subject to the provisions of the Magistrates' Courts (Recovery Abroad of Maintenance) Rules 1975, SI 1975/488, p 328 *ante*, in the same way as those rules apply in relation to a Convention country but with certain modifications.

1.   (1) This Order may be cited as the Recovery of Maintenance (United States of America) Order 1979.

(2) This Order shall come into operation on 1st January 1980.

2.   In this Order, unless the context otherwise requires—

"the Act" means the Maintenance Orders (Reciprocal Enforcement) Act 1972;

"specified State" means a State specified in the Schedule to this Order.

NOTES

Maintenance Orders (Reciprocal Enforcement) Act 1972   Halsbury's Statutes, 4th edn Vol 27, title Matrimonial Law (Pt 3) (3rd edn Vol 42, p 714 *et seq*).

3.   (1) The provisions of Part II of the Act shall apply in relation to a specified State as they apply in relation to a convention country, subject to the modification set out in paragraph (2) below.

(2) After section 26 (3) of the Act there shall be inserted the following subsection:—

"(3A) an application under subsection (1) or (2) above, for the purpose of recovering maintenance from a person in a specified State within the meaning of the Recovery of Maintenance (United States of America) Order 1979, and a certificate signed by a justice of the peace or, where the applicant is residing in Scotland, the sheriff, to the effect that the application sets forth facts from which it may be determined that the respondent owes a duty to maintain the applicant and any other person named in the application and that a court in the specified State may obtain jurisdiction of the respondent or his property, shall be registered in the court in the prescribed manner by the appropriate officer or, in, Scotland, by the sheriff clerk in the Maintenance Orders (Reciprocal Enforcement) Act 1972 register.".

SCHEDULE   Article 2
SPECIFIED STATES

[Alaska]	Montana
Arizona	Nebraska
Arkansas	Nevada
California	New Hampshire
Colorado	[New Jersey]
Connecticut	New Mexico
[Delaware]	New York
Florida	North Carolina
[Georgia	North Dakota
Hawaii]	Ohio
Idaho	Oklahoma
Illinois	Oregon
[Iowa]	Pennsylvania
Indiana	[Rhode Island
Kansas	South Dakota
Kentucky	Tennessee]
Louisiana	Texas
Maine	[Utah]
[Maryland	Vermont
Massachusetts]	Virginia
Michigan	Washington
Minnesota	Wisconsin
[Missouri]	Wyoming

NOTES
Amendment   The States of Delaware, Maryland, Massachusetts, Missouri, Rhode Island, South Dakota, Tennessee and Utah were added by SI 1981/606, and the States of Alaska, Georgia, Hawaii, Iowa and New Jersey were added by SI 1984/1824.

RECIPROCAL ENFORCEMENT OF MAINTENANCE ORDERS (HAGUE CONVENTION COUNTRIES) ORDER 1979
SI 1979/1317

NOTES
Authority   This Order in Council was made on 19 October 1979 under the Maintenance Orders (Reciprocal Enforcement) Act 1972, s 40, Halsbury's Statutes, 4th edn Vol 27, title Matrimonial Law (Pt 3) (3rd edn Vol 42, p 735).
Commencement   1 March 1980; see art 1.
Interpretation   See art 2.
Amendment   This Order in Council is printed as amended by the Reciprocal Enforcement of Maintenance Orders (Hague Convention Countries) (Variation) Order 1981, SI 1981/837, the Reciprocal Enforcement of Maintenance Orders (Hague Convention Countries) (Variation) (No 2) Order 1981, SI 1981/1545, the Reciprocal Enforcement of Maintenance Orders (Hague Convention Countries) (Variation) (No 3) Order 1981, SI 1981/1674, the Reciprocal Enforcement of Maintenance Orders (Hague Convention Countries) (Variation) Order 1983, SI 1983/885, and the Reciprocal Enforcement of Maintenance Orders (Hague Convention Countries) (Variation) (No 2) Order 1983, SI 1983/1523.
General   This Order in Council provides for the implementation in the United Kingdom of the Convention on the Recognition and Enforcement of Decisions Relating to Maintenance Obligations concluded at the Hague on 2 October 1973. It applies the Maintenance Orders (Reciprocal Enforcement) Act 1972, Part I, Halsbury's Statutes, 4th edn Vol 27, title Matrimonial Law (Pt 3) (3rd edn Vol 42, p 717 *et seq*), in relation to Convention countries as it applies in relation to reciprocating countries, subject to certain exceptions, adaptations and modifications.

1.   (1) This Order may be cited as the Reciprocal Enforcement of Maintenance Orders (Hague Convention Countries) Order 1979.

(2) This Order shall come into operation on 1st March 1980.

2.   In this Order, unless the context otherwise requires—

"Act" means the Maintenance Orders (Reciprocal Enforcement) Act 1972, as amended by or under any other enactment;

"court in a Hague Convention country" includes any judicial or administrative authority in a Hague Convention country;

"Hague Convention" means the Convention on the Recognition and Enforcement of Decisions Relating to Maintenance Obligations concluded at The Hague on 2nd October 1973;

"Hague Convention country" means a country or territory specified in Schedule 1 to this Order, being a country or territory (other than the United Kingdom) in which the Hague Convention is in force.

NOTES
Maintenance Orders (Reciprocal Enforcement) Act 1972   Halsbury's Statutes, 4th edn Vol 27, title Matrimonial Law (Pt 3) (3rd edn Vol 42, p 714 *et seq*).

3.   The provisions of Part I of the Act shall apply in relation to a Hague Convention country as they apply in relation to a reciprocating country, subject to the exceptions, adaptations and modifications set out in Schedule 2 to this Order, and accordingly Part I of the Act shall, in relation to maintenance orders made by courts in the United Kingdom against persons in a Hague Convention country and to maintenance orders made by courts in a Hague Convention country against persons in the United Kingdom, have effect as set out in Schedule 3 to this Order.

SCHEDULE 1   Article 2
HAGUE CONVENTION COUNTRIES
Czechoslovakia
[Finland]
France
[Italy
Luxembourg

Netherlands (Kingdom in Europe and Netherlands Antilles)]
Norway
Portugal
Sweden
Switzerland
[Turkey]

NOTES
Amendment This Schedule was amended by SI 1981/837 (adding the Netherlands to the list of countries to which the Order applies, SI 1981/1545 (adding Luxembourg), SI 1981/1674 (adding Italy), SI 1983/885 (adding Finland) and SI 1983/1523 (adding Turkey).

SCHEDULE 2

NOTES
This Schedule sets out the exceptions, adaptations and modifications referred to in art 3 of this Order, subject to which the Maintenance Orders (Reciprocal Enforcement) Act 1972, Part I, Halsbury's Statutes, 4th edn Vol 27, title Matrimonial Law (Pt 3) (3rd edn Vol 42, p 717 *et seq*), is to apply in relation to Convention countries. Certain provisions thereof are excluded and others amended. For the provisions of Part I of the Act as so adapted and modified, see Sch 3, which is not printed here but which may be found set out in Stone's Justices' Manual.

SCHEDULE 3

NOTES
This Schedule is not reproduced in this work but may be found set out in Stone's Justices' Manual; see note to Sch 2 *supra*.

MAGISTRATES' COURTS (RECIPROCAL ENFORCEMENT OF MAINTENANCE ORDERS) (HAGUE CONVENTION COUNTRIES) RULES 1980
SI 1980/108

NOTES
Authority These rules were made on 31 January 1980 by the Lord Chancellor under the Justices of the Peace Act 1949, s 15, as extended by the Magistrates' Courts Act 1952, s 122, and the Maintenance Orders (Reciprocal Enforcement) Act 1972, ss 2 (3), (4), 3 (5) (*b*), (6A), (6B), (6D), 5 (3), (4) (*b*), (*c*), (6), (7), (10), 6 (2), (3), (5), (6), (7), (8), (10), (11), (12), 8 (5), (6), 9 (3), (4) (*b*), (*c*), (6), (7), (8), 10 (1)-(5), (7), 11 (1) (*b*), 14 (1), 16 (1), 18 (1), Halsbury's Statutes, 4th edn Vol 27, title Matrimonial Law (Pt 3) (3rd edn Vol 42, p 718 *et seq*), as extended by the Reciprocal Enforcement of Maintenance Orders (Hague Convention Countries) Order 1979, SI 1979/1317, p 334, *ante*. The relevant provisions of s 15 of the 1949 Act and s 122 of the 1952 Act were repealed by the Magistrates' Courts Act 1980, s 154 (3), Sch 9, and the rules now have effect as if made under s 144 of that Act, Halsbury's Statutes, 4th edn Vol 27, title Magistrates (3rd edn Vol 50 (2), p 1565; for s 154 (3), Sch 9, see pp 1575, 1604).
Commencement 1 March 1980.
General These rules make provision, in relation to magistrates' courts, for the various matters which are to be prescribed under the Maintenance Orders (Reciprocal Enforcement) Act 1972, Part I, Halsbury's Statutes, 4th edn Vol 27, title Matrimonial Law (Pt 3) (3rd edn Vol 42, p 717 *et seq*), as modified by the Reciprocal Enforcement of Maintenance Orders (Hague Convention Countries) Orders 1979, SI 1979/1317, p 334, *ante*. The order: (*a*) provides that the justices' clerk is the prescribed officer; (*b*) specifies the matters to be included in an application under s 2 of the 1972 Act; (*c*) provides for the form of registration of a maintenance order; (*d*) lays down that certain documents to be served on the payee are to be sent by post; (*e*) prescribes the form of notice of registration of a maintenance order which has to be served on the payer and the form of notice to the payee that a maintenance order has not been registered; (*f*) requires a justices' clerk to send the Secretary of State written notice of a court's decision to set aside the registration of a maintenance order; (*g*) provides for the enforcement of sums due under a registered maintenance order; (*h*) provides for the taking of evidence needed for foreign proceedings; (*i*) requires the clerk to give notice of the cancellation or registration of a maintenance order; (*j*) requires the clerk to notify the Secretary of State of notices served on a payer who resides in a Hague Convention country; and (*k*) makes provision, in cases where proceedings are brought in a Hague Convention country against a person residing in England and Wales, for notice of the institution of those proceedings to be served on that person.

ATTACHMENT OF EARNINGS (EMPLOYER'S DEDUCTION) ORDER 1980
SI 1980/558

NOTES
Authority This order was made on 14 April 1980 by the Lord Chancellor under the Attachment of Earnings Act 1971, s 7 (4) (*a*), (5), Halsbury's Statutes, 4th edn Vol 22, title Judgments and Execution (3rd edn Vol 41, p 800).

Commencement   1 June 1980.
General   This order, which revokes the Attachment of Earnings (Employer's Deduction) Order
1975, SI 1975/1868, increases from 13p to 50p the additional amount which an employer making
a deduction from a debtor's earnings under an attachment of earnings order may make towards
his clerical and administrative costs.

RECIPROCAL ENFORCEMENT OF MAINTENANCE ORDERS (DESIGNATION OF RECIPROCATING COUNTRIES) ORDER 1983 SI 1983/1125

NOTES
Authority   This Order in Council was made on 27 July 1983 under the Maintenance Orders
(Reciprocal Enforcement) Act 1972, ss 1, 24, 45 (1), Halsbury's Statutes, 4th edn Vol 27, title
Matrimonial Law (Pt 3) (3rd edn Vol 42, pp 717, 739, 756).
Commencement   1 September 1983.
General   This Order in Council: (*a*) designates as reciprocating countries for the purposes of
the Maintenance Orders (Reciprocal Enforcement) Act 1972, Part I, Halsbury's Statutes, 4th
edn Vol 27, title Matrimonial Law (Pt 3) (3rd edn Vol 42, p 717 *et seq*), the countries or territories
contained in the Schedule hereto (for further orders so designating other countries and territories,
see SI 1974/556, p 319, *ante*, SI 1975/2187, p 331, *ante*, and SI 1979/115, p 332, *ante*); and (*b*)
amends the Reciprocal Enforcement of Maintenance Orders (Designation of Reciprocating Countries) Order 1974, SI 1974/556, p 319, *ante*, so as to extend the designation in respect of Manitoba
and New Zealand to maintenance orders generally.
    The Schedule to this order is in the following terms:

COUNTRIES AND TERRITORIES DESIGNATED AS RECIPROCATING COUNTRIES

(1) Country or territory	(2) Description of maintenance orders to which designation extends
Anguilla	Maintenance orders generally
Falkland Islands and Dependencies	Maintenance orders generally
Isle of Man	Maintenance orders generally
Nauru	Maintenance orders generally
Papua New Guinea	Maintenance orders other than provisional affiliation orders
St Helena	Maintenance orders generally

Zimbabwe	Maintenance orders other than—
	
	(*a*) affiliation orders; and
	
	(*b*) maintenance orders of the description contained in
	    paragraph (*b*) of the definition of "maintenance
	    order" in section 21 (1) of the Act of 1972 (orders
	    for the payment of birth and funeral expenses of
	    child).

    The reference to "section 21 (1) of the Act of 1972" is to the Maintenance Orders (Reciprocal
Enforcement) Act 1972, s 21 (1), Halsbury's Statutes, 4th edn Vol 27, title Matrimonial Law
(Pt 3) (3rd edn Vol 42, p 737).

Importation

INDEX

This Index follows the pattern of the Consolidated Index. References are given to the pages of the volume, and also, where appropriate, to the year and number of the instrument concerned.

Basutoland:
> maintenance orders, reciprocal enforcement . . 300; 318 (1959/377)
> marriage . . 201, 202

Bechuanaland:
> maintenance orders, reciprocal enforcement . . 300; 318 (1959/377)
> marriage . . 201, 202

Belgium:
> maintenance recovery . . 301; 328 (1975/423)

Belize. *See* British Honduras

Bermuda:
> maintenance orders, reciprocal enforcement . . 300; 331 (1975/2187)
> marriage . . 201, 202

Bicycles:
> racing on highways, conditions for authorisation . . 59; 61 (1960/250)

Borneo:
> maintenance orders, reciprocal enforcement . . 300; 318 (1959/377)
> *See also* Malaysia

Botswana:
> *See* Bechuanaland

Brazil:
> maintenance recovery . . 301; 328 (1975/423)

Bridges:
> orders as to reconstruction, improvement, etc:
>> applications for:
>>> Minister, to . . 60; 71 (1965/869, regs 3,4)
>>> notice to authorities and departments . . 72, 73 (1965/869, regs 5, 6)
>> draft order:
>>> objection to . . 73 (1965/869, reg 9)
>>> publication, etc . . 73 (1965/869, reg 8)
>> order, notice of making and inspection . . 74 (1965/869, reg 10)
> railway, load-bearing standards . . 60; 98 (1972/1705)
> *See also* Highway authorities; Local authorities

British Columbia. *See* Canada

British Gas:
> Corporation:
>> financial year . . 21 (1972/1737)
>> functions, etc . . 4
>> general regulations . . 4; 25 (1972/1879)
>> limitation of prices, compensation for . . 26 (1976/1108)
>> membership and proceedings . . 25 (1972/1879)
>> money deposited as security with, interest . . 26 (1982/655)
>> offshore:
>>> interests, further disposal of . . 34 (1983/1096)
>>> oilfields, disposal of . . 26 (1982/1131)
>> pension schemes, establishment and maintenance of . . 5
>> quality of gas supplied . . 5
>> rate of levy . . 26 (1982/548)
>> transfer of shares of subsidiaries . . 33 (1983/967); 37 (1983/1667)
> *See also* Gas

British Guiana:
> maintenance orders, reciprocal enforcement . . 300; 318 (1959/377)
> war marriages, divorce, etc, decrees . . 215

British Honduras:
> maintenance orders, reciprocal enforcement . . 300; 318 (1959/377)
> marriage . . 201, 202

British Solomon Islands. *See now* Solomon Islands

British Virgin Islands. *See now* Virgin Islands

Brunei:
> maintenance orders, reciprocal enforcement . . 300; 319 (1959/377)

Builders' skips, highways on, marking of . . 58; 126 (1984/1933)

Byelaws:
> new streets . . 55

St Christopher and Nevis:
    maintenance orders, reciprocal enforcement . . 300; 318 (1959/377)
St Helena:
    maintenance orders, reciprocal enforcement . . 300; 336 (1983/1125)
St Lucia:
    maintenance orders, reciprocal enforcement . . 300; 319 (1959/377)
    marriage . . 201, 202
St Vincent:
    maintenance orders, reciprocal enforcement . . 300; 319 (1959/377)
    marriage . . 201, 202
Sarawak:
    maintenance orders, reciprocal enforcement . . 300; 319 (1959/377)
    See also Malaysia
Saskatchewan. *See* Canada
Scilly Isles:
    local housing authority, defined as . . 145
    Refuse Disposal (Amenity) Act 1978, applied to . . 50 (1984/288)
    Road Traffic Regulation Act 1984, application to . . 49 (1971/256)
Scotland:
    maintenance orders, reciprocal enforcement . . 301
Secure tenants. *See* Housing, right to buy
Seychelles:
    maintenance orders, reciprocal enforcement . . 300; 319 (1959/377)
    marriage . . 201, 202
    war marriages, divorce, etc, decrees . . 215
Sierra Leone:
    maintenance orders, reciprocal enforcement . . 300; 319 (1959/377)
    marriage . . 201, 202
Singapore:
    maintenance orders, reciprocal enforcement . . 300; 332 (1979/115)
    marriage . . 201, 202
    See also Malaysia
Social Security and Housing Benefits Act 1982, commencement . . 148; 173–176 (1982/906)
Solomon Islands:
    maintenance orders, reciprocal enforcement . . 300; 319 (1959/377)
Somaliland:
    maintenance orders, reciprocal enforcement . . 300; 319 (1959/377)
South Africa:
    maintenance orders, reciprocal enforcement . . 300; 331 (1975/2187)
    war marriages, divorce, etc, decrees . . 215
Southern Rhodesia. *See* Zimbabwe
Spain:
    maintenance recovery . . 301; 328 (1975/423)
Special roads:
    maps:
        limits of deviation . . 95 (1971/1706, reg 4)
        scales of . . 94 (1971/1706, reg 3)
    opening, notice of . . 64 (1962/1320)
    schemes for, procedure . . 53; 61 (1962/1319)
Sri Lanka:
    maintenance recovery . . 301; 328 (1975/423)
    See also Ceylon
Stopping up of highways:
    statutory powers . . 54, 55
Straits Settlements. *See* Malaysia; Singapore
Street playgrounds, generally . . 57
Street works:
    generally . . 59
Streets:
    collection of money in . . 59
    new, by-laws for . . 55, 56
    private, making up of . . 56
    See also Roads